THE COURSE OF AMERICAN HISTORY: INTERPRETIVE READINGS

1607–PRESENT

EDITED BY

IRWIN UNGER
New York University

DAVID BRODY
University of California, Davis

PAUL GOODMAN
University of California, Davis

XEROX COLLEGE PUBLISHING

Waltham, Massachusetts / Toronto

The Course of American History: Interpretive Readings

1607–Present

ACKNOWLEDGMENTS

Footnotes have been omitted except where they are necessary for an understanding of the text.

DOUGLASS G. ADAIR, " 'Experience Must Be Our Only Guide': History, Democratic Theory, and the United States Constitution." Reprinted with permission of the Henry E. Huntington Library and Art Gallery.

BERNARD BAILYN, from *The Ideological Origins of the American Revolution*. Excerpted by permission of the publishers. Cambridge, Mass.: The Belknap Press of Harvard University Press. Copyright, 1967, by the President and Fellows of Harvard College.

THOMAS C. BARROW, "The American Revolution as a Colonial War for Independence." Reprinted by permission of the author.

BARTON J. BERNSTEIN, "America in War and Peace: The Test of Liberalism" from *Towards a New Past,* edited by Barton J. Bernstein. Copyright © 1968 by Random House, Inc. Reprinted by permission of Pantheon Books, a Division of Random House, Inc.

RAY ALLEN BILLINGTON, "Frontier Democracy: Social Aspects" from *America's Frontier Heritage* by Ray Allen Billington. Copyright © 1966 by Ray Allen Billington. Reprinted by permission of Holt, Rinehart and Winston, Inc.

JOHN MORTON BLUM, "President, Congress, and Control." Reprinted by permission of the publishers from John Morton Blum *The Republican Roosevelt,* Cambridge, Mass.: Harvard University Press. Copyright, 1954, by the President and Fellows of Harvard College.

JAMES MACGREGOR BURNS, excerpted from *Roosevelt: The Lion and the Fox,* © 1956 by James MacGregor Burns. Reprinted by permission of Harcourt Brace Jovanovich, Inc.

STOKELY CARMICHAEL, "Toward Black Liberation." Reprinted by permission of the University of Massachusetts Press.

WILLIAM N. CHAMBERS, "Parties and Nation-Building in America" from *Political Parties and Political Development,* eds. J. LaPalombara and Myron Weiner, Social Science Research Council (copyright © 1966 by Princeton University Press; Princeton Paperback, 1968).

DAVID DONALD, "A. Lincoln, Politician" from *Lincoln Reconsidered,* by David Donald. Copyright © 1956 by David Donald. Reprinted by permission of Alfred A. Knopf, Inc.

OSCAR HANDLIN, "Old Immigrants and New." Reprinted by permission of Collins-Knowlton-Wing, Inc. Copyright © 1956 Oscar Handlin. "The Significance of the Seventeenth Century" from *Seventeenth-Century America* by James Smith. Reprinted by permission of the University of North Carolina Press. Copyright © 1959 by the Institute of Early American History and Culture.

RICHARD HOFSTADTER, "Pseudo-Conservatism Revisited—1965" from *The Paranoid Style in American Politics,* by Richard Hofstadter. Copyright © 1965 by Richard Hofstadter. Reprinted by permission of Alfred A. Knopf, Inc. "Thomas Jefferson: The Aristocrat as Democrat" from *American Political Tradition,* by Richard Hofstadter. Copyright 1948 by Alfred A. Knopf, Inc. Reprinted by permission of the publisher.

KENNETH KENISTON, "You Have to Grow Up in Scarsdale to Know How Bad It Is." Copyright © 1969 by The New York Times Company. Reprinted by permission.

PAUL KLEPPNER, "The Politics of Realignment: The Reaction of the Toiling Masses." Reprinted with permission of The Macmillan Company from *The Cross of Culture* by Paul Kleppner. Copyright © 1970 by The Free Press, a Division of The Macmillan Company.

WALTER LAFEBER, "Epilogue." Reprinted from Walter LaFeber, *The New Empire: An Interpretation of American Expansion, 1860–1898.* Copyright © 1963 by the American Historical Association. Used by permission of Cornell University Press.

AUBREY C. LAND, "Economic Base and Social Structure: The Northern Chesapeake in the Eighteenth Century." Reprinted by permission of *The Journal of Economic History.*

Contents

Introduction

This collection is designed principally to meet the needs of the introductory survey of United States history. This course is currently undergoing considerable change on college campuses around the country. At one time the typical beginning survey strongly emphasized political history—but political history conceived in the narrowest way as the succession of presidential administrations. Though this approach may survive here and there, it is rapidly being replaced by classes stressing the social and intellectual dimensions of the American past. It seems less important to students and faculty today to talk about Jackson's Kitchen Cabinet than about the condition of women in Jacksonian times; it seems less interesting to focus on the details of the Kansas–Nebraska Act than on the plight of blacks under slavery; it appears pointless to deal with scandals in the Truman regime when we all want to know more about the roots of the cold war.

Recognizing the new concerns of both teachers and students, we have sought to devote half our space to articles on society and social events. We have not, however, neglected politics. Instead we have attempted to include important synthesizing articles that bring together material on an entire political epoch. Our purpose has been to provide the student with a liberal sampling of the very best of the new American history while at the same time furnishing readable and provocative special studies to supplement the narratives of paperback books and standard texts.

IRWIN UNGER
DAVID BRODY
PAUL GOODMAN

PART 1

The Early Years
1607-1815

The Transit of Civilization from the Old World to the New

Englishmen crossing the ocean to America expected to transfer to the new colonies the familiar institutions and arrangements under which men lived in the Old World. The forms of government, religious worship, economic activity, and family relationships that people knew at home became the basis for establishing new societies in a wilderness. But according to Oscar Handlin in the following selection, Englishmen failed to transfer intact the structure of society they left behind.

Establishing settlements proved to be full of surprises. The migration of people and institutions was selective. Few English aristocrats, for instance, were willing to migrate to an empty wilderness. Hence, the class structure in America lacked a hereditary aristocracy, such as occupied the top of the social pyramid in England. Similarly, colonists did not reproduce English political patterns. The Crown, which played a dominant role in English politics during the seventeenth century and was still a major force in the eighteenth century, was a remote and much weaker institution in the colonies. At a time when the tendency in England was for political authority to gravitate to London, in the colonies power became fragmented, dispersed among the gentry of dozens of towns and counties. Nor did Englishmen plant in America a productive system like that in England. There, most arable land was under cultivation and falling into the hands of fewer and fewer landowners as the wealthier, more progressive landlords pushed unneeded peasants off their estates. In America, a virgin continent awaited the axmen to clear the trees, and abundant lands made possible an ever-growing army of small freeholders who chiefly populated British North America. Religious institutions, no less than political and economic institutions, underwent alteration in America. Instead of supporting a state church, embodiment of the one true faith, the colonists spawned a dozen competing churches, none of which enjoyed the monopoly possessed by the Church of England. The result was that, though few came to America with the purpose of creating a new society, well before the American Revolution discerning observers realized a new society was emerging in the colonies inhabited by what one Frenchman described as "a new race of men."

FOR FURTHER READING:

BOORSTIN, DANIEL. *The Americans: The Colonial Experience.* New York: Random House, Vintage Books, 1958.*

HANDLIN, OSCAR. *The Americans: A History of the People of the United States.* Boston : Little, Brown & Company, 1963.*

VER STEEG, CLARENCE. *The Formative Years.* New York: Hill & Wang, Making of America Series, 1964.*

Asterisk denotes paperback edition.

The Significance of the Seventeenth Century   OSCAR HANDLIN

The historian is trained to see the past in its own terms. He studies the seventeenth century as the product of that which had gone before it, and he attempts to reconstruct the culture and society of the American colonies as those might have seemed to the men who lived in them.

This is the necessary perspective for an understanding of the period. An impressive body of recent studies has shown that the settlements along the coast of North America were elements of imperial systems that had their counterparts in many other regions of the world. We have learned that the institutional life of the colonies can only be understood against a background that reaches back to the medieval past. The labor system, the forms of government, even the modes of thought of the seventeenth century extended patterns that had long before been developing in Europe. To see in them the forerunners or prototypes of what would emerge in the eighteenth or nineteenth century is grievously to misinterpret them.

But our purpose in celebrating the 350th anniversary of the settlement of the Jamestown colony must be somewhat different. The seventeenth century should have general meaning, for we — and the historians along with the rest of us — live, after all, in the twentieth century; and we expect somehow that the experiences of the men who began to come off the ships at Jamestown have also a meaning for us in the twentieth century. A commemorative occasion is a time for retrospection — for looking backward from the present to take account of the way we have come. It has its picturesque and interesting aspects, of course. But its true value arises from the opportunity it offers us to acquire perspective on the present and the future. From that point of view, it is our obligation to look back to the seventeenth century for what it can reveal of the antecedents of our own culture.

In that respect the seventeenth century was immensely significant. In the decades after the settlement at Jamestown, three generations of Americans — the first Americans — began to shape the social order, the way of life, and an interpretation of their own experience that would influence much of subsequent American history. Pick up the story where you will — in the eighteenth or nineteenth century or in our own times — and invariably in these matters the threads lead back to the seventeenth century. It will be worth while to discuss each of these developments briefly.

The colonists who settled at Jamestown and elsewhere along the coast after 1607 brought with them fixed conceptions of what a social order should be like. Their whole effort thereafter was devoted to recreating the forms they had known at home. Yet in practice their experience persistently led them away from the patterns they judged desirable. The American social order that finally emerged was abnormal. That is, it not only diverged from the experience of the European society from which the newcomers emigrated, but it was also contrary to their own expectations of what a social order should be.

The settlers were loyal to the governments from which they emigrated, and they were conservative in their attitudes toward existing institutions. Repeatedly they ex-

Source: Oscar Handlin, "The Significance of the Seventeenth Century," in *Seventeenth-Century America*, ed. James M. Smith (Chapel Hill: University of North Carolina Press, 1959), pp. 3–12.

plained that their emigration was not intended to disrupt but rather to preserve and improve the society they left. Nevertheless they were constantly moving off on tangents through the force of circumstance and the pressure of the environment. A number of examples will clarify this point.

The forms of colonial government developed slowly and erratically. The first settlers transplanted two forms commonplace in the practice of Europeans in this period. The chartered commercial companies, as in Virginia and Plymouth, carried across to their plantations institutions that went back to the medieval boroughs. The proprietary colonies rested on old feudal precedents. Both efforts at imitation quickly proved unstable, however, and the colonies of either sort passed through a period of rapid change.

The problem of changing political forms was, of course, also troubling Europe in the seventeenth century. But in the Old World this era witnessed the emergence of the centralized bureaucratic state. Theory and practice moved in the same direction, toward the derivation of all authority from a single source, such as the Crown, however defined.

The colonies accepted the theory. Their most prominent men were surprisingly legalistic and had no inclination to dispute the authority under which their government functioned. But practice took another direction. Power tended to devolve to its local sources. Whether that involved the town, as in New England, or the local powers sitting in the vestry, as in Virginia, the characteristic political organization was decentralized. Whatever acknowledgment might be given to the authority of the Crown, political institutions were decisively shaped by the necessity of defining connections to local power. Significantly, the most stable colonies of this period were Connecticut and Rhode Island, where the organization of local government in the towns preceded and remained basic to the organization of central political institutions.

The dispersal of power to local sources was, however, characteristic of other, nonpolitical institutions also. The churches developed a *de facto* congregational form, despite the fact that their communicants theoretically held to a belief in centralized authority. Apart from the Plymouth Separatists, there was no disposition to challenge the traditional hierarchical and centralized structure of the church. Yet, the New England Puritans, once here, found themselves closer to the Separatists than to the Church of England of which they had expected to remain adherents. Most strikingly, the members of the Church of England throughout the colonies continued to acknowledge that a bishop was essential to the full practice of their religious duties. Yet in practice, delays, obstructions, and evasions prevented the emergence of an episcopate before the Revolution. Religious functions too seemed to devolve to their local sources.

These developments were related to the structure of the population, which was also anomalous in the sense that it ran contrary to the expectations of those who planted the colonies. The founders expected that their societies would consist of functionaries and peasants. The companies anticipated plantations populated by servants, that is, by soldiers and clerks, who would carry forth the business of trade and defense. The proprietors looked forward to a population of native or imported peasants who would reconstruct some sort of manorial system in the New World. This was evident, even toward the end of the seventeenth century, in the plans of the Carolina proprietors.

Instead, surprisingly, all the colonies developed a society of yeomen and artisans

— not by plan, and often, it seemed, simply through the want of an alternative. Yet the consequences were radical. There developed in the mainland colonies of the seventeenth century a wide variety of social types, a microcosm of the Old World as it were, ranging from slaves and servants at the bottom through yeoman farmers and artisans, to a gentry at the top. Within this variety of types there were both the recognition of actual stratification and a high degree of mobility. The fact that a servant was different from a yeoman and yet that a servant could become a yeoman led to the definition of a new concept of freedom and to the development of distinctive social institutions.

In the structure of the population, therefore, as in the evolution of governmental and other institutions, the seventeenth-century colonies followed an abnormal path, one which was different from the experience of Europeans at home or in other parts of the world and one which was contrary to their own expectations. The causes of this abnormality were complex. In part it was due to the extensive quality of the land to which these settlers came. They had pitched upon the edge of an almost empty continent; and the existence of open space to which men could withdraw remained a constant condition of their life. That in itself was an element tending toward looseness of social structure.

Furthermore, they encountered no going society with fixed institutions of its own. The Indians who inhabited the region had a culture, of course. But they were so few in number and so little prepared to resist as to have relatively little effect upon the whites. The Europeans of the same period in India or even in Africa were significantly influenced by the institutions they encountered there; those in America, hardly at all. Indeed the American colonists were often disappointed in their natives. The continued inclination to refer to the Indian kings, queens, and nobility reflected an eagerness to discover in the red men a fixity of forms that did not exist. Its absence was a further source of instability.

But most important, the institutional looseness of the seventeenth century was related to the way of life that developed in the colonies. The American seventeenth-century social order was disorderly by the expectations of normal men. But the settlers were not normal men. The terms of American existence compelled frequent and serious deviations from the norms of behavior accepted by the men who peopled the colonies. Every aspect of their existence combined to produce disorder.

The century was occupied by a succession of waves of immigration, so that the experience of transplantation was not limited to one group or to one moment, but was repeated again and again. And that experience caused enormous shocks in the personal and social relationships of those involved in it. The circumstances of the crossing at once threw these men and women into disorder. It takes an effort of the imagination to conceive of the conditions of life on the three ships which came to Jamestown in 1607. These vessels of 100, 40, and 20 tons, respectively, were laden with the gear and the supplies and provisions for the voyage and also with all that the plantations would at first require. Yet, there was also room on these tiny craft for 140 people. The settlers were almost five months in transit, at the mercy of the winds and weather and of the unknown sea. Later voyages involved larger ships — but not much larger; and the time spent in crossing shrank, although not dependably. But accommodations were never commodious and the experience was never pleasant. Few immigrants recovered quickly from the difficulties of crowded and uncomfortable weeks at sea in tiny ships that carried them to their strange destinations.

Many of those who made the crossing were people whose life was already in disorder. Often, they had already been displaced and compelled to move once; their stamina had already been tried. The residents of London who came to the colonies had, as likely as not, been born in the country and had drifted to the city. Others among the newcomers, like the Pilgrims, like the Finns who settled on the Delaware, like the German sectarians, were already uprooted and had already deviated from the settled life of stable societies.

Hard conditions of life compounded the disorder for a greater or lesser time in each of the colonies. Everywhere the settlers who survived could look back upon a starving time, a period when the margin between life and death narrowed perilously and when the very existence of the feeble societies hung by a thread. So, in retrospect, the Virginia burgesses looked back to the administration of Sir Thomas Smith and recalled:

> The allowance in those tymes for a man was only eight ounces of meale and half a pinte of pease for a daye the one & the other mouldy, rotten, full of Cobwebs and Maggots loathsome to man and not fytt for beasts; which forced many to flee for reliefe to the Savage Enemy, who being taken againe were putt to sundry deaths as by hanginge, shootinge and breakinge upon the wheele; & others were forced by famine to filch for their bellies, of whom one for steelinge 2 or 3 pints of oatmeale had a bodkinge thrust through his tongue and was tyed with a chaine to a tree untill he starved. Yf a man through his sickness had not been able tow worke, he had no allowance at all, and so consequently perished. Many through these extremities, being weery of life digged holes in the earth and hidd themselues till they famished. . . . So lamentable was our scarsitie that we were constrained to eat Doggs, Catts, ratts, Snakes, Toad-Stooles, horsehides and wt nott; one man out of the mysery he endured, killinge his wiefe powdered her upp to eate here, for wch he was burned. Many besides fedd on the Corps of dead men, and one who had gotten unsatiable, out of custome to that foode could not be restrayned, until such tyme as he was executed for it, and indeed soe miserable was our estate that the happyest day that eyer some of them hoped to see, was when the Indyands had killed a mare they wishing whilst she was boyling that St *Tho*: *Smith* [the Governor] was uppon her backe in the kettle.

Later prosperity never dimmed the memory of the early difficulties; and there remained always areas where the trying experience of survival was being repeated. As settlement spread, there was always at its edge a brutal and disorderly struggle for existence.

Some of the harsh features of pioneer life disappeared with the development of settled communities. But others endured for a long time. A high death rate remained constant and throughout the century embittered the personal relationships of the colonists. In the first winter at Plymouth, one-half the Pilgrims died. Between 1606 and 1623 about five thousand immigrants came to Virginia. They had children and raised families. Yet at the end of that period there were only one thousand left.

Nor was this cruel mortality simply a condition of initial settlement. It remained characteristic of seventeenth-century life. Infant mortality was murderous; and although many children were born, the number of survivors was distressingly low. It was rare in this century that a husband and wife should live into old age together. The frequency of remarriages by widowers and widows showed how familiar a factor in life was death.

More generally, constant nagging difficulties intruded in the management of the details of home or farm or shop. Old habits did not apply to new circumstances; and it was hard for individuals to fulfill the personal, family, religious, or communal roles they were expected to play. This, perhaps, explains the harsh judgments that the colonists were always making of one another. The lack of stability or orderliness even in the home was particularly troublesome. In the tight quarters of the seventeenth-century houses, large families had to learn to live with one another, and also with the Negroes and other strange servants. Emotional strains were inevitable and weak community discipline sometimes led to violence, desertion, or criminality. The lack of permanence, the constant mobility that shifted individuals and families about through the continent exacerbated all these tensions. By contrast, the old homes of the Old World in retrospect came to embody orderliness. Often, in thinking of what they had left in Europe, the colonists expressed a poignant sense of separation from the source of stability and culture.

Finally, their life was rendered harsh by the apparent hostility of the elements. The wilderness itself created problems for men accustomed to open spaces. In the folk literature of Europe the forests were peopled by wild, inhuman creatures often hostile to man. In America even the climate and the changes of the seasons were unfamiliar. Most important, the denizens of the wilderness were a constant threat to the flimsy structure of civilization. The Indians grew more and more fearsome as the century advanced; and on the borders French and Spanish Papists were a continuing threat. In the face of all these dangers, there was no security in the settlements. The precariousness of existence was at the root of the disorder that overwhelmed them. Everywhere from the moment they boarded ship the first Americans found risks of the greatest order inseparable from the conduct of their lives.

The native-born, that is, the second and third generations, were more at home in the wilderness and, never having known Europe, were less pressed by the necessity of making comparisons with that which had been left across the ocean. They had sources of instability of their own, in their heightened rootlessness and mobility. But they were likely to accept the disorder and precariousness that troubled their immigrant parents or grandparents as a way of life and to adjust to its conditions.

The men subject to so many elements of abnormality and disorder necessarily interpreted their own experiences in a distinctive way. They were constantly driven to ask questions that other men had no need to raise. People whose families had lived generations without end in the same village had no cause to wonder why they were where they were or to speculate on the significance of having been placed where they were. But the immigrants whose conditions of life and whose institutions had been driven so far from every ordinary course necessarily had to seek answers to such questions.

The necessity was particularly urgent in the seventeenth century when men ascribed to every event a deep meaning. Nothing that occurred was taken as simply random. Everything was the product of the intent of some mover. A tree did not fall; it was felled. If a monstrous child was born or a school of porpoises seen, that was a sign of something. In the same way, there was necessarily a significance to the painful shift of population that created colonial society. In an era in which men believed literally in signs, portents, curses, spells, and imprecations, to say nothing of witches, they had to seek a meaning to their own unusual experiences.

The first Americans continued the habit of explaining every occurrence in terms of a familiar dichotomy. On the one hand, they could see in some events good impulses, derived from God and reflecting a divine intent. But they also found abundant evidence of evil impulses or dark desires emanating from satanic intentions. The fearful men who lived with risk and disorder were constantly on the lookout for the means of identifying and interpreting what happened to them. As a simple matter of a guide to personal life, it was essential to know whether an incident was the product of divine or devilish interference.

The same confrontation of good and evil could be seen in the social world that surrounded the individual. There in the external wilderness, in the savagery of life without reliable guides, were the sources of corruption. Were not the Indians imps of Satan, and the Papists, creatures of the Devil, and was not therefore the whole American experience one which endangered man's salvation? On the other hand, was it not possible to identify that which lay across the ocean with that which was good and conducive to man's salvation? Europe, from the American perspective, was the source of morality, of law, of order, and of Christianity. But in that event, how was the colonist to explain his migration, away from order to disorder, away from law to savagery, away from Christianity to the spiritual perils of the New World?

The question thus raised could be answered on both the personal and the social level; and the answer on the one offers an analogy to the answer on the other. The character of this response may be discerned in the poem that a grieving grandmother wrote in the 1660's to explain to herself the death of three grandchildren within four years. All were under the age of four. Surely these tender innocents had been stricken down through no fault, no evil deed, of their own. There was, however, a reason. Anne Bradstreet explained:

> By nature Trees do rot when they are grown.
> And Plumbs and Apples thoroughly ripe do fall,
> And corn and grass are in their season mown,
> And time brings down what is both strong and tall.
> But plants new set to be eradicate,
> And buds new blown, to have so short a date,
> Is by his hand alone that guides nature and fate.

An unnatural misfortune of this sort was thus in itself evidence of a particular divine concern. While the nature of God's intentions might be inscrutable to men and closed to fallible human understanding, the event itself nevertheless was a sure indication of some particular purpose. It could even supply a kind of assurance of divine interest and oversight.

It was also true that a way of life out of the usual course was evidence of some particular design. The whole character of the plantation of these settlements, by its very abnormality, indicated that there had been some special purpose to the coming to America. The fact that this whole area had been withheld from previous human habitation indicated that there was some special intention for its use. The fact that their institutions and their course of life did not follow any usual pattern was itself a sign that these settlements had an unusual destiny.

As the immigrants examined their own coming, they could see evidence of a larger will in their own careers. Their migration was largely the product of their own helplessness, of social forces over which they had no control — persecution by the Established Church, changes in agriculture and the unavailability of land, the disruption of the wool trade and the growth in the number of men without employment. But on the other hand, the migration was also the product of their own choice. Not all those who were persecuted or displaced or unemployed had come. Migration stemmed from a compulsion that forced the emigrant to leave and also the positive act of will by which he decided to go. The emigrant might thus be compared to a legate dispatched on a mission by a potentate, a legate who accepted the errand voluntarily. The fact, too, that not all those who went arrived reflected a process of survival and seemed to imply a kind of selection of some from among the rest.

In no other way could these people account for the experience but by the conclusion that somehow they had been chosen to depart from the ways of ordinary men and to become in their own lives extraordinary for some special purpose.

Among some of the colonists this intention was spelled out with considerable sophistication. New England Puritans thought of themselves as led by Divine Providence to a new Canaan where they were to create a new kind of society that would be a model for the whole world. Their city upon a hill would ultimately be emulated by all other men. It was a part of the scheme of divine redemption, occupying the stage at a critical turn in the cosmic drama that had begun with the Creation, that had been continued in the Reformation, and that would end in the Second Coming.

Elsewhere the explanation was less sophisticated, less explicit, and less literate. But there nonetheless emerged again and again expressions of conviction in a sense of mission — to convert the Indians or to civilize the wilderness. The newness of a New World reserved for some ultimate purpose and waiting for those who would bring it under cultivation or use it as the setting for their own experiments in salvation confirmed the successive groups of immigrants, in the seventeenth century and later, in the belief that there was a profound importance to their coming.

The second and third generations were different in this respect also. They were natives, not subject to the strains of the decisions that had burdened their parents or grandparents. Indeed, in the eyes of the immigrants, the second generation seemed a ruder, less cultivated, and wilder people. That accounts for the complaints about declension and about the loss of the sense of mission that began to be sounded in the last quarter of the century.

But the second generation had actually not lost the sense of mission so much as transformed it beyond the recognition of their predecessors. The very fact that they were a wilderness people, at home in the New World, gave them a sense of power. They could deal with the forest and the savage as their parents could not. Out of contact with the standards of the Old World, they developed their own, and their ability to do so generated confidence in their own capacity for achievement.

Therefore they too, although in a different form, were moved by a conviction of the grandeur of their destiny; and they could link that conviction to the potentialities of the land, which was not alien to them as it had been to their parents. Pride in their own power and in the future greatness of their homes created for them a picture of themselves as a people destined to conquer, an idea to be eloquently expressed just after the turn of the century by Robert Beverley.

In a variety of forms, the sense of mission has remained a continuing theme in American life. In the eighteenth century Jefferson's generation gave it secularized liberal expression. The nineteenth century imbued it with the spirit of liberal reform. And at the opening of the twentieth century, it was woven into the ideology of imperialism. So, too, social disorder, the acceptance of risk, and the precariousness of life that developed in the seventeenth century long remained characteristic of America. It was the significance of the seventeenth century to bring into being peculiarities of character and institutions, the influence of which was long thereafter felt in the history of the United States.

The New England Way: Puritan Quest for Utopia

Most of those who left Europe for America came to improve their lot by acquiring a larger share of the world's goods. Settlers in colonial New England were no exception, but the Puritans who established the Massachusetts Bay Colony were also driven by a vision of recreating an archaic Christian commonwealth that had once existed when the Christian faith was young and uncorrupted. In the following selection, Alan Simpson explores the Puritan quest, explaining how the vision of establishing "a city upon a hill" in a wilderness shaped the settlement of New England and why that adventure ended in failure.

Puritans came to America to escape, not simply from persecution by English authorities, but because they had lost hope of purifying the church in England. This was a cause they regarded as the first step in the struggle to regain control over forces that were transforming England from a more stable, placid, and secure place in which to live into an unpredictable, rapidly changing modern society in which no one's position was secure, especially no one in middle classes. Neither the nobility, whose positions were fairly fixed, nor the poor peasantry, who pessimistically accepted as fixed their lowly position, proved as receptive to the voices spreading the gospel of the Protestant Reformation in Britain. But to middle-class folk, Protestantism was a compelling new vision.

Protestantism switched the burden of Christian salvation from the shoulders of the church, and placed it directly on those of the sinners. Since neither priest nor Pope could intercede with God, each man must be his own priest. Moreover, it insisted that God preordained each person's spiritual fate, yet no one could know for certain what that fate was — Heaven or Hell. The result was that the Christian pilgrimage was redefined as an endless search for signs of God's grace, for indications that one was among the saved, and evidence for this was man's capacity to resist temptation. Puritans could not rely on a merciful God who would forgive; they lived in awe of a stern God who demanded that men actively struggle, not only against sin in their personal lives, but in their society.

With such convictions, Puritans attempted to establish a Christian commonwealth in Massachusetts which made the welfare of the community superior to the wishes of the individual. By imposing communal constraints on settlement patterns and on all forms of individual enterprise, Puritans hoped to create a stable and just society modeled on their notions of God's design. Such an experiment could only be attempted in a wilderness where no kings or bishops could interfere, yet the empty spaces, the limitless abundance, and the weakness of authority spelled ultimate failure. The Puritans learned that even in America man could not escape the physical world.

FOR FURTHER READING:

HALL, DAVID, ed. *Puritanism in Seventeenth-Century Massachusetts.* New York: Holt, Rinehart & Winston, 1956.*

MILLER, PERRY. *Errand into the Wilderness.* New York: Harper & Row, Publishers, Torchbooks, 1956.*

MORGAN, EDMUND S. *The Puritan Dilemma: The Story of John Winthrop.* Boston: Little, Brown & Company, 1958.*

Asterisk denotes paperback edition.

The Covenanted Community

ALAN SIMPSON

The first chance to see what the Puritan saint would make of life, if he had the freedom to experiment, came in America. The early history of Massachusetts (together with that of Plymouth, Connecticut, and New Haven, for the differences are unimportant from our point of view) is the story of men who shared an ideal, left the Old World to realize it in the New, only to discover when the work of planting was done that the spirit had evaporated. Frustration was the fate which awaited every Puritan. In England, where the defeat came in war, it has all the features of tragedy; here, where there was no defeat but apparent success, it becomes a kind of ironic tale.

The Puritans who came to America continued to have much in common with those who stayed at home. Take, for instance, that apocalyptic view of their place in history which all Puritans shared and which can hardly be overemphasized if we want to understand the quality of their enthusiasm. We are all familiar today with the Communist's conviction that he is moving toward a preordained victory. His science tells him that the historical process is obeying a determinate logic, and, so far from the inevitability of this process slowing down his efforts, it acts as an enormous spur to them. The Puritan has a similar theory of history and the same sort of compulsion to cooperate with destiny. Admittedly, Divine Providence is a good deal more mysterious than dialectical materialism. But this unpredictability, if an argument in some situations for more patience than a Communist could admit in his timetable, always offers the possibility of a miraculous delivery. The winters of the church may be cruelly long; but when that frozen world thaws, as in the springtime of the Reformation, the whole earth seems to rush toward its harvest.

The Puritan thought of human history as the field in which God gathered his saints, saving the few from the fate which all had deserved and imparting to that few some knowledge of his Will. For reasons known only to himself, God had permitted ignorance of his Will to envelop the visible church between the age of the apostles and the age of the Reformation. These thirteen or fourteen centuries had seen a downward swing to the lowest depths of depravity; then a slow ascent had begun as God chose to reveal more and more of himself. Wave after wave of witnesses had been summoned to testify; country after country seemed likely to be the scene in which the destiny of the age would be fulfilled. On the crest of that movement stood the Puritan, with his "panting, longing, eager" desire to find the revelation com-

Source: Alan Simpson, *Puritanism in Old and New England* (Chicago: University of Chicago Press, 1955), chap. 2, "The Covenanted Community," pp. 19–38.

pleted in himself. These adjectives are not mine, nor are they those of some simple enthusiast. They might be Oliver Cromwell's or John Milton's. They are, in fact, the words of John Cotton, the leading intellectual among the founders of the New England Way.

Incidentally, the intellectual quality in the Puritan's piety can easily be overstated. When every compliment has been paid to Professor Miller's studies of Puritanism — and I yield to no one in my admiration for those ingenious works — at least one gentle criticism may be made. He has told us too much about the Puritan mind and not enough about the Puritan's feelings. If the seventeenth-century Puritan, with his formal training in scholasticism, usually tries to give a rational account of his faith, it is the stretched passion which makes him what he is. They are people who suffered and yearned and strived with an unbelievable intensity; and no superstructure of logic ought to be allowed to mask that turmoil of feeling.

It may be said, of course, that the Puritan was better prepared for disappointment than most men and therefore less disposed to commit himself to a utopian dream. It was some such thought as this that led Professor Miller to say that a disillusioned Puritan is impossible to conceive. Was it not the Puritan who had preached the arbitrariness of God and the depravity of man? Who was he to falter if the age missed what in his foolish pride he had allowed himself to believe was its destiny? I can only say this was not the mood of 1630, when the Pilgrims left England to build their Zion in the wilderness. It was not the mood of Oliver Cromwell when he told a Parliament of Puritan saints that they stood on the edge of the promises and the prophecies. It was the Puritan's compromise with defeat, and when he finally made it — either in the despairing cry of the English Puritan, "God has spit in our faces," or in the melancholy dirge of the American Puritan at the end of the century — the crusade was finished.

The founders of New England not only shared the apocalyptic view of history with the Puritans whom they left behind. Their confession of faith, their search for regeneration and sanctification, their techniques of self-trial and self-denial, all spring from the same community of experience. A series of New England sermons explaining how God calls, justifies, and sanctifies his elect; a New England diary recording an agonizing search for the evidence of this work in the diarist's soul; New England's advice to educators on the education of a saint or to businessmen on the duty of combining "diligence in business with deadness to the world"; New England's conviction that every man is his brother's keeper; New England's persuasion that a good joke ought to be balanced with some savory morsel to keep merriment in its proper bounds; New England's cultivation of the Puritan art forms: the biography of the saint, the record of divine judgments, the history which weaves both into a narrative of God's blessings and punishments — all this, and much else, can be matched on both sides of the water. Behind it shines that vision which a tinker living on the ecstatic fringe of the movement described for all Puritans in the *Pilgrim's Progress*.

The specialty of the New England Way only emerged as its founders came to grips with the problems of embodying the vision in institutions. It is suggested by that analogy which was not confined to them but which acquired a more concrete and durable form in their experience than elsewhere: the analogy between themselves and the first people who were admitted into a covenant of grace with God. New England was to be a New Israel — a covenanted community. Its founders, who had already experienced in their own lives the sensation of being offered, and of accepting, the covenant of grace, were to form themselves into a community of saints for the enjoyment of God's ordinances and the elevation of their colony into the status of a chosen people. Such seemed to be the opportunity which God, working through the secondary causes which made colonization possible at this juncture of history, was offering to the regenerate. The labor of explorers, the greed of merchants, the ambition of kings, the pressure of persecution, the incidence of economic hardship, every motive and every capacity for colonization was but a web of contrivance designed by invisible hands for ends which only the elect could fathom. The interpretation of those ends in terms of a covenanted community begins with the famous sermon by Governor Winthrop in mid-ocean and only ends among the disenchantments of the late seventeenth century after desperate efforts to recall the wandering pilgrims to a proper sense of their destiny.

Let me quote Governor Winthrop's own words. They are taken from the sermon called "A Modell of Christian Charity," which was delivered on board the *Arabella:*

> Thus stands the cause between God and us; we are entered into Covenant with him for this work; we have taken out a Commission; the Lord hath given us leave to draw our own Articles; we have professed to enterprise these actions upon these and these ends; we have hereupon besought him of favor and blessing. Now if the Lord shall please to hear us, and bring us in peace to the place we desire, then hath he ratified this Covenant and sealed our Commission, and will expect a strict performance of the Articles contained in it, but if we shall neglect the observation of these Articles which are the ends we have propounded, and dissembling with our God, shall fall to embrace this present world and prosecute our carnal intentions, seeking great things for our selves and our posterity, the Lord will surely break out in wrath against us, be revenged of such a perjured people, and make us know the price of the breach of such a Covenant.

What this decision came to mean was the tribalization of the Puritan spirit. The goals of regeneration and sanctification, common to Puritans everywhere, were to be sought within a tribal community. Let me sketch some of the implications of this conception as it appeared to its authors.

First, no diversity of opinion in fundamentals would be permitted within the tribe. Regenerate men, using that faculty of reason which grace had restored, and applying it to the Word of God as revealed in Scripture, could come to only one conclusion. Rightly informed consciences do not judge differently; they concur. What they perceive is that regenerate men must form their lives within an external discipline and cooperate in enforcing that discipline on the unregenerate. The mission of the elect is to uphold an orthodoxy.

The external discipline of the tribe would involve, in Winthrop's words, "a due form of ecclesiastical and civil government." So far as the first was concerned, all Puritans believed that the true form of ecclesiastical government had been prescribed in Scripture, and what these Puritans found in Scripture was authority for confining church membership to "visible saints." Churches would be composed of groups of converted souls who formed a covenant among themselves to create a church and who looked forward to a perpetual succession of saints who would enter the church covenant as the work of conversion continued. The orthodox idea of a church, whether in Anglican England or Presbyterian Scotland, was a body coextensive with the community, admission to which depended on baptism, subsequently confirmed by a profession of faith. But this New England church is going to be built out of the conversion experience, and it is assumed that a subjective experience can be detected by objective tests. However, there is one other class of members attached to the church besides the converted. God's covenant with Abraham had included not only Abraham but his seed. The children of the converted will be admitted to baptism, in the expectation that they will eventually be able to attest the conversion experience and qualify for full membership.

These churches, around which the New England towns will be built, are autonomous congregations. The powers of church government were not given by God to bishops, or to Presbyterian assemblies, but to them. However, no anarchic consequences need be feared from their autonomy. Rightly informed consciences reach the same conclusions; that is the essence of the promise. Congregations are expected to consult if they encounter difficulties, and erroneous consciences, persisting in their errors, will find themselves opposed by the massed forces of orthodoxy.

So much for the ecclesiastical discipline. But in a convenanted community the discipline of the state must also be directed by saints. It is true that all Puritans talk about the separation of church and state, and this is one of the things that distinguish them from all Anglicans. But nine out of ten Puritans only want to separate church and state in order to bind them together again. In other words, they have to break the indissoluble unity of church and state in Anglican England so as to get the church on its scriptural basis, Presbyterian or Congregational, as the case may be; but, once on that basis, they expect the state to uphold it, to be "the nursing father" of the church. Separation of church and state, in such a context, meant simply a division of functions between two partners with a tendency to reduce the state to a junior partner where the clergy claimed a superior insight into the Divine Will. In New England it was expected to be a partnership in unison, for church and state alike were to be dominated by saints.

The same compact among saints would underlie the civil government as it underlay the ecclesiastical government. The idea that political authority, while authorized by God, derives from the consent of the people was a familiar one in the English tradition, and Puritans invoked it to suit their purposes. The founders of Massachusetts were prepared to interpret their charter as a social covenant, and the communities which hived off from Massachusetts used the covenant device to launch their plantations. But the consent which is expressed in these compacts is not to be confused with any notion of popular sovereignty. Popular sovereignty is the grossest atheism in a Puritan universe governed by God. It is a consent to be governed according to the ordinances of God: an acceptance by saints of the political obligations of a chosen people.

These compacts do not commit them to any particular form of government. Forms of civil government, unlike forms of ecclesiastical government, are not prescribed in Scripture, and there is no reason why English representative institutions and English common-law principles should not be admitted into the holy community provided they do not prevent saints from governing that community, from protecting its church, and from making such changes as are necessary to bring English legal custom in line with the laws of God. However, this is some proviso. It means that in a remote corner of His Majesty's realm there will be a group of one-party states, where access to power depends on evidence of conversion. Party politicians will uphold the party preacher; laws will be modified to suit the party ethic; the administration of law will not be embarrassed by procedural safeguards; and all deviationists will either repent or suffer expulsion.

So much for "the due form of ecclesiastical and civil government." One further decision will be necessary to underpin the stability of the whole enterprise: a crucial decision about the qualifications of the prophet in the chosen community. The Puritan way of life had been worked out by a learned clergy, and learning — the learning of the schools — had been regarded as an indispensable means for the discovery and the application of the Divine Will in the lives of the regenerate. However, Puritanism had preached that without grace reason was helpless, that the pilgrim must await the miracle which no merit on his part could produce, and that, once this miracle had been bestowed, Christ was "ingrafted" in his heart. Could these regenerate spirits be held within any bounds? Could reason, which had begun by abdicating its authority, reassert itself so as to insure that one true discipline which was God's design for men — or even to insure any society at all? The whole history of Puritanism is a commentary on its failure to satisfy the cravings which its preaching had aroused. It was forever producing rebellions against its own teachers: rebellions within the learned camp and rebellions from outside that camp against the assertion that learned reason had anything to teach the illuminated spirit.

How much of this the founders of the covenanted community foresaw is open to question. The history of the Reformation had been full of it, and they were always being reminded by their enemies of the risks they ran; but in the nature of things these risks would not be fully revealed until the opportunity came for the saint to claim his privileges — the opportunity so delightfully expressed by that admirer of Anne Hutchinson who said to Edward Johnson: "I'll bring you to a woman that preaches better gospel than any of your black-coats that have been at the Ninneversity." However, whether they foresaw it or not, it is certain that they carried with them the ideal of a learned clergy, and everyone knows of their determination to reproduce on the frontier the basic intellectual institutions of the Old World: the school, the college, the library, and the press. What is less clear, perhaps, since Professor Morison wrote his history of Harvard, is the purpose of these institutions. The merits of that great work speak for themselves, but it has one small flaw. The author has tried, in devious ways, to redeem his alma mater from the suspicion of being too much troubled by sin. But the founders of Harvard College would hardly have thanked him for this carnal enterprise. What they aimed at producing was not Christian gentlemen with a liberal education but saints with a saving knowledge. The college was to be a school of prophets — learned prophets, certainly, but emphatically prophets. What else would a chosen people expect from its educational institutions?

I have tried to sketch the lines along which the vision would be embodied in these communities. Between 1630 and the mid-forties the work of planting and consolidating went on, until at last one species of Puritanism had been stabilized. Viewed simply as an achievement of order in the wilderness, out of human beings as potentially explosive as Puritans, this was certainly impressive. But it is no slight to the leadership to suggest that the problem of welding communities out of Puritan material was somewhat simplified for them.

The most obvious simplification was the opportunity to create a new community without having to tear an old one to pieces and to go on creating new communities if the first proved disappointing. These Puritans leave all their opponents behind them. They pass straight from settled life to the tasks of creating a new life without any disorderly interlude. When they reach the wilderness, work crowds in and danger binds them. If the worse comes to the worst, there is always the frontier. The deviationists can take their chances in Rhode Island. Thomas Hooker, who is no deviationist, but who may have felt that Massachusetts was too small for two such

redoubtable saints as himself and Mr. Cotton, can become the founder of Connecticut. The saints in England must often have sighed for some such *Lebensraum.*

The other great advantage might seem to be the preagreement about ecclesiastical
policy. Puritans had little difficulty in agreeing about doctrine. What they usually
disagreed about was the form of church government within which the elect should
fulfil their mission. When the Puritans came into power in England, they were prepared to fight a civil war over the rival merits of Presbyterianism, Nonseparating
Congregationalism, and Separatism. New England, although it shares part of this
experience in its contests with separatists like Roger Williams, rallies with surprising
ease around the principle of Nonseparating Congregationalism and has relatively
little difficulty with Presbyterianism. How did this happen?

It used to be thought that the adoption of Congregationalism was suggested by
the example of Plymouth which the main body of the colonists found when they got
there. It is now assumed that Professor Miller has conclusively demonstrated a pre-
engagement among the majority of the clergymen which can be traced back through
their Dutch experience to the original advocates of Nonseparating Congregationalism as a middle way between Presbyterianism and Separatism. However, Professor
Miller has to admit that some ministers were Presbyterians; that others, who had
not gone through the Dutch experience, might have been uncommitted, and that the
views of the secular leaders, at the time of their arrival, are largely unknown.

Doubtless the Congregationalists were in a position to take the initiative. But the
acquiescence in that initiative must certainly have been helped by the composition
of the Puritan population that came over here and by the frontier situation. Congregationalism aroused objections in England as an unsuitable organization for a community which was both hierarchical and centralized. It deprived the great Puritan
magnate of his power to appoint ministers. It seemed to place hereditary influence
at the mercy of the conversion experience, for, unless his children could attest it,
they would presumably find themselves deprived of both church membership and
political power. Worst of all, it looked like a dangerous loosening of the social
bonds to substitute a church of autonomous congregations for the corporate and
centrally controlled church of tradition. Just how dangerous was to become clear
enough in the Civil Wars when Congregationalism, in its separatist form, became
the medium through which every kind of radicalism found expression. But few of
these fears were realistic in New England. Puritan peers and very rich Puritans, the
backbone of English Presbyterianism, were conspicuous by their absence. The
lesser leaders who came over were reasonably insured against social, as distinct from
theological, unrest by their monopoly of talent and by the frontier opportunities
which took the sting out of class bitterness. And the communities to be administered were, after all, a handful of decentralized settlements as compared with a
highly integrated England. Congregationalism commended itself to clerical special-
ists like Cotton and Hooker as the one form of church government prescribed by
God for his saints; but, if the local situation had not made it a safe enough proposition, the Word would doubtless have seemed less clear.

So much for the New England Way viewed simply as an achievement of order.
But how far did it fulfil the expectations of its founders: that this covenanted people
would represent the ideal toward which all history was converging; that there would
be a succession of saints with the same intense piety as themselves; and that under
the rule of these saints the whole community would be held to the obligations of the
covenant and sanctified by its blessings?

Much of the frustration which follows is common to Puritans everywhere. They had dreamed of themselves as a united army forming the vanguard of history; but the army splinters into columns, battalions, and platoons, while history seems to be marching on. They had thought that conversion could become an institution, but they find themselves with church members where they had hoped for saints. They had devised one of the most formidable disciplines ever seen for keeping sin within bounds, but there seemed to be as much of it inside the covenant as outside. They had demanded an impossible tension from the elect and an impossible submission from the mass. Everywhere the taut springs relax, the mass rebels, and compromises eat away at a distinction on which the whole system was based.

The history of the New England Way is the history of a losing struggle to preserve the intensity of the experience of the saint and his authority over society. On the one hand, a church of visible saints, each of whom could attest the miracle of conversion, is gradually transformed into a church where membership depends on a profession of faith and a standard of Puritan morality. On the other hand, the church, thus formalized, is deprived of its organic control of political power and forced to depend for its control over society on the opportunity its clergy have had to make themselves a ruling class and the allies of ruling families.

The decay of spiritual intensity is the theme of almost all the founders as they survey the tribal community in their declining years. Few things are more moving than the comparisons drawn by a Bradford, a Winthrop, or a Shephard between the spirit that sustained them and the spirit they find around them.

Let me quote from Bradford — that simple hero who never forgot, in all the labor of planting a colony, that his true home was elsewhere. He had copied into his journal the claim which the leaders of their little church had made when they applied in 1617 for permission to settle in the New World:

> We are knit together as a body in a most strict and sacred bond and covenant of the Lord, of the violation whereof we make great conscience, and by virtue whereof we do hold ourselves straightly tied to all care of each other's good, and of the whole by every one, and so mutually.

When he read that entry in his old age, he wrote this confession on the back of the page:

> O sacred bond, whilst inviolably preserved! How sweet and precious were the fruits that flowed from the same, but when this fidelity decayed, then their ruin approached. O that these ancient members had not died or been dissipated (if it had been the will of God) or else that this holy care and constant faithfulness had still lived, and remained with those that survived, and were in times afterward added unto them. But (alas) that subtle serpent hath slyly wound in himself under fair pretenses of necessity and the like to untwist these sacred bonds and ties, and as it were insensibly, by degrees, to dissolve or in a great measure to weaken, the same. I have been happy, in my first times, to see, and with much comfort to enjoy, the blessed fruits of this sweet communion, but it is now a part of my misery in old age, to find and feel the decay and want thereof (in a great measure), and with grief and sorrow of heart to lament and bewail the same. And for others warning and admonition, and my own humiliation, do I here note the same.

What had happened to them is part of the common experience of all creative revivals, when the first generation hands over to the second, when the organizer follows the visionary, and habit replaces direct experience as the source of guidance. But, of course, it is colored by their own circumstances. There is little to keep alive their memories of persecution. There is less and less to sustain their sense of the

New World as a beacon for the Old when the progress of events in England reduces the New England Way first to a backwater of the Puritan spirit and later to a provincial anachronism. There is plenty of evidence that, in spite of all their precautions, worldliness is still with them and that saints who struggle to rule the world may find themselves ruled by it — especially the Puritan, who develops for religious purposes a type of character which can hardly fail to be a worldly success.

All this they see. What they fail to see is that the very work to which they have set their hands with so much resolution — the tribalization of the Puritan experience — is stifling its free spirit. Every repression of dissent, every insistence on the subordination of subjective experience to the judgment of the church, makes the work of enlisting zeal so much harder. They were probably right in thinking that order was possible on no other terms; but so was Anne Hutchinson when she accused them of substituting a covenant of works for a covenant of grace. Obedience to an external order, rather than immediate confrontation of God, was becoming, in spite of its formal theology, the criterion of New England Puritanism.

Before this first generation had passed away, it was obvious that the second generation would not be able to attest the conversion experience in sufficient numbers to perpetuate the succession of saints. It is some testimony to the severity of their standards that the fact was faced: that the second generation was held to be, and admitted itself to be, deficient in grace, though it was willing to support the church and to conform itself to its discipline. However, the sincerity of all parties only heightens the irony of a situation in which a chosen people cannot find enough chosen people to prolong its existence. Everything depended on saints. They composed the church and ruled the state. What would happen if the supply ran out? The escape was found through the famous halfway covenant, a device whereby the second generation was admitted to church membership, after making a profession of obedience, and so enabled to have its children baptized. The return to tradition had begun. Of course the effort to produce conversions among the children and grandchildren was not abandoned. The preachers kept reminding themselves, and the clans, that the covenant had included Abraham's seed. But somehow, in spite of all their struggles, the religious experiences of the first generation refused to become a hereditary endowment. "Doth not a careless, remiss, flat, dry, cold, dead frame of spirit, grow in upon us secretly, strangely, prodigiously?" We are hardly surprised to learn that the halfway covenant was in most cases just a halfway house between a church from which all but the saint had been excluded and one in which all but the flagrant sinner was admitted.

It was inevitable that this subsidence of the saints into a company of conformists should be reflected in the deterioration of Puritan piety. The congregations are not, of course, to be judged by the condemnations which the preachers heaped on them as part of the Puritan ritual during that prolonged jeremiad known to history as "God's controversy with New England." The deterioration is not a matter of crimes or misdemeanors. It is entirely compatible with the most persevering virtues. But it means contracted sensibility; gestures replacing feelings; taste subduing zeal; pride elbowing out humility; intellect playing a game; divided souls acting a part their ancestors have forced on them. It is the well-meant mimicries of Samuel Sewall which produce such farcical effects when compared with the old, high seriousness. The diarist who finds it "an awful yet pleasing treat" to review the coffins in his family vault has traveled a long way from Bradford or Winthrop. Equally far is the distance between the Puritan who knew the difference between spiritual and financial success and his descendant who sometimes confused them. The old Puritans had a grim description for this compromise with the covenant: they called it "the forms of godliness without the power."

Meanwhile, as a utopian church subsides into an established church, its grip over political power also relaxes. An early symptom was that pressure for a rule of law as opposed to a rule of discretion which distinguished the politics of Englishmen everywhere in the seventeenth century. Saints in power were always tempted to demand as free a hand for themselves as possible. A life-tenure for the trusted saint seemed to Cotton, as it later seemed to Milton, the best security for the holy commonwealth, and Winthrop's effort to keep a wide discretion in the hands of a chosen few has its counterpart in Cromwell's practice. But on both sides of the water the parliamentary tradition refused to be ousted by the theocrats. In Old England it was temporarily swept aside and then vindicated at the expense of the saints. In New England the saints discovered early that they would have to compromise with it if they hoped to control it. They were not even able to establish the system in Massachusetts without concessions to the principles of limited government which were extracted by the freemen in their struggles with the magistrates.

The intention, notwithstanding these concessions, was to maintain a theocracy within the forms of representative government, and the essence of the system was the restriction of political power to church members. In Massachusetts and New Haven this was achieved by confining the franchise to the elite. In Connecticut the same result could be expected without a formal restriction. But in the long run this monopoly of power was bound to be weakened by combined pressure from inside and outside: the pressure of expanding communities for a relaxation of religious tests and the pressure of imperial authority on a colonial theocracy. New Haven, the purest theocracy of the original settlements, had already suffered from its restrictive practices before its enforced absorption in Connecticut in 1662. Massachusetts, under pressure from England, went through the motions of liberalizing its religious tests at the same time. Finally, with the loss of the old charter in 1684, and the issue of a new one in 1691, the custodians of the Puritan ideal in Massachusetts were obliged to defend it under increasingly difficult conditions.

The power to choose their governor had passed to the Crown. Synods no longer advised legislatures. Boston flaunted the corruptions of a colonial court, the heresies of enforced toleration, and the sins of a thriving seaport before the eyes of the faithful, while the secularized culture of western Europe seeped in through a hundred different channels. No doubt all was far from lost. Preachers might keep their hold on rural communities by the combined force of personality and tradition. Conversions would certainly come back again; and the notion of a chosen people, still maintained in the pulpit, was only beginning its career in the world. But none of this should obscure the fact that an effort to escape from history into a utopia ruled by saints had suffered its usual failure.

The Plantation South

The United States was formed out of highly distinctive regions, so much so, that not until almost a century after the republic was born, did the nation establish, through civil war, its supremacy over its sections. The roots of sectionalism go back into America's colonial period. The New England, middle, and southern colonies each had enough common characteristics to distinguish them from one another. On the other hand, a heightened sense of sectional identity awaited the struggle for independence that propelled Americans into a national political arena where they competed and became more self-conscious of their differences.

Two institutions defined the American South before the Civil War, and both emerged in the colonial period: slavery and the plantation system. Slave labor made plantation agriculture possible. Most colonists were farmers, who relied principally on the labor of large families. Consequently, the amount of land they could cultivate was limited, since agricultural technology was still primitive. Plantations, however, employed capital and labor to produce commercial crops, such as tobacco and rice, on a large scale. Aubrey C. Land shows in the following essay that though there were relatively few plantations — that is, large-scale enterprises — there were many "planters."

The explanation of this paradox is that most southern farmers considered themselves planters even though they operated small family farms, occasionally with a slave or two. Yet almost all aspired to a life of ease and elegance on a large, impressive estate, with a great mansion and thousands of acres, tilled by hundreds of slaves. Few achieved this dream. Land was easy to acquire, but not many accumulated the necessary capital to buy slaves. Some tried by plowing back profits from tobacco or rice into acquiring more slaves. With these they could cultivate more land, raise larger crops, and buy still more slaves. Eventually, they could lift themselves into the ranks of the leading planters. But there were other, even more important, routes to the top. According to Professor Land, enterprising southerners also engaged in trade and manufacturing, practiced law, and speculated in land. Profits from these activities provided capital for the developing plantations. Still another important source came from wealthy English merchants who advanced credit to Americans while helping market southern exports overseas. Those most skillful and aggressive in taking advantage of these opportunities formed the plantation elite, proud of their elegant, gracious life and contemptuous of the commercial spirit that they ascribed to the money-grubbing, boorish Yankee sharpers.

FOR FURTHER READING:

MORTON, LOUIS. *Robert Carter of Nomini Hall: A Virginia Tobacco Planter of the Eighteenth Century.* Charlottesville, Va.: University Press of Virginia, 1964.*

PHILLIPS, ULRICH b. *Life and Labor in the Old South.* Boston: Little, Brown & Company, 1929.*

WOODMAN, HAROLD D. *Slavery and the Southern Economy: Sources and Readings.* New York: Harcourt, Brace & World, 1966.*

Asterisk denotes a paperback edition.

Economic Base and Social Structure: The Northern Chesapeake in the Eighteenth Century AUBREY C. LAND

The *Maryland Gazette* for 18 October 1749 carried an obituary of more than common interest:

> On the Eleventh Instant Died, at his Seat on Wye River in Queen Anne's County, Richard Bennett, Esq. in the Eighty-third Year of his Age, generally lamented by all that knew him. As his great fortune enabled him to do much good, so (happily for many) his Inclination was equal to his Ability, to relieve the indigent and distressed, which he did very liberally, without regarding of what Party, Religion or Country, they were. As he was the greatest Trader in this Province, so great Numbers fell in his Debt, and a more merciful Creditor could not be, having never deprived the Widows or Orphans of his Debtors of a Support; and when what the Debtors left, was not sufficient for that purpose, frequently supply'd the deficiency. His long Experience and great Knowledge in Business, as well as his known Candor and generosity, occasion'd many to apply to him for Advice and Assistance, and none were ever disappointed of what was in his Power, and several by his means, extricated out of great Difficulties. . . .

A later issue adds some particulars:

> On Wednesday last was solemnized the Funeral of Richard Bennett, Esq. of Wye River, in a very handsome and decent Manner, by the Direction of his sole executor, the Hon. Col. Edward Lloyd. Mr. Bennett, by his Will, has forgiven above one hundred and fifty of his poor Debtors, and has made Provision for the Maintainance of many of his Overseers, and other poor Dependents, and settled a Sum of Money to be paid annually to the Poor of a Parish in Virginia: and done many other Acts of Charity and Munificence. He was supposed to be the Richest Man on the Continent. . . .

Bennett's obvious virtues as a Christian gentleman need no underscoring, but two comments of the eulogist should be noted; his great wealth and his calling as a "trader." Perhaps the enthusiastic editor went beyond the exact truth in estimating Bennett's fortune, though probably not much. The field certainly included a few other candidates for the richest man. A neighbor across the Bay, Charles Carroll, counted his total worth at something like a hundred thousand pounds sterling, including £ 30,000 loaned at 6 per cent interest. Robert Carter, south of the Potomac in Virginia, could reckon himself worth nearly as much. The second William Byrd had left an impressive heritage which his son of the same name had already begun to dissipate. Even by the standards of London these were wealthy men.

All three alternate possibilities for the title of richest man are better known than Bennett, because they have had biographers, or because they played important political roles, or both. They belong to what has been variously called the aristocracy, the ruling oligarchy, or the squirearchy. The pejorative connotations of all three terms incline me toward a label suggested by a profound student of early American social and cultural history, "the southern agrarian leaders." We can understand them in a sense as leaders of an agrarian area. But when we inquire about the eco-

Source: Aubrey C. Land, "Economic Base and Social Structure: The Northern Chesapeake in the Eighteenth Century," *Journal of Economic History*, vol. 25 (1965), pp. 639–654.

nomic milieu in which they flourished or seek the mechanisms by which they acquired their dominant positions, we are faced with some difficulties.

The traditional historiography has leaned heavily on literary evidence, and when it does not ignore these questions often gives impressions that are positively misleading. As sources, personal letters, travel accounts, and memoirs have the great merit of being relatively easy to put into context and ideal to paraphrase. A few dozen up to a few thousand items of this kind can be quilted into interesting and convincing patterns. The procedure has the limitations of the sources. Even the most acute observer focuses on objects of high visibility. The high tor eclipses the molehill in the landscape until the king falls to his death because of the "little gentleman in black velvet."

In the eighteenth-century Chesapeake, the "great planters" were the element of high visibility. They held slaves, owned vast estates, and built magnificent houses that have survived as showpieces. Visitors came under the spell of these gracious livers and left charming accounts of their balls, their tables, and their luxury. Planters themselves contributed to the effect. They wrote letters and a few left diaries that have survived along with their great houses. Viewed through these sources they cut large figures and play the star roles in the arrangements that the people of the Chesapeake made for themselves in that period. These personages are accurately enough drawn, but they are a detail, though an important one, in the total production. Unfortunately the supporting cast and stage hands that made the production possible receive next to no attention, sometimes not even the courtesy of a billing. Just as *Hamlet* cannot be successfully staged without Hamlet, there can hardly be a play with Hamlet alone.

Not much literary evidence for the minor figures has come down; but another kind does exist and, even though bristling with difficulties and overawing in bulk, it can be compelled to yield some data for a fuller view. This body of material has been brought together in two despositories, the Maryland Hall of Records and the Virginia State Archives, and properly canvassed will fill in some gaps in our knowledge of Chesapeake affairs. It consists of inventories and accounts of the estates in personalty of all free men at the time of their death. The argument in this paper applies only to Maryland, for which a statistical analysis has been completed. The Virginia counties that have been analyzed give me the clear impression that differences between the areas north and south of the Potomac are not very great in respect of the basic contention here. Both were a part of a single economic region which political boundaries could not split asunder and were treated as a unit in contemporary British commercial records.

To obtain from the voluminous Maryland records a sample that faithfully reflects conditions in the northern Chesapeake, some of the usual economies are not possible. Geographical sampling by selected counties is ruled out. The process of carving new counties out of large older counties went on continuously from 1690 to the Revolution. Consequently the county of one decade is not necessarily the same unit in a later decade. Accordingly, all counties of the province are included. Over the entire eighty-year period 1690–1770 for which the records are reasonably complete the alternate decades from 1690–1699 to 1750–1759 have been tabulated. If it can be assumed that these sizable samples reflect with reasonable accuracy the spectrum of planters' estates, then we have some basis for understanding an otherwise shadowy aspect of the Chesapeake economy.

The profile of estates in the decade January 1, 1690, to December 31, 1699, shows an unexpected imbalance. Three quarters of these estates (74.6 per cent, to be precise) are of the magnitude £ 100 sterling or less. In the next bracket, £ 100 to £ 200, the percentage drops to 12.1, and in succeeding hundred-pound brackets to 5.5 per cent, 2.7 per cent, 1.4 per cent, 1.3 per cent, 0.6 per cent, and 0.3 per cent. After a break in the distribution, a meager 1.5 per cent at the top are valued at £ 1,000 sterling or greater.

Beyond the obvious fact that the less affluent far outnumber the better off, this analysis tells us little. The estates, small or great, are all those of planters — a handful of physicians, mariners, and clergymen specifically excepted. "Planter," then, simply describes an occupation without indicating economic status of the individual. To get at what this distribution means in terms of worldly goods, standard of living, and possibly social status, it is necessary to look at particulars in the inventories themselves. Here impressions become vivid.

The planters at the bottom of the scale, those with estates of £ 100 or less, have at best a "country living": a saddle horse or two, half a dozen or fewer cows, a few swine to furnish fresh or salt meat for the table according to the season, a modest assortment of household utensils — sometimes nothing more than a cooking pot or skillet, a few tools and agricultural implements. Many essentials of a household — for instance, plates and cups — are missing in fully half the inventories, an omission indicating that makeshifts such as wooden bowls and gourds took the place of these articles. The appraisers of estates overlooked no article, not even a cracked cup without a handle or a single glass bottle. In brief the standard of living might be described as rude sufficiency. The self-styled poet laureate of Maryland, Eben Cooke, calls planters at this level "cockerouses."

The inventories also speak to the productivity of these small planters. In those inventories made during the autumn and winter after the tobacco had been cut the appraisers carefully estimated the size of the deceased's crop. Crop entries range from twelve hundred pounds, a trifle over two hogsheads, up to three thousand pounds, or about six hogsheads. This represented the producer's cash crop, almost his entire annual income, excepting possibly the occasional sale of a heifer, a pig, or a few bushels of corn to a neighbor or local trader. Reckoning the price of tobacco at ten shillings a hundred, these small producers could count their disposable incomes at a figure between £ 6 and £ 15 a year.

Even taking into account the small planter's self-sufficiency in fresh vegetables from the kitchen garden, cereals from whatever field crops he grew besides tobacco, and meat from his own farm animals, an income of this size imposed iron limitations on him. Between investment and consumption he had no choice. Such necessities as thread, needles, powder and shot, coarse fabrics for clothing or featherbeds, and an occasional tool or a household utensil strained his credit at the country store until his crop was sold. For the small planter, provincial quitrents, church tithes, and taxes represented a real burden. He cast his ballot for a representative who could resist the blandishments of governors and hold public expenses to the barest minimum. In good part the pressures from men of his kind kept investment in the public sector to lowest dimensions, whether the object was a county courthouse, a lighthouse, or a governor's mansion. As a private person he could not invest from savings because he had none. With tobacco crops barely sufficient to cover his debt to the country merchant, a disastrous year could prostrate him. A lawsuit, the death of cattle in a winter freeze, or a fire in house or barn forced him to contract debts which had often not been paid at the time of his death and which ate up his entire personal estate, leaving his heirs without a penny. Not infrequently his administrator actually overpaid his estate in order to save trifling family heirlooms more precious than their valuation in the inventory. Investment in a slave or indentured servant to increase his productivity, though not completely out of the question, was very difficult.

The small planter clearly was not the beneficiary of the planting society of the Chesapeake. He bred his increase and added to the growing population that filled up vacant land from the shoreline to the mountains before the Revolution. In the language of the courts he qualified as a planter. Considering the circumstances of his life, it would stretch the usual meaning of the term to call him a yeoman, particularly if he fell in the lower half of his group.

In the brackets above £ 100, different characteristics of the estates immediately strike the eye. Sumptuary standards of planters above this line were obviously higher. Kitchens had ampler stocks of utensils; and for dining, earthenware and china replaced the gourds and wooden makeshifts that apparently were the rule on tables of families in the lowest economic bracket. Ticking stuffed with flock gave way to bedsteads and bedding. Even more striking is the prevalence of bond labor, both indentured servants and slaves, in this higher stratum. The transition comes abruptly. In estates below £ 100, servants or slaves rarely appear and then only in those within a few pounds of the line. In the estates at £ 100 to £ 200, the inventories of eight out of ten estates list bond labor — a higher percentage, actually, than in any of the succeeding £ 100 brackets up to £ 500.

In fact, these estates falling between £ 100 and £ 500 form a relatively homogeneous group. Altogether they comprise 21.7 per cent of all estates. Though existence for the planter is less frugal, his worldly goods show few signs of real luxury. Not a single estate was debt free, though fewer than a tenth had debts amounting to more than half the value of the inventory. The number of slaves in single estates does not run high: from one to five in 90 per cent of the estates that had them at all. Yet even this small number represented between half and two thirds of the appraised valuation. Reflecting the additional hands for husbandry, tobacco crops ran higher roughly in proportion to the number of slaves or indentured servants. Crops ranged from twelve hundred pounds (planters with no bond labor) up to nearly twenty thousand pounds, or from a little over two up to forty hogsheads. Again using ten shillings per hundred for transforming tobacco values to sterling, we can put the incomes from tobacco production alone between £ 6 and £ 100 a year. Other sources of income for families with bond labor should not be ruled out. Doubtless off-season occupations such as riving staves or shingles, sawing plank, and making cereal crops occupied some productive time. Unfortunately only occasional data on this type of product appear, enough to call for acknowledgment but insufficient for measurement.

Nevertheless, with annual incomes of these dimensions from their tobacco crops, planters in this group had alternatives not open to the lowest income group. As respectable citizens with community obligations to act as overseers of roads, appraisers of estates and similar duties, they might choose to lay by something to see their sons and daughters decently started in turn as planters or wives of planters. Or they might within the limitations of their estates live the good life, balancing consumption against income. Social pressure must have urged them in this direction, to a round of activities that included local politics and such country entertainments as dances, horseracing, and cockfights, occasionally punctuated with drinking brawls complete with eye-gougings and other practices not usually associated with the genteel life of the planter. Whatever the choice it is difficult to see how the planter in these circumstances could add appreciably to his estate in a short period of years, or even in a lifetime.

Still further up the scale, the estates appraised at sums above £ 500 form an even smaller percentage of the total. The five £ 100 brackets between £ 500 and £ 1,000 include altogether 2.2 per cent of all estates. At first glance this small group appears to be a plusher version of the preceding: somewhat more slaves, larger tobacco crops, more personal goods including some luxury items. These are planters of substance, much closer to the stereotype, as the character and contents of their inventories show. And in their activities they moved on a higher plane. One had represented his county for a term in the General Assembly and another had served on the county court as a justice of the peace. In the matter of indebtedness, however, some interesting differences appear. Just over half the inventories list debts owed to the estate among the major assets. In a few cases the portion of total assets in the form of debts owed the estate runs to half or more.

What I think we see here is an emerging business or entrepreneurial element, a small group of planters with sources of income other than planting alone. All were planters in the sense that they, or their bond labor, produced tobacco crops. But the appreciable number in the creditor category have other concerns. The nature of these concerns appear more clearly in the most affluent element, whose members can be studied individually as cases.

This element includes all persons with estates inventoried at more than £ 1,000 sterling. In the decade 1690–1699, they represent 1.6 per cent of the total. They were the "great planters" of the day.

The smallest estate in personalty, that of Nicholas Gassaway of Anne Arundel County, was inventoried at £ 1,017 14s. 11½d. sterling; the largest, that of Henry Coursey of Talbot County, at £ 1,667 17s. 1¼d. Perhaps estates of this size would have cut a mean figure beside those of the sugar planters of the West Indies. In the northern Chesapeake of the closing years of the seventeenth century, they loom high.

The composition of these largest estates varies a bit from what we might expect of the great planter's holdings. Slaves comprise less than a quarter of the assets and, in several, less than a fifth. It should be remembered that this decade lies in the transition period when slaves were displacing indentured servants as field labor. Even so, the numbers seem unimpressive — often no greater than slave holdings in estates a third as large. By contrast, the number and the amount of assets in the form of debts owed the estate are striking. Altogether they comprised between a quarter and a half of the assets in individual estates. In one of the largest estates, debts owed the deceased came to 78 per cent of the total assets.

The inventories themselves give some clues as to how these large planters had become creditors. Occasionally an industrious appraiser included information on how the debtor had incurred his obligation: for a pipe of wine, for a parcel of steers, for corn, for rent of a certain property, for goods. In short, the great planter had also become a "trader." Frequently a portion of the inventory is simply labeled "in the store" and the contents of that room or building listed under this heading. Then the origin of the debts becomes clear. Sometimes they ran well over a hundred major items and were carefully listed under captions "sperate debts" and "desperate debts."

Putting this cross section or sample against the general outlines of the Chesapeake economy, I suggest the hypothesis that the men of first fortune belonged functionally to a class whose success stemmed from entrepreneurial activities as much as, or even more than, from their direct operations as producers of tobacco. The Chesapeake closely resembles pioneer economies of other times and places. It was a region with a relatively low ratio of population to resources and an equally low ratio of capital to resources. External commerce was characterized by heavy staple exports and high capital imports. Internally this flow created a current of high capital investment, full employment, profit inflation, and rising property values. The tobacco staple did not lend itself to bonanza agriculture, as did sugar in the West India islands where fortunes could be made in a decade. Consequently the Chesapeake planters did not go "back home" to dazzle the populace with their wealth. Their returns derived in the first instance from tobacco production, which afforded a competence, and secondly from enterprise, which gave greater rewards. As entrepreneurs, they gave the Chesapeake economy both organization and direction. They took the risks, made the decisions, and reaped the rewards or paid the penalties. And they worked unremittingly at these tasks, which could not be performed in their absence by the small planter or by overseers.

It is not easy to analyze the activities of this economic elite into neat categories. They were at once planters, political leaders, and businessmen. The first two roles tend to obscure the last. Their role in politics is a textbook commonplace. As planters they lived in the great tradition, some even ostentatiously. On this point testimony is abundant and unambiguous. Had they depended solely on the produce of their tobacco fields, they doubtless would have lived up to or beyond current income. And some did. But in fact many among them increased their fortunes substantially and a few spectacularly, while still maintaining their reputations as good livers. During the early years of the eighteenth century, when the tobacco trade was far from booming, some of the first families of the Chesapeake established themselves as permanent fixtures. Several had come to the first rank, or very near it, both in politics and wealth by 1700: the Taskers, the Catholic Carrolls, the Lloyds, and the Trumans. Others, less well known but eventually architects of equal or greater fortunes, were rising in the scale within another decade: the Bordleys, the Chews, the Garretts, the Dulanys, the Bennetts, and the Protestant Carrolls. The secret of their success was business enterprise, though almost to a man they lived as planters separated from the kind of urban community in which their more conspicuously entrepreneurial counterparts to the north had their residences and places of business. An examination of the chief forms of enterprise discloses the mechanisms by which they came to the top of the heap.

One of the most profitable enterprises and one most commonly associated with the great planters of the Chesapeake, land speculation, appears early in the eighteenth century in both Virginia and Maryland. The Virginia Rent Roll of 1704, admitted as imperfect but the best that could be done at the time, shows half a dozen holdings that suggest speculative intent. After these tentative beginnings, speculators moved quite aggressively during the administration of Spotswood and his successors, when huge grants in the vacant back country became commonplace events for privileged insiders, with the governors themselves sharing the spoils of His Majesty's bounty. In the more carefully regulated land system of Maryland, agents of the Lords Baltimore made a few large grants to favored persons like Charles Carroll the Settler in the first two decades of the century. During these same decades other wary speculators took up occasional large grants. The Maryland system compelled speculators to be cautious, because it exacted some money for the patents and made evasion of quitrents nearly impossible. But by the 1730's, eager speculators had glimpsed a vision of the possible returns and kept the land office busy issuing warrants for unpatented areas. For a relatively modest outlay a small number of Marylanders obtained assets with which they experimented for years before discovering the last trick in turning them to account.

Speculators capitalized their assets in two chief ways, both enormously profitable. First, as landlords of the wild lands, they leased to tenants who paid rents and at the same time improved their leaseholds by clearing, planting orchards, and erecting houses, barns, and fences. Almost exclusively long-term leases, either for years (commonly twenty-one) or for lives, these instruments specified the improvements to be made. Tenants who could not save from current income thus under compulsion contributed their bit to capital formation to the ultimate benefit of the landlord. Literary sources give the impression that tenancy was not very widespread, but the records tell another story. Something over a third of the planters in the lowest £ 100 bracket in Maryland leased their land. Secondly, the large landholder sold off plantation-size parcels as settlement enveloped his holdings and brought values to the desired level. Not content to leave this movement to chance, many speculators hastened the process by encouraging immigration and by directing the movement of settlers toward their own properties. Jonathan Hagar in Maryland and William Byrd in Virginia are two among many who attempted to enhance the value of their properties in this way. It is difficult to determine profits even for single speculators except for short periods. Experience must have varied widely, and undoubtedly some speculators failed. But some of the successful ones made incredible gains in a relatively short span of years.

Even more ubiquitous than the planter-speculator was the planter-merchant. The inventories and accounts contain much evidence on the organization of commerce in the tobacco counties of the Chesapeake. Hardly a parish lacked one or more country stores, often no more than a tiny hut or part of a building on the grounds of a planter who could supply, usually on credit, the basic needs of neighboring small producers — drygoods, hoes and other small implements, salt, sugar, spices, tea, and almost always liquor. Inventories show some small stores with a mere handful of those articles in constant demand. Others had elaborate stocks of women's hats, mirrors, mourning gloves, ribbons, patent medicines, and luxury goods. The names of several great families are associated with country stores, particularly in the earlier generations of the line. Frequently, storekeeping duties fell to a trusted servant or to a younger member of the family as a part of his training. Occasionally, an apprentice from one of the county families came to learn the mysteries of trade by measuring out fabrics or liquors and keeping the accounts.

As with land speculation, determining profits of merchants is next to impossible. Consumers complained bitterly of high markups, and a few storekeepers boasted of them. Even so, the country merchant's profits were not limited to sale of goods alone. He stood to gain on another transaction. He took his payment in tobacco, the crops of the two- to six-hogshead producers. The small planter participated directly in the consignment system of the early eighteenth century only to a limited extent. His petty wants and his small crop hardly justified the London merchant's time and trouble in maintaining him as a separate account. His nexus to the overseas market was the provincial merchant, who took tobacco at prices that allowed at least a small profit to himself on every hogshead.

Closely allied to merchandising, moneylending presents almost as great problems of analysis. The Chesapeake economy operated on an elaborate network of credit arrangements. Jefferson's famous remark that Virginia planters were a species of property attached to certain great British merchant houses may have been true of some planters, as it was of Jefferson himself. But the observation has created a mischievous view of credit relations between England and the tobacco colonies and does not describe the debt pattern within the area at all accurately. A full account awaits the onslaught of an industrious graduate student armed with electronic tapes and computers. Meanwhile the accounts can tell us something. Country merchants had to be prepared to extend credit beyond that for goods purchased by their customers. They paid for some of their customers at least the church tithes, the tax levies, and the freedom dues of indentured servants who had served their terms. These petty book debts could be collected with interest in any county court. Loans to artisans — the shoemakers, tanners, and blacksmiths who multiplied in number toward mid century — were of a different order. For working capital, the artisan in need of £ 5 to £ 20 and upward turned to men of means, the "traders." Far from abating, the demand for capital increased as the century wore on.

Investment opportunities were never lacking for planters with ready money or with credit in England. As lenders, they squarely faced the conflict of the law and the profits. By law they could take interest at 6 per cent for money loans and 8 per cent for tobacco loans. One wonders why the Carrolls chose to loan their £ 30,000 sterling at 6 per cent, even on impeccable securities. Could the answer be in part that returns at this rate equaled those from further investment in planting? At any rate they did choose to lend, following the example of Bennett and a dozen or so others.

Far more profitable as an investment opportunity, manufacturing exercised an enduring fascination on imaginative men of the Chesapeake. During Virginia Company days, before the first settlement of Maryland, glass and iron had figured among the projects launched under Company stimulus. Although these had come to ruin in the massacre of 1622, Virginians never gave up hope of producing iron. Their success was limited; but in the upper reaches of the Bay a combination of easily worked ore, limitless forests for charcoal, oyster shell, and water transportation from the furnace site invited exploitation. British syndicates moved first to establish the Principio Works and later the Nottingham and Lancashire works. These remained in British hands until the Revolutionary confiscations. Last of the big four, the Baltimore Iron Works (1733) became the largest producer and the biggest money-maker. Five Maryland investors subscribed the initial capital of £ 3,500 sterling. The Baltimore enterprise was a triumph for native capital, though technicians and technology were both imported from Britain. After the first three years of operation the partners received handsome dividends but always plowed a substantial part of the profits back into the enterprise. By the early 1760's the share of each partner was valued at £ 6,000 sterling. The five partners were among the first fortunes in Maryland.

Beyond iron making, other forms of enterprise (mostly small-scale manufacturing or processing) attracted investment capital. In nearly all areas of the Chesapeake some shipbuilding, cooperage, and milling establishments provided essential local services or commodities. None of these required either the capital outlay or the organization of an ironworks. Consequently, as enterprises they were attractive to investors with modest capital but large ambitions. In the area of Baltimore, flour milling developed major proportions after mid century, as the upper counties of Maryland found grain more profitable than tobacco as a field crop.

An astonishing percentage of the personal fortunes of the northern Chesapeake had their roots in law practice. While not entrepreneurial in a technical sense, the rewards went to the enterprising. During the seventeenth century lawyers were neither numerous nor always in good odor. Private persons attended to their own legal business in the courts. By 1700, the fashion had changed as the courts insisted on greater formality in pleading and as the cumbersome machinery of the common law compelled the uninstructed to turn to the professional. Pleading "by his attorney" swiftly replaced appearances *in propria persona*. Still the legal profession remained trammeled. Laws strictly regulated fees attorneys could take and kept these at levels low enough that the ablest members of the Maryland bar went on strike in the 1720's. What lawyers lacked in size of fees they made up in number of cases. An attorney might, and frequently did, bring thirty or forty cases to trial in a three- or four-day session of a county court. Had these been litigation over land, an impression widely held by students who use the *Virginia Reports* and the *Maryland Reports*, attorneys might have spent their entire time in title searches, examining witnesses, and preparing their cases. The court proceedings at large, however, show fifty cases of debt collection for every case over land; and sometimes the ratio runs as high as a hundred to one. One traveler to the Chesapeake, remarking on the "litigious spirit," wryly concluded that this spectacle of everybody suing everybody else was a kind of sport peculiar to the area. In fact, the numbers of suits grew out of the very arrangements — a tissue of book debts, bills of exchange, and promissory notes — that kept the mechanism operating.

In this milieu the lawyer had an enviable position. From his practice he derived a steady income freed from direct dependence on returns from the annual tobacco fleet. In a phrase, he had ready money the year 'round. Furthermore, he had an intimate knowledge of the resources and dependability of the planters in the county — and, indeed, throughout the province if he also practiced at the bar of the superior courts. Consequently he could take advantage of opportunities on the spot, whether they were bargains in land, sales of goods or produce, or tenants seeking leases. He could besides avoid the costs of litigation that inevitably arose as he involved himself in land speculation, lending, or merchandising, as many did. As a rule the lawyers did well, and the most enterprising moved into the highest brackets of wealth. Perhaps the most spectacular example, Thomas Bordley, a younger son of a Yorkshire schoolmaster, came from an impecunious immigrant apprentice in a Maryland law office to distinction in the law, in politics, and in Maryland society within the span of a short lifetime. After his premature death in 1726 his executors brought to probate the largest estate in the history of the province to that time.

Quite commonly, lawyers added a minor dimension to their income from office holding. A fair percentage of Maryland offices were sinecures that could be executed by deputies for a fraction of the fees. Most carried modest stipends, but a few eagerly-sought prizes paid handsomely. Baltimore's provincial secretary received £ 1,000 per annum.

This is not the place to argue the returns from planting, pure and simple. Many planters did well without other sources of income. But impressive fortunes went to those who, in addition, put their talents to work in some of the ways described above. A few engaged in all. The list is finite, for we are referring here to a small percentage of planters, those with estates above £ 1,000: in the decade 1690–1699 to 1.6 per cent, in 1710–1719 to 2.2 per cent, in 1730–1739 to 3.6 per cent, and in 1750–1759 to 3.9 per cent. When tabulated and examined for group characteristics, they resemble functionally a type that could easily come under that comprehensive eighteenth-century term, merchant. They look very unlike the planter of the moon-light-and-magnolias variety. It is a commentary on the prosperity of the northern Chesapeake that, as this favored category increased in percentage and in absolute numbers, so did the magnitude of its members' individual fortunes. The sample taken just before the turn of the century shows top fortunes between £ 1,000 and £ 2,000, with none above. The sample decade 1730–1739 includes an appreciable number over £ 2,000. The two largest were those of Samuel Chew (£ 9,937) and Amos Garrett (£ 11,508), both merchants. Even these did not match the fortunes left by Dr. Charles Carroll and Daniel Dulany the Elder in the decade 1750–1759, nor that of Benjamin Tasker in the next.

The poor were not excluded, individually or as a group, from the general prosperity of the Chesapeake. Four individuals — Thomas Macnemara, Thomas Bordley, Daniel Dulany, and Dr. Charles Carroll — moved up the scale from nothing to the top bracket of wealth, two of them from indentured servitude. These were extraordinary men, but their careers indicate the avenues open to their combination of talents for the law, land speculation, moneylending, merchandising, and manufacturing in which they engaged. Of course all were planters as well.

But for the mass, advance was by comparison glacial. The composition of the base on which such performances took place changed more slowly. In the fourth decade of the eighteenth century the percentage of planters in the lowest economic group, those with estates of £ 100 or less, had fallen to 54.7 per cent, in marked contrast to the 74.6 per cent of the decade 1690–1699. Between the same two sample decades the percentage in the next higher category of estates (£ 100 to £ 500) had increased to 35.7 per cent from 21.7 per cent. If this means that the poor were getting richer, it also means for the great majority that they were doing so by short and slow steps. Together, these two lowest categories still made up 90.4 per cent of the planting families in 1730–1739, as compared with 96.3 per cent in the last decade of the seventeenth century. Nonetheless, the shift toward a higher standard of living within this huge mass of lesser planters is quite as important a commentary on the economic well-being of the Chesapeake as is the growth in numbers and magnitude of the great fortunes.

It is never easy to know just how much to claim for statistical evidence. Perhaps there is enough here to raise doubts about the descriptive accuracy of reports from Chesapeake planters themselves. These sound like a protracted wail of hard times, rising occasionally in crescendo to prophesies of impending ruin. Yet even during the early and least prosperous decades, the northern Chesapeake experienced some growth. During the second quarter of the century and on into the following decades the samples made for this study indicate a quickened rate. The results worked no magic change in the way of life or economic station for the small planter, the mass of Maryland. These were always the overwhelming percentage of the producers. As a social group they come in for little notice. Their lives lack the glitter and incident that has made the great planter the focus of all eyes. By the standards of the affluent society theirs was a drab, rather humdrum, existence bound to the annual rhythm of the field crop. The highest rewards were for those who could transcend the routine of producing tobacco and develop the gainful activities that kept the economy functioning.

Religion in the New World

"But it does me no injury for my neighbor to say there are twenty gods, or no God. It neither picks my pocket nor breaks my leg," wrote Thomas Jefferson in the 1780s. Few of those who settled America would have agreed with the Sage of Monticello. Most early European settlers, especially the middle classes and the peasantry, which supplied the bulk of the immigrants, believed that man's relations with God were the central experience of life. Yet by Jefferson's time, and increasingly so since, most Americans have been more preoccupied with life in this world than in the next. The emergence of a secular outlook facilitated the ultimate triumph of religious tolerance and the separation of church and state, since people who are indifferent toward religion are less likely to insist on conformity from dissenters and persecute them for heterodoxy, than those who are preoccupied with salvation and certain that their faith is the only true road to Heaven.

Tolerance and separation of church and state — two foundations of the American religious tradition — did not simply await the corrosive effects of secularism on religious belief, as Perry Miller explains in the following essay. Most colonists brought across the ocean the common assumption of the time that no well-ordered society could exist without an established church to which all people belonged, which all supported financially, and which all accepted as the "true" faith. The Protestant Reformation, however, had divided Christendom into dozens of competing denominations, each claiming to be the only authentic interpretation of Christianity. It also triggered a century of religious wars and persecutions that sent defeated minorities in search of refuge to America. Puritans came to Massachusetts, Catholics to Maryland, Quakers and German Lutherans to Pennsylvania. But the persecuted, with some exceptions, did not seek freedom for all men. Their formula was freedom for themselves, but not for others who were "heretics." Diversity, however, played havoc with efforts to create in the colonies state churches that tolerated no dissent. In some, as in Virginia and Massachusetts, dissenters became so numerous and influential that eventually the established churches grudgingly made concessions and later, during the Revolutionary era, lost their privileged positions. Elsewhere, such as in Pennsylvania, there was never a state church because the Quaker founders believed, as a matter of principle rather than of Jeffersonian expediency, that faith was a private and holy affair between man and God and that state involvement would only corrupt the church and oppress those seeking God.

FOR FURTHER READING:

GREENE, EVARTS B. *Religion and the State: The Making & Testing of an American Tradition.* Ithaca, N.Y.: Cornell University Press, 1959.*
MEAD, SIDNEY E. *The Lively Experiment.* New York: Harper & Row, Publishers, 1963.*
SWEET, WILLIAM W. *Religion in Colonial America.* New York: Cooper Square Publishers, 1942.*
Asterisk denotes paperback edition.

The Contribution of the Protestant Churches to Religious Liberty in Colonial America   PERRY MILLER

While endeavouring to formulate these remarks I have come to suspect that there may possibly lurk in the title of my paper a misleading implication. The word "contribution" would seem to connote on the part of the Protestant churches a deliberate and concerted effort toward the triumph of religious liberty. Those of us who prize ecclesiastical freedom would like to feel that our colonial ancestors of their own free will and choice undertook the march to liberty. Liberal-minded historians in particular are prone to sing the praises of this individual or that church for furthering this advance; they are inclined to gloss over or to apologize for the men and the institutions that hindered it.

Such an attitude, though inspired by the most admirable of motives, has been, I am convinced, an encumbrance to the student of history. There is no way to deny — and as far as I can see, no use in denying — that Protestants coming to this country in the seventeenth century were almost unanimous in their conviction that toleration was a dangerous and heathen notion. They came fresh from Europe of the Reformation, where experience had demonstrated that if two divergent churches were permitted to exist within striking distance of each other, it would only be a question of time before throats were cut. And Protestants were far from deploring this belligerency. If you believe, as men believed in that era, that you are altogether on the Lord's side, and that your enemies are and must be entirely on the devil's, you can see no virtue in the idea of tolerating them. Statesmen knew that a policy of toleration would not work; theologians were grimly determined that it never should work. As the Reverend Nathaniel Ward of Ipswich in Massachusetts Bay emphatically declared:

> He that is willing to tolerate any Religion, or descrepant way of Religion besides his own, unless it be in matters merely indifferent, either doubts of his own, or is not sincere in it. He that is willing to tolerate any unsound Opinion, that his own may also be tolerated, though never so sound, will for a need hang God's Bible at the Devil's girdle.

When a Protestant church came into a colony at the beginning of settlement, with no other churches on the ground, with a clear field before it, that church deliberately set up an exclusive régime, it conscientiously strove to establish one official church in absolute uniformity, it frankly employed the civil power to compel all inhabitants to conform and contribute. Both Virginia and Massachusetts furnish examples of this disposition. The Anglicans in the one colony and the Puritans in the other, entertaining utterly different conceptions of polity and theology, were at one in their philosophy of uniformity. Among the early enactments of the House of Burgesses was a statute demanding that there "be a uniformity in our Church as near as may be to the Cannons in England, both in substance and in circumstance, and that all persons yield obedience under pain of censure." Puritan ministers and the Puritan settlement at Nansemond were driven out, and in 1671 that picturesque and outspoken governor, Sir William Berkeley, reported with glowing pride that no free

Source: Perry Miller, "The Contribution of the Protestant Churches to Religious Liberty in Colonial America," *Church History,* vol. 4 (1935), pp. 57–66.

schools disgraced the landscape in Virginia: "I hope we shall not have [them] these hundred years: for learning has brought disobedience and heresy and sects into the world." This, quite clearly, is nipping religious liberty in the bud.

The Puritans were equally clear and decisive. Many writers have already called attention to the fact that though the Puritans came to New England to escape persecution, they did not come to bestow upon those who disagreed with them any such immunity within the confines of their colonies. John Cotton patiently explained their position to Roger Williams thus: anybody in possession of his senses must recognize what is true and what is false when a learned Congregational minister demonstrates truth and falsehood to him. If a man, after such instruction, then maintains certain errors, he deserves punishment, not for being in error, but for persisting in it. In his heart of hearts, his own better judgment must acknowledge as much, even if he won't admit it. Accordingly, the laws of Massachusetts and the explicit pronouncements of her apologists pile up incontrovertible evidence that the leaders of the Bay Colony were intentionally and consistently intolerant; the banishment of Williams and Anne Hutchinson, the fining of Dr. Child, the whipping of Obadiah Holmes, and the dangling bodies of four Quakers hanged on Boston Common attest the fidelity with which the Puritans scouted the idea of toleration.

Speaking still as a historian, I must confess my gratitude to such men as Berkeley and Cotton. We know, at any rate, where we stand with them. With many figures of this stripe for our authorities, we can confidently assert that the Protestant *intention* in America was not towards religious toleration, let alone liberty. Yet it is also true that the colonies of Virginia and Massachusetts were the exceptions; they were the only colonies in which a program of intolerance had any real success, the only colonies in which a religious uniformity was achieved, and even in them for a relatively short time. The colonial period witnessed a fairly steady growth of practical religious freedom. From time to time some men in one or another of the churches might foresee the end and even approve. But by and large, I can find very little evidence that the Protestant churches ever really entertained the conception of complete liberty as their ultimate goal, or that they often moved in that direction unless forced to do so by the pressure of events or by the necessities of the social environment. As I say, there are exceptions, notably of course Williams and Penn, but the contribution of the majority of the Protestant churches must in the final analysis be described as inadvertent.

My time is limited, and it would manifestly be impossible to relate the whole narrative here. I wish therefore only to indicate, however briefly, what seems to my mind to be three important factors determining the development of religious liberty in America. To enumerate them roundly, they seem to me to have been, first the practical situation of the sects in the colonies, second the influence and interference of England, and third the shift in issues and concerns produced by the introduction or development of both the rationalistic and evangelical temper in the eighteenth century.

Most of the colonies were not as fortunate as Virginia or Massachusetts; they did not begin with unsettled expanses, or they could not people them with men of only one persuasion. The proprietors of the Carolinas, for instance, intended some day to establish the Church of England in their domains, but from the beginning had to reckon with a hopeless variety of creeds, Puritans from England and from New England, Huguenots, Dutch Calvinists, Scotch Calvinists, Quakers and several sorts of Baptists. The uniformity for which the noble proprietors hoped was impossible, unless they were prepared to expel nine-tenths of their settlers. So religious principle gave way to economic interest; practical toleration became the rule. The official clique still contemplated a full establishment of the Anglican church and in 1704 felt themselves strong enough in South Carolina to enact legislation excluding dissenters from the assembly and establishing an ecclesiastical court. A revolution was averted only when these acts were annulled by Parliament and toleration was restored.

The story in New York is much the same. The Dutch had been fairly tolerant and hospitable, following the national policy at home. When the English took over the colony, the number of sects already flourishing precluded any effective establishment. As Governor Dongan complained in 1687:

> Here bee not many of the Church of England; few Roman Catholics; abundance of Quaker preachers, men and women especially; Singing Quakers; Ranting Quakers; Sabbatarians; Anti-Sabbatarians; some Anabaptists; some Independents; some Jews; in short, of all sorts of opinions there are some, and the most part of none at all. The most prevailing opinion is that of the Dutch Calvinists. . . . As for the King's natural born subjects that live on Long Island, and other parts of the Government, I find it a hard task to make them pay their Ministers.

The governors did what they could, but the best they could wring from a predominantly Dutch Calvinistic assembly was the peculiar Ministry Act of 1693, which established in four counties six Protestant churches, not necessarily Anglican. Very few denominations were clearly advocating religious liberty on principle in New York; they were all opposing an established church, and the result was that religious liberty in large measure they all had. Circumstances placed insuperable obstacles in the way of intolerance. Where a multiplicity of creeds checkmate each other, they find themselves to their surprise maintaining religious liberty.

Indeed, the reasons that made uniformity difficult or ineffective in the Carolinas or in New York ultimately made it impossible in Virginia and Massachusetts. The established order in Virginia was never a very efficient organization; as early as 1629 the Burgesses were endeavouring to stop the clergy from "drinking or ryott" or "playing at dice." Meantime the dissenters began trickling in, Quakers and Baptists, and then the Scotch-Irish with their militant Presbyterianism streamed down the Shenandoah. Many of these were valuable settlers, particularly on the frontier, and the government had to give them allowance, either by express enactment or by tacit agreement. In Massachusetts also Quakers and Baptists forced an opening, and Anglicans came to stay in the train of the royal governors. By the 1730's the province had to allow some dissenters from the established Congregational order to pay their rates to churches of their own persuasion.

Thus in the colonies a generous amount of liberty or at least of toleration had come to prevail by the time of the Revolution. But this situation was hardly the result of conscious and deliberate theory; it was the result of circumstances. Diversity of belief compelled it. Rhode Island is, of course, an exception to this statement, thanks to the teachings of Roger Williams. Inspiring a figure as Williams may be, he nevertheless devised theories that were not palatable to the majority of Protestant churches in his day. Williams may speak for the essentially individualistic tendency inherent in all Protestantism; in the perspective of time we may see that his was the only solution for the ecclesiastical problem in a Protestant world, but Protestants in the colonies did not want to think so. If we desire to state accurately the "contribution" of the Protestant churches in all colonies beside Rhode Island and Pennsylvania to the development of religious liberty, we are forced to say that they made it inevitable by their dogged persistence in maintaining their own beliefs and practices. They persisted so resolutely that the governments had either to exterminate them or to tolerate them. In this connection it is worth noting that once a sect was tolerated it was generally ready to thrust itself into intolerance if it could get the upper hand. The Anglicans in Maryland, for example, given toleration by the Catholic proprietor in 1649, spent every effort to secure a Protestant establishment and the disfranchisement of their benefactors. Once the Church of England was established in Maryland, we have the old story again; the dissenting sects that had opposed the proprietor's church at once banded together, with the Catholics this time, to antagonize the royal governor's. By 1776 the established church in Maryland had become a shadow. The New Side Presbyterians and the Baptists in eighteenth century Virginia brought down upon their own heads the official persecution to which they were subjected by their own scurrility in assaulting the deplorable established church. "They treat all other modes of worship with the utmost scorn and contempt," complained the broad-minded Governor Gooch in 1745. The Protestant churches in America finally accepted the idea of religious liberty because they had become habituated to it. Most of them had not moved toward it with intelligent foresight; they had been forced to accustom themselves to it, because experience demonstrated the futility of exclusive domination by any one church, because settlers were too valuable to be antagonized over-much by acts of conformity, and because there were simply so many Protestant organizations that no power on earth could whip them into a system of uniformity.

A second source of liberal developments in colonial America is to be found in the example of English opinion and English law. The many sects that sprang up like mushrooms in the frenzied years of the Civil Wars had banded together with the English Independents against the Presbyterians to demand toleration. The dissenters were finally given toleration by the Parliament and the Established Church in the act of 1689. Though this act by no means created religious liberty, it marked the demise in England of that philosophy of absolute uniformity and enforced conformity which had characterized all Protestant churches during the Reformation.

It is with this development of opinion in England that we are to connect the experiment of William Penn. The Quakers were one of the enthusiastic groups that came into being during the wars. They began their existence when the idea of toleration had already been embraced by the Independents. Although in the first flush of their zeal the Quakers had flung themselves against all other churches in a spirit that betrayed little comprehension of toleration, they soon aligned themselves with the Independents. Their peculiar theology made it possible for them to admit, much more easily than other creeds could do, that men might be holy and good even if they belonged to other organizations. In that spirit Penn founded his colony, on an explicit theory of liberty for all churches, though his conceptions were still not as broad as those of Williams and he would not enfranchise Jews or give harbor to atheists. His plan was a little too broad for the home government, so that in 1705 the colony yielded to compulsion from Queen Anne and required the test-oath to be taken by office-holders, thus excluding Catholics from official positions.

Yet if the English government was instrumental in curtailing religious liberty in Pennsylvania, the act of 1689 fashioned a weapon by which minority groups in other colonies could pry loose the laws of conformity. The dissenters of South Carolina successfully appealed to the Whigs in Parliament to block the exorbitant acts of 1704. Francis Makemie, by demanding a license to preach in Virginia under the terms of the act of 1699, compelled the Burgesses to incorporate them into Virginia law. Samuel Davies appealed to the act again in 1753 to procure liberty for itinerant ministers. The Royal charter of Massachusetts, drawn up in 1691, guaranteed that "there shall be liberty of conscience allowed, in the worship of God, to all Christians (except Papists)." When Connecticut in 1708 grudgingly gave toleration to dissenters from the Congregational system, it specifically cited "the act of William and Mary." Thus once more, liberty was forced upon the colonies from without. The Quakers were intentionally libertarian; the other churches used English principles and laws for self-protection. In the end they furthered the growth of religious liberty, but not with malice aforethought; they achieved that end in the course of securing relief and opportunities for themselves.

The eighteenth century saw a steady extension of toleration in the colonies until with the Revolution established churches collapsed, in Massachusetts and Connecticut somewhat belatedly. But again an examination of the activity and statements of the churches before the Revolution does not offer much evidence that they took the lead. In the shift of the general intellectual climate, and the pressure of one or two political factors, religious liberty came to seem attractive. A complete account of this transformation would entail a chapter in intellectual history that has yet to be written; lacking that chapter we can here only enumerate a few of the factors. Before the Revolution the dissenting churches were thrown into co-operation and alliance against the threat of an Anglican bishop; this served to lessen the hostility of one toward another. Furthermore, in this century the question of church-polity ceased to be a serious issue; the young Jonathan Edwards would as soon serve in a Presbyterian as in a Congregational parish. Probably the most irritating of controversies was thus minimized. Then also, the differences between the sects began to seem of minor significance in the face of the towering danger of scientific rationalism and deism, which threatened all traditional creeds alike. Against the spread of "infidelity" all the churches drew closer together. Finally the movement for religious liberty was carried to a speedy triumph in the Revolutionary decades because the leadership was taken by a rational aristocracy, shot through with deistical beliefs, willing to see any number of religions have their freedom because they believed in none of them. As Nathaniel Ward had said, nothing is easier than to tolerate when you do not seriously believe that differences matter. So the Adamses, Masons, Franklins, and Jeffersons could advocate dis-establishment and religious liberty in a spirit which is, from an orthodox Christian point of view, simply cynical. As James Madison cheerfully put it: "In a free government, the security for civil rights must be the same as that for religious rights; it consists in the one case in a multiplicity of interests and in the other in the multiplicity of sects." At the same time the transformation of religious issues wrought by the Great Awakening and the introduction of revivalistic evangelicalism had created a situation in which the new Protestant groups were able to see clearly that a policy of religious liberty offered them definite advantages. Evangelical Baptists and New Side Presbyterians, and eventually the Methodists, came to perceive that they were opposing conceptions of institutionalized civic religion inherited from the previous century; they had to demolish established churches along with intricate theological structures in order to have the track cleared for their own program of spiritual regeneration and impassioned zeal. I do not think it has ever been sufficiently emphasized, or that it can be too much stressed, that there is a subtle and close connection between the shift of vital religious interest from elaborate intellectual systems of theology to the simplified emotional fervor of the new revivalism and the turning of Protestant Americans from a concern with ecclesiastical exclusiveness to the demand for liberty to all churches. It is not only that two or three more militant minorities now existed to contend for privileges against vested institutions, but that the whole bent and temper of this evangelicalism required that organization, external regulation and formal discipline become subordinated to the reawakening of the spirit and the revivifying of morality. It is in Massachusetts where the ruling classes most stoutly resisted what they considered the crude mysticism of the camp meetings that the retention of an established church was the most protracted. Such apparent champions of religious liberty as the Baptists Backus and Manning, or the Presbyterian Davies, have about them an apparent liberalism which is inspiring to behold, which yet can easily be made too much of. The truth of the matter was that they understood the situation, they realized that old institutions had to be replaced by less systematized forms if the sort of religious incitement they prized was to have full opportunity. James Manning — symbolizing the vast difference of evangelical Protestantism in the eighteenth century from Puritanism of the seventeenth, as we have seen that Puritanism incarnated in Nathaniel Ward — said to the Massachusetts delegates to the Continental Congress in October, 1774, "Establishments may be enabled to confer worldly distinctions and secular importance. They may make hypocrites, but cannot create Christians." So for the time being such leaders often made common cause with the rational aristocracy to attack established order and medieval theology. Yet all the time they were perfectly aware that their cause would not be lost, but in reality furthered, if various denominations were allowed to practise it in various ways. In terms of an ideal of ethics rather than of evangelical emotion, the same ultimately became true of the Unitarians. As Professor Hall has remarked, "It was easier for Harvard College to take up Unitarianism than it would have been to introduce at that date sports on Sunday."

It therefore seems to me that it is possible to speak too glibly of the "contributions" of Protestant groups to religious liberty; we can be easily betrayed by our own approbation for the idea into prizing and unduly exalting such instances of advance as we can find in our forebears. It has often seemed to me that the worshippers of Roger Williams have done more harm than good not only to the Puritans of the Bay but to their hero himself by their extravagant laudation of his ideas without at the same time maintaining sufficient historical perspective upon the general intellectual background from which he so dramatically emerged. Exceptionally liberal men in Protestant ranks undoubtedly exist, and they deserve all honor and veneration; but by and large Protestants did not contribute to religious liberty, they stumbled into it, they were compelled into it, they accepted it at last because they had to, or because they saw its strategic value. In their original intention, Protestants were intolerant; because of the sheer impossibility of unifying colonies made up of a hodge-podge diversity, because of the example of toleration set and enforced by England, and because of a complete shift in the intellectual situation in the eighteenth century, whereby religious liberty became a perfect solution for new issues — for these reasons, the Protestant churches did not so much achieve religious liberty as have liberty thrust upon them.

Roots of the American Revolution

From the Revolutionary generation to the present, Americans have never ceased trying to explain why the American colonies, after more than 150 years as loyal outposts of Great Britain, suddenly revolted and established an independent republic. Americans at that time had a simple explanation: wicked English politicians sought to deprive them of their liberty, and the colonists manfully and successfully resisted. Later generations, skeptical of such simple black-and-white interpretations, discovered that the British taxes and regulations which triggered American resistance in the 1760s resulted from sincere, if not always wise, efforts to deal with difficult, indeed intractable, problems of imperial government that grew out of England's victory in the Seven Years' War (1754–1761). The need for a revenue and for tighter central control, as perceived by London, clashed with well-entrenched traditions of decentralized rule, from which Americans profited and which they were reluctant to give up. Still other historians have maintained that conflicting economic interests tore the Empire apart as British merchants and officials attempted to enrich themselves at the expense of the colonists. The following selection by Bernard Bailyn is an important recent major contribution to Revolutionary historiography. Bailyn argues that whatever the actual motives of British policy-makers, the Americans became convinced of a plot against their freedom.

The conspiratorial mentality — an irrational pattern of explanation that attributes dire events to hidden, malign forces — has appeared many times since in American history: in Andrew Jackson's War against the Bank of the United States, in the Populist crusade against Wall Street, and more recently in Senator Joe McCarthy's demagogic attack on supposed Communist subversion in high places. It made its first full-blown debut in America during the turbulent decade preceding the Revolution. It flourished then and later because people, living in times of rapid change, are often bewildered and do not understand why their lives are being disrupted. Americans, for instance, did not perceive the Stamp Act and other British measures as reforms in imperial governance. The new policies clearly departed from past ones and seemed to fly in the face of the long-accepted theory that the best way to advance the interests of the mother country was to permit the colonists ample freedom. Unable or unwilling to understand the real reasons for having to pay new taxes or submit to new trade regulations, Americans could only imagine themselves the victims of a wicked plot against their freedom.

Colonial political developments and English political thought further predisposed Americans to this view. The colonists did enjoy more freedom than any other people in the Western world; they regarded America, moreover, as a refuge to which victims of tyranny had fled. Their own experience as well as their study of history and politics taught them that, because man is inherently self-seeking, willing to enslave others for his own benefit, those who are free always live in danger from others. The chief danger came from the state, since the men who controlled it possessed a monopoly of force. The best defense against the abuse of authority was a properly balanced constitution that placed limits on rulers. Americans thought they lived under such a constitution until the 1760s. Then, Professor Bailyn argues, when they thought legislatures, courts, and churches to be under attack from England, they became convinced of a plot to subvert the British constitution and to destroy their liberty.

FOR FURTHER READING:

BAILYN, BERNARD. *Ideological Origins of the American Revolution.* Cambridge, Mass.: Harvard University Press, 1967.*
BILLIAS, GEORGE A., ed. *American Revolution: How Revolutionary Was It.* Magnolia, Mass.: Peter Smith, 1965.*
MORGAN, EDMUND G. *Stamp Act Crisis.* Chapel Hill: University of North Carolina Press, 1963.*
Asterisk denotes paperback edition.

From *The Ideological Origins of the American Revolution*   BERNARD BAILYN

. . . The colonists believed they saw emerging from the welter of events during the decade after the Stamp Act a pattern whose meaning was unmistakable. They saw in the measures taken by the British government and in the actions of officials in the colonies something for which their peculiar inheritance of thought had prepared them only too well, something they had long conceived to be a possibility in view of the known tendencies of history and of the present state of affairs in England. They saw about them, with increasing clarity, not merely mistaken, or even evil, policies violating the principles upon which freedom rested, but what appeared to be evidence of nothing less than a deliberate assault launched surreptitiously by plotters against liberty both in England and in America. The danger to America, it was believed, was in fact only the small, immediately visible part of the greater whole whose ultimate manifestation would be the destruction of the English constitution, with all the rights and privileges embedded in it.

This belief transformed the meaning of the colonists' struggle, and it added an inner accelerator to the movement of opposition. For, once assumed, it could not be easily dispelled: denial only confirmed it, since what conspirators profess is not what they believe; the ostensible is not the real; and the real is deliberately malign.

It was this — the overwhelming evidence, as they saw it, that they were faced with conspirators against liberty determined at all costs to gain ends which their words dissembled — that was signaled to the colonists after 1763, and it was this above all else that in the end propelled them into Revolution.

Suspicion that the ever-present, latent danger of an active conspiracy of power against liberty was becoming manifest within the British Empire, assuming specific form and developing in coordinated phases, rose in the consciousness of a large segment of the American population before any of the famous political events of the

---

Source: Bernard Bailyn, *The Idealogical Origins of the American Revolution* (Cambridge, Mass.: Harvard University Press, 1967), pp. 94–97, 98–101, 101–106, 107–110, 112–115, 117–120, 124–125, 129–130, 135–136, 138–143.

struggle with England took place. No adherent of a nonconformist church or sect in the eighteenth century was free from suspicion that the Church of England, an arm of the English state, was working to bring all subjects of the crown into the community of the Church; and since toleration was official and nonconformist influence in English politics formidable, it was doing so by stealth, disguising its efforts, turning to improper uses devices that had been created for benign purposes. In particular, the Society for the Propagation of the Gospel in Foreign Parts, an arm of the Church created in 1701 to aid in bringing the Gospel to the pagan Indians, was said by 1763 to have "long had a formal design to root out Presbyterianism, etc., and to establishing both episcopacy and bishops."

This suspicion, which had smoldered in the breasts of New Englanders and nonconformists throughout the colonies for half a century or more, had burst into flame repeatedly, but never so violently as in 1763, in the Mayhew-Apthorp controversy which climaxed years of growing anxiety that plans were being made secretly to establish an American episcopate. To Mayhew, as to Presbyterian and Congregational leaders throughout the colonies, there could be little doubt that the threat was real. Many of the facts were known, facts concerning maneuvers in London and in America. Anglican leaders in New York and New Jersey had met almost publicly to petition England for an American episcopate, and there could be little doubt also of the role of the Society for the Propagation of the Gospel in this undercover operation. For if the ostensible goal of the Society was the gospelizing of the pagan Indians and Negroes, its true goal was manifestly revealed when it established missions in places like Cambridge, Massachusetts, which had not had a resident Indian since the seventeenth century and was well equipped with "orthodox" preachers. Such missions, Mayhew wrote, have "all the appearance of entering wedges . . . carrying on the crusade, or spiritual siege of our churches, with the hope that they will one day submit to an episcopal sovereign." Bishops, he wrote unblinkingly in reply to the Archbishop of Canterbury, have commonly been instruments in arbitrary reigns of "establishing a tyranny over the bodies and souls of men," and their establishment in America would mark the end of liberty in Massachusetts and elsewhere. By 1765, when the final exchanges in this pamphlet war were published, it was commonly understood in New England and elsewhere that "the stamping and episcopizing [of] our colonies were . . . *only different branches of the same plan of power.*"

Fear of an ecclesiastical conspiracy against American liberties, latent among nonconformists through all of colonial history, thus erupted into public controversy at the very same time that the first impact of new British policies in civil affairs was being felt. And though it was, in an obvious sense, a limited fear (for large parts of the population identified themselves with the Anglican Church and were not easily convinced that liberty was being threatened by a plot of Churchmen) it nevertheless had a profound indirect effect everywhere, for it drew into public discussion — evoked in specific form — the general conviction of eighteenth-century Englishmen that the conjoining of "temporal and spiritual tyranny" was, in John Adams' words, an event totally "calamitous to human liberty" yet an event that in the mere nature of things perpetually threatened. . . . Fear of the imposition of an Anglican episcopate thus brought into focus a cluster of ideas, attitudes, and responses alive with century-old Popish-Stuart-Jacobite associations that would enter directly into the Revolutionary controversy in such writings as John Adams' *Dissertation on the Canon and Feudal Law* (1765) and Samuel Adams' "A Puritan" pieces published in the *Boston Gazette* in 1768. And more than that, it stimulated among highly articulate leaders of public opinion, who would soon be called upon to interpret the tendency of civil affairs, a general sense that they lived in a conspiratorial world in which what the highest officials professed was not what they in fact intended, and that their words masked a malevolent design.

Reinforcement for this belief came quickly. Even for those who had in no way been concerned with the threat of an episcopal establishment, the passage of the Stamp Act was not merely an impolitic and unjust law that threatened the priceless right of the individual to retain possession of his property until he or his chosen representative voluntarily gave it up to another; it was to many, also, a danger signal indicating that a more general threat existed. For though it could be argued, and in a sense proved by the swift repeal of the act, that nothing more was involved than ignorance or confusion on the part of people in power who really knew better and who, once warned by the reaction of the colonists, would not repeat the mistake — though this could be, and by many was, concluded, there nevertheless appeared to be good reason to suspect that more was involved. For from whom had the false information and evil advice come that had so misled the English government? From officials in the colonies, said John Adams, said Oxenbridge Thacher, James Otis, and Stephen Hopkins — from officials bent on overthrowing the constituted forms of government in order to satisfy their own lust for power, and not likely to relent in their passion. Some of these local plotters were easily identified. To John Adams, Josiah Quincy, and others the key figure in Massachusetts from the beginning to the end was Thomas Hutchinson who by "serpentine wiles" was befuddling and victimizing the weak, the avaricious, and the incautious in order to increase his notorious engrossment of public office. In Rhode Island it was, to James Otis, that "little, dirty, drinking, drabbing, contaminated knot of thieves, beggars, and transports . . . made up of Turks, Jews, and other infidels, with a few renegado Christians and Catholics" — the Newport junto, led by Martin Howard, Jr., which had already been accused by Stephen Hopkins and others in Providence of "conspiring against the liberties of the colony."

But even if local leaders associated with power elements in England had not been so suspect, there were grounds for seeing more behind the Stamp Act than its ostensible purpose. The official aim of the act was, of course, to bring in revenue to the English treasury. But the sums involved were in fact quite small, and "some persons . . . may be inclined to acquiesce under it." But that would be to fall directly into the trap, for the smaller the taxes, John Dickinson wrote in the most influential pamphlet published in America before 1776, the more dangerous they were, since they would the more easily be found acceptable by the incautious, with the result that a precedent would be established for making still greater inroads on liberty and property.

> Nothing is wanted at home but a PRECEDENT, the force of which shall be established by the tacit submission of the colonies . . . If the Parliament succeeds in this attempt, other statutes will impose other duties . . . and thus the Parliament will levy upon us such sums of money as they choose to take, *without any other* LIMITATION *than their* PLEASURE.

. . . To John Adams it seemed "very manifest" that the ultimate design behind the Stamp Act was an effort to forge the fatal link between ecclesiastical and civil despotism, the first by stripping the colonists "in a great measure of the means of knowledge, by loading the press, the colleges, and even an almanac and a newspaper with restraints and duties," the second, by recreating the inequalities and dependencies of feudalism "by taking from the poorer sort of people all their little subsistence, and conferring it on a set of stamp officers, distributors, and their deputies." This last point was the most obvious: "as the influence of money and places generally procures to the minister a majority in Parliament," Arthur Lee wrote, so an income from unchecked taxation would lead to a total corruption of free government in America, with the result that the colonies would "experience the fate of the *Roman* people in the deplorable times of their slavery."

But by then, in 1768, more explicit evidence of a wide-ranging plot was accumulating rapidly. Not only had the Townshend Duties, another revenue act, been passed by Parliament despite all the violence of the colonists' reaction to the Stamp Act, but it was a measure that enhanced the influence of the customs administration, which for other reasons had already come under suspicion. There had been, it was realized by the late 1760's, a sudden expansion in the number of "posts in the [colonial] 'government' . . . worth the attention of persons of influence in Great Britain" — posts, Franklin explained, like the governorships, filled by persons who were

> generally strangers to the provinces they are sent to govern, have no estate, natural connection, or relation there to give them an affection for the country . . . they come only to make money as fast as they can; are sometimes men of vicious characters and broken fortunes, sent by a minister merely to get them out of the way.

By the late 1760's, in the perspective of recent events, one could see that the invasion of customs officers "born with long claws like eagles," had begun as far back as the last years of the Seven Years' War and was now being reinforced by the new tax measures. The wartime Orders in Council demanding stricter enforcement of the Navigation Laws; the Sugar Act of 1764, which had multiplied the customs personnel; and the American Board of Customs Commissioners created in 1767 with "power," Americans said, "to constitute as many under officers as they please" — all of these developments could be seen to have provided for an "almost incredible number of inferior officers," most of whom the colonists believed to be "wretches . . . of such infamous characters that the merchants cannot possibly think their interest safe under their care." More important by far, however, was their influence on government.

For there was an obvious political and constitutional danger in having such "a set of *idle drones*," such "lazy, proud, worthless *pensioners* and *placemen*," in one's midst. It was nothing less than "a general maxim," James Wilson wrote,

> that the crown will take advantage of every opportunity of extending its prerogative in opposition to the privileges of the people, [and] that it is the interest of those who have *pensions* or *offices at will* from the crown to concur in all its measures.

These "baneful harpies" were instruments of power, of prerogative. They would upset the balance of the constitution by extending "*ministerial influence* as much beyond its former bounds as the late war did the British dominions." Parasitic officeholders, thoroughly corrupted by their obligations to those who had appointed them, would strive to "*distinguish themselves* by their sordid zeal in defending and promoting measures which *they know beyond all question* to be *destructive* to the *just rights* and *true interests* of their country." Seeking to "*serve the ambitious purposes of great men* at home," these "*base-spirited wretches*" would urge — were already urg-

ing — as they logically had to, the specious attractions of "SUBMISSIVE behavior."
They were arguing

> with a plausible affection of *wisdom* and *concern* how *prudent* it is to please the *powerful*
> — how *dangerous* to provoke them — and then comes in the perpetual incantation that
> freezes up every generous purpose of the soul in cold, inactive expectation — "that if
> there is any request to be made, compliance will obtain a favorable attention."

In the end, this extension of executive patronage, based on a limitless support of
government through colonial taxation, would make the whole of government
"merely a ministerial engine"; by throwing off the balance of its parts, it would destroy the protective machinery of the constitution.

But even this did not exhaust the evidence that a design against liberty was unfolding. During the same years the independence of the judiciary, so crucial a part
of the constitution, was suddenly seen to be under heavy attack, and by the mid-
1760's to have succumbed in many places.

This too was not a new problem. The status of the colonial judiciary had been a
controversial question throughout the century. The Parliamentary statute of 1701
which guaranteed judges in England life tenure in their posts had been denied to the
colonies, in part because properly trained lawyers were scarce in the colonies, especially in the early years, and appointments for life would prevent the replacement of
ill-qualified judges by their betters, when they appeared; and in part because, judicial salaries being provided for by temporary legislative appropriations, the removal
of all executive control from the judiciary, it was feared, would result in the hopeless
subordination of the courts to popular influences. The status of the judiciary in the
eighteenth century was therefore left open to political maneuvering in which, more
often than not, the home government managed to carry its point and to make the
tenure of judges as temporary as their salaries. Then suddenly, in the early 1760's,
the whole issue exploded. In 1759 the Pennsylvania Assembly declared that the
judges of that province would thereafter hold their offices by the same permanence
of tenure that had been guaranteed English judges after the Glorious Revolution.
But the law was disallowed forthwith by the crown. Opposition newspapers boiled
with resentment; angry speeches were made in the Assembly; and a pamphlet appeared explaining in the fullest detail the bearing of judicial independence on constitutional freedom.

In New York the issue was even more inflamed and had wider repercussions.
There, the judges of the Supreme Court, by a political maneuver of 1750, had managed to secure their appointments for life. But this tenure was interrupted by the
death of George II in 1760 which required the reissuance of all crown commissions.
An unpopular and politically weak lieutenant governor, determined to prevent his
enemies from controlling the courts, refused to recommission the judges on life tenure. The result was a ferocious battle in which the opposition asserted New York's
"*undoubted right* of having the judges of our courts on a constitutional basis," and
demanded the "liberties and privileges" of Englishmen in this connection as in all
others. But they were defeated, though not by the governor. In December 1761 orders were sent out from the King in Council to all the colonies, permanently forbidding the issuance of judges' commissions anywhere on any tenure but that of "the
pleasure of the crown. . . ."

"More and more," as the people contemplated the significance of crown salaries
for a judiciary that served "at pleasure," was it clear that "the designs of administra-

tion [were] totally to subvert the constitution." Any judge, the House in Massachusetts ultimately stated, who accepted such salaries would thereby declare "that he has not a due sense of the importance of an impartial administration of justice, that he is an enemy to the constitution, and has it in his heart to promote the establishment of an arbitrary government in the province. . . ."

The more one looked the more one found evidences of deliberate malevolence. In Massachusetts, Thomas Hutchinson's elaborate patronage machine, long in existence but fully organized only after the arrival of Governor Francis Bernard in 1760, appeared to suspicious tribunes like Oxenbridge Thacher and John Adams to constitute a serious threat to liberty. The Hutchinsons and the Olivers and their ambitious allies, it was said (and the view was widely circulated through the colonies), had managed, by accumulating a massive plurality of offices, to engross the power of all branches of the Massachusetts government thereby building a "foundation sufficient on which to erect a tyranny."

> Bernard had all the executive, and a negative of the legislative; Hutchinson and Oliver, by their popular arts and secret intrigues, had elevated to the [Council] such a collection of crown officers and their own relations as to have too much influence there; and they had three of a family on the superior bench . . . This junto, therefore, had the legislative and executive in their control, and more natural influence over the judicial than is ever to be trusted to any set of men in the world.

With encouragement, no doubt, from England, they were stretching their power beyond all proper bounds, becoming "conspirators against the public liberty. . . ."

Meanwhile an event even more sinister in its implications had taken place in the colonies themselves. On October 1, 1768, two regiments of regular infantry, with artillery, disembarked in Boston. For many months the harassed Governor Bernard had sought some legal means or excuse for summoning military help in his vain efforts to maintain if not an effective administration then at least order in the face of Stamp Act riots, circular letters, tumultuous town meetings, and assaults on customs officials. But the arrival of troops in Boston increased rather than decreased his troubles. For to a populace steeped in the literature of eighteenth-century English politics the presence of troops in a peaceful town had such portentous meaning that resistance instantly stiffened. It was not so much the physical threat of the troops that affected the attitudes of the Bostonians; it was the bearing their arrival had on the likely tendency of events. Viewed in the perspective of Trenchard's famous tracts on standing armies and of the vast derivative literature on the subject that flowed from the English debates of the 1690's, these were not simply soldiers assembled for police duties; they were precisely what history had proved over and over again to be prime movers of the process by which unwary nations lose "that precious jewel *liberty*." The mere rumor of possible troop arrivals had evoked the age-old apprehensions. "The raising or keeping a standing army within the kingdom in time of peace, unless it be with the consent of Parliament, is against the law," the alarmed Boston Town Meeting had resolved. It is, they said,

> the indefeasible right of [British] subjects to be *consulted* and to give their *free consent in person* or by representatives of their own free election to the raising and keeping a standing army among them; and the inhabitants of this town, being free subjects, have the same right derived from nature and confirmed by the British constitution as well as the said royal charter; and therefore the raising or keeping a standing army without their consent in person or by representatives of their own free election would be an infringement of their natural, constitutional, and charter rights; and the employing such army

for the enforcing of laws made without the consent of the people, in person or by their representatives, would be a grievance.

But the troops arrived, four regiments in all: in bold, stark actuality a standing army — just such a standing army as had snuffed out freedom in Denmark, classically, and elsewhere throughout the world. True, British regulars had been introduced into the colonies on a permanent basis at the end of the Seven Years' War; that in itself had been disquieting. But it had then been argued that troops were needed to police the newly acquired territories, and that they were not in any case to be regularly garrisoned in peaceful, populous towns. No such defense could be made of the troops sent to Boston in 1768. No simple, ingenuous explanation would suffice. The true motive was only too apparent for those with eyes to see. One of the classic stages in the process of destroying free constitutions of government had been reached.

To those most sensitive to the ideological currents of the day, the danger could scarcely have been greater. "To have a standing army!" Andrew Eliot wrote from Boston to Thomas Hollis in September, 1768, "Good God! What can be worse to a people who have tasted the sweets of liberty! Things are come to an unhappy crisis; there will never be that harmony between Great Britain and her colonies that there hath been; all confidence is at an end; and the moment there is any blood shed all affection will cease." He was convinced, he wrote, that if the English government "had not had their hands full at home they would have crushed the colonies." As it was, England's most recent actions tended only "to hasten that independency which at present the warmest among us deprecate." "I fear for the nation," he concluded, and his fears were shared not only by all liberty-minded Bostonians but also, through the stimulation of the "Journal of the Times," a day-by-day account of Boston "under military rule" that was, in effect, syndicated throughout the colonies, it was shared by politically and ideologically sensitive Americans everywhere. Time did not ease these anxieties; it merely complicated them. Fear and hatred became edged with contempt. "Our people begin to despise a military force," Eliot observed a year after the troops had first appeared; they coolly woo away the soldiers and drag offending officers before the courts — which, he grimly added, continue to function "notwithstanding all their efforts." But "things cannot long remain in the state they are now in; they are hastening to a crisis. What will be the event, God knows. . . ."

Unconstitutional taxing, the invasion of placemen, the weakening of the judiciary, plural officeholding, Wilkes, standing armies — these were major evidences of a deliberate assault of power upon liberty. Lesser testimonies were also accumulating at the same time: small episodes in themselves, they took on a large significance in the context in which they were received. Writs of assistance in support of customs officials were working their expected evil: "our houses, and even our bedchambers, are exposed to be ransacked, our boxes, trunks, and chests broke open, ravaged and plundered by wretches whom no prudent man would venture to employ even as menial servants." Legally convened legislatures had been "adjourned . . . to a place highly inconvenient to the members and greatly disadvantageous to the interest of the province"; they had been prorogued and dissolved at executive whim. Even the boundaries of colonies had been tampered with, whereby *"rights of soil"* had been eliminated at a stroke. When in 1772 the Boston Town Meeting met to draw up a full catalogue of the "infringements and violations" of the rights of the colonists, and of this province in particular, as men, as Christians, and as subjects," it approved a list of twelve items, which took seventeen pamphlet pages to describe.

But then, for a two-year period, there was a détente of sorts created by the repeal of the Townshend Duties, the withdrawal of troops from Boston, and the failure of other provocative measures to be taken. It ended abruptly, however, in the fall and winter of 1773, when, with a rush, the tendencies earlier noted were brought to fulfillment. In the space of a few weeks, all the dark, twisted roots of malevolence were finally revealed, plainly, for all to see.

The turning point was the passage of the Tea Act and the resulting Tea Party in Boston in December 1773. Faced with this defiant resistance to intimidation, the powers at work in England, it was believed, gave up all pretense of legality — "threw off the mask," John Adams said in a phrase that for a century had been used to describe just such climactic disclosures — and moved swiftly to complete their design. In a period of two months in the spring of 1774 Parliament took its revenge in a series of coercive actions no liberty-loving people could tolerate: the Boston Port Act, intended, it was believed, to snuff out the economic life of the Massachusetts metropolis; the Administration of Justice Act, aimed at crippling judicial processes once and for all by permitting trials to be held in England for offenses committed in Massachusetts; the Massachusetts Government Act, which stripped from the people of Massachusetts the protection of the British constitution by giving over all the "democratic" elements of the province's government — even popularly elected juries and town meetings — into the hands of the executive power; the Quebec Act, which, while not devised as a part of the coercive program, fitted it nicely, in the eyes of the colonists, by extending the boundaries of a "papist" province, and one governed wholly by prerogative, south into territory claimed by Virginia, Connecticut, and Massachusetts; finally, the Quartering Act, to take effect in all colonies, which permitted the seizure for the use of troops of all buildings, public and private, deserted and occupied.

Once these coercive acts were passed there could be little doubt that "the system of slavery fabricated against America . . . is the offspring of mature deliberation."

To the leaders of the Revolutionary movement there was, beyond question, "a settled, fixed plan for *enslaving* the colonies, or bringing them under arbitrary government, and indeed the nation too." By 1774 the idea "that the British government — the *King, Lords,* and *Commons* — have laid a regular plan to enslave America, and that they are now deliberately putting it in execution" had been asserted, Samuel Seabury wrote wearily but accurately, "over, and over, and over again." The less inhibited of the colonial orators were quick to point out that "the MONSTER of a standing ARMY" had sprung directly from "a PLAN . . . *systematically* laid, and pursued by the British *ministry,* near twelve years, for enslaving America"; the Boston Massacre, it was claimed, had been "planned by Hillsborough and a knot of treacherous knaves in Boston." Careful analysts like Jefferson agreed on the major point; in one of the most closely reasoned of the pamphlets of 1774 the Virginian stated unambiguously that though "single acts of tyranny may be ascribed to the accidental opinion of a day . . . a series of oppressions, begun at a distinguished period and pursued unalterably through every change of ministers, too plainly prove a deliberate and systematical plan of reducing us to slavery." So too the fastidious and scholarly John Dickinson, though in 1774 he still clung to the hope that inadvertence, at least on the part of the King, was involved, believed that "a plan had been deliberately framed and pertinaciously adhered to, unchanged even by frequent changes of ministers, unchecked by any intervening gleam of humanity, to sacrifice to a passion for arbitrary dominion the universal property, liberty, safety, honor, happiness, and prosperity of us unoffending yet devoted Americans." So too Washington, collaborating with George Mason in writing the Fairfax Resolves of 1774, agreed that the trouble had arisen from a "regular, systematic plan" of oppression, the English government "endeavoring by every piece of art and despotism to fix the shackles of slavery upon us"; he was convinced "beyond the smallest doubt," he wrote privately, "that these measures are the result of deliberation . . . I am as fully convinced as I am of my own existence that there has been a regular, systematic plan formed to enforce them. . . ."

The most common explanation, however — an explanation that rose from the deepest sources of British political culture, that was a part of the very structure of British political thought — located "the spring and cause of all the distresses and complaints of the people in England or in America" in "a kind of fourth power that the constitution knows nothing of, or has not provided against." This "overruling arbitrary power, which absolutely controls the King, Lords, and Commons," was composed, it was said, of the "ministers and favorites" of the King, who, in defiance of God and man alike, "extend their usurped authority infinitely too far," and, throwing off the balance of the constitution, make their "despotic will" the authority of the nation.

> For their power and interest is so great that they can and do procure whatever laws they please, having (by power, interest, and the application of the people's money to *placemen* and *pensioners*) the whole legislative authority at their command. So that it is plain (not to say a word of a particular reigning arbitrary *Stuarchal* power among them) that the rights of the people are ruined and destroyed by ministerial *tyrannical* authority, and thereby . . . become a kind of slaves to the ministers of state.

This "junto of courtiers and state-jobbers," these "court-locusts," whispering in the royal ear, "instill in the King's mind a divine right of authority to command his subjects" at the same time as they advance their "detestable scheme" by misinforming and misleading the people. . . .

Perhaps the most explicit and detailed explanation of the assault upon America by a conspiratorial ministry, encapsulating a century of opposition thought, came from the pen of a country parson in Connecticut writing "to enlighten the people of a country town not under the best advantages for information from the newspapers and other pieces wrote upon the controversy." Seeking to rouse the villagers "to a sense of the danger to which their liberties are now involved," the Rev. Ebenezer Baldwin of Danbury explained that during the last war "the state of the colonies was much more attended to than it had been in times past," and "a very exalted idea of the riches of this country" had been conveyed back to England by the returning officers and soldiers. This exciting information fitted the plans of the ministry neatly, for

> notwithstanding the excellency of the British constitution, if the ministry can secure a majority in Parliament who will come into all their measures [and] will vote as they bid them, they may rule as absolutely as they do in *France* or *Spain,* yea as in *Turkey* or *India.* And this seems to be the present plan: to secure a majority of Parliament, and thus enslave the nation with their own consent. The more places or pensions the ministry have in their gift the more easily they can *bribe* a majority of Parliament by bestowing

those places on them or their friends. This makes them erect so many new and unnecessary offices in America, even so as to swallow up the whole of the revenue . . . by bestowing these places — places of considerable profit and no labor — upon the children or friends or dependents of the members of Parliament, the ministry can secure them in their interest. This doubtless is the great thing the ministry are driving at, to establish arbitrary government with the consent of Parliament. And to keep the people of England still, the first exertions of this power are upon the colonies.

Thus the balance of the constitution had been thrown off by a gluttonous ministry usurping the prerogatives of the crown and systematically corrupting the independence of the Commons. Corruption was at the heart of it — the political corruption built on the general dissoluteness of the populace, so familiar in the history of tyranny and so shocking to observers of mid-eighteenth-century England. The evil, public and private, that had appalled Dickinson in 1754 had ripened, it seemed clear, in the subsequent decade. . . .

. . . "Liberty," John Adams wrote, "can no more exist without virtue and independence than the body can live and move without a soul," and what liberty can be expected to flow from England where "luxury, effeminacy, and venality are arrived at such a shocking pitch" and where "both electors and elected are become one mass of corruption"? It was not hard to see where England stood: it was, Adams declared, precisely at the point "where the Roman republic was when Jugurtha left it, and pronounced it 'a venal city, ripe for destruction, if it can only find a purchaser.'" The analogy to the decline and fall of Rome and its empire was intriguing and informative; others carried it further and became more specific. Like Rome in its decline, England, "from being the nursery of heroes, became the residence of musicians, pimps, panders, and catamites." The swift decline of her empire, which, it was observed, had reached its peak only between 1758 and the Stamp Act, resulted from the same poison that had proved so fatal to free states in classical antiquity: the corruption, effeminacy, and languor that came from "the riches and luxuries of the East" and led to a calamitous "decay of virtue" and the collapse of the constitution. Even Franklin, his old caution and careful optimism gone, agreed, writing in 1775 to his one-time political ally Joseph Galloway, that he would himself, reluctantly, have to oppose Galloway's plan for reconciliation.

. . . when I consider the extreme corruption prevalent among all orders of men in this old rotten state, and the glorious public virtue so predominant in our rising country, I cannot but apprehend more mischief than benefit from a closer union. I fear they will drag us after them in all the plundering wars which their desperate circumstances, injustice, and rapacity may prompt them to undertake; and their wide-wasting prodigality and profusion is a gulf that will swallow up every aid we may distress ourselves to afford them. Here numberless and needless places, enormous salaries, pensions, perquisites, bribes, groundless quarrels, foolish expeditions, false accounts or no accounts, contracts and jobs, devour all revenue and produce continual necessity in the midst of natural plenty. I apprehend, therefore, that to unite us intimately will only be to corrupt and poison us also. . . .

The fact that the ministerial conspiracy against liberty had risen from corruption was of the utmost importance to the colonists. It gave a radical new meaning to their claims: it transformed them from constitutional arguments to expressions of a world regenerative creed. For they had long known — it had been known everywhere in the English-speaking world in the eighteenth century — that England was one of the last refuges of the ancient gothic constitution that had once flourished everywhere in the civilized world. And now, in the outpourings of colonial protest, it was again repeated, but with new point and urgency, that by far "the greatest part of the human race" already lies in "total subjection to their rulers." Throughout the whole continent of Asia people are reduced "to such a degree of abusement and degradation"

> that the very idea of liberty is unknown among them. In *Africa,* scarce any human beings are to be found but barbarians, tyrants, and slaves: all equally remote from the true dignity of human nature and from a well-regulated state of society. Nor is *Europe* free from the curse. Most of her nations are forced to drink deep of the bitter cup. And in those in which freedom seem to have been established, the vital flame is going out. Two kingdoms, those of *Sweden* and *Poland,* have been betrayed and enslaved in the course of one year. The free towns of *Germany* can remain free no longer than their potent neighbors shall please to let them. *Holland* has got the forms if she has lost the spirit of a free country. *Switzerland* alone is in the full and safe possession of her freedom.

And if now, in this deepening gloom, the light of liberty went out in Britain too — in Britain, where next to "self-preservation, political liberty is the main aim and end of her constitution" — if, as events clearly portended and as "senators and historians are repeatedly predicting . . . continued corruption and standing armies will prove mortal distempers in her constitution" — what then? What refuge will liberty find?

"To our own country," it was answered, "must we look for the biggest part of that liberty and freedom that yet remains, or is to be expected, among mankind . . . For while the greatest part of the nations of the earth are held together under the yoke of universal slavery, the North American provinces yet remain *the country of free men:* the *asylum,* and the last, to which such may yet flee from the common deluge." More than that: "our native country . . . bids the fairest of any to promote *the perfection and happiness of mankind.*" No one, of course, can predict "the state of mankind in future ages." But insofar as one can judge the ultimate "designs of providence by the number and power of the causes that are already at work, we shall be led to think that the perfection and happiness of mankind is to be carried further in America than it has ever yet been in any place." Consider the growth the colonies had enjoyed in so short a time — growth in all ways, but especially in population: a great natural increase it had been, supplemented by multitudes from Europe, "tired out with the miseries they are doomed to at home," migrating to America "as the only country in which they can find food, raiment, and rest." Consider also the physical vigor of the people. But above all consider the moral health of the people and of the body politic.

> The fatal arts of luxury and corruption are but comparatively beginning among us . . . Nor is corruption yet established as the common principle in public affairs. Our representatives are not chosen by bribing, corrupting, or buying the votes of the electors. Nor does it take one half of the revenue of a province to manage her house of commons . . . We have been free also from the burden and danger of standing armies . . . Our defense has been our *militia* . . . the general operation of things among ourselves indicate strong tendencies towards a state of greater perfection and happiness than mankind has yet seen.

No one, therefore, can conceive of the cause of America as "the cause of a mob, of a party, or a faction." The cause of America "is the cause of *self-defense,* of *public faith,* and of the *liberties of mankind* . . . 'In our destruction, liberty itself expires, and human nature will despair of evermore regaining its first and original dignity.' "

This theme, elaborately orchestrated by the colonial writers, marked the fulfill-ment of the ancient idea, deeply embedded in the colonists' awareness, that America had from the start been destined to play a special role in history. The controversy with England, from its beginning in the early 1760's, had lent support to that belief, so long nourished by so many different sources: the covenant theories of the Puri-tans, certain strands of Enlightenment thought, the arguments of the English radi-cals, the condition of life in the colonies, even the conquest of Canada. It had been the Stamp Act that had led John Adams to see in the original settlement of the colo-nies "the opening of a grand scene and design in providence for the illumination of the ignorant and the emancipation of the slavish part of mankind all over the earth." And Jonathan Mayhew, celebrating the conclusion of the same episode, had envi-sioned future streams of refugees escaping from a Europe sunk in "luxury, debauch-ery, venality, intestine quarrels, or other vices." It was even possible, Mayhew had added, "who knows?" that "our liberties being thus established . . . on some future occasion . . . we or our posterity may even have the great felicity and honor to . . . keep Britain herself from ruin."

Now, in 1774, that "future occasion" was believed to be at hand. After the pas-sage of the Coercive Acts it could be said that "all the spirit of patriotism or of lib-erty now left in England" was no more than "the last snuff of an expiring lamp," while "the same sacred flame . . . which once showed forth such wonders in Greece and in Rome . . . burns brightly and strongly in America." Who ought then to sup-press as "whimsical and enthusiastical" the belief that the colonies were to become "the foundation of a great and mighty empire, the largest the world ever saw to be founded on such principles of liberty and freedom, both civil and religious . . . [and] which shall be the principal seat of that glorious kingdom which Christ shall erect upon earth in the latter days" ? America "ere long will build an empire upon the ruins of Great Britain; will adopt its constitution purged of its impurities, and from an experience of its defects will guard against those evils which have wasted its vigor and brought it to an untimely end." The hand of God was "in America now giving a new epocha to the history of the world."

In the invigorating atmosphere of such thoughts, the final conclusion of the colo-nists' logic could be drawn not with regret but with joy. For while everyone knew that when tyranny is abroad "submission is a crime"; while they readily acknowl-edged that "no obedience is due to arbitrary, unconstitutional edicts calculated to enslave a free people"; and while they knew that the invasion of the liberties of the people "constitutes a state of war with the people" who may properly use "all the power which God has given them" to protect themselves — nevertheless they hesi-tated to come to a final separation even after Lexington and Bunker Hill. They hesi-tated, moving slowly and reluctantly, protesting "before God and the world that the utmost of [our] wish is that things may return to their old channel." They hesitated because their *sentiments of duty and affection"* were sincere; they hesitated because their respect for constituted authority was great; and they hesitated too because their future as an independent people was a matter of doubt, full of the fear of the unknown.

What would an independent American nation be? A republic, necessarily — and properly, considering the character and circumstances of the people. But history clearly taught that republics were delicate polities, quickly degenerating into anar-chy and tyranny; it was impossible, some said, to "recollect a single instance of a nation who supported this form of government for any length of time or with any degree of greatness." Others felt that independence might "split and divide the empire into a number of petty, insignificant states" that would easily fall subject to the will of "some foreign tyrant, or the more intolerable despotism of a few American demagogues"; the colonies might end by being "parceled out, Poland-like."

But if what the faint-hearted called "the ill-shapen, diminutive brat, INDEPENDENCY" contained within it all that remained of freedom; if it gave promise of growing great and strong and becoming the protector and propagator of liberty everywhere; if it were indeed true that "the cause of America is in a great measure the cause of all mankind"; if " 'Tis not the concern of a day, a year, or an age; posterity are virtually involved in the contest, and will be more or less affected even to the end of time by our proceedings now" — if all of this were true, ways would be found by men inspired by such prospects to solve the problems of a new society and government. And so let every lover of mankind, every hater of tyranny,

stand forth! Every spot of the old world is overrun with oppression. Freedom hath been hunted round the globe. Asia and Africa have long expelled her. Europe regards her like a stranger, and England hath given her warning to depart. O! receive the fugitive, and prepare in time an asylum for mankind.

The Nature of the American Revolution

Periodically, newspaper reporters, without identifying the document, ask Americans if they would be willing to sign the Declaration of Independence. Typically most Americans refuse, some describing it as "Commie junk," others certain that "Somebody ought to tell the FBI about this sort of rubbish." A nation, conceived in revolution, thus seems fearful of acknowledging its revolutionary history, perhaps because revolution, in our own time, has become identified with turbulent worldwide conditions that many believe threaten American society. Yet America was a revolutionary nation, and its example once inspired the downtrodden elsewhere to fight for their liberty.

In the following essay, Thomas C. Barrow seeks to discover how revolutionary the American Revolution was, and to determine how it compares with other great revolutions in modern history, such as the French and Russian. Barrow argues that, at least at the outset, the American Revolution was a struggle against foreign rule, rather than an internal upheaval, as it occurred in France and Russia where the oppressed masses toppled their rulers in the hope of creating a more just social order. Such social revolutions stem from deep-seated and long-standing conflicts over the very nature of the social system. The American quarrel with Great Britain, however, was of a much more limited nature. It was essentially a demand for home rule. Moreover, the origins of the Revolution profoundly influenced the direction the new nation took. Though the American Revolution did bring about important changes in the social order, they were relatively modest compared to the transformations occurring in France after 1789, or Russia after 1917, or China after 1948.

The principal problem Americans faced after 1776 was not redistributing wealth or privilege, but coping successfully with the demands of nation-building. These included devising constitutions and governments that citizens would respect and obey, integrating diverse elements into a nation strong enough to defend itself against other nations, and promoting the general welfare even when it conflicted with parochial interests.

Yet the absence from the American Revolution of a reign of terror or of bloody purges of the ruling classes should not obscure its genuinely revolutionary character. In 1776, kings and aristocrats ruled almost everywhere. Few, except the Americans, believed that republican government, resting on a measure of popular control, was practical. Conventional wisdom held that men were too turbulent to be governed except by kings and noblemen, that liberty and order were incompatible, and that people must sacrifice freedom for the sake of stability. The Americans understood how perilous their experiment in republicanism was, but they were confident that they could discover how to reconcile liberty with order. Sustaining them during the early years, when the country was an untested beleaguered nation, was the faith, expressed by James Madison that "the citizens of the United States are responsible for the greatest trust ever confided to a political authority." That trust was to demonstrate to a skeptical world the practicality of a government based on the consent of the governed, a notion truly revolutionary in most of the world until recently.

FOR FURTHER READING:

GIPSON, LAWRENCE H. *The Coming of The Revolution.* New York: Harper & Row, Publishers, 1954.*
GREENE, JACK P., ed. *The Reinterpretation of the American Revolution.* New York: Harper & Row, Publishers, 1969.*
PALMER, R. R. *Age of Democratic Revolution: The Challenge.* Princeton: Princeton University Press, 1969.*

Asterisk denotes paperback edition.

The American Revolution as a Colonial War for Independence   THOMAS C. BARROW

The current historiographical controversies over the American Revolution owe much to Carl Becker. From Becker's day to the present, historians have debated the question of the existence or non-existence of an "internal revolution" in American society. Some historians, following Becker's lead, search for traces of internal social or political turmoil. Others, disagreeing with Becker, stress the continuity of institutions and traditions during the Revolution. At issue is the basic question of just "how revolutionary was the American Revolution," and in the failure of historians to agree on an answer to that question lies the source of controversy. And so the great debate continues.

Unfortunately, there is no adequate definition of a "revolution." The dictionary description of a revolution as a "total or radical change" certainly provides no effective guideline. Since history is the study of change in human society, locating a revolution according to that formula becomes a matter of appraising just how much change is involved in a given event, which inevitably comes down to a question of where one wants to place the emphasis. In any case, precise definitions are somewhat beside the point. When the word *revolution* is used today in connection with a political system, its meaning, if not its precise definition, is abundantly clear. The image called to mind is inescapably that of the French and Russian revolutions, which have provided us with our classic formulas for revolutionary re-structurings of society. A revolution in these terms represents the replacement of an archaic, repressive regime or regimes with something new, something more open, more flexible, more adaptable. In effect, in the interests of "progress," within the political system stability is replaced by instability until some new synthesis is achieved. Only then is stability restored, at which point the revolutionary drama is closed.

For generations now American historians have struggled to fit their "revolution" into this classic mold. The difficulties they have encountered in doing so are reflected in the present historiographical impasse. It is a problem that might have been avoided had we remembered that the American people were, until 1776, colonials. By its very nature, a colonial society must be, in certain vital ways, unstable. Unable to exercise complete political control, subject to continual external interven-

Source: Thomas C. Barrow, "The American Revolution as a Colonial War for Independence," *William and Mary Quarterly,* 3d ser., vol. 25 (1968), pp. 452–464.

tion and negative interference, a colonial society cannot achieve effective "maturity" — that is, cannot create and control a political system that will be suited to the requirements of the interests indigenous to that society. A colonial society is an "incomplete" society, and consequently an inherently unstable society. This was as true of American society prior to 1776 as it is today of the colonial societies left in our world. And, consequently, if instability is the given fact in American society at the beginning of the imperial crisis, it is hard to see how the classic pattern of "stability replaced by instability" can be imposed upon it. The answer, of course, is that it cannot, that in fact colonial wars for independence or "liberation" are generically different from revolutions of the French or Russian variety. And, after all, the American Revolution was just that — a colonial war of liberation. Given the widespread existence of such wars in today's world, it is odd that for so long a time we have overlooked the full implications of this fact.

Colonial wars for independence have an inner logic of their own. The first problem is to achieve self-determination. Once that is accomplished, it then becomes a matter of organization, about which, naturally, there always will be fundamental disagreement. What course this disagreement will take, and how bitter it will be, will be determined by the nature of the particular society. In former colonies which have emerged into nationhood in this century, the determining factor has largely been the heterogeneous nature of their societies; with little internal unity or coherence, these new nations generally have fallen back at first on authoritarian centralism. When this has proved incapable of solving the complex problems confronting the society, it has been replaced usually by some kind of collective leadership, often based on the only effective national organization in existence, the military. It is at this point that many of the emergent nations of today find themselves.

Americans were more fortunate in their escape from colonialism. Thanks to the nature of the First British Empire, with its emphasis on commercial growth rather than on imperial efficiency, its loose organization, and the high degree of self-government allowed to the colonists, Americans had developed effective political units which commanded the allegiance of most inhabitants and served as adequate vehicles for the transition from colonial status to nationhood. Given a common English inheritance and a common struggle against British "tyranny," these states made the transition with a minimum of disagreement and dissension. In effect, by 1760 self-government in America, while still incomplete, had gone far. A tightening of English imperial authority after the last war with France brought about a reaction within the colonies toward complete self-determination, which was achieved finally through military success.

Yet, whatever the difference of the American experience from other colonial wars of liberation, certain elements were of necessity shared in common. Within any colonial society there exists an establishment, a group of men whose interests and situation tie them to the existing structure and whose orientation is towards the preservation of the colonial status. When the issue of independence or self-determination begins to be debated, these men are caught in powerful crosscurrents. As natives to the society, they identify to some degree with its problems. At the same time, as beneficiaries of their privileged position within the existing colonial structure, they are not enthusiastic for change. Such men fall back on arguments of moderation, particularly stressing the economic benefits of association with the dominant country and also emphasizing the immaturity of their own society. The gains associated with independence are outweighed for them by the prospects of social and political disorganization. So these men cast their lot with their colonial rulers. Such a man was Thomas Hutchinson. So, too, were many of his Tory associates.

And men like Hutchinson found much to disturb them within American society. Actually, not only was American colonial society subjected to the instability normally inherent in colonial status but there were certain peculiar circumstances which complicated matters further. The melting-pot aspects of American society, the diversity of ethnic, religious, and cultural backgrounds to be found within it, created problems of communication. And, of equal importance, American colonial society was, after all, an artificial creation. Unlike most other historic colonial episodes, the American case was not a matter of an indigenous native society being expropriated and exploited by outsiders. In such instances, the pre-existing patterns of such native societies provide a degree of internal continuity and stability. But the English colonies in North America had at their disposal no such pre-existence. They were created specifically and artificially to perform certain functions in relation to the mother country. Most particularly, from the very beginning their economy was geared to production for distant markets over which they had no control and little influence.

At the same time, while there were sizable non-English elements within the colonial population which created special problems, nevertheless the majority of the colonists were of the same national origin as their "rulers." It was not an instance of a conquered native population forced to bow fatalistically before the superior skills and power of an alien culture. Rather, it was a case in large part of Englishmen being governed and exploited by Englishmen. The result was a high degree of friction between governed and governors — an insistence by the colonists on their rights as Englishmen — that gave a special flavor and complexity to colonial politics.

Thoughful colonials were well aware of and influenced by these problems. Thomas Hutchinson and John Adams — Tory and Whig — disagreed not so much on the question of the eventual independence of the American colonies as on the question of timing. Hutchinson's toryism sprang in part from his conviction that American society was too immature, too unstable, to stand alone. External force and authority, it seemed to him, would be required for many years to maintain internal order and stability in America. Realistically, he understood that eventually independence was probable: "It is not likely that the American Colonies will remain part of the Dominions of Great Britain another Century." But, Hutchinson added, until then, "as we cannot otherwise subsist I am consulting the best interest of my country when I propose measures for maintaining this subjection [to England]." What particularly disturbed Hutchinson about the changes in English policy after 1760 was that they tended to increase the instability and disorder inherent within American society: "Sieur Montesquieu is right in supposing men good or bad according to the Climate where they live. In less than two centuries Englishmen by change of country are become more barbarous and fierce than the Savages who inhabited the country before they extirpated them, the Indians themselves."

John Adams viewed American development in a different way. Contrasting the New World with the Old, he found the former far superior. The settlement of America had produced men who "knew that government was a plain, simple, intelligible thing, founded in nature and reason, and quite comprehensible by common sense. They detested all the base services and servile dependencies of the feudal system . . . and they thought all such slavish subordinations were equally inconsistent with the constitution of human nature and that religious liberty with which Jesus had made them free." The problem was that this purity of mind and behavior was always threatened by contact with the corruption of the Old World. Specifically, subordination of Americans to a distant Parliament which knew little of their needs and desires was not only frustrating but dangerous to the American experiment: "A legislature that has so often discovered a want of information concerning us and our country; a legislature interested to lay burdens upon us; a legislature, two branches of which, I mean the lords and commons, neither love nor fear us! Every American of fortune and common sense, must look upon his property to be sunk downright one half of its value, the moment such an absolute subjection to parliament is established." Independence was a logical capstone to such reasoning, although it took Adams some time to take that final step.

The differences between Hutchinson and Adams suggest that the divisions in American society between conservatives and radicals on the question of separation from Great Britain were related in part to a disagreement over the means to achieve coherence or stability within American society. For one side, continued tutelage under English authority was a necessity until such a time as maturity was achieved. For the other, it seemed that the major roadblock to maturity, to internal harmony and unity, was that self-same English authority. In effect, it was a disagreement on means, not ends. And disagreements similar to that between Hutchinson and Adams can be found within any society — whether in the eighteenth or twentieth century — which is in the process of tearing itself loose from its colonial ties.

It is possible, too, to suggest certain similarities between American intellectual development in these years and the experience of other colonial peoples. From his study of politics in eighteenth-century America, and particularly from his analysis of the pamphlet literature of the Revolutionary years, Bernard Bailyn has concluded that the "configuration of ideas and attitudes" which comprised the "Revolutionary ideology could be found intact — completely formed — as far back as the 1730's" and that these ideas had their origin in the "transmission from England to America of the literature of political opposition that furnished the substance of the ideology of the Revolution." Colonial societies are both fascinated and yet antagonized by the culture of the dominant exploiting nation. They tend to borrow much from their rulers. The English background of a majority of the American colonists in their case made such borrowing a natural and easy process, particularly for those who, for one reason or another, identified themselves with British rule.

However, in colonial societies even many of those who are anxious to assert, or preserve, their native interests or culture cannot resist that fascination exerted by the dominant "mother country." These "patriots" borrow, too, but they are likely to borrow from the dissenting tradition within the dominant culture, from the literature of "opposition," to utilize in their own defense the language and literature of those elements within the ruling society which are critical, or subversive, of the governing traditions. In this way the prestige of the "superior" society can be used against that society itself. On the evidence of Bailyn's research, it seems that the Americans followed just such a line of development, fitting the "opposition" tradition into the framework of their own evolving institutions and traditions — a process which was facilitated by the natural connections between the American religious dissenting traditions and the "opposition" traditions of eighteenth-century English society.

Again, once the movement for independence enters its final phase within a colonial society and becomes an open contest of strength, other divisions tend to become obscured. The most determined supporters of the colonial rule are silenced or forced to rely increasingly on the military strength of their rulers to maintain their position. On the other side, the advocates of independence submerge momentarily whatever differences they may have and present a common front. It is a time of common effort, of mutual support within the forces interested in achieving self-determination. At the same time the "patriot" groups develop special organizations capable of coercing those elements within society, often a majority of the population, which are inclined towards neutrality or moderation. Such were the Sons of Liberty in the American Revolution, and the evidence suggests that they performed their work effectively. Partly because of their efforts, and more generally because of the peculiar character of American colonial society and the nature of the imperial conflict, American society weathered the crisis with relative stability and harmony. As John Adams put it, "The zeal and ardor of the people during the revolutionary war, supplying the place of government, commanded a degree of order, sufficient at least for the temporary preservation of society."

With independence come altered circumstances for a former colonial society. Victorious patriots, confronted with the task of creating a permanent political structure, gradually begin to disagree among themselves as to how it can best be done. Since the only effective central direction came previously from the colonial rulers, the problem in each newly independent society is to fit the surviving local units into some coherent national structure. Here the forces of localism and centralism come into conflict. Those men or interests firmly entrenched in their positions at the local level see in increased centralism a threat to their existence and power. On the other hand, those men or interests of a more cosmopolitan nature, geared to extra-local activities and contacts, can see the benefits that would accrue to them through the introduction of the smoother flow of communications and transactions that effective centralization would bring. The disagreement pits the particularism of the entrenched local interests and individuals against the nationalism of the cosmopolitan interests and individuals. In most contemporary emergent societies these latter groups are by far the weaker. Fortunately, in America the cosmopolitan groups were stronger and more effective, partly again because of the unusual origin and nature of American colonial society. From the beginning the English colonies had been geared to production for European markets; it was the reason for their existence. The result was the development of an economy which had geographical variations but a common external orientation. Merchants and large-scale producers of items for export dominated this society. In the period after independence was achieved, these men provided a firm base for the construction of an effective national political system. Their success came with the substitution of the Constitution of 1787 for the Articles of Confederation.

Historians following the Becker-Beard approach put a different interpretation on the period following the achievement of de facto independence. For them, it was the moment of the triumph of radical democratic elements within American society. The wording of the Declaration of Independence, the constitutions of the new state governments, and particularly the drawing up of the Articles of Confederation represent for these historians the influence of a form of "radicalism." Yet, as Elisha Douglass has noted, in the formation of the governments for the new states, rather puzzlingly the one political reorganization that was subjected to the most democratic method of discussion and adoption — that of Massachusetts — turned out to be not only the most conservative of all the state constitutions but more conservative, in fact, than the previous system. Somehow in Massachusetts, at least, an excess of democracy seems to have led to an enthronement of conservatism. And, indeed, the new constitutions or systems adopted in all the states were remarkable generally for their adherence to known and familiar forms and institutions.

Obviously, given the disruption of the traditional ties to England, the interruption of the natural economic dependence on English markets, the division of American society into opposing Whig and Tory camps, and the presence on American soil of enemy troops (which occupied at different moments the most important commercial centers), some confusion and dissension was inevitable within American society. What is remarkable is how little upheaval and disagreement there actually was. Had American society been ripe for a social upheaval, had it been comprised of oppressing and oppressed classes, no better opportunity could have been offered. The conservative nature of the American response suggests that something other than a radical re-structuring of society was what was debated or desired.

Again, some historians have interpreted the decentralized political system created under the Articles of Confederation as a "triumph" of radical democracy. However, if instability, associated with colonial status and with the peculiar character of American colonial society, was a recurrent problem, and if inability to achieve positive control of their own political system was a major irritant, then the decentralization of the Articles was a logical development. In effect, if home rule was the issue and the cure, it was only natural that each local unit should seek as much autonomy within the national framework as possible. Seemingly, decentralization was the best method to bring coherence and stability, or maturity, to American society. Each local unit could look to its own needs, could arrange for the effective solution of its own special problems, could work to create that internal balance and harmony of conflicting interests that are the earmark of stability and maturity.

The problem with the Articles was not an excess of democracy. What brought about an effective opposition to them was their failure to achieve their purpose. The history of the states under the Articles, at least in the eyes of many contemporaries, suggested that decentralization, rather than being a source of stability, was a source of confusion and turmoil. James Madison explained the nature of the mistake in his Tenth Federalist. In spite of independence, under the system created by the Articles, wrote Madison, "complaints are everywhere heard from our most considerate and virtuous citizens . . . that our governments are too unstable." The problem, for Madison, was to control faction within society, and the most dangerous type of faction is that which includes a majority. Unfortunately, the "smaller the society, the fewer probably will be the distinct parties and interests composing it; the fewer the distinct parties and interests, the more frequently will a majority be found of the same party; and the smaller the number of individuals composing a majority, and the smaller the compass within which they are placed, the more easily will they concert and execute their plans of oppression." The solution is to enlarge the sphere, because if "you take in a greater variety of parties and interests," then "you make it less probable that a majority of the whole will have a common motive to invade the rights of other citizens . . . The influence of factious leaders may kindle a flame within their particular States, but will be unable to spread a general conflagration through the other States."

Nor was the opposition to the Constitution less concerned than Madison about order and stability within society. Again, disagreement was fundamentally over means, not ends. The anti-Federalists clung to the former ideas of local autonomy. They were, in fact, not more democratic than their opponents but more conservative. They were afraid of change: "If it were not for the stability and attachment which time and habit gives to forms of government, it would be in the power of the enlightened and aspiring few, if they should combine, at any time to destroy the best establishments, and even make the people the instruments of their own subjugation." The trouble was that the system created under the Articles was not yet sanctified by time: "The late revolution having effaced in a great measure all former habits, and the present institutions are so recent, that there exists not that great reluctance to innovation, so remarkable in old communities . . . it is the genius of the common law to resist innovation." George Clinton agreed with Madison on the dangers of faction: "The people, when wearied with their distresses, will in the moment of frenzy, be guilty of the most imprudent and desperate measures. . . . I know the people are too apt to vibrate from one extreme to another. The effects of this disposition are what I wish to guard against." It was on the solution to the problem, not on the nature of the problem, that Clinton differed from Madison. For Clinton, the powerful central government created by the Constitution might too easily become a vehicle for popular tyranny. It was this same sentiment which led eventually to the adoption of the first ten amendments, the Bill of Rights, with their reservations of basic rights and powers to local units and individuals.

It would not do to carry the comparison between the American Revolution and other colonial wars of liberation, particularly those of the twentieth century, too far. But there is enough evidence to suggest certain basic similarities between the American experience and that of other emergent colonial peoples — enough evidence, at least, to suggest that the efforts of historians to impose on the American Revolution the classic pattern of the French and Russian revolutions have led to a distorted view of our national beginnings. A French Revolution is the product of unbearable tensions within a society. The purpose of such a revolution is to destroy society as it exists, or at least to destroy its most objectional aspects, and to replace the old with something new. In contrast, a colonial "revolution" or war of liberation has as its purpose the achievement of self-determination, the "completion" or fulfillment of an existing society, rather than its destruction. A French Revolution is first of all destructive; a colonial revolution, first of all constructive. In either case the process may not be completed. In the instance of the French Revolution, the re-constructed society may contain more of the old than the original revolutionaries desired. And in the case of the colonial revolution, the process of winning independence and the difficulties of organizing an effective national political structure may open the gates to change, may create a radicalism that carries the original society far from its former course; the result may be more destruction than was originally envisaged. Yet, the goals of these two revolutions are fundamentally different, and their different goals determine a different process of fulfillment. The unfolding of the revolutionary drama, the "stages" of revolution, will be quite different, if not opposite.

For John Adams, the American Revolution was an epochal event, a moment of wonder for the world to behold and consider. At times his rhetoric carried him beyond the confines of his innate caution, and he sounded like a typical revolutionary: "The progress of society will be accelerated by centuries by this revolution . . . Light spreads from the dayspring in the west, and may it shine more and more until the perfect day." But, as Edward Handler has noted, "The truth is that if Adams was a revolutionary, he was so in a sense very different than that produced by the other great modern revolutions." Adams did indeed feel that his revolution had a meaning for the world but it was not related to the violent re-structurings of society. Rather its message, for Adams, was that free men can decide voluntarily to limit their freedom in the interests of mutual association, that rational men can devise a system that can at once create order and preserve liberty. The American success was in contrast to the traditional authoritarian systems of the Old World: "Can authority be more amiable or respectable, when it descends from accidents or institutions established in remote antiquity, than when it springs fresh from the hearts and judgments of an honest and enlightened people?"

Most wars of liberation are not so orderly as that of the American Revolution. Most, at least in this century, have led to increasing radicalism and division within the liberated society. National unity has not been easily achieved. That the American emergence from colonialism had a different ending is significant. A firm basis for unity obviously existed within American society, which, naturally, suggests that the reverse, too, was true — that such tensions and divisions as did exist within American society were relatively minor and harmless. It is no wonder that historians determined to find an internal social or political revolution of the French variety within the American Revolution have encountered such difficulties. Nor is it a wonder that the Revolution has become so beclouded with historiographical debates and arguments. The problem has been in our approach. We have been studying, it would seem, the wrong revolution.

The Founding Fathers: Democrats or Aristocrats?

The revolutionary generation learned that it was far easier to declare American independence in 1776 than to set up a viable republic. For almost fifteen years, Americans searched for a workable political structure that would give them a central government, powerful enough to promote those general interests and perform functions beyond the capacity of the states, without creating a monster which undermined local authority and ignored local concerns. Their experience with Britain taught Americans to fear centralized government, and so the first attempt at nation-building — the Articles of Confederation — left sovereign power in the hands of the states, while at the same time thrusting formidable responsibilities for foreign affairs, the conduct of war and public finance, on Congress. The Confederation proved inadequate and various schemes to strengthen it foundered.

Convened to repair the Articles, the convention which assembled in Philadelphia in May 1787 designed instead a wholly new framework for the Union. For generations, the intent of the Founding Fathers has been a source of controversy in the courts, in the political arena, and among historians.

Throughout most of the nineteenth century, Americans venerated the Founding Fathers as supreme statesmen, as men touched with semi-divine wisdom and blessed with impartial benevolence, who constructed the most perfect instrument of democratic self-government in the history of man. This view received a rude jolt more than fifty years ago from Charles A. Beard and other historians who argued that the founders were human beings, not demigods, and that like most humans, they followed the dictates of class interest. The Constitution, Beard argued, established a strong central government, attuned to the interests of wealthy merchants and public security holders, a government in which they would have a dominant voice. Such a government would protect them from tyrannical popular majorities in the states, which were endangering property interests. Beard discovered that the members of the Convention owned substantial amounts of public securities. These were bound to increase in value because the new federal government had the power to fund the national debt, a power which the Confederation had lacked.

This thesis, long accepted by sophisticated students of the American past, no longer seems adequate. Critics of Beard point out that neither the class origins nor the property-holdings of those who opposed the federal Constitution distinguished them from those who backed it. This fact raised serious doubts that the Constitution was the product of rival economic interests as Beard defined them. In the following essays, Douglass G. Adair further argues that the Founding Fathers were neither the democrats enslaved by nineteenth-century constitution worship nor the aristocrats unmasked by Beard. They were skeptical of relying entirely on popular majorities to govern wisely but they had no more faith in the wisdom or benevolence of the wealthy few. Rich and poor alike, majorities and minorities, were subject to all the passions that led men to injure one another in the pursuit of self-interest. The task was to devise a government that restrained man's baser nature and released his nobler impulses. As students of history and close readers of political theory, the founders had no illusions that Americans could easily escape the sad fate of earlier republics which had invariably succumbed to tyranny or oligarchy. But they believed that a properly balanced government, such as they attempted to contrive in Philadelphia, offered Americans a new hope.

FOR FURTHER READING:

BEARD, CHARLES A. *Economic Interpretation of the Constitution of the United States.* New York: The Macmillan Company, Free Press, 1969.*
GOODMAN, PAUL, ed. *The American Constitution.* New York: John Wiley & Sons, 1970.*
McDONALD, FORREST. *We the People, The Economic Origins of the Constitution.* Chicago: University of Chicago Press, 1958.*

Asterisk denotes paperback edition.

"Experience Must Be Our Only Guide": History, Democratic Theory, and the United States Constitution

DOUGLASS G. ADAIR

"The history of Greece," John Adams wrote in 1786, "should be to our countrymen what is called in many families on the Continent, a *boudoir,* an octagonal apartment in a house, with a full-length mirror on every side, and another in the ceiling. The use of it is, when any of the young ladies, or young gentlemen if you will, are at any time a little out of humour, they may retire to a place where, in whatever direction they turn their eyes, they see their own faces and figures multiplied without end. By thus beholding their own beautiful persons, and seeing, at the same time, the deformity brought upon them by their anger, they may recover their tempers and their charms together."

Adams' injunction that his countrymen should study the history of ancient Greece in order to amend their political behavior suggests two points for our consideration. First, John Adams assumed without question that history did offer lessons and precepts which statesmen could use in solving immediate problems. Secondly, Adams urged the study of the classical Greek republics as the particular history especially relevant, most full of useful lessons and precepts for Americans in 1787.

Adams, as is well known, practiced what he preached. Working at high speed between October 1786 and January 1787, in time stolen from his duties as United States Minister to Great Britain, he composed his *Defence of the Constitutions of the United States* — a 300-page book exhibiting for his countrymen the lessons of history. And though he included material from all periods of western civilization, a large part of his data was collected from the classical republics of antiquity.

Source: Douglass G. Adair, " 'Experience Must Be Our Only Guide': History, Democratic Theory, and the United States Constitution," in *The Reinterpretation of Early American History,* ed. Ray A. Billington (San Marino, Cal.: Huntington Library, 1966), pp. 129–144.

Nor did his American audience who read Adams' work in the weeks immediately prior to the meeting of the Philadelphia Convention deny his assumptions or purposes in urging them to study the lessons of Greek history. Benjamin Rush, for example, reporting to the Reverend Richard Price in England on the attitude of the Pennsylvania delegation to the Convention, gave Adams' study the highest praise. "Mr. Adams' book," he wrote, "has diffused such excellent principles among us that there is little doubt of our adopting a vigorous and compounded federal legislature. Our illustrious Minister in this gift to his country has done us more service than if he had obtained alliances for us with all the nations of Europe."

Do Adams and Rush in their view on the utility of history for the constitutional reforms of 1787 represent the typical attitude of the members of the Convention? Did the fifty-five men gathered to create a more perfect union consciously turn to past history for lessons and precepts that were generalized into theories about the correct organization of the new government? Did lessons from the antique past, applied to their present situation, concretely affect their actions at Philadelphia? The evidence is overwhelming that they did, although the weight of modern commentary on the Constitution either ignores the Fathers' conscious and deliberate use of history and theory or denies that it played any important part in their deliberations.

Max Farrand, for example, after years of study of the debates in the Convention concluded that the members were anything but historically oriented. Almost all had served (Farrand noted) in the Continental Congress and had tried to govern under the impotent Articles of Confederation. There is little of importance in the Constitution (Farrand felt) that did not arise from the effort to correct specific defects of the Confederation.

Robert L. Schuyler, an able and careful student of the Constitution, goes even further in denying the Convention's dependence upon history. "The Fathers were practical men. They lived at a time when a decent respect for the proprieties of political discussion required at least occasional reference to Locke and Montesquieu . . . but . . . such excursions into political philosophy as were made are to be regarded rather as purple patches than as integral parts of the proceedings. The scholarly Madison had gone extensively into the subject of Greek federalism . . . but it was his experience in public life and his wide knowledge of the conditions of his day, not his classical lucubrations that bore fruit at Philadelphia. . . . The debate . . . did not proceed along theoretical lines. John Dickinson expressed the prevailing point of view when he said in the Convention: 'Experience must be our only guide. Reason may mislead us.'"

Dickinson's statement on August 13th: "Experience must be our only guide" does indeed express the mood of the delegates; no word was used more often; time after time "experience" was appealed to as the clinching argument for a controverted opinion. But "experience" as used in the Convention, more often than not, referred to the precepts of history. This is Dickinson's sense of the word when he warned the Convention that "reason" might mislead. "It was not reason," Dickinson continued, "that discovered the singular and admirable mechanism of the English Constitution . . . [or the] mode of trial by jury. Accidents probably produced these discoveries, and experience has given a sanction to them." And then Dickinson, turning to James Wilson and Madison who had argued that vesting the power to initiate revenue bills exclusively in the lower house of the Legislature had proved "pregnant with altercation in every [American] State where the [revolutionary] Constitution had established it," denied that the short "experience" of the American

States carried as weighty a sanction as the long historic "experience" of the English House of Commons. "Shall we oppose to this long [English] experience," Dickinson asked, "the short experience of 11 years which we had ourselves, on this subject." Dickinson's words actually point to the fact that theories grounded in historical research are indeed integral parts of the debate on the Constitution.

For Dickinson is not alone in using "experience" in this dual fashion to refer both to political wisdom gained by participation in events, and wisdom gained by studying past events. Franklin and Madison, Butler and Mason, Wilson and Hamilton all appeal to historical "experience" in exactly the same way. "Experience shows" or "history proves" are expressions that are used interchangeably throughout the Convention by members from all sections of the United States. Pure reason not verified by history might be a false guide; the mass of mankind might indeed be the slave of passion and unreason, but the fifty-five men who gathered at Philadelphia in 1787 labored in the faith of the enlightenment that experience-as-history provided "the least fallible guide of human opinions," that historical experience is "the oracle of truth, and where its responses are unequivocal they ought to be conclusive and sacred."

Schuyler's insistence that the Fathers were "practical men" who abhorred theory, associates him with a standard theme of American anti-intellectualism that honors unsystematic "practicality" and distrusts systematic theoretical thought. His argument, undoubtedly too, reflects nineteenth-century theories of "progress-evolution" that assume the quantititative lapse in time between 400 B.C. and A.D. 1787 *a priori* makes the earlier period irrelevant for understanding a modern and different age. And, of course, what came to be called "sound history" after 1880 when the discipline came to roost in academic groves, is quite different itself from the "history" that eighteenth-century statesmen found most significant and useful. Modern historians have tended to insist that the unique and the particular is the essence of "real history"; in contrast the eighteenth-century historian was most concerned and put the highest value on what was universal and constant through time.

Eighteenth-century historians believed "that there is a great uniformity among the actions of men, in all nations and ages, and that human nature remains still the same, in its principles and operations. The same motives always produce the same actions; the same events follow from the same causes. Ambition, avarice, self-love, vanity, friendship, generosity, public spirit; these passions, mixed in various degrees, and distributed through society, have been from the beginning of the world, and still are the source of all the actions and enterprizes, which have ever been observed among mankind. Would you know the sentiments, inclinations, and course of life of the Greeks and Romans? Study well the temper and actions of the French and English." Thus David Hume, distinguished eighteenth-century historian and philosopher.

The method of eighteenth-century history for those who would gain political wisdom from it followed from this primary assumption — it was historical-comparative synthesis. Again Hume speaks: "Mankind are so much the same, in all times and places, that history informs us of nothing new or strange, in this particular. *Its chief use is only to discover the constant and universal principles of human nature,* by showing men in all varieties of circumstances and situations, and furnishing us with materials, from which we may form our observations and become acquainted with the regular springs of human action and behavior. These records . . . are so many collections of experiments, by which the politician or moral philosopher fixes the principles of his science, in the same manner as the physician or natural philosopher becomes acquainted with the nature of plants, minerals, and other external objects, by the experiments which he forms concerning them."

John Adams would echo Hume's argument and use the identical metaphor in the preface to his *Defence*. "The systems of legislators are experiments made on human life, and manners, society and government. Zoroaster, Confucius, Mithras, Odin, Thor, Mohamet, Lycurgus, Solon, Romulus and a thousand others may be compared to philosophers making experiments on the elements." Adams was too discreet to list his own name with the Great Legislators of the past, but in his own mind, we know from his *Diary* and letters to his wife, he identified himself with Moses, Lycurgus, and Solon as the Lawgiver of his state, Massachusetts, whose republican constitution, based on his study of history, he had written almost single-handed in October 1779. Now eight years later his *Defence* both justified the form of government he had prepared for his own state and "fixed the principles" — to use Hume's words — of the science of government that ought to be followed in modeling a more perfect union of the states. Adams' book, in complete accord with eighteenth-century canons, was a comparative-historical survey of constitutions reaching back to Minos, Lycurgus, and Solon.

History proved, Adams felt sure, "that there can be no free government without a democratical branch in the constitution." But he was equally sure that "Democracy, simple democracy, never had a patron among men of letters." Rousseau, indeed, had argued, as Adams pointed out, that "a society of Gods would govern themselves democratically," but this is really an ironic admission by "the eloquent philosopher of Geneva that it is not practicable to govern *Men* in this way." For very short periods of time pure democracy had existed in antiquity, but "from the frightful pictures of a democratical city, drawn by the masterly pencils of ancient philosophers and historians, it may be conjectured that such governments existed in Greece and Italy . . . [only] for short spaces of time." Such is the nature of pure democracy, or simple democracy, that this form of government carries in its very constitution, infirmities and vices that doom it to speedy disaster. Adams agreed completely with Jonathan Swift's pronouncement that if the populace of a country actually attempted to rule and establish a government by the people they would soon become their "own dupe, a mere underworker and a purchaser in trust for some single tyrant whose state and power they advance to their own ruin, with as blind an instinct as those worms that die with weaving magnificent habits for beings of a superior order to their own." It was not surprising then to Adams that when he surveyed contemporary Europe he found no functioning democracy. Indeed, governments that had even the slightest "democratical mixture" in their constitutions "are annihilated all over Europe, except on a barren rock, a paltry fen, an inaccessible mountain, or an impenetrable forest." The one great exception outside of the American states where a democratic element was part of the constitution was Britain, the great monarchical or regal republic. And as Adams contemplated the English Constitution, he felt it to be "the most stupendous fabric of human invention. . . . Not the formation of languages, not the whole art of navigation and shipbuilding does more honor to the human understanding than this system of government."

The problem for Americans in 1787 was to recognize the principles exemplified in Britain, Adams thought, and to frame governments to give the people "a legal, constitutional" *share* in the process of government — it should operate through representation; there should be a balance in the legislature of lower house and upper house; and there should be a total separation of the executive from the legislative power, and of the judicial from both. Above all, if the popular principles of government were to be preserved in America it was necessary to maintain an independent and powerful executive: "If there is one certain truth to be collected from the history of all ages, it is this; that the people's rights and liberties, and the democratical mixture in a constitution, can never be preserved without a strong executive, or, in other words, without separating the executive from the legislative power. If the executive power . . . is left in the hands either of an aristocratical or democratical assembly, it will corrupt the legislature as necessarily as rust corrupts iron, or as arsenic poisons the human body; and when the legislature is corrupted, the people are undone."

And then JohnAdams took on the role of scientific prophet. If Americans learned the lessons that history taught, their properly limited democratic constitutions would last for ages. Only long in the future when "the present states become . . . rich, powerful, and luxurious, as well as numerous, [will] their . . . good sense . . . dictate to them what to do; they may [then] make transitions to a nearer resemblance of the British constitution," and presumably make their first magistrates and their senators hereditary.

But note the ambiguity which underlies Adams' historical thinking. Science, whether political or natural, traditionally has implied determinism — scientific prediction is possible only because what was, is, and ever shall be. Reason thus might be free to discover the fixed pattern of social phenomena, but the phenomena themselves follow a pre-destined course of development. The seventeenth-century reason of Isaac Newton discovered the laws of the solar system, but no man could change those laws or the pattern of the planets' orbits; Karl Marx might in the nineteenth century discover the scientific laws of economic institutions, but no man could reform them or change the pattern in which the feudal economy inevitably degenerated into bourgeois economy, which in its turn worked inexorably toward its predetermined and proletarian end.

In the same fashion Adams' scientific reading of history commited him and his contemporaries in varying degrees of rigidity to a species of *political determinism*. History showed, so they believed, that there were only three basic types of government: monarchy, aristocracy, and democracy, or government of the one, the few, or the many. Moreover history showed, so they believed, that each of these three types when once established had particular and terrible defects — "mortal diseases," Madison was to call these defects — that made each pure type quickly degenerate: Every monarchy tended to degenerate into a tyranny. Every aristocracy, or government of the few, by its very nature, was predestined to evolve into a corrupt and unjust oligarchy. And the democratic form, as past experience proved, inevitably worked toward anarchy, class-conflict, and social disorder of such virulence that it normally ended in dictatorship.

On this deterministic-theory of a uniform and constant human nature, inevitably operating inside a fixed-pattern of limited political forms, producing a predictable series of evil political results, John Adams based his invitation to Americans to study the classical republics. This assumption of determinism explains the constant and reiterated appeal to Greek and Roman "experience," both during the Philadelphia Convention and in the State ratifying conventions. At the beginning of the Revolution Adams had invited his rebellious compatriots to study English history, for from 1765 to 1776 the immediate and pressing questions of practical politics related to the vices and corruption of the English monarchy. But after 1776 at which time Americans committed their political destinies to thirteen democratic frames of government loosely joined in a Confederation, English monarchical history became temporarily less relevant to American problems. The American States of 1776 in gambling on democratic republics stood alone in the political world. Nowhere in contemporary Europe or Asia could Americans turn for reassuring precedents showing functioning republican government. So, increasingly from 1776 to 1787, as Americans learned in practice the difficulties of making republican systems work, the leaders among the Revolutionary generation turned for counsel to classical history. They were *obliged* to study Greece and Rome if they would gain "experimental" wisdom on the dangers and potentialities of the republican form. Only in classical history could they observe the long-range predictable tendencies of those very "vices" of their democratic Confederacy that they were now enduring day by day.

It was these frightening lessons from classical history added to their own present difficulties under the Confederation that produced the total dimension of the crisis of 1787. Standing, as it were, in John Adams' hall of magic mirrors where past and present merged in a succession of terrifying images, the Founding Fathers could not conceal from themselves that Republicanism in America might already be doomed. Was it indeed possible to maintain stable republican government in any of the thirteen American States? And even if some of the States units could maintain republicanism, could union be maintained in a republican confederation?

The answer of history to both of these questions seemed to be an emphatic "no." As Alexander Hamilton reminded the Convention June 18th and later reminded the country speaking as Publius, "It is impossible to read the history of the petty Republics of Greece and Italy without feeling sensations of horror and disgust at the distractions with which they were continually agitated, and at the rapid succession of revolutions, by which they were kept in a state of perpetual vibration between the extremes of tyranny and anarchy. If they exhibit occasional calms, these only serby as short-lived contrasts to the furious storms that are to succeed. If now and then intervals of felicity open themselves to view, we behold them with a mixture of regret, arising from the reflection, that the pleasing scenes before us are soon to be overwhelmed by the tempestuous waves of sedition and party rage."

Hamilton along with Madison, Adams, Jefferson, and every educated eighteenth-century statesman thus knew from history that the mortal disease of democratical republics was and always would be the class struggle that had eventually destroyed every republican state in history. And *now* with the "desperate debtor" Daniel Shays, an American Cataline — an American Alcibiades — proving only ten years after independence, the class struggle was raising monitory death's-heads among the barely united republican States of America. If potential class war was implicit in every republic, so too did war characterize the interstate relations of adjacent republics. The only union that proved adequate to unite Athens and Sparta, Thebes and Corinth in one functioning peaceful whole was the monarchical power of Philip of Macedon; Rome, after conquering her neighbor city states, it is true, had maintained republican liberty for a relatively long period, in spite of internal conflict of plebes and patricians, but when the Empire increased in extent, when her geographical boundaries were enlarged, Roman liberty died and an Emperor displaced the Senate as the center of Roman authority. In 1787 the authority of scholars, philosophers, and statesmen was all but unanimous in arguing (from the experience of history) that no republic ever could be established in a territory as extended as the United States — that even if established for a moment, class war must eventually destroy every democratic republic.

These were the two lessons that Hamilton insisted in his great speech of June 18 the Constitutional Convention must remember. These were the lessons that were stressed in John Adams' morbid anatomy of fifty historic republican constitutions. This was the theme of Madison's arguments (which the Convention accepted) for junking entirely the feeble Articles of the Confederation in favor of a government that would, it was hoped, neutralize interstate conflict and class war. It was because these lessons were accepted by so many educated men in America that the commercial crisis of 1784–5 had become a political crisis by 1786, and a moral crisis by 1787.

Had the Revolution been a mistake from the beginning? Had the blood and treasure of Americans spent in seven years of war against England ironically produced republican systems in which rich and poor New Englanders must engage in bloody class war among themselves? Had independence merely guaranteed a structure in which Virginians and Pennsylvanians would cut each others' throats until one conquered the other or some foreign crown conquered both?

From our perspective, 179 years later, this may appear an hysterical and distorted analysis of the situation of the United States in 1787, but we, of course, are the beneficiaries of the Fathers' practical solution to this problem that *their* reading of history forced upon them. Americans today have the historic experience of living peacefully in the republic stabilized by their Constitution. History has reassured us concerning what only the wisest among them dared to hope in 1787: that the republican form could indeed be adapted to a continental territory. Priestley, a sympathetic friend of the American Revolution was speaking the exact truth in 1791 when he said: "It was taken for granted that the moment America had thrown off the yoke of Great Britain, the different states would go to war among themselves."

When Hamilton presented his analysis of the vices of republicanism to his acceptant audience in Philadelphia, he also offered the traditional remedy which statesmen and philosophers from antiquity on had proposed as the *only* cure for the evils of the three types of pure government. This remedy was to "mix" or "compound" elements of monarchy, aristocracy, and democracy into one balanced structure. There was, Hamilton reasoned, little danger of class war in a state which had a king vested with more power than the political organs of government representing either the rich or the poor. The "size of the country" and the "amazing turbulence" of American democracy made him despair of republicanism in the United States, without an elective monarch who once in office could not be voted out by majority rule. The people, i.e., the multitudinous poor, would directly elect the lower house of the legislature; a Senate to represent the rich would be elected for life; and to guard against the poison of democracy in the separate States, they would be transformed into administrative districts with their governors appointed by the elected King.

We mistake the significance of Hamilton's proposal of an elective monarch as a solution of the crisis of 1787 if we think of his plan as either *original* or *unrepresentative* of the thought of important segments of American opinion in 1787. The strength of Hamilton's logical position lay in the fact that his proposal was the traditional, the standard, indeed, as history showed the *only* solution for the specific dangers of interclass and interstate conflict that were destroying the imperfect Union. A. early as 1776 Carter Braxton had offered almost this identical plan as the ideal constitution for Virginia. In May, 1782, reasoning parallel to Hamilton's had emboldened Colonel Lewis Nicola to invite Washington to use the Army to set himself up as a King. And after Shays' rebellion voices grew louder, particularly in the New England and the Middle States, proposing two cures for the ills of America. One cure was to divide the unwieldy Confederation into two or three small units; the other was the creation of an American throne. We have Washington's word for it that the most alarming feature of this revival of monarchical sentiment was its appearance among staunch "republican character" — men who like Hamilton had favored independence in 1776 but who had become disillusioned about ever achieving order and security in a republic. Add to this group of new converts the large bloc of old Tories who had never forsaken their allegiance to monarchy, and it is easy to see why Washington, Madison and other leaders were seriously alarmed that Union would break up and that kings would reappear in the Balkanized segments.

Furthermore, at the very time the Philadelphia Convention was rejecting Hamilton's mixed-monarchy as a present solution for the vices of American democracy, leading members of the Convention most tenacious of republicanism accepted the fact that an American monarchy was inevitable at some future date. As Mr. Williamson of North Carolina remarked, on July 24, "it was pretty certain . . . that we should at some time or other have a king; but he wished no precaution to be omitted that might postpone the event as long as possible." There is a curious statistical study of Madison's which points to his certainty also, along with the precise prophecy that the end of republicanism in the United States would come approximately 142 years after 1787 — about the decade of the 1930's. John Adams' *Defence* contains the same sort of prophecy. "In future ages," Adams remarked, "if the present States become great nations, rich, powerful, and luxurious, as well as numerous," the "feelings and good snese" of Americans "will dictate to them" reform of their governments "to a nearer resemblance of the British Constitution," complete with a hereditary king and a hereditary Senate. Gouverneur Morris is reported to have argued during the Covention "we must have a Monarch sooner or later . . . and the sooner we take him while we are able to make a Bargain with him, the better." Nor did the actual functioning of the Constitution during its first decade of existence lighten Morris' pessimism; in 1804 he was arguing that the crisis would come sooner rather than later. Even Franklin, the least doctrinaire of the Fathers — perhaps with Jefferson the most hopeful among the whole Revolutionary generation regarding the potentialities of American democracy — accepted the long-range pessimism of the Hamiltonian analysis. Sadly the aged philosopher noted, June 2, "There is a natural inclination in mankind to kingly government. . . . I am apprehensive, therefore — perhaps too apprehensive — that the government of these States may in future times end in monarchy. But this catastrophe, I think may be long delayed. . . ."

The "precious advantage" that the United States had in 1787 that offered hope for a "republican remedy for the diseases most incident to republican government" — the circumstance which would delay the necessity of accepting Hamilton's favored form of mixed monarchy — lay in the predominance of small free-hold farmers among the American population. Since the time of Aristotle, it had been recognized that yeoman farmers — a middle class between the greedy rich and the envious poor — provided the most stable foundation upon which to erect a popular government. This factor, commented on by Madison, Pinckney, Adams and others, helps explain why the Convention did not feel it necessary to sacrifice either majority rule or popular responsibility in their new Constitution.

Of equal importance was the factor of expedience. Less doctrinaire than Alexander Hamilton, the leaders of the Convention realized that a theoretical best — and member after member went on record praising the British Constitution as *the best* ever created by man — a theoretical best might be the enemy of a possible good. As Pierce Butler insisted, in a different context, "The people will not bear such innovations. . . . Supposing such an establishment to be useful, we must not venture on it. We must follow the example of Solon who gave the Athenians not the best government he could devise, but the best they would receive."

Consequently the Constitution that emerged from the Convention's debates was, as Madison described it a "novelty in the political world" — a "fabric" of government which had "no model on the face of the globe." It was an attempt to approximate in a structure of balanced republican government the advantages of stability that such mixed governments as Great Britain's had derived from hereditary monarchy and a hereditary House of Lords.

It was an "experiment" as members of the Convention frankly admitted, but one about which most of the Fathers could be hopeful because it adapted to the concrete circumstances of the United States of 1787, the experience of mankind through all ages as revealed by history. Driven by the collapse of the Confederation, the depression of 1785–86, and Shays' Rebellion to take stock of their political situation six years after Yorktown had won for Americans the opportunity for self-government, the Fathers had turned to history, especially classical history, to help them analyze their current difficulties. Their reading of history, equally with their immediate experience, defined for them both the short-range and the long-range potentialities for evil inherent in a uniform human nature operating in a republican government. But their reading of history also suggested a specific type of government that would remedy the evils they already knew and those worse evils they expected to come. Utilizing this knowledge, building on the solid core of agreement which historical wisdom had helped supply, they created, by mutual concession and compromise, a governmental structure as nearly like mixed government as it was possible to approach while maintaining the republican principle of majority rule. And this they offered the American people *hoping* it would be ratified, *hoping* that after ratification their "experiment" with all its compromises of theory and interest would provide a more perfect union.

If there is substance in the argument offered in the foregoing paragraphs, it should throw some light, at least, on the intellectual confusion exhibited during the last half-century by many learned commentators in discussing the nature of our Constitution. This confused and confusing debate has focused in part on the question: "did the Fathers write a 'democratic' Constitution?" The answers given have been almost as "mixed" as the theory to which the Framers subscribed.

Part of the bother lies in the lack of precision with which the word *democracy* was used then, and the even more unprecise way that we use it now. The more a word is used the less exact its meaning becomes, and in our day *democratic/democracy* has been extended to describe art, foreign policy, literature, etc., etc. Thus, from being a somewhat technical word of political discourse, in 1787, it has become a perfect sponge of squashy vagueness. Luckily, the context of formal theory that mixed government did imply in 1787 does allow us to recognize certain rather concrete and specific features usually associated, then, with the democratic form of government. In the first place, the very concept of "mixture" implies a relativism that modern doctrinaire democrats often forget: a political system, in 1787, was thought of as more-or-less democratic, as possessing few or many democratic features. Only in the pure form was democracy an either/or type of polity. In the second place, the simple democratic form was almost always thought of as appropriate only for a tiny territorial area — Madison in *Federalist 10,* for instance, would only equate the word with the direct democracy of the classical city-state. Thirdly, the functional advantages and disadvantages of the pure democratic form of government were almost universally agreed upon. A government *by* the people (so it was thought) always possessed *fidelity* to the common good; it was impossible for a people not to *desire* and to *intend* to promote the general welfare. However, the vices of democracy were that the people, collectively, were not *wise* about the correct measures to serve this great end and that the people could be easily duped by demagogues, who, flattering their good hearts and muddled heads, would worm their way to unlimited power. It was this well-meaning stupidity, the capacity for thoughtless injustice, the fickle instability of the popular will, that led the classical theorists, whom the Fathers were familiar with, to designate "pure democracy" as a form doomed to a short existence that tended to eventuate, with a pendulum swing, in the opposite extreme of tyranny and dictatorship.

In dark contrast to this *fidelity* of the democratic many was the vice afflicting both monarchy and aristocracy: an inveterate and incorrigible tendency to use the apparatus of government to serve the special selfish interests of the one or the few. However, the aristocratic form offered, so it was believed, the best possibility of *wisdom,* in planning public measures, while monarchy promised the necessary *energy, secrecy,* and *dispatch* for executing policy.

It is in this ideological context that one can deduce some of the intentions of the authors of our Constitution. It is clear, I think, that the office and power of the President was consciously designed to provide the *energy, secrecy,* and *dispatch* traditionally associated with the monarchical form. Thus Patrick Henry, considering the proposed Chief Executive and recognizing that the President was not unlike an elective king, could cry with reason that the Constitution "squints toward monarchy." But it was equally possible for Richard Henry Lee, focusing on the Senate, to complain that the document had a "strong tendency to aristocracy." This was said by Lee six months before Madison, in *Federalists 62–63,* explicitly defended the Senate as providing the *wisdom* and the *stability* — "aristocratic virtues" — needed to check the fickle lack of wisdom that Madison predicted would characterize the people's branch of the new government, the Lower House. Nor were there other critics lacking who, recognizing that the Constitution ultimately rested on popular consent, who, seeing that despite the ingenious apparatus designed to temper the popular will by introducing into the compound modified monarchical/aristocratic ingredients, could argue that the new Constitution was too democratic to operate effectively as a national government in a country as large and with a population as heterogeneous as the Americans'. One such was William Grayson, who doubted the need of *any* national government, but who felt, if one was to be established, it ought to provide a President and a Senate elected for life terms, these to be balanced by a House of Representatives elected triennially.

It is, thus, significant that if modern scholars are confused and disagreed about the nature of the Constitution today, so, too, in 1787–1788, contemporary observers were also confused and also disagreed as to whether it was monarchical, aristocratic, or democratic in its essence.

My own opinion is that the Constitution of 1787 is probably best described in a term John Adams used in 1806. Writing to Benjamin Rush, September 19, 1806, Adams, disapproving strongly of Jefferson's style as President, bemoaned the fact that Jefferson and his gang had now made the national government "to all intents and purposes, in virtue, spirit, and effect a democracy." — Alas! "I once thought," said Adams, "our Constitution was *quasi* or mixed government" — but alas!

"Quasi," or better still "quasi-mixed" — for, given the American people's antipathy to monarchy after 1776, and given the non-aristocratic nature (in a European sense) of the American upper class of 1787, the Constitution at best, or worst, could only be "*quasi*-mixed," since there were not "ingredients" available in the United States to compose a genuine mixture in the classic sense. So what the Fathers fashioned was a "quasi-mixed" Constitution that, given the "genius" of the American people, had a strong and inevitable tendency that "squinted" from the very beginning towards the national democracy that would finally develop in the nineteenth century.

The First American Party System, 1790–1820

The modern political party, an institution vital to the conduct of democratic government in the modern world, was born in the United States in the decade following adoption of the federal Constitution in 1789. In the following essay, William N. Chambers explains why.

Before parties emerged in America, political organization revolved around small groups of powerful families in towns and counties. Though the suffrage was broadly distributed, voter turnout was low, reflecting the belief of most citizens that politics was the business of the "better sort." Moreover, the colonists or their ancestors had migrated from Europe where the majority was disfranchised, and government was the preserve of landed aristocrats and wealthy mercantile and financial groups. People, therefore, had little experience with political participation. Even in America, political passivity had prevailed except when the colonists had from time to time become aroused by threats to their interests or had desired to advance their welfare through political action. On the whole, however, elections went uncontested, and citizens did not conceive of politics as a way of furthering a program or a policy.

The first American party system changed all that. Growing out of controversies at the nation's Capital over the course to be followed by the government initiated in 1789, parties represented a new method of organizing political life. They were coalitions which cut across state and local boundaries and brought men together to nominate candidates and win office. The creation of a national political arena after 1789 in a large, diverse nation, necessitated some means of managing Congress and electing Presidents. The cement that held coalitions of diverse elements together — northerners and southerners, Deists and Baptists, merchants and farmers — were common interests and attitudes that shaped a party's ideology and program. Parties were thus instruments by which people sought power to make government sensitive to their needs.

At first, American politicians from President Washington on down condemned the emerging parties, even when they themselves were engaged in the process of party-building. The Founding Fathers had specifically sought to contain organized political conflict because they believed that the rivalry of factions posed the chief danger to liberty. But the parties that emerged in the 1790s were nothing like the factions the founders had in mind — small groups of men, willing to sacrifice the general good for private advantage, adept at manipulation, and flourishing where the indifference of the many gave a free run to the scheming of a few. The first parties were broad-based coalitions that had to serve many interests to gain power. They operated in the open, for the most part, and felt compelled to justify their policies as serving the general welfare. Finally, parties aroused the electorate as never before. Presented periodically with a choice between rival programs and personalities, Americans went to the polls in unprecedented numbers in the 1790s, to vote for newly-formed party organizations that employed propaganda, money, and party workers to win votes. In 1800, when the Republicans under Thomas Jefferson captured the Presidency from the Federalists, led by President John Adams, it was a triumph for party government which had provided a peaceful and orderly means of settling differences and transferring power.

FOR FURTHER READING:

BEARD, CHARLES A. *Economic Origins of Jeffersonian Democracy.* New York: The Macmillan Company, Free Press, 1965.*

CHAMBERS, WILLIAM N. *Political Parties in the New Nation: The American Experience.* New York: Oxford University Press, 1963.*

GOODMAN, PAUL, ed. *The Federalists vs. the Jeffersonian Republicans.* New York: Holt, Rinehart & Winston, 1967.*

Asterisk denotes paperback edition.

Parties and Nation-Building in America

WILLIAM N. CHAMBERS

Political parties emerge out of certain sets of conditions, confront certain problems or loads in the political system, and perform interrelated functions which may include functions contributing to political integration. What the conditions are determines in part the shapes party structures will take, the functions they will perform, and how they will perform them. Yet the way in which political elites and party leaders handle political loads also determines the result in part and the impact parties may have on political development in general. In short there is a reciprocal relationship between political development and loads on the one hand and the effects of party action on the other. This relationship carries profound consequences for the political system, particularly in the era of national formation or nation-building.

Once political parties emerge, they may take on stable structures and establish stable patterns of interaction which constitute party systems. It is probably more useful for analysis to think in terms of developing party systems rather than simply of parties. For the United States it is certainly true that the relationship between parties and national integration can be understood only in terms of the party system and the net balance of integrative and malintegrative consequences of that system as a whole. Approached in this way, early American experience provides a useful laboratory. The United States constituted the first modern "new nation" in the sense that the American people were the first to throw off colonial rule, establish an independent polity, and achieve a fresh national identity. It was also the United States that brought into being the first modern political parties and party system with the emergence of the Federalist and Republican formations within two decades of the assertion of independence. In short, American development presents a case study of nation-building and party-building of great potential use in general and compara-

Source: William N. Chambers, "Parties and Nation-Building in America," in *Politics, Parties and Political Development,* eds. Joseph LaPalombara and Myron Weiner (Princeton: Princeton University Press, 1966), pp. 79–106.

tive political analysis. The address to these phenomena here will be to discuss the context and conditions out of which early American parties arose, the shape parties took and the functions they performed, the character of the party system, and the net impact that system had on national integration. The effect of parties on integration was a kind of end-product of the totality of functions the parties performed and of their relationships with one another.

The discussion will focus on the Federalists and Republicans in the 1790's, the crucial party-building decade. Neither of these formations survived beyond the period around 1820, and the first American party system was followed by a second system in the Jacksonian era in the 1830's. Yet the parties of the 1790's marked the way for later Democrats, Whigs, and second Republicans and for the party systems they evolved. These parties and systems showed important similarities to their predecessors as well as some differences.

Basic Conditions in Party Development

Political parties in America did not spring from growing resistance to colonial rule from 1763 to 1776 in a manner that is familiar in many new nations in Asia and Africa today. In the revolutionary struggle sharp divisions did develop between Patriots and Loyalists. The Patriots established committees of correspondence in the thirteen colonies or states, formed the Continental Congress as a coordinating agency for the revolutionary effort and as a quasi-government thereafter, and undertook other means of agitation, cooperation, and action. Yet the Patriots did not become a party in the full sense and did not persist as a distinct political formation past the period of the struggle for independence. Cleavage between so-called Federalists and anti-Federalists appeared in the controversy over the ratification of the new Constitution in 1788–1789. Yet once again these alignments did not take on party form, and the actual contest over ratification was waged among a pluralistic congeries of leaders and groups that varied significantly from place to place in the thirteen state arenas involved. In the internal politics of the several states, moreover, the contest for power was waged by a variety of factional formations rather than by parties. Only relatively advanced Pennsylvania developed something like a party system.

Thus the first American parties, or national parties, emerged out of new conflicts only in the 1790's. In terms of economic groups, what distinguished Federalists from Republicans were cleavages between mercantile, investing, and manufacturing interests and certain segments of agriculture on the one side and most planting and agrarian interests on the other. Differences also arose out of disagreements over the degree to which power should be consolidated in the new national government; over proposed policies to promote economic growth and capitalist development through government action; and over the extent to which foreign policy should be oriented toward traditionalist-monarchist England or revolutionary-republican France. Lastly, conflict grew out of contentions between leading personalities such as the Federalists Alexander Hamilton and John Adams on the one hand and the Republicans James Madison and Thomas Jefferson on the other, contentions that were sometimes as petty as they were colorful; and out of cleavages among a variety of other group, sectional, religious, local, and personal interests and persuasions. The whole story does not require retelling in its historical detail. The Federalists and

Republicans also developed out of a set of basic conditions, which are more to the point here.

As a general theory or hypothesis, the most basic conditions associated with the development of political parties in the modern sense may be summarized under four major headings:

1. The emergence or prospect of a significant national or common political arena, within which influence or power may be sought with reference to the decision-making centers and the offices of a common political system.

2. The development of differentiation or complexity within the political system in terms of divergences in group structures and conflicts of interest and opinion and in terms of governmental structures and functions.

3. The emergence of social structures and of ideologies or utopias which permit or encourage some form of popular or mass politics and a substantial electorate.

4. A sense of felt need to develop political structures to establish relationships between leaders and popular followings if leaders are to win and hold power and governmental functions are to be performed.

This statement of conditions can readily be related to the American instance by mediating the general theory through statements of particular sets of conditions which, taken together, constitute an immediate-conditional or relative-historical explanation for the emergence of the first American parties. The recital of American conditions will be summarized as a set of middle-range generalizations about American political development.

1. A national political arena was opened with the ratification of the new Constitution and the establishment of the national government in 1789.

Even in the colonial years a considerable degree of intercolonial communication and what might be called continental consciousness, or proto-national identity, had begun to emerge on the American scene. This development at once helped to sustain and received new impetus from the Revolutionary War effort and the Continental Congress of 1775–1789. The limited powers of this Congress, however, together with the fact that it could not exercise direct power over citizens but was only a quasi-government which depended on the states, and the fact that the Congress consisted of delegates appointed by state legislatures rather than of representatives chosen by the voters, kept it from providing a truly national political arena. The new general government with its single indirectly elected executive and its representative two-house Congress did become the center of a rapidly developing national arena. It was in and around this government that groups, leaders, and parties struggled and the great issues of the day were fought out.

2. The indigenous pluralism within the American nation produced a high degree of differentiation among groups, social strata, and states or sections and a complex interplay of interests, loyalties, sentiments, and opinions; and most of these forces quickly found expression in politics and turned increasingly to the national scene.

The cross-currents which the pluralism of early American life threw up were complex indeed. There were small-freehold farmers and great planters owning thousands of slaves; merchants, shippers and shipbuilders, importers and exporters, investors, and struggling manufacturers; artisans or "mechanics"; varied ethnic stocks and different religious faiths; would-be "aristocrats" and nascent "democrats," and sanguine "Gallomen" and sober "Anglomen"; states competing with one another; and a host of subgroupings, such as near-subsistence farmers or farmers who looked to the market. There extended across the new nation a congeries of interests that had to be given expression and accommodated if the system was to sustain itself and perform its functions; and parties developed in considerable part as a response to such felt needs. Certain interstate comparisons are also revealing in connection with this condition for party formation. Indices are difficult to assign, but Pennsylvania exhibited a particularly high degree of differentiation in the interplay of interests, which helps to explain the fact that Pennsylvania alone developed a state party system in the 1780's and also moved rapidly toward shaping local units of the national parties in the 1790's. A significant degree of complexity might also be attributed to New York, for example, where the pace of national party development was second only to that of Pennsylvania; but in New York old patterns of domination by great families and clique politics, characteristics which were much less in evidence in Pennsylvania, impeded party development. It may be suggested as a hypothesis that the higher the degree of differentiation of group and other relationships is in a political system, the greater is the probability for the development of political parties, though this probability may be reduced by the presence of other impending conditions. Such differentiation certainly existed in American national politics by the 1790's, as various group interests took on nation-wide form and sought national expression.

Substantial differentiation also characterized the national government. It was not only formally separated into executive, legislative, and judicial branches with distinct prescribed powers but the two houses of Congress had different electoral foundations and constituencies and somewhat different functions. The Constitution also provided among the various organs of government an intricate set of checks or reciprocal relationships that in effect constituted a further differentiation of functions. Again, parties arose in part in response to the problems leaders faced in trying to operate this complex governmental machinery effectively.

3. Social structures and basic perspectives in the American experience provided a strong impetus for popular involvement in politics, demands for representation and mechanisms of consent, and the emergence of a substantial electorate.

In comparison with contemporary European societies American society was remarkably open, atomistic, affluent, and fluid. It was not bound to feudal traditions, graded structures of estates or classes, or old corporate configurations. Most men owned a piece of farm land or other property as a foundation for individual independence; a vast continent and its wealth of resources offered unprecedented opportunities; distances between rich and poor were not so great as they were in Old World societies; social distinctions and deference patterns were not so sharp or rigid, and there was no genuine aristocracy or fixed hierarchy; and social mobility was a frequent fact as well as a hope. Distinctions there were, particularly between great planters and lesser farmers and Negro slaves in the South; and where social gradations were particularly sharp and persistent, patterns of deference held on longer than they did elsewhere. Yet distinctions were generally on the wane, partly as a result of economic opportunity and partly because of the democratization that had accompanied the Revolution and swept many states in the 1780's. This development was furthered by the impact of the social outlook, *ethos,* or mood that Hartz has aptly called the American "liberal tradition." This fundamental perspective, with John Locke as its ideologue, was to develop steadily in American conditions from a utopia to an increasingly common general ideology and foundation for emerging consensus; and in drafting the Declaration of Independence, which became the basic statement of the American creed, Jefferson drew on Lockian ideas as "the common sense of the subject." The liberal tradition placed heavy stress on such important if sometimes conflicting values as free individualism, opportunity, individual achievement, equalitarianism, and liberal democracy. It is not surprising that movement toward democratic participation, representation, and consent was rapid, and it is also not surprising that these forces brought the emergence of an extensive electorate in state after state. In terms of interstate comparisons all of these forces and particularly the stress on equalitarianism and a mass base for politics were especially pronounced in Pennsylvania, where party action developed most rapidly. On the other hand equalitarianism and the extension of suffrage took hold more slowly in the Southern states, where full-scale party structures and action came comparatively late, although even there the impact of remaining tax or property qualifications on suffrage has been exaggerated by older historians.

It may be suggested as a further general hypothesis that the greater the degree to which equalitarian political ideologies and extended suffrage obtain, the greater is the probability that political parties will develop in the absence of other, impeding factors. Recent research findings for the American case indicate that after the Revolution the great majority of white adult males in an era of widely held agricultural property could vote. Not all of them did, but the democratic impulse and keen party competition brought voting participation in the period 1799–1802 and after to the substantial proportion of 39 per cent or more of white adult males in important elections, a level that was not to be exceeded until new party rivalry appeared in the Jacksonian era. Moreover access to other avenues to the political arena was comparatively open. Freedom of political belief, expression, and action was also generally accepted, despite important uncertainties and exceptions in the early years.

4. Within the context of these conditions, a sense of felt need gradually arose for efficient means to represent and combine interests, amass power, conduct elections, and manage government.

Innumerable obstacles stood in the way of party development, and no one set out to construct parties with a blueprint in mind. Men thought in terms of devices to meet immediate needs, or bickered about immediate interests; many important political figures including George Washington spoke out against the idea of parties. The process of party-building was one of groping expediences as well as brilliant innovations, and it was some time before leaders came to think consciously in party-building terms. Yet in the space of a few years after the ratification of the Constitution in 1789 stable structures were evolved, and the Federalist and Republican formations emerged as parties.

This analysis is hardly unique in its basic terms. It is consistent with suggestions contained in the classical work of Ostrogorski, with the emphasis Weber puts on the relationship between popular or mass politics and "parties of politicians," and with many of the ideas offered by Duverger. Yet the summary here is based primarily on investigation of the American instance. Circumstances will certainly reveal variations from context to context in the significance of any one condition in the development of political parties even though the general pattern of relevant conditions may remain constant. Indeed it may be argued that generic conditions as they affect the development of parties can be firmly established only in terms of comparative historical processes carefully analyzed through a theoretically oriented historiography or time-oriented science of political development. As V. O. Key puts it: ". . . a conception of the party system must take into account its dimension of time. It may be useful to think of the party system as an historical process rather than as patterned and static institutional behavior. . . . if the party process is viewed through time, additional aspects of the working of party [systems] may be identified." This, presumably, is the task of developmental political science or analytical history.

A possible factor in party development as it has operated in many new nations today should be noted. This is the effect of external influences on the peoples of developing areas who are seeking to achieve the modernization that most Western societies have already accomplished. The adaptation of foreign ideas or models as part of the European legacy, including general models for political parties, has played a significant part in political development in Asia and Africa today, although of course local conditions continue to have profound effects. Such mimetic elements were virtually absent in the early American experience. The terms "Whig" and "Tory" had been in use in England for a century or more, but they denoted broad persuasions and shifting alliances of factions or personal clique-"connexions," in the old spelling and the old style, rather than parties as such; suffrage remained extremely narrow; and these early English political formations did not develop continuing and pervasive structures to provide stable links between leaders at the parliamentary center and substantial popular followings in the nation as a whole. It was not until the rise of the Liberal and Conservative formations after the limited first Reform Act of 1832 that England may be said to have arrived at genuine political parties. Nor were modern party models available in the 1790's in other European countries. In short the Federalist and Republican formations in the United States had to find their own way toward party structure and party action.

Political Development, Party Structures, and Party Functions

The argument that American parties in the 1790's were the first modern parties is more than a mere historiographical contention. It involves conceptions of what a political party is and does and of how American parties were related to the whole question of political development, and a conceptual distinction between party politics and faction politics. Political development may be understood as a movement toward a political system which is capable of handling the loads it confronts, characterized by significant differentiation of structures and specificity of functions, increasingly centralized and able to maintain itself. It may not be as easy to measure political development as it would be to measure economic development, for example, yet one might argue that a highly developed political system is characterized by some measure of rationalized political efficiency, defined as a substantial degree of coherence in policy output and a capacity for innovation in the face of new problems. Parties and party systems may have an important impact on the course of such development.

In the American case the emergence of parties marked a significant elaboration of structures and a movement toward relative political efficiency. Before the advent of parties politics was a pluralistic, kaleidoscopic flux of personal cliques like those that gathered around the great magnate families in New York, caucuses of the sort that came and went in many New England towns, select and often half-invisible juntos in the capitals or courthouse villages in the Southern states, or other more or less popular but usually evanescent factions. All of these political formations in their pluralistic variety may be brought under the general heading of faction politics. With few exceptions such old-style "connexions" or multiple factions were characterized by lack of continuity from election to election, by tenuous or shifting relationships between leaders in government on the one hand and the electorate on the other, by comparatively narrow ranges of support from interest groupings, and thus by a confusing degree of raw, unaggregated pluralism in politics. One result was that it was difficult for the voters to hold any one group of men responsible for the direction of public policy. Another was that policy-making was generally erratic or incoherent except where it was under the control of a dominant "connexion," clique, or junto.

The advent of the Federalists and Republicans as comprehensive parties, on the other hand, brought a new dualistic order into politics. The parties emerged as durable, differentiated, visible, rationalized formations which developed stable operating structures. Continuing relationships were evolved between leaders and cadre at the center of government and between lesser leaders and cadre in the states, counties, and towns; and in turn between this structure and broad popular followings in the electorate. It is appropriate in the American instance to consider the structure of leaders and cadre as "the party," or party proper, and its supporters or adherents in the public as its following. At the beginning American parties accomplished little toward organization strictly construed as a regularized differentiation of internal functions and corresponding division of labor. Indeed the Federalists never achieved significant organization, although the Republicans by the late 1790's and early 1800's devised party caucuses, conventions, and committees in several states which foreshadowed the full development of organization proper in the Jacksonian era. Yet both party structures in the 1790's did reach out to amass stable popular followings of considerable range and density that carried them well beyond the fluid and limited support pre-party factions had enjoyed. Lastly, both parties developed distinctive sets of in-group perspectives with emotional overtones, or ideologies, that helped to bind party structures together and popular followings to the parties. In short the first American parties can be described as developing historical patterns of stable structures linked to broad popular followings, with distinguishing ideologies, and as structures that were able and ready to perform crucial political functions. It is in terms of this general idea of what a party is that the Federalists and Republicans may be thought of as the first modern parties.

In the functions they came to perform the first American parties exerted an important influence on the course of political development in general. In the process of nation-building any people is likely to face a number of interrelated problems which impose significant loads on the political system. Among the most salient of these we may list the following:

1. Establishing and maintaining a national authority, or the operating political system itself.
2. Expressing and aggregating interests as essential functions and, if possible, containing conflict within a spectrum which will prevent immobilism or disruption.
3. Meeting the "crisis of participation" and meeting related problems of coordinating political action in a politics of popular participation.
4. Recruiting and training at all levels new leaders who are capable of managing the problems or loads at hand.

5. Effecting a "pay-off," in Lipset's terms, or meeting the "crisis of distribution" in order to maintain the political system by convincing at least substantial segments of the population that it is an instrument through which they may accomplish their objectives.

6. Arriving at a position with reference to possible opposition to governing elites within the polity.

Each problem noted here certainly does not carry the same weight in every emerging nation, but the loads are sufficiently universal in political development to give an analysis of their impact a general relevance. How political parties affected the way each was met in the American instance can be recounted briefly.

First, although parties did not establish the national constitutional authority in the United States, they did much to assure its effective operation. Despite controversy over the balance of federal and state powers in the new political system, both Federalists and Republicans worked within it. Both parties also discountenanced periodic eruptions of violence for political purposes; thus, for example, party spokesmen did not take up the violence of the Whisky Insurrection of 1794 or the Fries Rebellion of 1799 as a weapon of opposition but condemned it instead. As time passed, parties and party leaders also came to manage the structures of the central government, establish informal connections between its separated agencies, and staff its offices. In short, the parties filled gaps in the constitutional structure of national authority in a constitutional manner and thus performed a crucial constitutional function.

Second, parties dealt effectively with one of the major problems of the new American polity in expressing and aggregating conflicting interests. Given the manifold pluralism and sectional divisions on the American scene, and given a continuation of the politics of raw group pressures and of factions, conflicts of interest might have brought immobilism in the political system along with severe strains or social disruption. Both the Federalists and the Republicans amassed followings which included national coalitions or combinations of interests and opinions, however, held together by working formulas of agreement or compromises, and the Federalists enjoyed at the outset a far wider range of group support than early historians were willing to attribute to them. Conflict continued in party channels, but within viable limits.

Third, early American parties helped to meet the load of popular participation and related problems. Many Federalists were far from happy at the prospect of having to curry votes in order to hold power, but they adjusted at least in part to the imperatives an increasingly open, liberal society imposed. Their Republican opponents meanwhile actively encouraged popular involvement in politics and made the emerging general ideology of liberal democracy a particular ideology for their party, thereby winning an increasingly large following that helped to make them a dominant party after 1800. Indeed the Federalists tended to remain a "party of notables," in Weber's phrase, maintained a condescending tone, and were inclined to view elections as referenda on the policies they had already forged in government. On the other hand the Republicans, partly a "party of notables" but also and increasingly a "party of politicians," revealed a responsiveness to sentiments and opinions among their followers and in the electorate which made them what may be called a "popular party," a party highly sensitive to such currents. Yet both parties turned to general propaganda to inform voters and influence public opinion, most significantly through partisan media at the capital like the *Gazette of the United States* (Federalist) and the *National Gazette* (Republican) and satellite newspapers in the states, although the Republican *Gazette* was soon replaced by the Philadelphia *Aurora* as a national party organ. Moreover both parties gradually evolved procedures to coordinate action in the nomination of candidates and the conduct of election campaigns, and to appeal to and bring out the vote.

Fourth, the parties brought up leaders or enlisted new cadres who helped to manage political business throughout the political system. The roster of major leaders includes such brilliant figures as Hamilton, Adams, Jefferson, and Madison at the party "point," in the capital; editor-politicians like John Fenno, Philip Freneau, Benjamin Franklin Bache, or Noah Webster; such Congressional leaders as Fisher Ames, Theodore Sedgwick, James Monroe, or Albert Gallatin; and scores of prominent local leaders like John Jay in New York or Alexander Dallas in Pennsylvania. Yet the parties, particularly the Republicans, also developed national behind-the-scenes cadre figures like John Beckley, who served the Republicans as a kind of informal national chairman, and untold legions of lesser cadre in the supportive echelons of the party phalanx, in the states, counties, and towns. Most early American party managers were young, and many were intellectuals to a greater or lesser degree. The average age of nine representative Federalist leaders in 1792, when incipient parties were beginning to take recognizable form, was 44, and the average age of thirteen representative Republican leaders was 36. Nearly all had attended college at a time when higher education was not common, and most had significant intellectual talents as writers or in other areas. One of the most remarkable devices for bringing forward political leadership came with the growth of indigenous Democratic or Republican societies as formal political associations in several states and cities. These societies had a short life and never became mass-membership units in the Republican party as such; but they provided a useful training ground for new political elites.

Fifth, parties also provided mechanisms to assure that the new political system produced a pay-off. They not only quickly developed to the point where they could provide representation for important interests, but as each party partly emerged out of controversy over important national issues each maintained different positions on these issues. On economic policy, for example, Hamilton and the Federalists advocated government measures to encourage hothouse capitalist development even at the expense of economic inequality within the society, while Jefferson and most Republicans were content to speak for a predominantly agricultural economy as the foundation of an equalitarian simple-republican order even at the cost of a slow pace of national economic growth. In the positions they took on these and other issues the two parties in effect provided the electorate with a choice. In the coherence and innovation they brought into government they also helped to shape reasonably consistent courses for public policy. A comparison of Congressional behavior before and after the development of national parties makes clear the transition from confusion to some measure of order and coherence in policy decisions. No group perhaps got all it wanted, but all important groups had some means to express their demands; and serious dysfunction was avoided.

Sixth, American parties arrived at the acceptance of opposition. To be sure, not only Hamilton but also many other Federalist leaders were suspicious or impatient of opposition, and the Alien and Sedition Acts of 1798, which Adams as well as extreme Federalists supported, were aimed at Republican critics. Yet no general program of repression was undertaken, and when the Republicans won the presidency and both houses of Congress in 1800 the Federalists yielded power in 1801 without recourse to force. Despite overheated rhetoric in the campaign and later Congressional maneuvers to make Aaron Burr president instead of Jefferson, it was the first instance of such a peaceful transition in modern politics. Meanwhile the Republicans in opposition had followed a wholly peaceful course, had carefully avoided overtones of disruptive separatism in the Kentucky and Virginia Resolutions of Jefferson and Madison that censured the Alien and Sedition Acts, and had come rather more readily than the Federalists to the acceptance of opposition after they won power. American parties achieved a *modus vivendi* of adjustment to opposition and peaceful rivalry instead of repression or violence.

In short, parties helped to meet many of the loads the new nation faced and did so in an ideological spirit of open, innovative, and pragmatic accommodation. Parties moreover contributed to political development as a whole by providing mechanisms for the rationalization of politics through the party structures and by helping to introduce a measure of political efficiency which faction politics could scarcely have achieved. Within the general scheme advanced by Almond and Coleman for the analysis of non-Western or under-developed as well as Western or developed societies, the first American parties may be said to have undertaken important aspects of the crucial functions of socialization, recruitment, interest articulation, interest aggregation, communication, and rule-making. The intricate machinery of the Constitution could scarcely have functioned as it did without the role parties and the party system played.

It is possible to offer a conceptual generalization based on the American experience. The American parties of the 1790's took the form of cadre structures rather than mass-membership parties, in Duverger's terms; and they did not perform as comprehensive a range of internal functions as many parties in new nations in Asia and Africa have undertaken today, or at least not so intensively point by point. Other differences in specific structure and function could be pointed out from party system to party system. Yet it may also be argued that the American experience lays bare useful generic aspects of the process of party development. If this is the case, all modern parties may be thought of, in a conceptual hypothesis, as historical instances of social formations directed toward the acquisition of governmental power whose definitive characteristics are stable structures, stable relationships linking leaders and popular followings, performance or an offer to perform a wide range of crucial functions in the political system, and the generation of in-group perspectives or ideologies. The specific shape of parties will vary with conditions, loads, and responses, but all modern parties seem likely to exhibit at an irreducible minimum the four general characteristics suggested by the American case.

Party Systems and Party Roles

The ultimate impact parties have depends on the party system. Whether there is one party or more than one makes a difference; the kinds of relationships that exist between parties where more than one appears also count; and so does the kind of leadership that develops within the parties. Thus one-party systems will have their own consequences; the impact of plural party systems may differ in societies characterized by widely-shared agreement as compared with societies riven by the centrifugal forces of bipolarized pluralism, and a party system marked by intransigence is likely to produce quite different results from one in which pragmatic adaptation is the mode. Few if any of these matters can be taken as wholly foreordained, at least in the early stages of political development.

Continuing competition between the Federalists and Republicans in the 1790's produced the first modern two-party system. The American experience suggests that the defining characteristic of stable competitive two-party systems is continuing interaction between the parties in which each must take the other into account in its conduct, particularly as it touches on their relations with the electorate in their bids for power and their relations to the centers of government authority. The character of this interaction may be put in terms of four interrelated criteria:

1. The existence of continuing conflict between parties, at once based on and implying the development of policy positions and ideologies which appear as "we-they" perspectives. Differences between parties in policy and ideology may be relatively broad or relatively narrow.

2. The provision of stable links or connections between elements in the public or electorate on the one hand and government on the other as the parties contend with one another.

3. The conduct of party conflict short of social disruption, with at least some degree of acceptance of the idea of a loyal opposition. If party conflict passes beyond the bounds of the spectrum suggested here, it is difficult to conceive of the parties as operating within a stable system, because the seeds of the breakdown of the system or its transition to a different kind of system would always be present. In a stable competitive party system there must at a minimum be some kind of agreement to disagree without recourse to repression or disruption.

4. The existence of a reasonable chance for "out" parties to win governmental power and become "in" parties, and therefore the possibility of the alternation of parties in power. Where one party holds an unassailably dominant position even though opposition exists, we can scarcely speak of a genuinely competitive system.

In the United States the first parties established a pattern of dual party competition. This pattern gave way in the 1800's to a period of Republican ascendency in which the Federalists grew less and less able to provide a significant national challenge to the governing party of Jefferson, Madison, and Monroe; and this pattern of one-party dominance in turn gave way to a new period of faction politics as the Republicans themselves suffered disintegration. In the Jacksonian era, however, new parties revived the pattern of dual party competition, and it has persisted in America despite periodic third-party challenges in the national arena and variations in state arenas. In its broad form the model of a stable competitive party system derived from the early-American experience and suggested here may serve as a basic model of such systems in general, within which variations in particular characteristics may be taken into account.

Political parties may also be thought of as tending toward democratic or plebiscitarian poles in their behavior and roles in the party system. The issue hinges on the different ways parties respond to the load of participation in the course of political development. On the one hand the attitude of political elites may be that mass involvement in politics is something to be contended with through manipulation or control. This may be accomplished through parties as directing and mobilizing but not responsive structures; by molding interests and opinions rather than by giving them open expression; and by elections as formal referenda rather than effective choices. On the other hand elites may adjust to or stimulate patterns of effective participation in the power structure, assume attitudes of responsiveness to a variety of freely expressed interests and opinions in the party system, and view elections as open choices on broad policy options, which in turn should have an effect on public policy. Given their inclination to look upon elections as referenda on policies they had already forged, the Federalists tended toward a plebiscitarian outlook — or a restricted plebiscitarian outlook if one includes their additional inclination to view with misgivings the emergence of a sizable electorate — while the Republicans moved toward an increasingly democratic response. Yet the bent of social structure, Lockian ideology, and the polity tended to push the party system as a whole along a democratic course. The fact that parties developed in a competitive system in which each party had to appeal to a substantial electorate if it was to gain power also provided an internal dynamic in the party system itself which moved it still further in a democratic direction. The existence of open and continuing Federalist and Republican rivalry at virtually all levels of government meant that the party system provided a choice for the public or electorate. This opportunity for choice became the fulcrum of democratic consent and control in the American experience.

Variations in structure between the Federalists and Republicans are also relevant to the question of democratic and plebiscitarian patterns. The Federalists persisted in their notabilistic structure; they were internally created, in Duverger's phrase, originating as they did in and building out from a powerful nucleus at the center of government; and they never developed great sensitivity to popular demands. Because the Republicans were relatively free from such notabilistic characteristics, they developed more and more as a "popular party." Although they too built out from the center of government, they were also in an important part externally created, out of indigenous elements in the states and localities, in a manner Duverger finds unusual for cadre parties; and they were inclined to see elections as expressions of the popular will even to the point of investing them with a Lockian mystique. In the relationships the Republican party evolved with its popular following important patterns of two-way communication emerged, and what was said at either end of lines of communication was likely to be heard and considered at the other, at the top as well as at the bottom. In part such relationships emerged out of the fact that the Republicans grew up in opposition and were faced with the necessity of mobilizing support to counter the advantages in power the Federalists enjoyed as a government party. The result, however, was a further impetus toward democratization of the American party system.

Lastly, the democratic bent in the development of American parties found expression in the manner in which the parties performed political functions. Their style was more specific than diffuse, more instrumental than affective, and their appeal more general than particular, although personal ties continued as an important undercurrent in party life; and American parties developed in a direction that stressed mass appeals and popular mobilization in elections. Moreover the fact that the parties had a comprehensive governmental structure to work through meant that they enjoyed significant opportunities to carry popular choices in policy into effect once they had won office. Indeed the Federalists and Republicans probably achieved a higher degree of efficiency on this count than later American parties have done when internal factionalism has worked against coherent translation of national electoral choices into governmental decisions.

For the democratic and plebiscitarian alternatives the crucial point is the role party systems as a whole play. They may provide channels for open recruitment, effective participation, and effective representation, or they may not; if they do, they may exhibit a substantial measure of intraparty democracy. They may provide meaningful, relatively orderly, continuing options on policy as well as leaders among which the public or electorate can choose, or they may not; if they do, they offer choices as the operative meaning of interparty democracy. It may be argued as a general hypothesis that competive dual-party systems carry a stronger probability not only of democratic consent but of democratic control than do pluralistic multi-party systems, in the sense of the translation of broad popular choices into public policy; whereas multiparty systems or dual systems with a high incidence of intra-party factionalism are less efficient in promoting democratic control because the clarity of either-or alternatives is lacking and parties or factions must enter into *ad hoc* coalitions to govern. Yet these features and problems on consent and control are not involved at all in any effective sense in plebiscitarian systems, where domi-nation replaces meaningful consent and manipulation replaces free choice.

Parties and National Integration

In an important sense nearly every aspect of the discussion of American nation-building and party-building here is related to the question of integration. It re-mains, however, to isolate and analyze the elements involved from the point of view of this particular aspect of political development.

Most broadly, national integration may be taken as a process of incorporating various parts of a society into a functioning whole. Where a relatively high degree of integration obtains, a political system can perform essential functions with a sub-stantial measure of acceptance, order, and efficiency. Integration also tends to pro-ceed by phases, meeting various problems, so to speak, as it moves from lower to higher stages. Among these we may note the growth of obedience and loyalties to the nation which transcend loyalties to its parts; the reduction of barriers between various parts of the whole, the opening of communication, and ultimately the tolera-tion of differences within unity; the emergence of faith in the political system; and the emergence of shared values and perspectives, or consensus. Where norms or promises of democracy exist, integration appears to require general access to effec-tive participation in the processes of the political system. Successful integration in a society of any complexity also appears to require some rationalization of political processes so that the variety of elements in the nation may be related effectively to a single government. These aspects of political development will be taken here not as integration itself, or as "participation integration" and "process integration"; but as requisites for national integration, construed as the process of incorporation of parts into a whole. This notion of integration in general has been put suggestively by Deutsch in a summary of possible stages: "Open or latent resistance to political amalgamation into a common national state; minimal integration to the point of passive compliance with the orders of such an amalgamated government; deeper political integration to the point of active support for such a common state but with continuing ethnic or cultural group cohesion and diversity; and, finally, the coinci-dence of political amalgamation and integration with the assimilation of all groups to a common language and culture. . . ."

National integration may be found in different dimensions at different junctures in time. Much also depends on the sequence and clustering of issues. If a developing polity faces all at once the loads of establishing legitimacy and achieving some measure of integration and also the problems of participation and distribution and of rationalizing political processes, serious strains are likely to occur. In the American case the timing of issues was fortunate. It was no easy task to amalgamate thirteen previously separate, often squabbling states into a single nation. Yet the emergence of communication among the colonies and various sections even before the Revolution, the development of a continental consciousness, the Revolutionary experience and American tribulations after 1783 as a lonely republic in a generally hostile world, the existence of a substantial measure of cultural as well as linguistic identity, the rise of economic interdependence, and the increasing sway of the liberal tradition all helped toward the development of national identity in a way that few new nations in Asia or Africa today have enjoyed. The federal character of the new national political system under the Constitution, with its explicit recognition of diversity within unity, marked another important step. Finally the charismatic legitimacy George Washington brought to the new government, and his refusal to allow his personal appeal to be converted into a foundation for perennial power, also did much to smooth a transition from personal foundations for legitimacy to rational foundations in a legal-constitutional order. It was only after most of these phases in the process of integration had been passed through or were underway that other loads came to the fore in the nation as a whole. There was already a significant development toward integration before national political parties appeared.

Many aspects of party action did more to hinder this development than to advance it. The Federalists and Republicans not only expressed but even exacerbated cleavage in their representation of conflicts of interest in the society and in their maneuvering for office and power; in the way in which they helped to pit men against one another "like two cocks," as Jefferson put it in describing his relations with Hamilton in the cabinet; and by contributing to a general heating-up of the political atmosphere. Indeed conflict is inherent in competive party systems as they have been described here because such systems provide open channels for the clash of interests, sentiments, and opinions which already exist in the population and introduce new elements of antagonism on their own in their continuing rivalry for power. The we-they perspectives of parties, the stress on the virtues of "our" leaders and policies and symbols and the evil of "theirs," are all likely to stir strident outcries among rival partisans. Moreover early American party cadres were not always above sharp dealing and even occasional fraud in elections in the scramble for power; there was at least one occasion in the 1790's when invective between partisans in the American Congress came to blows; the suspicion and partisan motives which spawned the Alien and Sedition Acts carried over into the partisan strains of the election of 1800; and party conflict exacerbated personal dislikes, leading Burr and Hamilton to a duel in which the latter was killed. It was such aspects of political rivalry that Washington condemned when he spoke out against "the spirit of party" as a spirit sure to "distract the public councils." There is no discounting the malintegrative impact of such aspects of party rivalry in the American case.

Yet it is important to note two additional elements in this connection, which may be expressed as general hypotheses. First, it may be that parties of the general American type, by channeling the conflicts which already exist within the society and subjecting them to mediating structures, reduce on the whole the amount of conflict that would otherwise occur even though they generate distinctively partisan cleavages on their own. Second, it may be that such parties by expressing conflict openly in a patterned manner within the rules of the political system promote integration by facilitating rhetorical modes of expression as channels of social and psychological catharsis, thereby drawing off potential strains in the political system as a whole. In any case the American polity weathered the storms of its formative period and has weathered all such storms but one that blew up over the most continually divisive issue in American life, the place of the Negro in the national community — and in that one the loosing of the national and integrative ties of the party system in 1860 was the prelude to civil war in 1861. Although parties in the 1790's scarcely ushered in a millennium of harmony, conflict was kept within peaceful bounds.

In this connection the place of ideology requires some specification. Federalists and Republicans were divided ideologically on many questions of domestic policy. Issues of world politics such as the Jay Treaty with England in 1795 touched off frenzies of logomachy in which each party hinted that the other verged on treason, and Washington thought that the Jay Treaty controversy agitated the public to a point that equaled the excitements of the revolutionary era itself. Extreme or "High" Federalists in the late 1790's could scarcely stomach the thought of the Republicans gaining power, and a few of them in the early 1800's even toyed with abortive schemes for the secession of New England from the union as an answer to Republican ascendency. Yet by and large ideology among party leaders took the form of giving vent to emotional release in rhetoric; and as a controlling element in behavior it did not reach the point of ultimate intransigence. Extremist Federalists remained a minority in the party as a whole, and John Adams as a party leader as well as President insisted on following a moderate course in foreign policy; Jefferson's conduct in office has been described as a triumph of practical adaptation over ideological inflexibility — "what is practicable," he himself commented, "must often controul what is pure theory." On the whole ideological divisions between Federalists and Republicans were sharper than they have usually been between major American parties, but not sharp enough to produce disruptive consequences in the polity.

In their competion, meanwhile, early American parties made significant contributions to some of the crucial requisites for national integration. They helped to fulfill the democratic promises of the American liberal tradition by providing effective channels for popular participation. They assisted in meeting the problem of distribution by their transmission to government of the demands of important groups across the nation and in the states and localities. They contributed to solving the problem of orderly management in a complex polity by their conduct of nominations and elections and by helping to manage the agencies of the national government. In short, parties helped to realize a measure of political efficiency which could never have been achieved through faction politics.

As integration was involved in the problem of establishing constitutional legitimacy and the evolution of a viable national consensus, parties also performed directly integrative tasks in their relation with the public in several ways:

1. By supporting the new constitutional order in its hour of uncertainty and testing, even in the face of disagreements over specific interpretation of the Constitution itself.

2. By strengthening and maintaining communication and a sense of shared stakes among different groups in the several states. Thus, for example, both Massachusetts men and Virginians could join across state lines in being either Federalists or Re-

publicans, though there were more of the former in Massachusetts and more of the latter in Virginia. Without national parties malintegration among the several states might have persisted far longer than it did.

3. By undertaking recruitment and socialization, or bringing up and training new elites to man posts in the political system and providing popular education in politics on an informal basis.

In these ways parties helped to promote a sense of political community and efficacy and thereby further strengthened the new government. If they did not perform a range of directly integrative functions comparable to those that parties have undertaken in many new nations today, this was in part because the American problem of integration was less demanding by the time parties appeared.

In the final analysis, however, the effect of parties on national integration depends on the role of the party system as a whole. The fruitful issue for analysis appears to be not a general either-or question of whether parties integrate or don't integrate. The question is: Under what conditions do party systems of what kinds promote a net balance of integration or of nonintegration, and in what ways? It is the contention here that the first American party system, despite the malintegrative results of certain aspects of party action, produced a net balance of integrative results. This was the case in large part because of certain salient features of the system itself and their consequences.

First, there is the fact that the Federalists and the Republicans took on the form of stable, broad-gauge parties as contrasted with shifting, narrow factions. Thus the parties and their followings operated as broadly inclusive combinations of interest groups. In the long-term interaction of the parties in competition for support these combinations could be held together only by political brokerage and compromise in the party structures and in their relations with their followings. The net result was that the party system turned group conflict from unlimited pluralistic into manageable dualistic channels before it reached the decision-making centers of government. As compared with the tensions of deadlock that might have ensued if indigenous pluralism had continued unchecked, party dualism reduced malintegrative strains.

Second, because the parties developed as formations given more to the practical pursuit of power and office than to ideological intransigence, they tended to conduct conflict within a moderate range. They did so in part as a result of the moderate bent of American politics generally and in part out of the exigencies of their interaction in the party system itself. Yielding too much to the views of extremist groups or leaders threatened the loss of important blocs of votes that were essential to political success. The result was a tendency to push the party system toward moderation or centralism and to limit the ambit of extremist elements. All of these forces combined to produce a net balance of integrative results, particularly as compared with the degree of malintegration that would have followed from constant extremes in party policy or action. In this context the party system also arrived at the acceptance and legitimization of a coordinated political opposition.

Third, by providing instruments for electoral consent and democratic choice the party system helped to drain off dissatisfaction before it reached the point of serious dissaffection. It opened avenues of expression for those who were at the moment out of power as well as in, gave hope to the "outs" that they might become "ins" as a result of electoral choices, provided concrete mechanisms through which the far-flung national electorate could hold someone responsible for the conduct of government, and offered working tools for a peaceful change of elites if the electorate wished it. It is hard to imagine how major national elections could have been managed in a satisfactory manner without the machinery of operating democratic choice the party system made available. By 1800, for example, widespread dissatisfaction with Federalist leaders and policies had built up within many important groups in the population, however much parties intensified it. If the party system had not existed to help effect a transfer of power to the Republicans in a way the dispersed mechanisms of faction politics could scarcely have done, dissatisfaction might have grown to seriously disruptive proportions or turned to violence, as earlier antagonisms toward ruling elites and their policies had done in the Regulator movement in North Carolina, in Shays' Rebellion in Massachusetts, or in the Whisky Insurrection and the Fries Uprising. On balance again, the party system may be said to have reduced potential disaffection and disruption, with a net gain for integrative over malintegrative consequences.

Lastly, parties in the party system operated within the rules of the developing polity as a whole, with the obvious integrative results which this fact entailed.

This analysis of the American experience suggests as a general hypothesis that a democratic two-party system can produce a net balance of integrative impacts on political development if the parties embrace a wide range of interests and opinions in their followings held together by pragmatic adjustment, if they keep conflict within moderate bounds, and if they are ready to operate within a larger basic agreement or an accepted set of fundamental rules. The hypothesis contains a substantial set of "ifs," however; and they raise a final important question.

Leadership, Purposes, and Political Styles

The net impact of early American parties on national integration was what it was to an important degree because of key features which the party system came to exhibit as a whole — notably the features just outlined here, and its pragmatic development in general. It remains to explore why, or how, the American party system took on these particular characteristics; why, or how, it came to operate within the rules.

A large part of the explanation lies in the comparatively narrow range of conflict American conditions produced and in the rise of the American liberal tradition toward national consensus. The distribution of interests and opinions tended to fall into a curve of dualistic centrality, with most interests and opinions encompassed in two central peaks of concentration which tapered off into much lower measures of extremes, as it were, rather than into a bimodal curve of disruptive extremes or a centrifugal scattering of disruptive drives. Such matters of social fact, prevailing ideology, a relatively limited spectrum of social conflict, and the distribution of interests may be taken as a necessary condition in any explanation of how the American party system came to perform as it did. Yet the explanation as a whole goes beyond such matters and brings us again to the responses of American party leaders to the conditions and loads they faced.

Particularly in a period of national formation, what leaders do and how they do it may have a crucial impact. In the American case the bulk of party leaders were guided by purposes and convictions which included a deep concern for the future of the new nation or the success of its "republican experiment," as well as by concerns for more immediate or particular political goals. Moreover they had before them the example and counsel of Washington, who served far more as a moderator than he did as a mobilizer or dramatizer, as many later prophet-leaders of nationalism have. In the long run American party leaders avoided pushing issues and ideologies to the breaking-point of violence or disruption, as they might have done, and upheld the Constitution and the rules of the polity; and when the test of 1800 came the Federalists as a whole accepted the result rather than resort to force to prevent it. In short, no major party leader was ready to chance the destruction of the new nation in order to gain partisan or factional advantage. The role of leadership in this connection is underscored by the fact that the story might have been quite different if men like the intransigent ultra-High Federalists of Connecticut, for example, had dominated in national party leadership.

Lastly, American party leaders developed unusual skills in intergroup adjustment and combination, in compromise, in aggregating as well as mobilizing interests, and in the practical rationalization of political methods and processes; and through such skills they helped to establish patterns of adjustment as well as of conflict in the party system. These crucial matters of purpose, commitment, and skill became the foundations of the basically pragmatic style the preponderance of American party leaders achieved. It is in important part the lack of such commitments, skills, and styles that has prevented many new nations in Asia or Africa today from establishing a viable measure of national integration and efficiency, and many nations in Latin America from managing peaceful transfers of power by democratic procedures. If there are lessons for developing nations today that may be learned from the early American experience in political development, they lie in large part here — in the area of leadership and in the manner in which leaders conduct politics in general and party politics in particular.

Considered as a whole, the response of American party leaders to the problems of nation-building and party-building was more than a reflex action to social conditions and emerging ideology. It was also a creative element operating in reciprocal interaction with these elements, an active and positive factor itself. It was forwarded by human purposes, modes of behavior, and shared hopes, notably the hope of building a strong nation and making the republican innovation work in a hostile world. Rivals though they were and spokesmen of strongly different points of view, Hamilton the Federalist and Jefferson the Republican were outstanding examples of this creative personal element, one by virtually inventing a program to point the nation toward economic growth, the other by embodying the spirit of American nationhood and liberal democracy. If the total historical process in its groping, its occasional pettiness, and its conflict as well as its creative aspects was by no means all smooth and orderly, it did bring the United States from uncertainty to stable nationhood, from faction politics to working party politics, and to a political system that was cohesive, internally legitimate, and autonomous, in Deutsch's terms. The measure of integration early America achieved was in part a byproduct of underlying forces. It was also in part the result of active responses to conditions and loads by political leaders.

The Enigma of Thomas Jefferson

The revolutionary generation produced a galaxy of great Americans each of whom reflected different aspects of American character. None has proved more fascinating, or so full of paradoxes as Thomas Jefferson. If any single individual can lay claim to being the Father of American Democracy, Jefferson is the strongest candidate. Few of his contemporaries expressed deeper faith in popular government or did more to demonstrate the possibility of enlightened leadership in a democratic society. In the following essay, Richard Hofstadter shrewdly picks his way through conflicting historical interpretations of the Sage of Monticello as well as through the apparent contradictions within Jefferson himself.

Jefferson believed that all men were created equal, yet he owned dozens of slaves; he idealized the yeoman farmer as God's chosen class on whose simple honesty and virtue the success of the American experiment rested, yet he and his closest associates were great planters, masters of broad estates and numerous bondsmen, living in stately mansions surrounded by luxury and elegance. He insisted that virtue could only flourish in the countryside and that vice found its natural habitat in cities, yet as minister of finance in the 1780s, as secretary of state in the 1790s and, afterwards, as leader of the Republican party he fought fiercely to defend America's maritime claims to sail the seas freely, claims on which the prosperity of the cities rested. Devoted to his native Virginia whose yeomen served as his model of the good citizen, he was the commonwealth's severest critic. A state in which most citizens were illiterate and political power was monopolized by the slaveholding planter elite hardly conformed to Jefferson's conception of a republican order. Though he sought to reform his native state early in his career, he met with only limited success in the face of the conservative opposition from his own class. Ultimately he found far greater success as an apostle of reform in Paris, New York, Boston, and Washington.

Professor Hofstadter suggests that the Jeffersonian contradictions grew out of the counterpoint in the Virginian's life between the ideal and the practical. An agrarian republic, he thought, was the ideal society, but he was too much the realist to imagine that men would forego the opportunities commerce and manufacturing offered. He had faith in the ability of the people to govern themselves, but he knew that they were not infallible and that wise, benevolent, and selfless leaders, such as he presented himself to be, were indispensable. An irrepressible optimist, he believed that slavery — the greatest blot on the republic — was declining because it had become economically unprofitable, at the very time when the sudden and rapid emergence of the Cotton Kingdom was riveting it on the South more firmly than ever. Yet none saw more clearly than Jefferson that slavery someday would plunge the Union into a holocaust. Realist and idealist, cunning politician and aloof intellectual, provincial Virginian and cosmopolitan, Jefferson's life and career were full of paradox. More perhaps than any other American, his life reveals the ambivalences and contradictions of America itself.

FOR FURTHER READING:

CHINARD, GILBERT. *Thomas Jefferson: The Apostle of Americanism.* Ann Arbor: University of Michigan Press, 1957.*

NOCK, ALBERT J. *Jefferson.* New York: Hill & Wang, American Century Series, 1960.*

PETERSON, MERRIL. *The Jeffersonian Image in the American Mind.* New York: Oxford University Press, 1960.*

Asterisk denotes paperback edition.

Thomas Jefferson: The Aristocrat as Democrat   RICHARD HOFSTADTER

The sheep are happier of themselves, than under the care of the wolves.   THOMAS JEFFERSON

The mythology that has grown up around Thomas Jefferson is as massive and imposing as any in American history. Although the bitterly prejudiced views of Federalist historians have never had wide acceptance, the stereotype perpetuated by such adherents of the Jeffersonian tradition as Claude Bowers and the late V. L. Parrington has been extremely popular. Jefferson has been pictured as a militant, crusading democrat, a Physiocrat who repudiated acquisitive capitalistic economics, a revolutionist who tore up the social fabric of Virginia in 1776, and the sponsor of a "Revolution of 1800" which destroyed Federalism root and branch. Although there is fact enough to give the color of truth to those notions, they have been torn down by shrewd Jefferson scholars like Charles A. Beard, Gilbert Chinard, and Albert J. Nock, and it is certainly not lack of good criticism that accounts for the dominant Jefferson legend. The issues of his time have been overdramatized, and Jefferson has been overdramatized with them.

It would have been strange if Jefferson had become one of those bitter rebels who live by tearing up established orders and forcing social struggles to the issue. He was born into an eminent place in the Virginia aristocracy. Peter Jefferson, his father, was a self-made man, but through his mother, Jane Randolph, who came from the distinguished Virginia family, he had an assured social position. Peter Jefferson died in 1757, leaving his son, then fourteen, over 2,700 acres and a large number of bondsmen. During most of his mature life Thomas Jefferson owned about 10,000 acres and from one to two hundred Negroes. The leisure that made possible his great writings on human liberty was supported by the labors of three generations of slaves.

Jefferson was a benevolent slavemaster, and his feeling for the common people was doubtless affected by an ingrained habit of solicitude for the helpless dependents who supported him. He prided himself on not being overprotective, once writing Dupont that the difference between their affections for the people was that Dupont loved them as infants who must be nursed, while he loved them as adults who could govern themselves. But no aristocrat, reared in a society rent by such a

Source: Richard Hofstadter, *The American Political Tradition, and the Men Who Made It* (New York: Alfred A. Knopf, 1948), chap. 2, "Thomas Jefferson: The Aristocrat as Democrat," pp. 18–43.

gulf between rich and poor, learned and unlearned, could be quite the democrat Jefferson imagined himself. As Charles M. Wiltse puts it, "He remains always aloof from the masses, and if he claims equality for all men, it is not because he feels that men are equal, but because he reasons that they must be so." An element of gentle condescension is unmistakable in his democracy; its spirit is caught in one of his letters to Lafayette:

> It will be a great comfort to you to know from your own inspection, the condition of all the provinces of your own country, and it will be interesting to them at some future day, to be known to you. This is, perhaps, the only moment of your life in which you can acquire that knowledge. And to do it most effectually, you must be absolutely incognito, you must ferret the people out of their hovels as I have done, look into their kettles, eat their bread, loll on their beds under pretence of resting yourself, but in fact, to find if they are soft. You will feel a sublime pleasure in the course of this investigation, and a sublimer one hereafter, when you shall be able to apply your knowledge to the softening of their beds, or the throwing of a morsel of meat into their kettle of vegetables.

Jefferson was educated at the College of William and Mary at Williamsburg, where in spite of his youth he was immediately accepted by the most brilliant and enlightened society. After graduation he fell into the expected pattern of the Virginia gentry, among whom political leadership was practically a social obligation. At twenty-four he was admitted to the bar, at twenty-six elected to a seat in the House of Burgesses, which he held for six years. At twenty-nine, a successful but unenthusiastic consulting lawyer, he married a young widow and settled at Monticello. His marriage brought large landholdings to add to his patrimony, but also a debt of four thousand pounds. Like many other Virginia planters, he developed from his own relations with British creditors a bilious view of the province's economic subordination to England and fell in with the anti-British group among the Burgesses. The ringing phrases he had learned from English republican philosophers began to take on more vivid meaning for him. In 1774 he wrote a bold tract applying the natural-rights doctrine to the colonial controversy, which won immediate attention throughout the colonies and gave him the reputation for literary craftsmanship that later made him the draftsman of the Declaration of Independence.

The Revolution found Jefferson in the prime of life and at the full flush of his reforming enthusiasm; during its first few years he did some of the most creative work of his life. Under his leadership the Virginia reformers abolished primogeniture and entail and laid the base for freedom of thought and religion by disestablishing the Anglican Church and forbidding legal or political disabilities for religious dissent. They also attempted, with paltry results, to found a good common-school system. Jefferson wrote the bills destroying primogeniture and entail, and on behalf of the bill for religious freedom drafted one of the most brilliant and trenchant pleas for free thought in the history of literature.

The accomplishments of this reform movement were considerable, but they have been subject to fantastic exaggeration by historians and biographers who look upon Jefferson and his colleagues as revolutionists putting through a sweeping program of social reform, destroying the Virginia aristocracy, and laying the foundations for democratic government. Even Jefferson, who was usually modest and accurate about his achievements, claimed too much when he said that these reforms "laid the axe" to the root of the Old Dominion's aristocracy. If the changes were actually so important, one would expect bitter resistance. The truth is that, with the exception of the bill for religious freedom (which, Jefferson testified, gave rise to "the severest contests in which I have ever been engaged"), the old institutions fell almost without a push. Jefferson wrote to Franklin that "this important transformation" was accomplished with the most remarkable ease; only "a half-dozen aristocratic gentlemen, agonizing under the loss of pre-eminence," had opposed it, and they "have been thought fitter objects of pity than of punishment."

The explanation of this "revolution by consent" is simple: there was no revolution. Primogeniture in the full meaning of the word did not really exist in Virginia. It was never mandatory upon the landowner. It applied only when he died without leaving a will disposing of his land. It was not regularly practiced by the landed families of the Old Dominion, for Virginians usually did leave wills dividing their land among their sons, and sometimes even among their daughters. Entail was actually a nuisance to the aristocracy because it interfered with the sale of estates they often found inconvenient to hold. During the years before 1776 petition after petition came into the Virginia legislature from leading families asking that their lands be exempted from entail.

Much has been made by rapt biographers of Jefferson's interest in abolishing slavery at this time. As a member of a committee to revise the legal code, he did draft a law for gradual emancipation, but never presumed to introduce it. "It was found," he explained, "that the public mind would not bear the proposition. . . . Yet the day is not distant when it must bear and adopt it, or worse will follow." Trying to force through any law, however desirable, which "the public mind would not bear" would have been thoroughly uncharacteristic of Jefferson's pragmatic political temperament.[1]

After a most unhappy experience as war Governor of Virginia, Jefferson, at thirty-eight, was eager for permanent retirement from politics, but the death of his wife drove him away from Monticello and back into furiously active service for the Congress. From 1785 to 1789 he was American Minister to France, where his experience may have been crucial in determining the direction of his political thinking. While his friends at home were watching the failure of the Articles of Confederation, looking anxiously upon the political advances of the dirt farmers, and turning rightward in their politics, he was touring Europe, taking the measure of feudal and monarchical institutions, observing the bitter exploitation of the workers of England and the peasantry of France, and confirming his republicanism. Appalled at the extremes of wealth and misery in European countries, he found kings, nobles, and priests "an abandoned confederacy against the happiness of the mass of the people," saw in the royalty of Europe only "fools" and "idiots," and described the treatment of the English laboring classes in the bitterest language. Europe fortified his conviction that America, with its republican government, broad distribution of landed property, agrarian economy, and oceanic isolation, was the chosen spot of the earth. Although he found much to admire in the European common people, they too brought him back to the political superiority of America. A lifelong prejudice is summed up in a few words from one of his letters to Lafayette: "The yeomanry of the United States are not the *canaille* of Paris."

In France during the early days of the French Revolution, Jefferson was naturally consulted by the moderate leaders of its first phase. Once he committed the indiscretion of allowing Lafayette and a few friends to meet at his house. He promptly apologized to the French Foreign Minister, Montmorin; but Montmorin, who evidently understood Jefferson well, answered that he hoped Jefferson "would habitually assist at such conferences, being sure I would be useful in moderating the warmer spirits and promoting a wholesome and practicable reformation only." When the King showed the first signs of a conciliatory state of mind, appearing in public with the popular cockade on his head, Jefferson concluded that the time had come for a compromise with the crown. But the draft of terms which he gave to his revolutionary friends was rejected — because it was too moderate.

What of the notion that Jefferson was an impractical visionary, that he was, as Charles Carroll of Carrollton called him, "a theoretical and fanciful man"? There is a sense in which this was true, but it has little to do with his public activity or his cast of mind. He *was* fatally generous, borrowed funds to give to beggars, entertained with a lavishness far beyond the capacities of his purse, and in his last years gave his declining fortunes the *coup de grâce* by signing the note of a floundering neighbor.

But did his mind run naturally to high abstractions? Did he spend his spare moments on them? On the contrary, when he found time to write at length, he turned his energies to such matter-of-fact projects as the encyclopedic *Notes on Virginia*, a parliamentary manual for the use of the Senate, a study of Indian languages, and his autobiography. He never attempted to write a systematic book of political theory — which was well, because he had no system and lacked the doctrinaire's compulsion to be consistent. Although he found time and energy for everything from epistemology to the mechanical arts, it was the latter that interested him most. He had an almost compulsive love of counting, observing, measuring. ("Not a sprig of grass shoots uninteresting to me," he once wrote to his daughter.) His standard of values was eminently practical. ("The greatest service which can be rendered any country is to add a useful plant to its culture.") He was the architect of his own home, ran his farm on a fairly self-sufficient basis, and made elaborate efficiency studies of his slaves' work. He invented a hempbeater, worked out the formula for a moldboard plow of least resistance, for which the French Institute of Agriculture of the Department of Seine-et-Oise gave him a prize, devised a leather buggy top, a swivel chair, and a dumbwaiter. He kept elaborate journals about the farms, gardens, social conditions, and natural phenomena he saw on his travels. Albert Jay Nock concludes that he "examined every useful tree and plant in western Europe and studied its cultivation." For long periods he kept daily thermometric and barometric readings. He was constantly studying new plows, steam engines, metronomes, thermometers, elevators, and the like, as well as the processing of butters and cheeses. He wrote a long essay for Congress on standards of weights and measures in the United States, and an excellent critique of the census returns, with detailed suggestions for collecting more minute information. On his travels he procured the plans of twelve large European cities, which he was able to lend L'Enfant to help him lay out the scheme of Washington. He conceived the American decimal system of coinage, demonstrating on this score his superiority to the financier Robert Morris. Such are the contributions to practical arts of this "theoretical and fanciful man."

What of the Jefferson who said that the tree of liberty must be watered periodically with the blood of tyrants, who thought that a rebellion every twenty years was an excellent thing, and who urged throughout his life that constitutions should be completely remade every twenty-five or thirty years? What of the Jefferson who was considered dangerous by so many conservative contemporaries, who was everywhere understood to be a strongheaded doctrinaire?

Jefferson was a complex person who must be measured in whole, not in part, in action as well as thought. There were deep ambiguities in his thinking, which made any effort at consistency impossible. Although Federalist historians have cited these ambiguities as evidence of a moral taint, a constitutional shiftiness of mind, they may in fact be traced to a continuously ambivalent personal and political history. He valued much more highly the achievements of his father, whom he intensely admired, than the high social status of his mother, whose influence he never acknowledged; but from the beginning he was aware of both the assurance of the aristocracy and the real merits and talents of men who came from unknown families. In his autobiography he remarked dryly of the Randolph genealogy: "They trace their pedigree far back in England and Scotland, to which let everyone ascribe the faith and merit he chooses." When he came to maturity, Jefferson was a slaveowner and yet a revolutionist, who could say that man's rights were "unalienable" at the very moment when he owned several dozen souls. All his life he circulated among men of wealth, learning, and distinction, and as befitted one who disliked acrimony he learned to accommodate himself to them — but he also absorbed the most liberal and questionable opinions of his age and associated on congenial terms with men like Thomas Paine and Joel Barlow. In American politics he became a leader of yeomen farmers — but also of great planters. He was the head of a popular faction that stood against the commercial interests — but it was also a propertied faction with acquisitive aspirations of its own. Well read in the best philosophical literature of his century, he accepted broad cosmopolitan ideas, but he was also an ardent American patriot. He was a pacifist in personal temperament and philosophy, a nationalist by training, and yet a Virginian with strong parochial loyalties. He wanted with all his heart to hold to the values of agrarian society, and yet he believed in progress. Add to all this the fact that he lived an unusually long life, saw many changes, and tried to adapt his views to changing circumstances.

Jefferson had warm impulses. His cosmopolitan mind refracted the most advanced and liberating ideas of his time. He believed in those ideas, and rephrased and reiterated them in language that has become classic; but he was not in the habit of breaking lances trying to fulfill them. The generous and emancipating thoughts for which his name is so justly praised are to be found almost entirely in his *private* correspondence; after he wrote the Declaration of Independence and the Virginia Statute for Religious Freedom he avoided expressing his more unacceptable ideas in public. He understood that in the workday world of public activity his most lofty ideals were chiefly valuable to indicate the direction in which society should be guided. He never really expected them to be realized in his time and preferred to place his hopes in progress, in the promise that mankind would consummate his ideals in some magnificent future. ("Your taste is judicious," John Adams once taunted him, "in liking better the dreams of the future than the history of the past.")

Jefferson's practical activity was usually aimed at some kind of minimum program that could be achieved without keen conflict or great expenditure of energy. He hated vigorous controversy, shrank from asserting his principles when they would excite the anger of colleagues or neighbors. He tried to avoid a wide circulation of his *Notes on Virginia* because he did not want Virginians to read his bitter remarks on slavery and a few tart observations on the province's Constitution. Jefferson did not lack courage — his futile embargo policy, carried out under bitter protest from every part of the country, proves that — but rather that hardihood of spirit which makes a political fight bearable. Although he had strong political prejudices and sometimes violent animosities, he did not enjoy power and could not bear publicity. He was acutely sensitive to criticism, admitting to Francis Hopkinson in 1789: "I find the pain of a little censure, even when it is unfounded, is more acute than the pleasure of much praise." Abnormally shy and troubled by a slight speech defect, he found it impossible to read his messages in person to Congress as Washington and Adams had done. He had not the temperament of an agitator, hardly even of a leader in the qualities that leadership requires under modern democracy. Not once did he deliver an exciting speech. His private life was one of enormous variety and interest, and there were many times when he would have been happy to desert public service to enjoy his farm, his family, and his books.

Jefferson's Federalist opponents feared, above all, power lodged in the majority. Jefferson feared power lodged anywhere else. In his First Inaugural Address he asked concerning the common observation "that man cannot be trusted with the government of himself": "Can he, then, be trusted with the government of others?" He would have agreed with Madison that power is "of an encroaching nature," and he was sure that power corrupts those who possess it. "If once the people become inattentive to the public affairs," he wrote Edward Carrington from Paris, "you and I and Congress and Assemblies, Judges and Governors, shall all become wolves. It seems to be the law of our general nature, in spite of individual exceptions."

Admitting that a majority will often decide public questions wrongly, Jefferson argued that "the duperies of the people are less injurious" than the self-interested policies of kings, priests, and aristocrats. He refused to be alarmed by popular uprisings like the Shays Rebellion. In the safety of his private correspondence he felt free to say that "honest republican governments" should be "so mild in their punishment of rebellions as not to discourage them too much." "A little rebellion now and then is a good thing, and as necessary in the political world as storms in the physical." The people are not always well informed, but it is better that they have misconceptions that make them restless than that they be lethargic — for lethargy in the people means death for republics.

Again and again Jefferson urged that the people be educated and informed through a broad common-school system and a free press. Although he had small faith in the power of republics to resist corruption and decay, he hoped that mass education would stem this degenerative process.[2] Education not only would give stability and wisdom to the politics of a commonwealth, but would widen opportunities, bring out the natural talents that could be found in abundance among the common people. Throughout Jefferson's life there runs this humane concern for "the pursuit of happiness," for the development of the individual without regard to limitations of class.

By and large, however, when Jefferson spoke warmly of the merits and abilities of "the people" he meant "the farmers." He did not see a town until he was almost eighteen, and he believed deeply that rural living and rural people are the wellspring of civic virtue and individual vitality, that farmers are the best social base of a democratic republic. "Those who labor in the earth are the chosen people of God, if ever he had a chosen people," he proclaimed in his *Notes on Virginia.* "Corruption of morals in the mass of cultivators is a phenomenon of which no age nor nation has furnished an example." [3]

. . . generally speaking, the proportion which the aggregate of the other classes of citizens bears in any State to that of its husbandmen, is the proportion of its unsound to its healthy parts, and is a good enough barometer whereby to measure its degree of corruption. While we have lands to labor then, let us never wish to see our citizens occupied at a work bench or twirling a distaff. . . . Let our workshops remain in Europe.

The American economy, then, should be preserved in its agricultural state. Manufacturers, cities, urban classes, should be held at a minimum. So Jefferson believed, at any rate, until the responsibilities of the White House and the conduct of foreign policy caused him to modify his views. He once went so far as to say that he hoped the United States would remain, with respect to Europe, on the same economic footing as China. Commerce he would encourage — it supplied the needs of agriculture — but this was the extent of his early concessions to the urban classes.

Thus far Jefferson, with his faith in the farmers, his distrust of the urban classes, and his belief in the long-range value of rebellions and social disturbances, seems at the opposite pole from the Constitution-makers — and so he might have been if his political theory had been elaborated into a coherent system. But he had more in common with the conservative thinkers of his age than is usually recognized. His differences with the political theory of the Constitution-makers were differences of emphasis, not of structure. He shared their primary fears. He did not think that political constitutions could safely rely on man's virtue. In a letter to Mann Page in 1795 he declared that he could not accept the idea of the Rochefoucaulds and Montaignes that "fourteen out of fifteen men are rogues." "*But I have always found that rogues would be uppermost,* and I do not know that the proportion is too strong for the higher orders and for those who, rising above the swinish multitude, always contrive to nestle themselves into the places of power and profit." It was the upper, not the lower orders of society that he thought especially unregenerate — but it was Jefferson, too, who could use words like "canaille" and "swinish multitude." [4]

Jefferson, of course, accepted the principle of balanced government and the idea that the people must be checked. "It is not by the consolidation, or concentration of powers, but by their distribution that good government is effected," he wrote in his autobiography. He designed a constitution for Virginia in 1776 which employed the principle of checks and balances and required property qualifications of voters. [5] Of the two houses of the legislature, only the lower was to be elected by the people: the senate was to be chosen by the house, as was the governor, so that two of the three parts of the lawmaking body were at one remove from the citizens. Five years later, criticizing the Constitution that had been adopted by Virginia instead of his own, he complained primarily of its lack of checks: the Senate and the House of Delegates were too much alike because both were chosen by the voters in the same way. "The purpose of establishing different houses of legislation is to introduce the influence of different interests or different principles." He continued:

All the powers of government, legislative, executive, and judiciary, result to the legislative body. The concentrating these in the same hands is precisely the definition of despotic government. It will be no alleviation that these powers will be exercised by a plurality of hands and not by a single one. One hundred and seventy-three despots would surely be as oppressive as one. . . . As little will it avail us that they are chosen by ourselves. An *elective despotism* was not the government we fought for, but one which should not only be founded on free principles, but in which the powers of government should be so divided and balanced among several bodies of magistracy, as that no one could transcend their legal limits without being effectually checked and restrained by the others.

This would have been accounted sound doctrine at the Philadelphia Convention of 1787. A government that does not divide and balance powers in a system of checks is precisely what Jefferson means by despotic; the fact that the governing body is chosen by the people does not qualify his complaint; such a government, without checks, is merely "an elective despotism." Jefferson, then, refused to accept simple majority rule, adopting instead the idea that "different interests or different principles" should be represented in government.

All this sounds close to the theories of Madison and Adams. In fact, Jefferson did not differ with them strongly enough to challenge their conservative writings of the constitutional period. In 1788 he wrote to Madison praising the *Federalist* as "the best commentary on the principles of government which ever was written." Two years later, advising his nephew Thomas Mann Randolph on a course of reading, Jefferson praised Locke's work as being "perfect as far as it goes," and then added: "Descending from theory to practice, there is no better book than the Federalist." In 1787 he told John Adams that he had read his *Defence* "with infinite satisfaction and improvement. It will do great good in America. Its learning and its good sense will, I hope, make it an institute for our politicians, old as well as young." [6]

When the text of the federal Constitution of 1787 reached him in France, Jefferson confessed to Adams that he was staggered at what had been attempted, but soon recovered his composure. He informed Madison that he saw many good features in it, but objected strongly to two things: the absence of a bill of rights (later included in the first ten amendments), and the eligibility of the president for more than one term. In the end he gave it a substantial endorsement: "It is a good canvas, on which some strokes only want retouching." His regard for it grew with the years.

As much as Madison or Morris, Jefferson disliked the idea of city mobs — "the panders of vice and the instruments by which the liberties of a country are generally overturned" — but he believed that they would not emerge in the calculable future because America's lands would be open to make substantial farmers of the ragged and discontented. In his First Inaugural he said that the land would last the American people "to the hundredth and thousandth generation"! The United States would be a nation of farmers, tilling their own soil, independent, informed, unexcitable, and incorruptible. Such a national destiny, he must have felt, would be secured by the Louisiana Purchase.

The future, then, would be founded on a propertied class in a propertied nation. Jefferson leaned strongly to the idea that a propertied interest in society is necessary to a stable political mentality. In 1800 he wrote a friend that he had always favored universal manhood suffrage; but this was one of those theoretical notions to which he was not firmly wedded. "Still I find some very honest men," he added, "who, thinking the possession of some property necessary to give due independence of mind, are for restraining the elective franchise to property." His 1776 draft of a constitution for Virginia had required that voters own either a freehold estate of twenty-five acres in the country or one fourth of an acre in town, or pay taxes within two years of the time of voting. Never did Jefferson try to introduce universal manhood suffrage anywhere.[7]

The outstanding characteristic of Jefferson's democracy as its close organic relation to the agrarian order of his time. It seems hardly enough to say that he thought that a nation of farmers, educated, informed, and blessed with free institutions, was the best suited to a democratic republic, without adding that he did not think any *other* kind of society a good risk to maintain republican government. In a nation of large cities, well-developed manufactures and commerce, and a numerous working class, popular republicanism would be an impossibility — or at best an improbability.

Certainly the balance of Jefferson's good society is a tenuous thing: the working class is corrupt; merchants are corrupt; speculators are corrupt; cities are "pestilential"; only farmers are dependably good. Sunder human nature from its proper or "natural" nourishment in the cultivation of the soil and the ownership of real property, and he profoundly distrusts it. Sunder democracy from the farm and how much more firmly does he believe in it than John Adams? Yet this is just what the relentless advance of modern industrial capitalism has done: it has sundered four fifths of society from the soil, has separated the masses from their property, and has built life increasingly on what Jefferson would have called an artificial basis — in short, has gradually emptied the practical content out of Jefferson's agrarian version of democracy. This process had its earliest beginnings during Jefferson's lifetime, and, as we shall see, he yielded a good part of his agrarian prejudices (like the pragmatic, undoctrinaire soul that he was) without sacrificing his democratic preferences. But although he clung to his humane vision of democracy, he left it without the new economic rationale that it required.

In after years Jefferson declared that the struggle between his party and the Federalists was one between those who cherished the people and those who distrusted them. But he had been associated with a number of men like Elbridge Gerry, Pierce Butler, Charles Pinckney, and Edmund Randolph who did not cherish the people in the least, and the differences in abstract principle were hardly intense enough to account for the fierceness of the conflict or for the peculiar lines along which it was drawn. Although democratically minded Americans did stand with Jefferson, the line of division was essentially between two kinds of property, not two kinds of philosophy.

The Federalists during Hamilton's service as Secretary of the Treasury had given the government a foundation of unashamed devotion to the mercantile and investing classes. Through his method of funding the national debt, through his national bank, and through all the subsidiary policies of the government, Hamilton subsidized those who invested in manufactures, commerce, and public securities, throwing as much of the tax burden as possible on planters and farmers. The landed interests, however, were in a majority, and it was only a matter of time before they could marshal themselves in a strong party of their own. Jefferson's party was formed to defend specific propertied interests rather than the abstract premises of democracy, and its policies were conceived and executed in the sober, moderate spirit that Jefferson's generation expected of propertied citizens when they entered the political arena.

When Jefferson was elected in 1800, the more naïve Federalists, frightened to the marrow by their own propaganda, imagined that the end of the world had come. Fisher Ames anticipated that he would soon scent "the loathsome steam of human victims offered in sacrifice." Among those who knew the President-elect, however, there was no such hysteria — especially not among insiders who had private knowledge of the circumstances under which he had been chosen.

The election of 1800 was unique in American history. Because no distinction had yet been made in the Constitution between ballots cast for presidential and vice-presidential candidates, Jefferson and his running mate, Aaron Burr, won the same number of votes in the electoral college. The tied contest was thrown into the House of Representatives, where it fell to Federalist Congressmen to choose between two Republicans. To some this seemed merely a choice of executioners; others, looking upon Jefferson as their supreme enemy, gravitated naturally toward Burr. Not so Alexander Hamilton, who had long been Burr's political rival in New York. In a remarkable letter to a Federalist Representative, Hamilton gave a shrewd estimate of Jefferson's character. He admitted that his old foe's views were "tinctured with fanaticism; that he is too much in earnest with his democracy." But it is not true, he continued, in an appraisal that is as penetrating in substance as it is unfair in phrasing,

> that Jefferson is zealot enough to do anything in pursuance of his principles which will contravene his popularity or his interest. He is as likely as any man I know to temporize —— to calculate what will be likely to promote his own reputation and advantage; and the probable result of such a temper is the preservation of systems, though originally opposed, which, being once established, could not be overturned without danger to the person who did it. To my mind a true estimate of Mr. Jefferson's character warrants the expectation of a temporizing rather than a violent system. . . . Add to this that there is no fair reason to suppose him capable of being corrupted, which is a security that he will not go beyond certain limits.

Not entirely satisfied with Hamilton's advice, Federalist leaders sought for assurance from Jefferson. The Virginian refused to commit himself in response to direct approach, but a friend who sounded him out informally was able to convey to the Federalists the comforting knowledge that Jefferson's intentions were moderate. That Jefferson abandoned any of his original plans, and in that sense bargained away any principles to win the office, is extremely unlikely; but when he entered the White House it was after satisfying the Federalists that he and they had come to some kind of understanding.

A little thought on the difficult position in which Jefferson now found himself should convince anyone that for a man of his moderate temperament there was small choice in fundamental policy. The Hamiltonian system, now in operation for twelve years, had become part of the American economy. The nation was faring well. To unscramble Hamilton's system of funding, banks, and revenues would precipitate a bitter struggle, widen the breach between the classes, and drive moderates out of the Republican ranks; it might bring a depression, perhaps even rend the Union. And when the strife was over, there would always be the need of coming to terms with the classes that carried on commerce and banking and manufactures. Further, even if the landed interests were charged with the burden of Hamilton's debts, there was always the probability that they were better off when the system was working smoothly than they would be after a ruinously successful assault upon it. Jefferson, in short, found himself in a position much like that of modern social-democratic statesmen who, upon attaining power, find themselves the managers of a going concern that they fear to disrupt. Just as they have been incapable of liquidating capitalism, so Jefferson found himself unable to keep it from growing and extending its sway over the agrarian masses. Instead he wisely confined himself to trimming carefully at the edges of the Hamiltonian system.

Jefferson's First Inaugural Address was a conciliatory document contrived to bind up the wounds of the bitter period from 1798 to 1800 and to attract moderate Federalists to his support. "We are all Republicans — we are all federalists," he declared. Soon the President was writing to Dupont de Nemours in words that show how well Hamilton had taken his measure:

> When this government was first established, it was possible to have kept it going on true principles, but the contracted, English, half-lettered ideas of Hamilton destroyed that hope in the bud. We can pay off his debts in 15 years: but we can never get rid of his financial system. It mortifies me to be strengthening principles which I deem radically vicious, but this vice is entailed on us by the first error. In other parts of our government I hope we shall be able by degrees to introduce sound principles and make them habitual. What is practicable must often control what is pure theory.

Jefferson kept his promises to friends and enemies alike. So successfully did he whittle away at the Federalist machinery by reducing expenditures that he was able to abolish the hated excise duties that had stirred up the Whisky Rebellion and still make great inroads on the public debt. He tried hard to tame the federal judiciary — the last arm of the national government still under Federalist control — but to little effect. Through the Louisiana Purchase he widened the area for agrarian expansion. In 1811, two years after his terms were over, his party also allowed the First Bank of the United States to die upon the expiration of its charter.

But no attack was made upon other vital parts of the Hamiltonian system. No attempt was made to curb such abuses as speculation in public lands; nor did the well-organized Republican machines try hard to democratize the mechanics of government in the states or the nation. Limitations on the suffrage, for example, were left untouched. Professor Beard observes that the Republican states were "no more enamored of an equalitarian political democracy" than the Federalist states. Had Jefferson suggested a broad revision of the suffrage, many of his state leaders who had no use for theoretical democracy would have looked at him askance; if he had been the crusading democrat of Jeffersonian legend he could not have been so successful a machine leader.

Since his policies did not deviate too widely from those of the Federalists, Jefferson hoped to win over the moderates from their ranks and planned to use the patronage in doing so. "If we can hit on the true line of conduct which may conciliate the honest part of those who were called federalists," he wrote to Horatio Gates soon after taking office, "and do justice to those who have so long been excluded from [the patronage], I shall hope to be able to obliterate, or rather to unite the names of federalists and republicans."

In politics, then, the strategy was conciliation; in economics it was compromise. Soon the Republican machines began flirting with the financial interests they had sworn to oppose. Republican state legislatures issued charters liberally to local banks, which, in turn, tended to cleave to the Republican Party in politics. Jefferson gave his benediction to this process of mutual accommodation. When the Bank of Baltimore applied to the administration for assistance, he wrote to Secretary of the Treasury Albert Gallatin:

> It is certainly for the public good to keep all the banks competitors for our favors by a judicious distribution of them and thus to engage the individuals who belong to them in support of the reformed order of things or at least in an acquiescence under it.

And:

> . . . I am decidedly in favor of making all the banks Republican by sharing deposits among them in proportion to the disposition they show. . . . It is material to the safety of Republicanism to detach the mercantile interest from its enemies and incorporate them into the body of its friends. A merchant is naturally a Republican, and can be otherwise only from a vitiated state of things.

John Adams, in the quiet of his retirement at Quincy, might have been amused to see a new elite, closely linked to the fiscal interests, emerging in the heart of the Republican Party, but the militant agrarian John Taylor was deeply discouraged. In 1811 he wrote:

> . . . those who clearly discerned the injustice and impolicy of enriching and strengthening the federalists by bank or debt stock, at the publick expense, will seldom refuse to receive a similar sinecure. In short, a power in the individuals who compose legislatures, to fish up wealth from the people, by nets of their own weaving . . . will corrupt legislative, executive and judicial publick servants, by whatever systems constituted.

The inability of the Republicans to follow a pure policy of democratic agrarianism was matched by their inability to fashion a positive theory of agrarian economics. The predominant strain in their economic thinking was laissez-faire, their primary goal essentially negative — to destroy the link between the federal government and the investing classes. Acute and observant, their economic writing was at its best in criticism, but it offered no guide to a specific agrarian program. They had no plan; indeed, they made a principle of planlessness.

Jefferson has been described as a physiocrat by many writers — among them V. L. Parrington — but there is little more substance to this notion than there is to the preposterous idea that he was influenced chiefly by French thought. He was naturally content to remain an eclectic in economics. "No one axiom," he wrote to J. B. Say in 1815, "can be laid down as wise and expedient for all times and circumstances." Their defense of free trade was responsible for whatever appeal the physiocrats had for Jefferson; but after he read *The Wealth of Nations* he became a convert to the doctrines of Adam Smith.[8]

Like other theorists of the "natural law" era, Jefferson was quite ready to believe that the "natural" operations of the system of self-seeking private enterprise were intrinsically beneficent and should not normally be disturbed by government. In his First Inaugural he called for "a wise and frugal government, which shall restrain men from injuring one another, *which shall leave them otherwise free to regulate their own pursuits of industry and improvement,* and shall not take from the mouth of labor the bread it has earned." [9] In a letter to Joseph Milligan, April 6, 1816, in which he discussed the proper limits of taxation, he concluded that the state ought not be aggressive in redistributing property:[10]

> To take from one, because it is thought his own industry and that of his fathers has acquired too much, in order to spare to others, who, or whose fathers have not exercised equal industry and skill, is to violate arbitrarily the first principle of association, "the *guarantee* to everyone a free exercise of his industry and the fruits acquired by it."

John Taylor, perhaps the cleverest of the agrarian writers, likewise believed that "it is both wise and just to leave the distribution of property to industry and talents."

This conception of state policy was not anti-capitalist but anti-mercantilist. Jefferson and his followers had seen the unhappy effects of British governmental interference in American economic affairs, and they regarded Hamilton's system of state economic activity ("the contracted, English, half-lettered ideas of Hamilton") as merely a continuation at home of English economic ideas. Hamilton had set the government to helping the capitalists at the expense of the agrarians. The Jeffersonian response was not to call for a government that would help the agrarians at the expense of the capitalists, but simply for one that would let things alone. Where modern liberals have looked to government interference as a means of helping the poor, Jefferson, in common with other eighteenth-century liberals, thought of it chiefly as an unfair means of helping the rich through interest-bearing debts, taxation, tariffs, banks, privileges, and bounties. He concluded that the only necessary remedy under republican government would be to deprive the rich of these devices and restore freedom and equality through "natural" economic forces. Because he did not usually think of economic relationships as having an inherent taint of exploitation in them, he saw no necessity to call upon the state to counteract them. It was not the task of government to alter the economic order: the rich were not entitled to it and the poor would not find it necessary.

Jefferson rejected from his political philosophy the idea that one man has any intrinsic superiority over another; but he implicitly and perhaps unwittingly took it back again when he accepted competitive laissez-faire economics with its assumption that, so long as men were equal in law, and government played no favorites, wealth would be distributed in accordance with "industry and skill." Such a philosophy seemed natural enough to American farmers and planters who were in their own rights entrepreneurs, businessmen, exporters, and often, in a small way, speculators with a weather eye on land values — men accustomed to stand on their own feet.

In due time, of course, Jeffersonian laissez-faire became the political economy of the most conservative thinkers in the country. Fifty years after Jefferson's death men like William Graham Sumner were writing sentences exactly like Jefferson's and John Taylor's to defend enterprising industrial capitalists and railroad barons from government regulation and reform. And one hundred years after the Jeffersonians first challenged John Adams at the polls, William Jennings Bryan, leading the last stand of agrarianism as an independent political power, was still striving to give his cause the color of respectability by showing that, after all, the farmer too was a businessman!

The practical conduct of foreign relations forced the Jeffersonians into a position no less frustrating than the maintenance of Hamilton's domestic system. In the East they found themselves almost as dependent on foreign commerce as were the sea traders of New England; their cheapest manufactured goods were bought abroad, and abroad their surplus was sold. In the West, where they looked about hungrily for new lands, fear of the Indians and of the closure of their trade outlet at New Orleans intensified their expansionist appetites. Expansion of their export market on the land and defense of it on the sea finally started them on a headlong retreat from Jeffersonian principles.

Jefferson himself was both a fierce patriot and a sincere pacifist. During the Napoleonic Wars, when England and France began to prey upon American commerce, he tried to retaliate by a pacifistic policy of economic coercion. In December 1807 Congress passed his drastic Embargo Act, which simply confined American ships to port. His aim was to bring both sides to terms by withholding food and other supplies. This was the one doctrinaire and impractical measure of his career, and it proved a miserable failure. The Embargo not only failed to force Britain and France to respect American rights on the high seas, but also brought economic paralysis to the trading cities of the Northeast and the farms and plantations of the West and South. Jefferson finally admitted that the fifteen months of its operation cost more than a war. At the close of his second term the Embargo was replaced by a Nonintercourse Act, which opened trade with the rest of Europe but continued the costly ban on England and France.

Although Jefferson's successor, James Madison, continued to be harried by the maritime controversy, it was expansionism — what John Randolph called "agrarian cupidity" — rather than free trade that in the end brought the War of 1812. Southern planters wanted the Floridas and Northern farmers wanted Canada. Jefferson, always an ardent expansionist, approved of both aims and accepted the popular clichés with which expansion was justified. ("The possession of Canada," he wrote Adams in the summer of 1812, "secures our women and children forever from the tomahawk and scalping knife, by removing those who excite them.") As Julius W. Pratt has shown, enthusiasm for war with England raged along the broad arc of the frontier; resistance to war was hottest in the old Federalist and mercantile sections.

But if the United States was to withdraw from Europe economically, as under Jefferson, or to lose its best market through war, as under Madison, it had to find a way of employing its energies and supplying its people with manufactured goods. Accordingly, capital, cut off from its normal investment outlet in overseas commerce, began to turn to manufacturing. The period of the Embargo and the War of 1812 proved to be the seedtime of American industrialism; Henry Adams remarked on the ironic fact that "American manufactures owed more to Jefferson than to northern statesmen who merely encouraged them after they were established."

Jefferson, of course, realized the immediate implications of his desire to pursue an independent economic course and as early as 1805 became a convert to the development of manufactures. "The spirit of manufacture has taken deep root among us," he wrote Dupont in 1809, "and its foundations are laid in too great expense to be abandoned." "Our enemy," he wailed to William Short in 1814, "has indeed the consolation of Satan on removing our first parents from Paradise: from a peaceable and agricultural nation he makes us a military and manufacturing one." To another he wrote: "We must now place the manufacturer by the side of the agriculturist." If the United States was to be peaceful, it must be self-sufficient, must end its dependence on foreign goods and overseas trade. The Napoleonic Wars destroyed the Jeffersonian dream of an agrarian commonwealth. Since Jeffersonian democracy, as embodied in measures of public policy, was entirely dependent upon the agrarian order, these wars also erased the practical distinction between Republicans and Federalists.

Manufactures, if they were to be maintained, needed tariffs, especially when British capitalists, hoping to crush their new competitors at once, began dumping goods in the American market at the close of the war. In 1816 the Republicans passed a much higher tariff than Hamilton's. They, not the Federalists, began the American protective system.

And war must be financed. Hard hit by the economic drain of military operations and the financial sabotage of the Northeast, the Republicans were confronted with a bitter dilemma: either they must go begging to the fiscal interests for support, or they must charter a new national bank to fill the vacuum they had created by letting Hamilton's bank expire. They chose the second course — and soon Republican newspapers were reprinting Alexander Hamilton's arguments in favor of the constitutionality of the First Bank of the United States! In vain did Jefferson rage in his letters against the banking system. A second bank, similar in structure to Hamilton's, was chartered by the Republicans in 1816. By the end of that year Jefferson's party had taken over the whole complex of Federalist policies — manufactures, bank, tariffs, army, navy, and all — and this under the administration of Jefferson's friend, neighbor, and political heir, James Madison. As Josiah Quincy complained, the Republicans had "out-Federalized Federalism." By 1820 they had driven the rival party completely off the field, but only at the cost of taking over its program. Federalism, Jefferson wrote to Albert Gallatin in 1823, "has changed its name and hidden itself among us . . . as strong as it has ever been since 1800." Nathaniel Macon, one of the last of the intransigent agrarians, lamented: "The opinions of Jefferson and those who were with him are forgot."

And Jefferson himself? He lived through his last years without bitterness or anger, certainly without a sense of defeat. His country, in spite of one short-lived depression, was growing and flourishing, and as he looked down upon it from his mountaintop he predicted hopefully that the process of civilization would continue to sweep across the continent from east to west "like a cloud of light." He busied himself answering his voluminous correspondence, interpreting for inquirers the history of his times, trading opinions with scientists and inventors, trying to steady his failing fortunes, and laying the foundations of the University of Virginia, which gave him special pride. He renewed his old friendship with John Adams, and once again argued with him the case of democracy. At the age of seventy-eight he wrote to the old man at Quincy: "I shall not die without a hope that light and liberty are on steady advance." When Adams asked if he would choose to live his life over again, he replied in the affirmative, at least for the greater part of it. "From twenty-five to sixty, I would say yes; and I might go further back, but not come lower down." "I enjoy good health," he went on, "I am happy in what is around me, yet I assure you I am ripe for leaving all, this year, this day, this hour. Nothing proves more than this that the Being who presides over the world is essentially benevolent."

Here speaks the antithesis of the tragic temperament. Through all Jefferson's work there runs like a fresh underground stream the deep conviction that all will turn out well, that life will somehow assert itself. Wherever he was, he managed to find it good, and in these last years he never felt the need of moving more than a few miles from Monticello. Life had always come more than halfway to meet him, just as visitors now came from everywhere in the Western World to find him out on his mountain. For him no defeat could ever be more than a temporary interruption in the smooth flow of things toward their beneficent end. It was not, after all, a system of economics or politics that he was leaving, not even a political party, but an imperishable faith expressed in imperishable rhetoric. It did not matter that his agrarianism was in retreat, that his particularism was falling into the hands of proslavery apologists whom he would have detested, that his individualism would become the doctrine of plutocrats and robber barons. His sense of values would survive. Men like Hamilton could argue that manufactures ought to be promoted because they would enable the nation to use the labor of women and children, "many of them at a tender age," but Jefferson was outraged at such a view of humanity. Hamilton schemed to get the children into factories; Jefferson planned school systems. While Hamilton valued institutions and abstractions, Jefferson valued people and found no wealth more important than life. If he had gone astray as to means, he had at least kept his eyes on his original end — the pursuit of happiness.

One of the last survivors among the founders, Jefferson lived to see himself become an object of veneration, and as his life ebbed out he might easily have observed with the dying Roman Emperor: "I feel myself becoming a god." But he had no desire that he and his contemporaries should become oracles to future generations. "The earth," he was fond of saying, "belongs to the living." The world changes, and truths cannot be embalmed.

NOTES

1. Jefferson was characteristically circumspect about attacking slavery in his own state, but more aggressive in intercolonial affairs when he could expect Northern backing. Thus he included a bitter attack upon the slave trade in the Declaration of Independence — which was struck out — and tried to get slavery banned from the Northwest Territory in his Ordinance of 1784.
2. In his Bill for the More General Diffusion of Knowledge (1779) he declared that "experience hath shewn, that even under the best forms [of government] those entrusted with power have, in time, and by slow operations perverted it into tyranny. . . ."
3. In 1787 he wrote: "I think our governments will remain virtuous for many centuries; as long as they remain chiefly agricultural; and this will be as long as there shall be vacant lands in any part of America. When they get piled upon one another in large cities, as in Europe, they will become corrupt as in Europe."
   After he had observed the machinations of the Federalists, his faith in the husbandman's monopoly on civic virtue became even more rigid than before, and a shrill note rang through his letters: "Farmers, whose interests are entirely agricultural . . . are the true representatives of the great American interest, and are alone to be relied on for expressing the proper American sentiments."
   In his belief that one economic class, the freeholding farmers, had more political virtue than the other orders, Jefferson made a significant breach in the abstract conception that human nature is everywhere the same, but he does not seem to have developed the implications of this insight.
4. Not long after the first edition of this volume was published, Mr. Charles Carroll Ransom, Jr., was kind enough to call to my attention that the phrase "swinish multitude" was in very common use among the Federalists in 1795, in connection with the controversy over Jay's treaty. Mr. Ransom suggests — I believe correctly — that Jefferson's own use of the phrase was ironic rather than literal. My original construction of his meaning seems therefore to have been incorrect. R.H.
5. And yet in his *Notes on Virginia* he voiced his displeasure with the limited suffrage of the state: "The majority of the men in the State who pay and fight for its support, are unrepresented in the legislature, the roll of freeholders entitled to vote not including generally the half of those on the roll of the militia, or of the taxgatherers."
6. Later he also endorsed heartily John Taylor's *An Inquiry into the Principles and Policy of the Government of the United States* (1814), which was in large part a headlong assault on Adams's theories. This of course was after the Federalist-Republican antagonism had ripened.
7. It is important to add, however, that in 1776 Jefferson proposed that Virginia grant fifty acres of land to every white of full age who had less than that amount. This would have made suffrage practically universal. It also illustrates his belief in broadening economic opportunities where free land made the policy possible, as well as the vital linkage in his mind between landed property and democracy. He was, at this time, more democratic in his conception of the economic *base* of government than in his conception of the *structure* of government.
8. Ultimately he came to prefer J. B. Say's adaptations of Smith as more lucid and readable, and showed much admiration for the work of Destutt de Tracy.
9. In his Second Inaugural, when he listed the things government should do, he asserted that it should maintain "that state of property, equal or unequal, which results to every man from his own industry or that of his fathers."
10. He added that if an individual's wealth becomes so overgrown that it seems a danger to the State, the best corrective would not be discriminatory taxation but a law compelling equal inheritance in equal degree by all the heirs.

PART 2

The Middle Period
1815-1914

The Frontier and American Society

One of the most impressive attempts to explain the special qualities of America and Americans was the frontier thesis of Frederick Jackson Turner. Long before Turner, observers of the United States had assigned a distinctive place to the West in the molding of American thought and institutions. But the brilliant analysis by Turner of that role in his 1893 paper "On the Significance of the Frontier in American History" raised the observations of commentators to the level of a powerful theory and profoundly influenced the way both historians and laymen thought about the American past.

Turner's thesis was that "the existence of an area of free land, its continuous recession, and the advance of American settlement westward, explain American development." This central fact explained American politics, for democracy, in its various manifestations, came from the frontier. It explained American affluence and social stability, for the West was a land of economic opportunity and a "safety valve" for the deprived and the unsuccessful. It explained American individualism, for in the new western communities each man had only himself to rely on for safety and survival. All these traits of character and mind and these institutional distinctions were what made America exceptional and what, Turner might well have said, made America better.

Turner's seminal essay, and its elaboration in a dozen or so articles and a number of books, swept away the earlier emphasis by historians on the continuities between America and the European, particularly the Anglo-Saxon, heritage. Even during his lifetime, Turner was not unchallenged, but at least half of the historians of the country, for the first thirty years of this century, might be labeled "Turner's disciples." During these years the history of the West and the frontier flourished, and analyses of American politics emphasizing East–West conflict became standard elements in textbooks. In the 1930s, Turner went into eclipse. The scholars' disenchantment with capitalism and individualism during the depression made them skeptical of Turner's belief in American uniqueness. They subjected his insights to close scrutiny and often found them seriously wanting. Democracy did not seem to flow from the West; universal manhood suffrage came earlier in the East. The safety valve did not operate; farm-making costs were too high for the unemployed labor of the cities to take advantage of unoccupied land. Individualism was not particularly western; the West often demanded cooperation and conformity for survival.

One of Turner's most persistent and intelligent followers is Ray Allen Billington of the Huntington Library in San Marino, California. Billington is by no means an uncritical disciple. He finds much in Turner's concept of frontier individualism that is exaggerated and simplistic. On the other hand, he sees more merit in the picture of the West as egalitarian and mobile, a region where men did not defer to rank and wealth, and where both were within grasp of the able and the lucky. In the end, he concludes, America has still not entirely lost some of the exceptional qualities it inherited from its frontier past.

FOR FURTHER READING:

BILLINGTON, RAY ALLEN. *America's Frontier Heritage.* New York: Holt, Rinehart & Winston, 1967.*
SMITH, HENRY NASH. *Virgin Land: The American West as Symbol and Myth.* New York: Random House, Vintage Books, 1957.*
TURNER, FREDERICK JACKSON. *On the Significance of the Frontier in American History.* New York: Frederick Ungar Publishing Co., 1963.*

Asterisk denotes paperback edition.

Frontier Democracy: Social Aspects

RAY ALLEN BILLINGTON

To understand the uniqueness of *American* democracy we must consider not only the form of government and the extent of popular participation, but the way in which the people of the United States view government and society as a whole. Do they regard the state as the master or servant of its citizens? Do they consider their fellow men as equals, or as inferiors and superiors? In seeking answers to these questions, our concern is not with what *is,* but with what is *thought* to be. If the image of the social order common among Americans differs from that usual among Europeans, and if the differences can be explained by the pioneering experience, we can conclude that the frontier has altered the national character as well as institutions.

In this quest, two concepts are especially important: that of "individualism" and that of "equality." Visitors from abroad feel that the people of the United States have endowed these words with distinctive meanings. In no other nation is the equality of all men so loudly proclaimed; in no other country is the right of individual self-assertion (within certain areas) so stoutly defended. Travelers have also noted the relationship between the two concepts. Because all men are judged to be equal, all are assured the same freedom of individual expression. "They are apt to imagine," wrote Alexis de Tocqueville in the early nineteenth century, "that their whole destiny is in their own hands." Tocqueville believed that this attitude was dangerous, threatening as it did the atomization of society.

His fears were groundless, for even as he wrote conformity was displacing individualism as a national cult, save in one important aspect. To Ralph Waldo Emerson and Henry David Thoreau society may have been the sum of atomized individuals, but to the generations that followed the emergence of an industrial-urban complex that made social interdependence essential to survival was one of the stark realities of life. In this integrated society, the fact of individualism, if not the *theory* of individualism, was gradually altered. In theory individualism meant the right of every person to make his own decisions and choices without regard to their effect on the

Source: Ray Allen Billington, *America's Frontier Heritage* (New York: Holt, Rinehart & Winston, 1966), chap. 7, "Frontier Democracy: Social Aspects," pp. 139–157.

social group. In practice, this was acceptable only in the sphere of economic activity. In that realm, a sink-or-swim philosophy gained acceptance and still prevails. If a man makes a wrong decision, and a business fails or a job is lost, no one is to blame but the person himself. If his decision is correct and he does well, we believe that he should be rewarded by advancement to positions of ever higher prestige. The direction in which he moves is his responsibility alone; the successful person enjoys a sense of his own greatness quite unrelated to those around him. Individualism in the economic world seems fair to Americans as long as equal and plentiful opportunity exists for all, and who can doubt its existence in a land of abundance? Social-security systems, unemployment benefits, Medicare, and a host of other security measures today challenge the fact of economic individualism, but the theory is still vigorously defended.

Individualism in its distinctly American usage does not apply to the noneconomic world. It grants no license for freedom of personal expression; no respectable citizen would dream of exhibiting a unique personality in the clothes that he wears, the manners he adopts, or the behavior that he exhibits in public. The Frenchman instinctively distrusts the outsider and shuns cooperation; the American instinctively follows the herd. "Americans," observed Peter Ustinov, "are always attempting to run away from conformity, but unfortunately they always start running in the same direction." Twentieth-century travelers have pointed out the monotonous uniformity of the streets, the towns, the cities, of the United States. "Not a single American," wrote one, "can distinguish Main Street in one town from Main Street in one of hundreds of others." Let a Hollywood actress or a spotlighted pop singer adopt a new hair style and women rush to their hairdressers to imitate her. Let a public figure appear in a novel hat, or trousers, or haircut, and men fall into line. Even political behavior is regimented, as Americans dutifully cast their ballots for Democratic or Republican candidates rather than for the dozens of parties that range across the political spectrum in Europe. And woe unto the American who defends a belief that is currently unpopular, either of the extreme left or the extreme right.

The oft-defended individualism of the United States is no guarantee of the individual's freedom of expression, but is manifested in two ways, each related to the other. One is a relative lack of respect for the law; the typical American is more inclined to flaunt regulations, or to whittle a few illegal dollars from his income tax, than his British cousins. The other is a resentment of governmental meddling in private affairs. Some Americans preached individual freedom when the Eighteenth Amendment told them what not to drink, and the bootleggers' paradise of the 1920s was the result. Some raised an umbrella of "rugged American individualism" over their heads when the regulatory measures of Progressivism or the New Deal threatened to interfere with their free use of property. Some, living in the Southern states, hoisted the banner of states' rights when federal agencies told them to integrate their schools, but what they really defended was the right of every individual to like or dislike persons of his own choice, whatever the effect on society. All were proclaiming their defiance of the government, and demanding that it cease telling them how to live or manage their affairs. The American is willing to conform if he personally decides to conform, as he does in adopting the style of his clothes or the brand of popular music that he will enjoy. But the American is not willing to allow his elected representatives to decide that conformity is for him. This is the essential difference between the individualism of the United States and that of Europe.

As long as we dwell in the realm of theory, nothing could be easier than to link this distinctly American faith with the frontier experience. The modern American believes that each person shall be allowed to rise or fall in the workaday world as his own grit and ability decrees; he also clings to the belief that the government should not interfere. Such a system could operate only in a land of equal opportunity, where the dispossessed could begin life anew without too much difficulty, where new jobs were being created to absorb an expanding population, and where resources were so abundant that all could share in their wealth without governmental intervention in the role of umpire. Only in frontier America did this combination of beatitudes exist. Hence American individualism is the product of the frontiering experience. So men reasoned in the nineteenth century, and so many believe today.

This myth has been fastened on the public mind by the plausibility of logic. Nothing is more obvious than that the pioneer would resent social controls, or that he would be able to escape dependence on society. He had, after all, fled his fellows to battle the wilderness alone. In his new home the solitude in which he lived, the vastness of the world about him, and the assurance that he acquired as he combatted nature, contributed to a spirit of self-reliance that was universal among pioneers. This was accentuated by the richness of the land, and the equally shared opportunity to exploit those riches. Where all were potential millionaires, property assumed a new importance, even to the propertyless. Men on the frontier, Americans of the nineteenth century believed, were so confident of affluence that they needed no help from society and wanted no meddling by society. "Here," wrote a visitor to the Colorado mines, "a man looks upon the wealth of others as held in trust for himself, and will suffer no diminution of its sanctity." This attitude fostered rugged American individualism in its truly American sense.

Just as persuasive was the frequent testimony of travelers and Westerners that the West actually was a land of unbridled liberty where men behaved according to the dictates of their consciences, and devil take their neighbors. "Liberty here," wrote an Englishman from the Kentucky backwoods, "means to do each as he pleases, to care for nothing and nobody." This was natural in the borderlands, where men were free to shape the course of their lives without nearby neighbors inflicting their wills or watchful officials meddling in their affairs. There every man was king, and kings could rule themselves. When passengers on a keelboat tried to stop a frontiersman from singing on the Sabbath they were heatedly informed that they were in a "land of liberty" and had no right to interfere. A recruit among the fur trappers of the Rocky Mountain country was told by an old-timer that he had only to mind his own affairs to get along. "If you see a man's mule running off," the newcomer was advised, "don't stop it — let it go to the devil; it isn't yourn. If his possibles sack falls off, don't tell him of it; He'll find it out." A pioneer who told a visitor that he was moving from Arkansas to Texas because he "had heern there was no sich thing as a government there, and not one varmint of a lawyer in the *hull* place" only personified what the United States believed to be the spirit of the whole frontier.

This nineteenth-century image of the West perpetuated the belief that the pioneer was opposed to all governmental regulation of economic activity. If steamboats had accidents that killed hundreds of persons yearly, nothing should be done, for steamboats were the lifeblood of the Mississippi Valley, and a few lives were a cheap price to pay for the economic activity that they fostered. If speculators absorbed the best lands, or miners appropriated mineral wealth, or lumbermen stripped away the forests, or "Sooners" illegally usurped the prime acreage in land openings, the social losses were insignificant compared to the benefits that accrued when the free-enter-prise spirit was unleashed amidst the West's resources. These were the tales spread across the nation by the frontiersmen and their visitors, until they became a part of the nation's folklore. The frontier was a land of individualism, and American individualism was its natural offspring. This was a myth accepted throughout the nineteenth century and beyond.

Actually, the legend of frontier individualism rested on what people thought should be true, rather than what was true. The West was in truth an area where cooperation was just as essential as in the more thickly settled East. The danger of Indian attack, the joint efforts needed to clear the forests or break the prairie sod, the community of labor required for the variety of enterprises necessary in establishing a settlement, all decreed that new communities be occupied by groups, and never by solitary individuals. "In a young country," noted a visiting Englishman, "they must assist each other, if they wish to be assisted themselves — and there always will be a mutual dependence." Alexis de Tocqueville expressed nothing less than the truth when he observed that "In no country in the world has the principle of association been more successfully used, or applied to a greater multitude of objects, than in America."

This "principle of association" was more essential on the frontier than in the East. Cooperative enterprise is instinctive among all groups, even of the most primitive tribesmen, for habits of mutual dependence developed by family life during infancy are extended as people realize that the benefits of joint activity compensate for the work involved. Cooperation is normal within every in-group, but accentuates when the in-group is in conflict with an out-group and group solidarity is strengthened. This was the situation in frontier communities, where conflicts with Indians, with raw nature, and with dominating Easterners heightened the spirit of interdependence. In the West social cohesiveness, standardized behavior, and restrictive limitations on individual freedom were more acceptable than in the East.

So closely knit were pioneer groups that privacy of person or mind was virtually unattainable. Where neighbors were relatively few and newcomers a treasured rarity, every stranger was of rapt interest and a heaven sent opportunity to relieve the tedium of existence. "You are in a house of glass," complained one annoyed traveler as he endured the probing of the frontiersmen; another added that "privacy, either in eating, sleeping, conversation, or government, seems quite unknown, and unknowable." So prevailing was the community spirit that no one dared express individuality; people lived and dressed and thought exactly alike. "Whoever ventures to differ essentially from the mass," recorded a newcomer to the Michigan frontier, "is sure to become the object of unkind feeling, even without supposing any bitter personal animosity." And Charles Dickens, vitriolic as usual in his impressions of the Mississippi Valley pioneers, complained of "such a deadly, leaden people; such systematic plodding weary insupportable heaviness." These may have been exaggerations, but they were accurate in the over-all estimate of the spirit of cohesiveness existing in pioneer communities. Amidst the anonymity of a city, a person might dare to be different; amidst the intimacy of the frontier, he did not.

Much of this spirit was rooted in the stark realities of backwoods life, for cooperation was as essential to survival as a "Kentucky" rifle or a Colt revolver. Men went west in groups to minimize the Indian danger and the hardships of travel. When the journey was long and difficult, they organized a walking republic, complete with administrative and judicial officials to whom they delegated needed authority. As soon as they reached their destination they provided for the common defense by building a blockhouse or forming a militia company. These log or adobe forts became the centers of neighborhood life, especially in time of danger when the whole community "forted up" and shared guard duty until the threat passed. "Their common security," a pioneer told a traveler, "locked them in amity." Years after the times of danger a frontiersman remembered the pleasure they had provided because "we were so kind and friendly to one another." Commonly shared perils were a cohesive force among the homesteaders of the Great Plains no less than among earlier pioneers, for there grass fires, grasshopper invasions, and cattle wars banded the people together to combat mutual enemies. Any who refused to share were banished as traitors to society; there was no place for the uncooperative eccentric in a land where joint effort was the key to survival.

Cooperation was just as essential in times of peace as in times of war. Needed goods were imported by mutually owned caravans. Neighbors assisted in the "cabin raisings" and "barn raisings" that provided every newcomer with a home, and in the "logrollings" that helped him clear his fields. They joined in "corn huskings" and "quilting bees" and "fulling parties" where newly woven cloth was prepared for the housewife's needle. Scarce an activity in a frontier community that did not lend itself to neighborhood enterprise; records of pioneer settlements bristle with accounts of spinning parties, goose pickings, apple parings, rag cuttings, carpet tackings, wool pickings, and a dozen more. "A life in the woods," observed a visitor from Britain, "teaches many lessons, and this among the rest, that you must both give assistance to your neighbor, and receive it in return, without either grudging or pouting." Little wonder that students of the frontier refer to the "principle of mutuality" when speaking of life in the West.

The community benefited no less than individuals from mutual enterprise, because the necessity of common labor for society's good was cheerfully accepted as a part of pioneer life. Was a new church required, or a new school to be built, all hands turned out with axes and adzes to buckle to the task. "The neighbors divided themselves into choppers, hewers, carpenters, and masons," recalled an Indiana settler. "Those who found it impossible to report for duty might pay an equivalent in nails, boards, or other materials." When a road was to be constructed, or a bridge thrown across a stream, all were expected to help, since on the frontier division of labor was little known. Communities organized "Claim Clubs" to guard land from or for speculators, and in the Great Plains country recruited members to drive cattle from planted fields. Pioneer farmers, wherever they lived, were not so wedded to individualism that they would scorn help when help was needed.

Even these crown princes of individualism, the ranchers and miners, depended far more on joint effort than on self-prowess. Cattlemen on the Great Plains lost no time in forming associations that not only supervised the semiannual roundups, but that seriously restricted private enterprise by regulating pasturage on the open range. Community activity also quickened in time of emergency, furnishing men and horses to hunt down herds scattered by fire or drought. Cowboys as well as ranchers recognized the value of group activity; in 1883 some 325 in Texas organized to demand a $20 monthly raise, which they won after striking five ranches at roundup time. So did miners. The lone prospector is a figure from fiction rather than reality, for no single man could live long in the rugged mountain country of the early West. Most prospecting was done in groups of five to twenty men, usually well-mounted and provisioned, and led by a miner sufficiently versed in geology that no time was wasted on unlikely spots. Mining was never an individual enterprise, but was conducted by partners or teams who divided the labor and shared the profits. The rugged individualist, defending his claim with a six-shooter, had no place in the real Far West. "The Americans," wrote a Scottish visitor to the California gold fields, "have a very great advantage, for . . . they are certainly of all people in the world the most prompt to organize and combine to carry out a common object."

On all frontiers community effort found particular expression in law enforcement. Renegades from society posed a problem in new settlements, attracted as they were by the hope of quick wealth and the absence of machinery to administer justice, but when they became sufficiently numerous to threaten life and property, the sober citizens banded together to meet the situation head on. Known variously as Regulators or the Regulation in the forested regions, as Anti-Horse-Thief Associations on the Great Plains, and as Vigilantes in the Far West, they served as law officers, courts, and executioners, rounding up the worst offenders, subjecting them to a summary trial, and either hanging them to the nearest tree or banishing them from the community. So effective were they that in one California mining district 500 miles long, occupied by a hundred thousand turbulent men who had riches to tempt the outlaw but neither government nor locks as protection, "there was," noted a visitor in 1850, "as much security of life and property as in any part of the Union." This security was won at a grim price; vigilantes sometimes degenerated into lynching mobs that took the life of many an innocent man. Yet the readiness of frontiersmen to cooperate for protection, and their instinctive skill in organizing, underlines the myth of frontier individualism.

This was made even more obvious by the willingness of pioneers to accept governmental regulations that might have aroused protests in eastern cities. Blue laws were commonplace in many areas, restricting private behavior in a manner reminiscent of seventeenth-century Boston. Ohio in 1816 levied heavy fines for swearing by God, Christ, or the Holy Ghost; shooting bullets across a stream; and running horses in towns. Still heavier penalties awaited anyone guilty of arranging a puppet show, wire dancing, or tumbling. Illinois decreed a fine of $25 for any person selling cards, dice, or billiard balls. Towns studded their statute books with laws forbidding the playing of ninepins, serenading, or making a noise with "drums, fifes, horns, pans, kettles or with anything whatsoever." Frontiersmen accepted infringements on individual freedom needed to protect the community against gambling, time-wasting entertainment, or sleep-disturbing noise, just as had the Puritans.

Less well known was the willingness of the pioneers to adopt laws governing economic behavior, at least in the infant urban communities of the Midwest. Citizens were required to sweep the streets before their doors, and to conform to certain standards in advertising their products. Trade was regulated more exactly than in the East, because firm measures were necessary in near-monopoly situations to protect the uncertain food supply, prevent speculative pricing in times of shortage, and force licensed merchants to compete honestly with each other. Chicago confined the sale of meats and vegetables to certain times and places where they could be inspected to protect the public health. Other pioneer cities fixed the price of bread, regulated fees of hackmen and carters, and regularly checked the accuracy of weights and measures. Not even private property was too sanctified to escape controls designed for the public good.

Regulation by state and national agencies was equally acceptable to the pioneer — when he judged the laws to be in his own interest. Texas in 1883 set up machinery to control railroad rates and force roads to haul cars of their competitors, although such a measure invaded property rights that had been held sacred. Texan cattlemen welcomed laws governing the conduct of drovers on the "long drives" to the Kansas railroads, even though their own liberties were threatened. A few years later the embattled farmers of the Great Plains raised the banner of Populism to demand governmental regulation of the railroads, a "socialistic" parcel post service, and the curbing of monopolies. To the frontier-oriented Westerner, the government could be a valuable ally as readily as a dangerous enemy, and should be viewed in either light as the immediate situation dictated.

On the basis of this analysis of Western opinion, we can now seek answers to two questions: Was frontier individualism a myth, and if not, how did it differ from traditional individualism? One conclusion is obvious: in the social realm the pioneer was a complete traditionalist, leaning on the community no less than his city cousins. Cooperation with his neighbors was commonplace for defense, the accomplishment of essential pioneering tasks, law enforcement, and a host of other necessities. In the economic realm the frontiersman's attitudes were less sharply defined. Consistency was not one of his sins, he favored regulation that seemed beneficial to his interests, and opposed regulation that threatened immediate or potential profits. His views were, in other words, comparable to those of Eastern business leaders who demanded from the government protective tariffs, railroad land grants, and federal subsidies, while mouthing the virtues of "rugged individualism."

Yet in one sense, the frontiersman moved somewhat beyond his counterparts in the East. He was, to a unique degree, living in a land where everyone was a real or potential capitalist. Nowhere could a stake in society be more easily obtained, and nowhere was the belief that this was possible more strongly entrenched. Moreover the frontier was developed largely by capital imported from the seaboard or from Europe. The fur trade, mining, and cattle raising prospered only because a flow of money from the East and abroad made prosperity possible. "The real peculiarity of our present Pacific civilization," wrote the editor of the *Overland Monthly* in 1883, "is that it is, perhaps, the most completely realized embodiment of the purely commercial civilization on the face of the earth." Dependent as they were on this flow of capital, and certain as they were that the humblest tenant farmers would someday enjoy wealth, Westerners were even more acutely conscious of the value of private property than Easterners, and more grimly determined to defend their right to use property as they wished. They would favor regulatory measures needed to attract capital or assure a healthy return on investments, but they would oppose laws that threatened profits even more vigorously than Easterners.

The frontiersmen, then, were opportunists rather than consistent theorists, but to an even greater degree than the capitalists of the seaboard. They had to be. Gambling against an unpredictable nature, they were willing to follow any path that promised success. If their ends could be achieved by individualistic effort, they preached individualism. If, more commonly, cooperative labor was necessary, or the use of governmental controls, they showed no reluctance in approving these devices. Their purpose was to make a profit, not prove a political theory, and their views swung with the circumstances. Yet the widespread property holdings in the West, and the belief that every man would achieve affluence, inclined the Westerner to insist on his right to profits somewhat more stridently than others. His voice spoke for individualism louder than that of his fellows, even though he was equally willing to find haven in cooperation when danger threatened or need decreed.

The rural Westerner's inclination toward individualism was strengthened by the fact that except in periods of danger or disaster he was somewhat less integrated into society than a city dweller, especially after the frontier on which he lived had passed its pioneer stage. The Easterner, living in a land where the economy was based on division of labor, was only a cog in a machine that must keep on operating if he were to survive. The Westerner, even though he leaned on his neighbors for defense and cabin raisings and husking parties, was relatively more self-sufficient. He harbored the belief that his self-sufficiency would increase, knowing that his own abilities would assure him a prosperous future as he exploited the natural resources about him. He might need government help to regulate rates of railroads that carried his grain to market or prices of manufacturers who sold him his implements, but he wanted no government interference with his freedom as he followed the road to riches.

To this extent, the frontiersman was an individualist, and his brand of individualism was remarkably like that which has persisted in the United States as a whole. The American follows the herd in his social habits, and he is eager to accept government aid that promises benefits to his business. But he is loudest in protest when regulatory measures threaten his profits or his economic freedom. Individualism, in the uniquely American sense, does seem to duplicate the individualism of the pioneer.

Basically, frontier individualism stemmed from the belief that all men were equal (excluding Negroes, Indians, Orientals, and other minority groups), and that all should have a chance to prove their personal capabilities without restraint from society. This seemed fair in a land of plenty, where superabundant opportunity allowed each to rise or fall to his proper level as long as governments did not meddle. Faith in the equality of men was the great common creed of the West. Only an understanding of the depth of this belief can reveal the true nature of social democracy on successive frontiers.

To European visitors, this was the most unique feature of Western life and thought: the attitude that set that region apart from Europe or the East. "There is nothing in America," wrote one, "that strikes a foreigner so much as the real republican equality existing in the Western States, which border on the wilderness." The whole attitude of the people was different; calmly confident of their own future, they looked on all men as their peers and acted accordingly. One Westerner who defined the frontier as a region where a poor man could enter a rich man's house without feeling uneasy or unequal was not far astray. Menial subservience was just as unpopular there as haughty superiority. Dame Shirley, writing from the California gold fields, felt the "I'm as good as you are" spirit all about her, and believed that only an American frontiersman could

> Enter a palace with his old felt hat on —
> To address the King with the title of Mister,
> And ask the price of the throne he sat on.

Everywhere men of all ranks exuded that easy air of confidence that went with complete self-assurance, meeting travelers on terms of equality that charmed those democratically inclined and shocked those of opposite prejudice. "The wealthy man assumes nothing to himself on account of his wealth," marveled one, "and the poor man feels no debasement on account of his poverty, and every man stands on his own individual merits." The spirit of Western democracy was captured by a cowboy addressing a disagreeable scion of British nobility: "You may be a son of a lord back in England, but that ain't what you are out here."

In the give and take of daily life, Western egalitarianism was expressed in the general refusal to recognize the class lines that were forming in every community. Some of the self-proclaimed "better sort" might hold themselves aloof and put on aristocratic airs, but they were atypical of the great mass of the people. The majority, in evaluating those about them, applied value judgments that differed from those in communities where tradition played a stronger role. Men were weighed on their present and future contributions to society, with total disregard for their background. Each played a role in the developing social order, and as long as he played it well he was respected. "To be useful is here the ruling principle," wrote a Swedish visitor to the West; "it is immaterial what one does so long as he is respected and does his work efficiently." Drones and aristocratic idlers were not bearing their fair share and were outcasts; men of menial rank were contributing to the community welfare and were respected. "There is in the West," noted an unusually acute observer during the 1830s, "a real equality, not merely an equality to talk about, an equality on paper; everybody that has on a decent coat is a gentleman."

Contemporaries speculated often on the reasons for frontier social democracy. Most agreed that the burgeoning Western economy was basically responsible, offering as it did a chance for the lowliest to acquire prestige through accumulated wealth. All had an equal chance to improve themselves, and so all should be treated as equals; conversely, the servant who believed that he would someday be a millionaire saw no reason to be servile to his temporary betters. This was common sense, since every new community boasted dozens of living examples of rags-to-riches success: the tenant farmer who was now a county judge, the mechanic newly elected to the legislature, the farmer grown rich by the sale of lands. As a British traveler saw, "the means of subsistence being so easy in the country, and their dependence on each other consequently so trifling, that spirit of servility to those about them so prevalent in European manners, is wholly unknown to them." Why be servile when the man above today might be the man below tomorrow? Why cling to traditional views of rank when the heir apparent to a British earldom could be seen mowing hay, assisted by two sons of a viscount, while nearby the brother of an earl was feeding grain into a threshing machine? Clearly standards on the frontier were different, and equality more nearly a fact of life.

The common level of wealth encouraged this spirit, for while differences did exist, the gulf between rich and poor was relatively less in frontier regions than in older societies. Poverty was rare in pioneer communities that had graduated from the backwoods stage; one governor complained that the number of dependent paupers in his state was "scarcely sufficient to give exercise to the virtue of charity in individuals." Wealth might and did exist on rural frontiers, but its presence was less obvious than in the East, for money would buy little but land and land was available to all. Ostentatious spending existed but was uncommon, partly because luxuries and leisure were largely unavailable, partly because it would breed hostility in neighbors who resented display. "Their wealth," it was observed, "does very little in the way of purchasing even the outward signs of respect; and as to *adulation*, it is not to be purchased with love or money." This leveling process underlined the sense of equality that was so typical of the frontier.

It was further emphasized by the fact that on the newer frontiers rich and poor lived, dressed, and acted much more alike than in the East. Most owned their own houses, though some might be of logs and some of bricks. Most dressed in homespun clothes and shunned the powdered wigs and knee breeches that were the badge of the gentry in the early nineteenth century; travelers frequently complained that it was impossible to distinguish the well-born from the lowly by the garments they wore. Most bore themselves proudly, scorning the humble mien that marked the lower classes in Europe. "The clumsy gait and bent body of our peasant is hardly ever seen here," wrote an Englishman from Kentucky in 1819; "every one walks erect and easy." When people looked and acted alike, as they did along the frontiers, treating them alike came naturally.

No less important in fanning the spirit of egalitarianism was the newness of the West, and the lack of traditional aristocratic standards there. No entrenched gentry governed social intercourse, setting the practices of those below them and closing their ranks against newcomers. Those who rose in station did not have to surmount the barrier of learning new customs as do those achieving higher status today, for conventions, deferences, and distinctions were rare among the "tree-destroying sovereigns" of the West. A man's ancestry and prior history were less important than the contribution that he could make to a new society badly in need of manpower. One Westerner who remarked: "It's what's above ground, not what's under, that we think on," and another who added: "Not 'What has he done in the East?' but 'What does he intend to do in Kansas and for Kansas?' " summed up the reasons for much of the social democracy that thrived along the frontiers.

This combination of causal forces — economic equality, commonly shared living standards, and the absence of traditional aristocratic values — enshrined belief in equality as the common faith of Western society. Class distinctions did exist, of course; innate differences in talent, ambition, and skill divided the various strata at an early stage in the evolution of every Western community. But relatively, these distinctions played a lesser role in the West than in the East. Instead belief in equality compelled frontiersmen to uplift the lowly and degrade the superior as they sought a common democratic level.

Elevation of the lowly was most commonly expressed by refusal to use terms designating class distinctions. Every man on the frontier, whatever his status in life, was a "gentleman," and every woman a "lady." Travelers from older societies were frequently amused to find the ragged wagoner or the ill-kempt seller of old bones addressed in this fashion; one who asked a tavern keeper in an infant settlement in New York to find his coachman was delighted when that worthy called out: "Where is the gentleman that brought this man here?" "Ladies" were as carelessly designated; one traveling in the West might hear, as did Mrs. Trollope, references to "the lady over the way that takes in washing," or "that there lady, out by the Gulley, what is making dip-candles." If titles could serve as social escalators, no one on the frontiers need stay long in menial ranks.

The leveling spirit of Western democracy sought not only to elevate the lowly but also to dethrone the elite. Any attempt at "putting on airs," was certain to be met with rude reminders of the equality of all men. New settlers were warned by guidebooks to mingle freely and familiarly with neighbors, and above all to pretend no superiority, if they wished to be accepted. They were told that nothing ruined a man's chances on the frontier so fatally as a suspicion of pride, which, once established, would ruin his reputation. "The cry of 'Mad Dog,' " wrote a Michigan pioneer, "is not more surely destructive. Travelers were also instructed to dress in simple fashion, and to avoid display in their clothes or their speech; those garbed as mechanics risked insults far less than those dressed as gentlemen. Those who failed to heed these warnings might be greeted with such remarks as: "Hold on, tha'r, stranger! When ye go through this yer town, go slow, so folks kin take you in," or in dry tones: "Mister, how much do you ask for it?" "For what, sir?" "Well, for the town; you look as though you owned it." One English newcomer who asked to be addressed as "Esquire" found that within a few days not only his host but the hired hands were calling him "Charlie"; another had the brass buttons unceremoniously ripped from his coat by a frontiersman who objected to such display. Texas rangers gambled or gave away the fancy uniforms issued to them, and stole the gold-braided suits of officers so that these aristocratic evidences of rank would not be seen. "Superiority," observed an English visitor, "is yielded to men of acknowledged talent alone."

Outward signs of social snobbery might arouse resentment in the West, but so did any conduct that seemed to suggest superiority. Families with sizable incomes found themselves better accepted if they lived and dressed as simply as their poorest neighbors; politicians soon realized that for success they must insist on being addressed as "Mister" or "Governor," and not as "Excellency." Even such a born-to-the-purple native aristocrat as Theodore Roosevelt took pains to understate his wealth and ancestry when on his Dakota ranch. When Colonel Thomas Dabney appeared at a frontier cabin raising in the Southwest with twenty slaves to do his work he was ostracized by the community; when a traveler had the good sense to dispose of expensive luggage, he was at last accepted on friendly terms. Natives and visitors alike learned that in the West refusal to drink with a stranger was interpreted as a sign of social superiority; unless they could convince their would-be hosts that they had "sworn off," even redeye whisky was preferable to the trouble that followed if word spread that they were "too good" for the community.

So strong was the spirit of equality along the frontiers that any deviation was met with resentment that was sometimes carried to ludicrous ends. Frontier housewives found themselves in disfavor if they kept their homes neater or cleaner than those of their neighbors; one who had waited three years for her first caller was told: "I woulda come before but I heard you had Brussels carpet on the floor." Another who offered to lend teaspoons for a party was rudely informed that no such luxuries were wanted, for the guests would not be used to them. Even those with a few choice possessions apologized; carpets were excused as "*one* way to hide the dirt," a mahogany table as "dreadful plaguy to scour," and kitchen conveniences as "lumberin' up the house for nothin'." When an Englishman remonstrated about the lack of ceremony in Western life he was told: "Yes, that may be quite necessary in England, in order to overawe a parcel of ignorant creatures, who have no share in making the laws; but with us a man's a man, whether he have a silk gown on him or not." The spirit of Western social democracy could have found no more eloquent expression than that.

In practice this spirit found its most outspoken expression in the attitude of hired workers. A "servant" in the traditional sense was impossible to find in the West because any form of servility was demeaning and hence intolerable; some of the most wealthy hosts and hostesses interrupted their dinner parties to wait on table or busy themselves in the kitchen. When servants could be drafted from the ranks of newly arrived immigrants or the families of less well-to-do pioneers they refused to accept that designation, but insisted on being called "helps," or "hired hands," or "ladies." The term "waiter" was equally unpopular, and was likely to call forth a spirited rejoinder from the person so addressed. Still more insulting was the word "master." A misguided traveler asking "Is your master at home?" would probably be told "I have no master"; one in the Wyoming cattle country was heatedly informed that "the son of Baliel ain't been born yet." So deep was the resentment against any implication of servility that young men and women preferred to labor at poor pay under bad conditions rather than accept a post as servant.

Those who did so guarded their respectability by abolishing all traditional symbols of servitude. Livery was never used; bells to summon servants in Western inns were unknown because the "helpers" refused to respond. All insisted on being treated as equals, dining with the family, meeting guests, and joining in all social functions under threat of immediate departure. One who had been told she must eat in the kitchen turned up her lip, announced "I guess that's cause you don't think I'm good enough to eat with you," and flounced from the house. Nor was this rebellious spirit peculiar to household help. The oft-heard remark: "If a man is good enough to work for me, he is good enough to eat with me" was literally applied. A family who had hired several carpenters to build a barn made the mistake of an early breakfast without them one day; the next day they left. A honeymooning couple were abandoned by their hired driver when they tried to eat alone just once. In public houses or conveyances the story was the same; travel accounts abound with tales of stewards who joined the card game after serving drinks, of waitresses who leaned over chairs to join in the conversation or borrow a guest's fan, of messengers who seated themselves and demanded a drink while serving their messages, of waiters in inns who joined their patrons when their tasks were done. In the West men felt equal, and acted the part.

Menial tasks were as resented by servants as were menial titles. Travelers were often forced to clean their own boots in frontier inns, or to rub down their own horses while "helpers" looked on disdainfully. One who asked to be awakened in the morning was answered "call yourself and be damned." On another occasion a titled Englishman in the Wyoming wilds was told to take a swim instead of a bath when he asked his hired helper to fill a tub; when he refused the angry helper shot the tub full of holes, shouting: "You ain't quite the top-shelfer you think you is, you ain't even got a shower-bath for cooling your swelled head, but I'll make you a present of one, boss!" Nor did servants alone resent the suggestion of servility. A pioneer Michigan housewife who tired of seeing a guest attack the roast with his own knife and offered to carve was rudely informed: "I'll help myself, I thankye. I never want no waitin' on."

Travelers who were shocked by these evidences of social democracy in the West were equally appalled by the democratic spirit which prevailed in frontier inns. There no "First Class" or "Second Class" accommodations separated patrons; tradesmen, slave dealers, farmers, congressmen, generals, fur trappers, and roustabouts ate side by side at the long tables, and all were treated the same. Sleeping accommodations were allotted on a first-come-first-serve basis, with governors and herdsmen, senators and farmers, rich and poor, clean and unclean, all crowded three or four to a bed. "It has been my lot," recorded an experienced traveler, "to sleep with a diversity of personages; I do believe from the driver of the stage coach, to men of considerable name." Complaints against these arrangements were summarily rejected by pioneer landlords; one visitor from overseas who objected to using a dirt-encrusted washbowl with a dozen other guests was told that "one rain bathes the just and the unjust, why not one wash-bowl"; another's protest that the sheets were dirty was answered with: "since *Gentlemen* are all alike, people do not see why they should not sleep in the same sheets." The frontier inn was, as one traveler put it, "a most almighty beautiful democratic amalgam."

The social democracy and frontier-type individualism that characterized America's growing period have not persisted unchanged into the twentieth century. Individualism has retreated before the advance of social cohesiveness essential in an urban-industrial society. The nation's folk hero may still be the rugged individualist, but the lone wolves of the past have found that they cannot fight the pack and that in cut-throat competition all throats are cut. At least since the 1890s the economic community had grudgingly accepted the regulation that the pioneer resisted save when it was to his advantage, and today cooperation and reliance on government are almost as commonplace in the United States as in the older countries of Europe. Yet American individualism differs from that of France or England in its continued insistence on a degree of economic freedom that has long since vanished in those countries, and in a glorification of the individual's ability to care for himself despite daily proof that joint effort alone will succeed in a society increasingly enmeshed.

Just as vestiges of frontier individualism remain to distinguish the social attitudes of modern America from those of modern Europe, so do remnants of pioneer democracy. The United States is no longer a country free of class distinctions and so wedded to egalitarianism that manifestations of wealth arouse public resentment. But its social democracy does differ from that of older nations, marked by its relative lack of class awareness, and by the brash assurance of the humble that they are as worthy of respect as the elite. The house painter who addresses a client by his first name, the elevator operator who enters into casual conversation with his passengers, the garage mechanic who condescendingly compares his expensive car with your aging model, could exist only in the United States. Their counterparts are unknown in England or on the Continent partly because America's frontiering experience bred into the people attitudes toward democracy that have persisted down to the present.

The Second Party System

Politics in America has been a game, a spectacle, a religion, a way of doing homage to heroes, and a way of expressing disapproval of one's neighbors. It has also been a dead-serious way of distributing wealth and power. American politics began as an extension of English politics, often in response to English political events. As the colonies matured, men had divided over local issues, but they had also organized around differing responses to the English ministry and to its representatives, the colonial governors.

Factions, rather than parties, continued to characterize the first years of independence. These were groupings often owing allegiance, not to a program or set of principles, but to a leader and his "interest." Factions were usually temporary, rising and declining as one powerful or charismatic political or social leader appeared or died. Often they lasted only for a single electoral campaign.

A full national party system with permanent machinery, an official program, and continuity from year to year emerged during the 1790s in response to a flock of new issues: local versus national authority, the financial measures of Alexander Hamilton, and the ideological issues generated by the French Revolution. Those supporting the use of national power to effect social and economic change, who endorsed the Bank of the United States and the Hamiltonian funding program, and who favored England over France, became Federalists. Their opponents followed the leadership of Jefferson and came, eventually, to be called Republicans or Democratic-Republicans.

While national issues dominated this "first party system," Americans divided politically over ethnic and religious antagonisms, over local conflicts of economic interest, and over what we today would call differing "life styles." On the local level, these were often more important than larger national questions in determining which of the two major parties men joined.

Between 1800 and 1815, the first party system faltered and collapsed. It had never been fully accepted as legitimate by Americans who had vainly hoped that the new nation would be free of party squabbling. When the early issues that divided Federalists from Republicans began to recede, the two bodies started to erode. The weaker of the two, the Federalist, disappeared first, leaving the field to its opponent. This Republican triumph was temporary, for the Republicans, in turn, began to lose support. The next few years represented an unusual hiatus in the American party system. Factions, centering around personalities rather than clear-cut issues, once again became the norm, though men continued to call themselves by the old Jeffersonian labels.

Beginning in 1824, a new political structure materialized. This "second party system" is the subject of Richard McCormick's essay that follows. McCormick is not interested in the parties of the period 1824–1860 for their individual characteristics. His concern is the party structure as it functioned in this period. Using some of the approaches and concepts of political scientists, he examines the origins, development, and operations of the parties during the era of Whig-Democratic strife, and distinguishes them from their Federalist-Republican antecedents. His intention is to suggest in what ways the two differed and what the new system meant for the political life of the country.

FOR FURTHER READING:

BENSON, LEE. *The Concept of Jacksonian Democracy: New York as a Test Case.* New York: Atheneum Publishers, 1964.*

McCORMICK, RICHARD P. *The Second American Party System: Party Formation in the Jacksonian Era.* Chapel Hill: University of North Carolina Press, 1966.*

SCHLESINGER, ARTHUR M., JR. *The Age of Jackson.* Boston: Little, Brown & Company, 1945.*

Asterisk denotes paperback edition.

Political Development and the Second Party System   RICHARD P. McCORMICK

Historians engaged in the study of political parties in the United States have commonly focused their attention on individual parties as distinctive entities or on the contests between parties. Studies of particular parties abound, both at the state level and in larger contexts, and much of our political history is written in terms of the clashing rivalry of Jeffersonian Republicans and Federalists, Whigs and Democrats, or Democrats and Republicans. This approach has tended to emphasize the differences between parties, especially in terms of their ideologies and their constituencies. Worthy, rewarding, and time-honored as this usual type of inquiry may be, there is an alternative — or complementary — approach that can be expected to yield important insights into American political development. We can view the parties in existence at any given time as comprising a party system; and with the party system, rather than individual parties, as the phenomenon under scrutiny, we can proceed to new categories of questions and hypotheses.

In studying individual political parties, for example, we may properly direct our attention to certain activities in which parties engage, such as nominating candidates, conducting campaigns, aggregating interests, formulating ideological positions, and managing governmental power. We may also be concerned with the structure, or pattern of organized relationships between leaders and identifiers, of a particular party. If on the other hand the party system is the object of our concern, we may endeavor to formulate understandings of how and under what circumstances party systems emerge, define the character of the party system in terms of various proposed typologies, and evaluate the contribution of the party system — as an element in the larger political system — to the handling of certain "problems" or the meeting of specified "crises." To the degree that we are able to develop suitable and meaningful concepts of broad applicability, we can engage in the comparative

Source: Richard P. McCormick, "Political Development and the Second Party System," in *The American Party Systems: Stages of Political Development,* eds. William Nisbet Chambers and Walter Dean Burnham (New York: Oxford University Press, 1967), pp. 90-116.

analysis of successive party systems within our own nation over a period of time as well as of party systems in different nations. By engaging in such comparative studies, we may hope to formulate and test hypotheses regarding the role of party systems in our culture.[1]

Proceeding within this frame of reference, we can say that in the period between the establishment of a new government under the federal Constitution in 1789 and the disruption of the Union in 1860, two party systems rose and declined and a third was in the process of being formed as the nation confronted the crisis of disunion. The first party system, properly recognized as the first modern party system in any nation, was formed in the 1790's, deteriorated after 1815, and in a loose sense came to an end in 1824. The second party system had its origins in the presidential contest of 1824, acquired its full dimensions by 1840, and began to disintegrate in the early 1850's. By 1856, with the sudden rise of the Republican party to national prominence, there were signs that a third party system was emerging, although the disunited condition of the opposition parties down through 1860 and the cataclysmic effects of the Civil War and the subsequent era of Reconstruction left the eventual outlines of this party system in doubt until the 1870's.[2]

These three party systems shared many attributes. They were all, for example, two-party systems. But they differed in the circumstances surrounding their origins — and in the cases of the first and second party systems in the circumstances associated with their disintegration — as well as in such important respects as the character of their sectional alignments, the comprehensiveness of their appeal to potential participants, and their apparent capacity for resolving conflicts. They are, however, comparable, and when sufficient descriptive studies become available, it should be fruitful to engage in a comparative analysis of all three. Then it may be possible to identify similarities and differences and advance hypotheses to explain them.

This brief introduction will suffice to establish the general conceptual framework within which my particular subject — the second American party system — is presented. My main concern will be to offer a descriptive account of the formation of this party system and its growth to maturity in the 1840's.[3] In order to place the subject in proper perspective, I shall deal briefly with some aspects of party development before 1824 and after 1840 and suggest some comparisons among the party systems under consideration.

By way of background, it is relevant to offer some very general observations on the conduct of politics before the emergence of the first party system. Unlike most nations of the world, the United States had considerable experience in operating representative institutions long before the advent of parties. Passing over the colonial period, which, as current research has demonstrated, was marked by a lively brand of politics inspired by an ideology that came to assume an increasingly democratic thrust, it should be recognized that even after 1776 republican governments functioned without political parties. In all of the states leaders were recruited, substantial proportions of the adult males were involved in the electoral process, stability was maintained, the legitimacy of governmental authority was recognized, and important conflicts were resolved. In this era of popular or semipopular non-party politics, independence was secured, grievous postwar problems were met, a new Constitution was adopted, and the federal government was established. Many of the obvious pre-conditions for the rise of parties existed in many of the states —

elected legislatures, broad suffrage provisions, open competition for offices, a society of differentiated interests sharing common goals — but there was no semblance of a national party system, and, with two or three interesting but questionable exceptions, no party formation at the state level. Politics remained essentially local in scope and factional in character, and was therefore readily managed through informal structures.

Any general approach to the comparative study of American party systems must surely include some analysis of this pre-party era, for only through such an analysis can we test adequately any hypotheses that may be advanced to explain the emergence of parties shortly after 1789. Similarly, by comparing how certain functions conventionally ascribed to parties were actually performed in the pre-party period and after the advent of parties, we may be able to obtain valid understanding of what parties have contributed to our political system. Or, to put the matter differently, what obvious deficiencies existed in the political system before the 1790's that were rectified by the formation of parties? These questions can only be raised at this point; not until we have available well-conceived studies of colonial and state politics before 1789 can they be answered with any assurance.

National parties did not form during the Confederation period, but within a few years after the establishment of the new federal government, and surely by 1795, there were clear signs that party formation was well under way at all levels of government.[4] The origins of these parties can be detected first in cleavages that developed within the highest level of the national administration. Next, comparable factions formed within Congress. The emergence of these congressional factions encouraged the formation of parties at the state level. Finally, successive contests for the presidency in 1796 and 1800 provided an additional stimulant and served to focus and reinforce party feelings.

In endeavoring to account for the creation of parties at this particular time, we are obliged to ask what new conditions arose in the 1790's that seemingly created an environment more favorable to the formation of national parties than had maintained a decade earlier. It is my view that the critical new factor was the creation of a national political arena as the result of the adoption of the federal Constitution. Politics assumed an entirely new dimension — a national dimension — and the informal techniques of political management that had sufficed previously were replaced by party techniques. In particular, the constitutional arrangements for electing a President encouraged co-operation among political leaders throughout the nation in behalf of particular candidates. In quite a different way, the election of members of the House of Representatives by popular vote served to relate state and national politics. As parties were delineated on this national basis, the same alignments became operative in contests for state and even local offices.

Overly simple as this formulation may appear, it is not without its complications. It would seem that down to 1796, at least, we are confronted with a fairly clear case of parties whose origins were of the "interior" type, or "internally created" parties, to employ Maurice Duverger's typology.[5] That is, parties were formed first within the Congress and then were extended to the electorate. The complication arises because almost at once — in 1796 — quite a different influence entered the scene; namely, the contest for the presidency. The rivalry between John Adams and Thomas Jefferson in 1796 and again in 1800 served not only to dramatize and polarize the emerging partisan cleavage: it also enlarged party strife beyond the bounds of congressional districts, bringing it to embrace entire states and, by extension, the whole nation. Without pausing to develop this admittedly crucial point, I would contend that it was the contest for the presidency that was to exert the determining influence on the structure of the American party system.

The first party system, launched with such enterprise and vigor in the 1790's, soon entered upon what might be termed a stage of arrested development. It did not become established in the newer states that entered the Union after 1796; it soon languished in the Southern states; and in some other areas it succumbed to factional discord. By 1824 the remnants of the first party system possessed some vitality in only five states — Maine, Massachusetts, New Jersey, Delaware, and Maryland — although there were numerous isolated instances elsewhere of Federalists still offering challenges to their Republican adversaries.[6] Vestiges of old party organizations survived in some cases and party identities lingered on, but elections were rarely contested within the framework of the party system.

The first party system, then, can be seen in terms of failure as well as success. It failed to achieve truly national dimensions and, quite obviously, it failed to survive; and it also came perilously close to recording an even more serious failing. As the party system matured it became increasingly unbalanced. That is, the Republicans achieved such a lopsided superiority on a national basis that their Federalist opponents could scarcely hope to compete. What rendered this situation especially ominous was that the Federalist strength was sectionally concentrated, chiefly in New England, and that strength could now scarcely be effective in national politics. In consequence, the Federalists experienced a keen sense of political frustration, amounting to a sense of loss of their political efficacy. Much of New England's disaffection during the War of 1812 can be related to this factor, and the Hartford Convention, with its demands for revision of the constitutional "rules of the game," and even its implied threat of a division of the Union, brought the tensions to a crisis. What the ultimate result might have been had Andrew Jackson's victory at New Orleans in 1815 not transformed popular reactions to the war and to the record of the national administration must remain problematical. It can at least be suggested that the first party system as of 1814 was failing lamentably in achieving national integration and was even bringing the very legitimacy of the government into question. In other terms, the first party system was a failure because the parties became excessively unbalanced and took on a sectional alignment to the point where one sectionally oriented party, feeling that it could not compete, would no longer play the game according to the recognized rules.

In sequel, the first party system in its latter years — after 1815 — can be held responsible for a peculiar example of a "crisis of participation." Having failed to secure a revision of the rules, and having lost any prospect of electoral success, the Federalists in many states simply withdrew entirely from the arena of politics. In New Hampshire, for example, where the Federalists ceased to contest for state offices after 1817, voter participation declined from a high of slightly more than 80 per cent of those eligible in the gubernatorial election of 1814 to a low of 44 per cent by 1822. In Connecticut, for similar reasons, voter participation dropped from 45 per cent in 1819 to 22 per cent by 1822; in Vermont there was a comparable decline from 66 per cent in 1818 to 25 per cent by 1821; and in Rhode Island there was an abrupt falloff from nearly 50 per cent in 1818 to 15 per cent in 1819.[7] In other states, as party competition languished, voter participation generally sank to a low level.

Why did the first party system disintegrate? If we could answer this question with complete authority we should no doubt possess an important key to understanding the nature of the system. Without attempting to offer a comprehensive explanation for the breakdown of the parties, we could propose the simple proposition that the failure of the Federalists to extend, or even maintain, the bases of support they held in 1800 brought about a condition of extreme party imbalance. At this point the Federalists confronted the alternatives of rebelling against the system or withdrawing from it. After experiencing failure with the first alternative, they adopted the second in most states. No longer confronted by a formidable opposition, the Republicans in most areas succumbed to internal factionalism.

Approaching the problem from even a narrower perspective, we could advance the hypothesis that the first party system disintegrated because the chief purpose for which it had been formed had lost its urgency. That is, the fact that the contest for the presidency subsided after 1800 deprived the party system of the main source of its vitality and even the reason for its existence. The fortuitous availability of the members of the "Virginia Dynasty," the succession of Jefferson, Madison, and Monroe, and the failure of the Federalists as politicians to grasp the full significance of the importance of the presidential contest, together with certain impediments that inhered in the existing constitutional and social environment, all combined to reduce and ultimately eliminate the contest for the presidency as the stimulus to party action. This hypothesis — that the contest for the presidency provided the first party system with its crucial function — would obviously require extensive testing. Here it can only be noted that in the absence of a contest for the presidency there was little tendency for parties to form within individual states for the purpose of competing for state and local offices. Moreover, there is no evidence to suggest that cleavages within the Congress, even after 1815, could provide the basis for the rehabilitation or reconstruction of the party system. Finally, the revival of the contest for the presidency after 1824 had the immediate effect of stimulating the formation of a new party system.

As the national party system disintegrated, especially after 1815, it is noteworthy that there was not much of a tendency toward the formation of state-oriented parties, that is, parties organized solely for the purpose of contesting offices at the state level. The obvious exceptions to this generalization were New York, with its Bucktail and Clintonian parties; Georgia, with its peculiar Troup-Clark alignments; and Kentucky, where Old Court and New Court parties carried on a brief struggle.[8] It is also significant, I believe, that divisions did not form within Congress to provide the basis for a new party alignment even when such crises as those attendant upon the economic depression of 1819 or the furor over the admission of Missouri to statehood agitated public feelings.

It would seem to be quite clear that the stimulus for the formation of the second party system was supplied by the revival of the contest for the presidency in 1824. With the expiration of Monroe's second term there was no notable Virginian to take his place; the weak and discredited Republican congressional caucus was unable to produce a disciplined solution to the problem of succession; and soon there were four candidates — all self-styled Republicans — contending for the presidency. Except in New England, where John Quincy Adams had virtually no opposition, the contest was extremely confused and did not at once produce new party alignments. Because it was so chaotic, and also because in many states one or another of the

candidates enjoyed overwhelming support from local political leaders, voter participation was remarkably low.

The most important consequence of 1824, in terms of party formation, was that it
projected Andrew Jackson to the fore as the rival to Adams. Looking ahead to
1828, rival political leaders from state to state began to calculate their courses of action with respect to what was termed the "presidential question." Obviously, many
considerations entered into their appraisals, but the fact that loomed largest, no
doubt, was the highly sectional nature of the appeal of the two candidates.

This sectional bias was clearly revealed in the election of 1828. Adams swept
New England, securing majorities of three-to-one or better in four of the six states.
Jackson was equally impressive in the South, and won commanding majorities in
most of the newer states of the West. Having no sectional candidate of their own in
the race, the Middle States provided the major battleground of the election, and —
except in Pennsylvania — the vote was extremely close. The party alignments that
formed in the Middle States by 1828 tended to be durable, as Table 1 shows,[9] al-

TABLE 1   Differential between Percentages of Total Vote
Obtained by Major Presidential Candidates, 1828–44

State	1828	1832	1836	1840	1844
Maine	20	10	20	1	13
New Hampshire	7	13	50	11	19
Vermont	50	10	20	29	18
Massachusetts	66	30	9	16	12
Rhode Island	50	14	6	23	20
Connecticut	50	20	1	11	5
New York	2	4	9	4	1
New Jersey	4	1	1	4	1
Pennsylvania	33	16	4	1	2
Delaware	—	2	6	10	3
Maryland	2	1	7	8	5
Virginia	38	50	13	1	6
North Carolina	47	70	6	15	5
Georgia	94	100	4	12	4
Kentucky	1	9	6	29	8
Tennessee	90	90	16	11	1
Louisiana	6	38	3	19	3
Alabama	80	100	11	9	18
Mississippi	60	77	2	7	13
Ohio	3	3	4	9	2
Indiana	13	34	12	12	2
Illinois	34	37	10	2	12
Missouri	41	32	21	14	17
Arkansas	—	—	28	13	26
Michigan	—	—	9	4	6
Average differential	36	36	11	11	9

though in both New York and Pennsylvania the anti-Jackson forces lacked cohesion
and were distracted by Antimasonry. With these important exceptions, we could
say that a new two-party system had emerged in the Middle States by 1828 and that
it had been given definition by the presidential contest. In New England, because of
the overwhelming loyalty to the sectional favorite, the opposition Jacksonian parties
were able to make little headway until after Adams had been defeated. But by 1829

the political balance had altered considerably, and the Jacksonians rapidly moved into a competitive position in most states. In the South and West — except for the very special case of Kentucky — the election of 1828 stimulated the temporary formation of parties. Once the election was over, however, the alignments did not persist and politics continued to be conducted in what was essentially an unstructured fashion.

Despite the large issues that presumably were involved, the election of 1832 had remarkably little effect on party formation. In the South and West there were feeble efforts to organize support for Henry Clay, but in most states he fared even less well than had Adams in 1828. In the Middle States, the close balance that had become evident in 1828 persisted. The most striking shift occurred in New England, where in every state the Jacksonians made tremendous gains and captured Maine and New Hampshire. Perhaps this remarkable upheaval can be attributed to the popularity of Jackson's policies regarding the bank, tariff, and internal improvements. Yet I am inclined to believe that the explanation is to be found quite simply in the fact that Clay lacked the strong sectional appeal that Adams had possessed.

How well developed, then, was the new party system by the end of 1832? In broad terms, it was well established in New England and the Middle States, despite the complications of Antimasonry. In every state the Jacksonians had acquired recognized leaders, constructed an elaborate party apparatus, and enlisted in their ranks multitudes of voters who identified with the Jackson party. The opposition, plagued by the lack of a persistent standard bearer, nevertheless managed to maintain a competitive position, whether under the Adams, National Republican, or Antimasonic label. The South, except for Kentucky, could best be described as politically monolithic. Where nearly all political leaders and candidates were nominally, at least, of the Jacksonian persuasion, there could scarcely be a functioning two-party system. In certain of the newer states of the West what can only be described as a dual party system existed. There were temporary party formations in 1828 and 1832 for the purpose of contesting the presidential election, but in state and congressional elections the contests were either conducted on a non-party basis or, in some instances, on the basis of alignments quite different from those that obtained in the presidential elections. It is common, in describing American politics in this era, to assert that by 1828 or by 1832 a functioning party system existed; but it would be my contention that in many states the crucial stage of party formation had not yet been reached.

Slight as was the effect of the election of 1832 on party formation, it did reveal an undercurrent that was soon to assume the proportions of a tidal wave. Although Jackson retained, and even increased, his huge majorities throughout the South, there were strong manifestations of dissatisfaction with his running mate and heir-apparent, Martin Van Buren of New York. In Virginia, North Carolina, Georgia, and Alabama, factions that professed loyalty to Jackson also launched organized efforts to oppose Van Buren's candidacy for the vice-presidency, and there were similar signs of restiveness in other Southern states as well. Some of these early anti-Van Burenites were admirers of John C. Calhoun, and others were appalled at the prospect of having to support a Northerner for the presidency. Still others, no doubt, were calculating how they might exploit anti-Van Buren sentiment to advance their political fortunes within their particular states.

What can best be characterized as a political explosion rocked the South from

Virginia to Mississippi in 1834 and 1835. With Jackson nearing the end of his tenure, the political consensus that seemingly had prevailed was abruptly replaced by a sharp cleavage in almost every state. Those who remained loyal to the Jackson party found themselves confronted with a virulent opposition that shared a common antagonism to Martin Van Buren. While some of those "antis" continued to profess their undying loyalty to Old Hickory and his policies, others declaimed against executive usurpation, the removal of bank deposits, and the tariff, or sounded the changes on states' rights. The new sides were drawn in the state and congressional elections of 1834 and 1835, and by 1836 the Southern opposition parties — often bearing the name Whig — had found their standard bearer in Hugh Lawson White of Tennessee.

In the Western states, too, the approach of the election of 1836 spurred the slow process of party formation. More-or-less well-organized Van Buren-Democratic parties faced bitter struggles with opposition parties pledged variously to a local hero — William Henry Harrison of Indiana — or to mixed White-Harrison tickets. In part because of the unprecedented personal campaign waged by Harrison, the election aroused considerable interest. The alignments that emerged in this election persisted, even though state elections in Illinois, Indiana, and Missouri continued for a few years to bear only a vague resemblance to party contests.

The least studied of all our presidential elections, the election of 1836, was of crucial importance in determining the ultimate outlines of the second party system. In marked contrast to the situation that had existed in 1832, there were now two parties contesting elections in every state, and — no less significantly — in the large majority of the states the parties were competitive. Although Van Buren eked out a victory in the 1836 election, the party that he headed had very different dimensions from the one that had twice swept Jackson into office. In the South, where Jackson had encountered little more than token opposition, Van Buren polled slightly less than 50 per cent of the popular vote. Jackson had won 100 per cent of the votes in Georgia and 95 per cent of the votes in Tennessee in 1832; Van Buren lost both of these states in 1836. In the West, too, Van Buren's strength was far less than that of Jackson. Only in New England did Van Buren enhance the strength of the Democratic party. In the evenly balanced Middle States there was no large shift.

In brief, the effect of Van Buren's candidacy was to end the monolithic character of Southern politics and delineate and strengthen alignments in the West, thereby giving a truly national dimension to the second party system. While in 1832 the victorious candidate had secured a two-to-one margin in eleven states, only one state remained in that category in 1836: New Hampshire, which Van Buren carried by a three-to-one margin. Fittingly enough, the state in which Van Buren found his weakest support was Vermont. Here, indeed, is a conundrum for political analysts.

The anti-Buren or Whig parties that had formed in the several states between 1834 and 1836, together with those in New England and the Middle States that had originated earlier, had yet to develop national cohesion and leadership. Such an achievement would be essential if they were to contest successfully for the presidency. Meeting at Harrisburg in December 1839, in one of the most astutely contrived conventions ever held, they performed the difficult feat by agreeing to unite on the best available hero, Old Tippecanoe Harrison, and by sedulously avoiding any semblance of a party platform. Thus effectively mobilized, the Whigs proceeded to put on a spectacular campaign that was to fix a new style in American political drama.[10] The exciting contest, waged furiously now in every state, stimulated an unprecedented outpouring of voters and sent Van Buren down to a crushing defeat in the electoral college, although the popular vote was far less lopsided.

The campaign of 1840 brought the second American party system at last to fruition. In every region of the country, and indeed in every state, politics was conducted within the framework of a two-party system, and in all but a handful of states the parties were so closely balanced as to be competitive.[11] In broad terms, it was the contest for the presidency that shaped this party system and defined its essential purpose. The same party system, however, was to be utilized as the framework within which competition for office at all other levels of government would be conducted. The two parties were similar in structure, employed similar campaign techniques, and performed similar functions. Although in specific features the parties remained somewhat differentiated from state to state, there had in fact occurred a nationalization of institutional forms and political styles. There was also a nationalization of political identities. Voters everywhere would respond to candidates and issues as Whigs or Democrats.

With this brief and even partial synopsis of party development in mind, it becomes possible to attempt some analyses of what it all signifies. We can approach this question by attempting some broad comparisons between the first and second party systems. But before engaging in this exercise, we might well pause to consider how politics was conducted in the absence of parties, for only with some understanding of this phase of our political history can we measure and evaluate the effects of parties.

Even after the appearance of the first party system, many states continued to conduct politics on a non-party basis. An example is Tennessee, which did so for roughly forty years.[12] With no vestige of political parties, the Tennessee brand of politics featured hard-fought contests for seats in the legislature and in Congress that not uncommonly brought over 70 per cent of the electorate to the polls. In the process, the state produced a host of outstanding political figures, including not only Andrew Jackson but James K. Polk, Hugh Lawson White, John Bell, and Felix Grundy as well. Reference could readily be made to a dozen other states where as late as the 1820's, or even 1830's, political parties were nonexistent. Leaving aside the intriguing question of why parties were not formed, at least for the purpose of conducting state politics, it would no doubt be illuminating if we could answer the question of what functions usually ascribed to political parties were not being performed in some manner in Tennessee and other non-party states. Probably none of us would insist that representative government was inconceivable without political parties, but we may readily err in attributing to parties a larger and more comprehensive role in the American political process than they in fact deserve. Unfortunately, we know even less about pre-party politics in the United States than we do about party politics, with the result that as yet we are not well prepared to make reliable comparisons between the two systems.

We are on slightly firmer ground when we endeavor to compare the first and the second party systems, although admittedly our knowledge of both is inadequate and the conceptual framework within which we structure our comparisons is incomplete. For the purposes of this essay, the comparative analysis must necessarily be kept within brief limits and deal only with large and readily visible attributes.

The first and second American party systems did not have precisely the same origins. It would seem that cleavages within Congress preceded and even forecast the formation of parties in the 1790's. In theoretical terms, it would be extremely important to be able to affirm that the first party system represented an "internally created" or "interior" type of party formation. Unfortunately, we cannot be sure how far this interior process of party formation might have proceeded, for superimposed on the impulse supplied by the congressional parties was the mobilization for the presidential contests in 1796 and 1800. It is my view that these contests for the presidency supplied a greater stimulus to party formation than did the congressional groupings. Nevertheless, the early existence of congressional alignments in the 1790's has no counterpart in the 1820's. Moreover, the parties of the 1790's possessed at the outset an issue-orientation that can hardly be discerned in 1824 or 1828. Finally, the first party system had a relatively rapid emergence, whereas the second was formed in stages over a period of roughly sixteen years.

Both party systems, the second more clearly than the first, were oriented toward contesting presidential elections. This orientation presents a striking contrast to the situation in other Western political systems, where parties have been oriented toward securing as large a representation as possible in the national legislature (although it must be noted that in most cases it has been the legislature that names the functioning executive in such systems). It is this peculiarity, among others, that makes it so difficult to conceptualize American party systems in terms that would be relevant to other nations. In organizational terms, the congressional district has presented awkward problems for our parties, quite unlike the parliamentary constituencies in Europe. Why should the executive rather than the legislative branch have been the focal point for the party system, especially in the first half of the nineteenth century? No doubt an extended answer to this question could tell us much about the special character of American parties.

There were pronounced differences in the organizational structures of parties in the first and second party systems. The caucus reflected in part the prominent role taken by legislators — national and state — in guiding early party development, and it was extensively employed as a management device under the first party system.[13] In most states, as well as at the national level, party members within the legislature, often joined by non-legislators, performed extensive nominating functions and — usually through such agencies as central committees — directed party affairs generally. In many states, conspicuously in New England and Virginia, the caucus and its agencies operated a highly centralized party apparatus, although in time local party units increasingly employed delegate conventions to nominate candidates for lesser offices. Two states, New Jersey and Delaware, were exceptional in that they instituted the state convention. Because of the great variations in constitutional structures from state to state, the precise forms of party organization and even the functions performed by the caucus differed widely; but in its most highly developed form — notably in Massachusetts — the caucus structure was highly integrated and extremely efficient. At the national level, party management was relatively weak. The Republican congressional caucus was a promising institution, which under slightly altered circumstances might have exerted a lasting influence on the structure of American parties, but for reasons that must be passed over it failed to develop and maintain its authority and grew increasingly ineffective, especially after 1816. The Federalists, with their small and geographically unrepresentative delegation in

Congress, could scarcely use the caucus as an authoritative national agency, and they had little success in developing the convention as an alternative.

Under the second party system, the caucus was almost completely replaced by the convention as the characteristic device for party management. The changeover, which has not yet been studied thoroughly, had great theoretical significance. In addition to reflecting demands for popular participation in party affairs the convention also represented a highly practical solution to problems facing party leaders at a time when party identities in legislative bodies were extremely confused, or when incipient parties had too few legislative representatives to organize a respectable caucus. Much might be made of the fact that the Antimasonic party, the first clear example of what Maurice Duverger calls an "externally created" or "exterior" type of party in the United States, was especially zealous in developing the convention technique and, as we know, held the first national party convention. Whether the extralegislative origins of the Jackson and Adams parties in most — but not all — states would justify our describing them as "exterior" parties could lead to considerable debate. What would seem to be indisputable is that the shift from caucus to convention implied a loss in the political authority of legislative bodies. While they were suffering this loss, they were also experiencing general curtailment of their elective functions, as evidenced by the trend toward the popular choice of electors, governors, and other state officials. Again, one would like to be able to understand fully why this downgrading of the legislative branch occurred and what implications it had for our system of politics.

The widespread adoption of the convention system in the 1830's, with its hierarchy of delegate conventions and party committees extending from the smallest electoral unit up to the national conventions, made for an exceedingly elaborate and complex organizational structure. Because candidates had to be nominated at so very many different levels of government, elections were held so frequently, and the party system embraced the entire range of offices, the organizations that had evolved in most states by the 1840's were marvels of ingenuity and intricacy and required enormous manpower to staff them. In contrast to the diversity of organizational forms under the first party system, there was now a high degree of uniformity throughout the nation and in both major parties.

It is possible that the shift from the caucus to the convention may have tended greatly to emphasize the purely electoral functions of the party apparatus. The members of a caucus, in their dual capacity as legislators and party managers, may have been more concerned with matters of program and policy than were the members of conventions. It would also appear that in its most centralized form, the caucus structure imposed a much higher degree of discipline than was to prevail under the convention system. Despite their elaborate organization, the new parties of the second party system were actually decentralized structures. The party apparatus at each level of government, or within each type of constituency, possessed considerable autonomy. Party mechanisms were better designed for achieving agreement on nominations than for formulating policies. Perhaps the very complexity and magnitude of the formal organizational structure contributed to the rise of the professional party manager and the informal leader, or boss.

In discussing any formal party structures, whether of the caucus or convention type, the problem inevitably arises as to whether the formal structure reflected the actual locus of power or influence. Superficially, the delegate convention system of the 1830's and 1840's resulted in the "democratization" of parties, but we have yet to determine the degree to which conventions were genuine decision-making bodies. Perhaps they were, but they must also be viewed as having what might be termed a cosmetic function; that is, they gave a democratic appearance to what might in fact have been decisions determined by a party oligarchy. Indeed, Ostrogorski used the term "democratic formalism" to describe the convention structure.

The two party systems could also be compared with respect to participation. The installation of the convention party structure unquestionably multiplied opportunities for party followers to assume roles as activists. This development was especially prominent in those states where previously there had been little or no formal party organization, but its effects could be noted everywhere. Moreover, intense interparty competition stimulated unprecedented levels of voter participation, not uncommonly rising to 80 per cent of the electorate, whereas prior to 1824 in a very large number of states it was exceptional for half of the eligible voters to participate regularly in elections.[14] Both in the comprehensiveness of their structures and in the universality of their appeal, then, the new parties could truly be characterized as mass parties.

One may properly speculate as to whether the measurable increase in voter participation had a direct influence on party programs and governmental actions. To put the question differently, when vast numbers of men who had formerly lacked the franchise or who had been apathetic entered the electoral arena, were there discernible shifts in party attitudes or public policy? Did the parties and the governments become more "democratic"? This would be an extremely difficult question to answer, but I have the impression that the "new" voters tended to divide between the two parties in much the same proportion as the "old" voters.[15] We might conclude that both parties accommodated the new voters by modifying their appeals and their programs. An alternative conclusion could be that because the new voters did not enter predominantly into one party and make it the instrument for achieving their political goals, they had no great effect on the parties. Any sure evaluation of the effects of enlarged participation must depend on further studies, but at least we might agree that the mass participation that we associate with the second party system did affect the style of politics.

The extended form of participation in politics in the era of the second party system can scarcely be comprehended in purely political terms — that is, only in terms of rivalry between opposing power elites or interest groups for dominance in the state and for control over public policy. It would be difficult to account for all the phenomena of the system within these limited concepts, and the varieties of experiences that parties in this era afforded to the electorate went beyond the political sphere.[16] Those tens of thousands of men and women who attended the mammoth Whig festival at Nashville in 1840; those untold millions who carried torches, donned uniforms, chanted slogans, or cheered themselves hoarse at innumerable parades and rallies; those puffed-up canvassers of wards, servers of rum, and distributors of largesse; and all those simple folk who whipped themselves into a fury of excitement and anxiety as each election day approached, were thrilling to a grand dramatic experience, even a cathartic experience. There was no spectacle, no contest, in America that could match an election campaign, and all could identify with and participate in it.

Innumerable foreign observers saw clearly this amazing dimension of American politics. As Michael Chevalier perceived it, the political campaign and all its attendant pageantry and exaltation meant to Americans what religious festivals had meant to the peoples of Catholic Europe. Witnessing a post-election celebration of New York City Democrats, he was struck by the resemblance.

> The procession was nearly a mile long; the democrats marched in good order to the glare of torches; the banners were more numerous than I had ever seen them in any religious festival; all were in transparency, on account of the darkness. On some were inscribed the names of the democratic societies or sections . . . others bore imprecations against the Bank of the United States; *Nick Biddle* and *Old Nick* here figured largely and formed the pendant of our *libera nos a malo.* Then came portraits of General Jackson afoot and on horseback . . . Those of Washington and Jefferson, surrounded with democratic mottoes, were mingled in all tastes and of all colors. Among these figured an eagle, not a painting, but a real live eagle, tied by the legs, surrounded by a wreath of leaves, and hoisted upon a pole, after the manner of the Roman standards. The imperial bird was carried by a stout sailor, more pleased than ever was a sergeant permitted to hold one of the strings of the canopy, in a Catholic ceremony. From further than the eye could reach, came marching on the democrats. I was struck with the resemblance of their air to the train that escorts the *viaticum* in Mexico or Puebla. . . . The democratic procession, also, like the Catholic procession, had its halting places; it stopped before the house of the Jackson men to fill the air with cheers, and halted at the doors of the leaders of the Opposition, to give three, six, or nine groans.
> . . . If these scenes were to find a painter, they would be admired at a distance, not less than the triumphs and sacrificial pomps, which the ancients have left us delineated in marble and brass; for they are not mere grotesques after the manner of Rembrandt, they belong to history, they partake of the grand; they are the episodes of a wondrous epic which will bequeath a lasting memory to posterity, that of the coming of democracy.[17]

Finally, the first and second party systems exhibited pronounced differences in their extent and their alignment. The parties of the 1790's had never really been extended to more than fifteen states, and in several of those they scarcely became rooted. The second party system comprehended every state, although there might well be some reservations about South Carolina. The first party system was, from one point of view, very badly aligned. Early in its history the New England states were heavily inclined toward the Federalist party, while in the South the Republicans possessed a lopsided supremacy. Although New England in time achieved a brief balance of parties, the South became virtually a one-party region. The second party system was extraordinary in that the two parties were fairly evenly balanced in every region.[18] Between 1836 and 1852, as in no other period in our history, each of the parties was truly national in its extent.

It would be possible and even profitable to explain why the two party systems differed in so many attributes, but such a disquisition would probably have to be very lengthy if it were to be at all persuasive. Within the limited compass of this essay it is appropriate to attempt no more than a brief reference to the most salient factors.

Of foremost importance in affecting the structures of parties as well as the specific tasks that elements within the party organization had to perform were certain fundamental changes in the constitutional and legal environment.[19] To put the matter simply, the rules under which the political game was to be played changed greatly between 1800 and 1840. The most obvious development was a trend from diversity to uniformity in governmental structures and electoral procedures from state to state. The magnitude and significance of this quiet revolution in the electoral environment has generally been ignored, except for a curious preoccupation with modifications in suffrage qualifications.[20] We have yet to assess adequately the relevance to our party system of the movements toward the popular, at-large election of presidential electors, the choice of congressmen by districts, the popular election of governors, and the multiplication in numbers of locally elected officials. In a related realm, the adoption of printed ballots, the creation of small voting districts, and the consolidation of elections on a single day had enormous consequences for political parties.

One general effect of this quiet revolution was to complicate the tasks of the parties. In a situation where, for example, members of a legislature were elected from the county as a unit and where the legislature in turn appointed the governor, presidential electors, and county officials, parties would have very limited tasks, as contrasted with a situation where members of each house of the legislature were chosen from different constituencies, and presidential electors, the governor, and county officials were popularly elected. Compelled to elaborate an intricate organization capable of making nominations and conducting campaigns within a bewildering variety of constituencies, and obliged at the same time to appeal for the broadest possible base of support, the new parties confronted a staggering challenge, especially when they might be called upon to engage in electoral combat two or three times within a single year. It is no wonder that they were reduced to little more than electoral machines.

If one change in the electoral environment loomed larger than all the rest it was the shift to the popular, at-large election of presidential electors. This development gave a popular dimension to the contest for the presidency, reduced the political authority of the state legislatures, called forth elaborate and intensive campaign efforts, facilitated the building of national parties, reduced the effectiveness of third parties, and made the presidential election the focal point of the party system — to suggest but a few consequences. How and through what influences this transformation of the process of choosing electors was brought about has yet to be studied, but a complete understanding of its implications might well be crucial to any conceptualization of the American party system.

The political environment was profoundly influenced not only by these constitutional and legal developments, but also by fairly obvious technological, economic, and social changes. Revolutionary improvements in means of transportation and communication made it feasible, for example, for parties to hold state and even national conventions and conduct nationwide campaigns. Rising economic expectations associated with the transformation and expansion of the economy gave new energy to democratic dogmas and spurred mass participation in politics. The entrance of new states into the union broadened the spatial dimensions of the party system, and the growth of urban areas and the sharp rise in immigration created new challenges. Above all, the increasingly egalitarian flavor of American society, now given voice in an incontestable rhetoric, compelled both parties to project the same democratic image.

These briefly enumerated changes in the constitutional and cultural environment may account for certain fairly obvious differences in organization and style between the first and second party systems. But they do not fully explain what was most distinctive about the latter, namely, its lack of sectional bias. As the second party system reached maturity in the 1840's, it scarcely reflected the fact that the basic cleavage within the nation, transcending all others, was that which may be vaguely defined as North-South sectionalism. The first party system had mirrored this tension to the degree that after 1800 the Federalists were very largely a Northern party. The third party system as it finally became aligned in the 1870's also contained a decided sectional bias, with its solidly Democratic South and its Northern-oriented Republican party. In attempting to explain how the second party system produced not sectional parties but parties that were remarkably well balanced throughout the nation, we are confronted with a paradox. In the successive contests for the presidency between 1824 and 1836 strong sectional loyalties shaped the responses of political leaders and voters in each region to the opposing candidates. But by 1836 the end result of the series of realignments was a sectionally balanced party system. In brief, the explanation for the paradoxical character of the second party system is to be found in the peculiar circumstances associated with the contests for the presidency.

To recapitulate, the second party system did not emerge suddenly; it developed in a series of stages, and at each stage it was shaped by the sectional identifications of the candidates. With Andrew Jackson and John Quincy Adams as the candidates in 1828, a highly sectionalized vote resulted; New England went almost as overwhelmingly for Adams as the South did for Jackson; only the Middle States were evenly divided. When Henry Clay was substituted for Adams, New England was no longer held together by its loyalty to a sectional favorite, and parties throughout the North came into balance. When Martin Van Buren was substituted for Jackson — and opposed by White and Harrison — the South and much of the new West ceased to be politically monolithic, as anti-Van Buren parties quickly mobilized. These sectional responses to the presidential candidates were crucial at the time of party formation. Once the parties had been formed and identities had been acquired by the voters, alignments tended to remain relatively firm. Thus highly sectional responses in a series of presidential elections resulted in the formation of non-sectional parties.

Merely to emphasize their distinctiveness, I have chosen to call these national parties "artificial" because their ultimate alignments bore no direct relationship to the realities of sectional antagonism. At maturity, each party sought to aggregate interests that were national in scope; and within each party almost equally powerful Northern and Southern wings contested for supremacy. Intra-party tensions were greater than the tensions between the two parties. The federalized character of our constitutional structure and the inability of any national party agency to exercise firm discipline made it all but impossible to restrain the intra-party tensions. Responsible leaders of both parties understood that such parties could be destroyed by issues that were sectional in character. The parties could indulge themselves in furious controversies over the "Monster Bank," but they might be rent asunder by such issues as expansionism or the status of slavery in the territories.

The second American party system was truly a wondrous creation. Emerging over a period of sixteen years from the circumstances associated with the successive contests for the presidency, it elaborated a complex organizational structure within which there could be orderly competition for offices of all levels of government. It also provided maximal opportunities for mass participation and produced a political style that took on the aspects of a democratic religion. It could perform a wide range of electoral functions, and it could resolve conflicts that were not highly charged with sectional antagonisms. But, like the first party system, it, too, met with failure.

Apparently it was still in a healthy condition down to about 1850. Then, under the strain of the sectional issues confronting the nation, it began to crumble. The first sign was the collapse of the Whig party in the lower South, and by 1856 the already altered Democratic party was confronted by the newly marshalled Republican party and, in some areas, by the short-lived American, or "Know-Nothing," party as well. At last, in 1860, the Democrats succumbed to a fateful division and the Civil War followed. Although in the North a viable new party system operated, it was not until the 1870's, with the nation reunited and the South released from the abnormal years of Reconstruction, that the third party system assumed national dimensions.

Why did the second party system fail? One answer could be that it was inadequate to cope with conflicts that arrayed section against section. The first party system had come perilously close to foundering on this rock in 1814; but the second party system, for the reason that its parties were truly national in scope and lacked a pronounced sectional bias, was presumably better designed to manage divisive pluralism. Here we face a dilemma. If in a democratic two-party system the parties became so aligned as to reflect crucial ideological, class, social, or sectional cleavages, and they therefore present the electorate with drastic alternatives, the strain on the political system as a whole, and particularly at the level of government, may be disruptive. If, on the other hand, each party is expected to mediate conflicting interests by aggregating the broad spectrum of those interests, the strain on the political system at the level of the parties may be disruptive. I have no solution to propose to this dilemma, other than to suggest that a party system that is *too* comprehensive — as was the second party system — may be potentially as explosive as a party system that is polarized around drastic alternatives — as was the third party system in its formative years.[21] Perhaps this is to say that threatening problems or the strains of crises must be shared between the party system and the government.

In conclusion, some crude assessments of the contributions of the party systems to American political development down to 1860 might be attempted. Such an appraisal must be extremely tentative because the concept of political development, as formulated by LaPalombara and Weiner or others, is awkwardly elusive.[22] And even if one accepts the notion that such problems as national integration, political participation, distribution, legitimacy, and management of conflict are relevant to political development, it is all but impossible to measure the specific contributions of party systems to the solution of those problems. Consequently, what follows must be regarded as impressionistic and even subjective.

We must begin with the understanding that the United States in the 1790's did not confront crises of the same kind and magnitude as those facing the newly emergent nations of today. An extensive experience with the operation of representative institutions that dated back to early in the seventeenth century gave the new nation a politically skilled leadership corps, a broad and alert electorate, and an informed respect for constitutional order. In addition to possessing a common language, a cultural heritage that stemmed largely from British origins, and a relatively homogeneous Protestant religious background, the former colonies had strengthened their sense of national identity through their struggle for independence and had reaffirmed their unity by adopting the federal Constitution. The legitimacy of the new government was not challenged by a party of disaffection, nor was it threatened with subversion by a hereditary elite, an entrenched bureaucracy, or a powerful military establishment. The economy seemed to be capable of gratifying the expectations of the citizens. In relative terms, a high degree of literacy existed; and a flourishing, free press sustained political communication. Not least of all, if we accept the persuasive formulation of Louis Hartz concerning the flowering of a liberal tradition in America, there was consensual agreement on basic national values.[23]

The new American republic was designed as a federal republic, however, in recognition of the sovereign authority held by the several states, and the powers assigned to the national government were explicitly limited. This intricate, carefully adjusted political system was decidedly experimental, and by its very nature it placed restraints on national integration and even permitted the possibility of contests over legitimacy between state and national authorities. Given the complex of factors that conditioned the formation of the national union, we can appreciate the virtues of these arrangements, but they were to occasion very special problems for American party systems. These problems were to become especially formidable as the nation expanded in size and — most ominously — as sectional interests diverged and took precedence over other cleavages.

In gross terms I would take the view that the first and second American party systems were not confronted with serious crises of participation, nor with major crises of distribution. Neither were they required to meet challenges to the legitimacy of the constitutional regime, unless we choose to regard the menace of secession as a threat to legitimacy rather than to national integration. The two areas in which the party systems might be expected to contribute to political development were in advancing national integration and in managing conflicts.

We know, of course, that internal conflicts were not successfully managed in the 1850's and that the nation disintegrated in 1860–61, after having somewhat fortuitously averted a similar crisis in 1814. Now two possible courses of argument are open to us. We might adduce evidence to sustain the position that the first two party systems, despite their defects, held the nation together and resolved a number of conflicts over a period of sixty years, only to fail when confronted by irreconcilable cleavages. Or we might defend the position that the party systems, perhaps because of the difficulties inherent in the federal system, were ill-adapted to resolving conflicts that were sectional in character and that in 1814 and again in 1860 they were malintegrative in their effects.

Whichever position seems to us most plausible, one conclusion is inescapable: the early American party systems are no less notable for their failures than for their successes. We may properly hail the ingenuity of the political architects who constructed the first modern party system in history, but we must record that that party system fell victim to a kind of entropy after 1815. We can marvel at the comprehensiveness and popularity of the second party system, and at the incredible technical proficiency of its professional corps of managers, but that system collapsed within a generation. And as the third party system began to form, the nation divided. Whatever the contributions of the party systems to American political development, they were not after all adequate to avert the disaster of civil war.

NOTES

1. My own interest in the comparative study of party systems has been influenced in various ways by Gabriel A. Almond and James S. Coleman (eds.), *The Politics of the Developing Areas* (Princeton, 1960); Maurice Duverger, *Political Parties: Their Organization and Activity in the Modern State* (New York, 1954); Seymour Martin Lipset, *The First New Nation* (New York, 1963); Sigmund Neumann (ed.), *Modern Political Parties* (Chicago, 1956); and Joseph LaPalombara and Myron Weiner (eds.), *Political Parties and Political Development* (Princeton, 1966). For an admirable and full bibliography, see the last work, pp. 439–64. William N. Chambers has broken new ground with his brilliant conceptualizations of American party systems in *Political Parties in a New Nation: The American Experience, 1776–1809* (New York, 1963); and in "Party Development and Party Action: The American Origins," *History and Theory, III* (1963), 111–17. I have found many of his formulations suggestive.
2. Two useful but outdated standard histories of American parties are Wilfred E. Binkley, *American Political Parties: Their Natural History* (New York, 1962); and Edgar E. Robinson, *The Evolution of American Political Parties* (New York, 1924).
3. Much of the material in this essay is drawn from my study, *The Second American Party System: Party Formation in the Jacksonian Era* (Chapel Hill, 1966).
4. In addition to Chambers's *Political Parties in a New Nation,* which provides the best summary account of early party formation, two outstanding works are Joseph Charles, *The Origins of the American Party System* (Williamsburg, Va., 1956); and Noble E. Cunningham, Jr., *The Jeffersonian Republicans: The Formation of Party Organizations, 1789–1801* (Chapel Hill, 1957); see also Manning J. Dauer, *The Adams Federalists* (Baltimore, 1953). I share many of the understandings that Paul Goodman has set forth in his essay on "The First American Party System," in this volume. In particular, I agree with his insistence that the creation of a national political arena and its particular character was the crucial factor in the array of preconditions for the formation of national parties.
5. Duverger, *Political Parties,* xxiii–xxxvii.
6. Contrary to some understandings, the Federalist party did not experience an abrupt demise in 1815. Indeed, it was still amazingly vigorous as late as 1826 in Delaware — see John A. Munroe, *Federalist Delaware, 1775–1815* (New Brunswick, N.J., 1954). Two of the best studies on the Federalists are David Hackett Fischer, *The Revolution of American Conservatism: The Federalist Party in the Era of Jeffersonian Democracy* (New York, 1965); and Shaw Livermore, *The Twilight of Federalism* (Princeton, 1962).
7. For the sources of these, and other voting data cited, see my *Second American Party System,* 373–9.
8. Although I recognize that some may contend that the formations in New York, Georgia, and Kentucky were not parties, I believe that they are entitled to this designation. The point to be emphasized, however, is that these formations were exceptional and that in the absence of the stimulus of the contest for the presidency, parties did not form around state issues or group cleavages within states.
9. See Table 1 for an index of the balance — or imbalance — of parties in each state for the presidential elections from 1828 through 1844. It will be observed that the average differential between the total vote obtained by the presidential candidates in 1828 was 36 points, which would mean an average percentage of 68 for the victor and 32 for the defeated candidate.
10. The story of this memorable campaign is ably detailed in Robert G. Gunderson, *The Log Cabin Campaign* (Lexington, Ky., 1957).
11. See Table 1. In twenty of the states in 1840 the margin between the two parties was 15 points or less and the average differential was only 11 points. Note the contrast between 1832 and 1840.
12. Tennessee might be called a "one-party" state in the sense that nearly all public figures, as well as voters, identified themselves as Jeffersonian Republicans, or — after 1824 — as Jacksonians. But there was no formal party structure, and vigorously contested elections were conducted without relevance to parties.
13. For interesting material on the caucus-style party organization under the first party system, see Cunningham, *Jeffersonian Republicans,* 162–6; Cunningham, *The Jeffersonian Republicans in Power: Party Operations 1801–1809* (Chapel Hill, 1963), 111–12, 127, 133, 137, 142, 145–6; and Fischer, *Revolution of American Conservatism,* 60–90 passim.
14. See my "New Perspectives on Jacksonian Politics," *American Historical Review, LXV* (1960), 288–301, for illustrative data on the increase in voter participation. In those states where the parties were competitive after 1800, it was not uncommon for 70 per cent or more of the adult white males to vote, and on occasion higher levels were reached. But in states where the parties were unbalanced, or where elections were not contested on a party basis, participation would usually be under 50 per cent. There are, however, curious exceptions to these generalizations. Alabama recorded the suspiciously high figure of 97 per cent in a gubernatorial election in 1819, and Tennessee reached 80 per cent in the gubernatorial election of 1817. These, and other data that could be cited, suggest that high participation could be achieved in the absence of parties, and even in the absence of the stimulus of a presidential contest.
15. See my "Suffrage Classes and Party Alignments: A Study in Voter Behavior," *Mississippi Valley Historical Review, XLVI* (1959), 397–410.

16. M. Ostrogorski, among other foreign observers, has some extremely perceptive comments on the "ritual character" of American parties in *Democracy and the Party System in the United States* (New York, 1910), 408–12.

17. Michael Chevalier, *Society, Manners and Politics in the United States* (Boston, 1839), 318–19.

18. See Table 1.

19. Constitutions and electoral laws, as demonstrated by the studies of Duverger and others, strongly conditioned the nature of party systems. This is not to maintain that all attributes of parties are explainable in these terms, and in seeking to account for cleavages between parties, political styles, or the characteristics of political elites, for example, relevant social factors must be considered. But I would agree with Lipset that "electoral laws determine the nature of the party system as much as any other structural variable." See Lipset, *The First New Nation,* 293.

20. There have been scarcely any comparative studies of constitutional change at the state level, although this field offers rich opportunities for scholars. For a pioneering study, which still stands alone, see Fletcher M. Green, *Constitutional Development in the South Atlantic States, 1776–1860* (Chapel Hill, 1930).

21. For an interesting discussion of the conditions under which a two-party system may be less able to resolve conflict than a multi-party system, see Lipset, *The First New Nation,* 308–12.

22. The discussion that follows draws upon some of the concepts advanced by LaPalombara and Weiner in *Political Parties and Political Development,* 399–435. Similar concepts have been perceptively applied to an analysis of American party development by William N. Chambers in an extremely important essay in the same volume, "Parties and Nation Building in America," 79–106. For a contrasting view, which minimizes the effects of parties as independent variables, see Morton Grodzins's essay, "Political Parties and the Crisis of Succession in the United States: The Case of 1800," in the same volume, 303–27. I would suggest that the election of 1824 is an even better illustration of Grodzins's point.

23. Louis Hartz, *The Liberal Tradition in America* (New York, 1955).

The Black Slave

If America was exceptional, it was so not only in positive but also in negative ways. By 1860, the "land of the free" was also the home of four million black slaves, who constituted 13 percent of the whole population. Some of these bondsmen were African by birth; many more were descended from the wretched victims stolen from Africa by slavers in the colonial period. By the eve of the Civil War, blacks had been in North America for as long as Europeans, yet the overwhelming majority were chattel slaves, a "peculiar species of property," whose status would become more controversial with each passing year.

Slavery in the ante-bellum South was not a benign institution. Most masters sought to avoid using the lash and the branding iron to enforce their will, but everywhere in the South some slaves were punished brutally and peremptorily. More important, slavery denied its subjects' fundamental human needs by weakening the ties between husband and wife, children and parents. It also wasted tremendous human potential. A few slaves were able to develop and exercise their minds and their skills, but most were locked permanently into a life of mindless, backbreaking, common toil.

Yet human beings can adjust to many frustrating and coercive experiences. Most bondsmen learned to survive within the system by virtue of avoiding its penalties as much as they were able. Slaves shirked their duties, or did them in the easiest, and often the most inefficient, way possible. They expressed their resistance to the regime by feigning clumsiness or stupidity, by breaking tools and equipment, by mistreating farm stock. They often ran away. Sometimes they struck back physically at the master, though the penalty for such behavior was savage and summary punishment. A number of times during the slave era, bloody slave uprisings took place, upheavals that sent tremendous shocks through all of southern society.

Though slavery was founded on coercion, it would be a mistake to assume that the average bondsmen encountered nothing but beatings and brandings in his day-to-day existence. Work, rather than force, was the most common experience of the slave. They were employed in almost every conceivable occupation and in almost every conceivable setting in the Old South. Bondsmen were used as house servants in every capacity, from butler and cook to laundress, housemaid, and stable boy. A few worked at the skilled trades — carpentry, masonry, blacksmithing, and numerous others — both on the plantation and in the towns. They were common laborers on canals and railroads and were even employed as operatives in the South's cotton mills and iron works.

But above all they were agricultural laborers. The South was overwhelmingly agrarian. By 1860, the North, particularly the Northeast, was beginning to industrialize. The South had some industry too, but was well behind New England and the Middle Atlantic states in the size, number, and output of its factories and workshops. In colonial times, southern slaves had grown tobacco, rice, and indigo along the Chesapeake and the Carolina and Georgia coasts. Tobacco and rice continued to be cultivated in these older regions by slave labor, but by the 1790s these were no longer expanding crops, and it looked to many men as if slavery were doomed. The slave population continued to expand by natural increase, but it became more and more difficult to find profitable labor for it. Then came cotton and the rapid spread of slavery through the entire lower South. Thousands of slaves were drawn off to the burgeoning cotton kingdom to grow the white fiber. Men got rich, slave prices rose, and slavery once more became a viable and profitable labor system. By 1830, the South was a prosperous part of the American and the world economy, fiercely committed to the perpetuation of the plantation system and the labor regime that sustained it.

In the selection that follows, Kenneth M. Stampp, of the University of California at Berkeley, describes the work of the slave on the plantations and in the homes and workshops of the South. Stampp does not sentimentalize slavery. His book *The Peculiar Institution* is deeply colored by his repugnance for chattel slavery. Although he seeks to evaluate the institution objectively, he refuses to believe that, at heart, it was more than a way of squeezing profits from the lives and toil of black men.

FOR FURTHER READING:

ELKINS, STANLEY. *Slavery: A Problem in American Institutional and Intellectual Life.* Chicago: University of Chicago Press, 1968.*

JORDAN, WINTHROP. *White Over Black.* Baltimore: Penguin Books, Pelican, 1969.*

PHILLIPS, ULRICH B. *American Negro Slavery.* Magnolia, Mass.: Peter Smith, 1966.*

Asterisk denotes paperback edition.

From Day Clean to First Dark

KENNETH M. STAMPP

The day's toil began just before sunrise. A visitor on a Mississippi plantation was regularly awakened by a bell which was rung to call the slaves up. "I soon hear the tramp of the laborers passing along the avenue. . . . All is soon again still as midnight. . . . I believe that I am the only one in the house that the bell disturbs; yet I do not begrudge it a few minutes' loss of sleep it causes me, it sounds so pleasantly in the half dreamy morning." [1] On James H. Hammond's South Carolina plantation a horn was blown an hour before daylight. "All work-hands are [then] required to rise and prepare their cooking, etc. for the day. The second horn is blown just at good day-light, when it is the duty of the driver to visit every house and see that all have left for the field." [2] At dusk the slaves put away their tools and returned to their quarters.

The working day was shorter in winter than in summer, but chiefly because there was less daylight, not because there was much less to do. Seldom at any time of the year was the master at a loss to find essential work to keep his hands busy. Those

Source: Kenneth M. Stampp, *The Peculiar Institution: Slavery in the Ante-Bellum South* (New York: Alfred A. Knopf, 1956), chap. 2, "From Day Clean to First Dark," pp. 44–85.

who planned the routine carefully saved indoor tasks for rainy days. An Alabama planter told his father in Connecticut that cotton picking continued until January, "and after that [we] gathered our corn which ripened last August. We then went to work with the waggons ha[u]ling rails and repairing and rebuilding fences, say two weeks, we then knocked down cotton stalks and pulled up corn stalks and commenced plowing. There is no lying by, no leisure, no long sleeping season such as you have in New England."³ The terse plantation records of the year-round routine of slaves whose principal work was growing cotton usually ran something like this:

January–February: Finished picking, ginning, and pressing cotton and hauling it in wagons to the point of shipment; killed hogs and cut and salted the meat; cut and hauled wood; cut and mauled fence rails; repaired buildings and tools; spread manure; cleaned and repaired ditches; cleared new ground by rolling and burning logs and grubbing stumps; knocked down corn and cotton stalks and burned trash; plowed and "bedded up" corn and cotton fields; planted vegetables.

March–April: Opened "drills," or light furrows, in the corn and cotton beds; sowed corn and cotton seeds in the drills and covered them by hand or with a harrow; replanted where necessary; cultivated the vegetable garden; plowed and hoed in the corn fields.

May–August: "Barred" cotton by scraping dirt away from it with plows; "chopped" cotton with hoes to kill weeds and grass and to thin it to a "stand"; "molded" cotton by "throwing dirt" to it with plows; cultivated corn and cotton until it was large enough to be "laid by"; made repairs; cleared new ground; "pulled fodder," i.e., stripped the blades from corn stalks; cleaned the gin house.

September–December: Picked, ginned, pressed, and shipped cotton; gathered peas; hauled corn and fodder; dug potatoes; shucked corn; cleaned and repaired ditches; repaired fences; cut and hauled wood; cleared new ground.⁴

Thus the operations of one growing cycle overlapped those of the next. There were, of course, variations from planter to planter and differences in the time of planting crops in the upper and lower parts of the cotton belt. Slaves who grew long-staple, or sea-island, cotton in the coastal areas of South Carolina and Georgia had to exercise greater care in picking, ginning, and packing this finer and more expensive variety. But these were differences only in detail. The routine work of cotton growers was essentially the same everywhere, and their basic tools were always the hoe and the plow.

Slaves who cultivated sugar, rice, tobacco, or hemp were involved in a similar year-round routine. They used the same basic tools and much of the time performed the same kinds of supplementary tasks. But each of the staples required special techniques in planting, cultivating, harvesting, and preparing for market.

Some slaves in Texas, Florida, Georgia, and other scattered places in the Deep South produced a little sugar, but those who worked on plantations lining the rivers and bayous of southern Louisiana produced ninety-five per cent of this crop. Most of them were attached to large estates whose owners had heavy investments in land, labor, and machinery. On sugar plantations in the late fall and winter the slaves prepared the land with plows and harrows; before the end of February they planted the seed cane in deep furrows. The shoots grew from eyes at the joints of the seed cane, or ratooned from the stubble of the previous crop. Then came months of cultivation with hoes and plows until the crop was laid by in July. Meanwhile, other slaves cut huge quantities of wood and hauled it to the sugar house, and coopers made sugar hogsheads and molasses barrels. Much heavy labor also went into ditching to provide drainage for these lands which sloped gently from the rivers toward the swamps.

The first cane cut in October was "matalayed" (laid on the ground and covered with a little dirt) to be used as the next year's seed cane. During the frantic weeks from then until December most of the slaves worked at cutting the cane and stripping the leaves from the stalks, loading it into carts, and hauling it to the sugar house. At the mill other slaves fed the cane through the rollers, tended the open kettles or vacuum pans, kept the fires burning, hauled wood, and packed the unrefined sugar into hogsheads. When the last juice was boiled, usually around Christmas, it was almost time to begin planting the next crop.[5]

Soon after the Revolution South Carolina planters abandoned the cultivation of one of their staples — indigo.[6] But to the end of the ante-bellum period rice continued to be the favorite crop of the great planters along the rivers of the South Carolina and Georgia Low Country. Slaves had turned the tidal swamps into fertile rice fields by constructing an intricate system of banks, "trunks" (sluices), and ditches which made possible periodic flooding and draining with the rising and falling tides. Throughout the year slaves on rice plantations devoted much of their time to cleaning the ditches, repairing the banks and trunks, and keeping the tide-flow irrigation system in efficient operation.

In winter the slaves raked the rice fields and burned the stubble. After the ground was broken and "trenched" into drills, the seeds were planted in March and early April. During the first flooding (the "sprout flow") other crops on higher ground were cultivated. When the rice fields were drained and dried they were hoed to loosen the ground and to kill grass and weeds. The next flooding (the "stretch flow") was followed by a long period of "dry growth" during which hoeing went on constantly. Then came the final flooding (the "harvest flow") which lasted until September when the rice was ready to be cut. The slaves cut the rice with sickles, tied it into sheaves, and stacked it to dry. After it had dried they carried the rice to the plantation mill to be threshed, "pounded" to remove the husks from the kernels, winnowed, screened, and packed in barrels.[7] The other crops grown on lands above the swamps were gathered in time to begin preparations for the next year's planting.

The Tobacco Kingdom stretched into the border states of Maryland, Kentucky, and Missouri, but in the ante-bellum period its heart was still the "Virginia District." This district embraced the piedmont south of Fredericksburg, including the northern tier of counties in North Carolina. Here the plantations were smaller than in the Lower South, because each hand could cultivate fewer acres and because the crop had to be handled with great care. The unique aspects of tobacco culture included the preparing of beds in which the tiny seeds were sown during the winter, the transplanting of the shoots in May, and the worming, topping, and suckering of the plants during the summer months. In the late summer the tobacco stalks were split, cut, and left in the fields to wilt. Then they were carried to the tobacco houses to be hung and cured during the fall and winter. The following year, when work had already begun on the next crop, the leaves were stripped from the stalks, sorted, tied into bundles, and "prized" into hogsheads.[8]

The Bluegrass counties of Kentucky and the Missouri River Valley were the chief hemp producing regions of the Old South. Slaves were almost always the working force on hemp farms, because free labor avoided the strenuous, disagreeable labor required to prepare a crop for market. After the ground was prepared, the seeds were sown broadcast in April and May and covered lightly with a harrow or shovel plow. Unlike the other staples, hemp required no cultivation during the growing season, and slaves were free to tend other crops. In late summer the hemp was cut, laid on the ground to dry, and then tied in sheaves and stacked. In November or December it was again spread out in the fields for "dew rotting" to loosen the fiber. A month or so later the hemp was stacked once more, and the lint was laboriously separated from the wood with a hand "brake." The fiber was taken to the hemp house where it was hackled or sold immediately to manufacturers.[9]

In 1850, the Superintendent of the Census estimated that 2,500,000 slaves of all ages were directly employed in agriculture. Of these, he guessed that 60,000 were engaged in the production of hemp, 125,000 in the production of rice, 150,000 in the production of sugar, 350,000 in the production of tobacco, and 1,815,000 in the production of cotton. Somewhat casually he observed that these slaves also produced "large quantities of breadstuffs."[10] This was scarcely adequate recognition of the amount of time they devoted to such crops, even on many of the plantations which gave chief attention to one of the five staples.

To be sure, some planters in the Lower South were so preoccupied with staple production that they grew almost nothing else — not even enough corn and pork to feed their slaves. This pattern was common in the Louisiana sugar district. One planter explained that when sugar sold for fifty dollars a hogshead, "it is cheaper to buy pork[,] for it is utterly impossible to raise hogs here without green pastures and plenty of corn[,] and all lands here fit for pasturage will make a hogshead [of] sugar pr acre — The great curse of this country is that we are all planters and no farmers."[11] An Alabama cotton planter was alarmed when pork failed to arrive from Tennessee: "All of our towns and most of our large Planters are dependent on Drovers for their meat." Even some of the cotton and tobacco planters in North Carolina bought food supplies for their slaves.[12] Such planters were convinced that it was most profitable to concentrate on the production of a single cash crop.

Most planters, however, did not share this point of view. Almost all of the hemp and tobacco growers of the Upper South planted many acres of food crops to supply their own needs — and frequently additional acres to produce surpluses for sale. A major feature of the agricultural revival in ante-bellum Virginia was an improved system of crop rotation with increased emphasis upon corn, wheat, and clover.[13] Many of the tobacco planters gave enough attention to these and other crops to approximate a system of diversified farming. Their field-hands often devoted less than half of their time to tobacco.

Few planters in the Deep South approached such levels of diversification, but most of them produced sizeable food crops for their families and slaves. In southern agricultural periodicals they constantly admonished each other to strive for self-sufficiency. They instructed their overseers to produce adequate supplies of corn, sweet potatoes, peas, and beans, and to give proper attention to the poultry, hogs, and cattle. A Mississippi planter warned his overseer "that failure to make a bountiful supply of corn and meat for the use of the plantation, will be considered as notice that his services will not be required for the succeeding year."[14] The average planter, however, was tempted to forgive a great deal if his overseer managed to make enough cotton. Interest in other crops tended to vary with fluctuations in cotton prices. Even so, most of the field-hands on cotton plantations were at least familiar with the routine of corn cultivation.

Though southern planters showed that slaves could grow other crops besides the five great staples, there was a widespread belief that it was impractical to devote plantations to them exclusively. But here and there in the Lower South a planter disproved this assumption. In Richmond County, Georgia, an owner of more than a hundred slaves successfully used his labor force to raise grain and meat for sale in Augusta.[15]

In the Upper South many large slaveholders grew neither tobacco nor hemp but engaged in diversified farming. In Talbot County, Maryland, Colonel Edward Lloyd worked his two hundred and seventy-five slaves on profitable farms which produced wheat, corn, hams, wool, and hides.[16] On Shirley Plantation on the James River, Hill Carter, like many of his Virginia neighbors, made wheat his major cash crop. An incomplete list of the products of a plantation in King and Queen County included wheat, corn, oats, rye, vegetables, Irish potatoes, sweet potatoes, wool, hogs, apples, and strawberries.[17]

In North Carolina, corn was the chief crop on a number of Roanoke River plantations. In Tyrrell County, Ebenezer Pettigrew annually shipped thousands of bushels of wheat and corn to Norfolk and Charleston.[18] Clearly, the slave-plantation system had greater flexibility and was less dependent upon the production of a few staples than some have thought.

There is a different tradition about the agricultural operations of farmers who owned less than ten slaves. Here a high degree of diversification is assumed — presumably the smaller farms were better adapted to this type of farming than to the cultivation of the staples. Thousands of slaveholders in this group did engage in what was almost subsistence farming with cash incomes well below five hundred dollars a year. Others, especially in the Upper South, marketed large surpluses of pork, corn, and wheat. The amount of commercialization in the operations of non-staple producing small slaveholders depended upon the quality of their lands, their proximity to markets and transportation, and their managerial skill.

But a large proportion of these slaveholding farmers depended upon one of the five southern staples for a cash crop. In Kentucky and Missouri many of them produced a few tons of hemp; there and in Virginia and North Carolina they often gave tobacco their chief attention. A few small slaveholders in the Deep South even planted rice and sugar — sometimes surprisingly large amounts — in spite of the handicaps they faced in trying to compete with the planters. In St. Mary Parish, Louisiana, for example, an owner of seven slaves in 1859 produced forty hogsheads of sugar. These small operators depended upon their neighbors' sugar making facilities or ran their own crude horse-driven mills.[19]

In cotton production those with modest slaveholdings faced no overwhelming competitive disadvantage. Some of the smaller cotton growers were as preoccupied with this staple as were their neighbors on the large plantations. Some even depended upon outside supplies of food. Many of them reported astonishing cotton-production records to the census takers, the number of bales per hand easily matching the records of the planters.[20]

Nevertheless, the majority of small slaveholders did engage in a more diversified type of agriculture than most of the large planters. Slavery could be, and was, adapted to diversified agriculture and to the labor needs of small farms. It did not necessarily depend upon large plantations or staple crops for its survival.

For the owner of a few slaves, labor management was a problem of direct personal relationships between individuals. For the owner of many, the problem was more difficult and required greater ingenuity. Both classes of masters desired a steady and efficient performance of the work assigned each day. They could not expect much cooperation from their slaves, who had little reason to care how much was produced. Masters measured the success of their methods by the extent to which their interest in a maximum of work of good quality prevailed over the slaves' predilection for a minimum of work of indifferent quality. Often neither side won a clear victory.

Slaveowners developed numerous variations of two basic methods of managing their laborers: the "gang system" and the "task system." Under the first of these systems, which was the one most commonly used, the field-hands were divided into gangs commanded by drivers who were to work them at a brisk pace. Competent masters gave some thought to the capacities of individual slaves and to the amount of labor that a gang could reasonably be expected to perform in one day. But the purpose of the gang system was to force every hand to continue his labor until all were discharged from the field in the evening.

Under the task system, each hand was given a specific daily work assignment. He could then set his own pace and quit when his task was completed. The driver's job was to inspect the work and to see that it was performed satisfactorily before the slave left the field. "The advantages of this system," according to a Georgia rice planter, "are encouragement to the laborers, by equalizing the work of each agreeable to strength, and the avoidance of watchful superintendence and incessant driving. As . . . the task of each [slave] is separate, imperfect work can readily be traced to the neglectful worker." [21]

The task system was best adapted to the rice plantation, with its fields divided into small segments by the network of drainage ditches. Outside the Low Country of South Carolina and Georgia planters occasionally used this system or at least experimented with it, but many of them found it to be unsatisfactory. For one thing, they could get no more work out of their stronger slaves than out of their weaker ones, since the tasks were usually standardized. The planters also found that the eagerness of slaves to finish their tasks as early as possible led to careless work. After using the task system for twenty years, an Alabama planter abandoned it because of evils "too numerous to mention." A South Carolina cotton planter, who also gave it up, noted with satisfaction that under the gang system his slaves did "much more" and were "not so apt to strain themselves." [22]

Actually, most planters used a combination of the two systems. Cotton planters often worked plow-hands in gangs but gave hoe-hands specific tasks of a certain number of cotton rows to hoe each day. Each hand was expected to pick as much cotton as he could, but he might be given a minimum quota that had to be met. Sugar, rice, and tobacco planters applied the task system to their coopers, and hemp growers used it with hands engaged in breaking or hackling hemp. Masters generally tasked their hands for digging ditches, cutting wood, or mauling rails.

Thus most slaves probably had some experience with both systems. From their point of view each system doubtless had its advantages and drawbacks. A strong hand might have preferred to be tasked if he was given an opportunity to finish early. But many slaves must have been appalled at the ease with which they could be held responsible for the quality of their work. The gang system had the disadvantages of severe regimentation and of hard driving which was especially onerous for the weaker hands. But there was less chance that a slave would be detected and held individually responsible for indifferent work. In the long run, however, the rigors of either system were determined by the demands of masters and overseers.

The number of acres a slaveholder expected each of his field-hands to cultivate depended in part upon how hard he wished to work them. It also depended upon the nature of the soil, the quality of the tools, and the general efficiency of the agricultural enterprise. Finally, it depended upon the crop. Cotton growers on flat prairies and river bottoms planted as many as ten acres per hand but rarely more than that. Those on hilly or rolling lands planted from three to eight acres per hand. Since a slave could ordinarily cultivate more cotton than he could pick, acreage was limited by the size of the available picking force. By the 1850's each hand was expected to work from nine to ten acres of sugar but seldom more than five acres of rice or three of tobacco, plus six or more of corn and other food crops.[23] The yield per acre and per hand varied with the fertility of the soil, the care in cultivation, the damage of insects, and the whims of the weather.

When calculating his yield per field-hand a slaveholder was not calculating his yield per slave, for he almost always owned fewer field-hands than slaves. Some of his slaves performed other types of work, and the very young and the very old could not be used in the fields. The master's diseased, convalescing, and partially disabled slaves, his "breeding women" and "sucklers," his children just beginning to work in the fields, and his slaves of advanced years were incapable of laboring as long and as hard as full-time hands.

Most masters had systems of rating such slaves as fractional hands. Children often began as "quarter hands" and advanced to "half hands," "three-quarter hands," and then "full hands." As mature slaves grew older they started down this scale. "Breeding women" and "sucklers" were rated as "half hands." Some planters organized these slaves into separate gangs, for example, into a "sucklers gang." Children sometimes received their training in a "trash gang," or "children's squad," which pulled weeds, cleaned the yard, hoed, wormed tobacco, or picked cotton. Seldom were many more than half of a master's slaves listed in his records as field-hands, and always some of the hands were classified as fractional. Olmsted described a typical situation on a Mississippi cotton plantation: "There were 135 slaves, big and little, of which 67 went to the field regularly — equal, the overseer thought, to 60 able-bodied hands."[24]

The master, not the parents, decided at what age slave children should be put to work in the fields. Until they were five or six years old children were "useless articles on a plantation." Then many received "their first lessons in the elementary part of their education" through serving as "water-toters" or going into the fields alongside their mothers.[25] Between the ages of ten and twelve the children became fractional hands, with a regular routine of field labor. By the time they were eighteen they had reached the age when they could be classified as "prime field-hands."

Mature slaves who did not work in the fields (unless they were totally disabled or extremely old) performed other kinds of valuable and productive labor. Old women cooked for the rest of the slaves, cared for small children, fed the poultry, mended and washed clothes, and nursed the sick. Old men gardened, minded stock, and cleaned the stable and the yard.

Old or partially disabled slaves might also be put to spinning and weaving in the loom houses of the more efficient planters. The printed instructions in a popular plantation record book advised overseers to adopt this policy: "Few instances of good management will better please an employer, than that of having all the winter

clothing spun and woven on the place. By having a room devoted to that purpose
. . . where those who may be complaining a little, or convalescent after sickness,
may be employed in some light work, and where all of the women may be sent in
wet weather, more than enough of both cotton and woolen yarn can be spun for the
supply of the place." [26] One planter reported that he had his spinning jenny "going
at a round rate[.] Old Charles [is] Spinning and Esther reeling the thread. . . .
Charles will in this way be one of my most productive laborers and so will several of
the women[.]" [27] Thus a master's productive slaves were by no means limited to
those listed as field-hands.

The bondsmen who were valued most highly were those who had acquired special
skills which usually exempted them from field work entirely. This select group of
slave craftsmen included engineers, coopers, carpenters, blacksmiths, brickmakers,
stone masons, mechanics, shoemakers, weavers, millers, and landscapers. The excellence of the work performed by some of them caused slaveowners to make invidious comparisons between them and the free artisans they sometimes employed. An
Englishman recalled an interview with the overseer on a Louisiana sugar plantation:
"It would have been amusing, had not the subject been so grave, to hear the overseer's praises of the intelligence and skill of these workmen, and his boast that they did
all the work of skilled laborers on the estate, and then to listen to him, in a few minutes, expatiating on the utter helplessness and ignorance of the black race, their in-
capacity to do any good, or even to take care of themselves." [28]

Domestic servants were prized almost as much as craftsmen. The number and variety of domestics in a household depended upon the size of the establishment and
the wealth of the master. They served as hostlers, coachmen, laundresses, seam-
stresses, cooks, footmen, butlers, housemaids, chambermaids, children's nurses, and
personal servants. On a large plantation specialization was complete: "The cook
never enters the house, and the nurse is never seen in the kitchen; the wash-woman
is never put to ironing, nor the woman who has charge of the ironing-room ever put
to washing. Each one rules supreme in her wash-house, her ironing-room, her
kitchen, her nursery, her house-keeper's room; and thus . . . a complete system of
domesticdom is established to the amazing comfort and luxury of all who enjoy its
advantages." [29]

But the field-hands remained fundamental in the slave economy. Though their
work was classified as unskilled labor, this of course was a relative term. Some visitors described the "rude" or "slovenly" manner in which slaves cultivated the crops,
how "awkwardly, slowly, and undecidedly" they moved through the fields.[30] But
other observers were impressed with the success of many masters in training field-
hands to be efficient workers, impressed also by the skill these workers showed in
certain crucial operations in the production of staple crops. Inexperienced hands
had their troubles in sugar houses and rice fields, in breaking and hackling hemp,
and in topping, suckering, sorting, and prizing tobacco. Even the neophyte cotton
picker soon wondered whether this was unskilled labor, as one former slave testified: "While others used both hands, snatching the cotton and depositing it in the
mouth of the sack, with a precision and dexterity that was incomprehensible to me,
I had to seize the boll with one hand, and deliberately draw out the white, gushing
blossom with the other." On his first day he managed to gather "not half the quantity required of the poorest picker." [31]

Field workers kept up a ceaseless struggle to make the lands fruitful, against the
contrary efforts of the insects and the elements. The battle seemed at times to be of

absorbing interest to some of the slaves, conscripts though they were. In a strange and uneasy kind of alliance, they and their masters combatted the foes that could have destroyed them both.

In 1860, probably a half million bondsmen lived in southern cities and towns, or were engaged in work not directly or indirectly connected with agriculture. Some farmers and planters found it profitable, either temporarily or permanently, to employ part of their hands in non-agricultural occupations. Along the rivers slaves cut wood to provide fuel for steamboats and for sale in neighboring towns. In swamplands filled with juniper, oak, and cypress trees they produced shingles, barrel and hogshead staves, pickets, posts, and rails. In North Carolina's Dismal Swamp slave gangs labored as lumberjacks.[32] In the eastern Carolina pine belt several thousand slaves worked in the turpentine industry. An owner of one hundred and fifty slaves in Brunswick County, North Carolina, raised just enough food to supply his force; he made his profits from the annual sale of thousands of barrels of turpentine. Many smaller operators also combined turpentine production with subsistence farming.[33]

Elsewhere in the South bondsmen worked in sawmills, gristmills, quarries, and fisheries. They mined gold in North Carolina, coal and salt in Virginia, iron in Kentucky and Tennessee, and lead in Missouri. On river boats they were used as deck hands and firemen. Slave stokers on a Mississippi River steamer bound for New Orleans, who sang as they fed wood to the boiler fires, intrigued a European traveler: "It was a fantastic and grand sight to see these energetic black athletes lit up by the wildly flashing flames . . . while they, amid their equally fantastic song, keeping time most exquisitely, hurled one piece of firewood after another into the yawning fiery gulf." [34]

Other slaves were employed in the construction and maintenance of internal improvements. They worked on the public roads several days each year in states which required owners to put them to such use. For many years slaves owned by the state of Louisiana built roads and cleared obstructions from the bayous. Slaves also worked for private internal improvements companies, such as the builders of the Brunswick and Altamaha Canal in Georgia and the Cape Fear and Deep River Navigation Company in North Carolina. In Mississippi a hundred were owned by a firm of bridge contractors, the Weldon brothers.[35]

Railroad companies employed bondsmen in both construction and maintenance work. As early as 1836 the Richmond, Fredericksburg, and Potomac Railroad Company advertised for "a large number" of slave laborers. In the same year the Alabama, Florida, and Georgia Railroad Company announced a need for five hundred "able-bodied negro men . . . to be employed in felling, cutting, and hewing timber, and in forming the excavations and embankments upon the route of said Rail Road." During the 1850's southern newspapers carried the constant pleas of railroad builders for slaves. Almost every railroad in the ante-bellum South was built at least in part by bondsmen; in Georgia they constructed more than a thousand miles of roadbed. In 1858, a Louisiana newspaper concluded: "Negro labor is fast taking the place of white labor in the construction of southern railroads." [36]

Bondsmen in southern cities and towns, in spite of the protests of free laborers, worked in virtually every skilled and unskilled occupation. They nearly monopolized the domestic services, for most free whites shunned them to avoid being degraded to the level of slaves. Many of the Southerners who owned just one or two slaves were urban dwellers who used them as cooks, housekeepers, and gardeners. The wealthier townspeople often had staffs of domestic servants as large as those of rural planters. Other domestics found employment in hotels and at watering places.

Town slaves worked in cotton presses, tanneries, shipyards, bakehouses, and laundries, as dock laborers and stevedores, and as clerks in stores. Masters who owned skilled artisans such as barbers, blacksmiths, cabinet makers, and shoemakers often provided them with shops to make their services available to all who might wish to employ them. Many white mechanics used slave assistants. In short, as a visitor to Natchez observed, town slaves included "mechanics, draymen, hostlers, labourers, hucksters, and washwomen, and the heterogeneous multitude of every other occupation, who fill the streets of a busy city — for slaves are trained to every kind of manual labour. The blacksmith, cabinet-maker, carpenter, builder, wheelwright — all have one or more slaves labouring at their trades. The negro is a third arm to every working man, who can possibly save money enough to purchase one. He is emphatically the 'right-hand man' of every man." [37] The quality of the work of slave artisans had won favorable comment as early as the eighteenth century. Among them were "many ingenious Mechanicks," wrote a colonial Georgian, "and as far as they have had opportunity of being instructed, have discovered as good abilities, as are usually found among people of our Colony." [38]

Some Southerners were enthusiastic crusaders for the development of factories which would employ slaves. They were convinced that bondsmen could be trained in all the necessary skills and would provide a cheaper and more manageable form of labor than free whites. "When the channels of agriculture are choked," predicted an industrial promoter, "the manufacturing of our own productions will open new channels of profitable employment for our slaves." Others thought that slavery was one of the South's "natural advantages" in its effort to build industries to free it from "the incessant and vexatious attacks of the North." [39] They believed that industrialization and slavery could proceed hand in hand.

Southern factory owners gave evidence that this was more than idle speculation. Every slave state had industrial establishments which made some use of slave labor. In Kentucky, the "ropewalks" which manufactured cordage and the hemp factories which produced cotton bagging and "Kentucky jeans" employed slaves extensively.[40] Almost all of the thirteen thousand workers in the tobacco factories of the Virginia District were bondsmen. The majority of them were employed in the three leading tobacco manufacturing cities — Richmond, Petersburg, and Lynchburg. These slave workers were not only a vital part of this industry but also a curiously paradoxical element in the society of the tobacco towns.[41]

From its earliest beginnings the southern iron industry depended upon skilled and unskilled slaves. Negro iron workers were employed in Bath County, Kentucky, and along the Cumberland River in Tennessee. In the Cumberland country the majority of laborers at the iron furnaces were slaves. Montgomery Bell, owner of the Cumberland Iron Works, engaged his own three hundred slaves and many others in every task connected with the operation of forge and furnace.[42] In the Great Valley of Virginia, where the southern industry was centered during the early nineteenth century, slaves constituted the chief labor supply.

Until the 1840's, the famed Tredegar Iron Company in Richmond used free labor almost exclusively. But in 1842, Joseph R. Anderson, then commercial agent of the company, proposed to employ slaves as a means of cutting labor costs. The board of directors approved of his plan, and within two years Anderson was satisfied with "the practicability of the scheme." In 1847, the increasing use of slaves caused the remaining free laborers to go out on strike, until they were threatened with prosecution for forming an illegal combination. After this protest failed, Anderson vowed that he would show his workers that they could not dictate his labor policies: he refused to re-employ any of the strikers. Thereafter, as Anderson noted, Tredegar used "almost exclusively slave labor except as the Boss men. This enables me, of course, to compete with other manufacturers." [43]

But it was upon the idea of bringing textile mills to the cotton fields that southern advocates of industrialization with slave labor pinned most of their hopes. In cotton factories women and children were needed most, and hence it was often argued that they would provide profitable employment for the least productive workers in agriculture. Though the majority of southern textile workers were free whites, and though some believed that this work ought to be reserved for them, a small number of slaves were nevertheless employed in southern mills.

Occasionally mill owners managed to work slaves and free whites together with a minimum of friction. A visitor found equal numbers of the two groups employed in a cotton factory near Athens, Georgia: "There is no difficulty among them on account of colour, the white girls working in the same room and at the same loom with the black girls; and boys of each colour, as well as men and women, working together without apparent repugnance or objection." [44] But even if some white workers would tolerate this, slaveowners ordinarily looked upon it as a dangerous practice.

The southern press gave full reports of cotton mills which used slave labor and ecstatic accounts of their success. A Pensacola newspaper cited the local Arcadia Cotton Factory, which employed only slaves, to prove that "with the native skill and ingenuity of mere labor — the labor of the hands — the negro is just as richly endowed as the white." The Saluda mill, near Columbia, South Carolina, operated on the "slave-labor, or anti free-soil system." The white managers testified to the "equal efficiency, and great superiority in many respects" of slaves over free workers.[45] During the 1830's and 1840's, a half dozen other cotton mills in South Carolina's Middle and Low Country employed bondsmen. Most other southern states could point to one or more mills which used this type of labor. To many observers the enterprises of Daniel Pratt at Prattsville, near Montgomery, Alabama, provided models for other Southerners to copy. Pratt worked slaves not only in his cotton mill but also in his cotton gin factory, iron foundry, sash and door factory, machine shop, and carriage and wagon shop.[46]

Actually, the ante-bellum South had relatively few cotton mills, and most of them were small enterprises manufacturing only the coarser grades of cloth. In 1860, the fifteen slave states together had only 198 mills each employing an average of 71 workers, whereas Massachusetts alone had 217 mills each employing an average of 177 workers. Many of the southern factories resembled the one owned by a small manufacturer in East Tennessee which contained only three hundred spindles operated by fourteen slave hands.[47]

Still, in these textile mills and in what little other industry existed in the Old South there was abundant evidence that slaves could be trained to be competent factory workers. The evidence was sufficient to raise serious doubts that slavery was tied to agriculture, as some defenders and some critics of the institution believed.

Each year, around the first of January, at southern crossroad stores, on the steps of county courthouses, and in every village and city, large crowds of participants and spectators gathered for "hiring day." At this time masters with bondsmen to spare and employers in search of labor bargained for the rental of slave property. Thus thousands of nonslaveholders managed temporarily to obtain the services of slaves and to enjoy the prestige of tenuous membership in the master class. Thus, too, many bondsmen found it their lot to labor for persons other than their owners. Hired slaves were most numerous in the Upper South; during the 1850's perhaps as many as fifteen thousand were hired out annually in Virginia alone. But slave-hiring was a common practice everywhere.[48]

In December and January southern newspapers were filled with the advertisements of those offering or seeking slaves to hire. Some of the transactions were negotiated privately, some by auctioneers who bid slaves off at public outcry, and some by "general agents" who handled this business for a commission. In Richmond, P. M. Tabb & Son, among many others, advertised that they attended "to the hiring out of negroes and collecting the hires" and promised to give "particular attention . . . through the year to negroes placed under their charge."[49]

Though slaves were occasionally hired for short terms, it was customary to hire them from January until the following Christmas. Written contracts specified the period of the hire, the kind of work in which the slaves were to be engaged, and the hirer's obligation to keep them well clothed. Usually an owner could spare only a few, but occasionally a single master offered as many as fifty and, rarely, as many as a hundred. Though most slaves were hired in the vicinity of their masters' residences, many were sent long distances from home. Hamilton Brown, of Wilkes County, North Carolina, hired out slaves in Virginia, Tennessee, and Georgia; and Jeremiah Morton, of Orange County, Virginia, hired out fifty-two of his Negroes through an agent in Mobile.[50]

A variety of circumstances contributed to this practice. If for some reason the owner was unable to use his slaves profitably, if he was in debt, or if he had a surplus of laborers, he might prefer hiring to selling them. Executors hired out slave property while estates were being settled. Sometimes lands and slaves together were rented to tenants. Heirs who inherited bondsmen for whom they had no employment put them up for hire. Many spinsters, widows, and orphans lived off the income of hired slaves who were handled for them by administrators. Masters often directed in their wills that slaves be hired out for the benefit of their heirs, or that cash be invested in slave property for this purpose. A widow in Missouri hired out most of her slaves, because she found it to be "a better business" than working them on her farm.[51] Occasionally a slaveowner endowed a church or a benevolent institution with slaves whose hire was to aid in its support.

In addition, urban masters often hired out the husbands or children of their female domestics. Both they and planters who had more domestics than they could use or afford disposed of them in this manner. It was also very common for urban and rural owners of skilled slaves to hire them to others at least part of the time. Planters hired their carpenters and blacksmiths to neighbors when they had no work for them and thus substantially augmented their incomes. A master sometimes hired a slave to a white artisan with the understanding that the slave was to be taught his skill. For example, a contract between a North Carolina master and a white blacksmith provided that the hirer was to work a slave "at the Forge during the whole time and learn him or cause him to be learned the arts and mysteries of the Black Smith's trade." [52]

A few Southerners bought slaves as business ventures with the intention of realizing profits solely through hiring them to others. Between 1846 and 1852, Bickerton Lyle Winston, of Hanover County, Virginia, purchased at least fifteen slaves for this purpose. Winston kept careful records of these investments, noting the purchase prices, the annual income from and expenses of each slave, and the net profit. The slaves Randal and Garland were his first speculations. Randal's record ended abruptly in 1853 with the terse notation: "Deduct medical and funeral expenses: $20." Four years later Winston recorded the fact that "Garland came to his end . . . by an explosion in the Black Heath Pits." [53] Some overseers pursued a similar course by investing in slaves whom they hired to their employers. A resident in Mississippi knew families "who possess not an acre of land, but own many slaves, [and] hire them out to different individuals; the wages constituting their only income, which is often very large." [54]

Farmers and planters frequently hired field-hands to neighbors for short periods of time. Cotton growers who finished their picking early contracted to help others pick their cotton for a fee. When a planter's crop was "in the grass" he tried to borrow hands from neighbors with the understanding that the labor would be repaid in the future. Small slaveholders sometimes made less formal agreements to help each other. A Virginia farmer lent his neighbor two mules and received in return "the labor of one man for the same time." [55] Many masters were generous in lending the labor of their slaves to friends.

The demand for hired slaves came from numerous groups. The shortage of free agricultural labor caused planters to look to this practice as a means of meeting their seasonal needs for additional workers. During the grinding season sugar growers hired hands from Creole farmers or from cotton planters after their crops were picked.[56] Small farmers who could not afford to buy slaves were well represented in the "hiring-day" crowds. Some landowners employed free Negroes, Indians, or poor whites, but they generally preferred to hire slaves when they were available.

The great majority of hired slaves, however, were employed by those who sought a supply of nonagricultural labor. Many urban families hired rather than owned their domestic servants. Advertisements such as these appeared in every southern newspaper: "Wanted immediately, a boy, from 14 to 19 years of age, to do house work. One that can be well recommended from his owner." "Wanted a Black or Colored Servant, to attend on a Gentleman and take care of a Horse." [57] Hotels and watering places hired most of their domestics; laundries, warehouses, shipyards, steamships, cotton presses, turpentine producers, mine operators, lumberers, and drayage companies all made considerable use of hired slaves. Free artisans seldom could afford to own bondsmen and therefore hired them instead. Even a free Negro cooper in Richmond for many years hired a slave assistant.[58]

In most cases southern railroad companies did not own the slaves they employed; rather, they recruited them by promising their owners generous compensation. Railroad builders obtained most of their hands in the neighborhood of their construction work, but they often bid for them in distant places. In 1836, the Alabama, Florida, and Georgia Railroad Company advertised for a hundred slaves in Maryland, Virginia, and North Carolina. The Florida Railroad Company, in 1857, announced that for the past two years it had been employing slaves from Virginia and the Carolinas and offered to give masters evidence "of the health, climate, and other points of interest connected with the country and work." [59]

An advertisement in a Kentucky newspaper for "twenty-five Negro Boys, from thirteen to fifteen years old, to work in a woolen factory" pointed to another source of the demand for hired slaves. Gristmills, sawmills, cotton factories, hemp factories, iron foundries, and tobacco factories used them extensively, especially the smaller enterprises with limited capital. In 1860, about half of the slave laborers in Virginia tobacco factories were hired.[60]

A small group of slaves obtained from their masters the privilege of "hiring their own time." These bondsmen enjoyed considerable freedom of movement and were permitted to find work for themselves. They were required to pay their masters a stipulated sum of money each year, but whatever they could earn above that amount was theirs to do with as they wished. Almost all of the slaves who hired their own time were skilled artisans; most of them were concentrated in the cities of the Upper South. Though this practice was illegal nearly everywhere and often denounced as dangerous, there were always a few slaves who somehow managed to work in this manner under the most nominal control of their owners.

By permitting a trusted slave artisan to hire his own time the master escaped the burden of feeding and clothing him and of finding employment for him. Then, as long as his slave kept out of trouble, the master's sole concern was getting his payments (which were almost the equivalent of a quitrent) at regular intervals. Frederick Douglass described the terms by which he hired his own time to work as a calker in the Baltimore shipyards: "I was to be allowed all my time; to make all bargains for work; to find my own employment, and to collect my own wages; and, in return for this liberty, I was required, or obliged, to pay . . . three dollars at the end of each week, and to board and clothe myself, and buy my own calking tools. A failure in any of these particulars would put an end to my privilege. This was a hard bargain." [61]

But whatever the terms, most slave artisans eagerly accepted this arrangement when it was offered to them. A Negro blacksmith in Virginia pleaded with his master for the privilege of hiring his own time: "I would . . . be much obliged to you if you would authorize me to open a shop in this county and carry it on. . . . I am satisfied that I can do well and that my profits will amount to a great deal more than any one would be willing to pay for my hire." [62]

This slave had his wish granted, but few others shared his good fortune. It was the lot of the ordinary bondsman to work under the close supervision of his master or of some employer who hired his services. For him bondage was not nominal. It was what it was intended to be: a systematic method of controlling and exploiting labor.

Mammy Harriet had nostalgic memories of slavery days: "Oh, no, we was nebber hurried. Marster nebber once said, 'Get up an' go to work,' an' no oberseer ebber said it, neither. Ef some on 'em did not git up when de odders went out to work, marster nebber said a word. Oh, no, we was nebber hurried." [63] Mammy Harriet had been a domestic at "Burleigh," the Hinds County, Mississippi, estate of Thomas S. Dabney. She related her story of slave life there to one of Dabney's daughters who wrote a loving volume about her father and his cotton plantation.

Another slave found life less leisurely on a plantation on the Red River in Louisiana: "The hands are required to be in the cotton field as soon as it is light in the morning, and, with the exception of ten or fifteen minutes, which is given them at noon to swallow their allowance of cold bacon, they are not permitted to be a moment idle until it is too dark to see, and when the moon is full, they often times labor till the middle of the night." Work did not end when the slaves left the fields. "Each one must attend to his respective chores. One feeds the mules, another the swine — another cuts the wood, and so forth; besides the packing [of cotton] is all done by candle light. Finally, at a late hour, they reach the quarters, sleepy and overcome with the long day's toil." [64] These were the bitter memories of Solomon Northup, a free Negro who had been kidnapped and held in bondage for twelve years. Northup described his experiences to a Northerner who helped him prepare his autobiography for publication.

Mammy Harriet's and Solomon Northup's disparate accounts of the work regimen imposed upon slaves suggest the difficulty of determining the truth from witnesses, Negro and white, whose candor was rarely uncompromised by internal emotions or external pressures. Did Dabney's allegedly unhurried field-hands (who somehow produced much cotton and one of whom once tried to kill the overseer) feel the same nostalgia for slavery days? How much was Northup's book influenced by his amanuensis and by the preconceptions of his potential northern readers?

And yet there is nothing in the narratives of either of these ex-slaves that renders them entirely implausible. The question of their complete accuracy is perhaps less important than the fact that both conditions actually did exist in the South. Distortion results from exaggerating the frequency of either condition or from dwelling upon one and ignoring the other.

No sweeping generalization about the amount of labor extracted from bondsmen could possibly be valid, even when they are classified by regions, or by occupations, or by the size of the holdings upon which they lived. For the personal factor transcended everything else. How hard the slaves were worked depended upon the demands of individual masters and their ability to enforce them. These demands were always more or less tempered by the inclination of most slaves to minimize their unpaid toil. Here was a clash of interests in which the master usually, but not always, enjoyed the advantage of superior weapons.

Not only must glib generalizations be avoided but a standard must be fixed by which the slave's burden of labor can be judged. Surely a slave was overworked when his toil impaired his health or endangered his life. Short of this extreme there are several useful standards upon which judgments can be based. If, for example, the quantity of labor were compared with the compensation the inevitable conclusion would be that most slaves were overworked. Also by present-day labor standards the demands generally made upon them were excessive. These, of course, were not the standards of the nineteenth century.

Another standard of comparison — though not an altogether satisfactory one — is the amount of work performed by contemporary free laborers in similar occupations. Independent farmers and artisans set their own pace and planned their work to fit their own convenience and interests, but they nevertheless often worked from dawn to dusk. Northern factory workers commonly labored twelve hours a day. This was arduous toil even for free laborers who enjoyed the advantages of greater incentives and compensation. Yet contemporaries did not think that slaves were overworked when their masters respected the normal standards of their day. Some slaveowners did respect them, and some did not.

Unquestionably there were slaves who escaped doing what was then regarded as a "good day's work," and there were masters who never demanded it of them. The aphorism that it took two slaves to help one to do nothing was not without its illustrations. After lands and slaves had remained in the hands of a single family for several generations, planters sometimes developed a patriarchal attitude toward their "people" and took pride in treating them indulgently. Such masters had lost the competitive spirit and the urge to increase their worldly possessions which had characterized their ancestors. To live gracefully on their declining estates, to smile tolerantly at the listless labor of their field-hands, and to be surrounded by a horde of pampered domestics were all parts of their code.

In Virginia, the easygoing manner of the patricians was proverbial. But Virginia had no monopoly of them; they were scattered throughout the South. Olmsted visited a South Carolina rice plantation where the tasks were light enough to enable reasonably industrious hands to leave the fields early in the afternoon. Slaves on several sea-island cotton plantations much of the time did not labor more than five or six hours a day.[65]

The production records of some of the small slaveholding farmers indicated that neither they nor their slaves exerted themselves unduly. These masters, especially when they lived in isolated areas, seemed content to produce little more than a bare subsistence. In addition, part of the town slaves who hired their own time took advantage of the opportunity to enjoy a maximum of leisure. The domestics of some wealthy urban families willingly helped to maintain the tradition that masters with social standing did not examine too closely into the quantity or efficiency of their work.

From these models proslavery writers drew their sentimental pictures of slave life. The specific cases they cited were often valid ones; their profound error was in generalizing from them. For this leisurely life was the experience of only a small fraction of the bondsmen. Whether they lived in the Upper South or Deep South, in rural or urban communities, on plantations or farms, the labor of the vast majority of slaves ranged from what was normally expected of free labor in that period to levels that were clearly excessive.

It would not be too much to say that masters usually demanded from their slaves a long day of hard work and managed by some means or other to get it. The evidence does not sustain the belief that free laborers generally worked longer hours and at a brisker pace than the unfree. During the months when crops were being cultivated or harvested the slaves commonly were in the fields fifteen or sixteen hours a day, including time allowed for meals and rest.[66] By ante-bellum standards this may not have been excessive, but it was not a light work routine by the standards of that or any other day.

In instructions to overseers, planters almost always cautioned against overwork, yet insisted that the hands be made to labor vigorously as many hours as there was daylight. Overseers who could not accomplish this were discharged. An Arkansas master described a work day that was in no sense unusual on the plantations of the Deep South: "We get up before day every morning and eat breakfast before day and have everybody at work before day dawns. I am never caught in bed after day light nor is any body else on the place, and we continue in the cotton fields when we can have fair weather till it is so dark we cant see to work, and this history of one day is the history of every day." [67]

Planters who contributed articles on the management of slaves to southern periodicals took this routine for granted. "It is expected," one of them wrote, "that servants should rise early enough to be at work by the time it is light. . . . While at work, they should be brisk. . . . I have no objection to their whistling or singing some lively tune, but no *drawling* tunes are allowed in the field, for their motions are almost certain to keep time with the music." [68] These planters had the businessman's interest in maximum production without injury to their capital.

The work schedule was not strikingly different on the plantations of the Upper South. Here too it was a common practice to regulate the hours of labor in accordance with the amount of daylight. A former slave on a Missouri tobacco and hemp plantation recalled that the field-hands began their work at half past four in the morning. Such rules were far more common on Virginia plantations than were the customs of languid patricians. An ex-slave in Hanover County, Virginia, remembered seeing slave women hurrying to their work in the early morning "with their shoes and stockings in their hands, and a petticoat wrapped over their shoulders, to dress in the field the best way they could." [69] The bulk of the Virginia planters were businessmen too.

Planters who were concerned about the physical condition of their slaves permitted them to rest at noon after eating their dinners in the fields. "In the Winter," advised one expert on slave management, "a hand may be pressed all day, but not so in Summer. . . . In May, from one and a half to two hours; in June, two and a half; in July and August, three hours rest [should be given] at noon." [70] Except for certain essential chores, Sunday work was uncommon but not unheard of if the crops required it. On Saturdays slaves were often permitted to quit the fields at noon. They were also given holidays, most commonly at Christmas and after the crops were laid by.

But a holiday was not always a time for rest and relaxation. Many planters encouraged their bondsmen to cultivate small crops during their "leisure" to provide some of their own food. Thus a North Carolina planter instructed his overseer: "As soon as you have laid by the crop give the people 2 days but . . . they must work their own crops." Another planter gave his slaves a "holiday to plant their potatoes," and another "holiday to get in their potatoes." James H. Hammond once wrote in disgust: "Holiday for the negroes who fenced in their gardens. Lazy devils they did nothing after 12 o'clock." In addition, slave women had to devote part of their time when they were not in the fields to washing clothes, cooking, and cleaning their cabins. An Alabama planter wrote: "I always give them half of each Saturday, and often the whole day, at which time . . . the women do their household work; therefore they are never idle." [71]

Planters avoided night work as much as they felt they could, but slaves rarely escaped it entirely. Night work was almost universal on sugar plantations during the grinding season, and on cotton plantations when the crop was being picked, ginned, and packed. A Mississippi planter did not hesitate to keep his hands hauling fodder until ten o'clock at night when the hours of daylight were not sufficient for his work schedule.[72]

Occasionally a planter hired free laborers for such heavy work as ditching in order to protect his slave property. But, contrary to the legend, this was not a common practice. Most planters used their own field-hands for ditching and for clearing new ground. Moreover, they often assigned slave women to this type of labor as well as to plowing. On one plantation Olmsted saw twenty women operating heavy plows with double teams: "They were superintended by a male negro driver, who carried a whip, which he frequently cracked at them, permitting no dawdling or delay at the turning." [73]

Among the smaller planters and slaveholding farmers there was generally no appreciable relaxation of this normal labor routine. Their production records, their diaries and farm journals, and the testimony of their slaves all suggest the same dawn-to-dusk regimen that prevailed on the large plantations.[74] This was also the experience of most slaves engaged in nonagricultural occupations. Everywhere, then, masters normally expected from their slaves, in accordance with the standards of their time, a full stint of labor from "day clean" to "first dark."

Some, however, demanded more than this. Continuously, or at least for long intervals, they drove their slaves at a pace that was bound, sooner or later, to injure their health. Such hard driving seldom occurred on the smaller plantations and farms or in urban centers; it was decidedly a phenomenon of the large plantations. Though the majority of planters did not sanction it, more of them tolerated excessively heavy labor routines than is generally realized. The records of the plantation regime clearly indicate that slaves were more frequently overworked by calloused tyrants than overindulged by mellowed patriarchs.

That a large number of southern bondsmen were worked severely during the colonial period is beyond dispute. The South Carolina code of 1740 charged that "many owners . . . do confine them so closely to hard labor, that they have not sufficient time for natural rest." [75] In the nineteenth century conditions seemed to have improved, especially in the older regions of the South. Unquestionably the ante-bellum planter who coveted a high rank in society responded to subtle pressures that others did not feel. The closing of the African slave trade and the steady rise of slave prices were additional restraining influences. "The time has been," wrote a planter in 1849, "that the farmer could kill up and wear out one Negro to buy another; but it is not so now. Negroes are too high in proportion to the price of cotton, and it behooves those who own them to make them last as long as possible." [76]

But neither public opinion nor high prices prevented some of the bondsmen from suffering physical breakdowns and early deaths because of overwork. The abolitionists never proved their claim that many sugar and cotton growers deliberately worked their slaves to death every seven years with the intention of replacing them from profits. Yet some of the great planters came close to accomplishing that result without designing it. In the "race for wealth" in which, according to one Louisiana planter, all were enlisted, few proprietors managed their estates according to the code of the patricians.[77] They were sometimes remarkably shortsighed in the use of their investments.

Irresponsible overseers, who had no permanent interest in slave property, were frequently blamed for the overworking of slaves. Since this was a common complaint, it is important to remember that nearly half of the slaves lived on plantations of the size that ordinarily employed overseers. But planters could not escape responsibility for these conditions simply because their written instructions usually prohibited excessive driving. For they often demanded crop yields that could be achieved by no other method.

Most overseers believed (with good reason) that their success was measured by how much they produced, and that merely having the slave force in good condition at the end of the year would not guarantee re-employment. A Mississippi overseer with sixteen years of experience confirmed this belief in defending his profession: "When I came to Mississippi, I found that the overseer who could have the most cotton bales ready for market by Christmas, was considered best qualified for the business — consequently, every overseer gave his whole attention to cotton bales, to the exclusion of everything else." [78]

More than a few planters agreed that this was true. A committee of an Alabama agricultural society reported: "It is too commonly the case that masters look only to the yearly products of their farms, and praise or condemn their overseers by this standard alone, without ever once troubling themselves to inquire into the manner in which things are managed on their plantations, and whether he may have lost more in the diminished value of his slaves by over-work than he has gained by his large crop." This being the case, it was understandably of no consequence to the overseer that the old hands were "worked down" and the young ones "over-strained," that the "breeding women" miscarried, and that the "sucklers" lost their children. "So that he has the requisite number of cotton bags, all is overlooked; he is re-employed at an advanced salary, and his reputation increased." [79]

Some planters, unintentionally perhaps, gave overseers a special incentive for overworking slaves by making their compensation depend in part upon the amount they produced. Though this practice was repeatedly denounced in the ante-bellum period, many masters continued to follow it nevertheless. Cotton growers offered overseers bonuses of from one to five dollars for each bale above a specified minimum, or a higher salary if they produced a fixed quota. A Louisiana planter hired an overseer on a straight commission basis of $2.75 per bale of cotton and four cents per bushel of corn. A South Carolina rice planter gave his overseer ten per cent of the net proceeds. And a Virginian offered his overseer "the seventh part of the good grain, tobacco, cotton, and flax" that was harvested on his estate. "Soon as I hear [of] such a bargain," wrote a southern critic, "I fancy that the overseer, determined to save his salary, adopts the song of 'drive, drive, drive.' " [80]

Masters who hired their slaves to others also helped to create conditions favoring ruthless exploitation. The overworking of hired slaves by employers with only a temporary interest in their welfare was as notorious as the harsh practices of overseers. Slaves hired to mine owners or railroad contractors were fortunate if they were not driven to the point where their health was impaired. The same danger confronted slaves hired to sugar planters during the grinding season or to cotton planters at picking time. Few Southerners familiar with these conditions would have challenged the assertion made before a South Carolina court that hired slaves were "commonly treated more harshly . . . than those in possession of their owner[s]." [81]

But the master was as responsible for the conduct of those who hired his slaves as he was for the conduct of the overseers he employed. Overworked slaves were not always the innocent victims of forces beyond his control; there were remedies which he sometimes failed to apply. A stanch defender of slavery described a set of avaricious planters whom he labeled "Cotton Snobs," or "Southern Yankees." In their frantic quest for wealth, he wrote indignantly, the crack of the whip was heard early and late, until their bondsmen were "bowed to the ground with over-tasking and over-toil." [82] A southern physician who practiced on many cotton plantations complained, in 1847, that some masters still regarded "their sole interest to consist in large crops, leaving out of view altogether the value of negro property and its possible deterioration." During the economic depression of the 1840's, a planter accused certain cotton growers of trying to save themselves by increasing their cotton acreage and by driving their slaves harder, with the result that slaves broke down from overwork. An Alabama newspaper attributed conditions such as these to "avarice, the desire of growing rich." [83]

On the sugar plantations, during the months of the harvest, slaves were driven to the point of complete exhaustion. They were, in the normal routine, worked from sixteen to eighteen hours a day, seven days a week.[84] Cotton planters who boasted about making ten bales per hand were unconsciously testifying that their slaves were overworked. An overseer on an Arkansas plantation set his goal at twelve bales to the hand and indicated that this was what his employer desired. On a North Carolina plantation a temporary overseer assured the owner that he was a "hole hog man rain or shine" and boasted that the slaves had not been working like men but "like horses." "I'd ruther be dead than be a nigger on one of these big plantations," a white Mississippian told Olmsted.[85]

Sooner or later excessive labor was bound to take its toll. In the heat of mid-summer, slaves who could not bear hard driving without sufficient rest at noon simply collapsed in the fields. In Mississippi a planter reported "numerous cases" of sunstroke in his neighborhood during a spell of extreme heat. His own slaves "gave out." On a Florida plantation a number of hands "fainted in the field" one hot August day. Even in Virginia hot weather and heavy labor caused "the death of many negroes in the harvest field." [86]

NOTES

1. Joseph H. Ingraham (ed.), *The Sunny South; or, The Southerner at Home* (Philadelphia, 1860), pp. 51–52.
2. Plantation Manual in James H. Hammond Papers.
3. Henry Watson, Jr., to his father, February 24, 1843 (copy), Henry Watson, Jr., Papers.
4. This is a generalized description obtained from the records of many slaveholders who grew cotton in widely scattered parts of the cotton belt.
5. J. Carlyle Sitterson, *Sugar Country: The Cane Sugar Industry in the South, 1753–1950* (Lexington, Kentucky, 1953), pp. 112–56.
6. Michael Gramling, a small planter in the Orangeburg District, who was still producing indigo as late as 1845 was a rare exception. Michael Gramling Ms. Record Book.
7. Duncan Clinch Heyward, *Seed from Madagascar* (Chapel Hill, 1937), pp. 27–44; J. H. Easterby (ed.), *The South Carolina Rice Plantation as Revealed in the Papers of Robert F. W. Allston* (Chicago, 1945), pp. 31–32; Phillips, *Life and Labor in the Old South,* pp. 115–18.
8. Joseph Clarke Robert, *The Tobacco Kingdom* (Durham, 1938), pp. 32–50.
9. James F. Hopkins, *A History of the Hemp Industry in Kentucky* (Lexington, Kentucky, 1951), pp. 24–30, 39–64; Harrison A. Trexler, *Slavery in Missouri, 1804–1865* (Baltimore, 1914), pp. 23–25.
10. *Compendium of the Seventh Census* (Washington, 1854), p. 94.
11. Kenneth M. Clark to Lewis Thompson, June 20, 1853, Lewis Thompson Papers.
12. Columbus Morrison Ms. Diary, entry for November 27, 1845; Rosser H. Taylor, *Slaveholding in North Carolina: An Economic View* (Chapel Hill, 1926), pp. 36–37.
13. Avery O. Craven, *Soil Exhaustion as a Factor in the Agricultural History of Virginia and Maryland* (Urbana, Illinois, 1926), pp. 122–61; Robert, *Tobacco Kingdom,* pp. 18–19.
14. *De Bow's Review, X* (1851), pp. 625–27.
15. Ralph B. Flanders, *Plantation Slavery in Georgia* (Chapel Hill, 1933), p. 158.
16. Records of sales in Lloyd Family Papers. See also Frederick Law Olmsted, *A Journey in the Seaboard Slave States* (New York, 1856), p. 10.
17. Shirley Plantation Ms. Farm Journal; John Walker Ms. Diary.
18. Pettigrew Family Papers; Bennett H. Wall. "Ebenezer Pettigrew. An Economic Study of an Ante-Bellum Planter" (unpublished doctoral dissertation, University of North Carolina, 1946), *passim; Farmer's Journal, I* (1852), p. 147.
19. Sitterson, *Sugar Country,* pp. 50–51.
20. This information about small slaveholders was derived from a study of their production records in representative counties throughout the South as reported in the manuscript census returns for 1860.
21. *Southern Agriculturist,. VI* (1833), p. 576.

22. Sellers, *Slavery in Alabama*, p. 67; Hammond Diary, entry for May 16, 1838.
23. These are generalized figures from a survey of many plantation records. See also *De Bow's Review, II* (1846), pp. 134, 138; *X* (1851), p. 625; Sydnor, *Slavery in Mississippi*, pp. 13–14; Gray, *History of Agriculture, II*, pp. 707–708; Sitterson, *Sugar Country*, pp. 127–28; Robert, *Tobacco Kingdom*, p. 18.
24. Olmsted, *Back Country*, p. 47; *id., Seaboard*, p. 433; *Southern Agriculturist, VI* (1833), pp. 571–73; Sydnor, *Slavery in Mississippi*, pp. 18–20; Sellers, *Slavery in Alabama*, p. 66.
25. [Joseph H. Ingraham], *The South-West. By a Yankee* (New York, 1835), *II*, p. 126; Charles S. Davis, *The Cotton Kingdom in Alabama* (Montgomery, 1939), p. 58.
26. Thomas Affleck, *The Cotton Plantation Record and Account Book* (Louisville and New Orleans, 1847–).
27. Gustavus A. Henry to his wife, December 3, 1846, Gustavus A. Henry Papers; Herbert A. Kellar (ed.), *Solon Robinson, Pioneer and Agriculturist* (Indianapolis, 1936), *II*, p. 203.
28. William H. Russell, *My Diary North and South* (Boston, 1863), p. 273.
29. Ingraham (ed.), *Sunny South*, pp. 179–81.
30. Henry Watson, Jr., to Theodore Watson, March 3, 1831, Watson Papers; Olmsted, *Seaboard*, pp. 18–19.
31. Solomon Northup, *Twelve Years a Slave* (Buffalo, 1853), pp. 178–79.
32. Gustavus A. Henry to his wife, December 12, 1848, Henry Papers; John Nevitt Ms. Plantation Journal; William S. Pettigrew to James C. Johnston, January 24, 1856, Pettigrew Family Papers; Olmsted, *Seaboard*, pp. 153–55.
33. Olmsted, *Seaboard*, pp. 339–42; Guion G. Johnson, *Ante-Bellum North Carolina* (Chapel Hill, 1937), pp. 487–88.
34. Fredrika Bremer, *The Homes of the New World* (New York, 1853), *II*, p. 174.
35. Joe Gray Taylor, "Negro Slavery in Louisiana" (unpublished doctoral dissertation, Louisiana State University, 1951), pp. 43–44, 115–17; Raleigh *North Carolina Standard*, June 6, 1855; August 13, 1859; Horace S. Fulkerson, *Random Recollections of Early Days in Mississippi*, (Vicksburg, 1885), pp. 130–31.
36. Richmond *Enquirer*, August 2, 1836; Sellers, *Slavery in Alabama*, pp. 200–220; Flanders, *Plantation Slavery in Georgia*, pp. 197–98; Taylor, "Negro Slavery in Louisiana," pp. 112–13.
37. [Ingraham], *South-West, II*, p. 249.
38. Quoted in Flanders, *Plantation Slavery in Georgia*, p. 47. See also Leonard P. Stavisky, "Negro Craftsmanship in Early America," *American Historical Review, IV* (1949), pp. 315–25.
39. *De Bow's Review, VIII* (1850), p. 76; *IX* (1850), pp. 432–33.
40. Hopkins, *Hemp Industry*, pp. 135–37; J. Winston Coleman, Jr., *Slavery Times in Kentucky* (Chapel Hill, 1940), pp. 81–82.
41. Robert, *Tobacco Kingdom*, pp. 197–203; Alexander MacKay, *The Western World; or Travels in the United States in 1846–47* (London, 1849), *II*, p. 74.
42. Coleman, *Slavery Times in Kentucky*, p. 64; Robert E. Corlew, "Some Aspects of Slavery in Dickson County," *Tennessee Historical Quarterly, X* (1951), pp. 226–29.
43. Kathleen Bruce, *Virginia Iron Manufacture in the Slave Era* (New York, 1931), pp. 231–38.
44. James S. Buckingham, *The Slave States of America* (London, [1842]), *II*, p. 112.
45. Pensacola *Gazette*, April 8, 1848; *De Bow's Review, IX* (1850), pp. 432–33.
46. E. M. Lander, Jr., "Slave Labor in South Carolina Cotton Mills," *Journal of Negro History, XXXVIII* (1953), pp. 161–73; Charles H. Wesley, *Negro Labor in the United States, 1850–1925* (New York, 1927), pp. 15–20; *American Cotton Planter and Soil of the South, I* (1857), pp. 156–57.
47. William B. Lenoir to William Lenoir, May 18, 1833, Lenoir Family Papers.
48. Frederic Bancroft, *Slave-Trading in the Old South* (Baltimore, 1931), pp. 404–405.
49. Richmond *Enquirer*, January 1, 1850; Bancroft, *Slave-Trading*, p. 149.
50. Hamilton Brown Papers; Memorandum dated December 15, 1860, in Morton-Halsey Papers.
51. S. F. Lenoir to her sisters, November 18, 1851, Lenoir Family Papers; Bancroft, *Slave-Trading*, pp. 145–47.
52. Contract between William Frew and R. S. Young, dated December 30, 1853, in Burton-Young Papers.
53. Rickerton Lyle Winston Ms. Slave Account Book.
54. [Ingraham], *South-West, II*, pp. 251–52.
55. Edmund Ruffin, Jr., Farm Journal, entry for September 7, 1843.
56. Sitterson, *Sugar Country*, pp. 61–62; Taylor, "Negro Slavery in Louisiana," p. 94.
57. Charleston *Courier*, August 16, 1852.
58. Copies of letters to "James Sims a Colored man," in Walker Diary.
59. Richmond *Enquirer*, August 8, 1836; Wilmington (N.C.) *Journal*, December 28, 1857.
60. Lexington *Kentucky Statesman*, December 26, 1854; Robert, *Tobacco Kingdom*, p. 198.
61. Frederick Douglass, *My Bondage and My Freedom* (New York, 1855), p. 328.
62. Charles White to Hamilton Brown, December 20, 1832, Hamilton Brown Papers.
63. Susan Dabney Smedes, *Memorials of a Southern Planter* (Baltimore, 1887), p. 57.
64. Northup, *Twelve Years a Slave*, pp. 166–68.
65. Olmsted, *Seaboard*, pp. 431–36; Guion G. Johnson, *A Social History of the Sea Islands* (Chapel Hill, 1930), pp. 124–25; E. Merton Coulter, *Thomas Spalding of Sapelo* (Baton Rouge, 1940), p. 85.

66. Gray, *History of Agriculture, I,* pp. 556–57.
67. Gustavus A. Henry to his wife, November 27, 1860, Henry Papers.
68. *Southern Cultivator, VIII* (1850), p. 163.
69. William W. Brown, *Narrative of William W. Brown, a Fugitive Slave* (Boston, 1847), p. 14; Olmsted, *Seaboard,* p. 109; *De Bow's Review, XIV* (1853), pp. 176–78; Benjamin Drew, *The Refugee: or the Narratives of Fugitive Slaves in Canada* (Boston, 1856), p. 162.
70. *Southern Cultivator, VIII* (1850), p. 163.
71. Henry K. Burgwyn to Arthur Souter, August 6, 1843, Henry King Burgwyn Papers; John C. Jenkins Diary, entries for November 15, 1845; April 22, 1854; Hammond Diary, entry for May 12, 1832; *De Bow's Review, XIII* (1852), pp. 193–94.
72. Jenkins Diary, entry for August 7, 1843.
73. Olmsted, *Back Country,* p. 81; Sydnor, *Slavery in Mississippi,* p. 12.
74. See, for example, Marston Papers; Torbert Plantation Diary; *De Bow's Review, XI* (1851), pp. 369–72; Drew, *Refugee;* Douglass, *My Bondage,* p. 215; Trexler, *Slavery in Missouri,* pp. 97–98.
75. Hurd, *Law of Freedom and Bondage, I,* p. 307; Flanders, *Plantation Slavery in Georgia,* p. 42.
76. *Southern Cultivator, VII* (1849), p. 69.
77. Kenneth M. Clark to Lewis Thompson, December 29, 1859, Thompson Papers.
78. *American Cotton Planter and Soil of the South, II* (1858), pp. 112–13.
79. *American Farmer, II* (1846), p. 78; *Southern Cultivator, II* (1844), pp. 97, 107.
80. *North Carolina Farmer, I* (1845), pp. 122–23. Agreements of this kind with overseers are in the records of numerous planters.
81. Catterall, *Judicial Cases, II,* p. 374.
82. Hundley, *Social Relations,* pp. 132, 187–88.
83. *De Bow's Review, I* (1846), pp. 434–36; *III* (1847), p. 419; Selma *Free Press,* quoted in Tuscaloosa *Independent Monitor,* July 14, 1846.
84. This is apparent from the records of sugar planters. See also Sitterson, *Sugar Country,* pp. 133–36; Olmsted, *Seaboard,* pp. 650, 667–68.
85. P. Weeks to James Sheppard, September 20, 1854, James Sheppard Papers; Doctrine Davenport to Ebenezer Pettigrew, April 24, 1836, Pettigrew Family Papers; Olmsted, *Back Country,* pp. 55–57, 202.
86. Jenkins Diary, entries for August 9, 1844; July 7, 1846; June 30, 1854; Ulrich B. Phillips and James D. Glunt (eds.), *Florida Plantation Records from the Papers of George Noble Jones* (St. Louis, 1927), p. 90; John B. Garrett Ms. Farm Journal, entry for July 19, 1830.

Lincoln and the Civil War

The sectional crisis that culminated in the Civil War elevated Abraham Lincoln to prominence. Lincoln was an enigma to many of his contemporaries, and he is an enigma to us today. On the one hand, he is America's secular saint; but he was also an opportunistic politician. He was the defender of the common man; but he was also a lawyer for the powerful Illinois Central Railroad. He was the Great Emancipator; but he was a southerner by birth with many of the racial prejudices of that section's poor white class. He was a rock of strength for the Union; but his own youth was full of uncertainties and self-doubts.

Much of our fascination with Lincoln grows out of these ambiguities in his career and personality. It also grows out of the drama of the Civil War. No event in our history has exerted the same allure as this great crisis of the Union. The very survival of the nation was at stake, and every twist and turn of events seems portentous. Even the intricacies of national finance, or military logistics, or diplomatic negotiations — historical details that often seem arid and tedious for other periods of time — take on a special interest for the Civil War. The man who stood at the helm in this American *Iliad* inevitably becomes a figure larger than life.

It is difficult sometimes to get behind this image to the man himself and to the realities of his achievements. One of the most successful attempts in brief compass is the following essay by Professor David Donald. Donald is obviously aware of Lincoln's greatness, but he also recognizes that part of this, indeed an essential prerequisite to it, was his ability to manipulate the political levers. Lincoln, in a word, was not only a "statesman," he was also that much-maligned figure in our political mythology, a clever politician. Part of that astuteness was his success in creating, even among his contemporaries, the illusion of simplicity, guilelessness, and utter sincerity. It is clear that some of the difficulties we experience in perceiving the real man we can blame on the careful work of Abraham Lincoln himself.

FOR FURTHER READING:

CURRENT, RICHARD N. *Lincoln and the First Shot.* Philadelphia: J. B. Lippincott Company, 1963.*
NEVINS, ALLAN. *The War for the Union.* 2 vols. New York: Charles Scribners' Sons, 1959, 1960.*
THOMAS, BENJAMIN. *Abraham Lincoln: A Biography.* New York: Random House, Modern Library, 1968.*

Asterisk denotes paperback edition.

A. Lincoln, Politician   DAVID DONALD

The statesmanship of Abraham Lincoln is so widely recognized as to require no defense. But it is not always realized that Lincoln's opportunities for statesmanship were made possible by his accomplishments as a politician. Perhaps it is too cynical to say that a statesman is a politician who succeeds in getting himself elected President. Still, but for his election in 1860, Lincoln's name would appear in our history books as that of a minor Illinois politician who unsuccessfuly debated with Stephen A. Douglas. And had the President been defeated in 1864, he would be written off as one of the great failures of the American political system — the man who let his country drift into civil war, presided aimlessly over a graft-ridden administration, conducted an incompetent and ineffectual attempt to subjugate the Southern states, and after four years was returned by the people to the obscurity that he so richly deserved.

Lincoln's fame, then, was made possible by his success as a politician, yet in many of the techniques used by present-day political leaders he was singularly ineffectual. He never succeeded in selling himself — to the press, to the politicians, or to the people. To a public-relations expert, the Lincoln story would seem a gift from heaven. Like a skillful organist playing upon the keyboard of popular emotion, he could pull out the sentimental tremolo for Lincoln's humble origins, for his hard-scrabble Kentucky and Indiana childhood, for his Illinois rise from rags to respectability. A good publicity man would emphasize Lincoln's sense of humor (but, as a recent campaign has demonstrated, he should not overemphasize it), his down-to-earth folksiness, his sympathy for the oppressed. Appealing to the traditional American love of a fighter, especially an underdog, he could capitalize upon the virulent assaults of Lincoln's political enemies. The whole campaign, if managed by a Batten, Barton, Durstine & Osborn agent, should have been as appealing, as saccharine, as successful as the famous 1952 television appearance of our current Vice President.

In Lincoln's case, however, astonishingly little use was made of these sure-fire appeals — and when they were used, they backfired. The President said that he was a man of humble origins — and his opponents declared that, as Southern poor white trash, he was still cowed by the slaveholders and afraid of vigorously prosecuting the war. Lincoln stressed his sense of humor — and even his supporters protested: " . . . I do wish Abraham would tell fewer dirty stories." Mrs. Lincoln regularly visited the wounded in Washington's hospitals — and hostile newspapers hinted that she was really passing along military secrets to the Confederates.

Lincoln never succeeded in making his own case clear. He had no sounding-board. While Congressmen orated in the Capitol, the President sat gagged in the White House. In the 1860's, convention had it that a President must pretend not to be a politician. After wirepulling for a lifetime to secure the nomination, the successful candidate must be surprised when a committee from his party officially notified him that he was the lucky man. In the campaign that followed, he was supposed to sit indifferently at home, pretending to be a Cincinnatus at the plow, while his fellow citizens, unsolicited, offered him the highest post in the land. And, once in the Executive Mansion, he was to be muffled and dumb.

Source: David Donald, *Lincoln Reconsidered* (New York: Random House, Vintage Books, 1956), chap. 4, "A. Lincoln, Politician," pp. 57– 84.

Like most self-made men, Abraham Lincoln was very conventional, and he never challenged the rules of the political game. A strict view of the proprieties prevented President Lincoln from going directly to the people. Although he had made his fame as a public speaker, he never once addressed the Congress in person, but, following Jefferson's example, submitted written messages that dreary clerks droned out to apathetic legislators. Rarely after 1861 did Lincoln make any speeches or public pronouncements. "In my present position," he told a Maryland crowd in 1862, "it is hardly proper for me to make speeches." Later, as candidate for re-election, Lincoln still further limited his utterances. "I do not really think," he said in June 1864, "it is proper in my position for me to make a political speech. . . ." ". . . I believe it is not customary for one holding the office, and being a candidate for re-election, to do so. . . ." During the four years of civil war, the people could hear every strident and raucous voice in America, but not the voice of their President.

The President's negative attitude discouraged support from the press. Although he gave a number of informal interviews, Lincoln held no press conference; reporters were still not considered quite respectable, certainly not worthy of private audience with the President. Newspapermen go where there is news. When a Washington correspondent found the White House well dry, he turned naturally to those running streams of gossip and complaint and criticism and intrigue, the Congressmen, whose anti-Lincoln pronouncements all too often agreed with the prejudices of his editor. Most of the leading American newspapers were anti-Lincoln in 1860, and they remained anti-Lincoln till April 15, 1865, when they suddenly discovered that the President had been the greatest man in the world. There were some notable exceptions, of course — the Springfield *Republican* and the New York *Times,* for example — but even these were handicapped by Lincoln's negative attitude toward the press. As one editor complained: ". . . it is our great desire to sustain the President, and we deplore the opportunity he has let go by, to sustain himself."

But most newspapers had no desire whatever to sustain the President, and they berated Lincoln with virulent obscenity that makes even the anti-Roosevelt campaigns of our own day seem mild. The sixteenth President was abused in the newspapers as "a slang-whanging stump speaker," a "half-witted usurper," a "mole-eyed" monster with "soul . . . of leather," "the present turtle at the head of the government," "the head ghoul at Washington."

President Lincoln was no more successful with the politicians than with the press. One of the saddest aspects of Civil War history is the sorry failure of Lincoln's appeals for bipartisan support. The Copperheads, outright antiwar Democrats, he could not hope to win, but the enormous mass of the Democratic party was as loyal to the Union as the President himself. On all crucial issues Lincoln was closer to George B. McClellan or Horatio Seymour than to many members of his own party. "In this time of national peril," Lincoln kept saying to such War Democrats, he hoped to meet them "upon a level one step higher than any party platform." He did not expect them to endorse every measure of a Republican regime, but he did wish that " 'the Government' [might] be supported though the administration may not in every case wisely act." So earnestly did he desire the support of an energetic War Democrat like Governor Seymour of New York that in 1862 he sent him a message: if the Governor would help "wheel the Democratic party into line, put down rebellion, and preserve the government," Lincoln said, "I shall cheerfully make way for him as my successor."

Such hopes for bipartisan co-operation were blighted at birth. Governor Seymour regarded Lincoln's offer as a trap, and he spent most of his term in Albany denouncing the corruption and the arbitrary methods of the Lincoln administration. Far from co-operating, Democratic politicians took out time to compare Lincoln with the "original gorilla," a baboon, and a long-armed ape; the more scurrilous elements of the opposition party suggested that the President suffered from unmentionable diseases or that he had Negro blood in his veins.

If the President's failure with the Democrats was to be expected in a country with a vigorous two-party tradition, his inability to influence leaders of his own party was a more serious weakness. In Washington, reported Richard Henry Dana, author of *Two Years before the Mast,* "the most striking thing is the absence of personal loyalty to the President. It does not exist. He has no admirers, no enthusiastic supporters, none to bet on his head." Republican critics openly announced that Lincoln was "unfit," a "political coward," a "dictator," "timid and ignorant," "pitiable," "too slow," a man of "no education," "shattered, dazed, utterly foolish." "He is ignorant, self-willed, & is surrounded by men some of whom are almost as ignorant as himself," historian George Bancroft declared. Republican editor Murat Halstead thought Lincoln "an awful, woeful ass," and a correspondent of the Chicago *Tribune* said that "Buchanan seems to have been a granite pillar compared to the 'Good natured man' without any spinal column. . . ." Republican Senator James W. Grimes of Iowa felt that Lincoln's "entire administration has been a disgrace from the very beginning to every one who had any thing to do with bringing it into power."

From the beginning the President and his own party leaders in Congress were often at loggerheads. Radicals and Conservatives, former Whigs and ex-Democrats, Easterners and Westerners, all viewed Lincoln with suspicion. Such a situation is, of course, fairly normal in American politics. As our major parties consist of conflicting interest groups bound together by political expediency rather than by ideology, a President is bound constantly to disappoint nine tenths of the voters who elected him. But in Lincoln's case the situation was more serious because he seemed unable to build up any personally loyal following. Nearly every important Republican leader — Chase, Sumner, Greeley, Stevens, Wade, Davis, Chandler, Browning, Grimes, Weed — doubted the advisability of a second term for Lincoln. When a Pennsylvania editor visited the Capitol in 1864 and asked to meet some Congressmen who favored the President's renomination, old Thad Stevens stumped over to Representative Isaac N. Arnold of Illinois, announcing: "Here is a man who wants to find a Lincoln member of Congress. You are the only one I know and I have come over to introduce my friend to you."

A failure with the press and the politicians, Lincoln is said by sentimentalists to have won the favor of the common people. This stereotype, so comforting to those who like to believe in the democratic dogma, started with Lincoln himself. When Congressmen and editors erupted in a frenzy of anti-Lincoln fury, the President liked to reflect that the "politicians" could not "transfer the people, the honest though misguided masses" to their course of opposition. Lincoln felt that he understood the mind of the masses. Day after day he greeted the throngs of visitors, petitioners, and office-seekers who besieged him in the White House, and he claimed that these "public-opinion baths" helped him sense the popular will. In return for his sympathy, the President felt, he received popular support. His private secretary, John Hay, echoed Lincoln's belief: "The people know what they want and will have it" — namely, a re-election of the President in 1864.

In fact, though, the evidence for Lincoln's enormous popular appeal during the war is sketchy and unreliable. One could quote, for instance, Congressman Lewis D. Campbell's opinion of the 1864 election: "Nothing but the undying attachment of our people to the Union has saved us from terrible disaster. Mr. Lincolns popularity had nothing to do with it. . . ." More convincing, however, than such impressionistic evidence are the actual election returns. Lincoln was a minority President in 1861. His party lost control of the crucial states of New York, Pennsylvania, Ohio, Indiana, and Illinois in the off-year elections of 1862. And in 1864 — when all the Southern states were out of the Union and, of course, not voting — Northerners, given a chance to demonstrate their alleged enthusiastic support for the President, cast forty-five percent of their ballots against Lincoln and for a Democratic platform that called both his administration and the war for the Union failures. A change of only eighty-three thousand votes — two per cent of the toal — could have meant Lincoln's defeat.

Although Lincoln failed to win the press, the politicians, and the people, he was nevertheless a successful politician. He kept himself and his party in power. He was the first President since Andrew Jackson to win re-election, and his administration began an unbroken twenty-four years of Republican control of the Presidency.

The secret of Lincoln's success is simple: he was an astute and dextrous operator of the political machine. Such a verdict at first seems almost preposterous, for one thinks of Lincoln's humility, so great as to cause his opponents to call him a "Uriah Heep"; of his frankness, which brought him the epithet "Honest Abe"; of his well-known aversion for what he termed the "details of how we get along." Lincoln carefully built up this public image of himself as a babe in the Washington wilderness. To a squabbling group of Pennsylvania party leaders he said ingenuously: "You know I never was a contriver; I don't know much about how things are done in politics. . . ."

Before breaking into tears of sympathy for this innocent among thieves, it is well to review Lincoln's pre-Presidential career. When elected President, he had been in active politics for twenty-six years; politics was his life. "He was an exceedingly ambitious man," his Springfield law partner wrote, "a man totally swallowed up in his ambitions. . . ." "Rouse Mr. Lincoln's peculiar nature in a point where he deeply felt — say in his ambitions — his general greed for office . . . then Mr. Lincoln preferred Abm Lincoln to anybody else." But during his long career in Illinois politics Lincoln had never been chosen to major office by the people of his state; state legislator and one-term member of Congress he was, but never Senator — though he twice tried unsuccessfully — and never governor. Lack of appeal at the polls did not, however, prevent him from becoming the master wirepuller who operated the state political organization first of the Whig party and, after its decay, that of the Republicans. Behind that façade of humble directness and folksy humor, Lincoln was moving steadily toward his object; by 1860 he had maneuvered himself into a position where he controlled the party machinery, platform, and candidates of one of the pivotal states in the Union. A Chicago lawyer who had known Lincoln intimately for three decades summarized these pre-presidential years: "One great public mistake . . . generally received and acquiesced in, is that he is considered by the people of this country as a frank, guileless, and unsophisticated man. There never was a greater mistake. . . . He handled and moved men remotely as we do pieces upon a chess-board."

Lincoln's Illinois record was merely finger exercises to the display of political virtuosity he was to exhibit in the White House. He brought to the Executive office an understanding of the value of secrecy. So close did Lincoln keep his ideas, it can be said that no one of his associates understood him. Herndon concluded that this man was "a profound mystery — an enigma — a sphinx — a riddle . . . incommunicative — silent — reticent — secretive — having profound policies — and well laid — deeply studied plans." Nobody had his complete confidence. His loyal Secretary of the Navy was kept as much in the dark about Lincoln's views as the veriest outsider. "Of the policy of the administration, if there be one," Welles complained, "I am not advised beyond what is published and known to all." Lincoln moved toward his objectives with muffled oars. After ninety years historians are still arguing whether Lincoln arranged for Andrew Johnson to be nominated as his vice-presidential running-mate in 1864. Impressive and suggestive evidence can be cited to show that the President picked the Tennessean — or that he favored someone else entirely.

Lincoln's renowned sense of humor was related to his passion for secrecy. Again and again self-important delegations would descend upon the White House, deliver themselves of ponderous utterances upon pressing issues of the war, and demand point-blank what the President proposed to do about their problems. Lincoln could say much in few words when he chose, but he could also say nothing at great length when it was expedient. His petitioners' request, he would say, reminded him of "a little story," which he would proceed to tell in great detail, accompanied by mimicry and gestures, by hearty slapping of the thigh, by uproarious laughter at the end — at which time he would usher out his callers, baffled and confused by the smoke-screen of good humor, with their questions still unanswered.

Akin to Lincoln's gift for secrecy was his talent for passivity. When he arrived in Washington, he was faced by a crisis not of his own making. Fort Sumter, provocatively located in the harbor of Charleston, the very hotbed of secession, had to be reinforced or evacuated. Reinforcement would be interpreted, not merely by the Confederates but also by large peace-loving elements at the North, as an aggressive act of war; withdrawal would appear to other Northerners a cowardly retreat on the part of a spineless administration. Lincoln considered both alternatives. Characteristically, he sought clear-cut written opinions from his Cabinet advisers on the course to follow — but left his own ideas unrecorded. Characteristically, the whole episode is muffled in a fog of confusion which has produced an interesting argument among later historians. But characteristically, too, Lincoln's final decision was neither to reinforce nor to withdraw; he would merely send food and supplies to the beleaguered Sumter garrison and sit back and wait. His passivity paid off. Confederate hotheads were unable to wait so long as the cool-blooded Northern President, and they fired the first shot at Sumter. To Lincoln's support all elements of Northern society now rallied. "At the darkest moment in the history of the republic," Ralph Waldo Emerson wrote, "when it looked as if the nation would be dismembered, pulverized into its original elements, the attack on Fort Sumter crystallized the North into a unit, and the hope of mankind was saved."

Repeatedly, throughout the war, Lincoln's passive policy worked politically. Because any action would offend somebody, he took as few actions as possible. Outright abolitionists demanded that he use his wartime powers to emancipate the Negroes. Border-state politicians insisted that he protect their peculiar institutions. Lincoln needed the support of both groups; therefore, he did nothing — or, rather, he proposed to colonize the Negroes in Central America, which was as near to nothing as he could come — and awaited events. After two years of hostilities, many even in the South came to see that slavery was doomed, and all the important segments of Northern opinion were brought to support emancipation as a wartime necessity. Only then did Lincoln issue the Emancipation Proclamation.

Along with secrecy and passivity, Lincoln brought to his office an extraordinarily frank pragmatism — some might call it opportunism. Often while in the White House he repeated an anecdote that seemed to have a special meaning for him — how the Irishman who had forsworn liquor told the bartender that he was not averse to having a spot added to his lemonade, "so long as it's unbeknownst to me." Again and again the President showed himself an imitator of his Irish hero. When the Pennsylvania miners broke out in open rebellion against the operation of the draft law in their section, worried Harrisburg officials inquired whether Lincoln would send troops to execute the law. Entrusting nothing to paper, Lincoln sent a confidential messenger to A. K. McClure, the aide of the Pennsylvania governor: "Say to McClure that I am very desirous to have the laws fully executed, but it might be well, in an extreme emergency, to be content with the appearance of executing the laws; I think McClure will understand." McClure did understand, and he made no more than a feeble effort to subdue the miners' revolt, but let the agitation die out of its own accord. Thus, the Lincoln administration won the credit both for preserving the peace and for enforcing the draft.

Lincoln enjoyed a similar pragmatic relationship with his unpleasant and irritable Secretary of War, Edwin M. Stanton. There was a sort of tacit division of labor between these two dissimilar men. Lincoln himself explained the system: ". . . I want to oblige everybody when I can; and Stanton and I have an understanding that if I send an order to him which cannot be consistently granted, he is to refuse it. This he sometimes does." The President then had the pleasant and politically rewarding opportunity of recommending promotions, endorsing pension applications, pardoning deserters, and saving sleeping sentinels, and Stanton, who was something of a sadist, took equal pleasure in refusing the promotions, ignoring the petitions, and executing the delinquent soldiers. While the Secretary received the blame for all the harsh and unpopular acts that war makes necessary, the President acquired a useful reputation for sympathy and generosity.

Valuable as were these negative traits of secrecy, passivity, and pragmatism, Lincoln understood that it was not policies or principles which would cause Congressmen to support his direction of the war. To mobilize votes in Congress, the Head of State must be a practicing Party Leader. Lincoln was a political realist, and he worked with the tools he had at hand. He understood that in a democratic, federal government like ours, patronage is the one sure way of binding local political bosses to the person and principles of the President, and for this reason he used and approved the spoils system.

Lincoln's entire administration was characterized by astute handling of the patronage. Even in picking his Cabinet, he took leaders from all factions of his own party, giving all groups hope but no group dominance. The result was that Cabinet members were so suspicious of each other that they hardly had time to be jealous of the President. It was not efficient administration, for the Secretary of State met with the President privately — to regale him, enemies said, with vulgar stories; the Secretary of War would not discuss his plans in Cabinet meeting because he thought — with some justice — that his colleagues could not be trusted with secrets; and the Secretary of the Treasury finally refused to attend the "so-called" Cabinet meetings at all. Of all these men, outstanding political leaders in 1860, not one ever became President; in Lincoln's Cabinet they ate one another up.

Even without such competition, a Cabinet officer found his political activity necessarily curbed. The fading of Salmon P. Chase's presidential hopes provides an illuminating insight into Lincoln's use of the appointing power. Self-confident, upright, and able, Chase thought that he had deserved the Republican nomination in 1860, and from the first the Secretary of the Treasury looked upon Lincoln as a well-meaning incompetent. He never saw reason to alter his view. Chase was not a modest man; he was sure of his ability and his integrity, sure that he would make an admirable President. As a senator said: "Chase is a good man, but his theology is unsound. He thinks there is a fourth person in the Trinity" — namely, himself.

The day he became Secretary of the Treasury, Chase began scheming for the 1864 nomination, but he found himself hampered by his ambiguous position in the Cabinet. If his financial planning went wrong, he received the blame; but whenever he achieved a success, in the issue of greenbacks or the sale of bonds, the credit went to the Lincoln administration, not to Chase alone. He converted his numerous Treasury agents into a tightly organized and highly active Chase-for-President league, but as long as he remained in the Cabinet, he could not openly announce his presidential aspirations. To relieve himself from embarrassment, to go into outright opposition to Lincoln, Chase needed to get out of the Cabinet, but an unprovoked resignation would be political suicide, a cowardly evasion of his duties. All through 1863 and 1864, then, Chase wriggled and squirmed. Time after time he cooked up little quarrels over patronage, squabbles over alleged slights, and the like, so that he would have an excuse for resigning. Every time Lincoln blandly yielded the point in dispute and refused to accept Chase's withdrawal. But in June 1864, just after the Republican national convention at Baltimore had renominated Lincoln, Chase once again tried his obstructionist tactics that had worked so well in the past, and he threatened to resign from the Cabinet. This time, to his vast chagrin, it was different, and Lincoln accepted his withdrawal. Now that the race was over, Chase was free to run.

If patronage could close a Cabinet member's mouth, it could open the lips of an editor. James Gordon Bennett, the sinful and unscrupulous editor of the New York *Herald*, was one of the most powerful newspapermen of his day. Spiced with sex and scandal, the *Herald* had the largest circulation of any American newspaper, and it was a potent agency in shaping public opinion. Bennett had opposed Lincoln in 1860, and throughout the war he kept up a criticism that was all the more painful to Lincoln because it was well informed and witty. In 1864 Bennett hoped that Grant would run for President, and he also flirted capriciously with the Democratic nominee, General McClellan. For Lincoln he had no use.

President Lincoln [read a typical *Herald* editorial] is a joke incarnated. His election was a very sorry joke. The idea that such a man as he should be President of such a country as this is a very ridiculous joke. . . . His inaugural address was a joke, since it was full of promises which he has never performed. His Cabinet is and always has been a standing joke. All his State papers are jokes. . . . His title of "Honest" is a satirical joke. . . . His intrigues to secure a renomination and the hopes he appears to entertain of a re-election are, however, the most laughable jokes of all.

The vote in New York was going to be close, and Lincoln needed the *Herald*'s support. Emissaries went up from Washington to interview the canny Scottish editor and ascertain his price. Bennett's terms were high. "The fact is B. wants attention," Lincoln's agent reported. "He wants recognition — & I think it will pay." A newspaperman before he was anything else, Bennett promised to give the administration's views "a thorough exposition in the columns of the Herald," provided Lincoln and his advisers "would occasionally confidentially make known to him [their] plans." Then, too, the editor, who was barred from polite New York society because of his flagrant immorality and was generally considered "too pitchy to touch," had a hankering for social respectability. When Lincoln's agents approached him, the editor "asked plumply, 'Will I be a welcome visitor at the White House if I support Mr. Lincoln?'" The answer was unequivocally affirmative, and, as proof of his good faith, the President promised to the totally unqualified Bennett an appointment as minister to France. Bennett did not want to go abroad, for he was too busy with his paper, but he did want the social recognition that such an offer implied; he wanted to be able to refuse. The bargain was complete, and the *Herald* abandoned its criticism of the President.

As a practical politician, Lincoln understood that election victories required more than the support of Cabinet officers or newspaper editors. Like a famous New York politician, he knew that "Parties are not built up by deportment, or by ladies' magazines, or gush." In the United States, party machinery is more important than public opinion, and patronage more influential than principles. In recent years American liberal historians, scorning the sordid realities of political life, have pictured Lincoln as somehow above the vulgar party apparatus that elected him, unconcerned with the greasy machinery of party caucuses, conventions, nominations, and patronage. This idea is the political equivalent of the doctrine of the immaculate conception. Lincoln himself would have been astonished at it. Politics was his life, and he was a regular party man. Long before he became President, Lincoln said that "the man who is of neither party is not, and cannot be, of any consequence" in American life. As Chief Executive, he was a party President, and he proudly claimed that his had "distributed to its party friends as nearly all the civil patronage as any administration ever did."

Lincoln believed in party regularity. In 1864 there was much discontent in New York with Representative Roscoe Conkling, a Radical Republican who sought reelection, and more moderate party members threatened to bolt the ticket. Conkling was no personal friend of Lincoln's. Boasting the "finest torso" in American political life, he used to descend upon the harried inmate of the White House and, with his wilting contempt, "his haughty disdain, his grandiloquent swell, his majestic, supereminent, turkey-gobbler strut," proceed to lecture the President on how to conduct the war. But Conkling in 1864 was the regular nominee of the New York Republican Party, and the President wrote a public letter to aid him:

> . . . I am for the regular nominee in all cases; . . . and no one could be more satisfactory to me as the nominee in that District, than Mr. Conkling. I do not mean to say that there [are] not others as good as he is in the District; but I think I know him to be at least good enough.

Lincoln made the politicos pay for his support. They could vote against administration bills and they could grumble in Capitol cloakrooms about presidential "imbecility," but he expected them to support his renomination. Those who refused were cut off from patronage and promotion. When Senator Samuel C. Pomeroy of Kansas tried to organize the Chase boom in 1864, every patronage plum in his state was snatched from his greedy hands. After a few months of dignified hostility, Pomeroy sidled up to the White House and begged forgiveness. But Lincoln, who could be so forgiving to sleeping sentinels and deserting soldiers, had no mercy for defecting politicians, and Pomeroy went hungry.

Using the sure goad of patronage, Lincoln's agents early in 1864 began lining up delegates to the Republican national convention. Before the other presidential hopefuls knew that the round-up had begun, Lincoln had corralled enough votes to insure his renomination. The work of the Lincoln men in a state like New Hampshire is instructive. Dignified Salmon P. Chase was making eyes toward this state where he had been born, but while he was still flirting at a gentlemanly distance, New Hampshire eloped with Lincoln. Shrewd Lincoln agents, dispensing patronage to the faithful and threats of punishment to the disobedient, moved in on the state convention at Concord in January 1864 and rushed through a resolution calling for Lincoln's renomination. They permitted New Hampshire Republicans to mention their native son, Chase, in the state platform — but only in order to urge that he clean up the corruption in his Treasury Department.

Everywhere it was the same — Connecticut, Pennsylvania, New York, and even Chase's own Ohio. From state after state Chase's friends protested: "I have never seen such an exhibition of office holders in any convention before." But, packed or not, these conventions chose the delegates to the national assembly at Baltimore. By March Lincoln's renomination was assured, and, with poor grace, Chase was compelled to withdraw from a hopeless contest.

Patronage had helped defeat Lincoln's enemies within the Republican party, and patronage would help defeat the Democratic nominee, George B. McClellan. No one knows how much money the Republicans spent in the 1864 campaign — indeed, no one knows how much either major party has spent in any campaign — but it is certain that a large part of the sum came from assessments levied upon Federal officeholders. A man who received a job from Lincoln might expect to contribute regularly ten per cent of his income to the Republican campaign chest; some gave much more. Henry J. Raymond, chairman of the Republican National Committee, planned systematically to levy upon war contractors, customs officers, and navy-yard employees. When the upright Secretary of the Navy protested this proposal "to take the organization of the navy yard into their keeping, to name the Commandant, to remove the Naval Constructor, to change the regulations, and make the yard a party machine for the benefit of party, and to employ men to elect candidates instead of building ships," Raymond summoned him into the President's office in the White House and gave the Secretary a little lecture on the political facts of life, with Lincoln silently approving each word.

In the long run, though, it took not merely delegates and money but votes to carry the election. During the summer of 1864 the war was going badly. "I am a beaten man," Lincoln said in August, "unless we can have some great victory." As late as October he calculated that he would carry the electoral college by only six votes — three of them from the barren desert of Nevada, which Lincoln leaders in Congress had providently admitted to the Union precisely for such an emergency.

Although propriety prevented him from campaigning, the President personally concerned himself with the turn-out of Republican voters in key states like Indiana, Ohio, Pennsylvania, and New York. Seeing that the Northwestern states were going to show a closely balanced vote, Lincoln wrote in September to General Sherman, whose army was in a tight spot in Georgia: "Any thing you can safely do to let [your] soldiers, or any part of them, go home to vote at the State election, will be greatly in point." Although he added: "This is, in no sense, an order," Lincoln was clearly giving a directive, and it was one that Sherman promptly obeyed. The Republicans carried the Northwest by narrow majorities.

In the East, too, the soldier vote was crucial. Pennsylvania Republicans, fearing defeat, persuaded the President to furlough thousands of soldiers just in time to return home and vote. When the ballots were counted, Lincoln had carried the state by only twenty thousand and would have lost it entirely but for the army. In New York the soldier influence on the election was somewhat different. There, allegedly to prevent rioting, daredevil Republican General Benjamin F. Butler was put in charge of Federal troops and, over the protests of New York officials, he stationed plainclothesmen at the polling-places and had four regiments of troops waiting on ferryboats, ready to "land and march double quick across the island" — just in case there were Democratic disturbances. Some years later, reviewing his career, Butler denied that he had earned his military laurels in the Louisiana campaign. ". . . I do not claim," he said modestly, "to be the hero of New Orleans. Farragut has that high honor; but I do claim to be the hero of New York city in the election of 1864, when they had an honest election, the only one before or since." A Democrat might question the "honesty" of the proceedings, but, under the protection of Federal bayonets, New York went Republican by seven thousand votes.

November 8 was a "rainy, steamy and dark" night in Washington, but politicians gathered in the War Department to await the telegraphic election returns. Most of the visitors were tense, but Abraham Lincoln was relaxed, "most agreeable and genial all the evening." At a little midnight supper he "went awkwardly and hospitably to work shoveling out the fried oysters" to others, and more than once he was reminded of a little story. A mishap to one of the guests brought to mind an anecdote about wrestling which began: "For such an awkward fellow, I am pretty sure-footed. It used to take a pretty dextrous man to throw me." His political management of the Civil War demonstrated that Abraham Lincoln was still sure-footed. By dominating his party, securing a renomination, and winning re-election, a superb politician had gained the opportunity of becoming a superb statesman.

Black Reconstruction in the South

Resuming full partnership within the Union was one half of the reconstruction process after 1865. The other half was reconstructing southern society to accommodate the changes the war had produced. Part of this was purely physical. Much of the upper South had been a battleground for the contending armies and had been devastated. Where Sherman's army had swung through Georgia and the Carolinas, it had created a blackened swath of destruction. Substantial towns like Columbia and Atlanta had been almost totally burned out. The South's railroads and factories had either been destroyed or had worn out from excessive use and poor maintenance. Financial loss was added to physical damage. Millions of dollars of paper assets were swept away with the bankruptcy of the Confederate government and the collapse of the banks.

More serious was the social disruption produced by emancipation and the end of slavery. As has often been noted, Lincoln's Emancipation Proclamation of 1863, applying as it did only to regions of the South out of reach of federal power, did not itself free a single slave. But Union armies did, in vast numbers, and by the time of Confederate surrender in April 1865, slavery was dead. This event profoundly disturbed the South's social and economic arrangements. Four million former slaves, without previous experience as citizens or as breadwinners, were suddenly told that they were on their own. The Freedmen's Bureau, it is true, attempted to provide some economic help and guidance for ex-slaves, but it was spasmodic, inconsistent, short-lived, and, as we would say today, underfunded. Political help came from so-called scalawags, southerners who embraced the new order, and carpetbaggers, northerners who came south to take advantage of it. Moved by both civic spirit and avarice, these white men helped organize the freedmen politically within the ranks of the Republican party. Joining with talented black leaders, these white radicals succeeded in modernizing and liberalizing the constitutions of the former Confederate states and in providing expanded social services and educational opportunities for all southerners, white and black.

But though the ex-slave was now a citizen, he was also still part of the labor force, and a part that was largely unskilled and illiterate. Could the blacks be reintegrated into the southern economy as free men without massive economic disruption? Slavery had done little to prepare them for the market economy the nation endorsed, and many white men were fearful that, under the new regime, ex-slaves would not be willing to work, and the southern economy would stagnate.

Interwoven with this was the social issue: Would the blacks become a wage-earning proletariat, or would they be encouraged to become owners of property? Prevailing Jeffersonian values hallowed the yeoman and the family farm, and held that both the political and economic health of society demanded that there be a large class of small landholders. The recent Homestead Act had embodied this Jeffersonian ideal, but the lands to which it applied were largely in the Northwest, far removed from the South and from the cotton culture that the ex-slaves knew best.

Given these circumstances, it would have surely been wise for the federal government to have provided land for the freedmen. A number of prominent Radicals saw this clearly and sought to redistribute the land of prominent Confederates among them. Some land actually passed to ex-slaves through the efforts of the Freedmen's Bureau. But on the whole, little was done by Congress to create a black yeomanry. In the following essay, Joel Williamson discusses the actual economic readjustments that occurred in one southern state, South Carolina, in the absence of federal guidance.

FOR FURTHER READING:

DuBois, William E. B. *Black Reconstruction in America, 1860–1880.* New York: Atheneum Publishers, 1969.*

Stampp, Kenneth M. *The Era of Reconstruction, 1865–1867.* New York: Random House, Vintage Books, 1965.*

Wharton, Vernon Lane. *The Negro in Mississippi, 1865–1890.* Harper & Row, Publishers, Torchbooks, 1965.*

Asterisk denotes paperback edition.

New Patterns in Economics

JOEL WILLIAMSON

Before the end of Reconstruction, the Negro in South Carolina found that the pattern of his employment was already well defined. In agriculture, he belonged to one or more of four distinct groups. Either he rented the land upon which he worked, labored for wages, sold his supervisory skills as a foreman or a manager, or owned his own land.

In the first days of freedom, the Negro agrarian usually found himself in one of the first two categories. His desire to rent land was strong and persistent. He was also averse to working for wages and, especially, to working in gangs under direct supervision. David Golightly Harris, visiting Spartanburg village on January 4, 1866, observed: "The negroes all seem disposed to rent land, & but few are willing to hire by the day, month or year." Occasionally, the desire to rent became a mania. "I am about renting some land on the aint (Aunt) Juriy Hemphill place to Bek, Smith Sam & Peggy," wrote a Chester County planter in November, 1869. "They have hardly corn for Bread & will make nothing but are rent Crazy & must be gratified."

In the first years after manumission, renting was poor economics for most freedmen. Few had the managerial experience, and fewer still had the capital necessary to succeed as independent renters. Moreover, the late 1860's was a period of agricultural depression. Landowners were aware of these problems and, in addition to their aversion to renting land to Negroes for social and political reasons, they op-

Source: Joel Williamson, *After Slavery: The Negro in South Carolina During Reconstruction, 1861–1877* (Chapel Hill: University of North Carolina Press, 1965), chap. 5, "New Patterns in Economics," pp. 126–163.

posed the practice as economically unsound. "Negroes will not do to rely upon as croppers," journalized David Harris in the spring of 1869. "They will not [look] far enough ahead to do any good." As buildings, fences, ditches, and lands deteriorated under the neglect of successive tenants, resistance to renting to either blacks or whites became stronger among landowners. In the spring of 1868, Harris recorded a complaint frequently heard: "I have no little trouble to get my renters to do such work [maintenance], & have almost determined never to rent again. I sometimes think that if I can [not] hire hands to work my land as I want it done, it shall not be worked at all."

Possibly, the Negro renter made his choice against the clear dictates of agrarian economy because he wanted to free himself from the pattern of life he had known as a slave. As a wage laborer, he would have continued to live in the plantation village and to work in gangs under the eye of the white man. As a renter, he labored independently and lived with his family upon his own farm, having either moved a cabin from the plantation village or, as frequently happened, having built a new one upon his plot of earth.

Statistically, the "rent crazy" Negroes often had their way. A generation after emancipation, 37 per cent of the Negro farmers in the state were renters, a large majority occupying plots of less than fifty acres. Indeed, renting became the usual form of land tenure in the upcountry. For instance, of thirty-four Negro farmers who testified on the subject before a Congressional committee in the spring of 1871, twenty-one were renters, eight were wage laborers, and five owned their own land. Further, renting existed in considerable degree in every part of the state. "The negroes who cultivated cotton, as a general rule, rented land from their former masters," reported one native several decades later.

Negro renters paid their landlords in a variety of ways, but, generally, the method of payment belonged to one of two broad categories. In South Carolina in 1880, about one-quarter of the farm operators of both races compensated landlords with a share of the crop. Renting land for a share of the proceeds tended particularly to pervade those areas where cotton was grown; and, even after the return of prosperity, many planters (or landowners) continued to adhere to the system, deeming it more profitable than slavery. This was especially true in the upcountry. "In the upper counties the negroes work better and the masters treat them fairly, so that in some cases farms are still worked on shares with a profit to both parties," reported a Northern correspondent in 1874.

The proportion of the crop paid for the use of land normally varied from one-half to three-quarters, depending largely on the goods and animals that the landlord supplied in addition to the land. The share arrangement was thus capable of endless variety and complexity. For instance, in Edgefield District in 1866, Alfred rented a certain acreage from his late master for one-third the expected crop. However, for the cultivation of another plot, Alfred was to get a tenth of the gross yield in payment for his services as stockminder, then the owner was to have a third of the remainder as rent, and the last two-thirds was to go to Alfred as wages.

In 1880, slightly less than a quarter of the farm operators in South Carolina were renters who paid their landlords a fixed-cash rental. Like share-renting, the term fixed-cash renting covered a wide variety of methods of payment. A common device was the payment of the rent by a specific quantity of a given crop. Thus, in St. Paul's Parish, Colleton District, in December, 1865, "Miles (a Freedman of Colour) and Alfred E. Stokes of the same place" agreed to rent sixteen acres of land from

Charles H. Rice for the coming season. The rental was to be paid in November, 1866, and consisted of sixty-four bushels of corn and a third of the "peace and fodder that may be made." Frequently, Negro renters paid a money rental for their land. For instance, a planter near Adams Run filled his plantation with renters at five dollars per acre, whereas another planter in St. Andrews Parish, in 1872, had difficulty finding renters at three dollars an acre. Occasionally, labor was given in total or partial payment of rent. In Spartanburg County, David G. Harris recorded the terms of a contract with a Negro renter for 1869: "Prince morris has built a house[,] garden[,] cut a ditch & cleared an small field. He gives me Sim's [his son's] labour this year for this land."

To meet the needs of the renter, the landlord, the crop, and of the land itself, rental arrangements often assumed a bewildering complexity as various methods of sharing and paying produce, cash, and labor were combined to provide a satisfactory rental. In 1871 in Colleton County, seven renters (two of whom may have been white) agreed to six different arrangements with the same landowner. Benjamin Kelley agreed to pay the owner a fourth share which was to be used by Kelley himself to improve the house on his rented plot. A pair of renters agreed to work a mule for the owner on a given field and to pay the owner a half of the yield from this field in addition to the fourth due from their main plot. Didemus Allen agreed to farm four acres and to pay the owner two bushels of corn per acre and a fourth of all else he grew. Jerry Smith, a Negro, agreed to pay on Christmas Day, 1871, $12.00 plus a fourth of the produce from a twenty-acre plot that he was allowed to use. In the following year, Jerry contracted with the owner to set up ten thousand turpentine boxes on his land and to divide the profits of the enterprise evenly.

Contrary to the general impression, the plantations of South Carolina did not at the end of the war immediately crumble into many small parts. Indeed, probably most plantations continued to be worked, on a reduced scale, as integral units using wage labor. In the rice districts, fragmentation was impossible since the production of that crop required dikes, ditches, and flood gates which could only be constructed and maintained by a number of laborers organized under a well-financed management. Although few rice plantations were restored to full productivity during Reconstruction, many of these were operated as units. On the other hand, many cotton plantations were indeed divided into small farms and operated under the rental system. Even in the cotton areas, however, some plantations continued to be operated as units for some time after the war, and many planters who rented portions of their lands to others frequently retained large "home places" which they managed themselves.

Employers placed restrictions upon Negro wage laborers that were much more onerous than those imposed upon renters by landlords. The amount, the time, and, frequently, the quality of the wage hand's labor were closely prescribed in his contract, and any delinquency in his performance was severely penalized by fines. In the early years of Reconstruction, the task — the unit of labor used in the slave period — was widely utilized. Ideally, a task was an amount of work which an adult Negro of average abilities could do well in a day's time. The contract signed by thirty-six wage laborers on the Peter B. Bacot plantation in Darlington District in 1867 was typical: "The said servants agreed to perform the daily tasks hitherto usually allotted on said plantation, to wit: 125 to 150 rails; cutting grain 3 to 6 acres; ditching & banking 300 to 600 feet; hoeing cotton 70 to 300 rows an acre long; corn 4000 to 6000 hills. In all cases where tasks cannot be assessed, they agree to labor diligently ten hours a day." While the task system of measuring labor tended to persist in the rice areas, elsewhere there was a general trend toward substituting a given number of hours of labor per day. Ten hours daily was the usual requirement, beginning at or shortly after sunrise and ending at sunset, with greater and lesser periods of freedom allowed for the noon meal as the days lengthened and shortened. Often, attempts were made to control the quality of labor by including in contracts provisions binding Negroes to work "as heretofore," or to "the faithful discharge of his duties as an industrious farm labourer doing whatever he is directed to do . . ." The fine for "absence, refusal or neglect" was everywhere fifty cents for each day lost, and illness gave no exemption from the penalty. Absence from the plantation without leave was subject to fine at the rate of two dollars a day. Persistent absence or misbehavior was punishable by expulsion from the plantation and forfeiture of any claim to wages at the end of the year.

Contracts also included a host of minor regulations designed to enhance the efficiency of the laborer. Typically, the laborer was "not to leave the premises during work hours without the consent of the Proprietor or his Agent," and "not to bring visitors without permission." On some plantations, laborers were committed to observe silence in their cabins after nine o'clock in the evening, "to bring no ardent spirits at any time upon the plantation," and not to have private livestock or pets or to converse with one another in the fields. Often, the laborers as a group were required to supply from their numbers a foreman, a nurse when sickness occurred, a stockminder, and a watchman for the harvested crop. Employers also sought to use the contract to enforce a proper demeanor upon their Negro employees. Thus, laborers were often bound to "perfect obedience," promptness, diligence and respectful conduct," or "to conduct themselves faithfully, honestly & civilly," or to be "peaceable, orderly and pleasant," or "reliable and respectful and to mind all directions," or "to be kind and respectful to Employer and Agent," or to "treat the Employer with due respect." Disrespectful behavior, evidenced by "impudence, swearing; or indecent and unseemly language," was often punishable by fines. Finally, the laborer was invariably bound to pay for the loss or injury of tools and animals either through neglect or by his willful act.

In return for his toil, the agricultural laborer was paid by combinations of goods, services, and cash. In the early postwar years, most received at the end of the season a share of the crop, commonly a third of the gross yield. As with share-renting, the proportion taken by the employer depended largely on the degree to which he maintained his employees. In 1869, an upcountry editor averred that contracts usually granted the laborer a third of the crop in lieu of wages. However, he added, if the employer fed the laborer a weekly ration of four pounds of meat and one peck of meal with small allowances of coffee, salt, sugar, and lesser items, the share granted was a fourth. Share-wage arrangements were often very complicated. For example, on the MacFarland plantation in Chesterfield District, in 1866, twenty-five Negro workers agreed to share evenly with the landowner the net profit of the year after a fourth of the cotton crop or seven bales, whichever was less, was deducted for rent and the overseer's wages and other expenses had been paid.

Neither the share nor the specific amount of money the laborers received for their share was the ultimate measure of the individual's wages. On virtually every plantation, wage laborers contracted as a group, and the share which they earned collectively was divided among them in proportion to the working capacity of each as agreed upon in the contract itself. Thus, a full hand was paid a certain amount, while three-quarter, half, and quarter hands received proportionately less. In addition, employers promised "to furnish each family with quarters on his plantation & a garden plot and the privilege of getting firewood from some portion of the premises indicated by the Employer . . ." Also, laborers were sometimes allowed an "outside crop." A. H. Boykin, in Kershaw County, in 1875, permitted his dozen workers to cultivate as much land as "each thinks he can work every other saturday . . ." Further, he promised to let each employee keep "one cow & one hog," not unusual concessions ten years after emancipation. Occasionally, special allowances were made for family chores. On Dean Hall plantation on the lower Cooper River, in 1866, the contract provided that "only half a day's work on Saturdays will be required of female employees who are heads of families." Employers usually agreed to advance goods and services to their employees, the costs of which were deducted from their share at the end of the season. Whether a part of the contract or not, most employers were forced to supply rations to their employees to enable them to finish the season. In addition, they often advanced other items: tobacco, salt, molasses, blankets, overcoats, shoes, taxes, medical care, and even, with striking frequency, preachers' salaries, coffins, and grave sites. Sometimes, too, the laboring force was required to pay a fraction of the cost of fertilizer, insurance, bagging, and rope — all of which were advanced in the same manner by the employer.

Although it was true that many impoverished planters had no other resort in the early postwar years when cash was scarce, there are indications that many planters and laborers deliberately elected, at first, to use the share system. "I found very few [planters] — not more than one or two, who were offering monthly wages," wrote the owner of extensive lands on the Cooper River in February, 1866. "All on the Cooper River as far as I could learn were offering a share in the crops whether from a want of ability to pay wages &c or because they believed an interest in the crop would secure a more steady course of labor and prevent stealage, I know not, perhaps both." Many Negro workers, themselves, preferred shares to cash wages. "The negroes will not contract for wages," reported a lowcountry planter in the winter of 1866. In the fall of the same year, the majority of a large meeting of Negro laborers gathered in Sumter rejected a suggestion to change to cash wages, clinging "to their preference for a moiety of the crops." One planter thought the Negroes preferred goods to money because they feared: "Maybe it git lak Confeddick money."

Nevertheless, the great majority of planters shifted to money wages within the first few years after the war. Even in 1867, the number of planters paying cash wages, either entirely or partly, greatly increased. A cotton planter on Cooper River who ran "ten steady plows & more as the necesity [sic] calls for them and 30 hoe hands" wrote to a friend in the spring of 1867 that "We pay money for our labour half cash at the End of Each month." A Northern correspondent reported in that year that the few Sea Island planters who could afford it had shifted to monthly wages; and another, writing in 1874, asserted that the share system had been "entirely abandoned" in the lowcountry a year or two after the war and that most planters "now pay their hands monthly wages."

A preference for cash wages also spread among Negro laborers. In June, 1874, a planter on the Combahee River reported that "The negroes now work for money & I have to send out & pick them up where I can get them, & am obliged to take what I can get in order to get along." Such was still the case in the following winter:

"Uncle Hawk is here with some hands that know how to work & will work here all the week, they work for money, exclusively, & don't draw from the Commissary." As described earlier, the Combahee Riots in 1876 were partly caused by the desire of Negro laborers for payment of their wages in cash.

Definitions of the amount of labor demanded of an employee who worked for cash and the manner in which his wages were paid varied widely. On the whole, however, both were much less complicated than share agreements, and the parties concerned often dispensed entirely with formal, written contracts. A Combahee planter described one of his arrangements in 1875: "I have hired John Barnwell to Plow & attend to the mules at $5.00 per month, & give him 2 lbs meat & a package of flour per week . . ." In the early postwar years, planters, suspicious of the constancy of Negro labor, were prone to withhold a portion of their employees' wages until the crop was harvested. In Newberry District, in 1866, for instance, an employer contracted to retain half the wages due his employees until "after summer work begins," and the other half until the end of the year to insure "faithful performance." By the end of Reconstruction, however, most wage laborers were paid daily, weekly, or monthly, had contracted with their employers individually rather than collectively, and had taken a giant step away from the organizational forms of slavery.

Cash wages were also paid for part-time labor. Employees working on shares were paid cash for extra work. For instance, in 1867, the owner of Dirleton plantation on the Pee Dee contracted to pay fifty cents per day in wages to those share-laborers who would do "plantation work," particularly "carpenter work," beyond the terms of their contract. Extra labor, on and off the plantation, was hired "to get the crop out of the grass," or to assist in its harvesting. Gathering in the cotton crop was a usual occasion for hiring additional laborers, and the standard rate of fifty cents per hundred pounds of cotton picked soon became the fixed wage. In the lowcountry, many Negroes owning or renting small plots worked as day laborers whenever they could. In 1868, the Reverend John Cornish was breakfasting with John Jenkins at Gardenia Hall near Adams Run when "quite a gang of negroes came up the avenue with their hoes in hand, looking for work — John sent them into his cotton field — gives them 20cts a task — if very hard 25cts. In this way John is cultivating 30 odd acres of cotton this year — has but one hand constantly employed, & that is his plough man — "

In the Sea Islands generally, and on some rice plantations on the Cooper River, the payment of wages by a combination of land allotments and cash called the "two-day system" came to be widely practiced. As applied to cotton on the Sea Islands, the system involved the laborer's giving two days of work a week (usually Monday and Tuesday) during the ten-month working season in return for quarters, fuel, and five to seven acres of land to work as he wished. Additional labor performed for the planter was paid for in cash at the rate of fifty cents a day or task. "Laborers prefer this system," asserted an agricultural expert in 1882. The system was also applied to rice culture. Gabriel Manigault, having just completed the 1876 season on Rice Hope on the Cooper River, urged his brother Louis, who had had an unsuccessful year in rice on a Georgia Sea Island, to exchange land for two days' labor a week and to hire workers for two more, thereby cutting his cash expenses from $5,000 to $3,000 a year and avoiding "the paying of wages at every step." The "two-day system," too, was capable of infinite variation. In 1868, for instance, rice planters near Adams Run were said to give two and a half acres of rice land, two pounds of bacon, and four quarts of corn in exchange for three days of labor each week. Here again, possibly, the preference of the Negro worker for the "two-day system" marked his desire for greater independence in economic pursuits.

A third class of Negro agricultural worker emerged under the title of "foreman," or, less frequently, "agent" or "manager." Functionally, the foreman was the all too familiar "driver" of the slave period trading under a new label. Francis Pickens inadvertently recognized this fact when he drafted his first contract to employ his ex-slaves as free laborers. In that document he, at first, bound his workers "to obey faithfully the Overseer or Driver." Having second thoughts, he crossed out the word "Driver" and substituted "Agent." The primary function of the foreman (as that of the driver had been) was the day-to-day assignment of tasks to individual laborers and seeing that they were properly done. Unlike the driver, however, the foreman did not carry a whip as his badge of office, and his demeanor was often in sharp contrast with that of the driver. In 1868, the mistress of El Dorado, a lowcountry plantation, noted this development with disgust. "The work here consists in going out at 9 & hoeing in a very leisurely manner till 12 — when they disappear for the day," she reported. "The 'foreman' escorts the women with an air of gallantry — & Mary P. one day heard him saying in the most courteous manner — 'Hide your grass, ladies, hide your grass.' " Further, the foreman frequently assumed the obligations of a full field hand, laboring alongside his charges and, thus, becoming more of a leader among equals than a superior. Contracts typically bound all hands to obey the foreman equally with the owner, and occasionally, foremen possessed the power to discharge "disrespectful and idle or unfaithful" employees. Foremen were doubtless numerous because plantations which continued to be farmed as a unit invariably relied upon the services of at least one member of this class.

The foreman sometimes earned only as much as a full hand, sometimes more. In 1866, H. L. Pinckney made James, an ex-slave who had not been a driver, foreman over some thirty-three field hands on his Sumter District plantation. For his trouble, James seems to have received only a full hand's share of the crop. Two years later, Pinckney broke his force into three groups of which James, Mitchell (another Negro), and the owner himself were the leaders. James and Mitchell, apparently, received only the shares due full hands. Francis Pickens, in contrast, was very liberal in compensating his foremen. In 1866, he agreed to pay Jacob, who had been one of his drivers in the slave period, $100 at the end of the year and to keep him and his five dependents "in the old fashion." Comparatively, two years later, Pickens employed a "field labourer" for the year at $60 and maintenance.

Largely out of the ranks of the foremen, there arose a higher level of agricultural supervisors who might be described collectively as the "managerial class." Managers differed from foremen in that their primary concern was with yearly, rather than daily, operations, though they usually performed both functions. In essence, the manager substituted for the absentee owner. He planned the crops, scheduled the various phases of cultivation and harvesting, executed the schedules, kept the records, attended to the health, welfare, and efficiency of the laboring force, and prepared, shipped, and frequently marketed the finished product. The manager might also do field work, but he was clearly more than a field hand. He was the fully authorized agent of the owner, filling an office which before the war was dominated by whites. Frequently, the manager received a special share of the profits from the owner. Occasionally, he became the lessee of the plantation and operated it for his own profit and, thus, passed into the entrepreneurial class where he competed directly with white men.

The Negro manager in action was personified by Adam R. Deas. He had been born a slave, the son of Robert, a driver on The Grove, a rice plantation near Adams Run belonging to John Berkeley Grimball. In July, 1863, during an inland raid conducted by Union gunboats and a portion of the First South Carolina Volunteers, he fled to the Union lines along with the entire Negro population of The Grove, including his father, his mother Amy, and his grandmother Sally. Like so many refugee families, they pre-empted a plot on Edisto Island in the spring of 1865 and remained there through 1866. In the spring of 1866, however, Robert contracted with Grimball to serve as caretaker of The Grove and an adjacent rice plantation, Pinebury, which was also owned by Grimball. In return, Robert was allowed to farm whatever portion of land he chose with a mule provided by Grimball. Adam's mother and grandmother, however, elected to remain on Edisto, partly because they had already begun a crop.

Through 1868, Grimball attempted unsuccessfully to resume profitable operations on his two rice plantations. In 1865 and 1866, he and his son, Arthur, were unable to induce their ex-slaves to return from their Edisto homes. In 1867, Robert persuaded a few Negroes to plant rice on The Grove, paying a third of the produce as a rental. Since Grimball did not provide seed rice and advances, some of these laborers had to earn expenses by working on neighboring plantations and the yield was both late and scanty. In 1868, Pinebury, the buildings of which had been razed and the fields neglected since 1863, was taken up by a Negro manager named Henry Jenkins with the same unsatisfactory results.

In November, 1868, Grimball sent for Adam Deas. Deas, in a letter written in his clear, squarish script, promised to come to Grimball in Charleston within a week. "I was at the Grove on Thursday afternoon," he wrote, catching a scene. "The people are all busy thrashing & I met my father cleaning out the house, expecting you up. I hope the family are all well." In Charleston, early in December, he called on Grimball and agreed to act as the owner's agent in restoring Pinebury to productivity. What happened to Pinebury during the next eleven years was adequate testimony to Deas's worth as a manager. On December 5, Adam returned to the country and on December 9 he wrote: "The time being so Short I was out from 6 oclock this morning up [to] 10½ oclock to night, the Place being in Such bad order & no Building. It is a hard Task for me to gat any one, but up to this date the 9th, I have the Promise of 15 hands who Expect to move Right on the Plantation." On December 21, while laborers were searching for places for the coming year, he again reported to Grimball: "Everybody & my Self are Standing quite Still at present Waiting for Jan . . . So you must allow me a little Chance, I cant go to Work With a Rush, because I have no money." In concluding, he advised Grimball to take any offer for the lease of The Grove which he might receive.

In January, 1869, Deas mustered a score of rice hands on Pinebury and by early February was hard at work. Apparently, however, he had located his family on the Gibbes' plantation, near Willtown, perhaps because there were no buildings remaining on Pinebury. ". . . I was down to the Plantation Purty Much all this Week, and We are trying to do the Best We Can," he informed Grimball. "Just now the men are Buisy Building & preparing Some Where to Put their Provision & Seed Rice." He rejected Grimball's idea of transferring some Pinebury acreage to the Grove. "I don't think Sir that you aught to take a way any of the Pinebury land to Put with the Grove because If We Should not be able to Plant all of It this Season We will Want It to put in order this Summer for the next Season and I am trying to get the Place full up." Several days later, Deas wrote that nothing had been done on the Grove for the coming season. On April 1, while some planters were still seeking laborers, he reported: "We are trying to Push things through in the Best Way We Can We have one Square under water & in a day or 2 We Will have 2 more." By the end of June, the crop was planted. "We have Planted 74 acres of Rice & 50 acres of Corn. We are Now trying to Keep the Grass out of What is Planted." During 1869, Deas acted as Grimball's "agent and nominal leasee" for Pinebury. The payment for his services was a fifth of Berkeley's rental fee of five bushels of rice for each acre of rice land planted and one bushel of rice for each acre of high ground cultivated. On October 26, Deas's commission produced $142.92 in cash.

In 1870, Deas worked on Pinebury under the same terms, but a better yield on increased acreage raised his income to $233.74. In 1871, he received $243.84 for his portion of the crop. In July, 1871, Deas journeyed to Charleston where he signed a three-year contract with Grimball to "cash" rent Pinebury himself for 1000 bushels of rice a year. Hardly had Deas returned to Pinebury when the area was lashed by a hurricane. Nevertheless, by September 3, he reported that the laboring force was hard at work and would soon repair the damage to flood gates, dikes, ditches, and the crop. In 1872, Deas actually leased Pinebury for himself, generously agreeing to pay Grimball the rental which the owner would have received under the previous system only if the plantation were under maximum cultivation. Deas, apparently, intended to profit by using the two-day system to pay his laborers, a system which Grimball had steadfastly refused to utilize. Deas's income from Pinebury in 1872 was about $800, roughly half the salary of a South Carolina circuit judge. By some means Grimball broke the three-year lease, and, in 1873, Deas agreed to manage Pinebury for two-thirds of the yield of 105 acres of rice to be planted. Grimball's share of the crop sold for $946 and Deas's for twice that amount. Deducting $600 in expenses, Deas's income for the year was approximately $1300. Thus, Deas, for the first time, derived a higher income from managing Pinebury than its owner received as a rental.

Grimball was unhappy with the contract for 1873. Even in April, 1873, he had pressed Deas to plant more than the 105 acres stipulated in the agreement. However, a scarcity of laborers prevented further expansion. On June 30, Grimball met Deas in the Charleston office of their marketing agent, Ingraham, and told him he would only agree to share equally both expenses and profits in 1874. In August, Grimball thought that Deas was unwilling to agree to these terms, "says he has made nothing by planting," and complained that even the present terms were too high. Deas was to write his decision. Ultimately, Deas offered Grimball a cash rental of $1200, due on December 1, 1874, and Grimball accepted. The rent was no longer fixed by the acreage planted, and Deas expanded to the fullest the area under cultivation. Perhaps with the benefit of information from the marketing agent, Grimball estimated that Deas's sales grossed $4975 in the year 1874. If this were true, after deducting the expense of planting the increased acreage, Deas's income for the year was about $3,000, a handsome figure in view of the fact that the governor of South Carolina earned only $3,500 during the same period. Grimball agreed to a cash rental in 1875 also, and Deas's profits were probably similar to those of 1874.

Again unhappy with the terms of the contract, Grimball offered, in the summer of 1875, to rent Pinebury to Deas in 1876 for either $1625 in cash or one-third of the net profits. Finally, they agreed to plant at least 150 acres in rice, and the owner was to get a third of the net profits. However, a poor crop and poorer prices produced only about $900 for Grimball and twice as much for Deas. In 1877, they agreed to share both expenses and profits equally. At the end of the year, Grimball resolved to offer Deas a straight 10 per cent commission on profits to act as his manager. It is not clear whether Deas accepted or not, but he did remain in control of Pinebury in 1878 and 1879.

Finally, on December 20, 1879, in a letter addressed to John Berkeley Grimball at 19 Lynch Street, Charleston, Deas severed his connection with Pinebury and gave the owner some parting advice: "It is true I don't expect to plant pinebury next year but things there are moving too slowly. Other planters are moving and you should too, otherwise you allow the hands to Scatter off And it is so much trouble to Get them together again. I know that you dont like to Commence your work until January, but you throw things to far back why Sir you ought [to] be Ploughing now, Giving the Lands to the Rain and Frost." Unfortunately for Pinebury, Grimball did not take Deas's advice. At the end of the year, he gave management of the plantation to his son Lewis, a physician and druggist who had been singularly and repeatedly unsuccessful in his profession. Grimball, himself, remained in Charleston, visiting old friends and being visited, presiding over sessions of the Charleston Library Society, ordering books for the Library, and writing over and over again ever-diminishing lists of the ill-paying stocks and bonds of his and his wife's estates.

A similar story could be told of Bacchus Bryan, a Negro who managed five other hands in planting rice, cotton, and provision crops on a plantation in the vicinity of Adams Run. From 1866 through 1876, Bacchus agreed with the owner, Reverend John Cornish, each year to pay half the yield in return for the use of the land and the advance of supplies. Bacchus's profits were much less spectacular than those of Adam Deas but were probably nearer those of the average manager. For instance, in 1869, Bacchus's share of the cotton crop sold for about $160, and this probably constituted nearly the whole of his cash income for the year.

The Negro manager was a persistent figure in post-Reconstruction South Carolina. In 1888, a Northerner returning to the Sea Islands twenty-five years after he had first come there as a teacher, found that Cuffee, who had been a foreman on one of the plantations, was managing a stock farm for a Northern firm. In 1900, however, there were only 180 farm managers among the 85,000 Negro farm operators in South Carolina, and probably most of these were less like the entrepreneurs Adam Deas and Bacchus Bryan than the salaried Cuffee.

"We all know that the colored people want land," cried the carpetbag delegate from Barnwell District to the members of the Constitutional Convention which assembled in Charleston in January, 1868. "Night and day they think and dream of it. It is their all in all." The speaker hardly exaggerated; yet, at that time, relatively few Negroes had entered the class of agricultural landholders. Some free Negroes had owned land (and, indeed, slaves) before the war, a negligible number had been given lands by their late masters after emancipation, and some two thousand had secured titles to lands on the Sea Islands. But, in view of the desires of Negro agrarians, these were, after all, mere tokens. Under the circumstances, it is hardly surprising that Negro agriculturalists simply shifted the focus of their expectations from the federal to the state government, and that local Republican leaders, mindful of where their strength lay, were anxious to accommodate them.

Doubtless, many Negro voters would have favored confiscation. "I know how hard it was to beat down that idea," declared a Massachusetts man on the floor of the Constitutional Convention. "It has been in their minds that government would some day present them with their old homes and old farms. There is no gentleman on this floor from the country who does not know how much he has had to contend with when he has had to oppose that desire which has been uppermost in the hearts of the people." A few of the most radical of Republican leaders endorsed confiscation. A scalawag delegate to the organizing convention of the Republican party, held in May, 1867, was "perfectly disgusted with the negroes, that they advocate confiscation of lands . . ."; and as late as the campaign of 1870, the scalawag boss of Laurens County was vigorously preaching confiscation with the result, one resident observed, that "none of the men want to work, all looking forward to next month when they expect to get land & houses." White anxiety concerning confiscation was partially justified, but much of the furor was generated by an overly timorous white community. In Spartanburg, in November, 1867, a prospective purchaser of a plot of land was too cautious when he reneged because he was "afraid of confiscation." Furthermore, there were Conservative politicians who were not above promoting and playing upon the anxieties of their friends. "Knowing that the Radicals had scared the Southern people with *Confiscation* by Congress, from the path of honor and patriotism, I thought I would scare them back again with *Confiscation* by the negroes," B. F. Perry wrote to one of his supporters in the spring of 1867. "You have lived long enough in the world . . . to know that most persons are influenced more by their *fears* than by their honor," concluded that gentleman of highly vaunted democratic reputation.

Confiscation met with the early, persistent, and successful opposition of the main body of Republican leadership. In the convention of the party in July, 1867, the idea was not even formally introduced; in the field, campaigners subsequently adopted the same attitude; and the Constitutional Convention of 1868 with the full assent of its Negro delegates pointedly asserted that "The only manner by which any land can be obtained by the landless will be to purchase it." Two years later, in a political meeting at Christ Church, native Negro A. J. Ransier was still answering the charge that Republicans had offered Negroes forty acres and a mule. "We had never," he declared, "promised any such thing, but on the contrary advised the people to buy lands by saving their money, and not to expect confiscation or the possession of lands that were not theirs, nor ours to give them . . ."

To some extent, Republicans rejected confiscation as inexpedient — that is, that titles conferred might be impermanent, that Congress might disallow such a measure, or that whites might be driven to violence. Primarily, however, they refused confiscation because they felt it was contrary to the natural laws of economic morality; it would be useless, they argued, even pernicious, to legislate against the fiats of classical economics. "The sooner the public mind is disabused of that impression, the sooner every man knows that to acquire land he must earn it," declared W. J. Whipper, a Northern-born Negro delegate, to the convention, "the sooner he feels the Government has no lands to dispose of or to give him the better. Do what is necessary to protect the laborer in his labor and you will effect the greatest possible good."

Republican leaders were strong in their rejection of confiscation, but by no means did they abandon the use of political power to achieve the popular goal of a division of large landed estates among their supporters. Ultimately, they settled upon two complementary but separate programs. One of these involved the purchase of lands by the state for division and resale to actual settlers. By the spring of 1869, acting upon an ordinance of the Constitutional Convention, the Republican legislature had created a Land Commission which was to purchase, by the issue of bonds guaranteed by the state, lands at public sales and "otherwise." Under a land commissioner these acquisitions were to be surveyed, divided into smaller tracts, and sold to settlers at the purchase price. The settler would pay taxes on the land and 7 per cent interest yearly on the principal of the loan. One half the plot was to be under cultivation within three years, at which time payments on the purchase price would begin and would extend over such period as the legislature directed.

Almost from its inception the land program was hamstrung by political involvement. At least some Radical politicians thought that the partisan purposes of the relocation scheme were as important as the economic goals. In October, 1869, for instance, a leading Republican concurred in a statement by the land commissioner that party interest dictated "That in the upper counties it is necessary to purchase large tracts, so that colonies may be planted of sufficient strength to help, & protect each other, and to be the nucleas [sic] of education &c &c &c. . . . We must draw the union people to points where they will be a power & mutual supporters." In addition, the office of land commissioner, itself, soon became a political pawn. The first incumbent was Charles P. Leslie, an aging, erratic, unscrupulous New Yorker who was given the office, it was said, to compensate him for losing the United States marshalship which he really wanted. Whatever talents Leslie may have possessed were turned immediately to filling his own pockets, an occupation at which he was very adept. Using $200,000 in bonds authorized by the legislature, Leslie began to buy land at a rapid rate.

A very few purchases were well made at sheriff's sales, from the executors of estates, and by conscientious agents with an eye for a bargain. For instance, Henry E. Hayne, an ex-sergeant of the First South Carolina, acting as Leslie's agent in Marion County, arranged to buy 1734 acres of land for $1,500. The tract contained, by Hayne's report, 200 acres of "good swamp land, a splendid range for cattle &c and good corn and grain land. The balance is good upland, a large portion of woodland. There is good water on the place, several good buildings." The tract was then rented for $100 yearly, suggesting that the offered price was reasonable. But more to the point: "A number of citizens are prepared to purchase small tracts of this property from the State."

Unfortunately, most purchases were made by men less reliable than Hayne. In Darlington County, Leslie's agent bought lands at a sheriff's sale supposedly for the land agency. He later changed the titles to indicate that he had bought them on his own account and then re-sold the land to the state at twice the price he had paid. Throughout the life of the commission, a suspiciously large number of purchases were made from men directly involved in Republican politics — including Governor Scott, himself.

The secretary of state, Francis L. Cardozo, a Negro, had never approved of the choice of Leslie as land commissioner and soon refused to participate as a member of the advisory board. As rumors of fraud and mismanagement in the Land Commission began to circulate, Cardozo and other Negro leaders — including Rainey, Whipper, Elliott, Ransier, and Nash — moved to force Leslie out of his post. Dominant in the legislature in the winter of 1870, these men refused to pass a proposed bill authorizing the issuance of an additional $500,000 in bonds for the use of the commission. Leslie and others were very anxious to win the new issue because they had already overspent the amount initially authorized. It was arranged, finally, that Leslie would resign and the legislature would sanction the new issue. According to the subsequent testimony of N. G. Parker, treasurer of the state until 1872, Leslie demanded and got $25,000 in return for his resignation and the surrender of his one-twelfth share in the Greenville and Columbia Railroad. To raise this money, Parker arranged the fraudulent purchase by the commission of some 27,000 acres (one portion of which was appropriately known as "Hell Hole Swamp") for about $119,000 nominally, but actually for much less. D. H. Chamberlain, then attorney-general, discovered that the title to one of these tracts was faulty and that Parker and his associates were aware of the fault. However, he did not expose his findings.

One of the demands of the Negro legislators was the appointment of a Negro as land commissioner. The stipulation was met, but the choice was unfortunate, falling upon R. C. De Large, a native Charlestonian, still young in 1870 and very ambitious politically. Parker later asserted that De Large was Scott's choice and that the latter arranged his appointment so that De Large could steal enough money to unseat scalawag Congressman C. C. Bowen of Charleston, Scott's most bitter personal and political enemy. True or not, De Large was in fact immediately caught up in a year-long, vitriolic campaign against Bowen from which he emerged victorious. During De Large's absence, the scalawag comptroller-general, apparently, took the lead in administering the land program. Again, most purchases were made at exorbitant prices through the agency of or directly from officers of the state, and by 1871 the funds of the commission were exhausted. They were never renewed, but the quality of lands purchased during De Large's tenure did improve somewhat. The improvement may have resulted from the closer scrutiny to which Cardozo and Chamberlain subjected prospective transactions. Since Cardozo, as secretary of state, had to record purchases and Chamberlain, as attorney-general, was responsible for the legitimacy of titles, each man was in a position to block suspicious transactions. During the De Large period, interested parties were, apparently, willing to solicit their approval for purchases and the degree of control which they exercised was considerable.

Criticism within the Republican party during the spring and summer of 1870 forced many officials to defend their connections with purchases made by the commission. Chafing under charges that professional politicians were obstructing the efficient administration of the land program, an aroused legislature ordered the land commissioner to report immediately, formed a joint committee to investigate the program, and passed legislation clarifying the conditions of settlement on state lands. Ultimately, the legislature assigned the duties of the land commissioner to the secretary of state, and, thus, Cardozo, himself, assumed responsibility for the program. A very able administrator, Cardozo quickly systematized the haphazardly kept records of the office, ascertained the location of the one hundred thousand acres in twenty-three counties which belonged to the state, investigated the degree to which these lands were settled, and arranged to receive regular payments from the settlers. In April, 1872, the advisory board permitted the commissioner to base the price of lots (those already sold, as well as those remaining unsold) upon their actual value rather than the price which the state had paid for them. Immediately, a wave of additional settlers moved onto state lands. On one state-owned plantation on St.

John's Island, for instance, fifteen lots which had lain barren for two years were promptly settled by Negro families.

Henry E. Hayne, who succeeded Cardozo as secretary of state in 1872, continued the good work. He improved the administration of the program still more by appointing a single agent, J. E. Green, to replace the many county agents. Green familiarized himself with each tract, encouraged settlement, and made collections. In 1874, Hayne reported that the administration of the program under the new system cost only 8 per cent of collections, whereas before expenses had often exceeded revenues. On one occasion, when settlers were about to be evicted from their Darlington County plots because of a fault in the title purchased by the state, Hayne used the resources of the commission to correct the deficiency. The humane policy of the state was further revealed in February, 1874, when the legislature, following a poor farming season in some areas and a money scarcity which generally prevailed after the panic of 1873, authorized the commissioner to postpone payments in cases where subsistence was endangered.

Strangely enough, although they did not buy new lands to perpetuate the program, the Redeemers continued and improved still further the administration of the Land Commission. Through litigation they added about 1300 acres to the program, the only addition made after 1870. Further, they refunded taxes paid by settlers before titles were granted, it being customary for titleholders to pay tax claims against real estate, in this case the state itself. In November, 1877, about 47,000 acres or one-half of the state's lands remained unsettled. The Redeemers reduced prices on unsold plots, surveyed tracts more suitably, allowed occupants to reduce the size of their farms to adjust to their ability to pay, and passed on the lands of those unable to pay to other settlers.

The end result was that by the late 1880's nearly all the state's lands had been disposed of to actual settlers; and by the early 1890's approximately 2,000 families had obtained titles to farms through the agency of the Land Commission.

Perhaps the most effective scheme of land redistribution implemented by Republicans in South Carolina was also the most subtle. In its earliest form, it was conceived as a heavy tax on unused land. This tax was expected to force owners of such lands either to bear the burden of the tax from their other resources, to put the land under cultivation and thus employ laborers or renters, or to allow the land to be sold either to the state for resale or directly to private parties. As it matured, the basic concept expanded. Not only would unused lands be heavily taxed, but all property, real and personal, used and unused, would be so burdened. Thus, all capital would be forced into full productivity, or, in essence, would be confiscated and sold. One anticipated result of the program was that a large quantity of land would be offered for sale at prices that the landless could afford to pay. Also, heavy taxation would support a prospective expansion of public services rendered by the state: internal improvements; care for the insane, orphans, and indigents; a modern penitentiary; a streamlined and efficient judiciary; and, most important, a system of public education from primary to university levels. Heavy taxation, then, was the core of the Republican program in Reconstruction South Carolina. It was a program designed to give its supporters land, educational opportunity, and other benefits that would imbue them with a spirit of loyalty to the party and insure its continuance in power.

From its birth, the Republican party in South Carolina consciously and deliberately advocated land division through taxation. "We must drive them to the wall by taxation," cried one carpetbagger to a Republican convention in the summer of 1867. While the convention was more circumspect in its choice of words, its resolution on the subject was commonly interpreted as an endorsement of a tax program which, as one Negro delegate observed, "would force owners of large tracts of waste lands to sell and give us a chance." As the campaign for the Constitutional Convention of 1868 proceeded, the tax program supplanted confiscation in popularity. Such a program, one observer noted, would be as effective as confiscation, "and yet avoid the strenuous opposition that any scheme of general land pillaging would infallibly meet with in the North." Perhaps, with this criticism in mind, the Convention itself decided to tax all real and personal property at a single, uniform rate based upon actual values. This amendment did not mean that the party had deserted the tax program. The carpetbag delegate who was soon to become the treasurer of South Carolina put the case succinctly:

> Taxes are always (at least in hard times) a burden, will be assessed yearly upon all lands, and they must be paid. The expenses of the State (constantly increasing, will be a continual drag upon those who attempt to carry on large landed estates with a small amount of money,) will alone force sufficient lands upon the market at all times to meet the wants of all the landless. This Convention will cost the State quite a large sum of money. A legislature will soon assemble, and that will cost money. Education, once limited, is to be general, and that will be expensive; and, to keep up with the age, it is fair to presume that the State tax will be greater next year than this, and increase yearly; this will be felt, and will be the stimulus to many for owning less land, and cause them to see the necessity for disposing of their surplus.

The Convention adopted other measures which were to supplement the tax program. It requested and obtained from the military authorities a stay law — or rather order — designed to delay forced sales of lands to allow the landless an opportunity to accumulate capital and the tax program time to depress land prices. Once the agriculturalist had acquired a small holding, the Convention sought to protect him against the direct effects of forced sales in civil actions by a constitutional provision that exempted from such sales a homestead worth $1000 and personal property worth $500. A suggested corollary to the tax program would have required state officers to subdivide all tracts sold for taxes into plots of 160 acres or less. This proposal met with the sympathy of the Convention, but the majority ultimately decided that no satisfactory defense could be made against monied men buying as many plots as they chose.

Once in power on the state level, Republicans hastened to carry out the tax program. The burden of taxation was shifted from mercantile interests to landed property, and the total tax bill increased rapidly to astounding heights. During Reconstruction, the amount of taxes levied and collected every year was well over a million dollars; before 1860 it had always been considerably less, and, during the Orr regime, had been only about $600,000 — less than one dollar each for every man, woman, and child in the state.

Some Republican politicians contended that the state tax rate in South Carolina was no more than in some Northern states. Such, indeed, was the case, but the whole story of taxation in South Carolina was not told by the *state tax rate.* Actually, the rate was kept deliberately low, but other variables in the tax equation were manipulated to raise the tax bill ever higher. In addition to the state levy, each county taxed its property owners for the administration of regular county affairs and for special purposes such as new buildings and roads. Furthermore, the school tax was often quoted separately. Thus, E. Gelzer, in Abbeville County in 1871, paid a state tax of only $59.64; but, at the same time, he paid a $25.56 county tax and an $8.52 school tax. Property owners residing in towns and cities paid municipal taxes as well. Census returns indicate that Carolinians paid $2,800,000 in state and local taxes in 1870, an enormous sum by prewar standards. Of this amount, $1,600,000, including the school tax, went to Columbia, while almost half was consumed locally.

A second variable in the tax equation was the value placed on property for tax purposes. Before the advent of the Republican regime, the tendency was to under-value property in assessing it for tax purposes; after, the tendency was drastically reversed. This weapon for increasing taxes was sharpened by the authority given to the governor to appoint and remove assessors within each county and by the creation of a State Board of Equalization with power to decrease or increase (two- or threefold if it wished) the assessment of a given county. There was abundant evidence that this power was abused during the first six years of Republican rule. A meeting of Conservative white leaders in Columbia in 1871 admitted that the state tax rate (about 1 per cent at that time) was not excessive but complained that assessments were unduly high. Wide fluctuations in the total of assessments between 1869 and 1873 show clearly that this power was freely used. For instance, in 1870, the figure was placed at $184,000,000. In the hard election year of 1872, it was reduced to $146,000,000, only to be raised again after the election. Even some Republicans deprecated such blatant unfairness. Martin R. Delany, the former major, stated in 1871 that lands were often sold at one-half to one-fourth of the assessed value. "Land in South Carolina is greatly depreciated," he declared, "while taxes have become proportionately higher." "Taxes are enormous," exclaimed a Northern businessman residing in Charleston, voicing a fact all too well known among his land-owning Carolina contemporaries.

Astonishing as the tax bill was in the aggregate, it was even more astounding to the individual taxpayer. In May, 1871, a Chester County planter lamented: "I have paid $400.00 Dollars of Tax this year & expect to pay about $300.00 in the fall making $700 in all. before the war my Tax was from 30 to 50 Dollars. Where does the money go?" By January 6, 1873, he had paid $365 in taxes for that year and would have to pay another large tax bill before the year ended. "I can go to some other place (say Augusta) & live comfortably on my Tax," he asserted.

Republican reform Governor Daniel H. Chamberlain, who held office from November, 1874, until he was ousted by Hampton in April, 1877, made a determined and partly successful attempt to reduce the tax burden. In this he was ably assisted by Secretary of the Treasury Francis L. Cardozo. In 1874, Chamberlain recommended to the legislature an across-the-board reduction in expenditures and, soon thereafter, executed a re-assessment of taxable property throughout the state which very nearly equalized assessed and market values. When the legislature passed a tax bill in the spring that exceeded his recommendations, Chamberlain courageously vetoed it, and in the legislative session of 1875–1876 he succeeded in reducing the rate of taxation from 13 to 11 mils.

Chamberlain won much praise and considerable support from the native white community for his efforts, but other circumstances were operating in the fall of 1875 to turn the tide of taxpayer sentiment against him. In the counties and cities where corruptionists remained entrenched, local tax rates were largely beyond the control of the governor. In spite of Chamberlain's reforms, these drove the total tax bill for their areas to great heights. In heavily agricultural Kershaw County, yearly taxes (county and education, as well as state) amounted to about 2 per cent of the total value of taxable property. Taxpayers, under such circumstances, were hardly impressed with the fact that Chamberlain had saved them from a 2.2 per cent levy. One upcountry editor queried, "Does this mean reform or confiscation?" Even in counties under native white control, where local levies had been kept at a consistent minimum, Chamberlain's moderate gains were more than offset by the decline in cotton profits and the increase in food costs which began in the fall of 1875. "Our crops are poorer, the prices range much lower than for years past, while flour and bacon are higher," complained an Anderson County editor early in December. When he learned that the tax rate for his county was to be about 1.5 per cent he cried, "Thus our worst fears are realized."

The results of the Republican tax program were everything that its authors anticipated — and more. Vast quantities of land were forfeited to the state every year, and others passed under the hammer to satisfy judgments rendered in civil suits. When the Republicans took office, the state held only about 23,000 acres of land forfeited for taxes. This figure dwindled into insignificance as tax foreclosures by the Radical government proceeded. In the early 1870's, the local press, particularly in the middle and lower counties, abounded in advertisements of tax sales. During the state fiscal year which ended October 31, 1873, officials reported 270,000 acres of land as forfeited for about $21,000 in taxes; and in the following year the figure rose to more than 500,000 acres. Interestingly, the twelve counties in which the most land was forfeited were precisely those dozen counties in which the proportion of Negro to white voters was highest.

White landowners in the lower counties were convinced that Republican tax collectors were, indeed, conspiring to "drive them to the wall." One Georgetown plantation owner complained in the spring of 1869 that the county tax collector had told him he did not know how much his tax would be or when it would be determined. "The scallawags and capt Baggers would no doubt like right well to see my place advertised and sold for taxes," he surmised. "I trust they will not be gratified." John Berkeley Grimball could have added that confiscation by hook was fully as possible as by crook. In the spring of 1873, he was surprised to see that Pinebury, which Adam Deas was operating, was up for sale within two weeks for delinquent taxes. Hasty inquiry revealed that his tax payment had gone astray and much ado at the county seat eventually brought rectification. In January of the following year, when the tax collector visited Charleston for the convenience of residents owning land in Colleton County, Grimball proceeded to the appointed place prepared to pay his dues, only to find that the collector had fled to avoid meeting a rival claimant to his office. For some days, he tried to locate the elusive collector, always arriving just after the tax agent had departed, pursued by his rival. Finally, he succeeded in passing the duty to the post office by resorting to the use of registered mail.

In the fall of 1875, as agricultural profits declined and the price of foods increased, economic distress began to spread into the white counties. In 1873, no land had been forfeited for taxes in Anderson County, and, in 1874, only two acres were lost to the state. In December, 1875, however, the editor of the local newspaper noted that "a very large amount of property was sold" at the monthly sheriff's sales for the execution of tax and civil judgments against property.

The losses of property owners were not entirely reckoned in the number of acres forfeited. Obviously, all labored under the burden of paying unusually high taxes on lands which had never yielded so little income. J. B. Grimball paid state and local taxes on Pinebury amounting to $119.36 in 1873 and $136.08 in 1874. During the same period, he received about $1200 yearly by leasing the plantation to Adam Deas. Thus, the tax on the property amounted to about 10 and 11 per cent of the gross income in 1873 and 1874 respectively, and, in terms of productivity, these were banner years for Pinebury. Taxpayers were also distressed by the extremes to which they were forced to save their lands from the sheriff. The widow of the most prominent Know-Nothing leader in ante-bellum South Carolina complained to a friend in 1874: "Having six pieces of property not yielding me one dollar, and those demons after taking my Plantation from me, have this year levied 50 per cent Taxes which I have had to sell Silver to pay." Similarly, in 1872, a Charlestonian, noting that the ownership of a plantation "will *cost* me a good deal" during the year, complained: "I don't think you cd get any attempt at resistance in any part of the Old State to an immediate Confiscation of all the property of the whites if the so called Legislature ordered it."

The price of land in South Carolina was depressed after the war and continued to decline until 1868. Even after prosperity returned, prices remained relatively low. In some measure, this was a result of the uncertain political situation; but, more particularly, it was the fruit of the Republican tax program. In 1870, one upcountry farmer painted the picture rather deftly:

> Our country is in a bad condition. Negroes have every thing in their own hands, and do as they please. The Legislature is radical out and out. All or nearly all of our County officers are negroes. The consequence is that lands and every other kind of property is taxed so high that they have decline twenty five percent in value since last fall. Every little negro in the county is now going to school and the public pays for it. There is a negro school near Billy Turners, with over fifty schollars and lands principally are taxed to pay for them. This is a hell of a fix but we cant help it, and the best policy is to conform as far as possible to circumstance . . .

It is evident that many Negroes took advantage of these conditions to acquire lands by purchase. Unfortunately, no census of Negro farm owners was taken in South Carolina before 1890, but in that year 13,075 Negro farmers owned farms of some size. Since only about 4,000 Negroes obtained lands through government agencies, roughly 9,000 Negro farmers must have bought farms through their own efforts during the generation that followed emancipation. A large portion of these realized their desire for land during the eight years of Republican rule. In 1870, Reuben Tomlinson, a Northern missionary who came to the Sea Islands during the war and remained to become a Bureau educator and a state legislator, declared on the floor of the House of Representatives that "If we could get together the statistics of the laboring men who have during the past year become land owners through their own exertions and industry, we would be perfectly astounded." Random evidence seems to bear out this assumption, for one cannot travel far into contemporary writings without encountering numerous incidental references to the sale of land to Negroes.

It is improbable that many Negroes acquired land through cooperative purchases, but on at least two occasions, Negroes formed associations for the purchase of lands. In January, 1868, in the low country, F. L. Cardozo described one such operation to his colleagues in the Constitutional Convention: "About one hundred poor colored men of Charleston met together and formed themselves into a Charleston Land Company. They subscribed for a number of shares at $10 per share, one dollar payable monthly. They have been meeting for a year. Yesterday they purchased 600 acres of land for $6,600 that would have sold for $25,000 or $50,000 in better times. They would not have been able to buy it had not the owner through necessity been compelled to sell." In 1872, a similar group acquired a 750-acre estate on Edisto Island.

The Negro generally paid his poll tax and his one- or two-dollar levy on personal property cheerfully, but once he had acquired lands, he was subject to the same adverse effects of the Republican tax program as his white neighbors. Contrary to the design of the politicians, small holders suffered equally with large. In 1874, a Northern traveler visited the home of a Negro farmer who had bought his land two years previously with two hundred hard-saved dollars. "Now the cabin has fallen into decay, the rain and wind come through great cracks in the walls of the one cheerless room, the man and his wife are in rags, and the children run wild about the parched and stony fields, clothed very much as they were when they first saw the light. Negro voters are not exempt from the visits of the tax gatherer, and it is almost certain that the poor fellow's place will, with many others, be forfeited to the State at the next sale for delinquent taxes." It is hardly surprising that Negro property owners were observed in one lowcountry community in January, 1877, paying taxes for the support of the Hampton government while a Republican still sat in the governor's office.

Native white resistance to the aggressive tax program of the Republicans was at first tentative and cautious. There was, after all, no assurance that Republican rule through Negro voters would ever end and an imprudent resistance might close doors which could never be re-opened. Nevertheless, almost as soon as the first Republican tax bills reached the taxpayers a quiet desperation crept into Conservative politics. "Negro laws will ruin any people," an upcountry farmer advised his brother during the summer of 1869, "those that was not broke by the old debts will be by tax my tax was 57 dollars & 30 cents. I have paid but how long I can do so I dont no but we still hope for better times we think in the year 1870 we will be able to change the law making power . . ." In 1870, native whites looked anxiously to the polls and placed their trust in a "Reform" Republican candidate for governor. "If the Radicals gain the day what is to become of us, I don't see how we can stay in the country," a Laurens resident wrote to her son on the eve of the elections "for our taxes will be increased, and we will be under the very heels of the Radicals." The election was lost and taxes rose as expected. Among John Berkeley Grimball's papers there is an artifact, a clipping from a March, 1871, issue of a Charleston paper. What Grimball saved was an article which concluded with the sentence: "This is a TAXATION which is tantamount to CONFISCATION." Several weeks later, an upcountry woman wrote to her cousin: "I have nothing of a political nature to communicate that would interest you, — nothing much talked of these days except Taxation & the Ku Klux."

It was characteristic of the native white community that their anxiety should lead to meetings and that meetings should soon assume some state-wide organization. The state-wide conference took place in May, 1871, under the name of the Taxpayers' Convention. Even though the convention included Negroes, carpetbaggers, and scalawags, as well as rising young professional politicians within the ranks of the Conservatives, it was dominated by the prewar aristocracy — men such as Chesnut, Kershaw, Aldrich, Trenholm, Porter, Trescot, Bonham, and Hagood. Indeed, it was generally conceded that no comparably distinguished body of men had met in the state since the Secession Convention. Nevertheless, the leadership remained cautious. The debates were temperate, no Republican officeholder was personally impugned, and the resolutions were innocuous: it was in essence a whitewash of the Republican regime.

The Moses administration (1872–1874) brought still higher taxes and consequent agitation among the whites. ". . . our tax this year is full one third higher than last year and it looks to me like that it will finally result in confiscation of the land by Taxation," wrote a Laurens planter in February, 1873. The whites called another Taxpayers' Convention for February, 1874. "Things are blue enough here & the taxation is practically confiscation," wrote a resident of Georgetown in January, "I trust there may be some good in the Taxpayer's [sic] Convention *this time.*" The desperation of the whites rapidly became less quiet, particularly as they began to read signs outside the state which suggested that Negro rule might not be perpetual. The tone of the convention of 1874 was radically different from that of 1871. An impressive delegation of gentlemen from the convention journeyed to Washington where they formally presented to both Grant and the House of Representatives a vigorous indictment of the Republican regime in South Carolina. "It has been openly avowed by prominent members of the Legislature," the memorial of the convention declared, "that taxes should be increased to a point which will compel the sale of the great body of the land, and take it away from the former owners." Perhaps the most important result of the convention was the legacy of organization which it left to the white community. Largely under the leadership of the "Bourbons," local Tax Unions were formed which were to function as the watchdogs of persons in office. These organizations were very active in the 1874 campaign and in supporting the reform programs of the Chamberlain administration. In the fall of 1875, however, the Tax Union rapidly lost ground to more radical elements among the native whites and, by 1876, had virtually ceased to exist.

During 1876, native whites stymied the Republican tax program by extra-legal means. In the fall of 1876, they refused to pay taxes to the Chamberlain government which claimed victory in the November elections while they voluntarily paid 10 per cent of the previous year's levy to the Hampton government. By general concert, native whites also refused to buy lands being sold for taxes. In December, 1876, in Charleston County numerous parcels of land had been forfeited for some $200,000 in taxes and costs, but not one single purchaser could be found for any of these. Once firmly in power, the Redeemers hastened to restore forfeited lands to the tax books and allow delinquents generous limits within which to repair their deficiencies.

Although the great mass of Negroes in Reconstruction South Carolina earned their living through agricultural pursuits, others worked as domestics, as skilled or unskilled laborers, and as business and professional men.

With the exception of agriculture, the domestic class was by far the most numerous economic group. These found employment in various capacities in the homes of the whites. Negro men became butlers, valets, coachmen, gardeners, and handy men. Negro women became housemaids, personal maids, cooks, laundresses, nurses, and serving girls. As described earlier, a general reduction in household staffs occurred immediately after the war. As Reconstruction progressed, further reductions ensued. Typical was the H. L. Pinckney plantation near Statesburg, in Sumter District, in June, 1866, where a unique arrangement prevailed in which ten domestics — two cooks, two houseboys, a house servant, a gardener, a nurse, a housemaid, a washer, and "Louisa — (little)" — were included with thirty-nine agricultural workers in a contract by which all would receive a third of the crop. By 1868, the total work force had been reduced to sixteen, only three of whom were domestics.

In relations with his employer, the Negro domestic experienced grievances similar to those felt by his agrarian contemporaries. His responses, too, were much the same. In a sense, however, he was freer to express his dissatisfaction since desertion — the ultimate reply to unsatisfactory conditions — could follow the daily or weekly payday and he need not forfeit or await the division of a crop. Occasionally, individual domestics revealed a persistent reluctance to remain with any single employer very long. In 1872, in Charleston a Negro cook told her employer that she was leaving the household, not because she was dissatisfied with her position but "because, ma'am, it look like old time to stay too long in one place." However, like their brothers in agriculture, most Negro servants adjusted to the new order during the first years of Reconstruction and established rather permanent relations with a single employer. For instance, in 1870, a lady residing in a large household in the village of Chicora wrote: "We have only made one change in our domestic arrangements since you left [a year previously] & that is in the outdoor department, the indoor servants are all with us still & we go on so smoothly & comfortably that I hope it will be long before we have to make any change."

A glimpse into the life of a servant girl working in one of the Campbell households in Charleston in 1868 is preserved in a letter from her to her aunt in Camden. The girl, Celia Johnson, was a member of a "free" Negro family living in Camden and had come to Charleston as a servant. To her aunt's invitation to visit Camden, she replied that she would like to, but it was too "hard to get away from Mrs. Campbell, and hard to get money." Not all of Celia's life was drudgery. "I spent last Sunday night with sister Mary Stewart, and went to a meetin to the African church. We heard a blind man preacher and had good times." But, there was work to be done. "Excuse this short letter as I am very busy ironing," she concluded. "All the way I will get to go home is to promise to come back in October. If I don't I will make hard feelings . . . I have been sleeping upstairs so long that you will have [to] get me an upstairs room when I get there. I don't know how to sleep down stairs."

In slavery, large numbers of Negroes had performed relatively unskilled labor in the lumbering and turpentine industries and in construction, particularly railroad construction. In freedom, many laborers continued the occupations which they had learned as slaves and these were joined by freedmen who had never before had an opportunity to leave the fields. Frequently, the choice was made even more attractive by the prospect of higher and certain wages in industry. In 1873, a resident of the once rice-rich county of Georgetown noted the growing profitability of the production of naval stores and commented: "The turpentine interest being very lucrative, controls a great deal of labor & the Rice fields suffer thereby." The war, itself, promoted the growth of the laboring population outside of agriculture. During and after the war, hundreds of Negro laborers found employment in the Quartermaster and Engineering departments of the army and in the Freedmen's Bureau. The dislocations of the war and of the months immediately following left large numbers of

Negroes in Charleston and in the towns and villages of the interior. These often earned a subsistence by working as stevedores, street cleaners, yardkeepers, porters, draymen, messengers, and at other unskilled jobs. The repair of war-worn and torn rail lines and a boom in the construction of new lines gave at least temporary employment to several thousand Negro laborers. Many others found jobs in a new and fantastically profitable industry — the mining of phosphates for processing into fertilizers. Some of the rock was dug from tidewater river beds by giant dredges, but large deposits lay on or near the surface of the land. These "land deposits" were mined with pick and shovel, wielded by Negroes under the supervision of white foremen. "A common laborer will raise a ton a day, for which he is paid $1.76," wrote an agricultural expert in 1882. "The product of the land rock is about 100,000 tons a year." Negroes struggling to retain their small farms in the Sea Islands during the hard years following emancipation must have viewed the rise of the phosphate industry as providential.

Many of the free Negroes of Charleston had long earned their living as artisans. A month after their liberation, the Negro tradesmen of the city participated in a parade, described earlier, which indicated the diversity of their occupations and the solidity of their organization. Free Negroes in other centers of population followed much the same pattern on minor scales. Further, emancipation freed numerous slaves who had been trained in the trades, particularly in those connected with plantation maintenance. Thus, literally thousands of more or less proficient blacksmiths, carpenters, wheelrights, masons, plasterers, millers, mechanics, and engineers (who had operated steam engines supplying power to rice threshers, cotton gins, sawmills, and flour mills) became "free" economic agents.

Many of these, of course, were only partially trained for their occupations, and many combined the practice of their trade with other pursuits (e.g., farming) in order to support themselves. Still, a few Negro tradesmen attained eminence as artists in their work. The Noisette family in Charleston, for instance, was nationally praised for the products of their nursery and the elder Noisette gained a creditable reputation as botanist. Ben Williams, a Negro shoemaker in Columbia, was awarded a premium in November, 1869, "for the second best lot of shoes" exhibited at the annual fair of the State Agricultural and Mechanical Society.

In Reconstruction South Carolina, Negroes tended to withdraw or abstain from entering certain trades, leaving them entirely to whites. "The well wishers of the negro race see with regret that they seem to have little inclination to take to mechanical pursuits," reported a Northern journalist from Charleston in 1870. ". . . it is a rare thing to find a negro adopting the trade of blacksmith, or carpenter, or any other requiring skilled labor." This particular gentleman was apparently suffering from myopia induced by the fact that he did not, in truth, wish very well for the Negro race, but he did glimpse a part of a large trend among tradesmen. The results of this retirement of the Negro tradesman is evident in the business directory of the state published in 1880. In the entire state, it listed no Negroes among the cigarmakers, coopers, or coppersmiths, and only one Negro dyer and cleaner was polled. Furthermore, outside of Charleston there were no Negroes listed as tailors, dressmakers, tinners, upholsterers, wheelwrights, or builders and repairmen; in Charleston about half of the tradesmen engaged in each specialty were Negroes. Although the evidence is by no means conclusive, for obviously many Negro tradesmen continued to serve white customers, there was also a trend toward Negro tradesmen serving Negro customers exclusively. In Spartanburg District, in the winter of 1867,

David Golightly Harris probably touched a deep reason for this tendency. Vexed at the inefficiency of the white man he had chosen to run his flour mill, he had reached the point of exasperation. "I have an idea of puting Paschal to the mill," he wrote. "But some say a negro will drive all the customers away. . . . Everything is a botheration." Charleston, again, was perhaps exceptional in this respect.

Probably most Negro tradesmen worked independently and a few worked for established white employers, but many were also businessmen in that they kept shops in which their goods or services were sold. In addition to those in the trades, a large number of Negroes engaged in small enterprises, such as the flourishing trade in supplying firewood to Charleston from the neighboring islands. More typical of small Negro-owned businesses, perhaps, were those of Beverly Nash who operated a produce stand in Columbia in 1867 and later opened a coal and wood yard, and of Samuel Nuckles, a political refugee from Union County, who, in 1871, operated a drayage wagon in the same city. Occasionally, Negroes embarked upon large-scale undertakings in business. For instance, in the spring of 1866, "The Star Spangled Banner Association" led by Tom Long, a veteran of the First South, raised $20,000 by $15 to $100 subscriptions with which they opened a store at Beaufort and acquired a steamer to operate along the coast under the captaincy of Robert Smalls. During the Republican ascendency, Negro politicians participated in ventures darkened in greater or lesser degree by partisan shadows. Thus, F. L. Cardozo and J. H. Rainey were two of the twelve stockholders in the Greenville and Columbia Railroad Company and, with several other Negro leaders, charter members of the Columbia Street-Railway Company. However, the most striking successes in business were made by individuals in private life who gradually accumulated capital and expanded the scope of their operations. John Thorne, who had apparently led in a cooperative land purchase on Edisto Island in 1872, ten years later owned 250 acres of land on the island, "an extensive store and storehouse," and a comfortable residence. "He also runs a gin-house with six gins, and last year ginned out upwards of 400 bags of cotton of 300 pounds each, for which work he received four cents per pound. He advanced largely to several colored planters, and is worth from $15,000 to $20,000."

Although not numerous, the Negro professional class was very influential during and after Reconstruction. Ministers, politicians, and lawyers led the professions, while teachers and medical doctors formed a rather weak second rank, both in popular influence and economic importance.

Social Mobility in Urban America

One of the most important components of social health in any nation is the degree of social mobility that exists. It has always been traditional to assert the extraordinary social fluidity of the United States in the era of the family farm. The most convincing statement of this fact is the Turnerian Safety Valve Thesis which we have noted previously. But even Turner was concerned when he observed the apparent disappearance of the frontier at the end of the nineteenth century. With the end of free land for would-be farmers, what could the nation expect but growing class rigidities and growing class strife?

What Turner and his followers failed to observe was the immense social impact of the cities in the late nineteenth century. This was the period of the most rapid urban growth in our history. Between 1860 and 1910, the cities of the country increased their population by 35 million, while during the same years the nation as a whole grew by some 61 million. Between 1880 and 1910, urban population trebled; rural population increased only one-third. Many of these new urban folk derived from the natural increase of the cities themselves. Many were European immigrants. The largest contingent was composed of native-born rural Americans who found the farms straitened and sterile places to live. Increasingly then, the cities were serving as the safety valve for excess rural population, rather than the other way around.

Obviously America permitted a good deal of geographical movement. But did it also allow much mobility in wealth, occupation, and status? We must, surely, assume that geographical mobility must also have encouraged social mobility. Men would not have continued to come to the cities from the farms unless they had been able rather consistently to improve their economic lot. No doubt, a good deal of the moving about from city to city that afflicted American families represented the ebb and flow of restless failures. This is one of the points that Thernstrom emphasizes in the following essay. But could the steady movement from country to town have persisted over generations without a fair degree of success for the movers? That the migrants to cities knew what to expect when they arrived is attested to by the acceleration of urban growth during prosperous periods and its deceleration during hard times.

This conclusion is deductive. Is there also direct evidence of social mobility? Thernstrom's essay, though based on incomplete and tentative evidence, concludes that there was a considerable amount of such social movement, though it was far less than unbiased boosters of America, both contemporary and modern, would have us believe. In the end, he thinks, it was this fluidity that made the American social order a stable entity in a time of rapid industrialization and urbanization.

FOR FURTHER READING:

McKelvey, Blake. *The Urbanization of America, 1860–1915*. New Brunswick, N. J.: Rutgers University Press, 1967.

Schlesinger, Arthur M. *The Rise of the City, 1878–1898*. New York: The Macmillan Company, 1957.

Thernstrom, Stephan. *Poverty and Progress: Social Mobility in a Nineteenth-Century City*. New York: Atheneum Publishers, 1969.*

Asterisk denotes paperback edition.

Urbanization, Migration, and Social Mobility in Late Nineteenth-Century America STEPHAN THERNSTROM

The United States, it has been said, was born in the country and has moved to the city. It was during the half-century between the Civil War and World War I that the move was made. In 1860, less than a quarter of the American population lived in a city or town; by 1890, the figure had reached a third; by 1910, nearly half. By more sophisticated measures than the mere count of heads, the center of gravity of the society had obviously tilted cityward well before the last date.

If to speak of "the rise of the city" in those years is a textbook cliché, the impact of this great social transformation upon the common people of America has never been sufficiently explored. This essay is intended as a small contribution toward that task. It sketches the process by which ordinary men and women were drawn to the burgeoning cities of post-Civil War America, assesses what little we know about how they were integrated into the urban class structure, and suggests how these matters affected the viability of the political system.

The urbanization of late nineteenth-century America took place at a dizzying pace. Chicago, for instance, doubled its population every decade but one between 1850 and 1890, growing from 30,000 to over a million in little more than a generation. And it was not merely the conspicuous metropolitan giants but the Akrons, the Duluths, the Tacomas that were bursting at the seams; no less than 101 American communities grew by 100 percent or more in the 1880s.[1]

Why did Americans flock into these all too often unlovely places? There were some who were not pulled to the city but rather pushed out of their previous habitats and dropped there, more or less by accident. But the overriding fact is that the cities could draw on an enormous reservoir of people who were dissatisfied with their present lot and eager to seize the new opportunities offered by the metropolis.

Who were these people? It is conventional to distinguish two broad types of migrants to the American city: the immigrant from another culture, and the farm lad who moved from a rural to an urban setting within the culture. It is also conventional in historical accounts to overlook the latter type and to focus on the more exotic of the migrants, those who had to undergo the arduous process of becoming Americanized.

This is regrettable. To be sure, immigration from abroad was extremely important in the building of America's cities down to World War I. But the most important source of population for the burgeoning cities was not the fields of Ireland and Austria, but those of Vermont and Iowa. The prime cause of population growth in nineteenth-century America, and the main source of urban growth, was simply the high fertility of natives living outside the city.

We tend to neglect internal migration from country to city, partly because the im-

Source: Stephan Thernstrom, "Urbanization, Migration, and Social Mobility in Late Nineteenth-Century America," in *Towards a New Past: Dissenting Essays in American History,* ed. Barton J. Bernstein (New York: Pantheon Books, 1968), pp. 158–175.

migrants from abroad seem exotic and thus conspicuous, partly because of the unfortunate legacy left by Frederick Jackson Turner's frontier theory, one element of which was the notion that the open frontier served as a safety valve for urban discontent. When there were hard times in the city, according to Turner, the American worker didn't join a union or vote Socialist; he moved West and grabbed some of that free land. This theory has been subjected to the rather devastating criticism that by 1860 it took something like $1,000 capital to purchase sufficient transportation, seed equipment, livestock, and food (to live on until the first crop) to make a go of it; that it took even more than $1,000 later in the century; and that it was precisely the unemployed workmen who were least likely to have that kind of money at their command. It is estimated that for every industrial worker who became a farmer, twenty farm boys became urban dwellers.[2] There was an urban safety valve for rural discontent, and an extremely important one. The dominant form of population movement was precisely the opposite of that described by Turner.

Since scholarly attention has been focused upon immigrants from abroad, upon Oscar Handlin's "Uprooted," it will be useful to review what is known about their movement to the American city and then to ask how much the same generalizations might hold for native Americans uprooted from the countryside and plunged into the city.

Immigration is as old as America, but a seismic shift in the character of European immigration to these shores occurred in the nineteenth century, as a consequence of the commercial transformation of traditional European agriculture and the consequent displacement of millions of peasants.[3] Compared to earlier newcomers, these were people who were closer to the land and more tradition-bound, and they generally had fewer resources to bring with them than their predecessors. One shouldn't overwork this; a substantial fraction of the German and Scandinavian immigrants had enough capital to get to the West to pick up land. But some of the Germans and Scandinavians, and most men of other nationalities, had just enough cash to make it to the New World and were stuck for a time at least where they landed — New York, Boston, or wherever. They swelled the population appreciably and the relief rolls dramatically, particularly in the pre-Civil War years, when they entered cities which were basically commercial and had little use for men whose only skill in many cases was that they knew how to dig. Eventually, however, the stimulus of this vast pool of cheap labor and the demands of the growing city itself opened up a good many unskilled jobs — in the construction of roads, houses, and commercial buildings, and in the manufacturing that began to spring up in the cities.

That they were driven off the land in the Old World, that they arrived without resources, immobilized by their poverty, and that they often suffered a great deal before they secured stable employment is true enough. But these harsh facts may lead us to overlook other aspects which were extremely significant.

One is that immigration was a *selective* process. However powerful the pressures to leave, in no case did everyone in a community pull up stakes. This observation may be uncomfortably reminiscent of the popular opinion on this point: that it was the best of the Old World stock that came to the New — the most intelligent, enterprising, courageous. But this should not lead us to neglect the point altogether. The traits that led some men to leave and allowed them to survive the harrowing journey to the port, the trip itself, and the perils of the New World, could be described in

somewhat different terms: substitute cunning for intelligence, for example, or ruthlessness for courage. Still, whatever the emphasis, the fact remains: as weighed in
the scales of the marketplace, those who came — however driven by cruel circumstance — were better adapted to American life than those who remained in the village or died on the way.

The other main point about the immigrants, and especially those who suffered the
most extreme hardships — the Irish in the 1840s and 1850s, the French Canadians
in the 1870s, the Italians and various East Europeans after 1880 — is that they appraised their new situations with standards developed in peasant society. Lowell
was terrible, with its cramped stinking tenements, and factory workers labored from
dawn till dark for what seems a mere pittance. Children were forced to work at a
brutally early age; the factories and dwellings were deathtraps. But Lowell was a
damn sight better than County Cork, and men who knew from bitter experience
what County Cork was like could not view their life in Lowell with quite the same
simple revulsion as the middle-class reformers who judged Lowell by altogether
different standards. It is not so much the objectively horrible character of a situation that goads men to action as it is a nagging discrepancy between what *is* and
what is *expected*. And what one expects is determined by one's reference group —
which can be a class, an ethnic or religious subculture, or some other entity which
defines people's horizon of expectation.[4] Immigration provided an ever renewed
stream of men who entered the American economy to fill its least attractive and
least well rewarded positions, men who happen to have brought with them very low
horizons of expectation fixed in peasant Europe.

That those Americans with greatest reason to feel outrageously exploited judged
their situation against the dismally low standards of the decaying European village
is an important clue to the stunted growth of the labor movement and the failure of
American Socialism. Working in the same direction was what might be called the
Tower of Babel factor. A firm sense of class solidarity was extremely difficult to develop in communities where people literally didn't speak each other's language.
Even in cases where groups of immigrant workers had unusually high expectations
and previous familiarity with advanced forms of collective action — such as the
English artisans who led the Massachusetts textile strikes in the 1870s — they found
it hard to keep the other troops in line; a clever Italian-speaking or Polish-speaking
foreman could easily exploit national differences for his own ends, and if necessary
there were always the most recent immigrants of all (and the Negroes) to serve as
scabs to replace the dissenters en masse.

A somewhat similar analysis applies to the migrants who left the Kansas farms for
Chicago. They were linguistically and culturally set apart from many of their fellow
workers; they too had low horizons of expectation fixed in the countryside and
brought to the city. The latter point is often missed because of the peculiar American reverence for an idealized agrarian way of life. As we have become a nation of
city dwellers, we have come more and more to believe that it is virtuous and beautiful to slave for fourteen hours a day with manure on your boots. Recently that
sturdy small farmer from Johnson City, Texas, remarked that "it does not make
sense on this great continent which God has blessed to have more than 70 percent of
our people crammed into one percent of the land." A national "keep them down on
the farm" campaign is therefore in the offing.[5] But it is damnably hard to keep them
down on the farm after they've seen New York (or even Indianapolis), and it was

just as hard a century ago, for the very good reason that the work is brutal, the profits are often miserably low, and the isolation is psychologically murderous. Virtuous this life may be, especially to people who don't have to live it, but enjoyable it is not — not, at least, to a very substantial fraction of our ever shrinking farm population.

This applies particularly to young men and women growing up on a farm. Their parents had a certain stake in staying where they were, even if it was a rut. And the eldest son, who would inherit the place eventually, was sometimes tempted by that. But the others left in droves, to tend machines, to dig and haul and hammer — or in the case of the girls, to sell underwear in Marshall Field's, to mind someone else's kitchen, or in some instances to follow in the footsteps of Sister Carrie.

There were some large differences between native-born migrants to the cities and immigrants from another land, to be sure. But the familiar argument that native workmen "stood on the shoulders" of the immigrant and was subjected to less severe exploitation is somewhat misleading. The advantages enjoyed by many America-born laborers stemmed more from their urban experience than their birth, and they did not generally accrue to freshly arrived native migrants to the city. The latter were little better off than their immigrant counterparts, but then they too were spiritually prepared to endure a great deal of privation and discomfort because even the bottom of the urban heap was a step up from the farms they had left behind. The two groups were one in this respect, and perceptive employers recognized the fact. In 1875, the Superintendent of one of Andrew Carnegie's steel mills summed up his experience this way: "We must steer clear as far as we can of Englishmen, who are great sticklers for high wages, small production and strikes. My experience has shown that Germans and Irish, Swedes and what I denominate 'Buckwheats' — young American country boys, judiciously mixed, make the most honest and tractable force you can find." [6]

The move to the city, therefore, was an advance of a kind for the typical migrant. Were there further opportunities for advancement there, or did he then find himself crushed by circumstance and reduced to the ranks of the permanent proletariat? Did his children, whose expectations were presumably higher, discover correspondingly greater opportunities open to them? Remarkably little serious research has been devoted to these issues. Historians who see American history as a success story have been content to assume, without benefit of data, that the American dream of mobility was true, apparently on the principle that popular ideology is a sure guide to social reality. Dissenting scholars have been more inclined to the view that class barriers were relatively impassable, an assumption based upon generalized skepticism about American mythology rather than upon careful empirical study. Some recent work, however, provides the basis for a tentative reappraisal of the problem.

We know most about mobility into the most rarified reaches of the social order regarding such elite groups as millionaires, railroad presidents, directors of large corporations, or persons listed in the *Dictionary of American Biography*. What is most impressive about the literature on the American elite is that, in spite of many variations in the way in which the elite is defined, the results of these studies are much the same. It is clear that growing up in rags is not in the least conducive to the attainment of later riches, and that it was no more so a century ago than it is today.[7] There have been spectacular instances of mobility from low down on the social scale to the very top — Andrew Carnegie for instance. But colorful examples cannot sustain broad generalizations about social phenomena, however often they are impressed into service toward that end. Systematic investigation reveals that even in the days of Andrew Carnegie, there was little room at the top, except for those who started very close to it.

Furthermore, this seems to have been the case throughout most of American history, despite many dramatic alterations in the character of the economy. It seems perfectly plausible to assume, as many historians have on the basis of impressionistic evidence, that the precipitous growth of heavy industry in the latter half of the nineteenth century opened the doors to men with very different talents from the educated merchants who constituted the elite of the preindustrial age, that unlettered, horny-handed types like Thomas Alva Edison and Henry Ford, crude inventors and tinkerers, then came into their own; that the connection between parental wealth and status and the son's career was loosened, so that members of the business elite typically had lower social origins and less education, and were often of immigrant stock. Plausible, yes, but true, no. It helped to go to Harvard in Thomas Jefferson's America, and it seems to have helped just about as much in William McKinley's America. There were the Edisons and Fords, who rose spectacularly from low origins, but there were always a few such. Cases like these were about as exceptional in the late nineteenth century as they were earlier. The image of the great inventor springing from common soil, unspoiled by book-larnin', is a red herring. It is doubtful, to say the least, that the less you know, the more likely you are to build a better mousetrap. And in any event it was not the great inventor who raked in the money, in most cases — Henry Ford never invented anything — but rather the organizer and manipulator, whose talents seem to have been highly valued through all periods of American history.

These conclusions are interesting, but an important caution is in order. It by no means follows that if there was very little room at the top, there was little room anywhere else. It is absurd to judge the openness or lack of openness of an entire social system solely by the extent of recruitment from below into the highest positions of all. One can imagine a society in which all members of the tiny elite are democratically recruited from below, and yet where the social structure as a whole is extremely rigid with that small exception. Conversely, one can imagine a society with a hereditary ruling group at the very top, a group completely closed to aspiring men of talent but lowly birth, and yet with an enormous amount of movement back and forth below that pinnacle. Late nineteenth-century America could have approximated this latter model, with lineage, parental wealth, and education as decisive assets in the race for the very peak, as the business elite studies suggest, and yet with great fluidity at the lower and middle levels of the class structure.

Was this in fact the case? The evidence available today is regrettably scanty, but here are the broad outlines of an answer, insofar as we can generalize from a handful of studies.[8] At the lower and middle ranges of the class structure there was impressive mobility, though often of an unexpected and rather ambiguous kind. I will distinguish three types of mobility: geographical, occupational, and property, and say a little about the extent and significance of each.

First is geographical mobility, physical movement from place to place, which is tied up in an interesting way with movement through the social scale. Americans have long been thought a restless, footloose people, and it has been assumed that the man on the move has been the man on the make; he knows that this little town doesn't provide a grand enough stage for him to display his talents, and so he goes off to the big city to win fame and fortune, *or* to the open frontier to do likewise. When you examine actual behavior instead of popular beliefs, however, you discover that things are more complicated than that.

It proves to be true that Americans are indeed a footloose people. In my work on Newburyport, a small industrial city, I attempted to find out what fraction of the families present in the community in the initial year of my study — 1850 — were still living there in the closing year, 1880, one short generation. Less than a fifth of them, it turned out — and this not in a community on the moving frontier, like Merle Curti's Trempealeau County, where you would expect a very high turnover. There the true pioneer types, who liked to clear the land, became nervous when there was another family within a half day's ride of them and sold out to the second wave of settlers (often immigrants who knew better than to try to tame the wilderness without previous experience at it). But to find roughly the same volatility in a city forty miles north of Boston suggests that the whole society was in motion.

The statistics bear out the legend that Americans are a restless people. What of the assertion that movement and success go hand in hand, that physical mobility and upward social mobility are positively correlated? Here the legend seems more questionable. It seems likely that some who pulled up stakes and went elsewhere for a new start did improve their positions; they found better land, or discovered that they possessed talents which were much more highly valued in the big city than in the place they came from. What ever would have happened to Theodore Dreiser in small-town Indiana had there been no Chicago for him to flee to?

But the point to underline, for it is less commonly understood, is that much of this remarkable population turnover was of quite a different kind. As you trace the flow of immigrants into and then out of the cities, you begin to see that a great many of those who departed did so in circumstances which make it exceedingly hard to believe that they were moving on to bigger and better things elsewhere. There is no way to be certain about this, no feasible method of tracing individuals once they disappear from the universe of the community under consideration. These questions can be explored for contemporary America by administering questionnaires to people and collecting life histories which display migration patterns, but dead men tell no tales and fill out no questionnaires, so that part of the past is irrevocably lost. But some plausible inferences can be drawn about the nature of this turnover from the fact that so many ordinary working people on the move owned no property, had no savings accounts, had acquired no special skills, and were most likely to leave when they were unemployed. They were, in short, people who had made the least successful economic adjustment to the community and who were no longer able to hang on there. At the lower reaches of the social order, getting out of town did not ordinarily mean a step up the ladder somewhere else; there is no reason to assume that in their new destinations migrant laborers found anything but more of the same. When middle-class families, who already had a niche in the world, moved on, it was often in response to greater opportunities elsewhere; for ordinary working people physical movement meant something very different.

That is a less rosy picture than the one usually painted, but I think it is more accurate. And we should notice one very important implication of this argument: namely, that the people who were least successful and who had the greatest grievances are precisely those who never stayed put very long in any one place. Students of labor economics and trade union history have long been aware of the fact that there are certain occupations which are inordinately difficult to organize simply because they have incessant job turnover. When only 5 percent or 1 percent of the men working at a particular job in a given city at the start of the year are still employed twelve months later, as is the case with some occupations in the economic underworld today (short-order cooks or menial hospital workers, for instance), how do you build a stable organization and conduct a successful strike?

An analogous consideration applies not merely to certain selected occupations but to a large fraction of the late nineteenth-century urban working class as a whole. The Marxist model of the conditions which promote proletarian consciousness presumes not only permanency of membership in this class — the absence of upward mobility — but also, I suggest, some continuity of class membership *in one setting* so that workers come to know each other and to develop bonds of solidarity and common opposition to the ruling group above them. This would seem to entail a stable labor force in a single factory; at a minimum it assumes considerable stability in a community. One reason that a permanent proletariat along the lines envisaged by Marx did not develop in the course of American industrialization is perhaps that few Americans have *stayed* in one place, one workplace, or even one city long enough to discover a sense of common identity and common grievance. This may be a vital clue to the divergent political development of America and Western Europe in the industrial age, to the striking weakness of socialism here, as compared to Europe — though we can't be sure because we don't definitely know that the European working-class population was less volatile. I suspect that it was, to some degree, and that America was distinctive in this respect, but this is a question of glaring importance which no one has yet taken the trouble to investigate.

When I first stumbled upon this phenomenon in sifting through manuscript census schedules for nineteenth-century Newburyport, I was very doubtful that the findings could be generalized to apply to the big cities of the period. It seemed reasonable to assume that the laborers who drifted out of Newburyport so quickly after their arrival must have settled down somewhere else, and to think that a great metropolis would have offered a more inviting haven than a small city, where anonymity was impossible and where middle-class institutions of social control intruded into one's daily life with some frequency, as compared to a classic big-city lower-class ghetto, where the down-and-out could perhaps huddle together for protective warmth and be left to their own devices — for instance, those Irish wards of New York where the police made no attempt to enforce law and order until late in the century. Here if anywhere one should be able to find a continuous lower-class population, a permanent proletariat, and I began my Boston research with great curiosity about this point.

If Boston is any example, in no American city was there a sizable lower class with great continuity of membership. You can identify some more or less continuously lower-class areas, but the crucial point is that *the same people do not stay in them.* If you take a sample of unskilled and semi-skilled laborers in Boston in 1880 and look for them in 1890, you are not much more likely to find them still in the city than was the case in Newburyport.[9]

The bottom layer of the social order in the nineteenth-century American city was thus a group of families who appear to have been permanent transients, buffeted about from place to place, never quite able to sink roots. We know very little about these people, and it is difficult to know how we can learn much about them. You get only occasional glimpses into the part of this iceberg that appears above the surface, in the person of the tramp, who first is perceived as a problem for America in the 1870s and reappears in hard times after that — in the 1890s and in the great depression most notably. But what has been said here at least suggests the significance of the phenomenon.

So much for geographical mobility. What can be said about the people who come to the city and remain there under our microscope so that we can discern what happened to them? I have already anticipated my general line of argument here in my discussion of migration out of the city — which amounted to the claim that the city was a kind of Darwinian jungle in which the fittest survived and the others drifted on to try another place. Those who did stay in the city and make their way there did, in general, succeed in advancing themselves economically and socially. There was very impressive mobility, though not always of the kind we might expect.

In approaching this matter, we must make a distinction which is obscured by applying labels like "open" or "fluid" to entire whole social structures. There are, after all, two sets of escalators in any community; one set goes down. To describe a society as enormously fluid implies that there are lots of people moving down while lots of others are moving up to take their place. This would obviously be a socially explosive situation, for all those men descending against their will would arrive at the bottom, not with low horizons of expectation set in some peasant village, but with expectations established when they were at one of the comfortable top floors of the structure.

Downward mobility is by no means an unknown phenomenon in American history. There have been socially displaced groups, especially if you take into account rather subtle shifts in the relative status of such groups as professionals.[10] But the chief generalization to make is that Americans who started their working life in a middle-class job strongly tended to end up in the middle class; sons reared in middle-class families also attained middle-class occupations in the great majority of cases. Relatively few men born into the middle class fell from there; a good many born into the working class either escaped from it altogether or advanced themselves significantly within the class. There is a well-established tradition of writing about the skilled workman, associated with such names as the Hammonds, the Lynds, Lloyd Warner, and Norman Ware, which holds the contrary, to be sure.[11] This tradition still has its defenders, who argue that with industrialization "class lines assumed a new and forbidding rigidity" and that "machines made obsolete many of the skilled trades of the antebellum years, drawing the once self-respecting handicraftsmen into the drudgery and monotony of factory life, where they were called upon to perform only one step in the minutely divided and automatic processes of mass production."[12] Rapid technological change doubtless did displace some skilled artisans, doubtless produced some downward mobility into semiskilled positions. But defenders of this view have built their case upon little more than scattered complaints by labor leaders, and have not conducted systematic research to verify these complaints.

Careful statistical analysis provides a very different perspective on the matter. Two points stand out. One is that as certain traditional skilled callings became obsolete, there was an enormous expansion of *other* skilled trades, and, since many of the craftsmen under pressure from technological change had rather generalized skills, they moved rapidly into these new positions and thus retained their place in the labor aristocracy.[13] Second, it is quite mistaken to assume that the sons of the threatened artisan were commonly driven down into the ranks of the factory operatives; they typically found a place either in the expanding skilled trades or in the even more rapidly expanding white-collar occupations.[14]

As for workers on the lower rungs of the occupational ladder, the unskilled and semiskilled, they had rarely drifted down from a higher beginning point. Characteristically, they were newcomers to the urban world. A substantial minority of them appear to have been able to advance themselves a notch or two occupationally, especially among the second generation; a good many of their sons became clerks, salesmen, and other petty white-collar functionaries. And the first generation, which had less success occupationally, was commonly experiencing mobility of another kind — property mobility. Despite a pathetically low (but generally rising) wage level, despite heavy unemployment rates, many were able to accumulate significant property holdings and to establish themselves as members of the stable working class, as opposed to the drifting lower class.[15]

It may seem paradoxical to suggest that so many Americans were rising in the world and so few falling; where did the room at the top come from? The paradox is readily resolved. For one thing, our attention has been fastened upon individuals who remained physically situated in one place in which their careers could be traced; an indeterminate but substantial fraction of the population was floating and presumably unsuccessful. By no means everyone at the bottom was upwardly mobile; the point is rather that those who were not were largely invisible. Furthermore, the occupational structure itself was changing in a manner that created disproportionately more positions in the middle and upper ranges, despite the common nineteenth-century belief that industrialization was homogenizing the work force and reducing all manual employees to identical robots. The homogenizing and degrading tendencies that caught the eye of Marx and others were more than offset, it appears, by developments which made for both a more differentiated and a more top-heavy occupational structure. Third, there were important sources of social mobility that could be attained without changing one's occupation, most notably the property mobility that was stimulated by the increases in real wages that occurred in this period. Finally, there was the so-called "demographic vacuum" created by the differential fertility of the social classes, best illustrated in the gloomy late nineteenth-century estimate that in two hundred years 1,000 Harvard graduates would have only 50 living descendants while 1,000 Italians would have 100,000. The calculation is dubious, but the example nicely clarifies the point that high-status groups failed to reproduce themselves, thus opening up vacancies which had necessarily to be filled by new men from below.

For all the brutality and rapacity which marked the American scene in the years in which the new urban industrial order came into being, what stands out most is the relative absence of colective working-class protest aimed at reshaping capitalist society. The foregoing, while hardly a full explanation, should help to make this more comprehensible. The American working class was drawn into the new society by a process that encouraged accommodation and rendered disciplined protest difficult. Within the urban industrial orbit, most of its members found modest but significant opportunities to feel that they and their children were edging their way upwards. Those who did not find such opportunities were tossed helplessly about from city to city, from state to state, alienated but invisible and impotent.

NOTES

1. C. N. Glaab and A. T. Brown, *A History of Urban America* (New York, 1967), pp. 107–11.
2. Fred Shannon, "A Post Mortem on the Labor-Safety-Valve Theory," *Agricultural History, XIX* (1954), 31–37.
3. For general accounts, see Marcus L. Hansen, *The Atlantic Migration, 1607–1860* (paperback ed.; New York, 1961); Oscar Handlin, *The Uprooted* (Boston, 1951).
4. For discussion of the sociological concepts of reference groups and the theory of relative deprivation, see Robert K. Merton, *Social Theory and Social Structure,* rev. ed. (Glencoe, Ill., 1957) and the literature cited there. The problem of assessing the level of expectations of any particular migratory group in the past is extremely complicated, and it is obvious that there have been important differences between and within groups. But the generalizations offered here seem to me the best starting point for thinking about this issue.
5. *Boston Globe,* February 5, 1967.
6. Quoted in Oscar Handlin, *Immigration as a Factor in American History* (Englewood Cliffs, N.J., 1959), pp. 66–67.
7. For a convenient review of this literature, see Seymour M. Lipset and Reinhard Bendix, *Social Mobility in Industrial Society* (Berkeley, Cal., 1959), Ch. 4.
8. The main sources for the generalizations which follow, unless otherwise indicated, are: Stephen Thernstrom, *Poverty and Progress: Social Mobility in a Nineteenth Century City* (Cambridge, Mass., 1964); Merle E. Curti, *The Making of an American Frontier Community* (Stanford, Cal., 1959); Donald B. Cole, *Immigrant City: Lawrence, Massachusetts, 1845–1921* (Chapel Hill, N.C., 1963)–for my reservations about this work, however, see my review in the *Journal of Economic History,* XXIV (1964), 259–61; Herbert G. Gutman, "Social Status and Social Mobility in 19th Century America: Paterson, N.J., A Case Study," unpublished paper for the 1964 meetings of the American Historical Association; Howard Gitelman, "The Labor Force at Waltham Watch During the Civil War Era," *Journal of Economic History, XXV* (1965), 214–43; David Brody, *Steelworkers in America: The Non-union Era* (Cambridge, Mass., 1960); Pauline Gordon, "The Chance to Rise Within Industry" (unpublished M.A. thesis, Columbia University); Robert Wheeler, "The Fifth-Ward Irish: Mobility at Mid-Century" (unpublished seminar paper, Brown University, 1967); and the author's research in progress on social mobility in Boston over the past century, in which the career patterns of some 8,000 ordinary residents of the community are traced.
9. Recent work suggesting that even the most recent U.S. Census seriously undernumerated the Negro male population may make the critical reader wonder about the accuracy of the census and city directory canvases upon which I base my analysis. Some elaborate checking has persuaded me that these nineteenth-century sources erred primarily in their coverage–their lack of coverage, rather–of the floating working-class population. For a variety of reasons it seems clear that families which had been in the community long enough to be included in one of these canvases–and hence to be included in a sample drawn from them–were rarely left out of later canvases if they were indeed still resident in the same city. A perfect census of every soul in the community on a given day would therefore yield an even higher, not a lower, estimate of population turnover for men at the bottom, which strengthens rather than weakens the argument advanced here.
10. The assumption that discontent stemming from social displacement has been the motive force behind American reform movements has exerted great influence upon American historical writing in recent years. See for instance David Donald, "Toward a Reconsideration of Abolitionists," *Lincoln Reconsidered* (New York, 1956), pp. 19–36; Richard Hofstadter, *The Age of Reform: From Bryan to F.D.R.* (New York, 1955). Donald's essay is easily demolished by anyone with the slightest acquaintance with sociological method. Hofstadter's work, while open to a very serious objection, is at least sufficiently suggestive to indicate the potential utility of the idea.
11. J. L. and Barbara Hammond, *The Town Labourer (1760 – 1832)* (London, 1917); Robert S. and Helen M. Lynd, *Middletown* (New York, 1929), and *Middletown in Transition* (New York, 1937); W. Lloyd Warner and J. O. Low, *The Social System of the Modern Factory* (New Haven, Conn., 1947); Norman J. Ware, *The Industrial Worker, 1840 – 1860* (Boston, 1924).
12. Leon Litwak, ed., *The American Labor Movement* (Englewood Cliffs, N.J., 1962), p. 3.
13. This is evident from aggregated census data and from my Boston investigation, but we badly need an American counterpart to Eric Hobsbawm's splendid essay on "The Labour Aristocracy in Nineteenth Century Britain," in *Labouring Men: Studies in the History of Labour* (London, 1964), pp. 272–315.
14. So, at least, the evidence from Boston and Indianapolis indicates; for the latter, see Natlic Rogoff, *Recent Trends in Occupational Mobility* (Glencoe, Ill., 1953).

15. The clearest demonstration of this is in Thernstrom, *Poverty and Progress,* Ch. 5. It might be thought, however, that the remarkable property mobility disclosed there depended upon the existence of an abundant stock of cheap single-family housing available for purchase. It could be that where real estate was less readily obtainable, laborers would squander the funds that were accumulated with such sacrifice in places where home ownership was an immediate possibility. It appears from Wheeler's unpublished study of nineteenth-century Providence, however, that the working-class passion for property did not require an immediate, concrete source of satisfaction like a home and a plot of land. The Irish workmen of Providence were just as successful at accumulating property holdings as their Newburyport counterparts; the difference was only that they held personal rather than real property.

The Bryan-McKinley Campaign of 1896

The politics of the Gilded Age has always been something of a puzzle to historians. They find it hard to understand what the parties did, how they differed, and who supported them and why. It has always been possible to point to Republican allegiance to positive government in the interests of business and the Democrats' Jeffersonian-agrarian tradition. But not all businessmen were Republican; in the South most were Democrats. Nor were all farmers Democrats; in the Midwest they were generally Republican. Clearly the simple Hamiltonian-Jeffersonian class dichotomy for the post–Civil War parties does not work very well.

Nor were their policies significantly different during these years. It is true that the Republicans favored the tariff, while the Democrats were friendlier to free trade. But there were many low-tariff Republicans and many high-tariff Democrats. Besides, how serious an issue was the tariff in these years? It produced a good deal of rhetoric, but did it really get to the heart of contemporary industrial problems? And was silver any better as a serious distinction? It did not neatly divide the parties either. From the time the money question first appeared after the Civil War in the guise of the greenback and specie resumption issues, it had been a political football. At certain times and at certain places, the two parties had taken opposite stands on greenbacks and then, later, on free silver. But they had not been consistent. Moreover, what has been said of the tariff can also be said of the money question: it did not get to the heart of the problems that were troubling America in this era. All told, it is hard to deny the view of many contemporaries that the two major parties differed about as much as tweedle-dee from tweedle-dum. At times, their main function seems to have been either ceremonial or diversionary. Simultaneously, they legitimized the political process by giving the electorate the appearance of political participation and provided them with an annual fall carnival on about the same level as the World Series. In real terms, victory of one seems to have meant no more in the lives of Americans than victory of the other.

The Presidential election of 1896 has always seemed different. This contest, pitting William Jennings Bryan against William McKinley, came at the nadir of the severe depression that began in 1893. For three years the economy had deflated. Farm prices, already chronically depressed before the 1893 panic, dropped still further. In cities and factory towns, thousands were thrown out of work, and sharp wage cuts for those who kept their jobs fomented bitter labor discontent. The Democrats had had the bad luck to be in office when the disaster struck. President Grover Cleveland, a conservative Democrat, had concentrated solely on preserving the threatened gold standard by inducing Congress to repeal the Sherman Silver Purchase Act and by negotiating with New York and European bankers for several gold loans. Both actions angered the party's silver wing, and by the time the Presidential convention met in Chicago they were in revolt.

It was in this atmosphere that Bryan, a relatively obscure Nebraska politician who had hitched his political fortunes to a quasi-Populist platform emphasizing free silver, stole the party Presidential nomination from the conservatives. At the Chicago convention, the well-prepared Bryan captured the insurgents by his electrifying Cross of Gold speech and won the nomination. The Democratic platform declared in favor of free and unlimited coinage of the old silver dollar to relieve the burden of debt and taxes and to revive the economy.

The actual appeal to the voters during the campaign, as Paul Kleppner notes, was class-oriented in a way that has seldom been matched in American politics. The Bryan strategy, as he shows, was intended to mobilize the "toiling masses" against the "monopolies" and the "money power," and to construct a winning coalition out of wage earners and farmers.

How well this departure from the well-trodden path of American party consensus worked is the subject of Kleppner's essay. Using the vigorous new approach of quantification, he ingeniously tests the proposition that the Bryan strategy of 1896 succeeded in giving American party politics a class basis and in providing for the first time since the Civil War, the electorate with a significant political alternative.

FOR FURTHER READING:

DURDEN, ROBERT F. *The Climax of Populism: The Election of 1896.* Lexington, Ky.: University Press of Kentucky, 1965.*
GLAD, PAUL. *McKinley, Bryan and the People.* Philadelphia: J. B. Lippincott Company, 1964.*
JOSEPHSON, MATTHEW. *The Politicos.* New York: Harcourt, Brace & World, 1963.*

Asterisk denotes paperback edition.

The Politics of Realignment: The Reaction of the Toiling Masses PAUL KLEPPNER

Farmers Versus Workers?

After three years of depression, political parties in 1896 were forced to offer an explanation of economic events and future prospects to the voters. The repudiation of the Democracy in the state and federal elections of 1893 through 1895 created a leadership vacuum within the Democratic party. The defeat of northern and midwestern Democrats in the 1894 congressional elections shifted the leadership roles to the southern and western representatives of the party. Political leaders from these sections, responding to constituency pressures, hoped to remake the image of the party. They hoped to create a political vehicle expressive of, and responsive to, the economic demands of the semicolonial depressed agricultural regions. Aware of this sectional discontent with the eastern party leadership, William Jennings Bryan assiduously cultivated the prospective delegates to the 1896 national convention from the southern and western states. His efforts were capped with the success he

Source: Paul Kleppner, *The Cross of Culture, A Social Analysis of Midwestern Politics, 1850–1900* (New York: Free Press, 1970), chap. 7, "The Politics of Realignment: The Reaction of the Toiling Masses," pp. 279–315.

had worked for; he was nominated by the Chicago convention as the party's candidate for the presidency. That nomination and the platform that the convention adopted gave the Democratic party's answer to the depression: commodity price inflation.

The Republicans had less difficulty in formulating their explanation of the depression and selecting a candidate whose image was consonant with it. Republican rhetoric following the 1890 defeats had so closely linked William McKinley with the tariff that, when that question assumed new importance, large numbers of party leaders immediately saw him as the "logical" nominee. McKinley encountered opposition from the party's eastern leaders, who were suspicious of his stand on the silver question. But through skillful utilization of his extensive network of personal contacts, and aided by Mark Hanna's organizational techniques, the "Napoleon of Protection" was able to secure his party's nomination for the presidency.

The ensuing contest was a dramatic one. As Bryan toured the country preaching the free silver gospel, McKinley waged an energetic "front porch" campaign for tariff protection and honest money. Both were concerned not just with the audience within earshot, but with the broader one that would be exposed to their rhetoric through the written reports of their comments. The Bryan strategy was both apparent and simple. He aimed at uniting the "toiling masses" against the vested interests who oppressed both farmer and laborer. Since, collectively, farmers and urban workers constituted the bulk of the electorate, the strategic aim was preeminently reasonable. The crucial question is how well he succeeded in implementing his strategy.

The question of whether Bryan's candidacy was received favorably by urban workers is one that has long been dealt with by historians. In 1933, Arthur M. Schlesinger, reacting against the fronter-section hypothesis espoused by Frederick Jackson Turner and his followers, argued that the contest was a "clash between two cultures — one static, individualistic, agricultural, the other dynamic, collectivistic, urban." [1] Several years later William Diamond launched an attack on the Schlesinger hypothesis. Opposing both the sectional and urban-rural interpretations, he offered one based on conflict between interest groups and classes. In an article that has had a remarkable impact on the historiography of the 1896 election, he argued that some cities gave Bryan a higher percentage than their rural hinterland, while the opposite was true of other cities. These variations were the result of the fact that the socioeconomic compositions and functions of the cities differed from each other. But cutting across these differences there was one common feature: all the cities had significant conflicts with their surrounding rural areas. The results of 1896 could be explained on this basis. [2]

A key conceptual weakness marred both these attempts at explanation. Neither Schlesinger nor Diamond attempted to deal with the 1896 results in an historical dimension; neither attempted to *compare* the Bryan vote with the vote Democratic candidates had previously received in both urban and rural voting units. By systematically ordering the relevant data, by employing a comparative analytical context, and by examining the data over time, we can test these hypotheses and determine the extent to which the Bryan candidacy elicited a favorable response from the Midwest's "toiling masses."

How did the Democratic vote divide in 1896 *compared with its normal division* by place of residence? Schlesinger's hypothesis suggests the cohesion of rural voters against urban ones. Empirical verification of this hypothesis would require that the data show that the two groups moved in opposite directions, and that Bryan drew heavier support from rural areas than Democratic candidates normally did. Table 35 presents the necessary voting data.

TABLE 35   Democratic Percentage Strength, Rural and Urban Areas, 1892–96

| | MICHIGAN | | OHIO | | WISCONSIN | |
	Rural	Urban	Rural	Urban	Rural	Urban
1892	47.8	49.7	45.9	49.2	47.4	49.8
1894*	29.6	37.1	42.1	42.2	38.8	34.0
1896	41.0	38.0	47.6	43.9	37.2	41.4

* The Ohio data are for 1893.

The data are not consonant with Schlesinger's hypothesis. Bryan received only a minority of the rural vote in each state, hardly indicating disproportionate rural support. The two percentages moved in opposite directions only in Wisconsin, and there the rural percentage *decreased* and the urban one *increased.* In Michigan and Wisconsin, Bryan's rural percentage was lower in 1896 than the Democratic rural percentage had been in 1892. In Ohio the rural percentage was above 1892, but the urban percentage had moved in the same direction, although at a slower rate. With the exception of Wisconsin, the data do suggest that Bryan's candidacy was relatively more favorably received by farmers than urbanites, but they do not confirm anything close to the solid cohesion that the Schlesinger hypothesis implies.

Diamond's hypothesis is both more subtle and more suggestive. He did not contend that all farmers moved in one direction and all urban workers in the other. He explicitly posited the possibility that one group of urban voters reacted negatively to Bryan and another positively. Regardless of the direction of the movement, it was prompted by negative reactions on the part of urban and rural voters against each other. In short, it was the outgrowth of an *increasing* level of urban-rural tension.

Diamond devised an ingenious measure to treat the problem of urban-rural voting tension, the "percentage ratio." This is an index number designed to represent the relationship between Bryan's percentage in urban areas and in rural areas. "The percentage ratio of a city is the ratio of Bryan's percentage of the votes in that city to the percentage of votes he received in the nonurban sections of the state. The percentage ratio of a state is the ratio of Bryan's total urban percentage to his rural percentage." The index number will be greater or less than one. If above one, Bryan's percentage of urban votes was greater than the proportion of the rural vote he received. If below one, he did better among the state's rural voters. Diamond also established cut-off points to distinguish between minimal and significant urban-rural tension: "Ratios from .9 to 1.1, while they show a clear-cut difference in urban and rural votes, will be called the range of low urban-rural tension. Ratios below .9 and above 1.1 will be regarded as representing a high degree of tension between city and country." [3]

Employing his percentage ratio, and examining the distribution of the vote over space, Diamond concluded that: "But whatever the basis of urban-rural antagonism, whatever the forces that accentuate or soften the clash of city and countryside, the fact remains that in the election of 1896 there was a high urban-rural tension." [4] But *high relative* to what? If the notion has any explanatory power relevant to the 1896 results, Diamond must have been implying that the level of urban-rural tension then was *greater than normal;* that the "Bryan campaign acted as a catalyst to intensify urban-rural political conflicts having their roots in persistent socio-economic antagonisms." [5] Stated in these terms, Diamond's argument can be taken as a hypothesis to be tested against the relevant empirical data. The verification of that hypothesis requires not merely the demonstration of a particular level of urban-rural tension, but an *increase* in that tension in 1896 when compared with earlier levels.

Before testing the hypothesis, it is necessary to introduce one clarifying notion. Diamond's percentage ratio is a *combined* measure of both the magnitude *and* the direction of urban-rural tension. The combination of these two components into one statistical measure was one of the major advantages Diamond saw in the use of the ratio. "It will be seen at once that the use of the percentage ratio has the advantage of telling at a glance not only whether there was a difference in the reaction of urban and rural areas but also how great that difference was and in what direction it went." [6] For some purposes the combination of the two components into a single statistic might be advantageous. It is questionable whether this is the case when one is attempting to deal *solely* with the magnitude of the urban-rural tension. The absolute amount of that tension is not directly shown by the index number. The *amount* of tension is equal to the absolute remainder resulting from the subtraction of the index number from unity. We can illustrate this, and the confusion which results when only the index numbers are used to describe magnitude, by reexamining some of Diamond's data.

In 1896 Connecticut had a percentage ratio of 1.295, and Kentucky one of 0.703. Despite the differences in the index numbers, both states exhibited about the same *amounts* of urban-rural tension: Connecticut's measure was .295 and Kentucky's .297. The fact that two states can have widely different index numbers, while displaying approximately the *same amounts* of urban-rural tension, although entirely different *directions* in that tension, simply confuses any attempt to compare magnitudes alone. This undoubtedly accounts for the erroneous conclusion Diamond drew from his own data. Following his examination of the percentage ratio and Bryan's percentage strength in each of thirty-two states, he concluded that "the correlation of the [amount of] tension with the Bryan vote is plain." In fact, that correlation is not only *not* plain, it is *nonexistent.* The correlation between the *amount* of urban-rural tension and Bryan's percentage strength is $-.117$.[7]

As we are here directly concerned with variations in the amount of urban-rural tension over time, it is necessary to treat the magnitude component of the index separately. Using the data in Table 35, we can compute the percentage ratios for each of these three states, subtract that from unity, and compare the amounts. Going beyond the short-term, we can use similar data to construct a comparison with every general election since 1876. We can then summarize these comparisons by computing the mean percentage ratio between 1876 and 1892, and subtracting that figure from unity. Table 36 presents these measures.

Diamond observed that only ratios between .9 and 1.1 were to be regarded as representing a high degree of tension between city and country. According to that criterion, none of these three states exhibited high tension in 1896. In fact only Michigan in 1894, with a percentage ratio of 1.253, had ever met the standard since 1876. In Michigan the *amount* of urban-rural tension in 1896 was appreciably lower than

TABLE 36   Amount of Urban-Rural Tension, 1876–96

	M̄ 1876–92	1892	1894	1896
Michigan	.084	.005	.253	.074
Ohio	.044	.071	.002	.078
Wisconsin	.120	.111	.006	.072

the 1894 level, and was slightly below the mean level between 1876 and 1892. In Wisconsin and Ohio the *amount* of tension in 1896 was higher than in 1894; but only in Ohio was it above the mean for the sixteen-year period. Urban-rural "conflict" had not been a significant determinant of political contests at any point since 1876, and the Bryan-McKinley battle did not change that situation. Only in Ohio was there any increase in the tension ratio compared with the "normal" level, but there, as in the other two states, the Democratic percentage in urban areas was below its 1892 level. Bryan did not run as well as Democratic candidates usually did in urban areas in any of these states, and in only one of them, Ohio, did he do as well in rural areas as Democrats normally had.

TABLE 37   Democratic Percentage Strength by Size of Place, 1892–96

	MICHIGAN			WISCONSIN		
	1892	1894	1896	1892	1894	1896
100,000	52.3	38.7	32.2	49.1	31.4	42.9
45,000–99,999	46.4	31.8	43.3	—		
25,000–44,999	53.7	45.9	46.4	45.3	30.0	36.9
10,000–24,999	46.9	33.9	39.7	51.6	40.1	38.0
5,000–9,999	47.1	31.7	38.4	55.5	44.4	39.0
2,500–4,999	44.6	30.8	37.3	48.4	41.7	38.3

We can extend the definition of "urban" to include all units with more than 2,500 population to see if there was any consistent pattern in the Bryan vote by size of place categories in Michigan and Wisconsin (see Table 37). In Michigan, with the exception of the city of Detroit, Democratic percentage strength was higher in 1896 than it had been in 1894 in urban areas, but in no case was it at the 1892 level. Wisconsin's pattern is more mixed. There the two largest size categories showed Democratic increases over 1894, but percentage strength levels below 1892. But the Democratic mean in cities below 25,000 continued to decline in 1896. In such areas Bryan was apparently not even able to win back those who had defected from the party in 1894. In similarly sized units in Michigan, Bryan was successful in recovering a portion of the earlier Democratic losses. But even in that state the Bryan percentage was higher than the 1892 Democratic percentage in only nine of fifty-five urban places. In Ohio only two of the twenty-two cities with a population of 10,000 or more registered a higher Democratic percentage in 1896 than in 1892.

Taken in combination, these data support the following generalizations. Bryan did not put together a solid bloc of rural voters to oppose those in cities. The level of urban-rural tension was no more important as a voting determinant than it had been since 1876. Bryan's percentage in urban areas, except in Wisconsin, was generally better than the 1894 Democratic percentage, but was only a fraction of the usual Democratic percentage in such units. With the exception of Ohio, the Democratic 1896 rural percentage was also below the normal level; but, except in Wisconsin, it did increase between 1894 and 1896 at a faster rate than the urban percentage. This suggests that Bryan's candidacy was relatively more favorably received by rural voters than by urban ones, but in neither case was there anything close to overwhelming or disproportionate support.

There still remains one important avenue to investigate. Conceivably these data could conceal a sharp voter polarization along class lines within both rural and urban units. That is, it is possible that Bryan drew a disproportionate degree of his support from working class urban residents, and that a shift of middle and upper class urban voters in the opposite direction concealed this movement. Bryan might have proven more appealing to poorer farmers than to richer ones, and the counterbalancing shifts would not be evident in the gross data. We can explore this possibility by examining the data at the ward and township levels, and in comparison with previous levels of Democratic strength.[8]

The data from major midwestern metropolitan areas do not support the view that Bryan had an unusually strong attraction for urban workers. In Chicago, for example, while the 1896 Democratic percentages were better in twenty-nine of the city's thirty-four wards than they had been in 1894, in none of these wards was that strength equal to that which the party had registered in 1892. The case becomes clear when we group the wards by class categories and inspect the Democratic mean vote within each category over time (see Table 38). With the exception of the upper

TABLE 38   Mean Democratic Strength by Class Categories,
Chicago, 1892–96

	1892	1893*	1894	1896
Upper class	44.7	37.4	28.7	27.2
Upper middle class	55.6	45.3	31.6	39.0
Middle class	44.6	40.5	30.2	32.7
Lower middle class	57.2	48.3	31.9	42.2
Lower class	63.0	56.9	40.6	48.6

* Data from special mayoralty election, December, 1893.

class wards, the Democrats were stronger in 1896 in all class categories than they had been in 1894. Their 8.0 percentage point increase in the lower class wards was not materially different from the 7.4 percentage point increase in the upper middle class wards. Regardless of class, the Democratic percentages were lower in all categories in 1896 than they had been in 1892, or even in December 1893. Bryan's inability to polarize the urban "toiling masses" is even more strikingly illustrated by noting the movement of the Republican mean in the laboring class wards. Despite the depression, the Republicans had not received more than a 45.1% mean in these wards in 1894. For the first time, in 1896 the Republican mean went above the majority mark as the party registered 50.1%.

Bryan was no more successful in mobilizing workers in Detroit than he was in Chicago. The Democratic mean in working class wards in Detroit in 1896 was even lower than it had been in 1894, and considerably below the 1892 level. The city's laboring class wards had returned a Democratic mean of 59.0% in 1892, 43.3% in 1894, and 41.2% in 1896. In contrast, the richest wards in the city showed a Democratic mean of 52.2% in 1892, 40.4% in 1894, and 41.2% in 1896. In both types of units Bryan's percentages were considerably below the 1892 Democratic strength, although in the "rich" wards he was able at least to improve on the disastrous 1894 levels.[9]

Superficially, the Milwaukee data offer a better case for laboring class cohesion behind Bryan than those for Chicago or Detroit. In 1892 the Democratic mean in laboring class wards was 51.0%; this fell in 1894 to 33.5%; and in 1896 it rose to 52.1%. But a more intensive examination of the data raises serious doubt as to whether this movement was a class phenomenon. First, the "better class" wards moved in the same direction. In these units the respective Democratic means were 41.7%, 29.9%, and 32.1%. Thus the voting pattern was not the product of a bipolar movement of class units. Second, Bryan's percentage was lower than the 1892 Democratic percentage in all but one of the city's wards. That ward was one of the working class wards, but in the other working class units his percentage was lower than the 1892 Democratic strength. It is instructive to notice that although Bryan ran behind the 1892 Democratic percentages in Polish and German Catholic and German Lutheran working class wards, he ran ahead of that percentage, and by 16.7 percentage points, in the city's strongest native Protestant ward.[10]

In Michigan and Wisconsin the same absence of class polarization persisted in smaller sized cities. An intensive analysis of the relevant ward data indicates that nowhere was Bryan able to unite workers *as an economic group* in his support. Where the workers consisted of a majority of traditional Democrats, e.g., Poles, German Catholics, and the like, his percentage was usually lower than the 1892 Democratic percentage; only where the majority of the workers were pietists, native or immigrant, were there any instances of his running better than the Democrats had in 1892.

The variations in receptivity to Bryan's candidacy that marked rural voting units were not related to degree of economic prosperity. Within the same county, units of approximately the same economic ranking reacted quite differently, and units with similar reactions quite often varied widely in their degree of prosperity.

In Hillsdale county, Michigan, Moscow and Wright townships were both "marginal" farming units. In both the Democratic percentages in 1896 were above those of 1894; but although Moscow's 28.7 percentage point gain put it 14.1 percentage points above the Democratic level of 1892, Wright remained 3.4 percentage points below the 1892 level. In Calhoun county the top-ranking economic unit, "very prosperous" Albion, and "poor" Clarendon, which ranked twentieth, both registered stronger Democratic percentages in 1896 than they had four years earlier; Albion was 14.2 percentage points stronger, and Clarendon 9.7. Two "prosperous" units, Homer and Fredonia, which ranked eighth and ninth in the county, reacted very differently. Homer voted 20.2 percentage points above its 1892 Democratic level; Fredonia was 2.9 percentage points below the normal Democratic vote. In Van Buren county "prosperous" Keeler, which ranked second among the county's farming units, had voted 22.2% Democratic in 1892, dropped to 9.3% in 1894, and gave 55.4% of its vote to Bryan's Democracy. The "very poor" farmers in Pine Grove township were much less enthusiastic over the Bryan candidacy. They had given the Democrats 39.1% of their vote in 1892, dropped to 25.2% in 1894, and increased to 43.2% in 1896.

In the eastern portion of the state, Washtenaw county's twenty rural townships exhibited a mixed pattern of reaction. Democratic percentage strength in six of the units dropped below the 1894 level; it rose above that level in the remaining fourteen, but in only four of the units was the Democratic strength in 1896 above that of

1892. Two "very prosperous" units, Freedom and York, showed a comparable dissimilarity in their voting behavior. In 1896 Democratic percentage strength in Freedom continued to decline, and the unit fell 18.7 percentage points below the 1892 level. York not only gained in Democratic percentage strength between 1894 and 1896, but moved to 4.5 percentage points above the strength which it had given to the Democracy in 1892.

This type of bipolar movement was not randomly distributed. It was associated with important social correlates. But for present purposes it is sufficient to emphasize that it was *not* associated with variations in degree of economic prosperity. Bryan's ability to attract rural voters was not an economic class phenomenon.

In Wisconsin, Bryan's rural percentage was actually lower than the percentage the Democrats had attracted in 1894. But particular types of rural units did show a marked propensity to shift to the Democrats, and to return levels of Democratic percentage strength above those that the party had polled in either 1894 or 1892. These units were not invariably, nor consistently, the poorer ones. In fact, there was no discernible relationship between receptivity to the Bryan candidacy and degree of economic prosperity.

In western Wisconsin, in Pierce county, two "marginal" units, Trenton and Rock Elm, reacted very differently. Rock Elm registered a Democratic decline between 1894 and 1896, and in the latter year was 5.9 percentage points below the Democratic strength of 1892; Trenton was 26.7 percentage points above its 1892 level of Democratic support. In Pepin county "marginal" Durand responded favorably to Bryan and gave the Democrats a level of percentage strength 5.1 percentage points above the 1892 mark. But "very poor" Frankfort responded negatively, declined even below the disastrous level of 1894, and reached a nadir of 13.7 percentage points below the Democratic vote of 1892. In Grant county, "very prosperous" Patch Grove responded enthusiastically to Bryan. It not only increased its degree of support for the Democracy over the 1894 level, but gave the party 15.4 percentage points more strength than it had in 1892. On the other hand, "poor" Harrison continued to display a Democratic decline, and its 1896 level was 11.2 percentage points below the mark attained by the Democracy in 1892.

In eastern Wisconsin Bryan scored gains that put the Democratic percentage above its 1892 level among the "very prosperous" farmers of Oakfield township, Fond du Lac county. But the "marginal" farmers in Osceola, in the same county, who had declined in Democratic percentage strength by only 0.2 of a percentage point between 1892 and 1894, dropped off by 12.3 percentage points in 1896. In Racine county the Bryan candidacy brought the level of Democratic percentage strength in the top-ranking economic unit, "very prosperous" Rochester, to 11.2 percentage points above the 1892 level. In the lowest-ranking economic unit in the county, "marginal" Dover, Democratic strength continued to decline and reached a level of 4.2 percentage points below the 1892 strength.

Two units in Green county, in eastern Wisconsin, dramatically illustrate both the absence of a meaningful pattern of association between the changes in the Democratic vote and relative degree of prosperity, and the complete reversal of voting patterns that frequently occurred. Both Cadiz and Mount Pleasant were "very prosperous" farming units. Cadiz in 1892 gave 35.2% of its vote to the Democrats; it moved to a slightly lower level in 1894, 32.4%, but reached its nineteenth-century Democratic apex with 56.8% in 1896. Mount Pleasant gave 51.5% of its 1892 vote to the

Democrats; that dropped to 48.6% in 1894, and continued to decline to 32.1% in 1896.

The 1896 rural Democratic vote in Ohio was slightly above the level the party had polled in rural voting units in 1892. But that slight improvement was not associated with the movement of poorer farmers into the Democratic lists. The pattern of movement was quite a mixed one. For example, in Belmont county seven of the twelve farming units returned Democratic percentages lower than those in 1892. The Democratic revival in this county began with the 1895 gubernatorial election. In that year the mean Democratic vote in the farming units increased by 7.6 percentage points over the 1894 level. In 1896 that mean increased only 4.9 percentage points above the 1895 level, and was only 1.2 percentage points higher than the 1892 mean. The Republican mean in 1896 was 3.9 percentage points stronger than it had been in 1892. The movement toward Bryan was not associated with degree of prosperity. "Very prosperous" Colerain increased its Democratic percentage strength by 9.3 percentage points between 1895 and 1896, but "poor" Wayne increased by only 1.4 percentage points and was still 4.7 percentage points below its 1892 level.

In Athens county the Democratic gain in rural units was stronger in 1896 than it had been in 1895. But units with very different degrees of economic prosperity reacted in about the same fashion to Bryan. The top-ranking economic unit, Bern township, showed a 9.2 percentage point increase in Democratic strength between 1895 and 1896. The lowest-ranking unit, Alexander township, registered an 11.6 percentage point gain.

Ohio's rural voting pattern in 1896 persistently appeared to be somewhat different from that of Michigan or Wisconsin. It was, for instance, the only one of the three states in which the Democratic rural percentage in 1896 was above the 1892 level. But that deviation from the pattern was more apparent than real. First, there was no greater association of the Bryan gains with class factors in rural Ohio units than in those of the other two states. Second, the fact that the Democratic rural percentage was above the 1892 level was misleading; so, too, was the Republican rural percentage, and by a greater amount. We can examine the changing relative positions of the two parties in Ohio, and the other states, by comparing the percentages for both parties in 1892 and 1896 (see Table 39). Though the 1896 Democratic rural

TABLE 39   Rural Party Percentages, 1892 and 1896

	DEMOCRATIC		REPUBLICAN	
	1892	1896	1892	1896
Michigan	47.8	41.0	47.6	54.9
Ohio	45.9	47.6	47.6	50.3
Wisconsin	47.4	37.2	46.2	60.8

vote in Ohio was 1.7 percentage points above the party's 1892 strength, the Republican vote had increased by 2.7 percentage points during the same period. That the Democratic vote showed an increase was not due to greater receptivity to the Bryan candidacy by Ohio farmers as an economic group, but was a product of the manner in which the minor party vote was distributed upon the collapse of those entities in 1896.

In each one of these states the Bryan strategy was aimed at eliciting a favorable response from the voters who constituted what he repeatedly referred to as the "toiling masses." A union of downtrodden urban workers and oppressed farmers would insure a Democratic victory. Workers and farmers might have seen themselves as downtrodden and oppressed, but even if they did they obviously did not see the Democracy of Bryan as a solution to their problems. As economic groups, neither urban workers nor farmers reacted favorably to the candidate and his gospel of commodity price inflation.

The Bryan vote does not show a greater degree of cohesion even when we examine its distribution among specific occupational groups. If any geographic area of the Midwest was ripe for drastic solutions to its equally drastic economic problems, it was Michigan's Upper Peninsula. Bryan recognized its potentialities and devoted considerable time to campaigning there. It was also an area in which there had never been any tradition of a sound, stable currency. Workers there were both accustomed and reconciled to payment in various kinds of "funny money," especially the kind issued by the lumbering companies or iron mines. This scrip was invariably accepted at par value by local merchants. The use of locally issued currency dated to the money shortages that had occurred during the Civil War and was a commonly accepted feature in the area. Against this sort of background, there was no particular reason why voters should look with doubt on proposals calling for the issuance of a different kind of federal money.[11]

Despite the impact of a severe economic depression and the absence of any sort of commitment to gold-backed currency, Bryan's appeal to the "common people" went unheeded by the Upper Peninsula's voters. Lumbering units there in 1892 had shown considerable variation in their voting patterns; in 1894, under the impact of the depression, all such units moved away from the Democracy. In 1896 the units moved in two opposite directions; one group continued to decline in Democratic percentage strength, and the other showed Democratic increases. The combined effect was almost counterbalancing: the Democratic mean in 1892 was 46.9%; in 1894 that fell to 24.6%; and in 1896 it was 24.8%.

The same sort of movement took place in the area's iron mining units. There the Democratic mean was 41.8% in 1892, 23.6% in 1894, and 17.4% in 1896. Copper mining units also continued to register Democratic declines. The party's mean dropped from 37.6% in 1892, to 22.8% in 1894, and to a nadir of 18.7% in 1896.

At first glance, Ohio's coal fields present the best case for laboring class cohesion behind Bryan. There the mean Democratic vote in mining units within the coal producing counties usually increased in 1896 over 1895, and the rate of increase was generally greater than that between 1894 and 1895. But several facts raise serious doubts concerning the extent to which Ohio coal miners united behind the Bryan candidacy. First, within the same county the range of the Democratic increases was quite wide. For example, in Perry county's mining units the 1895–96 Democratic increases ranged from + 1.0 to + 28.3 percentage points. Second, although the Democratic percentages were usually better than they had been in 1894, they were not consistently above the 1892 level. The Democratic mean in mining units moved in the same direction as that in the farming units within the same county. Lastly, the Republican mean in the mining units was consistently above the 1892 level.

In 1896 both parties offered the voters explanations of the depression and proposed solutions to the ills which it had caused. Both the explanations and the solutions were in complete contrast. The major parties chose candidates for the presidency whose ideologies and images were consonant with the party's view of the depression and its cures. The Bryan strategy aimed at mobilizing the "toiling masses." However the attempt might have fared elsewhere, in Michigan, Ohio, and Wisconsin it was a complete disaster.[12] Neither rural nor urban areas showed any tendency to offer disproportionate support to Bryan. Though rural voters were relatively more favorably disposed than urban ones, even in these units Bryan fell below the 1892 Democratic percentage in Wisconsin and Michigan; though his Ohio rural percentage was above the Democracy's strength of 1892, the McKinley percentage exceeded the 1892 Republican strength by an even greater amount. Neither coal miners, nor iron miners, nor lumbermen responded favorably, *as economic groups*, to his class-oriented appeals. A strategy that seemed so preeminently reasonable proved to be a complete failure.

Liberal historians, sympathizing with Bryan's class appeals and projecting their own ideologies to contemporary human actors, have resorted to ingenious explanations of the phenomenon. Taking campaign rhetoric at face value, they have accepted the charges of the Bryan partisans that urban workers were bribed, duped, and/or intimidated in 1896. The fact that Bryan was frequently stronger in such units than the Democrats had been in 1894, although generally below the Democratic levels of 1892, immediately casts doubt on this type of explanation. At the very least the fact suggests that the coercive elements, if any were present at all, must have been relatively less effective in 1896 than in 1894. In short, a series of percentage point declines *over time* cannot be explained by the intrusion of coercive elements at *one point in time*. Nor does this type of explanation even begin to touch the rejection of Bryan on the part of midwestern farmers. Indeed, not even the Bryan partisans alleged coercion or corruption in rural units.[13]

Bryan's inability to mobilize voters along class lines is perfectly explainable, although not in the usual ideological terms. Knowing now the extent to which Bryan's Democracy was rejected by both midwestern urban workers and midwestern farmers, we can turn to these pertinent analytical questions.

The Politics of Rejection

Two dimensions of the failure of the "toiling masses" to cohere in the support of Bryan's Democracy deserve consideration. First, Bryan was not able to restore even the usual levels of Democratic support. Second, he failed to attract workers and farmers *as economic groups*, i.e., he failed to produce a class polarization of politics.

Once we realize that the political configuration that Bryan envisaged did not involve an extension of the old social bases of political action but the creation of an entirely new one, Bryan's lack of attraction for traditional Democrats becomes understandable. Democratic partisan loyalties were not rooted in economic class distinctions, but in religious value systems. In election contests prior to 1896, Democratic strategists had recognized the basis of these traditional attachments and designed their rhetoric *both* to reactivate latent loyalties and to reinforce the proclivity of such voters to support the Democracy.

Current studies of political behavior demonstrate the importance of these types of appeals in a political campaign. One such study offers this assessment of the overall effects of the campaign on the vote intention: "This is what the campaign does: reinforcement 53%; activation 14%; reconversion 3%; partial conversion 6%; conversion 8%; no effect 16%." [14] The important point to observe is that the first three categories, reinforcement, activation, and reconversion, involve a "return," in one sense or another, of the voter to his traditional partisan attachment. These data also indicate the disproportionately important role these effects play in shaping the final voting intention: they sum to 70.0%.

The most obvious fact about the 1896 rhetoric is the absence of reactivating appeals. The Bryanites did not greatly concern themselves with appeals to the underlying bases of traditional Democratic attachments. On the contrary, they explicitly argued that the old bases of political divisions were no longer relevant and that they welcomed support from "old Democrats" only when that arose from an agreement with the party's new program and ideology. We should not, of course, take seriously the claim by Bryan supporters that they sought only votes motivated by complete ideological concurrence. What is important here is not the validity of the claim, but the image being projected to traditional Democrats by the fact that the claim was being made and the fact that the party's rhetoric was devoid of the customary and expected types of reactivating appeals. In brief, that image was one of a *new* and *different* Democracy. It was *not* the image of the traditional Democratic party, the image of negative government and of maximum "personal liberty." [15]

Nor was it merely Bryan's enemies, Republican or Democratic, who were responsible for projecting such an image. Indeed, Democratic organs that opposed Bryan reiterated the theme that he did not represent the Traditional Democracy. Their concern with this type of theme was a reflection of their awareness of the potency of party identifications in mobilizing voters. That anti-Bryan organs projected such an image to Bryan's Democracy was less important than the fact that this was *by design* the image the Bryanites projected of themselves. Their concern was not with the reactivation of *old* loyalties, but with the creation of a *new* configuration of political forces. That involved *conversion,* not mere reactivation and reinforcement of old loyalties.

Late nineteenth-century midwestern partisan identifications were not rooted in economic class identifications. Voting behavior was not significantly determined by differences in relative degrees of economic prosperity. Bryan's appeals were directed to class awareness and designed to polarize voters along economic lines. To produce such a configuration required that large numbers of voters not only accept a new set of priorities, ones that placed economic considerations above ethnic and religious ones, but that they structure entirely new political perspectives. Essentially, Bryan was asking Democrats to view their party not as a preserver of their religious value system, not in the way in which they had seen it since the 1850's, but as a vehicle through which they could implement class objectives. In formal terms, such rhetoric was *disruptive* rather than *reactivating.* That is, its objective was to orient traditional Democrats to a pattern of values and a basis of party identifications that was specifically in conflict with their time-honored political perspective and its attendant values and definitions. [16]

Since perception is a selective mechanism, and the nature of the selectivity has partisan overtones, numerous Democrats undoubtedly drew the candidate and his program closer to their own positions. But even this mechanism waas relatively *less effective* in 1896 than in earlier elections. Misperception requires a certain degree of ambiguity in the objective situation being perceived. In 1896 the objective situation was less ambiguous than usual in presidential contests. This, coupled with the disruptive impact of Bryan's rhetoric, resulted in his failure to poll even the normal levels of Democratic support.

Conceivably, however, the free silver rhetoric could have served as a reinforcing type of appeal, i.e., it could have provided partisans with a series of arguments with which both to answer their own questions concerning the current economic situation and to counter the opposing Republican arguments. By design it was intended, of course, to do much more than this. It was intended to mobilize the bulk of the "toiling masses," regardless of previous partisan identifications, behind the Bryan candidacy. As the empirical data demonstrate, it achieved neither effect. We can understand this failure by examining that rhetoric in relationship to the social context in which the voter arrived at his partisan decision.

As an economic group urban workers, even those who had previously supported the Democrats, did not respond in a disproportionately favorable way to Bryan. Historians have often explained this on the grounds that the free silver argument offered little advantage to wage earners. There is a large measure of validity in such arguments, but they usually have been posited within a faulty conceptual framework. The implication is that the voter clearly perceived the relationship between the economic effects of free silver and his own class interests. The assumption, in short, is that free silver constituted a substantive "issue" and was rejected, after considerable ratiocination, by issue-oriented voters.[17] There is no factual basis for such assumptions. This does not mean that the free silver rhetoric played no role in Bryan's rejection by urban workers. It means that we have to analyze that rejection within a more useful and realistic conceptual framework.

It is of little analytical value to consider free silver as a substantive issue. But is very meaningful to consider both the money question and the tariff as ideological instruments of voter mobilization and party combat. Both were intended by party strategists to provide voters with an explanation of the 1893 depression and the subsequent economic crisis. Both were designed to offer voters a structured response to their inquiries concerning future economic prospects. In this analytical context the question of whether the tariff or free silver was the major substantive issue in the 1896 election is an irrelevant one; "The important struggle during that campaign was not over two sides of an issue, but over whether or not one issue or the other should be the primary focus of attention. . . . Each [presidential candidate] tried to mobilize voters around explanatory ideological positions with which those voters could identify."[18]

Through the free silver ideology Bryan and his supporters tried to explain both the advent of "hard times" and the process through which prosperity would be restored. The explanations, however, were not consonant with either the experiences or the perceptions of urban workers. An examination of the three major themes of the ideology illustrates the point.

The Bryan rhetoric spoke of the "crime of 1873" and emphasized that "crime" as the underlying cause of all subsequent discontent. The demonetization of silver, the act of "a corrupt and corrupting set of abominable traitors," had "assassinated labor"; it had reduced the "toiling masses" to subservience to "the interest of avarice and greed."[19] The remonetization of silver would undo this great evil and free the "common people" from the yoke of oppression by restoring the pristine virtues and social relationships that had characterized the earlier era. This type of explanation hardly accorded with the experience of urban workers. They attributed their difficulties, not to a long-term price decline, but to the immediate and severe impact of unemployment and wage reductions that had begun in 1893. The story of twenty years of cumulating hardship hardly accounted for this experience. Nor did the promise of a return to the relationships of a simpler, less complex social system hold out much hope for the restoration of jobs and wages. Free silver, from this perspective, was not a forward-looking, adjustive ideology, not one attuned to the growing complexity of a modern industrial society, not one addressed to the immediate problems of urban workers.[20]

When Bryan and his supporters spoke in terms of immediate solutions they used a theme equally discordant to urban workers. Commodity price inflation was the solution offered to overcome the problems of "the producers of the nation's wealth." This type of explanation bore little relationship to urban workers' perceptions. The size of the job supply was probably more salient to them than that of the money supply, and wage increases more relevant than price increases. But more important was the fact that the explanation revealed the jarringly anachronistic perception the Bryanites held of the role that the wage earner played in the industrial system. To Bryan and his followers commodity price inflation, a producer-oriented solution, was not inconsistent with the best interests of urban workers precisely because the latter *were* producers. Their vision of what the worker *should be,* a petty entrepreneur, was some forty years out of date. The urban laborer, who had accepted the wage system and sought pragmatic adjustments within its confines, saw the normative dictum of the free silver ideology in conflict with the reality he daily experienced.[21]

The third major theme of the free silver rhetoric also created a problem of cognitive dissonance for urban workers. The Bryanites emphasized the primacy of agriculture over industry. They concentrated on the agricultural producer and his role in the creation of the moral and just society. When they turned themselves to the welfare of the urban worker, they attempted to link that directly with the welfare of the farmer. The type of nexus they emphasized was significant. The economic recovery of the farmer had to precede that of the urban worker. Bryan was doing more than displaying his oratorical prowess when, in his address before the Democratic National Convention, he claimed that "the great cities rest upon *our* broad and fertile prairies. Burn down *your* cities and leave *our* farms, and *your* cities will spring up again as if by magic; but destroy *our* farms and the grass will grow in the streets of every city in the country." [22] He was giving verbal expression to his view of the world about him, and enunciating a central theme of the free silver ideology. The relationship between urban workers and farmers that ideology stressed was more than one of mutual interdependence, it was one in which the worker's concerns had to be subordinate to those of the farmer.

It is a mistake, of course, to suggest, or imply, that contemporary human actors separated one theme of the free silver ideology from another. Voter reactions were not based upon such analytical distinctions. These themes were not separated, but fused into an explanatory ideology through which Bryan hoped to mobilize supporters. That urban workers were not significantly responsive to these attempts was the result of the fact that the free silver ideology was *relatively less* consonant with their experiences and perceptions than the competing ideology offered by the opposition.

The Republican tariff ideology explained the "hard times" in terms that accorded with the urban worker's experiences. Its focus was not on distant causes, but on the very immediate ones that had converted the prosperity of 1892 into the depression of 1893. It addressed itself directly to the immediate problems of the urban worker: employment and wages. It did not propose to solve these problems by increasing prices, or by expanding the purchasing power of *farmers,* but by protecting the laborer's job and his wage levels. It was an ideology which the urban worker could translate into personally relevant terms.

Republican strategists were cognizant of the role played by the tariff ideology, by the "tariff as wage and job protection." Historians have often called attention to the fact that anti-Bryan sources emphasized the harm that would befall the worker whose wages were paid in fifty-cent dollars. To provide their supporters with arguments with which to answer the claims of free silverites, Republicans did use such rhetoric. What is more significant is that in addition to attacking the free silver solution, in urban areas the Republican party newspapers offered a counter-solution. For example, both the *Chicago Tribune* and the *Milwaukee Sentinel* devoted relatively more of their worker-directed symbolism to extolling the necessity of "restoring prosperity by restoring the tariff," than they did to attacks on "funny money."

Midwestern farmers were relatively more responsive to the Bryan candidacy than urban workers, but as an economic group they failed to provide disproportionate support to his Democracy. Since the Bryanites were especially convinced of their strength among midwestern farmers, the failure is particularly significant. One analysis of the "farm vote" has attempted to explain Bryan's poor showing on the grounds that he was faced with the task of making inroads into a solidly Republican bloc of voters, "Bryan had to convert traditionally Republican farmers to the Democratic cause and convince them to forsake their regular party allegiance." [23] This hypothesis could serve as the basis for an extremely important explanation of the variations in the degree of rural receptivity to Bryan, were it not for the fact that it is in no way congruent with the empirical voting data. Midwestern farmers were not solidly Republican prior to 1896. As a group they had tended to divide rather evenly between the two major parties since at least 1876. Reacting negatively to the party of "hard times," they were more Republican than usual in 1894, but even then a *substantial* minority was anti-Republican. The hypothesis has two more crucial weaknesses. It cannot begin to explain his failure in Michigan and Wisconsin to capture even the normal *Democratic* rural percentage. Nor can it explain the fact that in all three states some of his most pronounced gains came in units that had been solidly and steadfastly Republican during every election in the preceding twenty years.

Bryan's failure to elicit a favorable response from rural voters involved more than farmers voting their traditional party identification. For present purposes, it is adequate to focus on one aspect of this analytical problem: Why didn't these midwestern rural producers, who had suffered from long-term price declines and the short-term impact of the depression, respond favorably to an ideology explicitly designed to attract rural support? No doubt the prospects of repaying their mortgage indebtedness in inflated currency, and of rising commodity prices, were attractive to midwestern farmers. But the farmer did not approach the 1896 election without his own explanation of the ills that had befallen him during the previous two decades. He had his own perception of both the nature of his problems and the possible solutions available to him. That he found little congruence between these perceptions and the free silver ideology resulted in Bryan's failure to translate rural dissatisfaction into a favorable partisan voting intention.

Although they all had been squeezed between falling commodity prices and rising costs, farmers in the Midwest, the East, the trans-Missouri West, and the South, did not define their problems in the same way. Those definitions varied because the structure of agriculture and the impact of the "overproduction crisis" differed among regions. While no region was similar to any of the others, and none was internally homogeneous, it is adequate here to focus on the ways in which the midwestern farmer's perception of his problems diverged from those held by rural producers in the South and the West.[24]

Producers in the latter areas saw their difficulties arising from exploitation by the financial interests of the East. Capital and credit shortages required the importation of eastern money, at what western producers saw as ruinous interest rates. The absence of nearby large urban centers required the shipment of their products to eastern markets and made them highly vulnerable to changes in transportation costs. Involvement in an impersonal price and marketing system controlled by easterners merely intensified their sense of powerlessness. While these and other particulars could be endlessly extended, it suffices to observe that southern and western producers explained their problems to themselves in terms of exploitation by avaricious easterners. To them, "Wall Street" became a potent symbolic expression of what was wrong with their world. The solution that they envisaged involved wresting political and financial control from the exploiters. Bryan's free silver ideology was addressed to precisely such perspectives.

Midwestern farmers lived in a region that had a different set of structural relationships with the East. They tended to see their world, to define their problems in entirely different ways; they came, as a result, to propose different genera of solutions.

When the midwestern farmer asked himself what was wrong with his world, why his prices were declining and his property depreciating in value, his response gave no consolation to his western counterpart. The principal problem was not exploitation by eastern capitalists, nor excessive railroad freight rates, but the "unfair" competition created by western production. The availability of cheap land frequently provided by the government, relatively lower taxes, and advantageous long-haul freight rates enabled the western producer to send his beef, hogs, corn, and wheat "to enter and compete in markets which by natural contact should belong to others." Midwestern farm leaders attributed the depression of agriculture to an oversupply of production, not to an undersupply of currency. The chief villain was not the eastern financier but the western farmer, who was responsible for the overproduction. The president of the Ohio Agricultural Society translated the causative sequence into directly and personally relevant terms when he claimed that, "It has been overproduction by the opening up of the great West . . . that has placed mortgages upon the farmers' homes of this state." [25]

The antagonism of interests that the midwestern farmer perceived between himself and his western brethren found expression in the frequent resolutions adopted by all types of agricultural organizations against continued government expenditures for western irrigation and reclamation projects. In what they frequently described as "an age of competition," it made little sense to the embattled midwestern farmer for the federal government to appropriate public funds to aid his competitor. Midwestern farmers showed little sympathy for what they viewed as "a scheme to bring in competition with the farmer east of the Mississippi all these vast acres of land at the expense of the general government." [26]

The midwestern farmer was not content with a monistic explanation of his difficulties. He constructed a litany of troubles. But this shared little in common with the southern and western ejaculatory recitation. When the midwesterner railed against the railroads, he more often than not criticized them for the role they played in abetting the "unfair" western competition. His focus of complaint was not so much that his rates were too high, but that rates on western shipments were *too low.* He attributed some portion of his difficulty to the tax structure, and supported legislation to reduce the tax levels on real property and increase those on personal property. He sought to eliminate the "unfair" competition created by "fraudulent" products, oleo and filled-cheese, through legislative proposals at both state and national levels to outlaw or severely restrict the sale of such products. Such attempts involved farmers in conflict and combat with *local* Grocers and Retailers Associations. When the farmer directed his ire against financial manipulators, it was not eastern capitalists, not "Wall Street," that fell under fire, but "the *local* Boards of Trade" that speculated in futures, coerced local dealers, and depressed prices. Finally, he raised his voice against the tariff: not to oppose its principle, but to demand the extension of its protection to the products of the farm. Though midwestern farmers frequently complained that manufacturing interests received relatively too great a measure of tariff protection, and demanded a counterbalancing increase in the level of protection afforded their own products, they did not oppose the principle of tariff protection for industry. To the contrary, this protection guaranteed full employment in cities and a nearby, lucrative market for farm products. The farmers' objective was to "protect" that market both by continued high employment and by eliminating the "unfair" competition of western producers and "fake goods." [27]

When the midwestern producer sought relief, he turned to measures designed to combat *his* problems. He pressed for I.C.C. rulings to increase the freight rates on shipments from the West. He advocated legislation to eliminate the tax disparity between real and personal property. He favored legislative enactments to reduce the power of his *local* enemies, the Grocers and Retailers Associations and the Boards of Trade. But he did not confine himself to suggestions aimed only at changing the roles played by others. His own role, too, had to change.

Western and southern producers blamed their depressed condition on eastern exploiters, but rural opinion leaders in the Midwest allotted a major portion of the responsibility to the farmer himself. Success required farmers doing more than "going over the same routine of work that their fathers have laid out before them." If the farmer was not receiving a just share of society's profits, it was not enough for him to "settle down to the role of the chronic grumbler." Nor should he expect solutions to be bestowed upon him by either a kindly providence or a munificent government. The remedy lay in self-help:

> How long O! Lord, how long will it take the average American farmer to learn that the Lord helps those who help themselves? . . . Go out of the ruts then ye grumblers. Go to work and do your full share in trying to remedy existing evils, and until you have done that, shut up, and let us hear no more of your unmanly grumbling.[28]

It was not a *general* self-help ideology that distinguished midwestern solutions from southern and western ones, but the *specific* approaches into which that ideology channelled rural energies. If the midwestern producer was squeezed between falling prices and rising costs, the solution was "to economize," to adopt improved production techniques and thus reduce his costs. When his products sell for less than usual, the practical farmer "does not waste his vitality in trying to raise prices by grumbling about the times, but immediately turns his attention to producing an article at less cost." Even at the height of the depression, some farmers were able to make a profit. These, the opinion leaders argued, were the farmers who had adopted and adapted the "new knowledge" to the practical task of farming; the ones who had emulated, rather than castigated, businessmen and their principles and practices. If all farmers would model themselves after these, if they would follow the much-admired methods of the business world, then "every farmer can make a living, no matter how low prices are." [29]

In the Midwest, rural opinion leaders used two themes to elaborate their self-help ideology. First, businessmen were not enemies to be fought, but exemplars to be followed. If the captains of industry enriched themselves in "the battle of life," if the number of millionaires in the country was growing, this was not evil: "Let us put ourselves in the places of the successful individuals . . . and methinks we should have done as they have done and thought it no crime, but an honor." The farmers could learn from these men, they could learn how to be successful; they could learn the efficient, business-like principles of management and operation that they, too, had to adopt in order to "get out of the ruts worn deep by the sluggish, slow motion of our fathers." Profitable farming required the producer to adopt such methods.[30]

The necessity of conducting the farm as a business operation dovetailed with the second theme, the need for a higher level of practical education among farmers. Rural opinion leaders of all types preached the doctrine of scientific farming. The farmer who did not take advantage of the "new knowledge" emanating from the experiment stations and agricultural colleges was the *"hayseed, long-haired, backwoods clod-hopper."* If he expected to convert his farm into a practical and profitable business operation, the farmer had to "keep step with the advancing progress of the age, [or] he may as well throw up the sponge." [31]

Of course, not all midwestern farmers would have structured the same rank-ordering of the sources of their economic difficulties. Nor did they all, or even a majority, idolize businessmen and revere the test tube as deeply as the plow. There was undoubtedly considerable animosity toward local merchants and middlemen; and probably the majority of farmers ridiculed "kid-glove" farming. The opinions and attitudes expressed in the rural press, agricultural journals, Grange meetings, the conventions of agricultural societies and dairymen's associations, and the farmers' institutes were those of a much more cosmopolitanly oriented group than the average "hayseed." Nor was there a one-to-one relationship between these attitudes and grass-roots sentiments.

But in the midst of a severe depression such attitudes served an important function to farmers who were not of the leadership strata. Reiterated over a twenty-year period, collectively they created a climate of opinion which conditioned the political response of midwestern farmers to the "hard times" of the 1890's. The severity of the depression created a set of conditions beyond the experience of most rural producers; it created a literally unstructured situation. Attempting to impart meaning to that situation, to explain it to himself, the farmer was more likely to turn first to those ideologies which struck familiar chords. "Practical, or scientific, farming," "business-like management," "the tariff": these were explanations whose terms and implications he could understand; these were ideologies through which his support could be mobilized.[32]

When the depression struck, and more farmers *actively* concerned themselves with seeking solutions to their problems, these ideologies channelled their discontent. It was no coincidence that the worst years of the depression, 1894–96, saw marked increases in the popularity of the farmers' institutes and in the circulation of the bulletins of the agricultural experiment stations. By 1896 experiment stations bulletins were reaching 70.0% more readers in Indiana than they had in 1892, 125.0% more in Michigan, and over 300.0% more in Wisconsin. The average attendance at sessions of the farmers' institutes more than doubled in every one of the five midwestern states during each year between 1893 and 1896, and the number of institutes held also increased. While even after 1896 the "farmer constituency anxious to bring science down out of the skies and hitch it to the plow" was probably still only a minority, those who *actively* sought solutions to the economic difficulties during the depression were relatively more responsive to familiar ideologies than they were to one that inveighed against unfamiliar enemies and promised its chief benefits to groups that midwestern farmers saw as competitors.[33]

Bryan's free silver ideology did not elicit a cohesive and favorable response from midwestern farmers precisely because they could see in it little that was consonant with their perceptions of either the nature of their problems or what constituted feasible solutions.

Although he preached the free silver gospel with the zeal of a Methodist circuit-rider, Bryan failed to polarize the vote of the "toiling masses" in his favor. But if he was unable to realign the social bases of partisan support along class lines, he did succeed in producing considerable political movement among other categories of social groups.

NOTES

1. Arthur M. Schlesinger, *The Rise of the City, 1878–1898* (New York, 1933), p. 302. For the frontier-section hypothesis of Frederick Jackson Turner, see *The Significance of Sections in American History* (New York, 1932), and especially "The Problem of the West," in *The Frontier in American History* (New York, 1950 ed.), pp. 205–11.
2. William Diamond, "Urban and Rural Voting in 1896," *American Historical Review,* XLVI (January, 1941), 281–305.
3. *Ibid.,* p. 283. Diamond confined his definition of "urban" to places with a population of 45,000 or more; I have extended the definition to all places with a population of 10,000 or above.
4. *Ibid.,* p. 304.
5. Lee Benson, "Research Problems in American Political Historiography," in Mirra Komarovsky (ed.), *Common Frontiers of the Social Sciences* (New York, 1957), p. 161; for his highly perceptive discussion of the Diamond hypothesis see pp. 155–71.
6. Diamond, "Urban and Rural Voting," *American Historical Review,* p. 283.
7. *Ibid.,* see p. 296 for the quotation; my interpolation is clear from the context. Diamond's data are in Table 10, p. 295. The correlation coefficient is a Spearman rank-order.
8. This sort of movement is, in fact, implicit in the class conflict interpretations of the Bryan candidacy. Unless one makes the somewhat suspect assumption that there were about as many "rich" farmers as "poor" ones, and about as many upper and middle class urban residents as laboring class ones, the type of polarization envisaged should show itself in the category totals. But an examination of the relevant data at a still lower level of aggregation removes any element of doubt.
9. I have used the vote for president for both 1892 and 1896. The 1896 gubernatorial percentages for the city overstate Republican party strength since Hazen Pingree, the Republican candidate, ran considerably ahead of McKinley. The election data are from Election Records MSS, Wayne County Archives, Burton Historical Collection, Detroit Public Library.
10. The Republican mean in the city's working class wards was 44.8% in 1892, 43.0% in 1894, and 45.7% in 1896. Between 1894 and 1896 three new wards were created in the city. Fortunately, these were carved from old ones and it presented no major difficulty to reaggregate the election data in order to guarantee congruence with the 1892 and 1894 units.
11. The term "drastic solution" predicated of the Bryan ideology should not be construed to be an implication of my acceptance of the view that the free silver ideology was a "radical" one. As changes in the monetary system have long been a part of the American political tradition, there is no *historical* reason for conceiving the groups that waged the battle for price inflation in 1896 as "radical" ones; see Lee Benson, "Research Problems," in Komarovsky (ed.), *Common Frontiers of the Social Sciences,* p. 168.

12. The attempt was equally disastrous in the East; see Samuel T. McSeveney, "The Politics of Depression: Voting Behavior in Connecticut, New York, and New Jersey, 1893–1896" (unpublished Ph.D. dissertation, University of Iowa, 1965), pp. 381–472.

13. In my opinion, the rhetoric was part of the broader Bryan campaign strategy and should not be construed as accurate factual description. Viewed functionally, and as an integral part of that campaign strategy, the claims concerning the coercion of workers were aimed at providing potential laboring class supporters with reasons for taking their employers as politically salient negative referents. For a discussion of the credibility of the charges, see Richard J. Jensen, "The Winning of the Midwest: A Social History of Midwestern Elections, 1888–1896" (unpublished Ph.D. dissertation, Yale University, 1966), pp. 56–67.

14. Paul F. Lazarsfeld, Bernard Berelson, and Hazel Gaudet, *The People's Choice: How the Voter Makes Up His Mind in a Presidential Campaign* (2nd ed.; New York, 1948), p. 103, and also see Table V, p. 102, for a more detailed breakdown of its effects by categories of "vote intention in May."

15. My description of the public image projected by Bryanites in 1896 is based upon a systematic content analysis of the relevant state and national platforms, Bryan speeches, numerous excerpts of which are in *The First Battle* (Chicago, 1896), and full texts of which are available in contemporary newspapers, and of more than 1,000 pro-Bryan newspaper editorials that appeared in September and October, 1896. For a complete listing of the newspapers used, see the appropriate section of the bibliography.

16. See Talcott Parsons, *Essays in Sociological Theory* (Free Press ed.; New York, 1964), ch. viii, "Propaganda and Social Control," pp. 142–76, and especially the distinctions given on pp. 171–72; also see James O. Whittaker, "Cognitive Dissonance and the Effectiveness of Persuasive Communications," *Public Opinion Quarterly, XXVIII* (Winter, 1964), 547–55.

17. While varying in the particular mode of their treatments, the most recent studies of the 1896 contest share this type of framework; see Paul W. Glad, *McKinley, Bryan, and the People* (Philadelphia, 1964), pp. 203–4; Stanley L. Jones, *The Presidential Election of 1896* (Madison, 1964), pp. 332–50; and J. Rogers Hollingsworth, *The Whirligig of Politics* (Chicago, 1963), pp. 84–107. For a much different type of approach, see the perceptive suggestions offered by Hollingsworth in "The Historian, Presidential Elections, and 1896," *Mid-America, XLV* (July, 1963), 185–92, and in "Populism: The Problem of Rhetoric and Reality," *Agricultural History, XXXIX* (April, 1965), 81–85.

18. Samuel P. Hays, "Political Parties and the Local-Cosmopolitan Continuum, 1865–1929" (unpublished paper delivered at Washington University Conference on Political Development, Spring, 1966), p. 13, and his discussion of the importance of conceiving such "proposals" as ideologies rather than substantive issues, pp. 12–14.

19. The quotations are from the *Milwaukee Advance,* October 31, 1896, and the *Monroe Sun Gazette,* September 4, 1896.

20. The concern here is with the public image of the free silver ideology, as that image can be reconstructed through a systematic content analysis of the relevant *public* sources. This is both conceptually and analytically a much different approach from that which Norman Pollack criticizes in *The Populist Response to Industrial America: Midwestern Populist Thought* (Cambridge, Mass., 1962), p. 6. Pollack inveighs against the line of reasoning that contends that "Populism did not adjust to industrialism" and was, therefore, "unrealistic." In my opinion the argument, regardless of which side one takes, is an ahistorical one. "Populism" is an abstraction and incapable of adjustment or nonadjustment. It is only through an illogical resort to reification that historians discuss it in such terms. It is more meaningful to speak of *particular* Populists, occupying *particular* positions in the social structure from which they derived *particular,* and often quite conflicting, perspectives. The homogenization of these differences, which is an integral part of Pollack's own research design and which he has combined with an *eclectic* use of both public and *private* qualitative sources, adds little to our understanding.

21. Since the 1860's laboring groups had been skeptical of monetary solutions to their difficulties; see Irwin Unger, *The Greenback Era: A Social and Political History of American Finance, 1865–1879* (Princeton, 1964), pp. 94–114 and 181–90.

22. The quotation is from Bryan, *The First Battle,* p. 205, I have added the emphasis. The divergent perspectives that rural and urban "reformers" held created tensions even at the leadership level; see J. H. Berker, August 27, 1894, James P. Corse, September 3, 1894, and L. B. Howrey, September 7, 1894, all to T. C. Richmond, in Richmond MSS, State Historical Society of Wisconsin; Chester McArthur Destler, "Consummation of a Labor-Populist Alliance in Illinois, 1894," *Mississippi Valley Historical Review, XXVII* (March, 1941), 589–602; and William F. Zornow, "Bellamy Nationalism in Ohio, 1891 to 1896," *Ohio History, LVIII* (April, 1949), 152–70.

23. Gilbert G. Fite, "Republican Strategy and the Farm Vote in the Presidential Campaign of 1896," *American Historical Review, LXV* (July, 1960), 804–5.

24. Lee Benson's analysis of the reaction of New York farmers to Populism is unusually perceptive and served as the basis for the following reexamination of the reaction of midwestern farmers; see "The New York Farmers' Rejection of Populism: The Background" (unpublished M.A. thesis, Columbia University, 1948). The explanation here overtly follows Benson's model.

25. The respective quotations are from *Annual Report of the Ohio Farmers' Institutes, 1891–92,* p. 47, and

the *Annual Report of the Ohio State Board of Agriculture, 1891*, p. 58. These, and the other sentiments described here, recurred frequently in the relevant agricultural sources. For more detailed documentation of all these matters, see Paul Kleppner, "The Politics of Change in the Midwest: The 1890's in Historical and Behavioral Perspective" (unpublished Ph.D. dissertation, University of Pittsburgh, 1967), pp. 476–85.

26. The quotations are from the *Proceedings of the Annual Meeting of the Illinois State Dairymen's Association, 1890*, p. 29, and *Annual Report of the Ohio State Board of Agriculture, 1890*, pp. 3–4.

27. For examples of such sentiments, see *Annual Report of the Indiana State Board of Agriculture, 1890–91*, pp. 419–20, *1891–92*, pp. 351–52, *1893–94*, p. 349; *Proceedings of the Annual Meeting of the Illinois State Dairymen's Association, 1890*, pp. 497–98, *1891*, p. 47, *1895*, p. 272; *Prairie Farmer* (Chicago), September 30 and November 13, 1893, and April 21 and August 4, 1894; *Annual Report of the Michigan State Board of Agriculture, 1890*, p. 483; *Transactions of the Michigan Dairymen's Association, 1895*, pp. 29, 34–35, 56–66, and 114, *1896*, pp. 16–17, 27, 28–32, 96, and 159; *Annual Report of the Ohio State Board of Agriculture, 1893*, p. 223, *1894*, pp. 192–94, *1895*, pp. 278–81; *Proceedings of the Annual Session of the Ohio Dairymen's Association, 1895*, p. 564; *Ohio Farmer* (Cleveland), January 2 and 23, 1886, September 14, and October 12 and 26, 1889, August 22 and 29, 1891, February 1 and 8, March 1, April 19, June 14 and 28, 1894, January 2 and 23, February 13, March 5, 1896; *Annual Report of the Wisconsin Dairymen's Association, 1894*, pp. 190–91, *1895*, pp. 35 and 170–72, *1896*, pp. 50–51 and 193–95; *Transactions of the Wisconsin State Agricultural Society, 1876*, p. 164, *1889*, pp. 281–82, *1892*, pp. 237–42, *1895*, pp. 260–76, *1896*, pp. 123 and 139–43; and *Hoard's Dairyman* (Fort Atkinson), January 3, 1896.

28. The quotations are from *Ohio Farmers' Institutes, 1890–91*, p. 117; *Prairie Farmer* (Chicago), February 15, 1890; and *Journal of Proceedings, Annual Session of the Illinois State Grange, 1889*, p. 22. Also see the responses of Wisconsin farmers to a question concerning the causes of agricultural distress, in *Seventh Biennial Report of the Bureau of Labor, Census and Industrial Statistics, State of Wisconsin, 1895–1896* (Madison, 1896), pp. 112–23.

29. Quotations are from *Wisconsin Farmers' Institutes, Session of 1889*, p. 82, and *Ohio Farmer* (Cleveland), October 1, 1896.

30. The quotations are from the *Journal of Proceedings, Annual Session of the Illinois State Grange, 1893*, p. 10, and *1894*, p. 13.

31. *Ibid., 1896*, p. 18, and *Transactions of the Wisconsin State Agricultural Society, 1891*, p. 229.

32. For useful insights see David O. Arnold and David Gold, "The Facilitation Effect of Social Environment," *Public Opinion Quarterly, XXVIII* (Fall, 1963), 513–16; James G. March and J. S. Coleman, "Group Influences and Agricultural Innovations," *American Journal of Sociology, LXI* (May, 1956), 588–94; and S. E. Asch, "Effects of Group Pressure Upon the Modification and Distortion of Judgments," in Harold Guetzkow (ed.), *Groups, Leadership and Men* (Pittsburgh, 1951), pp. 177–90.

33. The quotation is from Vernon Carstensen, "The Genesis of an Agricultural Experiment Station," *Agricultural History, XXIV* (January, 1960), 20; the estimates of the increase in circulation of agricultural experiment station bulletins and attendance at farmers' institutes are based on data in the annual reports of the experiment stations for the years 1892–96 and in the reports of the institutes for the same years.

Overseas Expansion

American expansionism antedated the Civil War, but not until after 1865 did the United States become seriously interested in regions not physically contiguous. In 1867, we acquired Alaska from Russia. In 1870/71, during Grant's administration, we began — unsuccessfully as it turned out — to negotiate for a part of Santo Domingo in the Caribbean. This expansionist impulse came to a crescendo in the 1890s with the Spanish-American War and the seizure of the Philippines, Puerto Rico, and the simultaneous acquisition of Hawaii. Thereafter, we obtained little additional territory, but our expansionism continued in the shape of economic penetration of Latin America and periodic military intervention in the domestic affairs of our Latin neighbors. This was done in the name of law and order and to protect American lives and investments.

Late-nineteenth-century American imperialism has been ascribed to many factors. For a long time, a favorite explanation was that we became a colonial power almost by inadvertence. As a great power, in an age when great powers were carving up the non-European world, the United States somehow slipped into imperialism. The impulse was not strong and the mood soon passed. Another common explanation emphasizes the psychic crisis of the 1890s. The depression after 1893 with its social disturbances, the end of the frontier, the mood of pessimism fashionable among late-nineteenth-century intellectuals and literati — all these supposedly pushed America into foreign adventures as an escape from troubles at home.

Still another approach focuses on the immediate motives for war with Spain. One of these, it is said, was the sensational yellow journalism of the Hearst and Pulitzer press, scaring up atrocities in Cuba for the sake of circulation. Another was the sincere humanitarianism of the American people, unable to look on indifferently while Spain sought by brutal means to pacify the insurgent island.

All of these have taken second place, however, to the economic interpretation of American imperialism. This last analysis comes in several versions. The Marxist variety fits the American colonial venture into the larger framework of imperialism as a stage of advanced capitalism. When a capitalist country reaches the point where it can no longer sell its output at home, and when returns on domestic investment decline, it can only reprieve itself through cartelization and imperialism. By concentrating economic power in the form of monopolies and by exploiting the masses of colonial possessions, it can stave off growing discontents of the domestic working classes and prevent social conflict and revolution. Monopoly capitalism, then, is expansionist to save itself from its own excesses.

In the following selection, Professor Walter LaFeber provides us with an economic analysis of American imperialism, free of the rigidities of orthodox Marxism, yet informed by some of its more valuable insights. LaFeber himself is a member of the New Left, but he refuses to allow his convictions to push him into strident attacks on the businessmen whom he holds ultimately responsible for our imperialist misadventures.

FOR FURTHER READING:

MAY, ERNEST. *Imperial Democracy.* New York: Harcourt, Brace & World. 1961.

MORGAN, H. WAYNE. *America's Road to Empire: The War with Spain and Overseas Expansion.* New York: John Wiley & Sons, 1965.*

PRATT, JULIUS. *Expansions of 1898: The Acquisition of Hawaii and the Spanish Islands.* Chicago: Quadrangle Books, 1964.*

Asterisk denotes paperback edition.

Epilogue   WALTER LaFEBER

In his classic autobiography, Henry Adams recalls sitting at John Hay's table and discussing "the Philippines as a question of balance of power in the East" with members of the British cabinet. Adams suddenly realized "that the family work of a hundred and fifty years fell at once into the grand perspective of true empire-building, which Hay's work [in the Far East] set off with artistic skill." In less than a century and a quarter the United States had developed from thirteen states strung along a narrow Atlantic coastline into a great world power with possessions in the far Pacific.

Until the middle of the nineteenth century this had been, for the most part, a form of landed expansion which had moved over a large area of the North American continent. The Louisiana Purchase in 1803 had been followed by further important acquisitions in 1819, 1848, 1853, and 1867. But when William H. Seward entered the State Department in 1861, the nature of American expansion had begun to change. Under the impact of the industrial revolution Americans began to search for markets, not land. Sometimes the State Department seized the initiative in making the search, as in the Harrison administration. Frequently the business community pioneered in extending the interests of the United States into foreign areas, as in Mexico in the 1870's and in China in the 1890's. Regardless of which body led the expansionist movement, the result was the same: the growth of economic interests led to political entanglements and to increased military responsibilities.

Americans attempted to build a new empire, an empire which differed fundamentally from the colonial holdings of European powers. Until 1898 the United States believed that its political institutions were suitable only for the North American continent. Many policy makers and important journalists warned that extra-continental holdings would wreck the American republic just as they had ruined the Roman republic. Such sentiment helped to prevent the acquisition of Hawaii in 1893.

In 1898, however, the United States annexed Hawaii and demanded the Philippines from Spain. These acquisitions were not unheralded. Seward had pushed his

---

Source: Walter LaFeber, *The New Empire: An Interpretation of American Expansion, 1860–1898* (Ithaca, N.Y.: Cornell University Press, 1963), "Epilogue," pp. 407–417.

---

nation's claims far out into the Pacific with the purchase of Alaska and the Midway islands. Fish, Evarts, Bayard, Blaine, and Cleveland had maintained a tight hold on Pago Pago in Samoa, although they strongly disliked the political entanglements with England and Germany which were necessarily part of the bargain.

One striking characteristic tied these acquisitions to the new territory brought under American control in 1898 and 1899, immediately after the war with Spain. The United States obtained these areas not to fulfill a colonial policy, but to use these holdings as a means to acquire markets for the glut of goods pouring out of highly mechanized factories and farms.

The two acquisitions which might be considered exceptions to this statement are Alaska and Hawaii. It is most difficult, however, to understand the purchase of "Seward's Icebox" without comprehending the Secretary of State's magnificent view of the future American commercial empire. This view did not premise a colonial policy, but assumed the necessity of controlling the Asian markets for commercial, not political, expansion. As the chairman of the House Foreign Affairs Committee commented in 1867, Alaska was the "drawbridge" between the North American continent and Asia.

Hawaii had become an integral part of the American economy long before Harrison attempted to annex it in 1893. Missionaries had forged strong religious and secular links between the islands and the mainland, but of much more importance were the commercial ties. After the reciprocity treaty of 1875 the United States possessed a virtual veto power over Hawaii's relations with foreign powers. American capital, especially attracted by the islands' fertility during the depression years that plagued the mainland in the 1870's and 1880's, developed sugar plantations whose prosperity depended upon the American consumer. Exports of finished industrial goods left United States ports in increasing amounts for Hawaiian consumers. When the 1890 tariff severely retarded the export of Hawaiian sugar, American exports moved without abatement into the islands. The economic expansion of the United States, in terms of both capital and goods, had tied Hawaii irrevocably to the mainland.

By 1893 only the political tie remained to be consummated. The United States enjoyed the benefits of Hawaiian trade without the burdens of governmental responsibilities. But in five years the situation changed. Regaining confidence in American political institutions as the depression lessened in severity, and fearful of Japanese control, the McKinley administration attempted to annex the islands in 1897–1898. But one other factor was also of prime importance. American interests in Asia suddenly assumed much significance. And in this new framework, the Isthmian canal project gained added importance and support, for many expansionists believed the canal to be absolutely necessary if the eastern and Gulf states hoped to compete in Asian markets. As Senator John T. Morgan, Alfred Thayer Mahan, and Senator Cushman Davis noted, Hawaii was essential if the United States was to safeguard the Pacific approaches to the canal. When the Senate Foreign Relations Committee issued its majority report in March, 1898, which advocated annexation by joint resolution, the committee argued that the strategic position of Hawaii was "the main argument in favor of the annexation" plan. This, the report explained, meant not only the shielding of the western coast of the United States, but the "efficient protection" of American commerce as well. This report also noted the irrelevance of one of the antiannexationist arguments, then combined the strategic factor with the fear of Japanese encroachment as reasons for annexation: "The issue

in Hawaii is not between monarchy and the Republic. That issue has been settled.
. . . The issue is whether, in that inevitable struggle, Asia or America shall have the
vantage ground of the control of the naval 'Key of the Pacific,' the commercial
'Cross-roads of the Pacific.' "

The administration forces finally won their objective during the summer of 1898.
By July both the business community and policy makers had fully realized the value
of Asia as a potential area for American financial and commercial expansion. The
operations of Admiral George Dewey in the Philippines had, moreover, taught
Americans that Hawaii was absolutely essential as a coaling station and naval base
if the United States hoped to become a dominant force in the Far East.

The Philippines marked the next step westward. In 1899 the Secretary of the
American Asiatic Association analyzed the reason for the annexation of these
islands in a single sentence: "Had we no interests in China, the possession of the
Philippines would be meaningless." Mark Hanna, a somewhat more objective observer of the Far East than the gentleman just quoted, also desired "a strong foot-
hold in the Philippine Islands," for then "we can and will take a large slice of the
commerce of Asia. That is what we want. We are bound to share in the commerce
of the Far East, and it is better to strike for it while the iron is hot." The interests of
missionaries and of investors who believed the islands had great natural wealth no
doubt encouraged McKinley to demand the Philippines. But it should be noted
that, when the President first formulated his peace terms, he wanted the islands to
"remain with Spain, except a port and necessary appurtenances to be selected by the
United States." He changed this view only when convinced that Manila would be
insecure and indefensible unless the United States annexed the remainder of the
islands. Mahan had followed similar reasoning to reach the same conclusion. The
key to the Philippine policy of both men was their view of Manila as a way station
to the Orient.

Throughout the 1890's, debate had raged around the desirability of annexing yet
another outlying possession. The growing desire for an American-controlled Isthmian canal partially explains the interest Hawaii held for some Americans. But it
should be emphasized that in the 1890's, at least, Americans did not define their interests in a future canal as military; they termed these interests as economic. Policy
makers viewed the control of strategic areas such as Hawaii or Guantánamo Bay in
the same light as they viewed the Philippines, that is, as strategic means to obtaining
and protecting objectives which they defined as economic. Few persons discussed
the military aspects of the canal, and to interpret American expansion into the
Pacific and the Caribbean as expansion for *merely* strategic objectives distorts the
true picture. Most of those who were concerned with a canal agreed with McKinley's statement in his annual message of 1897: the Nicaragua canal would be of
"utility and value to American commerce." The foremost advocate of a Central
American passageway, Senator Morgan, constantly discussed the canal's value in
economic terms.

American control of these areas followed logically if two assumptions were
granted: first, the general consensus reached by the American business community
and policy makers in the mid-1890's that additional foreign markets would solve the
economic, social, and political problems created by the industrial revolution; and,
second, the growing belief that, however great its industrial prowess, the United
States needed strategic bases if it hoped to compete successfully with government-
supported European enterprises in Asia and Latin America. The *Journal of Com-*

merce summarized opinion on the first point when it remarked in early 1895 that "within the last half century" the industrial and transportation revolutions had made it a fact that "we are a part of 'abroad.' " Commenting upon one aspect of the frontier thesis, this journal warned that the nation was no longer "a vast public domain awaiting agriculture"; as a result of this transformation, Americans could not afford "to imagine that we can maintain ourselves in isolation from the rest of the commercial world."

Almost all Americans agreed on this first assumption. It was only on the second (how the United States could best protect its commercial interests abroad), that important disagreement flared. Walter Quintin Gresham, Edward Atkinson, and Carl Schurz were three of the leaders of the antiannexationist cause, but they were also strong advocates of increased commercial expansion. This point became evident when Atkinson and Schurz had to defend their ideals after the Spanish-American War. Atkinson presented his case through the pages of his periodical, *The Anti-Imperialist.* He admitted at the outset that "the export demand is the balance-wheel of the whole traffic of this country," but he believed that the largest demand would be found in Europe, not in the Pacific area. He had to face the fact, however, that many Americans did believe the Far East to be of great importance, and he attempted to destroy their premises by pointing out that the Philippines bought only $100,000 worth of goods from the United States each year. This was quite beside the point as far as the new empire expansionists were concerned. Atkinson began to see the weakness of his argument and countered with an attack which struck closer to the annexationists' theme: the Philippines, Atkinson remarked, could be maintained as a "sanctuary of commerce" without American involvement. Once he had gone this far, however, he had granted the McKinley forces their major assumption.

Schurz developed his case in more detail. In a speech of August 19, 1898, he noted a report from the Foreign Commerce desk of the State Department which demanded more foreign markets. "I fully agree," Schurz said. "We cannot have too many. But can such markets be opened only by annexing to the United States the countries in which they are situated?" This was his first mistake. Few people, other than some missionaries, viewed the Philippines as a great market. Certainly the McKinley administration did not. Schurz then made his second mistake when he repeated his staple argument that if the Philippines remained neutral, "we shall not only be able to get coaling-stations and naval depots wherever we may want them, but we shall qualify ourselves for that position which is most congenial to our democratic institutions." Other Americans were not as certain that such naval bases could be protected in the face of European encroachment, and this doubt had become stronger since the continental powers had shown their hands in China in late 1897 and early 1898. Annexationists could legitimately ask Schurz what power the United States could use if other nations used force or discriminatory methods to exclude Americans from Asian markets. Schurz replied in a letter to McKinley on June 1, 1898, that the nation could use the immense moral power inherent in posing as "the *great neutral Power of the world.*" He could find no better answer, and to these policy makers, schooled in the theories of Mahan, the answer was insufficient. In their eyes Schurz had granted the common premise of the necessity for commercial expansion, and then had made the two crucial errors of, first, utterly confusing the strategic, new empire policies of McKinley with the colonial policies of European powers; and, second, believing that such commercial expansion could be continued without defensible strategic bases.

Thus when the debates began on the annexation of Hawaii and the Philippines, the antiannexationists had ironically undercut their own argument. When the minority of the House Foreign Affairs Committee declared that "political dominion" over Hawaii "is not commercially necessary," the majority report replied that a continuation of a protectorate meant responsibility without control, but by annexation the United States "would assume no more responsibilities, and would acquire absolute control." Under a protectorate, Hawaii would still remain an incubator of international friction. And when Senator Vest introduced a resolution condemning the annexation of the Philippines, probably the most important of the antiannexationist moves in the Senate, he made the mistake of saying that the federal government could not annex a whole area as a colony, "except such small amount as may be necessary for coaling stations." The McKinley administration could accept this argument and then ask how the coaling station of Manila, for example, could be useful without Luzon, and how Luzon could be defended or maintained without the remainder of the Philippines.

The principal antiannexationist argument, that the Constitution and traditional American society would be ruined by expanding to noncontiguous areas, was, in fact, quite irrelevant granted the common assumption of the need for commercial expansion. By agreeing that a constantly expanding trade was also vital to the economic and political well-being of the nation, the antiannexationists had opened themselves to the devastating counterargument that this trade could not find the crucial markets in Asia and Latin America without the security which the Philippines and Hawaii would provide.

As for the annexationist forces, Lodge could espouse "large policies," but correctly argue, "I do not mean that we should enter on a widely extended system of colonization." When Alfred Thayer Mahan urged the State Department to demand only Manila in the summer of 1898, he differed little from many antiannexationists. His studies had convinced him, however, that a naval base could be strong and secure only when the hinterland of the base was strong and secure. He would accept the political burdens of the hinterland if this was necessary in order to safeguard the naval base and the trade which depended upon that base. McKinley apparently arrived at the same conclusion in much the same way. The President actually occupied a middle-of-the-road position on the issue, for by the early summer of 1898 some business periodicals, military experts, and such politicians as "Fire Alarm Joe" Foraker of Ohio urged the annexation of other Pacific islands and wanted to renege on the Teller Amendment in order to annex Cuba. The administration's Cuban policy is one of the best examples of the new empire approach. Not wanting the political burdens or the economic competition inherent in annexation, the problem was neatly solved by the Platt Amendment, which gave the Cubans their independence; but the measure also gave to the United States the Guantánamo Naval Base as a safeguard for American interests in the Caribbean, created a Cuban tariff which opened the island to American agricultural and industrial products, and recognized the right of American military intervention in the event that Cuban political life became too chaotic.

It may be suggested that one fruitful way to approach the "imperialist versus anti-imperialist" clash in the 1890's is to view the struggle in terms of a narrow and limited debate on the question of which tactical means the nation should use to obtain commonly desired objectives. Schurz's view of overseas empire differed from that of Mahan's in degree, not in kind. Few Americans believed that the Latin-American and Asian markets were of little importance to the expansive American industrial complex. On the other hand, few agreed with Foraker's intimation that the United States should claim and occupy every piece of available land in the Pacific. The mass opinion fell between these two views, and within that consensus the debate was waged. The fundamental assumptions of the consensus were never fought out. The grace note to this was appropriately supplied by William Jennings Bryan, who first successfully urged that the Philippine annexation measure be passed by Congress, and then tried to use the Philippine issue in the 1900 presidential campaign. He discovered on election night that, whatever the effect of other issues in the campaign, the issue of "imperialism" was apparently of little importance to the voters. McKinley, having solved this problem during the two previous years, had moved so far ahead of Bryan that the distance could be measured in political light years.

By 1899 the United States had forged a new empire. American policy makers and businessmen had created it amid much debate and with conscious purpose. The empire progressed from a continental base in 1861 to assured pre-eminence in the Western Hemisphere in 1895. Three years later it was rescued from a growing economic and political dilemma by the declaration of war against Spain. During and after this conflict the empire moved past Hawaii into the Philippines, and, with the issuance of the Open-Door Notes, enunciated its principles in Asia. The movement of this empire could not be hurried. Harrison discovered this to his regret in 1893. But under the impetus of the effects of the industrial revolution and, most important, *because of the implications for foreign policy which policy makers and businessmen believed to be logical corollaries of this economic change,* the new empire reached its climax in the 1890's. At this point those who possessed a sense of historical perspective could pause with Henry Adams and observe that one hundred and fifty years of American history had suddenly fallen into place. Those who preferred to peer into the dim future of the twentieth century could be certain only that the United States now dominated its own hemisphere and, as Seward had so passionately hoped, was entering as a major power into Asia, "the chief theatre of events in the world's great hereafter."

Progressivism

The Progressive mood that seized America from 1900 to 1916 was a complex phenomenon. It was a political reform movement emphasizing the need to make government on every level more responsive to the public interest. It was a revolt against plutocracy identified with the large corporations and "trusts" that had grown up since 1890. It was an impassioned effort to extend the blessings of a rich society to its disadvantaged elements. It was a mood of dissent in intellectual life that stressed the social origin of ideas and values and encouraged evolutionary, rather than static ways of regarding law, philosophy, and social thought. Finally, it was an obsession with efficiency and the use of trained intelligence in the management of governmental affairs.

Though it borrowed from Populism, Progressivism diverged from that movement. It differed in its personnel. Populism had flourished in rural areas especially in the West and South. Progressives were mostly urban folk, and while many western states were Progressive strongholds, so were urban, industrial ones like New York, New Jersey, and Massachusetts. It also differed from Populism in its sophistication. As befitted a rural movement, the intellectual level of Populism was not consistently high. Progressivism, on the other hand, enlisted some of the most subtle and powerful minds in America. To match the William "Coin" Harveys and the Ignatius Donnellys, Progressivism could muster Walter Lippmann, Herbert Croly, John Dewey, and Charles Beard.

Where did the movement come from? Why were middle-class urbanites restless and questioning in the first decades of the twentieth century? The work of George Mowry, Richard Hofstadter, and other important historians writing in the 1950s emphasized the role of severe social tensions. The movement, they said, depended on the fear of displacement of the older elite by new groups. Confronted by the new corporate rich, by big labor, and by a mass of foreign immigrants, the college-educated, individualistic, old-stock elite became alarmed. As intelligent, well-educated men, they did not merely seek to turn back the clock in some sort of blind reflex action; they sought to remake society so as to tame and redirect the new forces to constructive ends.

The Mowry-Hofstadter approach dominated the historiography of Progressivism for over a decade. In the essay by David P. Thelen that follows, we encounter a new way of looking at the Progressives that points up class cooperation instead of conflict.

FOR FURTHER READING:

HOFSTADTER, RICHARD. *The Age of Reform from Bryan to FDR.* New York: Random House, Vintage Books, 1955.*

LINK, ARTHUR. *Woodrow Wilson and the Progressive Era.* New York: Harper & Row, Publishers, 1963.*

MOWRY, GEORGE. *The California Progressives.* Chicago: Quadrangle Books, 1963.*

Asterisk denotes paperback edition.

Social Tensions and the Origins of Progressivism   D A V I D P . T H E L E N

Recent historians have explained the origins of the Progressive movement in several ways. They have represented progressivism, in turn, as a continuation of the western and southern farmers' revolt,[1] as a desperate attempt by the urban gentry to regain status from the new robber barons,[2] as a thrust from the depths of slum life,[3] and as a campaign by businessmen to prevent workers from securing political power.[4] Behind such seemingly conflicting theories, however, rests a single assumption about the origins of progressivism: the class and status conflicts of the late-nineteenth century formed the driving forces that made men become reformers. Whether viewed by the historian as a farmer, worker, urban elitist, or businessman, the progressive was motivated primarily by his social position; and each scholar has painted a compelling picture of the insecurities and tensions felt by the group that he placed in the vanguard of progressivism. Pressures and threats from other social groups drove men to espouse reform. In these class and status conflicts can be found the roots of progressivism.

How adequately does this focus on social tensions and insecurities explain the origins of progressivism? Since some of these scholars have invoked concepts from social science to support their rejection of earlier approaches, the validity and application of some of the sociological and psychological assumptions which make up the conceptual framework for the idea that social tensions impelled the progressive require analysis. Is the focus on social classes relevant to the rise of political movements like progressivism? Is it useful to rely upon a narrow, untestable and unproved conception of motivation when other approaches are available? How much of a concrete situation does an abstract model explain?

First, theories borrowed from one discipline are not designed to encompass the data of another. In questioning the application of models from physiology and physics to psychology, the noted personality theorist George A. Kelly explained: "We are skeptical about the value of copying ready-made theories which were designed for other foci of convenience"; and he urged his fellow psychologists to resist the temptation of "poking about in the neighbors' back yards for methodological windfalls."[5] Just as physiology and physics encompass only part of the psychologist's realm, so psychology, sociology, and political science are concerned with only part of the historian's realm.

Those historians who have borrowed the idea that social stratification explains the rise of political movements like progressivism illustrate the dangers inherent in borrowing theories from other fields. Most sociologists and political scientists now doubt the relevance of social stratification to the emergence of political movements. Reinhard Bendix, for example, maintained that "the study of social stratification, whether or not it is adumbrated by psychological analysis, is not the proper approach to an understanding of the role of cumulative political experience."[6] In their pleas for more pluralistic approaches to political power, such political scientists

---

Source: David P. Thelen, "Social Tensions and the Origins of Progressivism," *Journal of American History*, vol. 56 (1969), pp. 323–341.

---

as Nelson W. Polsby and Robert A. Dahl have found that social stratification is largely irrelevant to the exercise of political power.[7] So severe were these criticisms of the assumption that social class determined political power that one sociologist, reviewing the literature of the field in 1964, concluded that "the problem has simply been dropped." [8]

But an even greater problem with placing emphasis on social tensions is that it is ahistorical. Even sociologists like Seymour M. Lipset and Bendix have complained about the "increasingly ahistorical" drift of the focus of this field.[9] After analyzing the major models of social change, another sociologist concluded that the fundamental error of these models was their failure to incorporate the dimension of time.[10] Few scholars would deny that social tensions exist at all times and in all societies.[11] For at least twenty years before 1900, various business groups had tried to take political power away from workers and bosses. But to focus on the social class motivation of businessmen is to obscure the basic historical problem of why progressivism emerged *when* it did. Conflicts between businessmen and workers were hardly unique to the years around 1900. The emphasis on social tensions obscures chronology. When sociologists are disturbed about this problem, historians should be wary indeed.

The assumption that progressivism derived from social tensions is at least as vulnerable to attack by psychologists. If the kinds of questions historians generally ask about the origins of political and social movements are reduced to the psychological level, then the theories of class and status motivation would seem to be premised on very debatable assumptions about individual motivation. Most historians would want to know the conditions that existed before a change occurred, why the change happened, and what were the results of that change.

The first problem — the conditions before a change occurred — reduces in psychological terms to the way an individual perceives himself, his self-image. Psychologists have approached this question in many ways, but a theory of change which assumes that social tensions were the basic cause implicitly accepts only one of these approaches. It assumes that an individual defines himself primarily in terms of his particular social role, that his behavior is motivated mainly by his class and status role perceptions. Only about one out of every three psychologists, however, would accept this premise to any real extent.[12] Even some sociologists and anthropologists, who have traditionally seen individual behavior as primarily determined by culture, have retreated from that position and now see a more symmetrical interaction in which personality also influences culture.[13] An overwhelming majority of psychologists have rejected role theory as an adequate explanation for the way an individual who enlists in a reform movement forms his self-image.

The second problem — why the change happened — reduces in psychological terms to the mechanism by which an individual feels impelled to join a political movement like progressivism. Here again those scholars who emphasize social tensions have implicitly chosen only one of several alternatives offered by psychologists. They assume that the threat from some other social group frustrated the would-be progressive who, in turn, reacted aggressively against that threat. Very few psychologists, however, would claim that social tensions are the main source of frustration. Furthermore, individuals are generally capable of reacting to new roles without experiencing any major frustrations. The different ways in which Theodore Roosevelt and Calvin Coolidge, for example, remade the role of the presidency to fit their own personalities suggest how flexible roles can be without deeply frustrating an individual. Furthermore, different members of the same social class will perceive social challenges in different ways; many will experience no frustration at all.[14]

Even if historians concede that social stresses can frustrate an individual, does it follow that he will react aggressively toward the source of that frustration? The frustration-produces-aggression model is one of the most debated propositions in psychology.[15] Extreme critics have called it "nonsensical." [16] Others have shown that frustration more often produces anxiety, submission, dependence, or avoidance than aggression.[17] Even presumably simpleminded creatures like rats and pigeons do not necessarily react aggressively when they are frustrated.[18] If some psychologists have shown that aggression is only one possible result of frustration, others have shown that frustration is only one possible source of aggression. Indeed, prior to 1939 most psychologists accepted Sigmund Freud's *Beyond the Pleasure Principle,* which contended that aggression derived from the Death Wish.[19] Others have found the source of aggression in neither frustration nor the Death Wish.[20] The assumption that social tensions will frustrate an individual and drive him to react aggressively has been riddled by the artillery of a great many psychologists.[21] For historians to continue to assume that men react primarily to social threats is to ignore an impressive body of psychological literature.

The third problem — what were the results of that change — reduces in psychological terms to the way an individual outwardly expresses the internal change. If an individual felt angry following threats from another social group, how would he express that anger? The idea that he will sublimate his aggressive propensities into cries for political reform is one which is endorsed by many Freudians who follow *Civilization and Its Discontents.*[22] But even some psychoanalysts claim that Freud never adequately explained sublimation. Other personality theorists have asserted that "everyone recognizes . . . that at present we have no theory which really explains the dynamics" of sublimation.[23] Many psychologists have seen sublimation as only one possible way of expressing aggressive proclivities. Political reform is only one of hundreds of directions an individual can channel hostile impulses. But most personality theorists are so unimpressed by the concept of sublimation that they simply ignore it in their own theories.[24]

By assuming that social tensions produced progressivism, historians have approached the basic questions about social and political movements from a very narrow psychological viewpoint. Even more important, the psychological underpinnings of this assumption are either disproved, disputed, ignored, or "untestable" by modern psychologists.

Moreover, the whole psychological framework which includes these theories has recently come under attack. Both behaviorists and psychoanalysts had previously assumed that individuals were motivated by "a state of tenseness that leads us to seek equilibrium, rest, adjustment, satisfaction, or homeostasis. From this point of view, personality is nothing more than our habitual modes of reducing tension." [25] Men became reformers to relieve tensions, perhaps impelled by class and status anxieties. Now, however, many psychologists contend that personality theorists too long overemphasized the irrational components in motivation.[26] As early as 1953 Gordon Allport reported that the trend in motivational theory was away from the tension reduction approach and toward an emphasis on the rational and healthy side of individuals.[27] By stressing the rationality of free choice, these psychologists have argued that a commitment to reform, for example, may in fact be the ultimate expression of a mature personality and reflect a man who is capable of getting outside of his self-preoccupation. Indeed, Erich Fromm has said that the revolutionary leader might well be the only "sane person in an insane world." [28] The decision to embrace progressivism may simply represent a conscious choice between alternative programs, not an attempt to reduce tensions which grew out of a man's efforts to maintain his social position.[29]

There is another problem in borrowing models: the more inclusive the model, the farther it is removed from the reality it is attempting to explain. The data must be squeezed and distorted to make them conform to the model. Many social scientists themselves have revolted against the top-heavy and abstract models which have prevailed in their fields. One student of social stratification, for example, concluded from a review of 333 studies that his field suffered from "the disease of overconceptualization." [30] Similarly, many psychologists have rejected the abstract personality constructs used to explain motivation because they are too far removed from the reality of individual people. Arguing for a focus on the "life style" of each person, Allport has attacked theories which emphasize "the abstract motivation of an impersonal and therefore non-existent mind-in-general," preferring "the concrete, viable motives of each and every mind-in-particular." [31] In a like vein, Kelly has argued that most psychological constructs ignore an individual's "private domain, within which his behavior aligns itself within its own lawful system." These abstract constructs can only account for the individual as "an inert object wafted about in a public domain by external forces, or as a solitary datum sitting on its own continuum." [32] Allport even charged that psychologists who build universal models to explain human motivation are seeking a "scientific will of the wisp"; the " 'irreducible unlearned motives' of men" they are seeking cannot be found because they do not exist.[33]

This is not a critique of any particular psychological theory or approach to behavior. Rather it is a plea to be aware of the dangers in building a conceptual approach to such a problem as progressivism upon so many rickety psychological foundations. Historians should recognize that psychologists are not that different; they are at least as divided in their interpretations as we are. For historians to accept the assumptions that underlie the idea that social tensions produced progressivism would be similar to a psychologist borrowing Frederick Jackson Turner's frontier hypothesis for his research. Many of us would complain that there are other explanations for the development of American history; and a great many psychologists, in effect, are shuddering at the weak psychological underpinnings of the assumption that their social backgrounds made men become reformers.

The real test for the soundness of any approach is not theoretical, of course, but empirical. In this case the inadequacy of the sociological and psychological ideas which inform the assumption that social tensions produced progressivism becomes obvious after an examination of the types of men who became progressives and conservatives. If social tensions were relevant to the rise of progressivism, then clearly the class and status experiences of progressives should have differed in some fundamental way from those of the conservatives.

How different, in fact, were the social origins of progressives and conservatives? Following George E. Mowry's publication in 1951 of *The California Progressives,* several scholars examined the external social class attributes of progressive leaders and concluded that the reformers were drawn from the young urban gentry.[34] But because they neglected to sample a comparable group of conservatives, these studies failed to prove their contention that class and status experiences impelled the progressives. Subsequent profiles of both progressive and conservative leaders in the election of 1912 and the legislative sessions of 1911 in Washington and 1905 in Missouri showed that both groups came from nearly the same social background.[35] Objective measures of their social origins failed to predict the programs and ideologies of political leaders.

Scholars may not accept this finding because they question whether the 1912 campaign reflected political ideologies so much as the personalities of leaders and the desire for office. The studies of legislatures in Washington and Missouri might be questioned because in a single session such extraneous pressures as the personality of a powerful governor or the use of bribes might have interfered with a legislator's expression of his natural preferences. Furthermore, neither Washington nor Missouri was ever noted as a banner progressive state. Perhaps the issues in these states were not as hotly contested — and hence did not reveal as sharp social tensions — as in the more radical states.

The following profile of Wisconsin legislators was designed to avoid some of the possible objections to the other studies. Since contemporaries and historians alike have agreed on the pivotal position of Wisconsin, it is an ideal state to test whether social tensions were important in the development of progressivism. This sample begins with the 1897 session because it was then, for the first time, that the Progressive Republicans identified in their speeches, platforms, and votes the issues which divided them from the stalwarts, and concludes with the 1903 session, when many of their programs were enacted. The index for "progressivism" was based on votes growing out of the campaigns for a more equitable distribution of the tax burden, for regulation of quasi-public corporations, and for purification of the electoral and legislative processes. These were the issues which gave the thrust and tone to Wisconsin progressivism and served as the dividing lines between the old guard and the insurgents.[36]

During these four sessions there were 286 roll calls on these issues. A "progressive" legislator was defined as one who voted for more than 75 percent of the progressive measures; a "moderate" favored between 50 and 75 percent of the progressive measures; and a "conservative" opposed more than half of the progressive measures. Of the 360 Republican legislators included in this profile, 40 percent were progressives, 38 percent were moderates, and 22 percent were conservatives.[37]

If social conflicts were important to the emergence of progressivism, the variable which would be most likely to reveal that fact would be the occupations of legislators. Convincing generalizations from the following chart would need to be based upon large statistical differences, since the relatively small sample is divided so many ways. Occupation clearly made little difference in a legislator's vote on progressive measures.

The extent of a man's education helps to locate his social position. In Wisconsin neither progressives (22 percent), moderates (24 percent), nor conservatives (27 percent) were dominated by college graduates. At a time and place where college degrees were rare, perhaps a better measure of educational aspirations would be the proportion of men who sought any kind of formal schooling — high school, business college, night school — beyond the level of the common school. Here again, however, the differences in achievement between progressives (58 percent), moderates (60 percent), and conservatives (66 percent) are insignificant.

TABLE 1

	FARMER	MERCHANT	PROFESSIONAL	MANUFACTURER	FINANCIER	WORKER
	Percent	Percent	Percent	Percent	Percent	Percent
Progressives	20	27	26	13	9	5
Moderates	22	24	29	6	13	6
Conservatives	12	27	32	16	10	3

The place of a man's birth also indicates his social background. But the nativity of Wisconsin's legislators failed to differentiate progressives from conservatives (see Table 2).

TABLE 2

	MIDWEST	EAST AND NEW ENGLAND	CANADA	EUROPE
	Percent	Percent	Percent	Percent
Progressives	47	29	6	18
Moderates	61	24	2	13
Conservatives	49	30	5	16

If the Wisconsin sample corresponds roughly to those of other states in the occupations, education, and nativity of political leaders, it differs from them in two other respects. Students of the 1912 election found the progressives to be considerably younger than the conservatives in both age and political experience, a fact which led them to see progressivism as a revolt of the young, would-be politicians. In Wisconsin, however, progressives and conservatives both had an average age of forty-eight, and the moderates averaged forty-six. The median ages of progressives (49), moderates (45), and conservatives (47) likewise fail to suggest the existence of any generational conflict between progressives and conservatives.

Nor were Wisconsin's progressives the most politically immature of the rival factions. While service in the legislature is only one measure of political experience, it does reveal the effectiveness of politicians in winning renomination from their local organizations. Although Wisconsin's conservatives had the longest tenure in the legislature, they contrasted not so much with the progressives as with the moderates. Table 3 indicates the number of previous sessions attended by legislators.

TABLE 3

	NONE	ONE	TWO OR MORE
	Percent	Percent	Percent
Progressives	52	28	20
Moderates	62	27	11
Conservatives	35	37	28

The social origins of Wisconsin legislators between 1897 and 1903 clearly suggest that no particular manner of man became a progressive. Such variables as occupation, education, nativity, age, and previous legislative experience fail to differentiate the average progressive from the average conservative. The theories that progressivism was motivated by status or class tensions felt by the urban gentry, the businessmen, the workers, the farmers, or the incipient politicians are challenged in Wisconsin by the fact that members of these groups were as likely to become conservatives as progressives. And the Wisconsin profile parallels other studies. To the extent that social class allegiance can be measured by such attributes as occupation, nativity, education, and age, social tensions were apparently irrelevant to the formation of progressivism since the "typical" progressive and conservative came from the same social background.

Collective statistical profiles can, however, obscure more than they reveal. The five more prominent early Wisconsin progressive leaders, the men who forged the issues which Robert M. La Follette subsequently adopted, were most noteworthy for their different social origins. The man contemporaries hailed as the "father of Wisconsin progressivism" was Albert R. Hall, a small dairy farmer in the western part of the state. Nephew of national Grange head Oliver Kelley, Hall was basically an agrarian radical who developed the reputation of a fearless enemy of the railroads and other large corporations.[38] No less important was John A. Butler, the lengthened shadow of the powerful Milwaukee Municipal League. A sharper contrast to Hall could scarcely be found than this independently wealthy and highly educated Brahmin who seemed to spend more time in his villa than he did in his Milwaukee law office.[39] Milwaukee also contributed Julius E. Roehr, organized labor's leading champion in the legislature. Born in New York City — the son of German immigrants — this hardworking lawyer and dissident Republican politician would have been extremely uncomfortable with the smells of either Hall's farm or Butler's villa.[40] James H. Stout, the most respected of the early progressives in the legislature, was born and raised in Iowa and educated at the University of Chicago. A fabulously wealthy lumber baron, Stout used his company town of Menomonie to pioneer in vocational education and in welfare benefits for his workers.[41] The orator of these early legislative progressives was James J. McGillivray, a self-made Canadian-born architect and manufacturer who lived in Black River Falls and authored the state's antitrust acts.[42] It would seem almost pointless to hunt for a common social "type" in these early progressives. A Brahmin man of leisure and self-made manufacturer, an agrarian radical who knew no workers and a lawyer who never lived outside a large city and was the workers' champion, young men and old men, Yankees and immigrants, these were the leaders who made common cause in Wisconsin and developed the progressive program.

The widely scattered backgrounds of the most prominent early leaders and the remarkable collective similarity between the average progressive and conservative confirm the weaknesses in the sociological and psychological framework for the assumption that progressivism was rooted in social tensions. The widespread emphasis on social tensions is unsound sociologically because it draws upon only a narrow spectrum of personality theory, and those models upon which it does draw are either unproved or unprovable. The statistical profiles from Wisconsin and elsewhere reveal empirically that the origins of progressivism cannot be found by studying the social backgrounds and tensions of progressive leaders. Remembering Kelly's injunction to avoid "poking about in the neighbors' back yards for methodological windfalls," historians must develop alternative approaches which encompass not only the realm of sociology and psychology but also that of history.

Such an alternative approach should at least restore chronology, a major casualty in the repeated emphasis on men's class and status feelings, to a more prominent position. At this point it is possible to offer a tentative explanation for the origins of progressivism when that movement is placed in the context of the chronological evolution of both industrialism and reform.

When the Progressive era is put against the backdrop of the growth of industrialism in America, the remarkable fact about that period is its relative freedom from social tensions. If conflicts between city and farm, worker and boss, younger and older generations, native-born and immigrant are more or less natural results of industrialization, then the years between the late 1890s and the early 1910s stand as a period of social peace when contrasted with either the Gilded Age or the 1920s, when those conflicts were raw and ragged. Not competition but cooperation between different social groups—ministers, businessmen, workers, farmers, social workers, doctors, and politicians — was what distinguished progressivism from such earlier reform movements as Mugwumpery, Populism, the labor movement, and civil service reform. To the extent that men and groups were motivated by tensions deriving from their class and status perceptions, they would have been unable to cooperate with men from different backgrounds. In focusing on the broadly based progressive thrust, the real question is not what drove groups apart, but what drove them together? To answer this question, progressivism must be located in the development of reform in the late-nineteenth century.

The roots of progressivism reach far back into the Gilded Age. Dozens of groups and individuals in the 1880s envisioned some change that would improve society. Reformers came forward to demand civil service reform, the eight hour day, scientific agriculture, woman suffrage, enforcement of vice laws, factory inspection, nonpartisan local elections, trust-busting, wildlife conservation, tax reform, abolition of child labor, businesslike local government, regulation of railway rates, less patronizing local charity, and hundreds of other causes which would subsequently be identified with progressivism. Younger social scientists, particularly economists, were not only beginning to lambast the formalism and conservatism in their fields and to advocate the ideas which would undergird progressivism but they were also seeking to force governments to accept their ideas. Richard T. Ely's work on the Maryland Tax Commission in the mid-1880s, for example, pioneered in the application of the new economics to government and generated many of the programs which future reformers and politicians would soon adopt.

But this fertility of reform in the Gilded Age did not conceal the basic fact that individuals and groups remained fragmented. There was no common program which could rally all groups, and the general prosperity tended to reassure people that industrialism might cure its own ills. As late as 1892 one editor, reflecting this optimistic frame of mind, could state that "the rich are growing richer, some of them, and the poor are growing richer, all of them." [43] Men and groups seeking major changes, whether elitists or Populists, were generally stereotyped as cranks who were blind to the vast blessings and bright future of industrialism. Circumscribed by such problems and attitudes reformers were understandably fragmented in the Gilded Age.

The catastrophic depression of 1893–1897 radically altered this pattern of reform. It vividly dramatized the failures of industrialism. The widening chasm between the rich and the poor, which a few observers had earlier called a natural result of industrialism, could no longer be ignored. As several tattered bands of men known as Coxey's Army tramped from town to town in 1894, they drew attention to the plight of the millions of unemployed and vividly portrayed the striking contrasts between the way of life of the poor and the "conspicuous consumption" of the rich. Furthermore, as Thorstein Veblen observed, they showed that large numbers of Americans no longer cherished the old gospel of self-help, the very basis for mobility in a democratic society.[44] As desperation mounted, businessmen and politicians tried the traditional ways of reversing the business cycle, but by 1895 they realized that the time-honored formulas of the tariff and the currency simply could not dispel the dark pall that hung over the land.[45] Worse still, President Grover Cleveland seemed utterly incapable of comprehending, let alone relieving, the national crisis.

The collapse of prosperity and the failure of national partisan politicians to alleviate the crisis by the traditional methods generated an atmosphere of restless and profound questioning which few could escape. "On every corner stands a man whose fortune in these dull times has made him an ugly critic of everything and everybody," wrote one editor.[46] A state university president warned his graduates in 1894 that "you will see everywhere in the country symptoms of social and political discontent. You will observe that these disquietudes do not result from the questions that arise in the ordinary course of political discussion . . . but that they spring out of questions that are connected with the very foundations of society and have to do with some of the most elemental principles of human liberty and modern civilization." [47] Was the American dream of economic democracy and mobility impossible in an industrial society? Would the poor overthrow an unresponsive political and economic system? Such questions urgently demanded answers, and it was no longer either wise or safe to summarily dismiss as a crank anyone who had an answer. "The time is at hand," cried one editor, "when some of the great problems which the Nineteenth century civilization has encountered are crying for a solution. . . . Never before in the history of the world were people so willing to accept true teaching on any of these subjects and give to them a just and practical trial." [48] A man's social origins were now less important than his proposals, and many men began to cooperate with people from different backgrounds to devise and implement solutions.

This depression-inspired search for answers sprouted hundreds of discussion groups at which men met, regardless of background, to propose remedies. These groups gave men the habit of ignoring previously firm class lines in the face of the national crisis. When Victor Berger urged the Milwaukee Liberal Club to adopt socialism as the answer, for example, his audience included wealthy bankers, merchants, and lawyers.[49] In the same city, at the Church and Labor Social Union, banker John Johnston urged a "new society" where "class privileges will be abolished because all will belong to the human family," and the discussion was joined by Populists and Socialists as well as clergymen and conservative editors.[50] In this context, too, all types of people sought the wisdom of the men who had made a career of studying the social and economic breakdown. No one was surprised when unions, Granges, women's clubs, and other groups wanted University of Wisconsin economists like Ely to address them.[51] Maybe they had an answer. The social unrest accompanying the depression weakened class and status allegiances.

The direct political effects of the depression also broke down the previous rigidity and fragmentation of reform. The depression created a clear sense of priorities among the many causes which Gilded Age reformers had advocated. It generated broadly based new issues which all classes could unite behind. One such program was the urgent necessity for tax reform. When the depression struck, individuals and corporations were forced to devise ways of economizing as property values, sales, and revenues declined precipitously. Caught between higher taxes to cover the rising costs of local government and their own diminishing revenues, many wealthy individuals and corporations began to hide their personal assets from the assessors, to lobby tax relief through local governments, and even to refuse to pay any taxes. The progressive program was forged and received widespread popular support as a response to these economies. Citizens who lacked the economic or political resources to dodge their taxes mounted such a crusade against these tax dodgers that former President Benjamin Harrison warned the wealthiest leaders that unless they stopped concealing their true wealth from the tax assessors they could expect a revolution led by enraged taxpayers.[52] The programs for tax reform —including inheritance, income, and ad valorem corporation taxes — varied from place to place, but the important fact was that most citizens had developed specific programs for tax reform and had now agreed that certain individuals and corporations had evaded a primary responsibility of citizenship.

A second major area which proved capable of uniting men of different backgrounds was "corporate arrogance." Facing declining revenues, many corporations adopted economies which ranged from raising fares and rates to lobbying all manner of relief measures through city and state governments. Even more important, perhaps, they could not afford necessary improvements which elementary considerations of safety and health had led local governments to demand that they adopt. Corporate arrogance was no longer a doctrinaire cry of reformers. Now it was an unprotected railway crossing where children were killed as they came home from school or the refusal of an impoverished water company to make improvements needed to provide the healthful water which could stop the epidemics of typhoid fever.[53] Such incidents made the corporation look like a killer. These specific threats united all classes: anyone's child might be careless at a railroad crossing, and typhoid fever was no respecter of social origins.

From such new, direct, and immediate threats progressivism developed its thrust. The more corporations used their political influence to resist making the small improvements, the more communities developed increasingly radical economic programs like municipal ownership or consumer-owned utilities and fought to overthrow the machines that gave immunity to the corporations. Political reforms like the initiative, direct primary, and home rule became increasingly important in the early stages of progressivism because, as William Allen White said, men had first to get the gun before they could hit anything with it.[54] But it was the failure of the political system to respond to the new and immediate threats of the depression that convinced people that more desperate programs were needed.

Perhaps there are, after all, times and places where issues cut across class lines. These are the times and places where men identify less with their occupational roles as producers and more with their roles as consumers — of death-dealing water, unsafe railway crossings, polluted air, high streetcar rates, corrupt politicians — which serve to unite them across social barriers. There are also universal emotions — anger and fear — which possess all men regardless of their backgrounds.[55] The importance of the depression of the 1890s was that it aroused those universal emotions, posed dramatic and desperate enough threats to lead men of all types to agree that tax dodging and corporate arrogance had to be ended and thereby served to unite many previously fragmented reformers and to enlist the support of the majority that had earlier been either silent or enthusiastic only about partisan issues like the tariff or symbols like Abraham Lincoln. The conversion of the National Municipal League showed how issues were becoming more important than backgrounds. Originally composed of elitists who favored such Mugwumpish concerns as civil service reform, the League by 1898 had become so desperate with the domination over political machines by utility companies that it devoted its energies to municipal ownership and to political devices which promised "more trust in the people, more democracy" than its earlier elitism had permitted.[56] The attitude of moral indignation, such an obvious feature of the early stages of progressivism, was not rooted in social tensions but in the universal emotion of anger.

Whether this emphasis on the results of the depression — unrest, new threats and new issues, and cooperation among social groups — has widespread relevance or validity remains to be seen, but it does help to explain the roots of progressivism in Wisconsin. The most important factor in producing the intensity of Wisconsin progressivism was the cooperation between previously discrete and fragmented social groups both in forging popular issues and getting reforms adopted. And the most important factor in defining the popular issues was the arrogance of certain corporations. In Milwaukee the traction and electricity monopoly between 1894 and 1896 alone, for reasons ranging from extreme overcapitalization to confidence in its political powers, raised both its lighting and streetcar fares, refused to arbitrate with its striking employees, enjoined the city from enforcing ordinances lowering its fares, and used its political power — the company's chief manager was the state's leading Republican boss — to cut its tax bill in half, kill an ordinance which would have prevented it from polluting the air, and thwart generally popular attempts at regulation. Each time the monopoly refused to obey an order, lobbied special favors from the city or state, or prostituted the Republican party to the company, the progressive coalition grew. By the end of the depression, the coalition drew together both ends of the economic spectrum — the Merchants and Manufacturers Association and the Chamber of Commerce as well as several labor unions and the Federated Trades Council. Politically it included the country Republican Club, the Democratic Jefferson Club, and the Socialists and Populists. The Mugwumpish and upper-class Municipal League was joined by German social clubs like the Turnvereine. So defiant was the company — so desperate were the people — that the traction managers became the state's most hated men by 1899; and humorist-politician George Peck observed that Wisconsin's parents "frighten children when they are bad, by telling them that if they don't look out," the traction magnates "will get them." [57] Four hundred miles away, in Superior, the story was remarkably similar. Angered by the repeated refusals of that city's water company to provide the city with healthful enough water to prevent the typhoid fever epidemics that killed dozens of people each year, and blaming the company's political power within both parties for the failure of regulation, labor unions and Populists cooperated with business and professional men and with dissident politicians to try to secure pure water and to overthrow the politicians owned by the company. In Superior, political debate had indeed narrowed, as an editor observed, to a fight of "the people against corporate insolence." [58] The water company, like the traction monopoly at Milwaukee, stood isolated and alone, the enemy of men from all backgrounds. In Wisconsin, at least, the community's groups continued to perform their special functions; and, by the end of the depression, they were all agreed that corporate arrogance had to be abolished. Their desperation made them willing to speak, lobby, and work together.

If, as the Wisconsin experience suggests, cooperation was the underpinning of progressivism, historians should focus on reformers not as victims of social tensions, but as reformers. At any given time and place, hundreds of men and groups are seeking supporters for their plans to change society and government. The basic problem for the reformer is to win mass support for his program. In Wisconsin a reformer's effectiveness depended on how well he manipulated acts of corporate and individual arrogance that infuriated everyone in order to demonstrate the plausibility of his program. Desperate events had made tax dodging, corporate defiance and control of politics the main political issues and had allowed this program to swallow the older reformers at the same time that they created a much broader constituency for reform. The question then becomes: Why did some succeed while others failed? North Dakota never developed a full-blown progressive movement because that state's progressives never demonstrated the plausibility of their programs.[59] Wisconsin's early progressives did succeed in drawing together such diverse groups as unions, businessmen, Populists, and dissident politicians because they adapted their program and rhetoric to the menacing events which angered everyone. Reformers operate in their hometowns and not in some contrived social background which could as easily apply to New York or Keokuk, and it is in their hometowns that they should be studied. Historians should determine why they succeeded or failed to rally the support of their communities to their programs; for the most significant criterion for any reformer is, in the end, his effectivenesss.

When the progressive characteristically spoke of reform as a fight of "the people" or the "public interest" against the "selfish interests," he was speaking quite literally of his political coalition because the important fact about progressivism, at least in Wisconsin, was the degree of cooperation between previously discrete social groups now united under the banner of the "public interest." When the progressive politician denounced the arrogance of quasi-public corporations and tax-dodgers, he knew that experiences and events had made his attacks popular with voters from all backgrounds. Both conceptually and empirically it would seem safer and more productive to view reformers first as reformers and only secondarily as men who were trying to relieve class and status anxieties. The basic riddle in progressivism is not what drove groups apart, but what made them seek common cause.

NOTES

1. John D. Hicks, *The Populist Revolt: A History of the Farmers' Alliance and the People's Party* (Minneapolis, 1931), 404–23; George E. Mowry, *Theodore Roosevelt and the Progressive Movement* (Madison, 1947), 3–35.
2. Influential statements of this view include George E. Mowry, *The California Progressives* (Berkeley, 1951), 86–104; George E. Mowry, *The Era of Theodore Roosevelt: 1900–1912* (New York, 1958), 85–105; Richard Hofstadter, *The Age of Reform: From Bryan to F.D.R.* (New York, 1955), 131–72.
3. J. Joseph Huthmacher, "Urban Liberalism in the Age of Reform," *Mississippi Valley Historical Review, XLIX* (Sept. 1962), 231–41.
4. Samuel P. Hays, "The Politics of Reform in Municipal Government in the Progressive Era," *Pacific Northwest Quarterly*, 55 (Oct. 1964), 157–69; James Weinstein, "Organized Business and the City Commission and Manager Movements," *Journal of Southern History, XXVIII* (May 1962), 166–82.
5. George A. Kelly, *A Theory of Personality: The Psychology of Personal Constructs* (New York, 1963), 22–23.
6. Reinhard Bendix, "Social Stratification and Political Power," Reinhard Bendix and Seymour Martin Lipset, eds., *Class, Status and Power: A Reader in Social Stratification* (Glencoe, 1953), 609. In the same article which Richard Hofstadter cited, Seymour Lipset and Reinhard Bendix averred that "the exercise of power cannot be fully explained by the facts of social stratification as this subject is conceived by American sociologists." Seymour M. Lipset and Reinhard Bendix, "Social Status and Social Structure: A Re-examination of Data and Interpretations: II," *British Journal of Sociology,* Two (Sept. 1951), 254.

7. Nelson W. Polsby, *Community Power and Political Theory* (New Haven, 1963), 98; Robert A. Dahl, *Who Governs* (New Haven, 1962).

8. M. Herbert Danzger, "Community Power Structure: Problems and Continuities," *American Sociological Review,* 29 (Oct. 1964), 711.

9. Lipset and Bendix, "Social Status and Social Structure," 246, 247. See also C. Wright Mills' review of W. Lloyd Warner and Paul S. Lunt, *The Social Life of a Modern Community,* in *American Sociological Review, VII* (April 1942), 267–68.

10. Max Heirich, "The Use of Time in the Study of Social Change," *American Sociological Review,* 29 (June 1964), 386–97.

11. See, for example, Wilbert E. Moore, "Predicting Discontinuities in Social Change," *American Sociological Review,* 29 (June 1964), 337.

12. Calvin S. Hall and Gardner Lindzey, *Theories of Personality* (New York, 1957), 26, 548. Gordon W. Allport, for example, attacked role theory in "What units shall we employ?" Gardner Lindzey, ed., *Assessment of Human Motives* (New York, 1958), 244–46.

13. See, for example, Melford E. Spiro, "Social Systems, Personality, and Functional Analysis," Bert Kaplan, ed., *Studying Personality Cross-Culturally* (New York, 1961), 93–128.

14. A. H. Maslow, "Deprivation, Threat, and Frustration," Chalmers L. Stacey and Manfred F. DeMartino, eds., *Understanding Human Motivation* (Cleveland, 1958), 259–61, argues that the threat from other groups must be extraordinarily deep before an individual will be frustrated. Saul Rosenzweig, "An Outline of Frustration Theory," J. McV. Hunt, ed., *Personality and the Behavior Disorders* (2 vols., New York, 1944), *I,* 383, claims that men can completely ignore a frustrating situation.

15. The original statement of the frustration-produces-aggression model is John Dollard, Neal E. Miller, and others, *Frustration and Aggression* (New Haven, 1939).

16. Karl Menninger, *Love Against Hate* (New York, 1942), 295.

17. Kenneth R. Wurtz, "Some Theory and Data Concerning the Attenuation of Aggression," *Journal of Abnormal and Social Psychology,* 60 (Jan. 1960), 134–36; John W. M. Whiting, "The Frustration Complex in Kwoma Society," *Man, XLIV* (Nov.–Dec. 1944), 140–44; Irving L. Janis, *Air War and Emotional Stress: Psychological Studies of Bombing and Civilian Defense* (New York, 1951), 4–66, 98–125; J. P. Scott and Emil Fredericson, "The Causes of Fighting in Mice and Rats," *Physiological Zoology, XXIV* (Oct. 1951), 280–81, 284, 307–08.

18. John P. Seward, "Aggressive Behavior in the Rat. III: The Role of Frustration," *Journal of Comparative Psychology,* 38 (Aug. 1945), 233; N. H. Azrin, R. R. Hutchinson, and D. F. Hake, "Extinction-Induced Aggression," *Journal of the Experimental Analysis of Behavior,* 9 (May 1966), 191–204.

19. O. H. Mowrer and Clyde Kluckhohn, "Dynamic Theory of Personality," Hunt, *Personality and the Behavior Disorders, I,* 112–13.

20. See, for example, Scott and Fredericson, "Causes of Fighting in Mice and Rats," 273–309; Seward, "Aggressive Behavior in the Rat," 235. Leonard Berkowitz, *Aggression: A Social Psychological Analysis* (New York, 1962), 29–36, reviews many experiments which showed that aggression has other sources than frustration.

21. Studies which accept the basic outlines of the frustration-aggression thesis while insisting on modifying it significantly are Berkowitz, *Aggression;* Nicholas Pastore, "The Role of Arbitrariness in the Frustration-Aggression Hypothesis," *Journal of Abnormal and Social Psychology,* 47 (July 1952), 728–31.

22. Menninger, *Love Against Hate,* 126–33.

23. Kurt Lewin, *A Dynamic Theory of Personality: Selected Papers* (New York, 1935), 181.

24. Of all the approaches analyzed by Hall and Lindzey, *Theories of Personality,* only those of Sigmund Freud, Carl Jung, Harry Stack Sullivan, Kurt Lewin, and Raymond B. Cattell incorporate sublimation.

25. Gordon W. Allport, *Becoming: Basic Considerations for a Psychology of Personality* (New Haven, 1955), 48–49.

26. Roy Schafer, "Regression in the service of the ego: The relevance of a psychoanalytic concept for personality assessment," Lindzey, *Assessment of Human Motives,* 119–48; Irving L. Janis, "The psychoanalytic interview as an observational method," *ibid.,* 149–81.

27. Gordon W. Allport, "The Trend in Motivational Theory," *American Journal of Orthopsychiatry, XXIII* (Jan. 1953), 107–19. See also Ernest R. Hilgard and Gordon H. Bower, *Theories of Learning* (3rd ed., New York, 1966), 430–33.

28. Erich Fromm, *The Dogma of Christ and Other Essays on Religion, Psychology and Culture* (New York, 1955), 165.

29. Martin B. Duberman has used the writings of some of these psychologists to argue that the abolitionists were not hopeless neurotics. Martin Duberman, "The Abolitionists and Psychology," *Journal of Negro History, XLVII* (July 1962), 183–91; Martin Duberman, "The Northern Response to Slavery," Martin Duberman, ed., *The Anti-Slavery Vanguard: New Essays on the Abolitionists* (Princeton, 1965), 406–13.

30. Harold W. Pfautz, "The Current Literature on Social Stratification: Critique and Bibliography," *American Journal of Sociology, LVIII* (Jan. 1953), 392.

31. Gordon W. Allport, "The Functional Autonomy of Motives," Stacey and DeMartino, *Understanding Human Motivation,* 81. See also Allport, *Becoming,* 19–101; Allport, "What units shall we employ?" 239–60.

32. Kelly, *Theory of Personality,* 39–40. See also George A. Kelly, "Man's construction of his alternatives," Lindzey, *Assessment of Human Motives,* 33–64.

33. Gordon W. Allport, "Motivation in Personality: Reply to Peter A. Bertocci," Stacey and DeMartino, *Understanding Human Motivation,* 111.

34. Mowry, *California Progressives,* 86–104; Mowry, *Era of Theodore Roosevelt,* 85–105; Alfred D. Chandler, Jr., "The Origins of Progressive Leadership," Elting E. Morison, ed., *The Letters of Theodore Roosevelt* (8 vols., Cambridge, 1954), *VIII,* 1462–65; Hoyt Landon Warner, *Progressivism in Ohio, 1897–1917* (Columbus, 1964), 22–23, 46. Gerhard E. Lenski, "American Social Classes: Statistical Strata or Social Groups?" *American Journal of Sociology, LVIII* (Sept. 1952), 139–44, finds these external traits to be valid measures of social class affiliation.

35. Richard B. Sherman, "The Status Revolution and Massachusetts Progressive Leadership," *Political Science Quarterly, LXXVIII* (March 1963), 59–65; William T. Kerr, Jr., "The Progressives of Washington, 1910–1912," *Pacific Northwest Quarterly,* 55 (Jan. 1964), 16–68; Norman M. Wilensky, *Conservatives in the Progressive Era: The Taft Republicans of 1912* (Gainesville, 1965), 32–39; David Rosenblatt, "1905 Missouri Legislature Statistical Profile" (seminar paper, University of Missouri, 1967). Jack Tager, "Progressives, Conservatives, and the Theory of the Status Revolution," *Mid-America, XLVIII* (July 1966), 162–75, found that social origins failed to distinguish progressives from conservatives in Toledo.

36. David P. Thelen, "The Social and Political Origins of Wisconsin Progressivism, 1885–1900" (doctoral dissertation, University of Wisconsin, 1967), 220–38, 249–52, 261–70, 272–316, 330–402, 445–57.

37. The handful of Democrats, who seldom comprised over one tenth of the legislators, were excluded because they contributed no programs to the development of Wisconsin progressivism and because they used their meagre numbers primarily to embarrass the conflicting Republican factions. Because absences could be interpreted in many ways, those legislators who were absent for more than 20 percent of the roll calls on these issues were also excluded from the sample.

38. George W. Chowen to Albert R. Hall, March 30, 1871; Hall's mother to Hall, June 7, 1873; Eugene Elliott to Hall, July 20, 1896; Sara M. Dodge to Caroline A. Hall, Oct. 29, 1909, Albert R. Hall Papers (State Historical Society of Wisconsin, Madison); Madison *Wisconsin State Journal,* April 16, 1895; Milwaukee *Sentinel,* Dec. 16, 1894; *Weekly Madisonian,* March 30, 1895; La Cross *Leader-Press,* June 6, 1905; Albert O. Barton, *La Follette's Winning of Wisconsin, 1894–1904* (Des Moines, 1922), 93–101; Nils P. Haugen, *Pioneer and Political Reminiscences* (Madison, 1930 [?]), 97, 126.

39. *National Cyclopedia of American Biography* (49 vols. to date, New York, 1898–   ), *XXI,* 55–56; John A. Butler to Jerome H. Raymond, Nov. 10, 1895, J. H. Raymond File, Extension Division Correspondence, University of Wisconsin Archival Series 18/1/1–4 (Memorial Library, University of Wisconsin).

40. *The Blue Book of the State of Wisconsin . . . 1909,* pp. 730–31; Milwaukee *Sentinel,* Aug. 25, 1896, Feb. 27, April 4, 1899; Madison *Wisconsin State Journal,* April 23, 24, 1897.

41. Madison *Wisconsin State Journal,* March 5, May 10, 1895, Jan. 22, May 8, 1897; Kathryn Saucerman, "A Study of the Wisconsin Library Movement, 1850–1900" (master's thesis, University of Wisconsin, 1944), 84–85; Ann M. Keppel and James I. Clark, "James H. Stout and the Menomonie Schools," *Wisconsin Magazine of History,* 42 (Spring 1959), 200–10; *Blue Book . . . 1901,* p. 737.

42. *Blue Book . . . 1901,* p. 738; Madison *Wisconsin State Journal,* Feb. 8, 1895.

43. Milwaukee *Sentinel,* Oct. 22, 1892.

44. Thorstein Veblen, "The Army of the Commonweal," *Journal of Political Economy, II* (June 1894), 456–61. See also Douglas W. Steeples, "The Panic of 1893: Contemporary Reflections and Reactions," *Mid-America, XLVII* (July 1965), 155–75; and Samuel Rezneck, "Unemployment, Unrest, and Relief in the United States During the Depression of 1893–1897," *Journal of Political Economy, LXI* (Aug. 1953), 324–45, for other aspects of the depression.

45. Walter LaFeber, *The New Empire: An Interpretation of American Expansion: 1860–1898* (Ithaca, 1963), 150–96, suggests that many businessmen recognized the failure of traditional methods when they began the aggressive search for world markets in 1895.

46. Superior *Evening Telegram,* March 21, 1896.

47. Milwaukee *Sentinel,* June 18, 1894.

48. Superior *Evening Telegram,* July 12, 1893.

49. Milwaukee *Sentinel,* March 4, 1895.

50. *Ibid.,* March 2, 1894.

51. W. A. Hilton to Richard T. Ely, Sept. 6, 1893; John O'Connell to Ely, Aug. 6, 1894; Jerome H. Raymond to Ely, Nov. 14, 1895, Richard T. Ely Papers (State Historical Society of Wisconsin, Madison); W. A. McEwan to Raymond, Nov. 13, 1895, Raymond File, Extension Division Correspondence; *Proceedings of the 24th Annual Session of the Wisconsin State Grange Patrons of Husbandry* (1895), 18–19.

52. Superior *Evening Telegram,* Feb. 22, 1898.

53. Henry F. Bedford, *Socialism and the Workers in Massachusetts, 1886–1912* (Amherst, 1966), 63–136, implies that such issues became the basis for early Socialist victories in Haverhill and Brockton.

54. William Allen White, "The Insurgence of Insurgency," *American Magazine, LXXI* (Dec. 1910), 170–73.
55. Robert H. Wiebe, *The Search for Order, 1877–1920* (New York, 1967), 111–32, argues that growing cooperation resulted not from the depression but from modernization in general and professionalization and bureaucratization in particular.
56. Edward W. Bemis to Ely, Dec. 29, 1898, Ely Papers.
57. John A. Butler, "Street Railway Problem in Milwaukee," *Municipal Affairs, IV* (March 1900), 212–18; Charles E. Monroe, "The Time to Deal with Corporations Asking Public Franchises," *Municipality, I* (Aug. 1900), 5–14; Milwaukee *Sentinel*, Nov. 24, 26, 27, Dec. 2, 8, 1897, Dec. 19, 1899, Jan. 4, 6, 1900; Thelen, "Origins of Wisconsin Progressivism," 330–402.
58. Superior *Evening Telegram*, Aug. 14, Sept. 4, 11, Oct. 23, 1895, March 12, 16, 18, 20, 27, 28, April 18, 21, 1896, Feb. 2, March 30, 31, April 1, 1898; Superior *Leader*, Aug. 15, 1895, March 15, 1896, March 27, 1898; Superior *Sunday Forum*, Feb. 6, 20, 27, 1898; Thelen, "Origins of Wisconsin Progressivism," 225–40.
59. Charles N. Glaab, "The Failure of North Dakota Progressivism," *Mid-America, XXXIX* (Oct. 1957), 195–209.

Theodore Roosevelt and Progressive Leadership

American political movements generally require a charismatic leader to succeed. Andrew Jackson's personal magnetism supplied much of the force behind the movement for equality and individualism that takes his name. The New Deal had the urbane, aristocratic charm of Franklin Roosevelt behind it. Progressivism fortunately had Theodore Roosevelt — along with Woodrow Wilson and Robert LaFollette — to humanize it and give it the added emotional force of hero worship. It was the tragedy, and perhaps the fatal flaw, of Populism that it produced no leader of sufficient national stature and unambiguous personal appeal.

Though TR did not create Progressivism, he helped give it wings. A peculiarly American combination of aristocrat and man of the people, he was an odd assortment of seemingly contradictory attitudes. Cosmopolitan and multilingual, he was also jingoistic and utterly convinced of America's rectitude. He combined within himself, John Morton Blum suggests, both the best and the worst of the American people, "the whole spectrum from practical enlightenment and sound moral judgment to sentimentalism and braggadocio." He devoted his youth and early manhood to sports and vigorous outdoor living to the end of overcoming childhood physical inadequacies, and through his later years he remained an obsessive apostle of action and the strenuous life. At the same time, he was one of the few American Presidents who not only read books but wrote them. A man of broad and human sympathies, he could also exhibit raw prejudice as when he ordered an entire battalion of black United States troops dishonorably discharged and disqualified for further military and civil service following a riot in Brownsville, Texas.

Part of Roosevelt's contribution to Progressivism was to dramatize it and legitimize it. To many Americans TR's support for a particular measure or approach made it seem reasonable and just. But he was also a master political strategist. As Blum shows in the selection that follows, Roosevelt was a highly skilled manipulator of the legislative machinery to effect the ends he sought. However moralistic his pronouncements, he never let them interfere with the practical necessities of getting things done.

FOR FURTHER READING:

HARBAUGH, WILLIAM. *Life and Times of Theodore Roosevelt.* New York: The Macmillan Company, Collier Books, 1963.*

MOWRY, GEORGE. *Theodore Roosevelt and the Progressive Movement.* New York: Hill & Wang, American Century Series, 1960.*

PRINGLE, HENRY F. *Theodore Roosevelt: A Biography.* New York: Harcourt, Brace & World, 1956.*

Asterisk denotes paperback edition.

President, Congress, and Control

JOHN MORTON BLUM

At no time was Theodore Roosevelt more intent on achievement, more attuned to opinion, or more conscious of the nice relationships within his party than in November 1904 when he had at last become President in his own right. "Stunned" though he may have been "by the overwhelming victory" he had won, he nevertheless turned at once to fashion a program for Congress. His pursuit of the objective in that program he most valued — a measure to regulate the railroads — demonstrated perhaps better than any other episode in his Presidency both his facility in dealing with Congress and his mature evaluation of the kind of public arrangement which would best permit necessary government control over industrial operations.

Roosevelt was never a speculative man. Thinking as he did primarily about specific issues, he understood and judged large problems in terms of their more limited parts. By his intent, furthermore, his actions spoke for him better than did his words. He made his points most convincingly when he dealt with situations instead of theories. His talents and his purpose are best understood, therefore, by examination of those activities he counted most significant. This was the importance of his railroad program. For it he exercised those qualities of executive leadership upon which successful Presidents must depend; with it he expected to provide the devices upon which the governing of an industrial society might depend.

On various occasions Roosevelt overcame the obstacles imposed by the American Constitution and party system. Again and again he arranged that his recommendations should embody or win the concern of party leaders who, reflecting conflicting regional and economic demands, often had little in common other than the desire to retain office. He maneuvered legislation past the gamut of committee hearings and congressional debates where powerful chairmen and adroit parliamentarians knew how to delay and divert, sometimes defeat, the consensus of the party. Prepared as he was to influence his party and Congress by mobilizing public opinion, careful as he was never to press his program beyond the limits he calculated as practicable, he nurtured bills for the inspection of meat-packing, for the definition and enforcement of pure food and drug standards, for the expansion of the navy. But of all the legislation Roosevelt proposed, he had to work hardest and most skillfully for his railroad program.

Conspicuous inequities in American industrial life drew Roosevelt's concentration to railroad regulation. Existing laws had failed to affect the practices by which railway managers, usually unwillingly, often solely to protect their properties, favored the largest, most ruthless industrial corporations. Faced, as they were, with enormous fixed costs — interest on huge bonded debts, depreciation on large and expensive equipment — railroads, to insure enough business to meet their overheads, acceded to the demands of such corporations as the Standard Oil Company, the Armour Company, and the American Sugar Refining Company for freight rates below those accorded to smaller shippers. Although the Elkins Act of 1903 forbade

Source: John Morton Blum, *The Republican Roosevelt* (Cambridge, Mass.: Harvard University Press, 1954), chap. 6, "President, Congress, and Control," pp. 73–105.

these discriminations, the law was continually violated outright. These violations the offenders could usually obscure by bookkeeping methods over which the Interstate Commerce Commission had no control. The Elkins Act, furthermore, was continually circumvented. Standard Oil and Armour, among many others, besides seeking rebates, obtained discriminatory favor by arranging to receive inordinately large fees from railroads for the use of private cars — such as oil or refrigerator cars — and private sidings and terminals which the corporations owned. Practices such as these helped large shippers to grow wealthier, to absorb their less-favored competitors, to increase thereby their control over markets, and consequently to set prices for their products higher than those that might otherwise have obtained. If the railroads suffered, they too often compensated for their losses by establishing seemingly excessive freight rates either on commodities — like grain and carbon black — whose producers were in no position to demand favors, or over routes where there was no competition for transportation services.

Determined to remedy these conditions, Roosevelt proposed that Congress give the Interstate Commerce Commission effective power over railroad accounts, over private railway equipment, and — most important — in modest degree, over railroad rates. To translate this recommendation into legislation, Roosevelt first created a controlled environment within his party and then adapted his views to parliamentary conditions. He established by his tactics a productive relationship between the executive and Congress. While his program was debated in the Senate, in the session of 1905–1906, Roosevelt defined explicitly the concepts of executive control essential to his more elaborate theses on political economy. During and immediately after the lame duck session of 1904–1905, by strategy as revealing of his purpose as was his later, more explicit definition, he committed the Republicans to railroad regulation and twice got through the House bills that embodied his policy.

Roosevelt's first negotiation necessitated the sacrifice of his announced intention to direct a revision of the tariff. It depended, however, on the continuing threat of tariff revision. The manner in which Roosevelt used tariff revision to advance railroad regulation and the reasons for which he subordinated the one issue to the other have meaning both as a revelatory instance of executive leadership and as an important indication of the central purpose of Roosevelt's political action.

Only two days after the election of 1904 Roosevelt informed Nicholas Murray Butler that he had "already begun the effort to secure a bill to revise and reduce the tariff." The President well understood the dimensions of this task. In his first term he had almost lost to the Republican standpatters his prolonged fight for reciprocity with Cuba. Yet even as his second term began he raised the whole tariff issue, because, he suggested in a heated moment, "we beat the Democrats on the issue that protection was robbery, and that when necessary we would amend or revise the tariff ourselves." This explanation, as Roosevelt knew, did violence to the facts. If the Republicans had any effective national issue in the campaign of 1904 other than Theodore Roosevelt and the Square Deal, it was certainly not tariff revision. The President had accepted a platform that complacently praised Dingleyism; he had strongly endorsed the principle of protection, chastised his Secretary of War for favoring tariff reduction in a campaign speech, and denounced the Democrats for their insistence that protection was robbery.

In his more candid and quiet moments, Roosevelt explained his position with less hyperbole and more effect. "I am convinced," he wrote, "that there is, among the good Republicans and among the masses of independent Democrats who supported us . . . a very strong feeling in favor of what I prefer to call an amendment rather than a revision of the tariff laws." "My own judgment," Roosevelt confessed, "is that it is dangerous to undertake to do anything, but that it is fatal not to undertake it . . ."

This assessment of political sentiment had some validity. The Republican differences on the tariff were major and real. A considerable minority, primarily composed of Western agrarians, favored a general reduction of schedules. Others, for the most part representing Minnesota and Massachusetts shoe, woolens, and flour manufacturers, advocated reciprocity agreements, particularly with Canada, under which their constituents would benefit by cheaper raw materials and larger export markets. These revisionists contended that the party had promised the voters adjustment, though not abandonment, of the protective system. Failing this, they warned, the Democrats, as they had in Massachusetts in 1904, would profitably exploit the tariff issue. They urged Roosevelt, therefore, to summon an extra session of Congress to deal with the tariff, preferably in the spring of 1905. Most Republican leaders, including the most powerful members of Congress, however, opposing any changes in the tariff and jealously guarding the principle of protection, asserted that the election returns evidenced popular satisfaction with the Dingley rates.

Sympathetic to the revisionists, Roosevelt also recognized their strength, but he lacked their conviction and, conscious of the greater strength of their opposition, he feared the divisive hostilities and probable futility that characteristically attended tariff debates. For him the tariff was a matter of expediency. Never willing to risk a division of his party that would endanger his favored measures on an issue about which he did not feel strongly, Roosevelt, in spite of his occasional hyperbole, approached revision with consummate caution. Yet because of the articulate minority support for revision, Roosevelt seized upon tariff discussions as a useful weapon. The prospect of revision, even of a tariff debate, alarmed the standpatters sufficiently to provide an effective disciplinary tool. For Presidential coöperation on the tariff, they were ultimately willing to reach an understanding with Roosevelt, perhaps even to strike a bargain, on railroad regulation.

To that end Roosevelt maneuvered skillfully. His problem was to talk of tariff revision firmly enough to frighten the Old Guard but gently enough not to alienate them. If in the process of negotiation and legislation he could arrange tariff modifications, the achievement would be welcome, but he considered it always incidental. From the very beginning the form of his tariff negotiations suggested that they were less an objective than a device. Roosevelt did not demand; he consulted. "When I see you," he informed the Republican whip in the House, "I want to take up the question of the tariff . . . It seems to me that our party ought to revise the tariff now, but of course I do not want to say anything about it unless the leaders of the House approve, because I realize thoroughly that the matter is primarily one for you all in the House." A week later he added that "an extra session, even if it was not held until the 1st of September [1905], would be most desirable," for, he feared, "if we wait until the regular session . . . the Democrats will talk the matter over for a year and then we shall be swamped at the Congressional elections." Yet he acknowledged to one senator that "there should be only a few and moderate changes"; and even as he labeled protection "robbery," he assured the president of the

American Iron and Steel Institute that he intended "of course, to abide by the general judgment of the party." Meanwhile Roosevelt's personal secretary had announced on November 19 that the President's forthcoming State of the Union message would not mention the tariff.

Clearly Roosevelt never considered the tariff worth a fight. Three weeks after telling Butler he had begun his "effort to secure" a revision, he confessed privately that the issue was practically dead. "The trouble," he explained, "is that there are large parts of the country which want no tariff revision, and of course their representatives are hostile to any agitation of the subject. They say, with entire truth, that neither in the platform nor in any communication of mine is there any promise whatever that there shall be tariff revision. They also say, with equal truth, that the tariff changes should not be great, and that those clamoring for tariff changes are certainly to be disappointed at whatever is done . . . I am going to make every effort to get something of what I desire . . . ; but I shall not split with my party on the matter . . ." Having shed all pretense that the party had a mandate for revision, Roosevelt several days later, again privately, admitted that he had no intention of tackling the tariff in the immediate future. "At present, . . ." he wrote Butler, "there is a strong majority against [amendment or reduction] . . . The minority . . . is entirely split up as to the articles on which the amendment should come . . . This means that unless circumstances change in the next sixty days it will be . . . worse than idle to call the extra session early."

It was not that Roosevelt had retreated. He had never really attacked. But before making his candid admissions to Butler, he had, with less candor, begun to bargain. Just before leaving Illinois for Washington, that archpriest of protection, Speaker of the House Joe Cannon, had received from Roosevelt a disturbing draft, dated November 30, of a special message on the tariff that the President proposed sending to Congress. "While it is above all things desirable that the present tariff law should be kept in its essence unchanged," the draft read, "there may well be certain points as to which it can be amended. There may be some schedules that . . . should be changed . . . If it were possible to provide for reciprocity by a maximum and minimum scale to be applied in the discretion of the Executive, this should be done . . . In any event some of the schedules should now be examined . . ." If these modest proposals could not alarm the Speaker, they were certain at least to worry him. Carefully Roosevelt mitigated even worry, observing that he sent the draft "merely for the sake of having something which can be worked out, after you have consulted the men fresh from the people . . ."

Roosevelt timed the dispatch of the draft nicely. The Speaker was not to be allowed to forget that the tariff issue remained, even though the annual message, opening the last session of the Fifty-eighth Congress, said nothing of revision. He could not be allowed to forget, for that message voiced aggressively Roosevelt's demand for railroad regulation. "The government," Roosevelt instructed Congress, "must in increasing degree supervise and regulate the workings of the railways engaged in interstate commerce; and such increased supervision is the only alternative to an increase of the present evils on the one hand or a still more radical policy on the other. In my judgment, the most important legislative act now needed as regards the regulation of corporations is this act to confer on the Interstate Commerce Commission the power to revise rates and regulations."

With these words Roosevelt set off the battle over railroad regulation. On this issue the party was as divided as on the tariff. And the division, to Roosevelt's advantage, followed similar personal and sectional lines. The advocates of revision and reciprocity were also the proponents of regulation. Speaking for Western agrarians and grain dealers and for Massachusetts manufacturers, they wanted federal review of freight rates which had been, from their point of view, increasingly discriminatory. On the other hand, the standpatters, speaking either for or with the big business interests, had long resisted any departures from nineteenth-century *laissez faire.*

For the railroad program, to which there was strong Republican opposition, Roosevelt had genuine concern. He consulted Congress less and demanded more. It was "unwise and unsafe from every standpoint," he had concluded, "to fail to give the Interstate Commerce Commission additional power of an effective kind in regulating . . . rates." This, he believed, was an essential ingredient for his basic determination "that the Government should effectively shape the policy [of the] . . . Square Deal."

Thus fervently committed, but confronting a powerful opposition, Roosevelt capitalized on the divisions in Congress produced by regional and economic self-interest. The low-tariff, antirailroad group was to have one reform, the high-tariff, prorailroad group to hold one redoubt. Saving what he considered vital by sacrificing what he considered marginal, Roosevelt for the sake of railroad regulation jettisoned the draft of the special message on the tariff that had worried Cannon.

Toward this decision Cannon, by his own account, exercised his influence. The Speaker, and perhaps also Senator Nelson Aldrich, may have struck a bargain with Roosevelt on railroad regulation. The circumstantial evidence that there was some bargain or understanding is overwhelming. The alignments of economic self-interest provided fertile ground which Roosevelt had cultivated for such an understanding. The diminuendo in Roosevelt's private letters to Butler on tariff revision suggests that the President had settled his course in early December. Roosevelt's tariff conferences continued through the first week of January when, according to Cannon's account, he told the congressional leaders that revision would await the election of his successor. Cannon exaggerated, but shortly after that conference Roosevelt defined his position to a friend. "I am having anything but a harmonious time about the tariff and about the interstate commerce . . ." he wrote. "On the interstate commerce business, which I regard as a matter of principle, I shall fight. On the tariff, which I regard as a matter of expediency, I shall endeavor to get the best results I can, but I shall not break with my party." And for the time being, with regard to the tariff, Cannon and the party were one. Two days later Roosevelt wrote Cannon: "Stop in here as soon as you can. I care very little for what the newspapers get in the way of passing sensationalism; but I do not want the people of the country to get the idea that there will be any split or clash between you and me on the tariff or anything else."

Roosevelt permitted no clash. He made no recommendation for specific or general revisions. Although he encouraged efforts for reciprocity arrangements with Canada and Newfoundland, he gave those efforts only desultory support in his dealings with Congress. At the other end of Pennsylvania Avenue, Cannon gave railroad legislation a clear track. The Speaker, it has been argued, saw to it that no bill passed until so late in the session that the Senate could not act. Actually Cannon had no need for such a scheme. The hearings of the House Committee on Interstate

Commerce, as much as the debates on the floor, delayed approval of the bill. When it did finally come to a vote, it passed with a decisive majority of 309. Had it passed earlier, judging by the course of the railroad bill at the following session, it would have failed to get through the Senate before adjournment. And during the following sessions Cannon again presented no obstacles to railway regulation.

In the months following the expiration of the Fifty-eighth Congress, Roosevelt continued to rely on the threat of tariff revision. During that Congress the Senate Committee on Interstate Commerce began to hold hearings that continued through most of May 1905. Railroad executives, mobilized by Samuel Spencer, the chief of J. P. Morgan's railway division, and encouraged by sympathetic senators, used these hearings as a sounding board for opposition to Roosevelt. Outside of the committee room the railroads underwrote an expensive publicity campaign in which various business organizations, including the National Association of Manufacturers, came to their aid. With increasing fervor they rehearsed the dangerous folly of the President's proposals. As this propaganda received wide dissemination in the press, the enemies of regulation seemed to be gaining an upper hand.

Yet Roosevelt in this period displayed a measured optimism. Perhaps he suspected that the railroads would, as they did, overreach themselves. Doubtless he foresaw that investigations of the Standard Oil Company and the beef trust then under way would furnish much evidence to sustain him. Surely he had confidence that his speeches and those of his advisers would counteract the railroad propaganda. The President was continually at the hustings. In the winter at the Philadelphia Union League Club, later in Texas and Colorado, at Chautauqua and Chicago, along the southeastern seaboard, he spoke to adulating audiences of the righteousness, and yet the reasonableness, of his cause. If, in part, the prestige of his office drew them to hear him, the fervor in his falsetto persuaded them to listen. The overdrawn counterpropaganda of the railroads, whatever its merit in logic, could scarcely compete in a society primed by the muckrakers with the explosive personality of the President. Assertively he equated his view of rate-making with his then regnant dictum of a square deal for every man. He would restrain the perverters of privilege who by their manipulations of rates and rebates purloined the just profits of their honest competitors and threatened to provoke by their excesses the menace of socialism. This was a crisis (Theodore Roosevelt coped constantly with crises), but he would shackle greed and, routing the proponents of nationalization, save the railroads from themselves.

But Roosevelt did not confine his energies to the podium. In May he reminded the Old Guard that the tariff could still be an issue. To emphasize the tariff-railroad understanding that the battle of propaganda might otherwise have obscured, Roosevelt thrust at the standpatters' most sensitive spot. One guardian of protection had admitted the previous fall that the "strongest argument" for revision was that American manufacturers sold goods in foreign markets for less than they received at home. This condition, he then pointed out, while perhaps inequitable, was irremediable, for "no revision of the tariff which still left a protective margin could prevent" it. To challenge the differential in the export and domestic prices of protected commodities was to challenge the whole principle of protection. This was precisely what Roosevelt did.

On May 16, 1905, while the railroad propaganda was at its peak, an announcement that the Isthmian Canal Commission had decided to purchase supplies for the construction of the canal in foreign markets immediately staggered the standpatters.

They were further shocked when Roosevelt flatly assumed all responsibility for the adoption of this "cheapest-market" policy. The New York *Times* called the announcement the "doom of Dingleyism." The steel industry's most active lobbyist and his reliable congressional echoes shared the view of the New York *Press* that the cheapest-market policy, repudiating the high-tariff mandate of 1904, was "a faithless service of outrage." The president of the National Association of Manufacturers and the secretary of the American Protective Tariff Association tersely labeled Roosevelt's action "un-American."

Less emotional observers noted that Roosevelt probably intended not to abandon protection but to call the attention of Congress to the whole subject of tariff adjustment. They were correct, for after succeeding admirably in just that, the President was satisfied. Three days after the announcement was made, Cannon conferred with Secretary of War Taft, who then rescinded the cheapest-market order, referring to the next Congress the question of canal purchases. Responsible, according to his own statement, for the order, Roosevelt must also have been responsible for the reversal.

The dramatic episode of the canal purchases served as Roosevelt's most forceful but not as his final reminder to the stand patters that the tariff remained a potential issue. In August, White House "leaks" inspired newspaper reports that the President contemplated calling an extra session of Congress to consider tariff revision. If he did not plant these rumors, Roosevelt at least used them. To his Secretary of the Treasury, an uncompromising protectionist, he wrote in the tone he had long used: "I entirely agree with all you say as to the dangers which accompany tariff revision — or any attempt at it, but as yet I am not sure whether there are not at least equal dangers in avoiding [it] . . . I want to go over the entire matter very carefully with all of the Congressional leaders before we decide which set of risks to take." Roosevelt quickly decided. It was scarcely necessary for him to consult his congressional leaders — they had understood each other for months. In mid-August, Taft, then in the Philippines, released a message from the President that there would be no extra session of Congress. The regular session, Roosevelt had already implied at Chautauqua and stated in private, would be, insofar as he could control it, devoted to rate regulation.

In December 1905, the Fifty-ninth Congress convened. During the fall, the campaigns in Massachusetts and Iowa had kept the tariff issue alive while Roosevelt, in the South, had focused on the railways. The President's annual message, silent, as it had been in 1904, on the tariff, made railroad regulation the central objective of the Administration. In the long struggle that ensued, the tariff once more provided a lever. In the House, a combination of Democrats and Administration Republicans passed a bill reducing the rates on Philippine products. Intended as an instrument of colonial policy, the measure was nevertheless considered by standpat Republicans to breach the principle of protection. Administration leaders in the Senate by their lassitude permitted it to die in committee while, like Roosevelt, they concentrated their energy and their power on the railroad bill. For this division of labor no explicit bargain need have been made, for all matters pertaining to the tariff continued in 1906 to be, as they had been since 1904, useful whips rather than real targets. By 1906 Roosevelt had abandoned all effort for tariff revision, yet essentially he abandoned only a bargaining instrument. At no time in his long public career did tariff revision much concern him. For eighteen months, however, he employed adroitly the specter of tariff agitation.

By defining tariff revision as a matter of expediency and railroad regulation as a matter of principle, Roosevelt established his own position. His life, he felt, was a quest for the moral. What he meant by morality was not always clear, but the concept had obvious components. In some cases, that which was moral was that which could be accomplished. Given two paper trusts to bust, Roosevelt had attacked the less offensive but legally vulnerable pool and ignored the more oppressive but legally secure holding company. By this criterion, railroad regulation was in 1904 more moral than tariff revision, for public and political opinion on the railways divided on nonpartisan lines and the Republican party was less committed to the Elkins Act as a line of defense than to the Dingley Act. That which was moral was also often that which was popular. In making a crucial test of the Sherman Antitrust Act, Roosevelt had prosecuted neither the largest nor the most monopolistic holding company. He had chosen, rather, a railroad merger that had been born of a discreditable stockmarket battle, that consisted of units long unpopular with shippers in the areas in which they ran, that had already been challenged by state authorities. Unlike Justice Holmes, Roosevelt wanted to bring the voice of the people to bear on decisions. Showered as they were in 1904 by private and official disclosures of the iniquities of rebates, the evils of Armour, the machinations of Standard Oil, most of the people, particularly middle-class people, were less interested in the tariff than in direct controls of big business, especially the railways.

But Roosevelt's morality was not simply opportunistic. He felt that the central issue of his time pivoted on the control of business because this control determined conduct, and morality was for him a matter of conduct. He feared not the size but the policies of big business. He cared not about profits but about the manner of earning profits. This was the essence of the Square Deal. Roosevelt fought for railroad regulation because it was designed to control process. By his standard, tariff schedules — static matters — were as unimportant as an administrative agency overseeing day-by-day business arrangements was essential.

These dimensions of morality — practicability, popularity, and especially preoccupation with process — characterized Roosevelt's emergent progressivism. They permitted him to yield, when necessary, on details in order to advance his favored measures. They also persuaded him for reasons of policy as well as of tactics to arrange the understanding on tariff revision and railroad regulation that prepared the way for perhaps the most significant legislation of his Presidency.

Railroad rates could not be regulated, however, until Roosevelt, having committed the House to his policy, slowly brought the Senate also into line. In that second task, as in the persuading of the House, he exercised artfully the resources of office and person by which a President can lead Congress, in spite of the separation of powers imposed by the Constitution, to consummate his policies. Roosevelt's impressive ability to work within the structure of government, like his facility in managing the party, depended less on his arresting manner than on his appreciation of the institutions that shaped American political life. Like Edmund Burke, perhaps the greatest of British conservatives, Roosevelt valued the long wash of historical development, sometimes controlled, sometimes accidental, that had given form to the political society in which he lived. Both were wisely careful never to set up a system of their own. Like Burke, Roosevelt delighted in the processes by which political achievement and further institutional development were made possible. Both considered political peace the breathing-time which gave them leisure further to contrive. As he guided his railroad program through the Senate where formidable obstacles blocked his way, Roosevelt needed and took his daily gladness in situations "of power and energy," in government — as Burke described it — "founded on compromise and barter."

Behind all the political manipulation, beneath all the legalistic forensics, the issue was control. Theodore Roosevelt intended that an administrative agency should have the authority to rectify the inequities in the business of transportation. Nelson Aldrich, the resourceful leader of the President's opposition, intended that it should not. Roosevelt demanded that the Interstate Commerce Commission be invested with power to revise railroad rates. Here, he felt, lay the key to control. Aldrich, when he drew his lines, sought to transfer the final decision on rates from the commission to the courts, to leave the judiciary in its traditional, ineffectual, disorderly role of monitor of the price of transportation. President and senator, sensitive always to each other's strength, delighting in the test, came slowly to a crisis.

"I am well aware," Roosevelt stated in his annual message to Congress of 1905, "of the difficulties of the [railroad] legislation that I am suggesting, and of the need of temperate and cautious action in securing it. I should emphatically protest against improperly radical or hasty action . . . [But] the question of transportation lies at the root of all industrial success, and the revolution in transportation which has taken place during the last half-century has been the most important factor in the growth of the new industrial conditions . . . At present the railway is [the highway of commerce] . . . and we must do our best to see that it is kept open to all on equal terms . . . It is far better that it should be managed by private individuals than by the government. But it can only be so managed on condition that justice is done the public . . . What we need to do is to develop an orderly system, and such a system can only come through the gradually increased exercise of the right of efficient government control."

A year earlier Roosevelt had sent Congress only a paragraph on railroad legislation. Now he spelled out the elements of what he considered an orderly system of control. These he had derived from the accumulated findings of the Bureau of Corporations and the Interstate Commerce Commission and from the expert advice of the lawyers and railroad men in his Cabinet. Their recommendations, embodied in the Hepburn Bill with Administration guidance substantially as Roosevelt had announced them, covered every aspect of the railroad problem then recognized by the foremost authority on railroad economics in the United States. Grounded as it was on thorough study by essentially conservative men, much of Roosevelt's program provoked little congressional dissent.

The area of agreement was large. The Elkins Antirebate Act of 1903 had failed utterly to prevent the discriminations it explicitly forbade. Alive to this, and to the public's growing displeasure over the outrageous practices of Armour and Standard Oil, practices as harmful to the railroads as to the competitors of the favored, Congress shared the President's opinion that "all private-car lines, industrial roads, refrigerator charges, and the like should be expressly put under the supervision of the Interstate Commerce Commission . . ." Conscious of the experience of the government in investigating both railways and industrial concerns, Congress, like Roosevelt, had reached the commonsense conclusion that standardized records open to official inspection were a prerequisite for the determination of adequate policies of regulation as well as for the prevention of familiar abuses in corporation management. Congress was also willing, by providing for expeditious action in cases arising under the commerce act, to destroy "the weapon of delay, almost the most formidable weapon in the hands of those whose purpose is to violate the law."

Had Roosevelt recommended and Congress agreed to nothing else, these provisions would in themselves have been worth-while but inadequate achievements. They did not fundamentally alter the existing relationship between the federal government and the railroads. They established no new device of regulation. The restriction of rebates, now strengthened, had earlier existed; the inspection of records, now facilitated, had long since begun; the expedition of trial for suits involving infractions of the Interstate Commerce Act had already been provided for suits arising under the Antitrust Act. Roosevelt's orderly system of efficient government control depended not on these precedents but on an innovation to which many in Congress were still openly hostile. The President proposed that the I.C.C. be given limited authority to make rates. As he carefully defined it, this was his central objective.

Roosevelt took his first and final position on rates in his annual message of 1904. He there considered it "undesirable . . . finally to clothe the commission with general authority to fix railroad rates." "As a fair security to shippers," however, he insisted that "the commission should be vested with the power, where a given rate has been challenged and after full hearing found to be unreasonable, to decide, subject to judicial review, what shall be a reasonable rate to take its place; the ruling of the commission to take effect immediately." The "reasonable rate," Roosevelt implied by his reference to the Supreme Court's interpretation of the Interstate Commerce Act, was to be only a maximum rate. This meaning he made explicit in 1905 when he requested that the commission receive power "to prescribe the limit of rate beyond which it shall not be lawful to go — the maximum reasonable rate, as it is commonly called."

Roosevelt's Attorney General had advised that legislation empowering the commission to set definite rate schedules — the objective of many Democratic and some Western Republican senators — might be declared unconstitutional. "The one thing I do not want," Roosevelt explained to one critic, "is to have a law passed and then declared unconstitutional." Furthermore, he argued, the authority to prescribe a maximum rate, while perhaps short of the ultimate ideal, promised immediate, substantial improvement in existing conditions. "If the Commission has the power to make the maximum rate that which the railroad gives to the most favored shipper, it will speedily become impossible thus to favor any shipper . . ." If, after a test, it should prove inadequate, he would then be willing to try to secure a definite rate proposition. "I believe," he explained to the impatient, "in men who take the next step; not those who theorize about the two-hundredth step."

Roosevelt intended primarily to protect individual shippers from excessive or discriminatory rates. He agreed that the maximum rate provision would afford little remedy for discrimination between commodities or between localities, but such discriminations seemed to him relatively impersonal. He cared less about freight classification and long and short haul differentials because he could not readily associate those matters with a doer of evil and a victim. Discriminations against a small shipper or exorbitant rates the President understood and despised. They were, he was sure, immoral. His interest had also political meaning, for the spokesmen of the shippers' organizations concentrated on the problems that a maximum rate provision could begin to resolve. They neglected to mention, and Roosevelt did not apparently recognize, that no recommendation in the annual messages or provision in the Hepburn Bill prevented shippers or their consignees from passing on rate burdens originating in any discriminatory device to the still unorganized, essentially undiscerning consumers.

The maximum rate proposal, in many respects inadequate, properly labeled so by liberals of the time, nevertheless earned for Roosevelt the opprobrious criticism of a large part of the business community and the tenacious opposition of a near majority of the United States Senate. Modest as the proposal was, it challenged the most cherished prerogative of private management, the most hoary tenet of free private enterprise — the ability freely to make prices. This threat gave Roosevelt a reputation, persisting still among railway executives, of being a scandalous advocate of something closely akin to socialism. A more radical proposition, the President well knew, would have had no chance for success.

Roosevelt had constructed the Hepburn Bill with practiced care. Including as it did just enough to satisfy his purpose, it contained nothing that would alarm the marginal supporters without whom it could not survive. This was the last in a series of calculated tactics by which Roosevelt had prepared the parliamentary environment for his railroad program. "I have a very strong feeling," he acknowledged, "that it is a President's duty to get on with Congress if he possibly can, and that it is a reflection upon him if he and Congress come to a complete break." Avoiding a break, understanding his situation, he made the powers of his office and the talents of his person the instruments of viable leadership.

He had begun by trading tariff reform for railroad regulation. He had continued, after the adjournment of the lame duck session of the Fifty-eighth Congress, by taking his railroad issue, then the foremost national political problem, to the people. At the hustings his vigorous pleading won enthusiastic acclaim. His "plain people," for the most part, heard only the voice of their champion. Significantly, however, more careful, more cautious listeners, disregarding his dramatic allusions, at once could ascertain the moderation of his demands. Roosevelt's message was simple. His demands were not new. Indeed, Roosevelt added nothing to the principles or to the histrionics of the Granger and Populist railroad regulators of years gone by. But he did bring to their long-rejected national program a new respectability, an incomparable personal vitality, and assurances, impressive to thoughtful conservatives, that he, unlike his predecessors, would direct regulation to constructive ends.

The last was particularly important. By the fall of 1905 such reliable Republican senators from the West as Allison of Iowa and Spooner of Wisconsin, traditionally conservators of the status quo, now sensitive to the growing complaints of the farmers and shippers whose protests had preceded and exceeded Roosevelt's, realized that their political life rested upon an unprecedented capitulation to their constituents. In the President they recognized a safe sponsor for reform. If his language seemed at times extravagant, if his central purpose was a genuine departure from the past, he nevertheless, they knew from experience, guarded their party and, in the largest sense, their principles. This knowledge may also have comforted others who deeply distrusted the emotions Roosevelt evoked. Before the Fifty-ninth Congress convened, the roar of the President's crowds penetrated, perhaps, the cold quiet where Nelson Aldrich, by preference undisturbed, made policy. That master of the Senate, in any case, was thereafter willing to make a conciliatory gesture toward Roosevelt and his allies.

The President had set his stage. Reminded of the arrangements by which the tariff remained inviolate, the new House in February 1906, with only seven adverse votes, passed the Hepburn Bill. It provided for every objective of the Administration. The most thoughtful member of the I.C.C., Commissioner Prouty, told Roosevelt that it represented "an advance so extraordinary that he had never dared to suppose it would be possible to pass it." The President judged that it was "as far as we could with wisdom go at this time." Politically he was surely correct. Although an aroused constituency cheered the champions of the bill in the Senate, Nelson Aldrich, as debate began, had yet to surrender command of the chamber he had so long dominated. Roosevelt, until this time the aggressor, had now to adjust to the strength and the tactics of a talented oppositionist.

How unlike the President in many ways his adversary was: so urbane, so controlled, so indifferent to manifestations of approval, so patently disdainful of the string-tie statesmanship surrounding him; but, like Roosevelt, so bemused by the endless adventure of governing men! Did his friend Allison have, of a summer, to explain himself in ponderous periods from a rural podium? How dreary for Allison. Aldrich preferred the politics that the caucus controlled, the constituents one met graciously over liqueurs, the measured exchanges between mutually respectful equals who understood the manners and the meaning of their power. For all that, Aldrich was not the less discerning, not the less tenacious. Many of the dreadful things that Theodore did, the senator knew, he had to do. The people, after all, could vote. The railroads were unpopular. Roosevelt could have his bill, but not the way he wanted it. A gesture now, a delaying action — then, perhaps, the worst would pass. Perhaps, again, it would not pass; the comfortable world was changing. In that case, delay had of itself some value. And the means to resist were familiar and strong.

Aldrich had a corps of allies: among the Republicans, the intractables, all reliable, some expert parliamentarians, some outstanding men. There were also among the Democrats those who regularly resisted any reform and others, bound by quixotic tradition confounded with visions of miscegenation, who could be made to shy at any extension of the federal executive power. These were less reliable. Yet Aldrich in the past by prestige and by persuasion had combined these parts into a solid phalanx to front, unbudging, the bills that carried change.

Aldrich, disingenuous, moved quietly to bring the Hepburn Bill with its objectionable clause on rates into the arena where he and his allies had long had their way. While the measure lay before the Committee on Interstate and Foreign Commerce he labored at a disadvantage. There, with few exceptions, his trusted assistants had no seat. There Roosevelt's friends, making the President's moderation their own, seemed capable by coöperation with the Democratic committeemen of carrying crucial votes. There Jonathan Dolliver, the junior senator from Iowa, then beginning the progressive period of his career, ably pleaded the case of the Administration. Dolliver's continuing intimacy with Roosevelt and Attorney General Moody made him as informed as he was ardent. If Dolliver could with the Democrats model the bill to Roosevelt's satisfaction and then bring it out of committee as a party measure, he would have thereafter a tactical advantage. In these parts, Aldrich did not try to shape the bill in committee. He could not have persuaded a majority to go his way, but he could and did persuade a majority to ease his way. Seeming to yield, disarming Dolliver, Aldrich permitted the Hepburn Bill to be reported unamended. Then, supported by Democratic votes on which Dolliver had counted, he secured a motion reserving to each committee member the right to propose amendments from the floor. The issue, still unresolved, was now before the whole Senate.

The same Democratic votes sustained Aldrich's next move. Had Dolliver, as he expected, been designated to guide the measure on the floor, he would still have been an asset to the President and the bill might still have been presented as the party's. Almost the senator from Iowa could see the "Hepburn-Dolliver Act" engraved in history. The Democrats, however, desiring some credit for regulating railroads, preferred that half that title belong to them. This preference Aldrich exploited. He had won the Democrats in the committee to reporting the bill for amendment from the floor by arranging to name as its floor leader one of their party, Benjamin Tillman of South Carolina. With that serpent-tongued agrarian as its guide, the bill could not be labeled "Republican." For Dolliver this was a staggering personal blow; for Aldrich, a beguiling triumph; for Roosevelt, an embarrassing problem in communication. The President and Tillman had long loathed each other. Only recently the senator had made one of his calculated, insulting attacks on Roosevelt's character. For years they had not spoken. Now Aldrich had forced them either to coöperate or to endanger the policy they both espoused. Whatever their course, furthermore, Aldrich had moved the bill into a position where he and his collaborators had an excellent chance of neutralizing it by amendment. "Aldrich," Roosevelt concluded irritably, had "completely lost both his head and his temper." The President had lost the first round.

Well before the Hepburn Bill reached the Senate, Aldrich and his associates had determined on the nature of their attack. Perhaps out of deference to the electorate, they refrained from a direct assault on the maximum rate clause. Instead, they concentrated on amendments by which they intended to endow the judiciary, the least mobile of the branches of government, with the authority to nullify and to delay the rate rulings of the I.C.C. In behalf of these amendments they debated not the economics of rate-making or the proprieties of privilege, but the constitutionality of the regulatory process, the orderly system that the President proposed to create.

Roosevelt had noted with care that the I.C.C. or a substitute commission "should be made unequivocally administrative." To an administrative body as opposed to an executive department, Congress could, he believed, within the meaning of the Constitution on the separation of powers, delegate the authority to fix maximum rates. This has become a commonplace assumption, the basis of a proliferation of alphabet agencies, but in 1906 men of disinterested conviction as well as those who were sheer obstructionists questioned the legality of combining in one body the quasi-legislative power of determining rates, even maximum rates, the quasi-judicial authority of deciding upon the validity of rates, and the quasi-executive function of investigation and enforcement. The unsuccessful railroad bill of 1905, attempting to resolve this constitutional difficulty, had included a clause, briefly resuscitated in 1910 by the Mann-Elkins Act, establishing a special court of commerce to review the rate decisions of the I.C.C. The Hepburn Bill as it emerged from the House, however, made no similar provision. Dodging the whole issue of judicial review, it said nothing at all about jurisdiction in cases arising under it.

On the question of judicial review, the proponents and the opponents of Roosevelt's program drew their lines. Contrasted to the large and varied significance of the whole railroad measure, this deployment seems at first almost chicane. Yet since the debates on Hamilton's reports, American legislators had persisted in clothing their differences in constitutional terms. Nor, in the case of the Hepburn Bill, was this lawyers' legacy meaningless. Roosevelt envisioned a new kind of federal executive power to control the complex processes of an industrialized state. He anticipated the methods of the future. His opponents in the Senate, seeking to perpetuate the method or lack of method of the past, relied upon the prevailing dicta of the American courts to prevent the executive from interfering in the day-by-day operations of American business. In government based on law, this was in 1906 still a legal as well as an economic issue. Both sides assiduously spoke the Constitution fair.

The President by no means denied the right of judicial review. He did not believe that any legislation could "prevent . . . an appeal" from a ruling of the I.C.C. "The courts will retain, and should retain, no matter what the Legislature does," he had asserted, "the power to interfere and upset any action that is confiscatory in its nature." Yet Roosevelt also preferred that judicial review should be limited essentially to procedural questions — to a determination, in any mooted case, of whether the commission's method of reaching the decision had been fair to the carrier. His opponents, on the other hand, hoped to emasculate his program by providing explicitly for broad judicial reinterpretation of the facts of each case. This would have given the courts, considered friendly by the railroads, rather than the commission, which the railroads feared, the real authority over rates.

By its reticence on the matter, the House's version of the Hepburn Bill left to the courts themselves the determination of the scope of review. Roosevelt expressed his satisfaction with this evasion. Attorney General Moody, however, advised him that the measure, in order to pass the test of constitutionality, needed an amendment affirming the right of the railroads to have the courts review the commission's decisions. Roosevelt then considered it only desirable but not essential that the bill provide narrow review. As he began negotiations with the leaders of the Senate, he sought not a limitation to procedural review but only an ambiguous declaration, consonant with the evasion in the unamended version, of the right of review.

Inherent in, but in Roosevelt's opinion subordinate to, the problem of the scope of judicial review was the question of the time at which the rate decisions of the I.C.C. should become effective. Roosevelt had asked that they take effect "immediately," a stipulation the Hepburn Bill fulfilled to his satisfaction by making them effective in thirty days. But if the railroads took to court a decision of the commission, the long process of litigation would postpone indefinitely the application of the revised maximum rate. The House had avoided this problem. In the Senate, while the friends of the railroads wanted just such a delay, the advocates of regulation endeavored to construct some amendment that would prevent the use of injunctions to suspend, pending the outcome of litigation, the rulings of the commission. Roosevelt when debate began preferred, but, as on the question of narrow review, did not insist that the use of injunctions be restricted.

Against the President's moderate, almost uncertain, position the prorailroad senators launched an offensive. Philander Chase Knox, who had while Attorney General seemed to endorse Roosevelt's program, refused in a conference with Moody to reach an agreement on an amendment pertaining to judicial review. Moody's draft, supported by the President, protected the constitutionality of the Hepburn Bill without increasing the appellate jurisdiction of the courts. This was not enough for Knox. In conference he stated that he preferred the House's bill to Moody's amendment. To the Senate he proposed in February that the courts pass on the "lawfulness" of the commission's orders — a term Moody considered so vague as to invite continuing litigation on the economic details and constitutional implications of each rate order. Knox's broad definition of review, carrying as it did the prestige of its author, provided in compelling form precisely the objective of Aldrich and his allies. To graft upon the Hepburn Bill Knox's amendment or one just like it, Aldrich had maneuvered the measure out of committee and onto the floor.

Roosevelt, while Aldrich deployed, had not been idle. From the time the Hepburn Bill reached the Senate, even as it lay in committee, the President had begun to confer with his Republican associates about amendments. Like Aldrich, he had able collaborators. Most helpful of these were William B. Allison of Iowa and John C. Spooner of Wisconsin who, in other years, had with Aldrich and the now deceased O. H. Platt composed the Senate's inner council of control. Allison, of that Four the most sensitive to the tolerances of public opinion and the most skillful negotiator, "rendered," Roosevelt later recalled, "unwearied and invaluable service in the actual, and indispensable, working out of legislative business." Spooner, scarcely less gifted, had a large personal stake in the satisfactory resolution of the problem of regulation, for his home bastion rattled before the guerrillas of the insurgent La Follette. Allison and Spooner brought with them a loyal corps of lesser Western Republican veterans for whom freight rates had assumed pressing political importance. The President could also rely upon, though he would not confide in, the intense Republican left. Could these men clearly demonstrate their strength, others in the party would reluctantly go their way. Finally, there were the Bryan Democrats, Tillman, Bailey of Texas, and a few more cautious in thought and less erratic in deportment who would probably damn Roosevelt's bill but give it their votes.

So positioned, Roosevelt planned at first to carry the bill by sponsoring amendments which would attract the Republican center without alienating the bipartisan left. Throughout February and much of March, while the bill lay in committee, he sought only to perpetuate explicitly the ambiguities implicit in the House's version. The plan seemed feasible so long as the committee might fashion a party measure. But Aldrich's coup, preventing this, also permitted the senator to vitiate Roosevelt's influence with the uncertain. Naturally like Aldrich disposed to trust the judiciary to brake change, the Republican center, relieved of party discipline, now looked more favorably on broad review. Tillman as floor leader for the bill was scarcely fit by temperament or inclination to dissuade them. The President, consequently, had to adjust his strategy to Aldrich's *démarche*.

Roosevelt acted at once. As his personal, unofficial representative in the Senate he selected Allison, who could reach and convince a larger number of Republicans than could have any other possible agent. He arranged also to communicate with Tillman through ex-Senator William E. Chandler, a mutual friend and advocate of regulation. By this clumsy device, with Tillman's help and through Allison's negotiations, Roosevelt then set out to construct a new coalition. "Inasmuch as the Republican leaders have tried to betray me . . ." he explained, "I am now trying to see if I cannot get . . . [the bill] through in the form I want by the aid of some fifteen or twenty Republicans added to most of the Democrats." For this purpose, involving as it did both the enthusiasm of Tillman and the loyalty of Allison, Roosevelt had to move cautiously but clearly to the left of his original position.

Largely to Allison fell the difficult task of seeking a formula which would solve the problems of judicial review and the use of injunctions to the satisfaction of the divers partners to the potential coalition. Aldrich, if not surprised, must have been a little hurt to find his friend working the other side of the aisle. The work was tedious. Senator after senator contributed to the dozens of amendments under consideration. Three of these sufficiently reveal the nature of Allison's predicament. That of Senator Long of Kansas, the well-advertised product of a White House conference held just at the time Roosevelt decided to rely upon a coalition, prevented, according to the consensus of the Senate, judicial reconsideration of the facts of a case. In endorsing it, the President, no longer equivocal, won the favor of the coalition's Republicans and populist Democrats. Yet this was not enough. Senator Bailey of Texas, Tillman's closest associate, and other persistent Jeffersonians opposed the amendment, as Aldrich expected they would, because it seemed to them an unwarranted extension of executive power. Both Tillman and Bailey, moreover, considered the injunction issue more important than judicial review. The Texan had introduced an amendment, endorsed by most Democrats, which deprived the courts of authority to issue temporary writs suspending rate orders. Although this proposal effectively prevented delay in the application of rate rulings, it seemed to Roosevelt and his harassed lieutenants to be clearly unconstitutional. As negotiations proceeded, the President feared that Aldrich might adopt Bailey's plan or any of several like it in order with Democratic support to write a law that the courts would promptly nullify. Roosevelt and Allison therefore sponsored as an alternative an amendment drafted by Spooner. It provided that whenever a court suspended a rate order the amount in dispute between the carrier and the commission should be placed in escrow pending the outcome of litigation. Spooner's plan at once prevented confiscation of railroad property without due process of law, protected the shippers, and eliminated any advantage for the railroad in seeking litigation simply to cause delay.

Had Roosevelt and Allison been dealing only with resilient men, such ingenuity as Spooner's might, in time, have permitted them to devise a winning compromise. Bailey, for one, began to trim toward Allison. But a few Republicans and Tillman Democrats remained so adamantly for narrow review, many other Democrats so firmly for broad review, that Spooner's promising solution for injunctions never commanded the serious attention of either extreme. Before Allison had a chance to homogenize these stubborn parts, Aldrich precipitated crisis. He, too, had been active across the aisle. On April 18, as he predicted, the Democratic caucus refused to follow Tillman and Bailey. Roosevelt's attempt at coalition had failed.

Aldrich, the second round his, doubtless hoped that Roosevelt would either capitulate or, as he had a few weeks earlier, move further left. The President could have consolidated a noisy defense by throwing in his lot with the La Follette Republicans and Tillman Democrats. He could with them have swelled the rising voices of protest. He might, by such a move, have earned a popularity beyond even that already his. But he would have lost his bill. Seeing this as clearly as did Aldrich, Roosevelt had already prepared once more to redeploy.

Six days earlier, sensing defeat, the President had begun to hedge. If he could not win with Tillman, he might still win on his own original terms without the Democrats. "I am not at all sure," he then wrote Allison, "but that the easy way will be to come right back to the bill as it passed the House, and with very few unimportant amendments to pass it as it stands." On April 22 Roosevelt told Knox, again his confidant, that this opinion was "evidently gaining ground." Indeed it was, for Nelson Aldrich turned toward Roosevelt after the Democrats turned away. The leaders of the President's Republican opposition by early May ceased to insist on an explicit statement for broad review. Perhaps Aldrich became impatient with the continuing delay in the work of the Senate brought about by the everlasting debate on regulation. Perhaps he decided that Republican solidarity was more important than Roosevelt's purpose was dangerous. Probably, however, he saw that he had miscalculated. When Roosevelt, refusing to list with the left, reverted doggedly to the ambiguous center where he had first stood, he impelled Tillman, La Folette, and their likes, his erstwhile allies, into embittered opposition. Their protestations, couched in their inevitable vocabulary of revolt, attested to the safe reasonableness Roosevelt had ever claimed as his own. The uncertain minds of the wavering Republican center might now hear Allison out — might now, as Allison and Spooner had, see in Roosevelt safety. By some new alignment, like that he had hoped Dolliver would muster, the President with time in *Thermidor* might triumph. At least, so Aldrich may have reasoned. In any case he retreated.

He may also have drafted the amendment which, introduced by Allison, won a majority vote and thereby secured the enactment of the Hepburn Bill. Whether or not Aldrich drafted it, Allison's amendment, leaving the bill in effect as the House had written it, gave Roosevelt what he had started out to get. The authorship of the amendment, like the working of Aldrich's mind, remains obscure. Whoever wrote it, Allison guided it. His activities in the two weeks following the Democratic caucus may be accurately surmised. Leaving no records, the "unwearied and invaluable" senator from Iowa, camped in the cloakroom where he excelled, had fashioned for the President a compromise that satisfied enough Republicans to save the bill.

The Allison amendment covered both judicial review and the use of injunctions. With purposeful obscurity, it granted jurisdiction in cases arising under the Hepburn Act to the circuit courts but left the definition of the scope of review to the courts. In a flood of oratory over the meaning of the amendment, each senator interpreted it to suit himself and his constituents. Both sides claimed victory. Insofar as the amendment was described as a victory for either narrow or broad review, the claims were nonsense. The question of review remained in May as unsettled as it had been in February. Roosevelt had then asked for no more. Ultimately the Supreme Court, which he trusted so little, in the first decision involving rate rulings made his preference law by refusing to review the facts of the case.

The Allison amendment did affirmatively settle the matter of injunctions by empowering the courts to "enjoin, set aside, annul, or suspend any order" of the I.C.C. It also prescribed that appeals from the orders of the I.C.C. were to go directly to the Supreme Court with the calendar priorities of antitrust cases. The amendment did not, however, specify the grounds for suspension or establish an escrow scheme. There remained, consequently, the possibility of considerable delay before rate rulings took effect. Roosevelt had constantly expressed his preference for an arrangement less favorable to the railroads, but he had also continually indicated that he would accept a solution like that of the Allison amendment. On this matter Tillman and Bailey, but neither Aldrich nor Roosevelt, had been defeated.

Roosevelt was "entirely satisfied" with the Allison amendment, he pointed out, because he was "entirely satisfied with the Hepburn bill." The amendment, he informed a less satisfied representative of midwestern shippers, was "only declaratory of what the Hepburn bill must mean, supposing it to be constitutional . . . I should be glad to get certain [other] amendments . . . ; but they are not vital, and even without them the Hepburn bill with the Allison amendment contains practically exactly what I have both originally and always since asked for."

Characteristically, Roosevelt overstated his case. "Always since" did not apply, for in his maneuvers of late March and April, although only at that time, the President had asked for more. Tillman and Bailey, who had joined him then, with rankling disappointment attacked him for returning to what he had originally requested. Their attacks, often repeated by their friends, have persuaded two generations that Roosevelt, irresolute and insincere, deserting his friends, yielding to Aldrich, lost the battle for regulation. Surely his detractors felt this, but they erred. Roosevelt had made overtures to Tillman and Bailey only for tactical reasons. He had, temporarily and for parliamentary support, enlarged his earlier demands. When this did not produce sufficient support, he reverted for tactical reasons to his first position. In so doing he deserted his temporary allies, but he did not compromise his policy. Tillman and Bailey, proud veterans of the Senate, perhaps resented most the knowledge that they had been used. Doubtless their pain gave Aldrich, who had made Roosevelt woo them and leave them, some amused satisfaction.

His objective attained, Roosevelt exulted. "No given measure and no given set of measures," he believed, "will work a perfect cure for any serious evil; and the insistence upon having only the perfect cure often results in securing no betterment whatever." The Hepburn Act was not perfect. But, Roosevelt maintained, it represented "the longest step ever yet taken in the direction of solving the railway rate problem." This was a fair assessment. With his clear perception of political situations, Roosevelt had set the highest practicable goal. By his mastery of political devices, in contest with another master, he had reached it. The Senate, in the end, supplied the federal executive with authority beyond any antecedent definition to mitigate the maladjustments of a growing industrial society.

The Hepburn Act endowed the Interstate Commerce Commission with power commensurate with its task. By informed, expert decisions, it could at last alter the artificial configurations of a market that had long since ceased, in the classic sense, to be free. The courts inexpertly had judged transportation by criteria which, however precious in jurisprudence, bore little relation to the economics of the process. Released from the inhibition of judicial reinterpretations (the bond that Aldrich had sought to supply), endowed with weapons the carriers respected, the I.C.C. began to develop after 1906 the techniques of effective supervision. The need for further change of course remained. But the Hepburn Act provided the precedent, accepted by the courts and enlarged by later Congresses, by which federal regulatory agencies have promoted the national welfare. Now vastly ramified, government by administrative commission remains, though somewhat shabby, a useful part of American political arrangements.

For a troubled people in a complex time perhaps only the executive could have become steward. Aldrich, in that case, fought history and Roosevelt only accelerated what no man could have prevented. But Roosevelt's reputation rests securely even in acceleration, for the inevitable sometimes takes too long, and he knew just what he did. His efforts in behalf of the Hepburn Act — a measure meaningful but moderate — demonstrated his skilled concern for creating the instruments he thought the nation needed. For an orderly administrative system, for the right of efficient federal controls, for the positive government of an industrial society, he mobilized in a crucial first skirmish the full powers of his office. And he won.

Only continuous, disinterested administrative action, Roosevelt believed, not intermittent lawsuits or intermittent legislation, not the dicta of the bench or the dicta of partisan and sectional politics, could properly direct the development of American industrial society. This conviction related intimately to his feelings about power and its uses. These in their general implications — both domestic and international — must now be elaborated and explored.

Immigration after the Civil War

In the century between 1815 and the outbreak of World War I, some 30 million Europeans crossed the Atlantic to the United States. They came from every part of the old continent and represented every stratum of European population. Preponderantly, however, they were the little men, the peasants and the common laborers, leavened a bit by businessmen, professionals, and middle-class political refugees. Their goal was a better life for themselves and their families, and the magnets that drew the great majority of them was cheap land and high wages.

They did not come in a homogeneous, steady stream. Between 1815 and 1830 their numbers were small. During the 1830s, the number swelled to 600,000, followed by the deluge of 1.7 million in the 1840s, and 2.3 million in the following decade. The Civil War discouraged immigrants from coming, but the later 1860s and early 1870s, until the hard times following the 1873 panic, saw a tremendous additional burst. Another revival in the 1880s was followed by another decline during the lean years of the following decade. From 1900 through 1915, all-time yearly peaks were reached with the total number of arrivals soaring to over one million in each of six years during the fifteen-year period.

The reception these immigrants received on our shores was not uniform. While Americans often took pride in their open door, they were also frequently appalled at the foreign "hordes" that arrived. The immigrants not only peopled this empty land and did the hard work of building the nation physically, they also brought crime, and poverty, and alien ways. Protestant North Europeans — Germans, Scandinavians, and above all the English — groups whose cultural patterns most closely approximated those of the United States were most welcome. The Britons, particularly, who spoke English were scarcely noticed and quickly merged with the native-born population. Other groups did not receive as friendly a greeting. Before 1860, the Irish-Catholics were regarded as "a noisy, drinking and brawling rabble," whose Catholic faith was a danger to free institutions. Though nothing was done to restrict their coming, they found themselves treated as outcasts, their position in society and economy fixed, not only by their relative lack of skill, but also by bigotry and intolerance.

The Civil War period was a time of healing in the relations between natives and foreign-born. Though the Irish, particularly, were often skeptical of Republican policies, the immigrants' performance in the war, and the patriotism they exhibited in defense of the Union, resulted in ethnic reconciliation. Then, in the 1880s, a new wave of foreign arrivals from southern and eastern Europe upset the equilibrium. Except for the Jews these were largely Slavs, Hungarians, Greeks, and Italians who, like the Irish, were mostly peasants and Catholics. Once more native Americans became alarmed, and nativism began to flourish as an intellectual and social force.

As in the past, much of this nativism was fed by religious and especially anti-

Catholic prejudice. In the 1890s, the American Protective Association encouraged anti-Catholic feelings by playing on the economic fears of Protestant workingmen during the economically bad years after 1893. At one point, the organization disseminated a bogus Papal encyclical purporting to absolve Catholics from any oath of loyalty to the United States and encouraging them "to exterminate all heretics."

This crude religious bigotry was only effective among the ignorant and the simple-minded. Unfortunately, a more subtle and sophisticated force, racism, soon began to feed the fires of intolerance. Racism was not new to America. In the form of Negrophobia it had thrived in the pre–Civil War period when it had been used to justify slavery. The post–Civil War version of racism, however, was broader in its rejections and was buttressed by science, or rather pseudo-science, derived from "biology" and anthropology. Included now among the proscribed groups were southern and eastern Europeans who were held to be inferior intellectually and morally to the Nordic stock of northern Europe. The Nordic races had been the truly creative peoples of the world, declared men like Madison Grant, and America was allowing itself to be debased by permitting the mobs of inferior whites, "Alpines" and "Mediterraneans," to invade its shores.

The way in which racist thinking was applied to American immigration policy by the Immigration Commission in the early years of the twentieth century is the subject of Oscar Handlin's essay. A key assumption of immigration restrictionists, he notes, was the concept that the "old immigration" of the years before 1880 was Nordic and superior, that of the post–1880 period, the "new immigration," non-Nordic and inferior in talent, health, character, and the inherent ability to assimilate American democratic values.

FOR FURTHER READING:

ERICKSON, CHARLOTTE. *American Industry and the European Immigrant, 1860–1885.* New York: Russell & Russell, Publishers, 1967.
HIGHAM, JOHN. *Strangers in the Land.* New York: Atheneum Publishers, 1963.*
RISCHIN, MOSES. *The Promised City, New York's Jews, 1870–1914.* New York: Corinth Books, 1964.*

Asterisk denotes paperback edition.

Old Immigrants and New OSCAR HANDLIN

Between 1917 and 1924 American immigration policy took a sharp and decisive turn. From the earliest days of the republic until the First World War the United States had deliberately permitted newcomers of whatever origin to enter freely through its gates. Unrestricted immigration had significantly furthered national development. Yet suddenly this long-standing tradition yielded to a new attitude which thereafter was so firmly fixed in the American consciousness that it has not yet been shaken off.

A combination of circumstances was responsible for the abrupt shift. The fears

Source: Oscar Handlin, *Race and Nationality in American Life* (New York: Doubleday & Company, 1957), chap. 5, "Old Immigrants and New," pp. 73–110.

and distrust bred by the war and the unsuccessful peace nurtured suspicion of all that was foreign, of immigration as well as of the League of Nations. In addition some groups within the United States had come to consider their interests imperiled by the newcomers. The old Yankee families of New England, for instance, viewed with misgivings the rising percentage of foreign born about them. The organized labor movement, made up predominantly of skilled workers, had become convinced that only a sharp limitation of the labor supply could protect its interests. In the first decade of the twentieth century substantial blocs of Southerners, former Populists and Progressives, each for its own reasons, came to regard the continuation of immigration as undesirable. The gradual accretion of strength in these groups contributed to the ultimate shift in policy.

Prior to 1910 there was no indication that all these dissatisfied groups would see the solution to their own problems in the restriction of immigration in the actual form restriction took. For the new policy aimed not simply to limit the total numbers of entrants; it intended also to select among them. The new policy drew a sharp distinction between the immigrants of northern and western Europe and those from southern and eastern Europe. In the minds of those who framed the laws of 1917–1924 that distinction was more important than restriction itself.

Basic to that distinction was a "scientific" assumption, one that subsequently proved false, but that was sincerely and conscientiously held in the early decades of this century. That assumption seemed for a time to have been validated and confirmed by the report of a governmental commission which devoted a great deal of time and energy to its investigation. Since vestiges of that assumption still influence our laws, it is imperative that we look closely at the commission which gave it authoritative expression. To do so will also clarify some of the problems of science as an instrument for directing government policy.

One fundamental premise lay behind the immigration legislation of 1917–1924 and animated also the McCarran-Walter Act of 1952. Embodied in the quota system, this premise held that the national origin of an immigrant was a reliable indication of his capacity for Americanization. It was averred, and science seemed to show, that some people, because of their racial or national constitution, were more capable of becoming Americans than others. Furthermore, it was argued that the "old immigrants," who came to the United States before 1880, were drawn from the superior stocks of northern and western Europe, while those who came after that date were drawn from the inferior breeds of southern and eastern Europe.

There was a demonstrable connection between the diffusion of this assumption and the course of immigration legislation in the first quarter of the century. Those who argued in favor of a restrictionist policy did so not merely, perhaps not primarily, because they wished to reduce the total volume of immigration, but, more important, because they wished to eliminate the "new" while perpetuating the "old" immigration. This was the logic of the literacy test. Writing in the midst of the battle for its enactment, one of its leading proponents, Prescott F. Hall, pointed out that the test furnished "an indirect method of excluding those who are undesirable, not merely because of their illiteracy, but for other reasons." After all, Hall noted, "the hereditary tendencies of the peoples illiterate abroad . . . cannot be overcome in a generation or two." And, looking back at the accomplished fact, the Commissioner General of Immigration pointed out in 1923 that the widespread popularity of the literacy test was "based quite largely upon a belief . . . that it would reduce the stream of new immigration . . . without seriously interfering with the coming of the older type."

The literacy law, passed over President Wilson's veto in 1917, did not, however, accomplish what had been expected of it. The end of the war brought a resumption of immigration and, with it, a renewed demand that the objective of keeping out the "new" while admitting the "old" immigrants be attained through the national-origin device. The result was passage of the Johnson Act of 1921. The intent of the act was clear. On the question of whether the base year should be 1910 or 1920, for instance, Representative Box pointed out that "the number of the older and better immigrants coming has been relatively much smaller during the last 10 years, and the number from southern Europe, Italy, and Russia much greater, which will be reflected in the 1920 census. The making of the 1910 census the basis will give us more of the better and less of the less desirable immigration than if it were based on the census of 1920." The act of 1924, which pushed the base quota year back to 1890 and consolidated the theory of national origins, was motivated by similar convictions as to the inferiority of the "new" immigrants. Congressman Vestal, arguing in favor of the measure, put the idea clearly: the southern and eastern immigrants of Europe, he said, "have not been of the kind that are readily assimilated or absorbed by our American life."

It thus becomes a matter of considerable importance to ascertain how the conception originated and gained currency that the peoples of southern and eastern Europe were inferior to those of northern and western Europe. At root this concept could be traced to the racist beliefs, freely expressed in the 1890's, that the peoples of the Mediterranean region were biologically different from those of northern and western Europe and that the difference sprang from an inferiority of blood and could be observed in certain social characteristics.

The argument was given forceful expression by the distinguished anthropologist of the American Museum of Natural History in an enormously popular book, one adjudged by *Science* a "work of solid merit." In *The Passing of the Great Race* (1916), Madison Grant adopted the line of Gobineau and insisted that the new immigrants were not "members of the Nordic race as were the earlier ones. . . . The new immigration contained a large and increasing number of the weak, the broken, and the mentally crippled of all races drawn from the lowest stratum of the Mediterranean basin and the Balkans, together with hordes of the wretched, submerged populations of the Polish ghettos. Our jails, insane asylums, and almshouses are filled with this human flotsam and the whole tone of American life, social, moral, and political, has been lowered and vulgarized by them."

These theories were bitterly and inconclusively debated through the early years of the twentieth century. The decisive turn in the argument came when they seemed to receive validation from the reports of two governmental investigations. The first was the detailed study by the Immigration Commission under the chairmanship of Senator Dillingham. The second was a report by Dr. Harry H. Laughlin of the Carnegie Institution, "the expert eugenics agent" of the House Committee on Immigration and Naturalization.

These reports had a direct impact upon subsequent legislation, for they supported theoretical opinions privately held with what appeared to be official and presumably scientific proof. The Immigration Commission, appointed in 1907, presented its conclusions in 1910 in an impressive forty-two-volume report. Widely quoted, the report figured prominently in the deliberations which produced the Johnson Act of 1921. Congressman Box thus took for granted that "the great immigration commission, which some years ago spent hundreds of thousands of dollars in investigation and study of this great question," had produced "conclusive reasons why we should encourage the coming in of the class which has been extolled so highly as an element which has contributed so much to our life and why it should discourage that which comes from Russia and southern Europe." In the same way the Laughlin report, presented in 1922 and printed in 1923, laid the groundwork for the legislation of 1924. This latter report was widely quoted in quasi-scientific articles and entered prominently into the debate as a result of which the act of 1924 was enacted. It therefore becomes a matter of prime importance to investigate the preparation of these reports and the soundness of their conclusions.

The Dillingham Commission was the outgrowth of a renewed attempt to enact a literacy test in 1906. The opponents of that measure hoped to block it, or at least to postpone immediate action, by calling for a commission to study the whole problem. Congressman Bartholdt, who proposed the creation of such a body, undoubtedly had in mind a congressional committee such as those which had already conducted similar investigations in 1891 and 1892. This was also the expectation of Speaker Cannon, who opposed any airing of the immigration question on the ground that it was an issue likely to divide the Republican party politically.

Although the question was one primarily for congressional action, it also deeply concerned President Theodore Roosevelt. In part he was moved by such considerations as influenced Speaker Cannon. In part he was also concerned because he was even then engaged in delicate diplomatic discussions with the Japanese. Ultimately these negotiations would lead to the controversial Gentlemen's Agreement to limit Japanese immigration by the voluntary action of the Tokyo government. At the moment Roosevelt feared that agitation of the general question of immigration might upset these negotiations. Finally, the President had great faith in the efficiency of fact-finding agencies as devices to evade the necessity for clear-cut political decisions.

Although Theodore Roosevelt accepted and supported the idea of such a commission, he subtly modified the conception of what it should be and do. He proposed to the Congress that the study be entrusted not to the usual congressional investigating committee, but rather to a number of experts, whom he would himself appoint. While the question was still being debated in Congress, he confidentially requested Commissioner of Labor Neill to proceed at once to "as full an investigation of the whole subject of immigration as the facilities at hand will permit."

As enacted on February 20, 1907, the law was a compromise between presidential and congressional wishes. It provided for an investigating commission of nine, three to be chosen by the President of the Senate, three by the Speaker of the House, and three experts by the President. In this form the proposal secured the acquiescence of all parties to the debate and also drew the support of a great number of social workers and social theorists attracted by the idea of an impartial, scientific investigation as an instrument of the social engineering of which there was then much talk.

At this stage, therefore, there was a widespread expectation that out of the deliberations of the commission would come a body of verified and indisputable facts which would supply the groundwork for future action. President Roosevelt summed up these expectations in a private message to Speaker Cannon when he expressed the hope that from the work of the commission would come the information that he could then use "to put before the Congress a plan which would amount to a definite solution of this immigration business."

The circumstances of its establishment account for the great hopes that were held out for the report of the commission and the prestige that was ultimately attached to its findings. That prestige was certainly added to when the commission took more than three years to investigate, spent a million dollars, employed a staff of about three hundred, and published its results in forty-two impressive volumes.

A view of the actual circumstances of the compilation and of the methods used shows, however, that the commission's report was neither impartial nor scientific, and that confidence in it was not altogether justified. No public hearings were held, no witnesses cross-examined by the members of the commission. Largely the study was conducted by experts who each compiled voluminous reports which were not printed until *after* the commission had reached its conclusions. It is doubtful whether the senators and congressmen on the commission ever had the time to examine the bulky reports in manuscript. It is most likely they were compelled rather to rest their judgment upon a two-volume summary prepared for them by a group of experts on the staff. The final report was "adopted within a half hour of the time when, under the law, it must be filed." The identity of the experts must therefore be of some significance.

The key individual was the economist Jeremiah W. Jenks. Jenks was chosen because he had served for a decade in a similar capacity on other fact-finding investigations set up to deal with trusts and other questions. He had already expressed himself on the subject of immigration; and, as a teacher, had long argued the necessity of restricting the number of newcomers along the lines the commission would later recommend. The other public members were Commissioner of Labor Neill and William R. Wheeler, active in Republican politics in San Francisco, which was then being shaken by the Japanese question. The crucial post of secretary was given, on the recommendation of Senator Henry Cabot Lodge, an outspoken restrictionist, to Morton E. Crane, described by the senator as "absolutely safe and loyal" on the immigration question. Roosevelt was perhaps less concerned with impartiality than with the likelihood of producing a tactically safe report. In any case, he warned Jenks, "Don't put in too many professors."

Despite its scientific pretensions, therefore, the report began by taking for granted the conclusions it aimed to prove — that the new immigration was essentially different from the old and less capable of being Americanized. This assumption is clearly stated at the very beginning of the report:

> The old and the new immigration differ in many essentials. The former was . . . largely a movement of settlers . . . from the most progressive sections of Europe. . . . They entered practically every line of activity. . . . Many of them . . . became landowners. . . . They mingled freely with the native Americans and were quickly assimilated. On the other hand, the new immigration has been largely a movement of unskilled laboring men who have come . . . from the less progressive countries of Europe. . . . They have . . . congregated together in sections apart from native Americans and the older immigrants to such an extent that assimilation has been slow.

The assumption with which the commission started conditioned the preparation of the whole report and made it certain that the conclusions would confirm the prejudgment. To quote the commission's own words:

> Consequently the Commission paid but little attention to the foreign-born element of the old immigrant class and directed its efforts almost entirely to . . . the newer immigrants.

The notion that the old immigration stood clearly apart from the new was directly reflected in the techniques through which the commission operated. There was no effort to give a time dimension to its data; there was some talk of including a history of immigration, but such a study was never prepared. There was therefore no opportunity to trace the development of various problems or to make comparisons between earlier and later conditions. For the same reason the commission made no use of any information except that gathered by its own staff at the moment. The enormous store of data in the successive state and federal censuses was hardly touched. For fifty years state bureaus of labor statistics had been gathering materials on the conditions of industrial labor; the commission disregarded those entirely. Instead it planned, but never finished, a mammoth census of all industrial workers. It overlooked similarly the wealth of information contained in almost a century of investigations by other governmental and private bodies.

Finally, the commission consistently omitted from its calculations and judgments the whole question of duration of settlement. Time and again it assumed that a group which had lived in the United States for five years could be treated on the same footing as one that had lived here for thirty-five. In a few cases there was enough information to make out the distortions that followed upon that premise. In most cases, however, the commission did not even possess the data on which a reasoned judgment could be based.

Taking for granted the difference between old and new immigrants, the commission found it unnecessary to prove that the difference existed. In most cases the individual reports — on industry, crime, nationality, and the like — did not contain the materials for a proper comparison of old and new. *But in the summary the commission followed the procedure of presenting the introduction and conclusion of each individual report, together with its own interpretive comments, which supplied the judgment on the inferiority of the new immigrants.* Those comments sprang from its own a priori assumption, not from any evidence — whatever that was worth; sometimes, indeed, they ran altogether against such evidence.

The substance of the report fell into a number of general categories. Volumes I and II were summary volumes. Volume III, a statistical survey of immigration, 1819–1910, and Volume XXXIX, an analysis of legal provisions, were noncontroversial. Volume XL was a study of immigration in other countries, with no bearing upon the general conclusions.

The critical material in the other volumes fell into nine general categories:

1. A Dictionary of Races. Volume V, summarized in Volume I, 209 ff.
2. Emigration Conditions in Europe. Volume IV, summarized in Volume I, 165 ff.
3. Economic Effects of Immigration. Volumes VI–XXVIII, summarized in Volume I, 285 ff.
4. Education and Literacy. Volumes XXIX–XXXIII, summmarized in Volume II, 1 ff.
5. Charity and Immigration. Volumes XXXIV–XXXV, summarized in Volume II, 87 ff.
6. Immigration and Crime. Volume XXXVI, summarized in Volume II, 159 ff.
7. Immigration and Vice. Volume XXXVII, summarized in Volume II, 323 ff.
8. Immigration and Insanity. Volume II, 223 ff. Complete report.
9. Immigration and Bodily Form. Volume XXXVIII, summarized in Volume II, 501 ff.

It will be profitable to scrutinize each of these categories individually.

The Dictionary of Races

In considering the monumental *Dictionary of Races* compiled by the commission it is necessary to take account of the views of race held by its expert, Dr. J. W. Jenks, and by the anthropologist, Daniel Folkmar, who was charged with the responsibility for preparing that section of the report. Neither man consciously accepted the notion that such people as Italians or Armenians were set apart by purely biological distinctions; such a notion could not have been applied to differentiate among the masses of immigrants. But both agreed that there were innate, ineradicable race distinctions that separated groups of men from one another, and they agreed also as to the general necessity of classifying these races to know which were fittest, most worthy of survival. The immediate problem was to ascertain "whether there may not be certain races that are inferior to other races . . . to discover some test to show whether some may be better fitted for American citizenship than others."

The introduction to the *Dictionary of Races* explained that while mankind may be divided into five divisions "upon physical or somatological grounds," the subdivision of these into particular races is made "largely upon a linguistic basis." According to the dictionary, this linguistic basis of classification was not only practical, in the sense that immigrant inspectors could readily determine the language spoken, but it also had "the sanction of law in immigration statistics and in the census of foreign countries."

Yet, in practice, the dictionary concerned itself with much more than a classification by language. Through it ran a persistent, though not a consistent, tendency to determine race by physical types, to differentiate the old from the new immigrants racially, and to indicate the superiority of the former to the latter.

■ **The Biological Sources of Race.** Although the dictionary presumably rested upon a linguistic basis, it often considered biological inheritance the critical element in determining racial affiliation. The following examples will illustrate:

The Finns, it stated, linguistically belonged to the Finno-Tartaric race, along with the Hungarians, Turks, and Japanese. But the western Finns, who actually came to the United States, though they spoke the same language, were descended from "the blondest of Teutons, Swedes."

The Armenians linguistically "are more nearly related to the Aryans of Europe than to their Asiatic neighbors," but "are related physically to the Turks, although they exceed these . . . in the remarkable shortness and height of their heads. The flattening of the back of the head . . . can only be compared to the flattened occiput of the Malay."

Although "English has been the medium of intercourse for generations," the dictionary defined as Irish those descended from people whose "ancestral language was Irish."

Among the Japanese, who all spoke the same language, "the 'fine' type of the aristocracy, the Japanese ideal, as distinct from the 'coarse' type recognized by students of the Japanese to-day," was due to "an undoubted white strain." The "fine" type were the descendants of "the Ainos, the earliest inhabitants of Japan . . . one of the most truly Caucasian-like people in appearance."

■ **The Differentiation of Old and New Immigrants.** All these racial identifications were confused by the evident desire of the commission to demonstrate that the old immigration was different in racial type from the new. Thus Jewish immigrants, though in language and physical characteristics akin to the Germans, were reckoned among the Slavs or eastern Europeans. In the same way it was suggested that a large part of the Irish were "English or Scotch in blood, Teutonic ('Nordic') in type rather than 'Celtic.'" The Dutch were the "Englishmen of the mainland."

■ **The Inferiority of the New Immigrants.**   Throughout the dictionary and its summary were sprinkled reflections in scattered phrases and sentences upon the lesser capacity of the new immigrants to be Americanized. The English and the Irish came to the United States "imbued with sympathy for our ideals and our democratic institutions." The "Norse" make "ideal farmers and are often said to Americanize more rapidly than do the other peoples who have a new language to learn. . . . There is no need to speak of peculiarities in customs and the many important elements which determine the place of the German race in modern civilization." For "the German is too well known in America to necessitate further discussion." By contrast, the Serbo-Croatians had "savage manners," the South Italians "have not attained distinguished success as farmers" and are given to brigandry and poverty; and although "the Poles verge toward the 'northern' race of Europe," being lighter in color than the Russians, "they are more high-strung," in this respect resembling the Hungarians. "All these peoples of eastern and southern Europe, including the Greeks and the Italians . . . give character to the immigration of today, as contrasted with the northern Teutonic and Celtic stocks that characterized it up to the eighties. All are different in temperament and civilization from ourselves."

It need hardly be said there was no evidence in the report to support these characterizations. If the material in the dictionary proved anything, it proved that the people of Europe were so thoroughly intermixed, both physically and linguistically, that they could not be separated into distinct races. Nevertheless, the dictionary significantly established a pseudoscientific basis for the designation of various races. In the balance of the report the reservations and conditional statements in the dictionary dropped away, and the various immigrant groups were treated as fixed races, with well-defined characteristics. Furthermore, throughout, the commission proceeded on the assumption that these races could be combined into the two clearcut categories, the old and new.

Emigration Conditions in Europe

The commission studied the background of immigration by an extensive tour of Europe and through the examination of some of the relevant documents. It was interested in the causes of emigration, the surrounding conditions, the selective factors that operated in it, and the means by which the movement was effected.

In this section of its work, too, the commission deprived itself of the means of making appropriate comparisons between the old and the new immigrants, and then proceeded to make such comparisons to the disadvantage of the new immigrants, without the necessary evidence.

In approaching the subject the commission "was not unmindful of the fact that the widespread apprehension in the United States relative to immigration is chiefly due" to the shift in the source of immigration from the northwestern regions to the southeastern regions of Europe. It therefore "paid particular attention" to the latter group. Almost three hundred pages of the report dealt with the situation in Italy,

Russia, Austria-Hungary, and Greece. These discussions were, on the whole, fair and factual. But they were preceded by a general survey of some hundred and thirty pages which drew less fair inferential comparisons between the emigration from these places and that from western Europe. The extensive account of the difficulties of life in the countries of the new emigration and the omission of any such account for the countries of the old emigration left the impression that the circumstances which caused the one differed from those which caused the other.

In the general survey the old and the new immigrations were said to differ on four main points—permanence of settlement, sex distribution, occupation, and the causes of emigration. In the summary (Volume I) these differences were stated even more strongly than in the more extended report in Volume IV. It will be worth examining each of these differences in turn.

■ **Permanent or Transient Emigration.** The matter of permanent or transient emigration was important because the commission presumed that those immigrants who came with the intention of staying made better citizens and residents than the "birds of passage" who came merely with the intention of working for a few years, then to depart. The commission stated flatly, "In the matter of stability or permanence of residence in the United States there is a very wide difference between European immigrants of the old and new classes." This conclusion it proved by comparing the number of arrivals in 1907 with the number of departures in 1908 as follows:

	Immigrants Admitted 1907	Aliens Departing 1908
Per cent of old immigration	22.7	8.9
Per cent of new immigration	77.3	91.1
Total	100.	100.

If, however, the same data is taken for particular groups and presented in terms of the relationship of the number of departures to the number of arrivals, the case is by no means so clear. Such peoples as the south Italians and the Croatians would still show a high rate of departures; but, on the other hand, such "old" groups as the English, the Germans, and the Scandinavians would show higher rates of departure than such "new" groups as the Armenians, the Dalmatians, the Hebrews, and the Portuguese.

Taken even at its face value, this data would not justify a correlation between old immigration and permanence of settlement and between new immigration and transience of settlement. Indeed, the commission had available other kinds of data which pointed to the completely contrary conclusion. Most important of all, the discussion did not take account here of various conditioning factors, such as recency of migration. As an agent of the committee pointed out in another place:

> It is true, no doubt, that most of the recent immigrants hope at first to return some day to their native land, but . . . with the passing years and the growth of inevitable ties, whether domestic, financial, or political, binding the immigrant to his new abode, these hopes decline and finally disappear.

■ **Sex Distribution of Immigrants.** The identical criticism applies to the commission's opinion that the new immigration contained a higher proportion of single men than did the old. Again, that judgment was superficially supported by throwing all the old and all the new immigrants together into two distinct groups; that is the basis of the commission's table:

Per Cent of Males Among Immigrants, 1899–1909	
Old immigration	58.5
New immigration	73.0

But the specific groups of immigrants, taken individually, show no such clear-cut demarcation:

Per Cent of Males Among Immigrants, 1899–1909	
Irish	47.2
Hebrew	56.7
Bohemian	56.9
French	58.6
Portuguese	59.0
German	59.4
Scandinavian	61.3
English	61.7
Scotch	63.6
Welsh	64.8
Dutch	65.5
Finnish	65.8
Syrian	68.2
Polish	69.2
Slovak	70.0

Here, too, the factor of recency of immigration affected the validity of the generalizations. But even taking the data as presented it is significant that such new groups as the Hebrews, the Bohemians, and the Portuguese stand better than such old ones as the Germans, Scandinavians, and English.

■ Occupations. The commission attempted to prove that the new immigration brought to the United States a significantly larger percentage of unskilled laborers than did the old. Its data did not show this. For the purposes of this discussion only, therefore, the Hebrews were defined as not part of the new immigration. That still, however, did not account for the large proportion of servants among the old immigrants. Furthermore, an examination of the specific immigrant groups once more reveals that the Germans and Scandinavians among the old immigrants boasted fewer skilled laborers than such new groups as the Armenians, Bohemians, Hebrews, and Spanish; and the Irish were lower in the list than the south Italians. There was certainly no basis here for the commission's distinction between old and new.

■ The Causes of Emigration. By confining the discussion of economic pressures on emigration to the countries of southern and eastern Europe the commission left the inference that the new immigration was more conditioned by such factors than the old. Thus the report stated, "a large proportion of the emigration from southern and eastern Europe may be traced directly to the inability of the peasantry to gain an adequate livelihood in agricultural pursuits." The statement could just as well have been applied to the peasantry of northern and western Europe.

Similarly the summary in the report asserted, "the fragmentary nature of available data relative to wages in many European countries makes a satisfactory comparison with wages in the United States impossible. It is well known, however, that even in England, Germany, France, and other countries of western Europe wages are below the United States standard, while in southern and eastern Europe the difference is very great." Actually the report itself made it clear in another place that the only evidence the commission had was on the disparity between wages in the United States and those in France, Germany, and Great Britain. It admitted that there was no data on southern and eastern Europe. Yet by assuming that wages in the latter places were necessarily lower than in the former, the data on the old immigration was made to prove the inferiority of the new.

Economic Effects of Immigration

This section of the subject absorbed the major portion of the commission's attention. Fully twenty (*VI–XXV*) of the forty-two volumes were devoted to it. The commission's agents accumulated an enormous store of data in all parts of the country; they examined twenty-one industries intensively, and sixteen others only slightly less so. Much of the material so gathered was, and remains, useful. But the conclusions drawn from it by the commission were often unsound and misleading, almost invariably so when it came to comparisons between the old and the new immigrants.

The commission began with the dubious assertion that:

> the older immigrant labor supply was composed principally of persons who had had training and experience abroad in the industries which they entered after their arrival in the United States. . . . In the case of the more recent immigrations from southern and eastern Europe this condition of affairs has been reversed. Before coming to the United States the greater proportion were engaged in farming or unskilled labor and had no experience or training in manufacturing or mining.

By the commission's own figures this statement was untrue; less than twenty per cent of the old immigrants (1899–1909) were skilled laborers, and the percentage in earlier periods was probably smaller still. Starting with the misapprehension that there was a correlation between the old immigration and skilled labor and between the new and unskilled, the committee proceeded to draw from its material far-reaching conclusions as to the effects of the new immigration upon native and old-immigrant labor, unionization, industrial methods, new industries, unemployment and depressions, and agriculture.

■ **Effects of the New Immigration upon Native and Old-Immigrant Labor.** The commission wished to demonstrate the adverse effects of the new immigration upon the existing labor supply. At one point it actually suggested that the new immigration diminished the volume of the old and reduced the native birth rate. But it did not push that suggestion far.

Instead it argued that in many industries the "new" immigrants *pushed out* the old labor force. It could not, however, explain this "racial displacement" by the mere willingness of newcomers to work at lower wages, for the commission discovered that in the case of the industries covered by its investigation it was not usual "for employers to engage recent immigrants at wages actually lower than those prevailing at the time of their employment." The line of argument took another course, therefore. The presence of the newcomers, it was said, produced unsafe working conditions and lowered the standards of labor to a degree that "the Americans and older immigrants have considered unsatisfactory." To have proved that would have called for a historical investigation of the industries concerned from which evidence might be drawn for the presumed deterioration of conditions. There was no such study and no such evidence. Indeed, this section seems to have been inserted into the summary arbitrarily, for it did not correspond with any section of the extended report itself.

On the other hand, the report did contain material, not used by the commission, that threw a different light upon the process of displacement. The investigators discovered that "the chief reason for the employment of immigrants" was "the impossibility of securing other labor to supply the demand caused by the expansion of the industry. Without the immigrant labor supply, the development of the cotton-goods industry to its present status in New England and other North Atlantic States could not have taken place." All these changes were part of the complex development of the American economy. The rapid industrial expansion of the half century before the investigation had been accompanied by a swift technological transformation which mechanized many aspects of production and thereby eliminated the skill of the old craftsmen. That accounted for the displacement. But the commission also found that those displaced, in large measure, moved upward to better-paying jobs made available by the rapid expansion of the economy. To the extent that immigrants contributed to that expansion they actually helped to lift the condition of the laborers they found already there.

In any case, no connection was established between the specific qualities of the new immigrants and the whole process of displacement. Indeed, the report itself pointed out that the shifts in the labor force went back to early in the nineteenth century and had once involved such old groups as the Irish. That might have suggested to the commission, but unfortunately did not, that what was involved was not some peculiarity of the immigrants from southern and eastern Europe, but rather a general factor characteristic of all immigrants, and varying with the recency of the group.

■ **Unionization.** The commission made the blanket accusation that "the extensive employment of southern and eastern European immigrants in manufacturing and mining has in many places resulted in the weakening of labor organizations or in their complete disruption." This statement was made without a shred of evidence. The commission did not include in its report any data on union membership, either for the country as a whole or for specific industries or specific unions. It had no way of knowing what the trend of union membership was, or what the relationship of immigration was to that trend.

The accusation quoted above derived not from evidence, but from the commission's assumption as to the nature of the new immigration:

> The members of the larger number of races of recent entrance to the mines, mills, and factories as a rule have been tractable and easily managed. This quality seems to be a

temperamental one acquired through present or past conditions of life in their native land.

The lengths to which the commission was willing to go to maintain views of the effects of immigration on unions in accord with its prejudices emerge from a comparison of the account of the labor organizations in the cotton industry as it appeared in the extended report of the investigators with the same account "summarized" in the summary by the commission.

Speaking of the cotton-goods industry, the original report pointed out that unions were confined to the skilled branches of the trade while the immigrants were largely unskilled. The latter occupations "are not organized, and the coming of the foreigner there does not concern the textile unions." Since the organized branches of the trade were "protected, by the long time required to attain proficiency, from any sudden or immediate competition of unorganized foreigners, these unions are not strongly opposed to the immigrants gradually working into their trades." But "they manifest little interest in the immigrant employees until they have advanced to the occupations controlled by the labor organizations." Though the mass of laborers thus remained outside the union, the report continued, "all the operatives are strongly union in their sympathies and in the case of labor troubles have stood with the union people."

How was this summarized? Only an extended quotation will show the extent of the distortion:

The more recent immigrant employees from southern and eastern Europe and Asia, however, have been a constant menace to the labor organizations and have been directly and indirectly instrumental in weakening the unions and threatening their disruption. . . . The recent immigrants have also been reluctant to identify themselves with the unions.

This dictum inserted into the summary, in direct contradiction to the evidence, while the conclusions of the original report were omitted, demonstrated the total unreliability of the commission's observations on the question of unionization and immigration.

■ **Industrial Methods.** The commission's finding that an increase in the number of accidents was one of the effects of employing the new immigrants in industry has already been mentioned above. In addition reference should be made to the careful examination of the commission's conclusions on the subject by Dr. I. A. Hourwich (*Immigration and Labor* [2d. ed., N.Y., 1922], 458 ff.). Dr. Hourwich showed that the commission merely accepted the mine operators' point of view, which was to ascribe all accidents to employee negligence rather than to deficiencies in equipment. Reconstructing the history of mine accidents, Dr. Hourwich showed that their incidence varied with the output of industry rather than with the character of the labor force; and a comparison of mines in Oklahoma, Tennessee, and Alabama, which employed very few immigrants, with those of Pennsylvania, where the bulk of the miners were immigrants, exposed clearly the falsity of the commission's views. The commission, eager to reach its own final judgments, considered none of these types of evidence.

The conclusions of the commission also contained numerous miscellaneous statements as to the deterioration of the conditions of labor and of wages as the results of immigration. In this connection it is necessary only to emphasize again the fact that the commission had no evidence whatsoever to support these contentions. Such evidence could have come only by a comparative historical study which would actually trace the development of labor conditions over a substantial period. The commission made no such study. The hypothetical and speculative nature of its conclusions is evident in the following example:

Acknowledging that there was no evidence that immigrants actually worked at lower wages, the commission went on to say, "It is hardly open to doubt, however, that the availability of the large supply of recent immigrant labor prevented the increase in wages which otherwise would have resulted during recent years from the increased demand for labor."

■ **New Industries.** The commission drew another unfavorable comparison between the old and the new immigration with regard to the capacity of the latter for stimulating economic innovation. The arrival of the newest comers, it argued, did not result "in the establishment of new industries of any importance." But, "by way of contrast, it will be recalled that a large proportion of the earlier immigrant laborers were originally induced to come to this country to contribute their skill and experience toward the establishment of new industries, such as mining and textile, glass, and iron and steel manufacturing." This assertion sprang from the unreal fantasy to which the commission clung, that the old immigration was largely made up of skilled artisans. It disregarded also the obvious difference between industrial conditions in the United States in 1840 and 1900. It was, indeed, easier to create new industries at the earlier date; but that reflected the undeveloped economy of the country rather than the quality of the immigration.

■ **Unemployment and Depressions.** The conclusions of the report also contain a number of statements implying a relationship between the new immigration and unemployment and depressions. These are nowhere proved. In any case, as elsewhere, the commission found it unnecessary to show that the old immigration had stood in a different relationship; it took that for granted.

■ **Agriculture.** Here the discussion centered on a fairly sympathetic survey of many communities of recent immigrants. But the summary was preceded by an introduction, not particularly related to the report itself, which drew an invidious distinction between the old and the new immigrants with regard to the likelihood of their entry into agriculture. The comments disregarded two critical factors: first, that the number of farmers increased with the prolongation of a group's experience in the United States (this was revealed quite clearly in the commission's data, which showed that for all groups there was a greater percentage of farmers among the second than among the first generation); and second, that the American economy had changed after 1890. With industrialization there came a general growth of urban at the expense of rural population; even the sons of native farmers were being drawn to the city. Whatever difference existed between the old and the new immigrants was not the product of their inherent characteristics but of the conditions they had found and the length of time they had lived in the United States.

Education and Literacy

The agitation for the literacy test that occupied popular attention while the commission worked gave particular importance to its discussion of literacy and education, and to its attempt to establish a difference, in this regard, between the old and the new immigration.

The background was established in the account of emigration conditions in Europe, which clearly indicated a substantial difference in the rate of illiteracy. The original report examined the various reasons for the high rate of illiteracy in southern and eastern Europe and concluded, "But probably the most apparent cause of illiteracy in Europe, as elsewhere, is poverty. The economic status of a people has a very decided effect upon the literacy rate." It then went on to predict a steady improvement in the future. The commission's own investigators abroad thus recognized that the inability to read was a product of environmental rather than of racial deficiencies. The summary, however, omitted this optimistic discussion and instead made the sweeping suggestion that the high rate of illiteracy among the new immigrants was due to "inherent racial tendencies."

The commission also labored the point that the new immigrants in the United States were less literate than the old. The supporting documentation was nowhere brought systematically together; it was instead scattered through the reports on industries and agriculture. Criticism in detail is therefore difficult. But the general fallacy of the argument is evident enough.

The commission almost everywhere failed to take account of duration of settlement in arriving at the conclusion that "a much higher degree of illiteracy prevails among the immigrants of recent years from southern and eastern Europe than among those of old immigration from Great Britain and northern Europe." That is, in comparing the natives of Italy in the United States with the natives of Scotland, it calmly disregarded the fact that the former had lived in the country for a far shorter period than the latter. Yet that circumstance was of critical importance, as may be gathered from the data on the ability of employees in clothing manufacture to learn English, which does take account of it:

Percentage of Foreign-Born Employees Who
Speak English by Years in the United States

Years in the United States	Per Cent
Under 5	38.8
5 to 9	66.5
10 or over	83.0

The failure of the commission to reckon with the duration of settlement invalidated its whole comparison of old and new immigrants.

Its difficulties with the more general problems of education were even more obvious. The commission had apparently thought it would be possible to measure the capacity of the old and new immigrants to be schooled. Discussing the question, Jenks had pointed out, "Anyone who has observed, even in a small way, the different classes of people that come into this country knows that some are very much inclined toward making the best possible use of our schools, while others make no attempt whatever to get in touch with our educational system." The commission planned to make such measurements through an elaborate investigation of more than two million school children in order to discover which races were most likely to be retarded.

Although four volumes of tables came forth from this investigation, they proved nothing. To begin with, the data was defective since it was based upon questionnaires sent to teachers who did not understand them. "In a considerable proportion of cases," the commission acknowledged, "the teachers have assigned a 'cause of retardation' for pupils who are the normal age or even younger than the normal age for the grade." The commission nevertheless used the bulk of material gathered in its elaborate tables on "retardation," the very meaning of which many teachers did not understand.

The volumes of statistics that the commission reprinted thus reflect not the care and accuracy of the survey, but, rather, the fact that it was not able to shape its material to the conclusions at which it wished to arrive.

There was no basis in the data for dividing the old from the new immigrants on the performance of their children in schools. But the information in the tables did show a wide variation from place to place in the achievements of children within any given group. Thus 55 per cent of the German children in St. Louis were retarded, but only 21.2 per cent in Scranton; similarly the English showed 56.2 per cent in St. Louis, 19.1 per cent in Scranton, and 13.9 per cent in Worcester.

That might have suggested that the quality of schools and the social environment were more significant variables than parentage. But not to the commission.

Too, through the tables there ran a good deal of material that emphasized the importance of recency of settlement, so much so that the original report pointed out:

> Length of residence in the United States has an important bearing on progress of pupils. It can hardly be expected that children of immigrants who have been in the United States only a few months or even years can make the same progress as children of those who have been here long enough to become more or less adjusted to their new surroundings.

But this reasonable comment did not seem worthy of inclusion in the summary.

Charity and Immigration

The data on pauperism, dependence, and admissions to institutions did not provide the basis for any general comparisons between the old and new immigration, except insofar as the old were more subject to alcoholism than the new.

Immigration and Crime

"Statistics show," said the commission, "that the proportion of convictions for crimes according to the population is greater among the foreign-born than among the native-born." Furthermore, it concluded that "the proportion of the more serious crimes of homicide, blackmail, and robbery, as well as the least serious offences, is greater among the foreign-born." These statements followed smoothly from the conception of racial propensities defined in the *Dictionary of Races*. But to support them with statistical evidence was more difficult.

When the commission turned to the only existing body of information, the *United States Census Report on Prisoners*, it discovered a disconcerting situation. This data, gathered by a body which did not have to prove any conclusions, showed that "immigration has not increased the volume of crime to a distinguishable extent, if at all"; indeed, that the percentage of immigrants among prisoners had actually fallen between 1890 and 1904, and that native Americans "exhibited in general a tendency to commit more serious crimes than did the immigrant."

Obviously such statistics would not do. The commission proceeded to gather its own. For its study the commission accumulated a very large number of cases, fully 1,179,677, extracted from court records over a period of seven years. These were, however, derived from relatively few sources. Of them some 1,130,000 were drawn from New York and Chicago, the two cities with the largest number of foreign-born in the United States, and 30,000 more came from Massachusetts, also a state of high immigrant density. (The remainder were the 12,000 aliens in federal institutions.) Apparently it was unnecessary to sample the experience of such places as New Orleans, Memphis, San Francisco, or Atlanta.

No inferences drawn from this partial data could possibly support the sweeping generalizations of the conclusions. Such a sampling would hardly be illuminating for the country as a whole, nor could it measure the pressure of the immigrant in the national crime problem. At most it might throw light on the peculiar problems of the two cities from which the bulk of the cases were taken.

The commission did not, however, use the source material as if it applied only to the communities from which it was drawn; if it had, its conclusions could not stand. Nor did it examine the frequency of crime relative to the number of the foreign-born and the natives. To attempt such a correlation, it felt, would not be feasible. Instead the commission organized the data to show how immigration had changed the character of crime in the United States. Its evidence, the commission imagined, proved that immigration had increased:

the commission of offenses of personal violence (such as abduction and kidnaping, assault, homicide, and rape) and of that large class of violations of the law known as offenses against public policy (which include disorderly conduct, drunkenness, vagrancy, the violation of corporate ordinances, and many offenses incident to city life) . . . [as well as] offenses against chastity, especially those connected with prostitution.

It must be emphasized again that at no point did the commission have the evidence to support its general conclusions that the immigrants committed a higher proportion of crimes than did the natives. Furthermore, it *did not* show that such a result had followed upon immigration. It had, indeed, no basis at all for comparison with earlier periods.

What it did was quite different. It traced the distribution of various types of crimes attributable to each group of immigrants and to the much larger group of native Americans. Within each group it compared the incidence of each specific type of crime with the total number of crimes in that group. That is, it reckoned up all the crimes charged to Italians and then computed what percentage of that number were homicides, larcenies, and the like. It did the same for every other group by nativity and then compared the resultant percentages for larceny or homicide. When, therefore, it said that the foreign-born were more prone than the natives to crimes of personal violence, it did not mean that the foreign-born committed *more such crimes* than the natives either absolutely or relative to their percentage in the total population. It meant only that such crimes accounted for a larger part of the total criminality of the group.

One illustration will suffice to show the meaning of this difference. The New York county and Supreme courts, in 1907 and 1908, showed the following cases of assault, by nativity:

Country of Birth	Number
United States	630
Italy	342
Russia	73
Austria-Hungary	62
Germany	47
Ireland	38
Canada	15
Poland	14
England	8

This data was presented by the commission in a table headed "Relative Frequency" of such offenses, as follows:

Country of Birth	Per Cent of Total
Italy	28.9
Austria-Hungary	15.0
Poland	14.6
Ireland	13.7
Canada	12.1
Russia	11.3
Germany	9.1
United States	8.7
England	5.0

Only the wariest reader could avoid concluding from this tricky presentation that Italians committed more such crimes than the natives, whereas the exact opposite was true.

The table last cited could be accurately understood only if one remembered that "per cent of total" meant per cent of crimes of this category of the total number of crimes committed by the nativity group concerned. The high position of the Italians, for example, was not due to the fact that they perpetrated more assaults than the natives, but to the fact that they were responsible for fewer crimes of other types. In almost every instance the low rating of natives of the United States seemed due to the fact that the total number of crimes they committed was much larger than that of other groups. As the commission presented this data, it was never very meaningful, often misleading, and in no case supported the commission's general contentions.

Immigration and Vice

The commission's finding on the "white slave traffic" was moderate in tone and factual in content. It was on the whole free of the conjectural elements that marred so much of the rest of the report. Perhaps the only objection to it was the failure adequately to place the problem in its context. Dealing exclusively with the immigrants, it gave the impression, unintentionally, that prostitution was largely a responsibility of the foreign-born, although fragmentary data in the report indicated that the immigrants were only a minor element in a more general American problem.

Immigration and Insanity

The commission did not make a firsthand investigation of this subject. Its data was drawn from the census and other sources. While the available information seemed to indicate that the foreign-born supplied more than their share of the insane, it also indicated that it was the old, rather than the new, immigration that was chiefly responsible. The Irish, the Germans, and the Scandinavians showed the greatest relative responsibility, or, as the report put it:

> It appears that insanity is relatively more prevalent among the foreign-born than among the native-born, and relatively more prevalent among certain immigrant races and nationalities than among others. In general the nationalities furthest advanced in civilization show, in the United States, a higher proportion of insane than do the more backward races.

Changes in Bodily Form among the Descendants of Immigrants

The commission considered within the scope of its inquiry the whole problem of the physical characteristics of the immigrants. To the *Dictionary of Races,* which rested upon information gathered from other sources, it wished to join its own findings on the physical characteristics of immigrants and their descendants. This was an important question because it was theretofore assumed that such characteristics of a race as bodily form were fixed and permanent. It was not imagined that they would change in the course of immigration; and if they did not, that might conspicuously affect the assimilation of the immigrants.

Professor Franz Boas of Columbia University, the distinguished anthropologist charged with responsibility for the study, discovered surprising results, however. It appeared that:

> the head form, which has always been considered one of the most stable and permanent characteristics of human races, undergoes far-reaching changes due to the transfer of the people from European to American soil. . . . This fact shows . . . that not even those characteristics of a race which have proved to be most permanent in their old home remain the same under the new surroundings; and we are compelled to conclude that when these features of the body change, the whole bodily and mental make-up of the immigrants may change. . . . All the evidence is now in favor of a great plasticity of human types.

The commission was certainly surprised with these results. It perforce quoted them—but cautiously, and with the reservation that a good deal more study was needed before they could be accepted. The commission, however, did not allow these findings to influence the materials in the *Dictionary of Races* or to stand in the way of its allusion to the fixed nature of the temperaments of the races it discussed through the body of the report.

Summary Evaluation of the Commission's Findings

In summary it may be said the commission did not use the opportunity afforded it to make the open, objective study of the problem it might have. It began with preconceived ideas as to the difference between the old and the new immigration. It did not find the evidence to substantiate that assumption. But it devoted much of its effort to bending what evidence it could find to that end. Its conclusions were largely invalidated by those distortions and offered an unsound basis for the legislation that followed.

Less than a decade after the submittal of the Dillingham Commission's report the proponents of more restrictive legislation sought further scientific support for their theories. They found it in the "Analysis of America's Modern Melting Pot," by Dr. Harry Laughlin, a highly qualified geneticist associated with the Eugenics Records Office. This inquiry, commissioned by the government, was designed to correct the inability of the earlier investigation to demonstrate conclusively the social inferiority of the new immigrants. Laughlin's report originated in a hearing of the House Immigration Committee (April 16, 17, 1920), which asked him to study the relationship of biology to immigration, particularly as that bore on the problems of social degeneracy.

Laughlin's analysis was presented to the committee in November 1922. Congressman Albert Johnson, chairman of the committee, examined the report and certified that "Dr. Laughlin's data and charts . . . are both biologically and statistically thorough, and apparently sound." Whatever the chairman's competence to pass upon these matters, he was satisfied that the investigation had proved the inferiority of the new immigrants.

The opinions that were before long to be reflected in legislation were summarized by Dr. Laughlin:

> The outstanding conclusion is that, making all logical allowances for environmental conditions, which may be unfavorable to the immigrant, the recent immigrants as a whole, present a higher percentage of inborn socially inadequate qualities than do the older stocks.

This conclusion was accompanied by the assurance that it was based upon "data and conditions," and not on "sentiment or previous attitudes."

Before advancing to an examination of that data it will, however, be worth making note of Dr. Laughlin's own sentiments as he explicitly stated them to the committee:

> We in this country have been so imbued with the idea of democracy, or the equality of all men, that we have left out of consideration the matter of blood or natural inborn hereditary mental and moral differences. No man who breeds pedigreed plants and animals can afford to neglect this thing.

Dr. Laughlin thus purported to be studying the "natural inborn hereditary" tendencies of the new immigrants to the significant social disorders. His method was to examine the distribution of various national stocks in 445 state and federal institutions in 1921.

This procedure was inherently defective, for commitments to public institutions did not actually measure the hereditary tendencies Dr. Laughlin presumed he was measuring. In the case of insanity, for instance, the standard of commitment was most inadequate, since the availability of facilities in various sections varied greatly, as did the willingness of certain social, economic, and ethnic groups to make use of those facilities in preference to private institutions or to home care. All the generalization based on such data must be dubious.

Furthermore, Laughlin's sample was faulty and he treated his material crudely, failing to make corrections for occupational, age, or sex distribution. His critical statistical device, "the quota fulfillment plan of analysis," was based upon a comparison of committal records of 1921 with the distribution of population in 1910, *al-*

though the census data of 1920 was available to him. By this means he certainly magnified the relative number of the immigrants among the socially inadequate.

But all these methodological faults, grave as they are, shrink in importance when compared with a more basic criticism. *The data, faulty as it is, simply does not say what Laughlin says it says.* His conclusions can find support, of a sort, only by throwing together all forms of inadequacy in a few gross, and arbitrary, divisions, as follows:

	Per Cent of Quota Fulfillment
Native white, native parentage	84.33
Native white, foreign parentage	109.40
Native white, mixed parentage	116.65
Northwestern Europe immigrants	130.42
Southeastern Europe immigrants	143.24

Laughlin's own materials do not support his conclusions if the various national groups are treated separately, whether for inadequacy as a whole or for particular types of inadequacy. In the chart which follows, the various nationalities are ranked according to their order in Laughlin's rating of quota fulfillment for each category and for the total. The ranking is in the order of descending desirability, that is, those at the top are most desirable, those at the bottom, least.[1]

Feeblemindedness

1. Ireland
2. Switzerland
3. All Asia
4. Greece
5. France
6. Germany
7. Scandinavia
8. Austria-Hungary
9. Canada
10. Rumania
11. Italy
12. Great Britain
13. Turkey
14. Russia and Poland
15. Bulgaria
16. U.S., native parents
17. U.S., foreign parents
18. U.S., mixed parents
19. Australia
20. Serbia

Insanity

1. Japan
2. Switzerland
3. U.S., native parents
4. Rumania
5. U.S., mixed parents
6. U.S., foreign parents
7. Canada
8. All Asia
9. Austria-Hungary
10. Great Britain
11. Italy
12. France
13. Greece
14. Germany
15. Scandinavia
16. Turkey
17. Russia and Poland
18. Bulgaria
19. Ireland
20. Serbia

Crime

1. Switzerland
2. Ireland
3. Germany
4. Scandinavia

Epilepsy

1. Scandinavia
2. France
3. Switzerland
4. All Asia

Crime

5. Great Britain
6. Canada
7. Austria-Hungary
8. U.S., native parents
9. U.S., foreign parents
10. U.S., mixed parents
11. France
12. Russia-Poland
13. Rumania
14. Japan
15. Italy
16. Turkey
17. All Asia
18. Greece
19. Bulgaria
20. Serbia

Epilepsy

5. Greece
6. Austria-Hungary
7. Germany
8. Canada
9. Italy
10. U.S., native parents
11. Turkey (European)
12. Ireland
13. Russia-Poland
14. Rumania
15. Great Britain
16. U.S., foreign parents
17. U.S., mixed parents

Tuberculosis

1. Switzerland
2. Germany
3. Austria-Hungary
4. Great Britain
5. U.S., native parents
6. Canada
7. U.S., mixed parents
8. U.S., foreign parents
9. Italy
10. Ireland
11. All Asia
12. Russia-Poland
13. Scandinavia
14. Greece

Dependency

1. Austria-Hungary
2. Italy
3. All Asia
4. Russia-Poland
5. Scandinavia
6. U.S., mixed parents
7. U.S., foreign parents
8. U.S., native parents
9. Switzerland
10. Germany
11. Greece
12. Canada
13. Great Britain
14. France
15. Turkey
16. Ireland

All Types of Social Inadequacy

1. Switzerland
2. Japan
3. U.S., native parents
4. Austria-Hungary
5. Canada
6. Rumania
7. Germany
8. U.S., foreign parents
9. Great Britain
10. U.S., mixed parents
11. Scandinavia
12. France
13. All Asia
14. Italy
15. Russia-Poland
16. Greece
17. Turkey
18. Ireland
19. Bulgaria
20. Serbia

A candid examination of these rankings will reveal that, whatever their intrinsic value, they did not show any consistent order of superiority or inferiority among the various nationality groups concerned. Furthermore, they certainly did not show that the new nationalities could, in any sense, conceivably have been said to rank below the old nationalities. All the inferences of the Laughlin report should therefore have been categorically rejected.

They were not. Instead they were widely accepted and significantly influenced American policy. The newspaper reader, like the member of Congress, took their results uncritically and without question. The one jarring note, struck by the Boas investigation into bodily forms, was quietly disregarded and not, for several decades, further pursued. Unfortunately the means of critical appraisal of these biased reports had long since been dulled by science itself, which had already led men to expect the results Dillingham and Laughlin found.

The studies that have here been examined have a historical interest insofar as they have contributed to the adoption of the national-origins quota system, which is still a part of American immigration legislation. By giving governmental and scientific validation to existing prejudices against the new immigrants, they helped to justify the discriminations against them in the laws of 1921 and 1924.

But these studies have also a larger significance: they show how vulnerable science was, at the beginning of the twentieth century, to penetration by images and conceptions charged with popular emotions. Those emotions sprang from a deep uneasiness in the hearts of disturbed men. To understand the hatreds and the fears that spilled over into the laboratories and that biased the computing machines, it will be necessary to look beyond the world of science at the human condition from which they sprang.

NOTES

1. Not all Laughlin's entries are included, and Negroes are excluded, so that "native" refers to native white.

PART 3

Recent America
1914-Present

America's Role as Neutral, 1914–1917

The outbreak of war in Europe in 1914 opened the modern era of world conflict. American intervention in 1917 also marked the country's entry into the international arena as a great power. Since the way the United States entered the World War helped define the world role it would play, that initial event has been of absorbing interest to historians.

Generally speaking, historians have tended to be harsh in assessing United States entry into World War I. The "realists" have taken it as a prime example of blind American adherence to idealism in a world order ruled by power and interest. Others have found in Woodrow Wilson's idealism merely a mask for the advancement of selfish American ends, whether defined in the narrow economic terms of the revisionist historians of the 1930s, or the somewhat broader ones of recent New Left scholars.

William L. Langer, dean of European diplomatic historians, takes a fresh tack in a lecture given in honor of the centennial of Woodrow Wilson's birth. He confronts the crucial question head on: What was Wilson's objective during the neutrality period preceding April 1917? To be the initiator of a durable peace, Langer insists. Wilson felt he could do this because of America's idealism and the absence of a direct interest in the conflict. These ideas, far from demonstrating Wilson's naiveté, in fact provided the basis for a strategy of the highest realism. Only by having pure and disinterested motives, Wilson reasoned, could he serve as mediator between the belligerents. Lasting peace required a concert of nations — a League of Nations. But of more immediate importance to Wilson was that the war end in a "peace without victory," that is, a negotiated settlement in which neither side dictated terms. The intransigent resistance of all the belligerents to this idea foiled Wilson's persistent efforts, and when Germany resumed unrestricted submarine warfare, the United States went to war. That act not only ended Wilson's peace offensive, but tragically, by his own logic, doomed any hope for a durable peace. For a peace without victory depended on a disinterested America, and America could no longer be disinterested, once it entered the war. Wilson failed; and it still remains to assign the blame for that failure. But the failure was not due to any blindness on his part about the requirements for permanent peace. In that sense, Wilson had a clearer vision than any other world leader. He demonstrated, Langer argues, "statesmanship of a high order."

FOR FURTHER READING:

LINK, ARTHUR S. *Wilson the Diplomatist.* Baltimore: The Johns Hopkins Press, 1957.*
MAY, ERNEST R. *The World War and American Isolation.* Chicago: Quadrangle Books, 1966.*
OSGOOD, ROBERT E. *Ideals and Self-Interest in America's Foreign Relations.* University of Chicago Press, 1953.*

Asterisk denotes paperback edition.

From Isolation to Mediation

WILLIAM L. LANGER

It seems to me that for us and for the whole contemporary world what is important about Woodrow Wilson's foreign policy is its bearing on the eternal question of war and peace, for our reconsideration of which the first World War and the Paris Peace Conference provide the necessary backdrop.

At the very outset one is bound to be struck by the fact that Mr. Wilson, though an authority on American history and a leading educator, had at best but a superficial knowledge of and nothing more than a general interest in foreign affairs when he succeeded to the presidency in 1913. He had, it is true, already recognized that the passing of the frontier in the 1890's was bound to make the conditions of life in the United States more difficult, and that in the future the country would have to abandon its cherished isolation in order to seek in the larger world arena the needed outlets for the expansive impulses which he regarded as the natural expression of mature national strength. But he had not followed up this general proposition with any specific suggestions or programs. In fact, his interest remained concentrated on domestic issues. From time to time he might visit the British Isles, but on only one occasion, in 1903, did he stray as far afield as France and Italy. His papers and records contain nothing to suggest close study of particular foreign issues or even much preoccupation with the broader aspects of international relations.

Like most Americans of his time, Mr. Wilson considered the United States unique among the nations — a land of liberty, equality and opportunity whose greatness depended not so much upon its material wealth as upon its spiritual strength. During the period of its growth the country had, he believed, rightly held aloof from the sordid rivalries and everlasting conflicts of Europe. But now, in the days of its splendid maturity, the United States had a sacred mission to provide leadership to other nations. It should stand as the champion of freedom, justice, and peace, and should be prepared to serve selflessly the interests of humanity. The President's response to the crisis of July, 1914, which was to eventuate in the Great War, was to express publicly the hope that the world would turn to the United States for "those moral inspirations which lie at the basis of all freedom" (Fourth of July Address, 1914). When, presently, the storm broke over Europe, Mr. Wilson, like most of his countrymen, regarded this newest and most terrible conflict merely as the latest manifestation of the crass materialism, the ruthless ambition, the political immorality and the baleful power politics which had always sullied the history of the Old World. It looked like "a natural raking-out of the pent-up jealousies and rivalries of the complicated politics of Europe," he remarked on a later occasion.

Mr. Wilson knew little and evidently cared less about the origins and causes of the cataclysm. After two years of life-and-death struggle he could still state publicly that he and his countrymen were not concerned to search for the obscure foundations from which the stupendous flood had burst. He had always hated war and regarded it as a barbarous method of settling international issues. The conflict in Europe, he once remarked, was like "a drunken brawl in a public house." It was a most disgusting spectacle, but as between the antagonists his sympathies were de-

Source: William L. Langer, "From Isolation to Mediation," in *Wilson and the World of Today*, ed. Arthur Dudden (Philadelphia: University of Pennsylvania Press, 1957), pp. 23–46.

cidedly with Britain and France. He was easily persuaded that Germany had been guilty of aggressive trade policies and that German philosophy was essentially selfish and devoid of spirituality. On the other hand, Britain and France were democracies, defending liberty and popular government against the forces of German militarism and autocracy. Was not France the victim of attack, and was not Britain fighting in fulfillment of a moral obligation to defend Belgian neutrality? Such observations and queries were not very profound and hardly exhausted the crucial problem of responsibility for the Great War. But they evidently satisfied the President, who seems never to have been troubled by serious doubts about these matters.

Colonel Edward M. House, Mr. Wilson's intimate adviser, as well as prominent American diplomats like Walter Hines Page and James W. Gerard held the same views but were more sophisticated and articulate in their partisanship. From the outset they were convinced that the Germans, if victorious, would eventually move against Latin America or even the United States itself. It was therefore in the American interest to support the Allied powers in every way possible, if need be even by force of arms. They expounded this thesis to the President time and again, but Mr. Wilson was reluctant to believe in the threat to American security. He agreed that the victory of Prussian militarism and autocracy would bode ill for the future of democracy, but he never really despaired of the ultimate victory of Britain and France.

This was in general the sentiment of the country also. Even those who recognized the importance for American security of the maintenance of the British position did not regard the defeat of the Allies as imminent or even probable. It is easy, therefore, to understand the absence of any marked sentiment for American intervention in the war. Neutrality was the natural expression of the country's traditional attachment to isolation. For the President, however, neutrality soon came to take on a special significance: it meant to him the maintenance of the strictest impartiality so that, when the time was ripe, the United States might serve as mediator, to bring the antagonists together and ensure the conclusion of a just peace. In short the war, hateful though it was, might provide a unique opportunity for that selfless service to humanity of which Mr. Wilson dreamed. America was, he felt, peculiarly fitted for the role of mediator, for it was "the mediating nation of the world," as he declared in April, 1915. "We are compounded of the nations of the world. . . . We are, therefore, able to understand all nations. . . . It is in this sense that I mean that America is a mediating Nation." Already he envisaged himself attending the eventual peace conference as the exponent of America's spiritual leadership, already he was interesting himself in projects for an association of nations to safeguard the world against further armed conflict.

In my opinion it was this basic attitude toward the European War that determined the President's entire policy during the period of American neutrality. I do not mean to belittle the gravity or importance of his long disputes with Britain as well as with Germany over the well-worn issue of freedom of the seas. Neither do I mean to ignore the thesis, so popular in the period between the two World Wars, that the President and the American people were duped by British propaganda and victimized by powerful munitions and banking interests who, in their anxiety to forestall the defeat of Britain and France and protect the huge American investment in those countries, finally engineered the intervention of the United States just as the Allied cause was beginning to fail. These matters are certainly of great interest and importance, but they have been so thoroughly and judiciously treated by Professor Charles Seymour in his essays on *American Neutrality, 1914–1917* (New Haven,

1935) and by other writers that, so far as I can see, little if anything remains to be said. My time being limited, I have elected to analyze and evaluate certain less familiar aspects of American policy.

It is important for my argument to realize that Mr. Wilson, though he regarded the British and French as the defenders of liberty and democracy against militarism and autocracy, as nations standing "with their backs to the wall, fighting wild beasts," did not for that reason intend to show partiality in the conduct of American relations with the belligerents. Some critics have taxed him with unwarranted tolerance of British violations of the freedom of the seas. But it should be noted that, however reluctant to hamper the British war effort, Mr. Wilson was frequently irritated and at times positively infuriated by British disregard of international law. Personally, I do not agree with those who contend that his numerous notes of protest to London were mere window dressings. On the contrary, I think he intended them as detailed specifications of American claims to be presented when the war was over.

On the assumption, then, that Mr. Wilson meant to hold the British as well as the Germans accountable for their methods of warfare, it was nevertheless an inescapable fact that British violations of international law involved only property rights, whereas Germany's unrestricted submarine warfare inevitably entailed the loss of human lives. It has often been argued, with undeniable cogency, that the Germans, subjected to rigid blockade and exposed to possible starvation, could hardly be blamed for resorting to any weapon in their effort to break the grip of British sea-power. The submarine was a new weapon, for which existing international law made no provision. The rules of cruiser warfare were hardly adequate, for a submarine attempting to stop and search a merchant ship on the high seas ran the risk of being immediately rammed or sunk by gunfire. The armament which merchant ships were permitted to carry for defense against cruisers could be used with great effect for offensive action against submarines. The submarine commander had therefore but little choice. Unable to bring his prize to port, he had to sink it. In the interest of his own and his crew's safety, he had to sink it with little or no warning.

Secretary of State Bryan, Senator William J. Stone, and many others argued from these simple facts that the only way to prevent loss of American lives on belligerent ships was to forbid American citizens from traveling on them and to prohibit American-flag ships from entering declared war zones. But the rights of neutrals were clear and the President refused to surrender them. Thereupon Mr. Bryan resigned, but Senator Stone and some of his colleagues pressed the issue. Whatever the legal rights of Americans, Stone contended, it was "foolhardiness amounting to a sort of moral treason against the Republic," for citizens to risk their lives on armed belligerent ships. To this President Wilson replied in a well-known letter that "no group of nations has the right, while the war is in progress, to alter or disregard the principles which all nations have agreed upon in mitigation of the horrors and sufferings of war, and if the clear rights of American citizens should very unhappily be abridged or denied by any such action, we should, it seems to me, have in honor no choice as to what our course should be. For my own part, I cannot consent to any abridgment of the rights of American citizens in any respect. The honor and self-respect of the nation is involved. . . . Once accept a single abatement of right and many other humiliations would certainly follow, and the whole fine fabric of international law might crumble under our hands piece by piece." The rights of neutrals, he held, were among the "inalienable rights" of mankind. The United States was therefore contending for nothing less high and sacred than the rights of humanity. Refusing all compromise, then, the President notified Berlin that the Imperial Government would be held "strictly accountable" for the loss of American lives. Following the sinking of the *Sussex* (March 24, 1916) he threatened American intervention to force the Germans to stop sinking merchant ships by submarine without prior warning and without due provision for the safety of passengers and crew.

The President's attitude on the submarine issue was determined in part by his larger aims. Over and over again in his so-called preparedness speeches of early 1916, he stressed the fact that Americans were "a body of idealists, much more ready to lay down their lives for a thought than for a dollar"; that they were the "trustees of the moral judgment of the world," and that other nations looked to them "to keep even the balance of the whole world's thought." There was, therefore, a price too high to pay even for peace and that was the price of self-respect, of duties abdicated, of glorious opportunities neglected. Everything points to the conclusion that to his own mind the President was defending the right as against all violators. In the case of the Germans, however, human rights as well as neutral rights were involved. When finally he felt obliged to ask Congress to declare war on Germany, it was primarily because the Imperial Government by overt acts had demonstrated its readiness to override international law in a desperate drive for victory.

The President has often been criticized for having pitched American policy on the high plane of general principles. He should have seen, it is said, that Germany threatened the security of the sea lanes between the United States and Britain, that our national interest required the continued existence of Britain and that it therefore forbade the domination of Europe by an unfriendly Germany. For that reason if for no other he should much sooner have committed the United States to active participation in the war.

As a matter of fact this facet of the problem was obvious to discerning minds in both official and unofficial circles, and I find it difficult to believe that the President was entirely unaware of it. But, as I have said before, hardly anyone, not even the exponents of a "realistic" policy, considered the threat of German victory imminent. The position of the Allies, militarily and economically, was believed to be better than we now know it to have been, and the whole trend of public thought was so averse to intervention for anything but the highest motives that even so uncompromising a realist as Theodore Roosevelt felt impelled to explain the entry of the country into the war in terms of the struggle for democracy against autocracy, for liberty against tyranny, and for right against wrong. Analyzing the popular attitude in April, 1917, the British agent, Sir William Wiseman, stated in a report approved by the President: "It is important to realize that the American people do not consider themselves in any danger from the Central Powers. It is true that many of their statesmen foresee the danger of a German triumph, but the majority of the people are still very remote from the war. They believe they are fighting for the cause of Democracy and not to save themselves."

Since the national security did not appear to require American intervention in the European War, the President felt entirely justified in maintaining neutrality, in acting as trustee of the moral judgment of the world and as defender of human rights. Above all, he was prepared and eager to provide good offices for the settlement of the conflict, as well as leadership in the organization of the world for peace.

This was the crux of his policy. It required, first and foremost, the maintenance of neutrality so as to retain the freedom of action necessary "to do the high thing we intend to do." The President hated war and would not resort to it except under extreme provocation: he was too proud to fight for anything but the highest values. "It would be a calamity to the world at large," he wrote Colonel House after the sinking of the *Arabic* (August 19, 1915), "if we should be drawn actively into the conflict and so deprived of all disinterested influence over the settlement." The same thought recurs much later, when the German decision to resort to unrestricted submarine warfare was already known in Washington and war had become all but inevitable. It would be a crime, said the President to Colonel House, to become involved in the conflict to such an extent that later the United States would be unable to save Europe. On the very eve of American intervention Mr. Wilson was still hoping that neutral powers would unite to support the American position and so induce the German government to reverse its fateful decision. Surely it is no exaggeration to say that one of the major objectives of neutrality was to fulfill the requirements of mediation.

Hardly less prominent in the President's mind was the concept of peace without victory. Obviously, if either side were to win a decisive victory, it would not desire nor would it accept American mediation. The chances were great that total victory would produce a harsh, punitive peace. "Victory," said the President in his great programmatic address to the Senate on January 22, 1917, "would mean peace forced upon the loser, a victor's terms imposed upon the vanquished. It would be accepted in humiliation, under duress, at an intolerable sacrifice, and would have a sting, a resentment, a bitter memory upon which terms of peace would rest, not permanently, but only as upon quicksand." He saw all too clearly that upon such a foundation it would be impossible to erect a new international order. He therefore clung to the principle of a compromise settlement, concluded between equals.

It was not the President's idea, however, that the United States should take a hand in drafting the terms of the European peace settlement. It might aid in bringing the antagonists together, but the latter would then have to find their own settlement of the issues in dispute. The interest of the United States would be solely in the establishment of a new concert of power, a universal association of nations to guarantee the settlement, if it were a just one, and to provide for common action against any nation which in future should resort to war. Such at least was Mr. Wilson's initial conception, as he expounded it to the League to Enforce Peace on May 27, 1916. Before long, however, he came to see that the United States, if it were to undertake large responsibilities for the preservation of world peace, would of necessity be deeply interested in the nature and even the details of the peace settlement. The treaties ending the war, he told the Senate on January 22, 1917, "must embody terms which will create a peace that is worth preserving, a peace that will serve the several interests and immediate aims of the nations engaged." Since a decisive victory held little promise of such a settlement, he laid increasing emphasis on the need for a compromise peace, that is, a peace without victory. Furthermore, he began to advance the thesis that the new international system should be set up first of all, so that the erstwhile belligerents, their security guaranteed by the concert of nations, would have no further need to seek security through the imposition of punitive measures.

The evolution of the President's thinking no doubt reflected his disillusioning experiences as a would-be peacemaker. In the initial days of the war he had tendered his good officers in an effort to end hostilities. Both sides had declined, and soon after, at the end of September, 1914, the British rejected an American suggestion that discussions looking toward peace be held by the ambassadors of the belligerent powers in Washington. On this and on subsequent occasions the Germans expressed a readiness to engage in negotiations. In fact, they at times urged the President to mediate. But they did so only when the military situation was in their favor. Postwar studies of German objectives and above all the extremely harsh terms imposed on Bolshevik Russia in the Treaty of Brest-Litovsk (March, 1918) leave no shadow of doubt that the Germans until the time of their imminent military defeat were willing to discuss peace only on their own terms.

It was perhaps natural that the President should look primarily to the British for co-operation in bringing the war to an end and establishing a new and better world order. Common traditions, common outlook, and common language should all have facilitated understanding. But the British were in this respect to prove a grave disappointment. They showed little if any desire for guidance or salvation. Sir Edward Grey, the Foreign Secretary, was an early convert to the idea of a League of Nations and expressed readiness to make peace as soon as there were real promise of a durable settlement. He expressed doubt whether it would be either feasible or desirable to crush Germany, and averred that Britain and France, if victorious, would negotiate a fair and reasonable settlement with their fallen foe. But only if and when a military victory proved impossible would Grey and his countrymen welcome friendly American mediation.

Sir Edward was, so it seems, just about as anxious to circumvent mediation as the President was to secure its acceptance. Yet the British Foreign Secretary was probably more favorably disposed toward the American policy than most of his cabinet colleagues or than the British public at large. Most newspapers were violently opposed to neutral mediation. A few Liberal organs like the *Economist,* the *Nation,* the *Contemporary* and the *Manchester Guardian* stood with Grey as advocates of a reasonable peace and at times even expressed a desire for American mediation. But the other newspapers and journals denounced and abused them for their pains. Mr. Asquith, the Liberal Prime Minister, had sounded the keynote of British policy when, on November 9, 1914, he declared in his Guildhall speech: "We shall not sheathe the sword . . . until the military domination of Prussia is fully and finally destroyed."

It must have been disheartening to the President and Colonel House to have their high-minded proposals meet so cool a reception. But they considered the question of peace much too important to be shelved. In January, 1915, Colonel House went to London as Mr. Wilson's personal representative to see if he could discover, in intimate discussions, whether there was a possibility of initiating peace talks. But again British leaders, from King George to Sir Edward Grey, left their visitor in no doubt that peace efforts were useless and that American mediation was not wanted. Grey, however, made every effort to convince his visitor that Britain shared the President's high ideal of a new world order in which war would be outlawed and disarmament would become possible. The important thing, he argued, was that America should commit itself to participate fully in future world affairs.

It would be both interesting and instructive to follow in detail the ensuing phases of this problem. I have time, however, only to touch upon the main developments and to underline the more important features. House's second wartime visit to Europe, in the early months of 1916, satisfied him that there was no disposition in Berlin to make concessions and that in London too, "peace discussions at this time would be about as popular . . . as the coronation of the Kaiser in Westminster

Abbey." The British desired the United States to enter the war, but only on the issue of German submarine warfare, so that the Allies might remain free with respect to future peace terms. So anxious was House to stage a peace conference and so intent were the British not to offend or estrange the Americans, that Grey eventually agreed to a memorandum submitted by House with the approval of President Wilson.

This Grey-House Memorandum was a truly remarkable document, for it specified that, on hearing from Britain and France that the moment was opportune, President Wilson should demand the convocation of a conference to put an end to the war. Should the Allies accept and the Germans refuse, the United States would "probably" enter the war against Germany. It was House's opinion that if such a conference met, it would establish peace on terms "not unfavourable" to the Allies; if it failed to secure peace because of German unreasonableness, the United States would ("probably" was added by Mr. Wilson) leave the conference as a belligerent on the side of the Allies.

If this loosely worded agreement meant anything, it meant that President Wilson and Colonel House were so eager to end the war and establish the new world order that they were prepared to act in collusion with the Allies to compel the Germans to attend a peace conference and accept terms "not unfavourable" to the Allies, on pain of having the United States enter the war against them. The British, who were as much opposed to American mediation as ever, were not called upon for any commitment. Indeed, the whole scheme was to go into operation only when they gave the word. In other words, they could appeal to the President if their situation became positively desperate, and could rely upon the United States to ensure them "not unfavourable" terms.

As a matter of fact the British never took advantage of what on its face appears to have been a most attractive offer. Possibly they doubted whether the Congress would in any contingency vote for war. Possibly they had but a poor opinion of the military contribution the United States could make within any reasonable period. More likely, however, they still regarded American mediation as the least desirable solution of their problem. British opinion was still firmly opposed to all outside interference and equally set against a negotiated peace.

The plan embodied in the Grey-House Memorandum was the brain child of Colonel House rather than of the President, and we may assume, I think, that Mr. Wilson went along with it only for want of some better method of attaining his objective before it was too late. Still he was disappointed by the obstinate refusal of the British to accept American direction. In a public address on May 27, 1916, he announced the readiness of the United States to become a partner in a League of Nations and outlined his ideas as to the nature of such an association. In no uncertain terms he bade farewell to isolation: "We are participants, whether we would or not, in the life of the world. . . . The interests of all nations are our own also. We are partners with the rest. What affects mankind is inevitably our affair as well as the affairs of the nations of Europe and Asia."

Yet even this epoch-making pronouncement was vehemently attacked by the British press. Mr. Wilson, in speaking of the war, had remarked: "With its causes and objects we are not concerned." To the British, even to those in high circles, these words revealed a lack of understanding not only of the origins, but also of the objectives of the struggle. Some even suggested that the President had fallen a victim to German "peace claptrap."

It is easy to understand the "emotional reaction" of the President, to which Mr. Seymour several times refers in his work on the House papers. Mr. Wilson was disgusted as well as discouraged. It was at this time that he spoke of the war as "a drunken brawl in a public house," and privately referred to the British leaders as "poor boobs." On another occasion he told House that he could see no justification for helping the Allies "to destroy Germany politically and economically, so that France and Russia might divide the dictatorship of the Continent and Great Britain be rid of German naval and commercial competition."

Months passed by without noticeable change in the British attitude. On September 16, 1916, the *Spectator* denounced all ideas of a "great, flat, flabby, overgrown international Pow-wow . . ."; and presently Mr. Lloyd George declared that "the fight must be to the finish — to a knock-out"; intervention by other powers in behalf of peace, he added, would not be tolerated. These uncompromising words cannot be dismissed as an irresponsible outburst, for they were followed up by equally stiff statements from the Prime Minister and the Foreign Secretary (October 11, 23). Perhaps the clearest and most succinct definition of the British position appeared in a memorandum prepared by Sir Edward Grey for the Cabinet at the end of November: "As long as the naval and military authorities believe that Germany can be defeated and satisfactory terms of peace can eventually be dictated to her, peace is premature, and to contemplate it is to betray the interests of this country and of the Allies."

During the closing months of 1916 the German government was doing its utmost to induce the President to arrange discussions for peace. The German military situation was still favorable, but it was becoming increasingly clear that a decisive German victory could be won only through the reintroduction of unrestricted submarine warfare. The High Command realized that such a move would bring the United States into the war against Germany, but was perfectly confident that Britain could be brought to its knees long before American aid could become effectual. The civil authorities, however, remained opposed to the submarine program and hoped that peace could be attained on acceptable terms before the final, fateful decision was made.

The President, on his part, firmly refused to make any further moves until after the November election, the result of which he could interpret as an expression of public support for his foreign policy. But the situation in the Allied countries at the end of 1916 was anything but propitious for mediation. Anglo-American relations had reached their nadir as a result of British interference with American trade and mail, and the announced British intention of fighting on to a knockout spelled the doom of any further American effort to mediate. Yet the President felt that he must act to forestall further bloodshed such as had marked the offensive on the Somme, and to ensure a new order of international affairs before either side was completely exhausted.

His initial thought seems to have been simply to demand that the belligerents cease hostilities on pain of American intervention. But this variant on Colonel House's earlier program depended so greatly on the sheer military power by which it could be backed that it must have seemed to the President impracticable. Eventually, on December 18, 1916, he simply called on both sides for a statement of the terms on which they would be prepared to conclude the war and of the arrangements they would deem satisfactory as a guarantee against its renewal or the kindling of a similar conflict in the future. He disclaimed any effort at mediation and, though he offered his services if desired, he insisted that he had no wish to determine the method or the instrumentality. He warned, however, that the United States, while not at liberty to suggest terms, had a genuine interest in the conclusion of peace, lest its position as a neutral become intolerable. Furthermore: "If the contest must continue to proceed toward undefined ends by slow attrition until one group of belligerents or the other is exhausted; if million after million of human lives must continue to be offered up until on the one side or the other there are no more to offer; if resentments must be kindled that can never cool and despairs engendered from which there can be no recovery, hopes of peace and of the willing concert of free people will be rendered vain and idle."

The President's note was less pretentious than his earlier proposals. He seems to have had real difficulty in formulating his suggestion and evidently hastened its completion because the German government itself had a week before proposed a conference of the belligerents. Mr. Wilson was much concerned lest the British, by turning down the German proposal, should bang the door on peace. Perhaps he was also disturbed by the possibility, however slight, that the belligerents might make peace without American participation and without providing guarantees for the preservation of peace in the future.

In his haste Mr. Wilson again allowed an infelicitous statement to slip into his note: "The objects which the statesmen of the belligerents on both sides have in mind in this war are virtually the same as stated in general terms to their own people and to the world." The ensuing passage shows clearly that by this the President meant simply that the belligerents had stated their aims in general terms and that it might be well now to present specifications. But the first part of the questionable sentence was bitterly attacked in the Allied countries. King George is said to have wept as he expressed his surprise and depression, while nothing would deter the new Prime Minister, Mr. Lloyd George, from airing his feelings in a public speech (December 19) in reply to the German overture. In no uncertain terms he declared that peace could be obtained only on the basis of "complete restitution, full reparation, and effectual guarantees." What this signified was spelled out in greater detail in the official British reply to the President's note (January 10, 1917) which left no doubt that the Allies meant to fight on until victory made possible the imposition of Draconian terms. Small comfort was to be derived from the statement that, while the Allies desired to shield Europe from the covetous brutality of Prussian militarism, the extermination and the political disappearance of the German peoples had never formed part of their designs.

Despite the fact that the German government had expressed its preference for direct negotiations with its enemies, and despite the uncompromising attitude of the London government, the President decided to press on with his program, for he knew that important decisions were in prospect on the German side and that time was probably running out. In one of his great addresses to the Senate (January 22, 1917) he asserted that in making his proposal for a statement of peace terms he was speaking "on behalf of humanity and of the rights of all neutral nations." It was true, he continued, that the United States would have no voice in establishing the concrete terms of peace, but it would certainly have a voice in deciding whether or not peace should be made lasting by the guarantees of a universal covenant, the need for which all parties recognized. It was not enough to say, as statesmen of both belligerent groups had said, that it was no part of their purpose to crush their antagonists. A durable peace could not be based on a victor's terms, but could only be a "peace without victory." "Only a peace between equals can last. Only a peace the very principle of which is equality and a common participation in a common benefit. The right state of mind, the right feeling between nations, is as necessary for a lasting peace as is the just settlement of vexed questions of territory or of racial and national allegiance."

Once again the British found in the President's words grounds for protest, this time with reference to the phrase "peace without victory." But on this occasion their indignation was superfluous, for within a week the President was notified of the German decision to resume unrestricted submarine warfare on February 1. Berlin's repudiation of its earlier engagements made the severance of diplomatic relations inevitable, yet Mr. Wilson still hoped that a common front of neutral states could be formed and that the Imperial government might give way to combined pressure. At all events he would await overt acts on the part of the Germans before asking Congress to declare war.

The sinking of several American ships and the resulting loss of life left the President no choice but to accept the German challenge. Still, in explaining the situation to Congress (April 2, 1917), he made no effort to conceal his disappointment and grief. The German government, by resorting to a form of warfare which he described as "warfare against mankind," had compelled the United States to take up arms "to vindicate the principles of peace and justice in the life of the world as against selfish and autocratic power. . . ." Despite the latest disheartening developments, however, his own thought, he said, had not been driven from its habitual and normal course. He did not blame the German people, for whom he felt nothing but sympathy and friendship. Not they, but their ruthless and irresponsible rulers had brought the world to this pass. Clearly no autocratic government could be trusted to keep its faith. If there were ever to be a concert for peace, it could only be a partnership of democratic nations. The world, therefore, had to be made safe for democracy.

It is impossible to read the historical record for this period without sensing what a blow to Mr. Wilson's dearest hopes was the German proclamation of unrestricted submarine warfare. He felt that it had forced him to take his country into the war at the very time when the prospect for peace negotiations and American mediation seemed at long last to be growing brighter. Now the whole picture had changed: the United States as a party at interest could no longer serve as impartial mediator, and there was real danger that an Allied victory, to which the United States was now bound to contribute, would eventuate in a punitive peace which, in turn, would make impossible a new world order of justice and co-operation.

America's entry into the Great War obliged the President, therefore, to undertake a thorough reconsideration of his policy. The ensuing changes I should like to examine in my second lecture, but in closing tonight I trust you will permit me to restate the leading theme of my argument.

President Wilson has been taken to task for his failure to recognize the requirements of American security and for basing his foreign policy on moral principles and the idea of selfless service to mankind rather than on the simple demands of national interest. Though this thesis has been seriously overworked, it certainly has some validity. I have tried to explain it by recalling the traditional American attitude of aloofness and superiority to the sordid politics of Europe. Woodrow Wilson set his countrymen a higher goal and a nobler mission than any they had yet envisaged. Everything we can learn of public opinion at that time indicates that the

American people gladly shared his aspirations and loyally supported his policies.

Furthermore, it appeared to the country, as it did to him, that the United States, having no territorial or other selfish aims and being in no way threatened by developments in Europe, had a real obligation to further its high ideals. Those who hold that in the interests of national security the President should at an early date have taken the country into the war against Germany overlook the fact that relatively few people at that time recognized the eventual threat involved in a German victory. Even the historians, whom the general public seems to think can look forward as well as backward, were for the most part blind. Long after the war many of them still argued that American intervention was a mistake, no matter what the shape of things to come in Europe.

It was just because the President believed that the United States had nothing to fear and had no axe to grind that he hoped to mediate, to aid in arranging a just peace and above all to provide leadership in organizing a new international order that would prevent war in the future. He had dreamed of something like this since early manhood. To play the role of peacemaker would have been infinitely gratifying to him. But to qualify for the part he had to stand immovable by the international law on which he hoped to build the new order. Furthermore, he had to keep his country out of the conflict if at all possible. And finally, he had to induce and if necessary force the belligerents to accept neutral mediation and abandon the idea of a fight to the knockout. To me it is clear that Woodrow Wilson, for all his lack of knowledge and interest in concrete European issues, saw more clearly than most that a decisive victory would almost inevitably produce a punitive peace and that such a peace could not possibly serve as the foundation for a society of nations. This, I submit, was statesmanship of a high order.

Intolerance in the 1920s

In the aftermath of World War I, the Ku Klux Klan experienced a phenomenal revival. Nearly moribund for the first five years after its resurrection in 1915, the KKK suddenly exploded into life in 1920. By 1925, it had recruited perhaps five million men into its hooded ranks. Identical to the Klan of Reconstruction days in regalia and ritual, the KKK of the 1920s actually drew on a much broader base of support. The object of its hatred now included many others than the black man, and its strength extended far outside the South. During the first half of the decade, the Klan exerted immense power, dominating the politics of some states and imposing its standards of "Americanism" far more widely. The downward slide was no less swift, however. By the end of the 1920s, the Klan had become a negligible force and would remain so until the civil-rights revolution called it forth for a second resurrection in the modern era.

The Klan of the 1920s, Robert Moats Miller argues in the following essay, must be treated not as an aberration, but as part of the American mainstream. On the one hand, it drew on dark strains of intolerance, authoritarianism, and violence deep-rooted in the nation's history. The Klan attracted its clientele not primarily from America's blackguards and dispossessed, but from its decent, God-fearing citizenry. On the other hand, the Klan expressed the deep anxieties about the social revolution taking place in the country. For the American drawn to the Klan—Anglo-Saxon, fundamentalist, rural at least by birth—the 1920s seemed a time of profound and threatening change. A massive stream of immigrants, supposedly unassimilable and inferior, had poured into the country; the dreaded Roman Catholics constituted a third of the population; city dwellers were about to become a national majority; manners and morals had grown loose and impure. All of these threats to the older America, no less than the continuing determination to preserve white supremacy, had stimulated the growth of the KKK. Its equally fast decline was a sign of easing tensions, either through adjustment to the new world or, as in the case of the political radical and the black man, through suppression of the danger. By his analysis, Robert Miller rescues the KKK from the realm of historical curiosity. The hooded organization becomes rather a key for understanding the American experience in the 1920s.

FOR FURTHER READING:

CHALMERS, DAVID M. *Hooded Americanism.* New York: Doubleday & Company, 1965.*
HIGHAM, JOHN. *Strangers in the Land.* New York: Atheneum Publishers, 1963.*
MURRAY, ROBERT K. *Red Scare: A Study in National Hysteria.* New York: McGraw-Hill Book Company, 1964.*

Asterisk denotes paperback edition.

The Ku Klux Klan   ROBERT MOATS MILLER

The Ku Klux Klan of the 1920's is a study in anxiety rather than in abnormality. The citizens of the Invisible Empire were deeply anxious men, but they were not, save for the psychotic few, moral monsters; and to dismiss these five million hooded Americans as peculiarly depraved is to blink away the banality of evil. The Klan illuminates the need of mediocre men to flee to the mysticism of the primitive collectivity, and serves, therefore, to remind us that Americans are implicated in the totalitarian temper of the modern world. To discern more than a casual relationship between the Klan and twentieth-century collectivism, however, is not to say that the Klan is a study in un-Americanism. These True Believers of the twenties were not converts to an alien ideology; rather, they confessed to a creed shared, in whole or in part, by many Americans in every generation. The Klan illuminates the persistency of dark strains in American history, strains that have been eased but never entirely erased by faithfulness to the countervailing ideals of decency and fair play. Why, however, should these strains become acutely manifest in a decade fondly deemed the apogee of "normalcy"? Admitting that all men in the modern world bear the burden of anxiety, acknowledging the racism, nativism, and irrationalism flawing the American past, it remains our task to comprehend what there was in the social and psychic air of the early 1920's making many Americans so terribly anxious as to compel them to seek release in a secret, hooded order which, if spawned in Europe, would have carried the designation "fascist."

Any attempt to resolve this paradox must begin with the understanding that the Klan was a many-splintered thing or, less invidiously, a many-splendored thing. The Knights were troubled souls, but that which tried their souls varied from region to region and, indeed, from Knight to Knight. It was as though an outraged citizenry participated in a gigantic police line-up to identify the enemies of society, with each "good" American fingering a different suspect: uppity Negro, conspiratorial Catholic, avaricious Jew, dirty Mexican, wily Oriental, bloody-handed Bolshevik, scabrous bootlegger, fancy "lady," oily gambler, fuzzy internationalist, grafting politico, Sabbath desecrator, wife-beater, home-breaker, atheistic evolutionist, feckless-faithed Modernist, scoffing professor, arrogant intellectual, subversive socialist, slick urbanite, simpering pacifist, corrupt labor organizer. Of necessity, the line of suspects was endless because the evils threatening America appeared legion: miscegenation, mongrelization, Romanism, socialism, urbanism, skepticism, secularism, paganism, modernism, radicalism, internationalism, materialism, Freudianism, relativism, surrealism, alcoholism, sexualism.

These myriad dangers appeared more clear and present in some regions and to some citizens than others; consequently, it is imprecise to speak of *the* Klan of the 1920's. Rather, there existed many local Klans operating as virtually autonomous units, and each unit ranked the dangers in some order of priority, just as each Knight was motivated (whether consciously or not) by his life experiences.

Fragmented and amorphous, the Klan was yet a fellowship of belief, knitted together by a shared anxiety about tomorrow and a shared longing for the return of yesterday. Perhaps, after all, there was only one great enemy: *change!* Made bewil-

Source: Robert Moats Miller, "The Ku Klux Klan," in *Change and Continuity in Twentieth-Century America: The 1920's,* eds. John Braeman et al. (Columbus, Ohio: Ohio State University Press, 1968), pp. 215–238, 246–253.

dered and fearful by the swift and surging forces reshaping "their" country, unwilling or unable to understand this strange, new century, men banded together to offer resistance. Essentially, then, the Klan was a counter-revolutionary movement. Its core appeal was to those Americans who, through consideration of rational self-interes or unconscious emotional needs, dreamed that the clock might be stopped; and who, as they donned their white dream robes, knew a momentary identification with a fanciful older and purer community.

The older and purer community of the Klansman's dream was, of course, a white man's community. "I believe in the Klan. I don't believe the thing to do at this moment is to go out and shoot a nigger in the street. But when the time comes — when it comes — we'll take them down by the busload, by the trainload, that's what we'll do. By the busload. By the carload! . . . We don't hate Negroes. We love 'em, in their place — like shinin' shoes, bell-hoppin', street-sweepin', pickin' cotton, diggin' ditches, eatin' possum, servin' time, totin' buckshot, river-floatin', etc." Thus spoke the voice of the Klan in 1965, as articulated by a Jacksonville, Florida, barber. "Our main and fundamental objective is the MAINTENANCE OF THE SUPREMACY OF THE WHITE RACE in this Republic." Thus spoke the voice of the Klan in 1867, as articulated by the delegates to the organizational meeting of the Reconstruction Klan in Nashville.

Because the Negro was the central target of both the Reconstruction and mid-twentieth-century Klans, because both saw the untrammeled Negro as the nation's greatest menace, the temptation is to interpolate and conclude that the same Negrophobia dominated the Klan of the twenties. Perceptive historians have not succumbed to this temptation, realizing that the Klan that flowered after World War I reflected the coalescence of many different fears and loyalties. Indeed, students of the Klan in the Southwest, Far West, and Midwest deem the black man an inconsequential factor in the growth of the white-robed order. We may concur that the movements of the 1860's, 1920's, and 1960's, although sharing a common name and ritual, were substantively different. We may even concur that in great areas of the country where the Klan was powerful the Negro population was insignificant, and that, in fact, it is probable that had not a single Negro lived in the United States, a Klan-type order would have emerged, such was the pervasive anxiety of the post-Versailles years.

Yet having escaped the errors of simplism and "presentism," perhaps in this very sophistication the principle of Ockham's Razor has been forgotten: complex and refined explanations of observed phenomena must not obscure the simple and evident. Just as there is no more demonic theme in American history, so there is none more persistent than that America was a white man's country. White supremacy was an article of faith with almost all modern Europeans and their descendants in the northern New World. Until almost today it was a faith seemingly supported by much scientific and scholarly evidence. Kluxers of every generation have feared the Negro — and consequently have hated him. And Kluxers in every generation have enjoyed the covert endorsement of large numbers of citizens too timid or too hypocritical to enlist under the banner of the fiery cross. The Klan of the 1920's was first, if not foremost, a movement to keep the black man in his place — if necessary, by digging his grave. Its founder, Colonel William Joseph Simmons, was an Alabaman who with a band of Georgians on Thanksgiving night, 1915, ascended Stone Mountain near Atlanta to call "from its slumber of half a century" that Invisible Empire that once had saved the prostrate South from mongrelization. "The present

Klan," testified Simmons, "is a memorial to the original organization. In a sense it is the reincarnation among the sons of the spirit of the fathers." As gallant southerners had galloped with torch and mask to the defense of their society imperiled by conquering Yankee and former bondsmen, so their sons would band to resist with equal success the present pretensions of "darkies" who, said Simmons, were "getting pretty uppity." Childhood cloudy fantasies of redeeming Klansmen were given sharper focus on the screen of the darkened Atlanta theater as the good Colonel saw repeated performances (on scrounged passes) of that tarnished epic, *The Birth of a Nation,* a film that wrote "history with lightning," to use Woodrow Wilson's words of mindless approbation; and in both fantasy and film Simmons identified the redemption of his beloved South with the preservation of the existing caste system. It is, therefore, not surprising that all prospective Knights vowed to "faithfully strive for the eternal maintenance of white supremacy." Nor is it a matter of astonishment that when Simmons was maneuvered from control, his successor, Hiram Wesley Evans, reaffirmed the ancient dogma that "God Almighty never intended social equality for Negro and white man," and who, with a coterie of Dallas disciples, implemented the Almighty's wishes by branding with acid the initials KKK across the forehead of a Negro bellhop. As the Klan was reborn in Georgia by southerners determined to rekindle with fiery cross the resistance spirit of their fathers, so it was in Dixie in 1920, 1921, and 1922 that the movement first gained strength. To be sure, presently the Klan penetrated other sections and exploited other anxieties, but its southern "style" and essential Negrophobia was never totally lost. And the 1960's have reminded us of the historic fact that white men in the North when put to the test are scarcely color-blind.

The period immediately following World War I was a time of testing for the white man and a time of terror for the Negro. Even as the guns on the Western Front quieted, racial violence in America exploded. Service overseas gave Negro soldiers a taste of equality and a sense of pride. The migration of thousands to northern cities engendered a feeling of independence. And the millions who remained in the South hoped that President Wilson intended to include American Negroes among the beneficiaries of his new world of democracy. By 1920 their hopes had been shattered and their pretensions corrected. America was to remain, as it always had been, a white man's country. This was the hard lesson learned of a thousand floggings, a hundred lynchings, and a score of race riots in the months following the Armistice — a lesson administered over the land from Washington to Omaha and from Chicago to Longview, Texas. Further, it was an instruction to be repeated throughout the 1920's for the benefit of forgetful Negroes by the revived Ku Klux Klan.

If many Americans were made fearful by the rising tide of color, it is possible that an even greater number trembled over the menace of Rome. In truth, the shadow of the Pope seemed darker than that of the Negro, and anti-Catholicism was the key to the Klan's growth in the Far West and Midwest and, though not initially, perhaps in the South as well. Although Colonel Simmons dreamed of resurrecting the Reconstruction Klan, he in fact reawakened two other resistance movements, the Know-Nothings of the 1840's and 1850's and the American Protective Association of the 1880's and 1890's. In these movements there raged the fever of anti-Catholicism, the oldest and stubbornest variety of the disease called "nativism," a disease far too common in the United States to be diagnosed a foreign or un-American strain. If the conquest of America by Rome seemed a freightening possibility to nineteenth-century Protestants, to their twentieth-century sons it was an imminent probability and, in the great northern cities, an actuality. In the twenty-five-year period preceding the incident atop Stone Mountain, the Catholic church gained in membership 114.1 per cent, and in 1920, the year of the Klan's great surge, Catholics comprised 36 per cent of the American religious population. The power, the prestige, the "arrogance" of Catholicism was everywhere evident in American life; and when Alfred Emanuel Smith made his first bid for the presidency in 1924, the last, worst fear of Protestants was at hand: the "Dago of the Tiber" (to borrow a Klansman's characterization of the pope) would now take up residence on the Potomac.

It is impossible to understand the enormity of the peril and consequently the enormous appeal of the Klan unless we comprehend the historic identification between Protestantism and Americanism. Since the first settlements, Protestants had prided themselves on being the senior partners in the American enterprise, and in the nineteenth century the American nation and the Protestant denominations had marched to greatness together. This was entirely appropriate, for there was no discernible tension between the evangelical churches and society, between piety and patriotism. The Protestant way of faith and the American way of life were one. What was good for the churches was good for the country. To be sure, this resulted in a "culture-Protestantism" wherein the churches paid a tragic price for their comfortable relationship with American culture; rarely was it found necessary to cry, "Let the Church be the Church!" The churches were not merely domesticated, they were virtually emasculated, and like the eunuchs of old, served as ornaments without seriously disturbing their master's establishment.

Thus, the prideful cry of the Ohio Klan leader was repeatedly uttered: "We want the country ruled by the sort of people who settled it. This is *our* country and we alone are responsible for its future." Protestants viewed the growing power of Catholicism as not only a threat to their religion but also to their beloved nation. Indeed, since Protestantism and Americanism were inseparable, it was impossible to assault the one without wounding the other. Therefore, the Klan attracted patriots as well as bigots, appealing to nationalist loyalties as well as to religious prejudices. Even irenic-spirited Protestants saw (or thought they saw) in the authoritarian structure of the Catholic church objective reasons for opposing its spread in a democratic society. As in wartime true citizens willingly lay down their lives in defense of their free institutions, so patriots in peacetime should freely spend of themselves in the fight against internal subversion. It is instructive that the "Klan verse" of the New Testament is Romans 12:1: "I beseech you therefore, brethren, by the mercies of God, that ye present your bodies a living sacrifice, holy, acceptable unto God, which is your reasonable service." Perhaps we can now understand why the Klan tapped anti-Catholic hostilities even in areas, such as rural Indiana, where the Catholic population numbered less than 2 per cent. Social conflict between Protestants and Catholics over such matters as schools, local politics, prohibition, and censorship heightened tension in many communities; but even where abrasive contact was absent, patriotic Protestants yet feared for the future of "their" nation.

The very name *Roman* Catholic church was suggestive of sinister foreign influence, underscoring the essential Americanism of the Protestant denominations. The very militancy of Catholicism transmuted Protestant tolerance from a virtue to a weakness. And the very authoritarianism of the Church of Rome sharpened the revelation of Protestantism's fragmentation, rendering efforts to quench the conflagration of Catholicism sweeping the land as feeble and ill-directed as the spray from a leaky hose. The Klan carried the hope of Protestant unity and the promise of Protestant militancy. At long last God-fearing men could know, as they assembled around the blazing hillside cross, identification with a mighty supradenominational movement. Like all crusaders, these Klansmen without conscious hypocrisy could cry, "For God and country," and in their righteousness have no sense of shame as they battled the enemies of their faith and nation. "I've attended a lot of church gatherings and conventions," remarked an Exalted Cyclops after the Klan's 1924 national convention, "but I never attended one where the revival spirit was as pronounced as it was at the Klan Klonvocation."

The operative words are "revival spirit," for though anxiety over Catholicism's growth and ambitions was widespread, few liberal Protestants could bring themselves to join the Klan. Thus, far from being a unifying force, the Klan further sharpened the cleavage between Modernists and Fundamentalists. Though not all Fundamentalists were Klansmen, virtually all Klansmen — aside from the obvious charlatans — were Fundamentalists. Fundamentalism and the Klan were perfectly mated in their anti-intellectualism, their morbid compulsion to destroy that which they did not understand, their passion for emotional release, and their frustration, as well as in their blind faith and total commitment. At the same time we should note the national leadership of American Protestantism, including almost every minister of reputation and every theologian of significance, denounced the hooded order, as did almost every national governing body of the larger denominations. Thus the Klan was not an instrument of American Protestantism in the sense, say, that the Inquisition was of the medieval church. It is crucial to understand that the Protestant denominations did not call forth the Klan; rather, the Klan sought desperately to become identified by Protestants as an ally, and it did so by tapping the historic anti-Catholic bias learned by Protestant children in cradle and conventicle and by exploiting the prideful Protestant assumption that they were the darlings of American history.

The Klan made the identification in many ways. Its symbol was a cross, and "The Old Rugged Cross" became almost the official hymn, sometimes with the alteration, "I will cherish the bright Fiery Cross. . . ." Its Kreed "reverentially" acknowledged the majesty of God. Its code of conduct was drawn from the Ten Commandments. The *Kloran* declared that "the living Christ is a Klansman's criterion of character," and Klan pamphlets bore such titles as "Christ and Other Klansmen." Every Klavern had a chaplain called a Kludd, who opened each meeting with a prayer and closed with a benediction. The fervent religiosity of the meeting reached a crescendo as the Knights gathered before the altar to sing the "Kloxology." And perhaps as they marched from the Klavern to burn a warning cross atop a nearby hill, their voices broke forth in the militant "Onward, Christian Solders." Perhaps, too, a few thoughtful members quieted their troubled consciences with the words from another much loved hymn, "God moves in mysterious ways, His wonders to behold."

Little wonder, then, that the Klan succeeded in attracting thousands of evangelical ministers, men already disturbed by the passing of "Old-Time Religion" and made uneasy by their own declining community status. When a Kleagle entered an area, almost invariably he made his first overtures to the local preachers, offering them membership free of the usual ten-dollar fee. Often a co-operating clergyman was thanked or a stiff-kneed one threatened by a sudden Sunday visitation of white-robed and masked Klansmen who silently entered the sanctuary, marched down the aisles, congregated in front of the pulpit to present a purse of perhaps forty dollars. Additional hundreds of ministers were on the Klan payrolls as organizers, lecturers, and officers; and without their active labors and without the tacit endorsement of a numerically impressive element of the ministry, the Klan could not have flourished. The obscene spectacle of men of God gathered about a cross ignited by their hands is perhaps tempered only by a sense of pity for Christians possessed by such anxiety.

"My country in 1900 is something totally different from my own country of 1860. I am wholly a stranger in it." The writer continued: "The child born in 1900 would . . . be born into a new world which would not be a unity but a multiple." This lament and this prediction were made by that purest of patricians, Henry Adams, grandson and great-grandson of presidents; but the words might have been uttered by the most banal of Klansmen, for the opening years of the twentieth century saw the older Americans overwhelmed by a sense of estrangement as "their" land was flooded by a sea of new immigrants. Historians of immigration make much of the shock of alienation experienced by the "uprooted" as they migrated from the psychological security of their familiar European villages to the unknown New World. These insights are altogether valid, for the immigrant's ordeal was seldom physically easy and never emotionally painless. The obverse side of the coin, however, has been examined by fewer students. How does a man accustomed to power and prestige respond when strangers enter the land to dethrone him — and if perchance the dethronement is only in the man's imagination, it does not lessen the fear.

Between the year William McKinley enlisted as a private in the 23rd Ohio Volunteer Infantry in the Civil War and his assassination at the hands of a twenty-eight-year-old Polish-American with the "sinister" name of Czolgosz, fourteen million people came to the United States, "new" immigrants from southern and eastern Europe accounting for over 50 per cent of the total by the 1890's. In the opening fifteen years of the new century the torrent accelerated rather than slackened, an average of 1,000,000 entering annually, and now the "new" immigrants accounted for 72 per cent. The impulse was temporarily stemmed by the war, but with the coming of peace, it renewed. From June, 1920, to June, 1921, more than 800,000 individuals entered, and consuls in Europe reported that additional millions were planning to leave. Then, in one of the most momentous enactments in American history, Congress virtually closed the gates, and the Statue of Liberty lost all relevance save for returning tourists — and a handful of immigrants. (Probably the whole twenty-five-year period after 1925 saw fewer immigrants to the United States than the single year 1907.)

There was more than a casual relationship between this surge of immigration and the resurgence of the Ku Klux Klan. These "new" immigrants, these "beaten men of beaten races," these mongrel worshipers of Bacchus or Baal or Marx, seemed no less threatening to the cherished America of yesteryear than insolent blacks and arrogant Romans. Inquired Colonel Simmons in explaining the growth of the Klan: "What were the dangers which the white men saw threatening to crush and overwhelm Anglo-Saxon civilization? The dangers were in the tremendous influx of foreign immigration, tutored in alien dogmas and alien creeds, flowing in from all climes and slowly pushing the native-born white American population into the center of the country, there to be ultimately overwhelmed and smothered." The Colonel's successor, Evans, elaborated: "When the Klan first appeared the nation was in the confusion of sudden awakening from the lovely dream of the melting pot, disorganized and helpless before the invasion of aliens and alien ideas. After ten years of the Klan it arms for defense." Nordic Americans, he continued, finally

> decided that even the crossing of salt water did not dim a single spot on a leopard; that an alien usually remains an alien no matter what is done to him, what veneer of education he gets, what oath he takes, nor what public attitudes he adopts. They decided that the melting pot was a ghastly failure, and remembered that the very name was coined by a member of one of the races — the Jews — which most determinedly refuses to melt. They decided that in every way, as well as in politics, the alien in the vast majority of cases is unalterably fixed in his instincts, character, thought and interests by centuries of racial selection and development, that he thinks first for his own people, works only with and for them, and never an American. They decided that in character, instincts, thought, and purposes — in his whole soul — an alien remains fixedly alien to America and all it means.

It is again necessary to insist on a hard point. As the Klan tapped rather than created Negrophobia and anti-Catholicism, so it did not so much inspire as reflect a pervasive Anglo-Saxon racism. The Klan can be understood only in the context of the tribalism of the times: the lynching of Leo Frank and the judicial execution of Sacco and Vanzetti; the subtle anti-Semitic discrimination instituted by eastern clubs, resorts, and universities and the crude slanders leveled at Jews by Henry Ford; the superman notions of Jack London and the elitist concepts of Irving Babbitt; the "Yellow Peril" warnings of Homer Lea and the anti-Oriental practices of native Californians; the findings prideful to Anglo-Saxons and diminishing to other "races" of the Army intelligence tests administered during the war and the conclusions implicit in "objective" sociological studies; and the consensus seemingly reached by geneticists such as Henry Fairfield Osborn, geographers such as Ellsworth Huntington, psychologists such as William McDougall, and a host of pseudo scholars such as Madison Grant, that the American grain was being choked by alien chaff.

It is disconcerting to note the similarities between this xenophobia and European fascism. Both stressed racial purity, a return to a primitive community of one blood, and the purging of alien minority groups. And if the Klan preached 100 per cent Americanism, was this not the national goal during World War I? If the Klan sought to save the country from mongrelization, was this not the intent of the Congressional restriction laws of 1921 and 1924, laws as ardently supported by many patricians, populists, and progressives as by hooded Knights?

John Higham has given a very serviceable definition of nativism: an intense opposition to an internal minority on the ground of its foreign (i.e., "un-American") connections; and he has discerned three major themes each with a separate history reaching back before the Civil War: anti-Catholicism, Anglo-Saxon racism, and antiforeign radicalism. We have seen how the Ku Klux Klan reflected and exploited two of these manifestations. Almost equally central to the Klan's purposes was the stamping out of radicalism in all its variants. Throughout American history, patriots have feared their nation endangered by imported radical ideologies. The Birchites and McCarthyites of the mid-twentieth century experience an apprehension as old as that which impelled the Alien and Sedition acts during the anti-Jacobin hysteria of the 1790's. And when in the 1960's Klansmen proclaim "FIGHT COMMUNISM," the injunction is no more imperative than that given by their fathers to "FIGHT BOLSHEVISM." Today the enemy within is deemed less the alien immigrant than the native-born "fellow traveler" seduced by alien ideas. Following World War I, however, the stereotype of the immigrant radical knew its most tarnished hour.

During the war all Americans, irrespective of race or religion or ethnic background, had rallied 'round the flag, save only for some Socialists, Industrial Workers of the World, and other elements of the left wing. Thus radicalism was equated with wartime treason, the dissenter identified with the Hun. Scarcely had the United States been saved, despite the radicals' activities, than there loomed the menace of Bolshevism. And in America the advance agents of the Comintern were quite obviously aliens who somehow owed a double allegiance to Germany and Russia. Surely alien agitators were responsible for the massive labor unrest, the Seattle general strike, the Boston police strike, the "Great Steel Strike," and the thousands of additional strikes involving millions of workers in 1919 and 1920. Surely no true American laborer, unless deranged by Bolshevik propaganda, would march in May Day parades or shout, "To hell with the United States!" or join the new Communist and Communist-Labor parties. And certainly only foreigners were capable of the bombings and attempted assassinations of public officials that seemed proof positive of a vast revolutionary conspiracy.

Such was the peril, it was not enough to bar future immigration or patiently instruct foreigners in the meaning of Americanism. Heroic surgery was immediately required to cut out the cancerous growth. The "Great Red Scare" was a time of unparalleled intimidation, suppression, imprisonment, deportation — at the local, state, and federal level — because at no time in American history, either before or since, had the American people been seized by such a collective failure of nerve. It is, therefore, altogether fitting that the most feared nativist movement in American history, the revived Ku Klux Klan, should date its take-off point from the "Great Red Scare." The Klan never articulated an economic program, and capitalism was not mentioned in its constitution; but it is evident that the Klan saw Americanism and radicalism in irreconcilable tension and that at least some elements in the business community supported the order as an ally in the war against all forms of radicalism, including as it happened, labor unions.

Hopefully, the anatomy of the revived Ku Klux Klan is becoming discernible. Far from being a uniquely reprehensible episode in an otherwise sunny American pageant, it was the archetype of nativist movements, the receptacle for nativist themes flowing from the distant American past. Far from being an isolated, ugly phenomenon in an age of wonderful nonsense, it reflected the tensions of an age of revolution and embodied the anxieties of a people convulsed by change. Far from being a membership entirely of society's failures, it embraces many citizens who historically had enjoyed power and prestige, the prerogatives of the nation's senior partners. To repeat a point made earlier, the Klan may best be understood as a counterrevolutionary movement called into being by sober individuals to resist a world they neither made nor admired — nor understood. The Klan adopted as one of its mottos the command attributed to George Washington: "Put none but Americans on guard tonight!" Alas, Klansmen would not acknowledge — indeed, could not bear to acknowledge — that Negroes, Catholics, immigrants, or "radicals" had any rightful claim to the coveted title "American."

In 1927 in the southern Alabama farm country of Crenshaw, a group of Klansmen led by a Baptist minister, L. A. Nalls, flogged a divorcée, the mother of two children, who had married a divorced man. After the whipping the Reverend Nalls offered the consoling sermon: "Sister, you were not punished in anger this evening; you were punished in a spirit of kindness and correction, to set your feet aright and to show your children how a good mother should go." A collection for the woman was taken up among her assailants and the resulting three dollars and fifty cents were given her along with a jar of Vaseline for her wounds. This incident and these words reveal still another color of the chameleon-like Klan: its moral authoritarianism, its vigilantism, and its sadism.

Recent scholarship has demonstrated what must have been self-evident to the victims of the Klan's wrath at the time: the hooded Knights, who took as their motto, "Not for self, but for others," regarded themselves as perfect knights, *sans peur et sans reproche,* and therefore the proper guardians of public virtue and private morality. And in the postwar years, public corruption and private depravity seemed endemic. Is it necessary to explicate this point? Is it mandatory to refer once again to Hemingway's heroes and Fitzgerald's heroines and all the beautiful and the damned of the Lost Generation of the Roaring Twenties? The quips about rising skirts and falling morals and the times being out of joint when the word "neck" abruptly became a verb are not merely surface manifestations of a society that remained at its core stable. Bootleggers, speak-easies, rumrunners, syphilitic gangsters, organized gambling, open prostitution, lurid movies, salacious literature, Sabbath sports, easy divorce, family disintegration, sexy dances, purchased politicians, bought policemen — these things, of course, were not unique to the twenties. Yet a social and moral revolution, already apparent before the war, was in fact dislocating the old nineteenth-century Victorian structure. The acids of modernity were in truth dissolving the old verities of piety, patriotism, and moral purity, reverence for church, country, and home. To older Americans this revolution was as menacing as the rising tide of Negroes, Catholics, aliens, and radicals. Indeed, the strangers in the land (together with the proverbially sexually depraved blacks) had introduced these evils into a formerly chaste society, and now, obviously, even the sons and daughters of the American Revolution were being infected.

Read a Klan handbill: "Every criminal, every gambler, every thug, every libertine, every girl runner, every home wrecker, every wife beater, every dope peddler, every moonshiner, every crooked politician, every pagan Papist priest, every shyster lawyer, every K. of C., every white slaver, every black spider — is fighting the Klan. Think it over. Which side are you on?" In torchlight parades white-robed men (and it probably is not happenstance that white, the emblem of purity, was chosen for the robes) carried signs: LAW AND ORDER MUST PREVAIL. COHABITATION BETWEEN WHITES AND BLACKS MUST STOP. BOOT-LEGGERS, PIMPS, HANGERS-ON, GET RIGHT OR GET OUT. WIFE-BEATERS, FAMILY-DESERTERS, HOME-WRECKERS, WE HAVE NO ROOM FOR YOU. LAW VIOLATORS, WE ARE WATCHING YOU. BEWARE. GO JOY RIDING WITH YOUR OWN WIFE. THE SHERIFFS OF BOWIE AND MILLER COUNTIES HAVE MORE DEPUTIES THAN CARRY COMMISSIONS. PURE WOMENHOOD. CRAP SHOOTERS BEWARE. LOVE THY NEIGHBOR AS THYSELF, BUT LEAVE HIS WIFE ALONE. Although the evidence is fragmentary, it is quite possible that the majority of individuals flogged, tarred and feathered, branded, emasculated, and otherwise tortured and intimidated by the Klan were those who had in some way transgressed morally.

When the Klan proclaimed its opposition to "Jew, Jug, and Jesuit," its intimate relationship to Prohibition was merely underscored. There were millions of prohibitionists, of course, who never became Klansmen, but almost all Klansmen *claimed* to be as dry as a powder flask. The harsh, repressive spirit of Prohibition represented a souring of the original humanitarian passion of the early temperance reformers. Just so, the moral passion of the Kluxers was a perversion rather than a denial of progressivism's vision of a redeemed society.

And so it came to pass that thousands of good, decent citizens, genuinely alarmed by civic corruption and moral decay, failed initially to discern the Klan's own corrupt nature and welcomed it as an agency of reform. And seemingly many a community *was* rid of gamblers, bootleggers, and prostitutes because of the Klan's presence. Exulted the editor of a Texas newspaper: "It cost Goose Creek just $1200 to clean up. It cost the boys down there $1200 in fines assessed for flogging to transform a rough and tumble oil camp into a progressive and God-fearing community of industrious toilers. . . . The Ku Klux Klan has made a new and different town of Goose Creek." After one visit from Klan regulators, it was said, a tough town became "almost a Sunday School class." Vigilantism is, after all, as much a sign of a desire for law and order as it is a manifestation of lawlessness. In America vigilantism was an old and not always dishonorable tradition. In fact, in 1920 and 1921 masked farmers roamed the countryside with lighted torch in order to check the sale of cotton, and their acts of intimidation, however justified, provided an example for the Klan to follow.

The dangers of men taking the law into their own hands, the arrogance of men appointing themselves as civic censors, the voyeurism and prurience implicit in Comstockery, the sadism in the act of stripping and whipping "fallen" women, the temptation to exact personal vengeance in the name of "morality" — these things are no less true because obvious. As Sartre observed, "It is *fun* to be an anti-Semite." Undoubtedly, the Klan attracted cranky professional moralists, village vigilantes, local busybodies, prudish Pecksniffs, old ladies of both sexes haunted (as Mencken sneered) by the fear that someone, somewhere, might be happy. But even Klansmen of the purest conscious motives and highest community status failed to heed the words of George Santayana: "Neither prosperity nor empire nor heaven can be worth the winning at the price of a virulent temper, bloody hands, an anguished spirit, and a vain hatred of the rest of the world." In our effort to understand the Klan we might heed the words of John Higham: "Perhaps, in the pageant of American history, the white-robed Klansmen should stand in the place of Santayana's genteel New Englander as the Last Puritan."

When a Klansman addressed a Catholic priest, "You, who wears his collar backwards like a mule," his audience caught the allusion, for they were steeped in agrarian life and lore, and when they dreamed of the past it was of a pastoral community, a virgin land, inhibited by sturdy yeomen, unspotted by the urban world. But urbanization had come to the United States. In fact, the revived Klan emerged at the precise moment when the tides of population, power, and prestige were running heavily to the city, and at the end of the twenties only 40 per cent of the population still lived in rural areas. There is more than a casual correlation between this demographic change and the Klan's rise. Yet it is not a simple relationship.

Most students interpret the Klan as a rural, village, and small-town phenomenon. This is true less in a statistical than in a psychological sense. The Klan was reborn in Atlanta. It enjoyed great strength in the booming cities of the Southwest: Shreveport, Dallas, Tulsa, Little Rock (but not cosmopolitan New Orleans). The Milwaukee unit was the first and largest in the state of Wisconsin, and Detroit was the center of the Klan's power in Michigan. It was strong in Indianapolis, Chicago,

Dayton, and Pittsburgh in the heartland of America, and on the eastern shore in Norfolk and on the West Coast in Portland. Cities as diverse as Denver, Tampa, and Philadelphia were spawning beds. It is therefore misleading to presume that city dwellers were protected by some invisible *cordon sanitaire* from the virus of the Invisible Empire. Yet it remains essentially correct to identify the Klan with the older agrarian angle of vision.

For one thing, the Klan *was* in fact a force in the villages and small towns dotting the land. For another, there had migrated to the cities farmers and villagers who, regardless of how they might be located for census purposes, retained their rural mentality. They were America's own uprooted, as lost and dislocated as the European immigrant. Stripped of their identity by the externalization, impersonalization, and depersonalization of urban industrial life, they sought desperately to define themselves by clinging to the values of their fathers and perhaps of their own childhood. The Klan had held the hope that men might preserve their ancient, agrarian values even as they now lived in an urban environment. Indeed, it was imperative that these values be imposed on the cities. Thus when Klansmen spoke of redeeming the country, in reality they meant saving the great cities of the nation, for rural and village America had not yet been lost. It was in the cities, dominated by alien hordes and ruled by politicians subservient to their wishes, that there flourished gangsterism, alcoholism, skepticism, radicalism, sexualism — in brief, the paganism that threatened to break forth from the metropolitan centers and engulf the entire land. The very enormity of the challenge heightened the Klansman's anxiety and dictated the extremism of his response.

Just as Klansmen were in the twentieth century but dreamed they were not of it, so they hoped their country somehow could be in the world but not of it. The Klan clearly drew from the wellsprings of nineteenth-century American exceptionalism and isolationism. Equally discernible is its marriage with the mood of disenchantment and bitterness that followed the Great Crusade. It is unnecessary to explicate this point at length. The Klan opposed American membership in the World Court and, at least after 1920, in the League of Nations. It did not favor the reduction of war debts or disarmament, and it loathed pacifism. (However, the Klan did not agitate for intervention in Mexico, a foreign adventure associated with the Catholic hierarchy.) It was the old story of American innocence and European wickedness. Klansmen would have concurred in Ben Hecht's sentiment, if not in his imagery, in comparing Wilson at Versailles among the crafty Old World diplomats to "a long-faced virgin trapped in a bawdy house and calling in violent tones for a glass of lemonade." Once again it must be remarked that the spirit of the Klan fused intimately with the general temper of the 1920's. In its ethnocentrism, provincialism, and inability to accept the facts of twentieth-century life, the Klan mirrored perfectly the notion of Fortress America, a nation whose strength was the strength of ten because its heart was pure. And America's purity could be preserved only in isolation. Alas, the Klan's Manichaean view of the international scene was as murky as its vision of an America divided between the children of light and the children of darkness.

Men who see things in this fashion, who make simplistic judgments and draw sharp distinctions between right and wrong, good and evil, who think in terms of stereotypes and moralisms, tend to be prejudiced. They also tend to be anti-intellectual. Ambiguity, irony, paradox, relativism, contingency, skepticism, suspended judgment, speculation, open-mindedness — these are the attributes of the intellectual's glory (and perhaps the source of his misery). The average Klansman was neither blessed nor cursed by them; the intellectual as Klansman was atypical. Indeed, we are of the conviction that while the Klan appealed to an entire host of Americans, poor and prosperous, disinherited and establishment-secure, southerner and Yankee, farmer, villager, and urbanite, scarcely a single intellectual claimed citizenship in the Invisible Empire. Thus the Klan both perpetuated the pervasive anti-intellectualism in American history and illuminated the growing estrangement in the 1920's between artists and scholars and the commonalty. Hiram Wesley Evans put it pointedly and poignantly:

We are a movement of the plain people, very weak in the matter of culture, intellectual support, and trained leadership. We are demanding, and we expect to win, a return of power into the hands of the everday, not highly cultured, not overly intellectualized, but unspoiled and not de-Americanized, average citizen of the old stock. Our members and leaders are all of this class — the opposition of the intellectuals and liberals who hold the leadership and from whom we expect to wrest control, is almost automatic.

This is undoubtedly a weakness. It lays us open to the charge of being "hicks" and "rubes" and "drivers of second-hand Fords." We admit it. Far worse, it makes it hard for us to state our case and advocate our crusade in the most effective way, for most of us lack skill in languape. . . .

Every popular movement has suffered from just this handicap. . . .

The Klan does not believe that the fact that it is emotional and instinctive, rather than coldly intellectual, is a weakness. All action comes from emotion, rather than from ratiocination. Our emotions and the instincts on which they are based have been bred into us for thousands of years; far longer than reason has had a place in the human brain. . . . They are the foundations of our American civilization, even more than our great historic documents; they can be trusted where the fine-haired reasoning of the de-natured intellectuals cannot.

Thus spoke the spirit of fundamentalism with its repression through anti-evolution laws and heresy trials and textbook censorship of all in modern science and scholarship threatening to a faith made truly blind by ignorance. Thus spoke the spirit of fascism with its appeal to primitive instincts and tribal symbols. Thus spoke mediocre men maddened by the epithet's "yahoo," "boob," and "Babbitt" flung at them by all the sneering Menckens of the "Smart Set." Thus spoke Klansmen in an age when not only were ancient truths questioned, the very existence of Truth itself was coming to be doubted. . . .

Inevitably the Klan entered politics, and invariably it became a divisive and sinister force. At no time did it sponsor or support a third-party movement, but this fact heightened rather than diminished its malevolent influence. A Klan leader justified this political concern: "Everybody knows that politicians nowadays cater to all kinds of 'elements' mostly selfish, some corrupt, and some definitely anti-American. They cater to the German vote, the Catholic vote, the Jewish vote, the Italian vote, the boot-leg vote, the vice vote, and sometimes even to the violently criminal vote. What the Klan intends to do is to make them pay some attention to the American vote, the Protestant Christian vote, and the decent, God-fearing, law-abiding vote." Candidates were expected to certify their adherence to the Klan's definition of "Americanism" and their sympathy for the Invisible Order — or suffer the consequences. Neither unadvisedly nor lightly could politicians afford (as one of them lamented) to "withstand an incalculable impact, of indefinite forces, from an invisible source, and at an unexpected time."

The Klan became a terrible element in state and local politics from North Carolina to California and from Indiana to Texas. It elected governors in Georgia and

Oregon; a United States senator in Texas; congressmen in several states. In Arkansas it was so politically powerful that it held its own primaries. In Oklahoma it impeaced the hostile governor after a struggle reflecting little credit on either side. In Indiana under Stephenson the Klan was the state. In communities throughout the South, Southwest, Midwest, and Pacific Coast whole municipal establishments, literally from mayor to dogcatcher, were Klansmen or subservient to the order. And the Klan's role in the presidential nominations and elections of 1924 and 1928 suggest that the Invisible Empire came perilously close to achieving the status coveted for it by Imperial Wizard Evans, that of a "great militant political organization."

The cast of Klan leaders seems incredible; that is, until we remember that the scenario was shot in the 1920's. The star of the production, albeit a dim and flickering one, was Colonel William Joseph Simmons, whose fevered imagination called the Klan "from its slumber of half a century to take up a new task." Big and hollow, pious and prissy yet profane, genteely attired in rump-sprung britches and diamond stick pin, laden with lodge badges and heavy gold watch chain, breathing a hopefully deceptive mixture of cloves and bourbon, fond of poker and the ladies (his wife was an invalid), this amiable fraud, this "engaging old reprobate," was as "full of sentiment as a plum is full of juice." What made "Doc" Simmons run? He pursued the same light as Jay Gatsby and Sammy Glick (though he would not have approved of the company) as preacher, drummer of ladies' garters, and professional lodge man (he claimed membership in twelve or fifteen fraternal orders). With his Klan, "The World's Greatest Secret, Social, Patriotic, Fraternal, Beneficiary Order," with its membership, raiment, and life-insurance fees, he whiffed at last the sweet smell of success. Oleaginous, mellifluous, lazy yet lovable, vacuous yet sly, he disarmed the American people as he did investigating congressmen with platitude, piety, and pomposity. "Are we the only people that use a mask?" he asked of his inquisitors. "If so, what about Mardi Gras celebrations in this country, and what about Hallowe'en celebrations? . . . Our mask and robe, I say before God, are as innocent as the breath of an angel." Not even Warren G. Harding could have improved on that. And is it unsporting to inquire what sort of man the sovereign citizens of the United States elected to their highest office in 1920, the precise year of Simmons' ascending star?

Simmons' star ascended in 1920 (until that year his Invisible Empire after a struggling half-decade remained almost literally invisible) because he had the wit to tap the wits of two professional promoters, Edward Young Clarke and Mrs. Elizabeth Tyler. Eyeing the main chance, these inelegant hucksters transformed Simmons' easygoing southern fraternity of patriotic whites into a violently aggressive national organization of chauvinistic native-born white Protestants. It is a compliment to their promotional abilities to say Klan membership skyrocketed under their shrewd guidance. It is a commentary on the Klan to say that in 1919 the dubious duo had been arrested, while drunk and undraped, and fined for disorderly conduct; that Clarke deserted his wife before being deserted by the divorced Mrs. Tyler; that in 1923 Clarke was arrested for transporting whisky, and in 1924 he pleaded guilty to violating the White Slave Act. Perhaps in their way Ed Clarke and Mrs. Tyler were as at home in the Jazz Age as the organization they promoted.

In November, 1922, Simmons (and soon Clarke) was pressured out of power in a palace revolution led by a Dallas dentist, Hiram Wesley Evans. Plumpish, moonfaced, spectacled, benign, platitudinous, Evans called himself the "most average man in America." Evans testifies to the banality of evil, to the sinister consequences of a blind sincerity, to the unhappy fact that sobriety and chastity are not incompatible with bigotry and fanaticism. Like another American in the 1920's, Calvin Coolidge, Evans was a "Puritan in Babylon." The country would not have missed the leadership of either "average" man. As for the gross, tough, amoral David C. Stephenson, it is sufficient to observe that had he exchanged roles with Al Capone, neither Chicago nor Indiana would have been the loser — or the winner.

By late 1924 the KKK claimed a membership of four million, perhaps even five million, though most certainly not eight million as one authority estimates. "They just threw the doors open," complained a once dedicated Knight, "and every man that had the money, they took him in just to get his vote. . . . " It was really not a very exclusive fraternity. One needed only to be white, Protestant, and native-born — and willing to part with $10.

The Klan attracted good men, sincerely anxious about the future of "their" country, seemingly imperiled by Negroes, Catholics, aliens, and radicals. It was a godsend to the frustrated and insecure, unconsciously seeking scapegoats for their sense of failure. Weak men joined because their wills were unequal to the community pressures to conform. The Klan carried enormous appeal to lonely men who would join any fraternal order to erase the monotony of daily existence. Political opportunists saw the Klan as the highroad to power. To hucksters, the society spelled "Ku Klux Kash."

> For it's order and trumpet and anger and drum
> And power and glory command you to come;
> The graves shall fly open and let you all in,
> And the earth shall be emptied of mortal sin.
>
> (W. H. AUDEN, "Danse Macabre")

Yet the membership melted away like chilled aspic on a warm summer afternoon. Immigration no longer seemed a threat after the restriction act of 1924. The task was now one of Americanization through education rather than the immediate intimidation and repression of a once ceaseless flow of new aliens. A Negro rebellion had not materialized, and by the late 1920's the black man was again his docile self. Although the U.S.S.R. failed to wither away, the feeble and feckless condition of both labor unions and socialist parties by the middle of the decade suggested that the fires of radicalism in the United States had now been banked. The general prosperity and the coolness (not to say placidity) of the Coolidge era drained reform ardor. Many Klansmen, like many prohibitionists and, for that matter, progressives, said farewell to reform. Ardor gave way to apathy. Or, perhaps, to a feeling of resignation.

Decent citizens drew back in horror as the evidence of the order's indecency mounted. How could the good people of Indiana, for instance, continue to believe in the moral authority of the Klan after Grand Dragon Stephenson's imprisonment? In fact, everywhere Klan leadership proved either weak or obscene. Internal wrangling was endemic. Unlike fascist movements in Europe, the KKK threw up no charismatic Mussolini or Hitler.

Official American Protestantism with increasing firmness rejected the Klan's representation of itself as a great, militant supradenominational agency. The world of journalism was almost uniformly hostile. Anti-Klan riots, anti-mask bills, and counterboycotts intimidated the timid membership. And prudent politicians increasingly learned that the Klan's blessing was a kiss of death. (After all, native-born white Protestants were themselves in many communities a minority group, as the politician recognized when he arranged to have a cross burned in front of *his* home.) Moreover, when the Klan proved unable to dominate either major party, its failure to found a third party became fatal. But, then, how could the order survive politically when it championed not a single *concrete* economic or social reform. Its appeal was essentially negative, and if it played a part (minor, we think) in the defeat of Smith in 1928, more crucial is its failure to prevent his easy nomination in the first instance. The fact of religious pluralism in America, confirmed in the life of John F. Kennedy, was foreshadowed in the career of Al Smith.

To be sure, most Klansmen remained loyal to their exclusive and prideful definition of Americanism, and they continued to cherish their dreams of an older and purer America. But they lost hope in the Klan as the agency of redemption. They were largely unmoved by rational persuasion or moralistic preaching that they had been wrong, and their drift from the Klan represented a rejection of the order itself, but not necessarily of its ideals.

Ultimately, however, the Knights unmasked and dismounted because an even larger number of Americans recalled and honored Abraham Lincoln's indictment of the Know-Nothing party:

> How could I be [a member]? How can any one who abhors the oppression of Negroes, be in favor of degrading classes of white people? Our progress in degeneracy appears to me to be pretty rapid. As a nation we began by declaring that *'all men are created equal.'* We now practically read it 'all men are created equal, *except Negroes.'* When the Know Nothings get control, it will read, 'all men are created equal except Negroes, *and foreigners, and Catholics.'* When it comes to this I should prefer emigrating to some country where they make no pretence of loving liberty — to Russia, for instance. . . .

The Reform Response to the Great Depression

The Great Depression confronted the American democratic system with perhaps the greatest crisis in its history. Beginning with the stock market crash in the fall of 1929, the economy foundered and sank to an unprecedented trough of inactivity: in 1932, national income was less than half of 1929; industrial production fell from an index of 110 in 1929 to 57 in 1932; at least 12 million Americans — one out of four — were unemployed. As the inadequate sources of relief dried up, suffering grew intense. By 1932, probably only a quarter of the jobless were actually on relief. By then nobody seemed to know what to do. America's business leaders, those vaunted men who had laid claim to the brilliant economic successes of the 1920s, offered no answers now; and the Hoover administration had exhausted its bag of tricks. The next act in the drama was not chaos or dictatorship, but the New Deal. A historical event, after it has happened, seems natural and inevitable. (That is one of the tricks history plays on us.) In the case of the New Deal, indeed, the current tendency is to emphasize, not Roosevelt's achievement in fashioning a workable response to the depression, but rather his failure to bring about more thoroughgoing reform and more complete social justice.

Arthur M. Schlesinger's essay, which follows, restores to us the perspective of 1932. He emphasizes the rigidity with which political leaders, in Europe no less than in America, viewed the economic crisis. Caught in the trap of abstract dogma, they insisted that the only choice was between unregulated capitalism and socialism, between old-fashioned liberalism and dictatorship. This was a counsel which, in the end, froze governments into inaction. It was, Schlesinger argues, Franklin D. Roosevelt's great virtue to be free of Hoover's dogmatism, to refuse to be enchained by "either/or." The willingness to experiment was at the heart of the New Deal. Necessarily, the end result lacked intellectual consistency, fell short of success, in many ways — not the least of which was the failure to bring about genuine economic recovery — and distributed its benefits unequally. But if, as Schlesinger contends, the alternative was dogmatic inaction, the New Deal ought rightly to be judged by its partial success rather than its partial failure.

Why was not the New Deal frozen by the same doctrinal consistency that afflicted the traditional political parties both in America and western Europe? Putting aside the intangible element of Roosevelt's personality, Schlesinger argues that the New Deal drew on the experimentalism inherent in American reformism. He and other historians have elsewhere traced the roots of the New Deal in populism and progressivism. Here, however, Schlesinger emphasizes timing. Beneath the surface of normalcy during the 1920s, a new reform wave was gathering force, Schlesinger suggests, and, even without the depression, would have struck the country in the 1930s. So Roosevelt had ready at hand the resources of American reform when he set about erecting the New Deal. The hypothesis is interesting but, as Schlesinger himself acknowledges, highly speculative. For one thing, an emerging reform impulse during the 1920s remains to be proved. And, without the economic crisis to give it direction, would this reformism have been at all comparable to the New Deal? Might it not, indeed, have been the kind of attack on American culture and values that the country is in fact experiencing today?

FOR FURTHER READING:

HOFSTADTER, RICHARD. *The Age of Reform: From Bryan to FDR.* New York: Random House, Vintage Books, 1955.*

ROMASCO, ALBERT U. *The Poverty of Abundance: Hoover the Nation, the Depression.* New York: Oxford University Press, 1965.*

SCHLESINGER, ARTHUR M., JR. *The Crisis of the Old Order.* Vol. 1 from *The Age of Roosevelt.* Boston: Houghton Mifflin Company, Sentry Editions, 1957.*

Asterisk denotes paperback edition.

Sources of the New Deal

ARTHUR M. SCHLESINGER, JR.

In the background of any historical episode lies all previous history. The strands which a historian may select as vital to an understanding of the particular episode will vary widely according to his interest, his temperament, his faith and his time. Each man must unravel the seamless web in his own way. I do not propose here any definitive assessment of the sources of the New Deal. I doubt whether a final assessment is possible. I want rather to call attention to certain possible sources which may not have figured extensively in the conventional accounts, including my own — to the relation of the New Deal to the ebb and flow of American national politics and then its relation to the international dilemma of free society in this century.

Such relationships are speculative; nonetheless, an attempt to see them may perhaps cast light on some of the less discussed impulses behind the New Deal itself. To begin — and in order to make a sharp issue — let me ask this question: would there have been a New Deal if there had been no depression? Without a depression, would we have had nothing but a placid continuation, so long as prosperity itself continued, of the New Era of the Twenties?

I would answer that there would very likely have been some sort of New Deal in the Thirties even without the Depression. I think perhaps our contemporary thinking has come too unreflectively to assume depression as the necessary preliminary for any era of reform. Students of American history know better. The fight against depression was, to be sure, the heart of the New Deal, but it has not been the central issue of traditional American reform: it was not the heart of Jeffersonian democracy nor of Jacksonian democracy nor of the anti-slavery movement nor of the Progressive movement.

What preceded these other epochs of reform was an accumulation of disquietudes and discontents in American society, often non-economic in character, and producing a general susceptibility to appeals for change — this and the existence within so-

---

Source: Arthur M. Schlesinger, Jr., "Sources of the New Deal," *Columbia University Forum,* vol. 2 (Fall 1959), pp. 4–12.

ciety of able men or groups who felt themselves cramped by the status quo and who were capable of exploiting mounting dissatisfaction to advance policies and purposes of their own. This combination of outsiders striving for status and power and a people wearying of the existing leadership and the existing ideals has been the real archetype of American reform.

The official order in the Twenties presented perhaps the nearest we ever came in our history to the identification of the national interest with the interests, values and goals of a specific class — in this case, of course, the American business community. During the generation before Harding, the political leaders who had commanded the loyalties and the energies of the American people — Theodore Roosevelt and Woodrow Wilson — expressed strains in American life distinct from and often opposed to the dominant values of business. They represented a fusion of patrician and intellectual attitudes which saw in public policy an outlet for creative energy — in [Walter] Lippmann's phrase, they stood for mastery as against drift. In the service of this conception, they led the people into great national efforts of various sorts, culminating in the convulsive and terrible experience of war. Two decades of this — two decades under the glittering eyes of such leaders as Roosevelt and Wilson, Bryan and La Follette — left the nation in a state of exhaustion.

By 1920 the nation was tired of public crisis. It was tired of discipline and sacrifice. It was tired of abstract and intangible objectives. It could gird itself no longer for heroic moral or intellectual effort. Its instinct for idealism was spent. "It is only once in a generation," Wilson himself had said, "that a people can be lifted above material things. That is why conservative government is in the saddle two-thirds of the time." And the junior official to whom he made this remark, the young Assistant Secretary of the Navy [FDR], also noted soon after his unsuccessful try for the Vice-Presidency in 1920, "Every war brings after it a period of materialism and conservatism; people tire quickly of ideals and we are now repeating history." John W. Davis, the Democratic candidate in 1924, said a few years later: "The people usually know what they want at a particular time . . . In 1924 when I was a candidate what they wanted was repose."

A nation fatigued with ideals and longing for repose was ready for "normalcy." As popular attention receded from public policy, as values and aspirations became private again, people stopped caring about politics, which meant that political power inevitably gravitated to society's powerful economic interests — the government of the exhausted nation quite naturally fell to the businessmen. And for nearly a decade the business government reigned over a prosperous and expanding country.

Yet, for all the material contentment of the Twenties, the decade was also marked by mounting spiritual and psychological discontent. One could detect abundant and multiplying symptoms of what Josiah Royce, after Hegel, used to call a self-estranged social order. The official creed began to encounter growing skepticism, and even opposition and ridicule, in the community at large. Able and ambitious groups, denied what they considered fitting recognition or opportunity, began to turn against the Establishment.

If the economic crash of 1929 astonished the experts, a spiritual crash was diagnosed well in advance. "By 1927," reported Scott Fitzgerald, "a widespread neurosis began to be evident, faintly signalled, like a nervous beating of the feet, by the popularity of crossword puzzles." In the same year Walter Lippmann pointed more soberly to the growing discrepancy between the nominal political issues of the day and the actual emotions of the people. If politics took up these real issues, Lippmann said, it would revolutionize the existing party system. "It is not surprising, then, that our political leaders are greatly occupied in dampening down interes. in obscuring issues, and in attempting to distract attention from the realities of American life."

What was wrong with the New Era was not (as yet) evidence of incompetence or stupidity in public policy. Rather, there was a profound discontent with the monopoly of power and prestige by a single class and the resulting indifference of the national government to deeper tensions. Those excluded from the magic circle suffered boredom, resentment, irritation and eventually indignation over what seemed the intolerable pretensions and irrelevancies of their masters. Now it is the gravest error to underrate the power of boredom as a factor in social change. Our political scientists have pointed out convincingly how the human tendency toward inertia sets limits on liberalism; I wish they would spend equal time showing how the human capacity for boredom sets limits on conservatism. The dominant official society — the Establishment — of the Twenties was an exceedingly boring one, neither bright nor witty nor picturesque nor even handsome, and this prodded the human impulse to redress the balance by kicking up heels in back streets.

All this encouraged the defection of specific groups from a social order which ignored their needs and snubbed their ambitions. Within the business community itself there were dissident individuals, especially in the underdeveloped areas of the country, who considered that opportunities for local growth were unduly restrained by Wall Street's control of the money market. The farmers felt themselves shut out from the prevailing prosperity. Elements in the labor movement resented their evident second-class citizenship. Members of foreign nationality groups, especially the newer immigration and its children, chafed under the prevalent assumption that the real America was Anglo-Saxon, Protestant, middle-class and white. In time some of the younger people of the nation began to grow restless before the ideals held out to them; while others, in accepting these ideals, acquired a smug mediocrity which even depressed some of their elders.

Gravest among the symptoms was the defection of the intellectuals: writers, educators, newspapermen, editors — those who manned the machinery of opinion and who transmitted ideas. The fact of their particular estrangement and discontent guaranteed the articulation, and thus, to a degree, the coordination of the larger unrest. The intellectuals put the ruling class in its place by substituting for its own admiring picture of itself a set of disrespectful images, which an increasing number of people found delightful and persuasive; the insiders, who had before been seen in the reverent terms of Bruce Barton and the *American Magazine,* were now to be seen less reverently through the eyes of H. L. Mencken and Sinclair Lewis. Satire liberated people from the illusion of business infallibility and opened their minds to other visions of American possibility. The next function of the intellectuals was precisely to explore and substantiate those other visions. They did so with zest and ingenuity; and the result was that, beneath the official crust, the Twenties billowed with agitation, criticism and hope. Dewey affirmed man's capability for social invention and management; Beard argued that intelligent national planning was the irresistible next phase in history; Parrington insisted that Jeffersonian idealism had a sound basis in the American past and, indeed, expressed a truer Americanism than did materialism. Together the satirists and the prophets drew a new portrait of

America — both of the American present and of the American promise — and the increasingly visible discrepancy between what was and what might be in America armed the spreading discontent.

The well of idealism was rising again; energies were being replenished, batteries recharged. Outsiders were preparing to hammer on the gates of the citadel. The 1928 election, in which an Irish Catholic challenged Yankee Protestant supremacy, illustrated the gathering revolt against the Establishment. And, though Hoover won the election, Samuel Lubell has pointed out that "Smith split not only the Solid South but the Republican North as well." Smith carried counties which had long been traditionally Republican; he smashed the Republican hold on the cities; he mobilized the new immigrants. In losing, he polled nearly as many votes as Calvin Coolidge had polled in winning four years before. He stood for the vital new tendencies of politics; and it is likely that the prolongation of these tendencies would have assured a national Democratic victory, without a depression, in 1932 or certainly by 1936. And such a Democratic victory would surely have meant the discharge into public life of able and ambitious people denied preference under a business administration — much the same sort of people, indeed, who eventually came to power with the New Deal; and it would have meant new opportunities for groups that had seen the door slammed in their faces in the Twenties — labor, the farmers, the ethnic minorities, the intellectuals.

The suspicion that a political overturn was due even without a depression is fortified, I think, by the calculations of my father in his essay of some years back "The Tides of National Politics." In this essay he proposed that liberal and conservative periods in our national life succeed themselves at intervals of about fifteen or sixteen years; this alternation takes place, he wrote, without any apparent correlation with economic circumstances or, indeed, with anything else, except the ebb and flow of national political psychology. By this argument, a liberal epoch was due in America around 1934 or 1935, depression or no.

In short, the New Deal was, among other things, an expression of what would seem — to use a currently unfashionable concept — an inherent cyclical rhythm in American politics. The Depression did not cause the cycle: what the Depression did was to increase its intensity and deepen its impact by superimposing on the normal cycle the peculiar and unprecedented urgencies arising from economic despair. One might even argue — though I do not think I would — that the Depression coming at another stage in the cycle would not necessarily have produced a New Deal. It is certainly true, as I said, that depressions did not induce epochs of reform in 1873 or in 1893. I think myself, however, that the magnitude of the shock made a political recoil almost certain after 1929. still, the fact that this recoil took a liberal rather than a reactionary turn may well be due to the accident that the economic shock coincided with a liberal turn in the political cycle.

In any event, the fact remains that the historical New Deal, whether or not something like it might have come along anyway, was after all brought into being by the Depression. It assumed its particular character as it sought to respond to the challenge of economic collapse. And, in confronting this challenge, it was confronting a good deal more than merely an American problem. Mass unemployment touched the very roots of free institutions everywhere. "This problem of unemployment," as Winston Churchill said in England in 1930, "is the most torturing that can be presented to civilized society." The problem was more than torturing; it was something civilized society had to solve if it was to survive. And the issue presented with particular urgency was whether representative democracy could ever deal effectively with it.

Churchill, in the same Romanes lecture at Oxford in 1930, questioned whether it could: democratic governments, he said, drifted along the lines of least resistance, took short views, smoothed their path with platitudes, and paid their way with sops and doles. Parliaments, he suggested, could deal with political problems, but not with economic. "One may even be pardoned," Churchill said, "for doubting whether institutions based on adult suffrage could possibly arrive at the right decisions upon the intricate propositions of modern business and finance." These were delicate problems requiring specialist treatment. "You cannot cure cancer by a majority. What is wanted is a remedy."

The drift of discussion in the United States as well as in Britain in the early Thirties revealed an increasingly dour sense of existing alternatives; on the one hand, it seemed, was parliamentary democracy with economic chaos; on the other, economic authoritarianism with political tyranny. Even more dour was the sense that history had already made the choice — that the democratic impulse was drained of vitality, that liberalism was spent as a means of organizing human action. Consider a selection of statements from American writers at the time, and their mortuary resonance:

> The rejection of democracy is nowadays regarded as evidence of superior wisdom. (Ralph Barton Perry)
> The moral and intellectual bankruptcy of liberalism in our time needs no demonstration. It is as obvious as rain and as taken for granted. (Nathaniel Peffer)
> To attempt a defense of democracy these days is a little like defending paganism in 313 or the divine right of kings in 1793. It is taken for granted that democracy is bad and that it is dying. (George Boas)
> "Liberalism is dead." So many people who seem to agree upon nothing else have agreed to accept these three sweeping words. (Joseph Wood Krutch)
> Modern Western civilization is a failure. That theory is now generally accepted. (Louise Maunsell Fields)
> Why is it that democracy has fallen so rapidly from the high prestige which it had at the Armistice? . . . Why is it that in America itself — in the very temple and citadel of democracy — self-government has been held up to every ridicule, and many observers count it already dead? (Will Durant)

Only the most venerable among us can remember the creeping fear of a quarter of a century ago that the free system itself had run out of energy, that we had reached, in a phrase Reinhold Niebuhr used as a part of the title of a book in 1934, the "end of an era." What this pessimism implied for the realm of public policy was that democracy had exhausted its intellectual and moral resources, its bag of tricks was played out, and salvation now lay in moving over to a system of total control.

In affirming that there was no alternative between laissez-faire and tyranny, the pessimists were endorsing a passionate conviction held both by the proponents of individualism and the proponents of collectivism. Ogden Mills spoke with precision for American conservatives: "We can have a free country or a socialistic one. We cannot have both. Our economic system cannot be half free and half socialistic . . .

There is no middle ground between governing and being governed, between absolute sovereignty and liberty, between tyranny and freedom." Herbert Hoover was equally vehement: "Even partial regimentation cannot be made to work and still maintain live democratic institutions." in such sentiments, Hoover and Mills would have commanded the enthusiastic assent of Stalin and Mussolini. The critical question was whether a middle way was possible — a mixed system which might give the state more power than conservatives would like, enough power, indeed, to assure economic and social security, but still not so much as to create dictatorship. To this question the Hoovers, no less than the Stalins and Mussolinis, had long since returned categorical answers. They all agreed on this, if on nothing else: no.

As I have said, economic planning was not just an American problem. Great Britain, for example, was confronting mass unemployment and economic stagnation; moreover, she had had since 1929 a Labor government. In a sense, it would have been hard to select a better place to test the possibilities of a tranquil advance from laissez-faire capitalism to a managed society. Here was a Labor leadership, sustained by a faith in the "inevitability of gradualness," ruling a nation committed by tradition and instinct to the acceptance of empirical change. How did the British Labor government visualize its problem and opportunity?

The central figures in the Labor government of 1929 were Ramsay MacDonald, now Prime Minister for the second time, and Philip Snowden, his sharp and dominating Chancellor of the Exchequer. Both were classical Socialists who saw in the nationalization of basic industry the answer to all economic riddles. Yet in the existing political situation, with a slim Labor majority, nationalization was out of the question. With socialism excluded, MacDonald and Snowden — indeed, nearly all the Labor party leaders — could see no alternative to all-out socialism but nearly all-out laissez-faire. A capitalist order had to be operated on capitalist principles. The economic policy of the Labor government was thus consecrated as faithfully as that of Herbert Hoover's Republican administration in the United States to the balanced budget and the gold standard — and, far more faithfully than American Republicanism, to free trade.

Socialism across the Channel was hardly more resourceful. As the German Social Democrat Fritz Naphtali put it in 1930, "I don't believe that we can do very much, nor anything very decisive, from the point of view of economic policy, to overcome the crisis until it has run its course." In this spirit of impotence, the democratic Socialists of Europe (until Léon Blum came to power some years later) denied the possibility of a middle way and concluded that, short of full socialization, they had no alternative but to accept the logic of laissez-faire.

The assumption that there were two absolutely distinct economic orders, socialism and capitalism, expressed, of course, an unconscious Platonism — a conviction that the true reality lay in the theoretical essences of which any working economy, with its compromises and confusions, could only be an imperfect copy. If in the realm of essences socialism and capitalism were separate phenomena based on separate principles, then they must be kept rigorously apart on earth. Nor was this use of Platonism — this curious belief that the abstraction was somehow more real than the reality, which Whitehead so well called the "fallacy of misplaced concreteness" — confined to doctrinaire capitalists and doctrinaire socialists. The eminent Liberal economist Sir William Beveridge, director of the London School of Economics, braintruster for the Lloyd George welfare reforms before the First World War, spoke for enlightened economic opinion when he identified the "inescapable fatal danger" confronting public policy in the Depression as "the danger of mixing freedom and control. We have to decide either to let production be guided by the free play of prices or to plan it socialistically from beginning to end . . . Control and freedom do not mix." Beveridge, encountering Donald Richberg in Washington in the glowing days of 1933, asked a bit patronizingly whether Richberg really believed that there was "a half-way between Wall Street and Moscow." as for Britain, "there is not much that anyone can do now to help us," Beveridge said. "We must plan to avoid another crisis later. We shall not by conscious effort escape this one."

So dogma denied the possibility of a managed capitalism. But could dogma hold out in Britain against the urgencies of depression? Some Englishmen dissented from the either/or philosophy. In the general election of 1929, for example, John Maynard Keynes and Hubert Henderson had provided the Liberal party with the rudiments of an expansionist policy, based on national spending and public works. As unemployment increased in 1930, so too did the pressure for positive government action. That year Sir Oswald Mosley, a member of the Labor government, proposed to a cabinet committee on unemployment an active program of government spending, accompanied by controls over banking, industry and foreign trade. But he could make no impression on the capitalist orthodoxy of the Socialist leaders; Snowden rejected the Mosley memorandum. Another minister suggested leaving the gold standard; Snowden covered him with scorn. To the party conference of 1930, MacDonald said, "I appeal to you to go back to your Socialist faith. Do not mix that up with pettifogging patching, either of a Poor Law kind or Relief Work kind." In other words, socialism meant all or — in this case — nothing!

As economic pressure increased, more and more had to be sacrificed to the balancing of the budget; and the implacable retrenchment meant more governmental economy, reduction in salaries, reduction in normal public works, until, in time, the frenzy for economy threatened the social services and especially the system of unemployment payments on which many British workers relied to keep alive. The summer crisis of 1931, after the failure of *Kreditanstalt,* weakened the pound; and to Snowden and the Labor government nothing now seemed more essential than staying on the gold standard. To keep Britain on gold required American loans; American loans would not be forthcoming unless satisfactory evidence existed of a determination to balance the budget; and the evidence most likely to satisfy J. P. Morgan and Company, which was arranging the American credit, was a cut in unemployment benefits.

In August 1931, MacDonald and Snowden confronted the cabinet with this dismal logic. Arthur Henderson made it clear that the whole cabinet absolutely accepted Snowden's economic theory: "We ought to do everything in our power to balance the Budget." But MacDonald's proposal for a cut in the dole seemed downright wrong; the Labor government fell. MacDonald soon returned to office as head of a National government. The new government, slightly more adventurous than its predecessors, took Britain off gold in a few weeks. Sidney Webb, Labor's senior intellectual, provided the Labor government its obituary: "No one ever told *us* we could do that!"

The Labor government having immobilized itself by its intellectual conviction that there was no room for maneuver, no middle way, now succeeded through its collapse in documenting its major premise. Then the experience of 1931 displayed the Right as too hardboiled ever to acquiesce in even the most gradual democratic change. "The attempt to give a social bias to capitalism, while leaving it master of the house," wrote R. H. Tawney, "appears to have failed."

If piecemeal reforms were beyond the power of the Labor government, as they were beyond the desire of a Tory government, then the only hope lay in the rapid achievement of full socialism; the only way socialism could be achieved seemed to be through ruthlessness on the Left as great as that on the Right. Such reasoning was responsible for the lust for catastrophic change that suffused the British Left and infected part of the American Left in the early Thirties. No one drew more facile and sweeping conclusions than Harold Laski. The fate of the MacDonald government, Laski wrote, was "tantamount to an insistence that if socialists wish to secure a state built upon the principles of their faith, they can only do so by revolutionary means."

From this perspective Laski and those like him quite naturally looked with derision on the advocate of the middle way. In December 1934, for the perhaps somewhat baffled readers of *Redbook* magazine, Laski debated with Maynard Keynes whether America could spend its way to recovery. Public spending, Laski said with horror, would lead to inflation or heavy taxation or waste; it would mean, he solemnly wrote, "an unbalanced budget with the disturbance of confidence (an essential condition of recovery) which this implies": it would bequeath a "bill of staggering dimensions" to future generations. "Government spending as anything more than a temporary and limited expedient," he concluded, "will necessarily do harm in a capitalist society." This was, of course, not only the argument of Ramsay MacDonald but of Herbert Hoover; Laski's novelty was to use it to defend, not a balanced budget and the gold standard, but — socialist revolution.

One way or another, the British Left began to vote against liberal democracy. Sir Oswald Mosley, who had championed the most constructive economic program considered within the MacDonald government, indicated the new direction when, with John Strachey and others, he founded the authoritarian-minded New Party in 1931. Mosley's excesses soon led him toward fascism and discredit; but plenty of others were reaching similar conclusions about the impossibility of reform under capitalism. Sidney and Beatrice Webb abandoned Fabianism for the mirage of a new civilization in the Soviet Union. All peaceful roads to progress seemed blocked. After a visit with Roosevelt in Washington, [Stafford] Cripps wrote, "My whole impression is of an honest anxious man faced by an impossible task — humanizing capitalism and making it work." "The one thing that is not inevitable now," said Cripps, "is gradualness."

Both Right and Left — Hoover and Stalin, John W. Davis and Mussolini, Ogden Mills and Stafford Cripps — thus rejected the notion of a socially directed and managed capitalism, of a mixed economy, of something in between classical free enterprise and classical socialism. And the either/or demonstration commanded considerable respect in the United States — self-evidently on the American Right; and to some degree on the American Left. So Laski had made clear in *Democracy in Crisis* that the American ruling class would be as tough and hopeless as any other:

> What evidence is there, among the class which controls the destiny of America, of a will to make the necessary concessions? Is not the execution of Sacco and Vanzetti, the long indefensible imprisonment of Mooney, the grim history of American strikes, the root of the answer to that question?

In 1932 both Right and Left thus stood with fierce intransigence on the solid ground of dogma. In so doing, they were challenging an essential part of the American liberal tradition. When Professor Rexford G. Tugwell of the Columbia University economics department, on leave in Washington, revisited his campus in 1933, he rashly bragged of the New Deal's freedom from "blind doctrine," and the *Columbia Spectator,* then edited by a brilliant young undergraduate named James Wechsler, seized on this boast as the fatal weakness of Tugwell's argument and of the whole New Deal. "This is the crux of the problem," the *Spectator* said; "the blind stumbling in the most chaotic fashion — experimenting from day to day — without any anchor except a few idealistic phrases — is worthless. It is merely political pragmatism."

Merely political pragmatism — to ideologists, whether of Right or of Left, this seemed conclusive evidence of intellectual bankruptcy. As the conservatives had said that any attempt to modify the capitalist system must mean socialism, so the radicals now said that any attempt to maintain the capitalist system must mean fascism. "Roosevelt's policies can be welded into a consistent whole," wrote I. F. Stone, "only on the basis of one hypothesis . . . that Mr. Roosevelt intends to move toward fascism." "The essential logic of the New Deal," wrote Max Lerner, "is increasingly the naked fist of the capitalist state."

Convinced of the fragility of the system, the radicals saw themselves as the forerunners of apocalypse. "American commercial agriculture is doomed," wrote Louis Hacker; capitalism was doomed, too, and the party system, and the traditional American way of life. In 1934 Sidney Hook, James Burnham, Louis Budenz, V. F. Calverton, James Rorty and others addressed "An Open Letter to American Intellectuals." "We cannot by some clever Rooseveltian trick," the letter warned,

> evade the unfolding of basic economic and political developments under capitalism . . . Let us not deceive ourselves that we shall not have to face here also the choice between reaction, on the one hand, and a truly scientific economy under a genuine worker's democracy on the other.

In 1935 *The New Republic* stated with magisterial simplicity the argument of the radicals against the New Dealers, of New York against Washington, of the Marxists against the pragmatists.

> Either the nation must put up with the confusions and miseries of an essentially unregulated capitalism, or it must prepare to supersede capitalism with socialism. *There is no longer a feasible middle course.*

Both radicalism and conservatism thus ended in the domain of either/or. The contradictions of actuality, which so stimulated the pragmatists of Washington, only violated the proprieties and offended the illusions of the ideologists. While they all saw themselves as hardheaded realists, in fact they were Platonists, preferring essence to existence and considering abstractions the only reality.

The great central source of the New Deal, in my judgment, lay precisely in the instinctive response of practical, energetic, and compassionate people to those dogmatic absolutes. This passion to sacrifice reality to doctrine presented a profound challenge to the pragmatic nerve. Many Americans, refusing to be intimidated by abstractions or to be overawed by ideology, responded by doing things. The whole point of the New Deal lay in its belief in activism, its faith in gradualness, its rejection of catastrophism, its indifference to ideology, its convention that a managed and modified capitalist order achieved by piecemeal experiment could combine personal freedom and economic growth. "In a world in which revolutions just now are coming easily," said Adolf Berle, "the New Deal chose the more difficult course of moderation and rebuilding." "The course that the new Administration did take," said Harold Ickes, "was the hardest course. It conformed to no theory, but it did fit into the American system — a system of taking action step by step, a system of regulation only to meet concrete needs, a system of courageous recognition of change." Tugwell, rejecting laissez-faire and communism, spoke of the "third course."

Roosevelt himself, of course, was the liberal pragmatist *par excellence.* His aim was to steer between the extremes of chaos and tyranny by moving always, in his phrase, "slightly to the left of center." "Unrestrained individualism," he wrote, had proved a failure; yet "any paternalistic system which tries to provide for security for everyone from above only calls for an impossible task and a regimentation utterly uncongenial to the spirit of our people." He constantly repeated Macaulay's injunction to reform if you wished to preserve.

Roosevelt had no illusions about revolution. Mussolini and Stalin seemed to him, in his phrase, "not mere distant relatives" but "blood brothers." When Emil Ludwig asked him his "political motive," he replied, "My desire is to obviate revolution . . . I work in a contrary sense to Rome and Moscow." He said during the 1932 campaign:

> Say that civilization is a tree which, as it grows, continually produces rot and dead wood. The radical says: "Cut it down." The conservative says: "Don't touch it." The liberal compromises: "Let's prune, so that we lose neither the old trunk nor the new branches." This campaign is waged to teach the country to march upon its appointed course, the way of change, in an orderly march, avoiding alike the revolution of radicalism and the revolution of conservatism.

I think it would be a mistake to underestimate the extent to which this pragmatic attitude was itself a major source of New Deal vitality. The exaltation of the middle way seems banal and obvious enough today. Yet the tyranny of dogma was such in the early years of the Great Depression that infatuation with ideology blocked and smothered the instinctive efforts of free men to work their own salvation. In a world intoxicated with abstractions, Roosevelt and the New Dealers stood almost alone in a stubborn faith in rational experiment, in trial and error. No one understood this more keenly than the great English critic of absolutes; Keynes, in an open letter to Roosevelt at the end of 1933, stated the hopes generated by the New Deal with precision and eloquence. "You have made yourself," Keynes told Roosevelt,

> the trustee for those in every country who seek to mend the evils of our condition by reasoned experiment within the framework of the existing social system. If you fail, rational choice will be gravely prejudiced throughout the world, leaving orthodoxy and revolution to fight it out. But, if you succeed, new and bolder methods will be tried everywhere, and we may date the first chapter of a new economic era from your accession to office.

The question remains: why did the New Deal itself have the pragmatic commitment? Why, under the impact of depression, was it not overborne by dogma as were most other governments and leaders in the world? The answer to this lies, I suspect, in the point I proposed earlier — in the suggestion that the New Deal represented, not just a response to depression, but also a response to pent-up frustrations and needs in American society — frustrations and needs which would have operated had there been no depression at all. The periodic demand for forward motion in

American politics, the periodic breakthrough of new leadership — these were already in the works before the Depression. Depression, therefore, instead of catching a nation wholly unprepared, merely accelerated tendencies toward change already visible in the national community. The response to depression, in short, was controlled and tempered by the values of traditional American experimentalism, rather than those of rigid ideology. The New Deal was thus able to approach the agony of mass unemployment and depression in the pragmatic spirit, in the spirit which guaranteed the survival rather than the extinction of freedom, in the spirit which in time rekindled hope across the world that free men could manage their own economic destiny.

The New Deal in Action

Given a depression crisis beyond the capacity of existing doctrine to handle, Franklin D. Roosevelt took office in March 1933 with one overriding advantage: his freedom from dogmatism. This made action possible. But it did not prescribe what it should be. The programs that we call the New Deal were constructed ultimately of several elements. One was the pragmatic determination to relieve, in a direct way, the suffering of the unemployed and the dispossessed. Another was the broad range of ideas and proposals that jostled one another within the administration. But, probably more important than anything else was the political vision that Roosevelt cherished. This vision James MacGregor Burns calls the "politics of the broker state." Roosevelt attempted to set himself up as President of all the people, above partisanship or identification with any one set of interests. From this vantage point, he would seek to mediate among contending groups in the national interest; government programs would incorporate the proposals of private interests and require their cooperation. The cornerstone measures of the early New Deal — the NRA and the AAA — both exemplified this mode of operation.

Roosevelt intended, Burns argues, to follow a middle course. Implemented by his immense political talents, he assumed that this centrism would hold the adherence of all, save those on the extreme left and right. But Roosevelt was wrong. For reasons that puzzled him then and have fascinated historians ever since, business turned decisively against the New Deal. On the other hand, agitation from the likes of Father Coughlin and Huey Long, plus the growing power of labor developed pressures from the left, greater than Roosevelt had anticipated. FDR was not thereby radicalized, Burns contends, but he did, in his flexible way, respond to this flow of events. The result was a definite move leftward in the mid-1930s. This was the point at which the New Deal received its progressive cast. Even so, no ideological apparatus emerged; and Roosevelt himself never thought he had abandoned his original purposes and mode of operation.

Broker politics thus resulted in a curious shift in emphasis. Not so much Roosevelt himself, as a variety of contending interests and developing events shaped the New Deal. Roosevelt played a crucial role, of course, but as *presiding* influence, not as determining one. Indeed, in so key a New Deal measure as the Wagner Act, which gave labor the right to organize and engage in collective bargaining, success occurred more in spite of, than because of Roosevelt. Broker politics had important shortcomings. It tended to leave out the least organized and least vocal. For all the reforms that it permitted, it was a poor way to come to grips with the underlying economic problems — the New Deal never did bring about recovery — and, from a radical's standpoint, it, of course, frustrated basic social change. Nevertheless, broker politics was Roosevelt's masterstroke, for it perfectly matched his experimental philosophy. Given his lack of faith in doctrinal answers to the economic crisis, Roosevelt created an arena in which a variety of American forces and ideas might contend and evolve a response to the depression. This was the essence of the New Deal, and broker politics was the operational method.

FOR FURTHER READING:

CONKIN, PAUL K. *The New Deal.* New York: Thomas Y. Crowell Company, 1967.*

HAWLEY, ELLIS W. *The New Deal and the Problem of Monopoly.* Princeton: Princeton University Press, 1966.*

LEUCHTENBERG, WILLIAM. *Franklin D. Roosevelt and the New Deal.* New York: Harper & Row, Publishers, Torchbooks, 1963.*

SCHLESINGER, ARTHUR M., JR. *The Coming of the New Deal.* Vol. 2 from *The Age of Roosevelt.* Boston: Houghton Mifflin Company, Sentry Editions, 1959.*

————. *The Politics of Upheaval.* Vol. 3 from *The Age of Roosevelt.* Boston: Houghton Mifflin Company, Sentry Editions, 1960.*

Asterisk denotes paperback edition.

From *Roosevelt: The Lion and the Fox*   JAMES MacGREGOR BURNS

During the first half of his first term Roosevelt tried a Grand Experiment in government. He took the role of national father, of bipartisan leader, of President of all the people. Playing this role with consummate skill, he extracted from it the last morsel of political power and government action. Eventually his biparty leadership was to falter, and he would turn in new directions. But during these first two years, 1933 and 1934, he savored the heady feeling of rising above parties and groups and acting almost as a constitutional monarch armed with political power.

The New Deal, the President told a Wisconsin crowd in August 1934, "seeks to cement our society, rich and poor, manual worker and brain worker, into a voluntary brotherhood of freemen, standing together, striving together, for the common good of all." Such government would not hurt honest business, he said; in seeking social justice it would not rob Peter to pay Paul. Government, he told a convention of bankers two months later, was "essentially the outward expression of the unity and leadership of all groups." His own role as president? It was "to find among many discordant elements that unity of purpose that is best for the Nation as a whole." Throughout Roosevelt's speeches of 1934 ran this theme of government as conciliator, harmonizer, unifier of all major interests. He was the master broker among the many interests of a great and diverse people.

As president of all the people Roosevelt tried to stay above the political and ideological battles that raged all around him. Insisting that he did not want to be drawn into controversy, he asked his supporters to take over the burden of answering attacks on the New Deal from the extreme right or left. He was forever acting as umpire between warring administrators or congressmen. When his advisers differed over policy he time and again ordered: "Put them in a room together, and tell them no lunch until they agree!" When Tugwell and Senator Copeland were at swords' points over food and drug legislation, the President suggested that they battle it out

---

Source: James MacGregor Burns, *Roosevelt: The Lion and the Fox* (New York: Harcourt, Brace & World, 1956), pp. 183–185, 191–197, 205–208, 218–226.

---

together while he sat in and held the sponge. He told his agency chiefs that he was operating between the 15 per cent on the extreme left and the 15 per cent on the extreme right who were opposing him for political reasons or "from pure cussedness." He insisted that he was going neither right nor left — just down the middle.

The country enjoyed a brief era of good feelings, and presiding jauntily over the era was Roosevelt himself. While the New Deal came in for some sharp criticism, everybody, it seemed, loved the President. William Randolph Hearst was a guest at the White House. The Scripps-Howard newspapers lauded his New Deal. Pierre Du Pont and other businessmen wrote him friendly letters. Farm leaders rallied to the cause. "To us," wrote Ed O'Neal of the American Farm Bureau Federation, "you are the Andrew Jackson of the Twentieth Century, championing the rights of the people. . . ." Father Coughlin defended him. William Green and other leaders of labor had little but words of praise for the man in the White House. Across the seas a man who seemed to love nobody had a good word for him. "I have sympathy with President Roosevelt," remarked Adolf Hitler in mid-1933, "because he marches straight to his objective over Congress, over lobbies, over stubborn bureaucracies."

Some Democrats could not understand Roosevelt's nonpartisan line. When one of them naïvely suggested early in 1934 that the President come to a celebration for the Democratic party's patron saint, the President gently rebuked him. He would take no part in Jefferson Day celebrations that year: "Our strongest plea to the country in this particular year of grace," he said, "is that the recovery and reconstruction program is being accomplished by men and women of all parties — that I have repeatedly appealed to Republicans as much as to Democrats to do their part." Much as he loved Jefferson, it would be better if "nonpartisan Jefferson dinners" should be held, with as many Republicans as Democrats on the banquet committees. He made no objection to a nationwide tribute to himself on the occasion of his birthday, in the interest of crippled children.

Republican party leaders were perplexed too. During the first months they were content to mute their protests and to bask in the patriotic posture of "country before party." But slowly the party emerged from its torpor. Its task was formidable at best. Republican leadership had been decimated in two national elections. Living almost in oblivion, Hoover was a scapegoat even for his own party, and the Republican leaders in Congress seemed pedestrian and heavy-footed next to the lustrous, fast-moving figure in the White House. By early 1934 they were trying hard to act as a real opposition party.

But what were they to oppose? A cardinal aspect of Roosevelt's nonpartisanship was his quarterbacking now on the right, now on the left, now down the center of the political field. As in the 1932 campaign, he did not leave an opening at either end of his line through which the Republicans could try to carry the ball. Indeed, the Grand Old Party itself tended to split into factions to the right and to the left of the President's erratic middle-of-the-road course. Despite their minority position in the party, the progressive Republicans like Norris and McNary had the advantage of White House smiles and favors.

A remarkable aspect of this situation was that Roosevelt continued in 1934 to take a more moderate and conservative stand on policy than did the majority of congressmen. On silver, on inflation, on mortgage refinancing, on labor, on spending, Congress was to the left of the President. In contrast with later periods, Roosevelt's main job in 1933 and 1934 was not to prod Congress into action, but to ride the congressional whirlwind by disarming the extremists, by seeking unity among the blocs, and by using every presidential weapon of persuasion and power. . . .

The Broker State at Work

If the New Deal had circus-like qualities during the first years, the center ring was occupied by the National Recovery Administration, and the ringmaster presented a fresh new visage on the American scene. General Hugh S. Johnson looked like the old cavalry man that he was; he had a hard, leathery face, squint eyes, and a rough bark of a voice, but underneath, curious qualities crowded one another: he was a sentimentalist, an old hand with businessmen and business ways, a West Pointer, and as mercurial and picturesque as a sideshow barker. Although Johnson's long-time boss Bernard Baruch rated him as only a "good No. 2 man," the general impressed the President enough to win the job of running the biggest experiment in peacetime governmental control of the economy that America had ever seen.

Johnson's main task was to induce businessmen to draw up codes of fair competition, which on the President's approval had the full force of law. Administered under the general's supervision by a code authority in each industry, the codes were supposed to stop wasteful competition, to bring about more orderly pricing and selling policies, and to establish higher wages, shorter hours, and better working conditions for workers. Antitrust policies would be softened so that businessmen could co-operate in setting up the codes. Johnson had expected to administer the vast public works section of the bill too, but at the last minute Roosevelt put this under Ickes. So furious was the general that he threatened to quit the whole business then and there; the President asked Miss Perkins to "stick with Hugh and keep him sweet," which she did by driving him for hours around Washington until he mastered himself and promised to go on with his part of the job.

And a job it was. Within weeks the NRA burst on the American people like a national call to arms. The NRA eagle was suddenly in every shop window, on magazine covers, in the movies, on girls in chorus lines. Rushing from city to city in an army plane, issuing pronunciamentos at every stop, Johnson orated, politicked, wisecracked, coaxed businessmen into signing codes drawn up by industry representatives hurriedly collected in Washington. The general became the symbol of recovery; for hours he reviewed a climactic parade up Fifth Avenue, trying desperately to greet the endless river of humanity without appearing to give the despised Mussolini salute. Not since 1917 had the whole nation savored such a throbbing sense of unity, of marching together.

But marching where? Almost at the start the President had virtually lost control of the NRA. He told the cabinet one day how Johnson, coattails standing out behind, had rushed into his office, and handed the President three codes to sign. As Roosevelt was signing the last one, Johnson looked at his watch, said he had five minutes to catch his plane, and dashed out, the codes in his pocket. "He hasn't been seen since," Roosevelt added brightly. The President was hardly more than a front man in whose name an elaborate re-employment agreement was arranged and a thousand other actions taken. Johnson himself had to delegate huge policy-making powers to hastily summoned businessmen who might or might not be representative of the myriad interests in their industries. And in the first flush of enthusiasm the NRA coverage was extended so far that the machinery was nearly swamped. An extreme case was the St. Louis bootblack who signed the re-employment agreement, cut his hours to forty a week, and promptly asked the NRA to make up his pay.

The NRA was essentially an expression of the broker state — that is, of the government acting for, and mediating among, the major interest groups. The NRA was the institutional expression of Roosevelt's plan for a partnership of all groups, achieved through friendly co-operation between the government and group leaders. But who were the leaders? It was not surprising that in the haste and confusion Johnson dealt with the business and labor leaders closest at hand, those who were most vocal, best organized, most experienced in dealing with politicians and bureaucrats. Who could speak for that amorphous group, the consumers? A Consumers' Advisory Board was set up but was eased to one side; a member quit indignantly within a few weeks of its establishment.

By the end of 1933 the NRA eagle was fluttering through heavy weather. "N.R.A. is the worst law ever passed," some disillusioned Cleveland grocers wired the President. "N.R.A. means National Run Around," read a labor placard hoisted by a Baltimore picket line. Protests rose in Congress. William Connery, chairman of the House Labor Committee, asked Roosevelt to tell Johnson to work with "true representatives" of labor. Roosevelt answered patiently that as one "a great deal older than you" he advised the Congressman not to overstate his case. "Most of us who consider ourselves liberals have the same ultimate objective in view. . . ." But the President could not ignore the protests. In March 1934 he appointed a review board under the old reformer and defense attorney Clarence Darrow, which soon was reporting that the codes had allowed the more powerful interests to seize control or extend their control of industries. Roosevelt trimmed NRA's powers, limited its jurisdiction, eased Johnson out, and put a more domesticated chief, Donald Richberg, in his place. But by the time the Supreme Court administered the *coup de grâce* shortly before NRA's second birthday, it was near administrative and political collapse.

If NRA was the mainspring of the New Deal in shop and factory, the Agricultural Adjustment Act was its counterpart on the farm. The object of the measure was to restore farm prices to parity — to the relationship, that is, they bore to nonagricultural prices in the years 1909 to 1914. To reach this goal, processing taxes were to be levied equal to the difference between the actual prices and parity. The money raised was to finance restriction of production either by renting land and keeping it out of production or by paying benefits to farmers in return for their agreement to reduce production — "to kill every third pig or plow every third row under," as the newspapers were soon putting it. But like the NRA, Triple-A was soon revealing the insuperable problems of Roosevelt's middle way.

The act bore telltale marks of its birth pangs. It was drawn up by spokesmen from the larger farm organizations and the farm journals, under the direction of Henry Wallace. The viewpoint of the larger commercial farmers, organized in the American Farm Bureau Federation and the National Grange, had the most weight in the early, vital policy-making process, while the Farmers Union, generally embracing the smaller farmers on more marginal land, and inheriting the old Populist tradition, was scarcely represented. Millions of farmers belonged to no organization at all; they could not afford the dues, they lacked the time, they could not travel fifty miles to meetings. And no real organization even existed for countless farm laborers on vast Middle Western farms, southern sharecroppers, illiterate farm hands, and migratory workers following the crops in battered Model-T Fords. Dirt farmers, rough in speech and countenance, returned from Washington deriding the men in neckties and white shirts they had seen testifying for the AAA bill.

Growers of "basic" crops covered by the act, such as wheat, cotton, corn, and to-bacco, got quick benefits from the federal checks handed out in return for crop limi-tation. On other farmers the only effect of the program was to raise their hopes and expectations. By fall Roosevelt admitted that the West was seething with unrest. A letter from a Minnesota farmer named Olson to Eleanor Roosevelt poignantly illus-trated the agricultural situation.

Painfully scrawling on cheap scratch paper, Olson described his "tradgety." "I am trying to hold my farm and get food for my children but it is hard this year. Money is scarce and hard to get. . . ."

Eleanor Roosevelt showed her husband this letter. "I am glad you wrote . . ." the President replied to him. "You are absolutely right that many things which the farmers raise have not by any means reached a proper level. . . ." He mentioned his own cattle raising in Georgia, and expressed the hope that AAA coverage would be extended. "All I can ask you to do is to believe that we are honestly trying to do our best, and that we think we are slowly but surely improving conditions."

Roosevelt's reassurances were partly justified. AAA benefits were extended to new crops in 1934, and farm prices and prosperity advanced. But discontent re-mained. The "big boys" — the large commercial farmers, farming corporations, banks and insurance companies — seemed to be getting more than their share of the take. Even worse, it was charged, AAA checks enabled recipients to buy machin-ery; by "tractoring" hired hands off the land and "plowing every third row under" farm managers cut down the need for farm labor. Vainly the Farmers Union de-nounced "scarcity economics" and insisted that the trouble with agriculture was not overproduction but underconsumption.

"The government wouldn't let us plant," tenant farmers complained, "so we had to go on relief."

Roosevelt knew that the acid test of the New Deal was recovery. During 1933 and 1934 he watched the ups and downs of the nation's economic temperature like a doctor following the condition of a feverish patient.

He was delighted when employment rose sharply the first four months after he took office. He proudly showed reporters a chart from which farm prices had dropped clear off the bottom of the sheet — the line had now reappeared and was headed up. But in July came a stock market crash and, even worse, a drop in pro-duction. The President dismissed the crash as due to gamblers: "everybody got to speculating and things went too fast; that got a perfectly natural corrective," he told reporters. Anyway, he said, employment looked good. By fall of 1933 he was wor-ried about employment too: "There aren't nearly enough people back at work," but he thought things were improving. He wrote Garner about this time that business was "not nearly as badly off as the New York crowd is howling about, but unem-ployment is still serious."

It was all so strange. Things seemed better — the NRA was going strong; the breath of recovery filled the air — yet the prosaic gauges of recovery — wages, prices, spending, employment — were moving up erratically and unpredictably where they were moving up at all. The situation looked so serious that in September 1933 the President instructed Secretary of War Dern to make ready army rolling kitchens for feeding the needy where local relief was inadequate. By the end of 1933 the alarmed and disconcerted President was looking for scapegoats. Prices had dropped, he said, because some people had not approved of NRA codes and because "some of our foreign friends" were deliberately trying to increase the exchange value of the dollar. Curiously, the President was almost embracing the idea of foreign causes of depression — an idea he had lambasted when Hoover used it in 1932.

Casting about for a solution, Roosevelt took up a notion that George F. Warren, a Cornell professor, had been pressing for some time. Drawn from the old quantity theory of money, the idea was that an increase in the value of gold would be the decisive factor in restoring higher prices. In October 1933 the President decided on this approach. In what has been called probably the "boldest attempt ever made to give the widest public a brief instruction in complicated economic doctrine and maneuver," Roosevelt told the people in a fireside chat about his plan to buy gold. "This is a policy and not an expedient," he said defensively. But while a government market for gold became a lasting policy, the Warren theory proved an abortive one; raising the price of gold did not boost commodity prices.

"Our troubles will not be over tomorrow, but we are on our way and we are headed in the right direction," the President said in his radio talk. During 1934 employment did improve somewhat. The cause lay largely in programs that Roosevelt viewed as essentially humanitarian rather than recovery-producing.

The first of these programs was run by Hopkins, more driving and sharp-tongued than ever. Told by Roosevelt to get help to the people fast, he had sat down at his desk while it was waiting in a hallway to be moved into his office, and in a few hours authorized millions of dollars of relief. Spurring and goading his subordinates, infuriating state politicians while playing his own brand of New Deal politics, ignoring bureaucratic protocol, Hopkins spent several hundred millions through the states during the early months of the New Deal and almost a billion on "quicky" projects through the Civil Works Administration in late 1933 and the first half of 1934.

Hopkins' main concern was to act fast. Told of a project that would work out in the long run, he answered bitingly that people "don't eat in the long run — they eat every day." Operating at a much slower pace was Ickes and his Public Works Administration. Suspicious, cantankerous, stubborn, "Honest Harold," as he was called to his discomfiture, authorized projects only after he had satisfied himself as to their legal propriety, economic value, and engineering practicality. But by 1934 money was moving out through PWA into the hands of contractors, manufacturers, engineers, laborers, truckers, carpenters, architects, and deep into the arteries of the economy.

Other agencies added to this outpouring of money. The Reconstruction Finance Corporation, continued from the Hoover days, was lending more money than ever. The TVA, beginning its vast development program in the Tennessee Valley, was converting an area that had been a drain on the economy into a source of economic stimulation. The AAA put into farmers' hands money that quickly found its way to Sears, Roebuck and the local hardware store, and thence to manufacturers, banks, workers.

Roosevelt used all these instruments; he put full reliance on no single one of them. As leader of all the people, as broker among major organized interests, he would take the middle way. He adopted spending policies, but only as a temporary measure until the budget was balanced. He favored tariff reduction, but not where it hurt major American interests. He wanted a "reflationary" price rise, but not an "inflationary" one. He was favorable to organized labor, but only to the point consistent with a partnership of industry, labor, and farmers with government.

Nowhere was the President's role as buffer among major interests, as conciliator of rival viewpoints, more sharply revealed than in a statement he made to a press conference in December 1933: "Douglas' job is to prevent the Government from spending just as hard as he possibly can. That is his job. Somewhere between his efforts to spend nothing . . . and the point of view of the people who want to spend ten billions additional on public works, we will get somewhere, and we are trying to work out a program. . . ."

In his first two years in office Roosevelt achieved to a remarkable degree the exalted position of being President of all the people. Could it last? Could he keep a virtually united people behind him?

He could not. Even during his first year there were subdued rumblings of discontent. In 1934 opposition was taking organized form, especially on the right.

The opposition on the right was a mixture of many elements. It was compounded in part of a national reaction to certain elements of the New Deal: the reaction of nineteenth-century individualists to the collectivism of NRA and AAA; of believers in limited government to the leviathan that Roosevelt seemed to be erecting; of champions of thrift to government spending; of opponents of labor organization to politicians who admitted union leaders into high places in the new partnership; of fanatic believers in the sanctity of the gold standard. But there must have been a deeper, more pervasive explanation for the hatred of Roosevelt on the part of people who in many cases had benefited from the New Deal. In the outcries of the anti-Roosevelt sections of business and industry was a sharp, querulous note betraying loss of status, class insecurity, lessened self-esteem.

The President was remarkably sensitive to pinpricks from the right, especially from people in his own class. Writing to a Boston banker and Harvard classmate, he went out of his way to mention remarks that he had heard his friend had made, and concluded "because of what I felt to be a very old and real friendship these remarks hurt." Roosevelt's ire rose at reports of conversations about him in business circles. "I wish you could have heard the dinner-party conversations in some of the best houses in Newport," he wrote to a business friend. He talked caustically to reporters about "prominent gentlemen" dining together in New York and criticizing him.

Ironically enough, Roosevelt made the same complaint against his critics that they directed against him. He said they were doctrinaire, impractical. When his friend James P. Warburg broke with the New Deal because of its monetary policies, Roosevelt wrote Warburg that he had read the latter's book with great interest. He then urged Warburg to get a secondhand car, put on his oldest clothes, and make a tour of the country. "When you have returned, rewrite 'The Money Muddle' and I will guarantee that it will run into many more editions!" The President made much of the fact that conservatives were criticizing the New Deal without offering constructive alternatives.

It was one thing to deal with malcontents off in New York — the "speculators," as Roosevelt called some of them disdainfully, or "that crowd." It was something else when opposition developed among his own advisers. His anger rose to white heat when Treasury Adviser O. W. M. Sprague, who he felt had offered no constructive advice toward recovery and who had evidently tried to call protest meetings against New Deal financial policies, resigned late in 1933. Scribbling on some scrap paper, the President wrote Sprague a scorching letter, in which he told him that he would have been dismissed from the government if he had not resigned, and that Sprague's actions had come close to the border line of disloyalty to the government. The letter was never sent, however. Other advisers resigned: Peek of the AAA, Douglas, Acheson.

Roosevelt seemed almost relieved when the conservative opposition coalesced and organized in the broad light of day. In August 1934 the American Liberty League was chartered, dedicated to "teach the necessity of respect for the rights of persons and property," the duty of government to protect initiative and enterprise, the right to earn and save and acquire property. Not only were there industrialists like the Du Ponts, automobile manufacturers like William S. Knudsen, oil men like J. Howard Pew, and mail-order house magnates like Sewell L. Avery among its members or spokesmen; there were also illustrious Democratic politicians such as Al Smith, Jouett Shouse, John W. Davis, and Bainbridge Colby. At a press conference the President said amiably that Shouse had been in and had pulled out of his pocket a couple of "Commandments" — the need to protect property and to safeguard profits. What about other commandments? Roosevelt asked. What about loving your neighbor? He quoted a gentleman "with a rather ribald sense of humor" as saying that the League believed in two things — love God and then forget your neighbor.

"There is no mention made here in these two things," the President went on, "about the concern of the community, in other words the government, to try to make it possible for people who are willing to work, to find work to do. For people who want to keep themselves from starvation, keep a roof over their heads, lead decent lives, have proper educational standards, those are the concerns of Government, besides these points, and another thing which isn't mentioned is the protection of the life and liberty of the individual against elements in the community which seek to enrich or advance themselves at the expense of their fellow citizens. They have just as much right to protection by government as anybody else. I don't believe any further comment is necessary after this, what would you call it — a homily?"

By the fall of 1934 Roosevelt's break with the Liberty League conservatives seemed irreparable. His own feelings were sharpening. He told Ickes that big business was bent on a deliberate policy of sabotaging the administration. When an ugly general strike broke out in San Francisco, he blamed "hotheaded" young labor leaders, but even more the conservatives who, he said, really wanted the strike. The President's thoughts must have been far from the grand concert of interests when, referring to his inaugural address, he told reporters, "I would now say that there is a greater thing that America needs to fear, and that is those who seek to instill fear into the American people." His hopes must have been far from a partnership of all the people when he wrote Garner, after a visit to the Hermitage in November 1934, "The more I learn about old Andy Jackson the more I love him."

Such was the beginning of the rupture on the right. Much more momentous were the forces of unrest gathering on the left. . . .

If Roosevelt failed to see the potentialities of an enlarged labor movement for the political coalition behind the New Deal, the reason lay in part in his attitude toward labor. He looked on labor from the viewpoint of a patron and benefactor, not as a political leader building up the labor flank of future political armies. He was concerned about their wages, hours, and conditions; he saw them as people with concrete troubles. It is significant that when he talked with reporters about a visit auto workers had paid him, he said nothing about the union situation in this vital industry but quoted line by line his conversation with the men about their problem of making ten dollars a day but working only sixty-five days a year.

The supreme test of Roosevelt's leadership in this area was his handling of the Wagner Act. This was the most radical legislation passed during the New Deal, in the sense that it altered fundamentally the nation's politics by vesting massive economic and political power in organized labor. Unlike much of Roosevelt's reform and relief program, the act cut through the heart of existing labor-management relations. It had an essential part in building powerful unions that in turn would furnish votes, money, and organization to future liberal coalitions.

Yet for months Roosevelt was cool to the Wagner bill; he threw his weight behind the measure only at the last moment, when it was due to pass anyway. He long showed a special indifference, even obtuseness, to the cardinal question of employee representation. In May 1934 he told reporters with some irritation that the workers could choose as representatives whomever they wished — including the Ahkoond of Swat, or the Royal Geographic Society, or a union, or the Crown Prince of Siam. He failed to see that the essence of the problem was whether or not workers could still be represented by company unions and by a variety of minority and craft spokesmen whose disunity would weaken the workers in dealing with employers and in forging a new political arm.

When Wagner went ahead and introduced his National Labor Relations bill into Congress in February 1935, he not only got no help or encouragement from the President, but it was all he could do to stop Roosevelt from lining up with Senators Robinson and Harrison in the latter's efforts to stall the bill to death. Questioned in press conferences, Roosevelt was invariably cool or evasive. Almost singlehanded Wagner shaped political strategy, won grudging acceptance of the bill from the AFL old guard, fought the bill through the Senate against a hostile press and indifferent leadership. The bill passed the Senate, 63–12, on May 16, 1935.

Eleven days later the Supreme Court invalidated the Recovery Act, including whatever legal support the act had given unionization. It might be logically supposed that it was this action, knocking the props from under the President's collective bargaining policy, that forced him into Wagner's camp. But no; on May 24, three days *before* the court decision, Roosevelt came out for the bill. Why? The explanation lies largely in his simple, pragmatic reaction to the immediate situation. The bill's top-heavy majority in the Senate made House passage seem certain. By coming out for the bill Roosevelt could influence some important provisions still open, and he could wangle his way out of what might be called an administration defeat. He may have been influenced, too, by the fact that Chamber of Commerce leaders, who had been generally sympathetic to his program, openly broke with him early in May. The Supreme Court decision simply reinforced a decision already made.

With typical Rooseveltian agility, he dropped his weight heavily on the scales, once he had decided to jump. By June the Wagner measure was a "must bill." Roosevelt helped push the bill over the hurdles in the House; he ignored the frantic entreaties of businessmen to stop the measure. After the bill passed the House without a roll call, the President congratulated Chairman Connery of the House Labor Committee, adding, "It is a tremendous step forward."

In this curious way Roosevelt and labor first became partners.

Left! Right! Left!

Roosevelt's sudden reversal on the Wagner Act was symptomatic of his policy-making during 1935. The first session of the Seventy-fourth Congress stands as one of the strangest examples of presidential leadership and congressional followership in modern times. That session had passed several mild New Deal measures and was apparently coming to an end when it suddenly showed a burst of energy and enacted, during the hot summer of 1935, some of the most significant measures of Roosevelt's first term. But if the President's course seemed erratic, the explanation was clear. He was picking his way, step by step, among great pressures, now forced left and now right as he faced specific problems, always moving toward a goal that was fixed only generally in his mind.

The President's State of the Union speech to Congress in January 1935 had given little foretaste of the stormy days ahead. Despite references to the need for more social justice, it was moderate in tone and called for a rather limited program. "We can, if we will," said the President, "make 1935 a genuine period of good feeling, sustained by a sense of purposeful progress." He told the receptive legislators that he was ready to submit a broad security program, embracing natural resources, unemployment insurance, old-age insurance, and better homes. He promised an extensive new program of public works and work relief. He mentioned briefly other needed measures such as extending the NRA and improving taxation "forms and methods." The New Deal, evidently, was to be clarified, improved, and consolidated, rather than extensively broadened.

This attempt by the President to follow a wobbling way between the left and right threatened for months to mire his program in a legislative swamp. The *via media* still would not work.

The huge work relief bill sharply etched the difficulties of the middle way. "The Federal Government must and shall quit this business of relief," the President told Congress. He was not willing that the vitality of the people should be further sapped by handing out cash or market baskets or by giving a few hours' work cutting grass or raking leaves. The most exciting thing about the bill was Roosevelt's request for $4,880,000,000 — a sensational sum for peacetime — but this sum was actually about halfway between the nine billions urged by progressives in the Senate and the small "dole" favored by some conservative legislators. Roosevelt also took the precaution of having the director of procurement, rather than the controversial figures Ickes and Hopkins (who would administer it), present the bill to the House Committee.

Steered firmly by the House leaders, the bill went through the lower chamber with relative ease. In the Senate the story was different. With unlimited debate at their disposal, groups on the right and left ripped into the bill. The goal of the conservatives was simple: to reduce the appropriation and turn the bill into poor relief. The labor bloc wished to expand the bill's coverage, but, above all, they hoped to write in a provision that labor would be given the prevailing wage paid by private employers in the area. This provision the President flatly opposed; he preferred a "security wage" of perhaps fifty dollars a month, partly to spread relief farther, partly to appease private employers' fears of wage competition. Lining up first with the left and then with the right were inflationists, Senators mainly concerned with converting the program into a pork barrel that they could open up back home, and adventurers like Long. Muddying the waters further were Ickes and Hopkins as they enlisted legislators to back their own favorite provisions.

Joining in a policy of opportunism, these disparate groups pushed a prevailing wage amendment through by one vote. Roosevelt's response was to have the resolution temporarily killed by being sent back to committee. The President was finding his course hard going. Ickes felt that he was dispirited, looking tired, and lacking his usual fighting vigor and buoyancy. In the Senate, Long was cock of the walk. While the White House tried to find a compromise on the prevailing wage, the Kingfish taunted: "I see by the newspapers that some votes are being switched on the prevailing wage amendment. I resent anyone calling on anybody for a trade without calling on me first. . . . I might cut the price a little bit." He rambled on. "I am a dyed-in-the-wool party man. I do not know just what party I am in right now, but I am for the party."

By compromising with the liberal-labor bloc the administration was finally able to stave off crippling amendments and push the bill through. Passage was due less to Roosevelt — who was cruising on the *Nourmahal* during the latter stages and complaining that the Senate was a "headache" and the whole situation "too childish for grownups" — than to administration leaders on the Hill and to the legislators' willingness to compromise on certain issues by leaving them to the President. Roosevelt had to accept some losses: most notably a provision requiring senatorial confirmation for employees under the measure who earned more than $5,000 a year.

By early April when the relief bill passed, Roosevelt had only this victory in three months. He had appealed to the Senate to ratify United States adherence to the World Court, but the effort had failed amid a deluge of hostile telegrams, many of them stirred up by Coughlin. His social security bill, which would commit the nation to a program of assisting the jobless and the poor through federal and state action, was floundering between the same forces that had almost ground the relief bill to death: the liberals were sorely disappointed by its limited coverage and by the reliance it put on state participation; the conservatives thought it went too far. A veterans' bonus bill had passed the House with more than enough votes to override the expected presidential veto.

Never had Roosevelt been so squeezed among opposing political forces as during the spring of 1935. Spokesmen of the United States Chamber of Commerce sharply attacked the administration. Meeting with the President in mid-May, progressive senators La Follette, Wheeler, Norris, and Johnson, backed up by Ickes and Wallace, urged him to assert the leadership that the country, they said, was demanding. Roosevelt's old adviser Felix Frankfurter reported that Justice Louis Brandeis had sent word that it was the eleventh hour. La Follette reminded the President that Theodore Roosevelt had taken open issue with members of his own party.

Roosevelt indicated to the progressives that he would take a firmer stand. But despite the pressure from left and right, and from the agitators of discontent, he was not yet ready to jettison the middle way. He was still pinning his hopes on an extension of NRA for two years. The NRA was not Little Orphan Annie, he told reporters, but "a very live young lady" and he expected the two-year extension to go through.

Then, late in May, came the unanimous decision of the Supreme Court invalidating the NRA, mainly on the grounds that Congress had exercised power beyond the scope of the interstate commerce clause and had delegated too much of this power outside its own reach. It was a jolting blow to the heart of Roosevelt's middle way.

For four days the President was silent, while the country waited expectantly. Then, on May 31, he gave his answer in a carefully staged performance. As the reporters trooped up to his desk, they saw an open copy of the high court's opinion on one side, and on the other a dozen or more telegrams. Eleanor Roosevelt was there, knitting on a blue sock. The President leaned back in his chair, lighted a cigarette, jestingly asked, as he so often did, whether the reporters had any news. Did he care to comment on the NRA? a reporter asked.

"Well, Steve, if you insist. That's an awful thing to put up to a fellow at this hour of the morning just out of bed." But the President was eager to talk. And talk he did, for almost an hour and a half.

His monologue was not that of a liberal outraged by a tory court. It was a long dissenting opinion by a man who had been following a moderate course helping and mediating among businessmen, workers, and farmers alike, and now to his surprise finds the props knocked from under him. One by one he quoted from the pile of telegrams. These "pathetic appeals," as he called them, came not from unemployed workers or from desperate farmers but from businessmen — drugstore proprietors in Indiana, a candy seller in Massachusetts, a Georgia businessman, a large department store owner, a cigar store operator. Pushing the telegrams aside, the President paused dramatically. What were the implications of the decision? It simply made impossible national action, collective action, the great partnership. Clearly he was attacking the decision not because it was conservative or antilabor but because it thwarted action by the national government to help all groups, including business.

Again and again the President insisted it was not a partisan issue. Where to go next? "Don't call it right or left; that is just first-year high school language, just about. It is not right or left. . . ." Then he slashed at the Court again. A "horse-and-buggy definition of interstate commerce." And he let the reporters quote that phrase.

FDR — "HORSE-AND-BUGGY DECISION" shouted next day from front pages across the nation. Most people took this remark figuratively as a New Dealer's attack on conservative judges. Actually Roosevelt was speaking literally — he was dissenting with judges who thought that national problems could be solved by forty-eight separate states. Pressed by reporters as to how he would cope with the effect of the decision, the President said, "We haven't got to that yet."

Then began the second Hundred Days.

Congress, which had been idling for weeks and had come to a standstill after the court decision, was galvanized into action. Roosevelt threw himself into the legislative battle. No longer was he squeamish about putting the lash to congressional flanks. Now he was bluntly telling congressional leaders that certain bills *must* be passed. Administration contact men ranged amid the legislative rank and file, applying pressure. Late in the afternoon they would report back to the President. When they mentioned a balking congressman, the big hand would move instantly to the telephone; in a few moments the President would have the congressman on the wire, coaxing him, commanding him, negotiating with him. To scores of others

Roosevelt dictated one- or two-sentence chits asking for action. He and his lieutenants, working late into the night, acting in close concert with friendly leaders on Capitol Hill, stayed one or two jumps ahead of the divided opposition. Congressmen complained, balked, dragged their heels, but in the end they acted.

The Wagner Labor Relations Act went through with a rush before the end of June, and the President signed it enthusiastically. The Social Security Act was passed, also by heavy majorities. Banking and Tennessee Valley legislation were strengthened. The AAA was modified in an attempt to protect it against judicial veto. The holding company bill, which was designed to curb the power of giant utility holding companies over their operating subsidiaries, and which Roosevelt had been urging since January, went through under intensified administration pressure. And a controversial tax bill became law despite intense opposition from business and grumbling among congressmen that the President was pushing them too hard.

Nothing better showed Roosevelt's sudden change of direction than the tax bill. He had said nothing about such a measure in his January message; his budget message had suggested that no new taxes would be needed. He had toyed with a "share-the-wealth" scheme of the Treasury's in February, but as late as May 22 he seemed to be sticking to his January position. Unexpectedly on June 19 the President asked Congress for an inheritance tax as well as the estate tax, gift taxes to balk evasion of the inheritance tax, stepped-up income taxes on "very great individual incomes," and a corporation income tax graduated according to the size of corporations, with a dividend tax to prevent evasion. Leaving Congress "tired, sick, and sore, and in confusion," as one Senator said, the President then departed for the Yale-Harvard boat races.

What had happened? Had the President turned left?

Viewed in retrospect, Roosevelt's course seemed to many a sudden and massive shift leftward, away from the *via media* of the first two years to a commanding position on the left. From such a view it was an easy step to the further assumption that Roosevelt had shifted left to meet the rising hurricanes among labor, farmers, Long, Coughlin, Townsend & Co. The trouble with this theory is that it does not fit the way Roosevelt actually behaved. His reaction to the hurricanes set off by agitators of discontent was to outmaneuver the leaders and to give way a bit to the blast, not to steal the ideological thunder of the left. He did not exploit the potentialities of encouraging and allying himself with the new millions of labor.

What did happen was the convergence of a number of trends and episodes at a crucial point — June 1935 — that left Roosevelt in the posture of a radical. The Supreme Court demolished the main institutional apparatus of the middle way by invalidating NRA. In filling this void, Roosevelt salvaged 7a (in the form of the Wagner Act) and other NRA provisions that had been concessions to the left. The Court's decision made impossible the resurrection of the code features that had been the NRA's attraction for certain business and industrial groups. The result of this situation was that merely carrying on prolabor elements of the NRA meant a leftward shift.

This was one reason for Roosevelt's new posture; another was the practical effect of dealing with Congress. Following a middle way between the progressive and conservative factions had not been as easy in 1935 as it had been earlier. For one thing, Congress had shifted leftward in interest and ideology after the November 1934 election. In the early months of 1935 Roosevelt's program had been bombarded from right and left, and narrowly escaped destruction. The exigencies of congressional politics pulled him to a more liberal program, and it was significant that his new position, harmonizing more smoothly with the majority in Congress on the left, resulted in an even more important array of measures than those of the first Hundred Days.

But the main reason for the new posture was the cumulative impact of the attacks from the right. He had been following a middle way; "as he looked back on it all," recalled Moley, who was watching him closely during this period, "he was, like Clive, amazed at his own moderation." The undercover attacks of business, the criticism that filled most of the press, the open desertion of big businessmen as symbolized in the Liberty League and smaller businessmen as represented in the Chamber of Commerce, the drifting away of conservative advisers like Moley — all these played their part. The desertion of the right, especially in the NRA decision, automatically helped shift Roosevelt to the left.

The theory that Roosevelt executed a swing left for ideological reasons as a result only of the NRA decision runs hard up against other strands of Roosevelt's development. His program had always embraced liberal measures as well as orthodox ones. Social security had long been in the works — Roosevelt in 1930 had been the first leading politician to advocate unemployment insurance — and it was put off to 1935 mainly because of administrative and drafting difficulties. The President urged the holding company bill throughout the session. He lined up for the Wagner Act before the NRA decision was announced. The speech he planned to give if the Supreme Court ruled against the abrogation of the Gold Clause would, except for the Court's 5–4 majority for the government, have precipitated a grave constitutional crisis in February 1935.

Roosevelt, in short, made no consciously planned, grandly executed deployment to the left. He was like the general of a guerrilla army whose columns, fighting blindly in the mountains through dense ravines and thickets, suddenly converge, half by plan and half by coincidence, and debouch into the plain below.

That Roosevelt had made no final ideological commitment to the left was made clear in an exchange of letters between the President and newspaper publisher Roy Howard shortly after Congress adjourned. Certain elements of business, Howard warned, had been growing more hostile to the administration, and considered the tax bill an attempt at revenge on business. They hoped for a breathing spell for industry, a recess from further experimentation. In a cordial response Roosevelt defended the tax measure and spoke for a "wise balance" in the economy. But, he added, the administration's basic program had now reached substantial completion. The "breathing-spell" was here — "very decidedly so." The zig had been followed by another zag.

Possibly Roosevelt really meant what he wrote to Howard. But events have ways of committing leaders to new positions. The great legislative victories of 1935 had unloosed forces that were to carry Roosevelt further from the middle way toward partisanship and party leadership. The second Hundred Days pointed the way toward the triumph of 1936 — and toward the defeats that lay beyond.

The American Entry into World War II

Why did the United States go to war in 1941? The question has provoked sharp debate among American historians. In the years after the war, revisionist scholars, among them Charles A. Beard and Charles C. Tansill, laid the blame on the United States. They accused President Roosevelt and his advisers of dragging the country, either blunderingly or deliberately, into a war that was neither in the national interest nor desired by the American people. In this thoughtful essay, Dexter Perkins, a veteran diplomatic historian, seeks to place the revisionist analysis in perspective. His argument develops on two levels. First, he makes a shrewd historiographical assessment of the nature of revisionism. Then he confronts the substantive issues raised in that analysis.

The central fact regarding the European war, Perkins argues, was the shift in public opinion away from the isolationism of the mid-1930s. Quite clearly, Roosevelt's policies after 1938 were not neutral and, indeed, grew progressively more provocative from the standpoint of Germany. But, far from acting without a mandate, the President was in fact reflecting national sentiment that was growing increasingly hostile to the prospect of a Nazi triumph.

Because Japan did not seem to pose nearly so formidable or evil a threat, assessment of American policy in the Far East becomes more complicated. Perkins stresses three points. First, owing to Roosevelt's deep concern over European developments, he was not bent on provoking a war with Japan. Second, because of a historic commitment to China that, well founded or not, could not be dodged, the United States stood athwart Japanese ambitions on the Asian mainland. Finally, the irreducible fact was that Japan was the aggressor, and increasingly so as the militarists gained the upper hand in Tokyo. In the intricate game of thrust and counterthrust between the two countries after 1937, clearly there were things that the United States did or left undone that hastened the day of Pearl Harbor. But, as Perkins sees it, the United States had much less leeway than the revisionists are willing to grant. Above all, evidence indicates that President Roosevelt welcomed a war with Japan.

The debate that occasioned Perkins's essay has waned since 1954. The focus of attention has shifted from polemics to careful scrutiny of the events that led to war. But Perkins's reasoned analysis remains as valid and persuasive today as when it was written in the mid-1950s. It is, in addition, an excellent illustration of the kind of historical wisdom that can come only from a lifetime of scholarship.

FOR FURTHER READING:

DIVINE, ROBERT. *The Illusion of Neutrality.* Chicago: Quadrangle Books, 1968.*
FEIS, HERBERT. *The Road to Pearl Harbor.* New York: Atheneum Publishers, 1962.*
LANGER, WILLIAM L., and GLEASON, EVERETT S. *Undeclared War, 1940–1941.* Magnolia, Mass.: Peter Smith, 1953.*
———. *The Challenge to Isolation.* 2 vols. Magnolia, Mass.: Peter Smith, 1953.*

Asterisk denotes paperback edition.

Was Roosevelt Wrong? DEXTER PERKINS

Revisionism may be defined as an after-the-event interpretation of American participation in war, with the accent on the errors and blunders that provoked the struggle and on the folly of the whole enterprise. If we accept this definition, we shall certainly agree that there has been plenty of revisionism in the course of our history. The war of 1812 has sometimes been judged to have been futile and sometimes described as a war of intended conquest. The Mexican War has come in for harsh treatment as a war of unnecessary aggression. James G. Randall, one of the foremost students of the Civil War period, suggests that a less passionate view of the sectional problem might have made the conflict avoidable. Again and again it has been stated by reputable historians that William McKinley might have prevented the war of 1898 had he stressed in his message to Congress the very large concessions that had been made by Spain. The First World War was brilliantly represented by Walter Millis as the product of a blundering diplomacy and of economic pressures not entirely creditable. And since 1945 we have had a crop of historians, headed by so eminent a member of his historical generation as Charles A. Beard, attempting to show that the maddest folly of all was our entry into the conflict that ended less than a decade ago. Clearly, revisionism is an American habit; though, in saying this, I do not mean to imply that it is unknown in other lands.

The roots of the revisionist tendency are worth speculating about. Such a point of view, I take it, is particularly apt to find expression in a country where peace is highly treasured and where the glorification of war is relatively uncommon. Just as many Americans easily put away the hates and resentment of war at the end of the struggle and display a tendency towards reconciliation with the vanquished, so they tend to forget the passions that animated them and drove them into the conflict, and to view what at the time seemed reasonable and natural as something that with a little more forbearance or wisdom could have been avoided. And there are other factors that reinforce this point of view. Wars are apt to end in disillusionment. After the glorious hopes of the years 1917 and 1918 came the clash of national selfishnesses at Versailles, and a distraught and threatened world. In 1945 the defeat of Hitler and Japan was soon seen to have left grave problems ahead. In the East, the American defense of China and the hopes of a strong democratic nation in the Orient ended in the victory of the Chinese Reds. And in Europe, though the peril from the ambitions of Hitler was exorcised, the United States found itself face to face with a new totalitarianism, far-ranging in its ambitions like the old. In such a situation it was natural to forget the menace that had been defeated, and to ask whether there might not have been a better solution to the problems that ended with the capitulation ceremonies at Rheims and on the deck of the *Missouri*.

After every large-scale war, moreover, there is a reaction against that strong executive leadership which is almost inevitably associated with periods of crisis in the life of the nation. This was true in 1920; and it was true after 1945. During the conflict the personality of Mr. Roosevelt loomed large, and almost immune from attack. But under the surface there was hostility, and this was to take the form of criticism of his war policies. Sometimes this criticism came, as in the case of Frederic R. San-

Source: Dexter Perkins, "Was Roosevelt Wrong?" *Virginia Quarterly Review,* vol. 30 (1954), pp. 355–372.

born in his "Design for War," from one who had a strong animus against the New Deal, and who approached the record of the administration in the field of foreign policy with this animus. Sometimes, on the other hand, as in the case of Charles A. Beard, it came from one who regarded the Roosevelt diplomacy as jeopardizing and perhaps wrecking far-reaching programs of internal reform. In these two cases, and in virtually every other, strong emotions entered into the account. It has been a satisfaction to the revisionists to tear down the President; and there has always been — and it was inevitable that there should be — a reading public to fall in with this point of view, either from personal dislike of Roosevelt or from partisan feeling.

Revisionism, then, has roots in the very nature of the case. But, if we analyze it coolly, what shall we think of it? This is the question I propose to examine in this essay.

It seems to me fair to say at the outset that it is impossible to avoid the conclusion that revisionism is essentially history by hypothesis. It suggests — indeed in some instances it almost claims — that the world would have been a better place, or that at any rate the present position of the United States would have been happier, if this country had not intervened in the Second World War. Such a proposition can be put forward, but it cannot be established like a theorem in geometry. We cannot go back to 1939 or 1941 and re-enact the events of those stirring and tumultuous years. In a sense, we are bound by the past.

None the less, it seems worth while, even though we are in the realm of speculation rather than scientific history, to state the revisionist point of view. First, with regard to Germany, the point of view is advanced that the United States was in no essential danger from Adolf Hitler, that he demonstrated no very great interest in the American continents, that he desired until almost the day of Pearl Harbor to keep out of trouble with the United States, that there is no reliable evidence that he meditated an assault upon the New World. It is possible for the revisionist to go further. The ambitions of Hitler, it would be maintained, would have been checked and contained within limits by the presence of the great totalitarian state to the East. The two colossi would act each as a restraint on the other. It needed not the intervention of the American government to preserve the safety of the New World. As to Asia, the argument runs somewhat differently. Less emphasis is placed on the question of national security and more on a certain interpretation of national interest. The United States, we are told, had only a meager interest in China; its trade and investments there were insignificant, and were likely to remain so. They were distinctly inferior to our trade and investments in Japan. The shift in the balance of the Far East that might come about through a Japanese victory over Great Britain was no real concern of the United States. As to the Philippines, they might have been left alone had we stayed out of the war, or conversely, they were not worth the sacrifice involved in maintaining our connection with them. Such are the assumptions, implied, if not always expressed, in the revisionist view of the problem of the Orient.

Now some of the assertions in this rationale are unchallengeable. It is true that Hitler desired to avoid a clash with the United States until just before Pearl Harbor. It is true that the economic interests of the United States in China were inferior to our interests in Japan. These are facts, and must be accepted as facts. But there still remain a good many questions about the revisionist assumptions. For example, was there in 1940 and 1941 no danger of the destruction of British naval power, and would that destruction have had no unhappy consequences for the United States? Granted that the documents show great reluctance on the part of the Fuehrer to challenge the United States, would this reluctance have outlasted the fall of Great Britain? Granted that the Kremlin might have exercised a restraining influence on the Germans, is it certain that the two powers might not have come to an understanding as they did in 1939, and had at other periods in the past? Just how comfortable a world would it have been if the psychopathic leader of Germany had emerged from the Second World War astride a large part of the Continent, with the resources of German science at his command? There are questions, too, that can be asked about the Orient. Did the United States have no responsibility for the Philippines, and would the islands have been safe for long if the Japanese had dominated the Far East? Could the United States divest itself of all concern for China, abandoning a policy of nearly forty years duration and a deep-seated American tradition? Was the destruction of British power in this part of the world a matter of no concern to this country? Could the defeat of Britian in the East be separated from the fate of Britain in the world at large? These are extremely large questions, and it is a bold man who will brush them aside as inconsequential or trivial, or who will reply to them with complete dogmatism. Indeed, it is because they raise so many problems cutting to the root of our feelings, as well as our opinions, that they arouse so much controversy. Nor is there any likelihood that we can ever arrive at a complete consensus with regard to them.

We must, I think, seek a somewhat narrower frame of reference if we are to answer the revisionists with facts, and not with speculations. One of the ways to answer them, and one particularly worth pursuing with regard to the war in Europe, is to analyze the policy of the Roosevelt administration in its relation to public sentiment.

Foreign policy, in the last analysis, depends, not upon some logical formula, but upon the opinion of the nation. No account of American diplomacy in 1940 and 1941 can pretend to authority which does not take into account the tides of sentiment which must always influence, and perhaps control, the course of government. It is not to be maintained that a President has no freedom of action whatsoever; he can, I think, accelerate or retard a popular trend. But he does not act independently of it; the whole history of American diplomacy attests the close relationship between the point of view of the masses and executive action. A peacefully-minded President like McKinley was driven to war with Spain; a President who set great store by increasing the physical power of the nation, like Theodore Roosevelt, was limited and confined in his action; and Franklin Roosevelt himself, when, in the quarantine speech of October, 1937, he sought to rouse the American people against aggression, was compelled to admit failure, and to trim his sails to the popular breeze. These things are of the essence; to fail to observe them is to fail to interpret the past in the true historical spirit.

Let us apply these conceptions to the period 1939 to 1941. It will hardly be denied that from the very beginning of the war public sentiment was definitely against Germany. Indeed, even before the invasion of Poland, the public opinion polls show a strong partiality for the democratic nations. As early as January, 1939, when asked the question whether we should do everything possible to help England and France in case of war, 69 per cent of the persons polled answered in the affirmative, and the same question in October produced a percentage of 62 per cent on the same side. No doubt this sentiment did not extend to the point of actual participation in the war, but it furnished a firm foundation for the action of the President in calling Congress in special session, and in asking of it the repeal of the arms embargo on shipments of war in the interest of the Allies. The measure to this effect was introduced in the Congress towards the end of September; and it was thoroughly debated. There are several things to be said in connection with its passage. The first is that after its introduction there was a consistent majority of around 60 per cent in the polls in favor of passage. The second is that, though there was a strong partisan flavor to the debate, the defections when they came were more numerous on the Republican than on the Democratic side. It is true that, without the leadership of the President, the repeal could not have been enacted. But also it did not fly in the face of public sentiment (so far as that can be measured), but on the contrary reflected it.

With the fall of France there took place a deep and significant development in public opinion. This change the revisionists usually do not mention. They prefer to treat of American policy as if it were formed in a vacuum without regard to the moving forces that have so much to do with the final decisions. Yet the evidences are ample that in June of 1940 the American people were deeply moved. Take, for example, the action of the Republican nominating convention. There were several outstanding professional politicians in the running in 1940, Senator Taft, Senator Vandenberg, Thomas E. Dewey. Each one of these men represented a policy of caution so far as Europe was concerned. Yet what did the convention do? It turned to a relatively unknown figure, to a novice in politics who had, however, more than once declared himself as advocating extensive assistance to the democracies. The choice of Wendell Willkie as the Republican candidate for the Presidency is a fact the importance of which cannot be denied. It is worth while calling attention to other like phenomena. One of these is the overwhelming majorities by which the Congress appropriated largely increased sums for the armed forces, not only for the navy but for the army and the air force as well. Perhaps the American people, or the representatives of the American people, ought not to have been perturbed at what was happening in Europe. But the fact is that they were perturbed. They were perturbed in a big way. And the votes in the legislative halls demonstrate that fact.

Or take another example. The movement for a conscription law in time of peace developed rapidly after June of 1940. It developed with very little assistance from the White House. It cut across party lines. And it resulted in a legislative enactment which reflected the excitement of the public mind. How can we interpret the measure otherwise? Was there not a substantial body of opinion in the United States that feared a German victory?

Another important factor to be noted is the formation in June of 1940 of the Committee to Defend America by Aiding the Allies. It is highly significant that this movement arose at all. It is doubly significant that it found a leader in a Kansan Republican such as William Allen White. It is trebly significant that, once initiated, it spread like wild-fire, and that by September there were more than 650 chapters in the United States. And it is also to be noted that in New York there soon came into being a more advanced group, the so-called Century Group, which advocated war if necessary to check the aggressions of Germany.

And it is further to be observed that out of the Committee to Defend America came an agitation for what was eventually to be the bases-destroyer deal of September 2, 1940. This deal, by the way, was approved by 62 per cent of the persons polled on August 17, 1940, two weeks before it was actually consummated.

Let us go further. The next important step forward in American policy was the lend-lease enactment of the winter of 1941. This measure, it would appear from the polls, was based on a very distinct evolution of public sentiment. In July of 1940, 59 per cent of the persons polled preferred to keep out rather than to help England at the risk of war, and 36 per cent took the contrary view. In October the percentages were exactly reversed: they were 36 to 59. By January of 1941, 68 per cent of those interviewed thought it more important to assist Great Britain than to keep out of war. And the lend-lease enactment, when presented to the Congress, passed the Lower House by the impressive vote of 317 to 71 and the Senate by 60 to 31. As in the legislation of 1939, though the vote again had a partisan flavor, there were more defections from the Republicans in favor of the measure than of Democrats against it. And there is something more to be added to the account in this instance. By the winter of 1941 the America Firsters had appeared upon the scene. A counter-propaganda was now being organized against the administration. Yet this new group, despite its vigorous efforts, failed signally to rally majority opinion. And Senator Taft, who represented the most thoughtful opposition to the administration, himself proposed a measure of assistance to Great Britain.

I shall treat a little later of the various measures requiring no legislative sanction which the President took in the course of the year 1941. But it is important to observe that throughout the period there was a strong public sentiment that believed that it was more important to defeat Germany than to keep out of war. This view was held, according to the polls, by 62 per cent of those interrogated in May of 1941 and by 68 per cent in December of 1941. As early as April, 1941, 68 per cent of the pollees believed it important to enter the war if British defeat was certain.

We should next examine the legislation of the fall of 1941. By this time the Congress was ready to authorize the arming of American merchant ships, and this by a heavy vote. The measure was passed by 259 to 138 in the House and the Senate amended it and passed it by 50 to 37. Congress was ready, more reluctantly, to repeal those provisions of the neutrality acts which excluded American vessels from the so-called war zones. It was moving in the direction of fuller and fuller engagement against Hitler. We shall never know, of course, what the next step would have been had not that step been taken by Germany. It was the dictator of the Reich who declared war on the United States, not the American national legislature that declared war on the Fuehrer and his minions. But in the period between 1939 and 1941 it seems safe to say that the foreign policy of the Roosevelt administration was in accord with the majority public opinion of the nation. It seems incontestable that the President was acting on assumptions which majority opinion accepted, and pursuing a course of action which majority opinion approved.

This circumstance is naturally either ignored or obscured in the revisionist literature. And what makes it easier to forget is the undeniable fact that Franklin Roosevelt was unhappily sometimes given to equivocation and shifty conversation. Very early, it is true, as early as the quarantine speech of October, 1937, he sounded the alarm against the totalitarians. Very often he stated his conviction that their continued progress presented a threat to the United States. On occasion he took his courage in his hands as, when at Charlottesville in June of 1940, in an election year, he came out frankly in favor of aid to the democracies, or in the declaration of unlimited emergency in the address of May 27, 1941. There is little doubt that he deemed the defeat of Hitler more important than the avoidance of war (as did many other Americans, as we have seen). Yet he was often less than frank in his approach, and the emphasis he laid on his devotion to peace was often excessive. He shocked even his ardent admirer, Robert Sherwood, in the election of 1940. His presentation of the case for lend-lease does not at all times suggest candor; indeed, the very phrase seems a bit of cajolery. With regard to the question of convoy, in the spring of 1941, he was clever and, though verbally correct, hardly wholly open in his approach to the problem. In the famous episode of the *Greer* (an attack by a German submarine on a vessel which was reporting its position to a British destroyer), he misrepresented the facts, or spoke without full knowledge of them. All this it is only right to admit. Yet we must not exaggerate the importance of these considerations. The country knew where it was going with regard to Germany. It accepted lend-lease as desirable. Of the patrolling of the ocean lanes which followed, the President spoke candidly in the speech of May 27, 1941. There was nothing clandestine about the occupation of Greenland or Iceland. The pattern in the fall of 1941 would most probably not have been much altered if Roosevelt had been more scrupulous with regard to the *Greer*. In the last analysis we come back to the essential fact that Roosevelt represented and expressed in action the mood of the country with regard to Germany.

The question is, I believe, more difficult when we come to examine American policy towards Japan. We can say with some assurance that the denunciation of the treaty of commerce of 1911, undertaken by the administration in July of 1939 as an indication of American displeasure with Japanese policy, was distinctly well received. Indeed, if the State Department had not acted, the legislature might have. We can also say that in August of 1939 there was an overwhelming feeling against sending war materials to Nippon. When in September of 1940, an embargo on the export of scrap iron was imposed, 59 per cent of the persons polled on this issue approved the step that had been taken. And in 1941 the number of persons who believed that some check should be put on Japan even at the risk of war rose from 51 per cent to 70 per cent between July and September, and stood at 69 per cent at the time of Pearl Harbor.

But we have fewer indications of the direction of public sentiment in the action of Congress, and no actual votes on which to base our estimate of how the representatives of the American people felt with regard to the important problem of our course of action in the Orient. We must, I think, speak less confidently on this question of public opinion than in the case of Germany. We must turn rather to an analysis of the policy of the administration, and to revisionist criticism of that policy.

First of all, let us look at some of the uncontroverted facts. We know that there were militarist elements in Japan. We know that as early as 1934 Japan proclaimed its doctrine of a Greater East Asia in the famous Amau statement. We know that in the same year it upset the naval arrangements made at Washington and London. We know that it set up a special régime in North China in 1935. We know that it became involved in a war with China in 1937. This, of course, was only prelude. The outbreak of the European conflict in Europe, and the collapse of France, offered to the sponsors of further aggressive action a great opportunity. The occupation of Northern Indo-China followed. In the summer of 1940, the impetuous and aggressive Matsuoka came to the Foreign Office. On September 27, 1940, there was signed a tripartite pact with Japan, which bound Nippon to come to the assistance of the Axis powers if they were attacked by a power then at peace with them. In other words, the Tokyo government sought to confine and limit American policy.

In April of 1941 came a neutrality pact with Russia which freed the hands of the Japanese militarists for a policy of advance towards the South. In July came the occupation of the rest of Indo-China. The occupation of *northern* Indo-China made some sense from the point of view of blocking the supply route to the Chinese Nationalists. The occupation of *southern* Indo-China made no sense, except as the prelude to further acts of aggression. And in due course the aggression came.

Admittedly, this is only one side of the story. The question to be examined is, did these acts take place partly as a result of American provocation? Was it possible for a wiser and more prudent diplomacy to have avoided the rift that occurred in December, 1941? Revisionist criticism of our Oriental policy has been expressed in a variety of ways. In its most extreme form, it suggests that the President and his advisers actually plotted war with Japan. In its less extreme form, it directs its shafts at a variety of actions, of which I shall examine the most important. They are the conversations with the British as to the defense of the Far East, the commitments made to China, the severance of commercial relations, the failure to accept the proposals of Prince Konoye for direct conversations with the President, and the breakdown of the modus vivendi proposal of November, 1941. I shall examine each of these briefly, but let us first turn to the accusation that American policy was directed towards producing and not avoiding an armed conflict in the Orient.

It seems quite impossible to accept this view on the basis of the documentation. During the greater part of 1940 and 1941, it was certainly not the objective of the Roosevelt administration to bring about a clash in the Far East. On the contrary such a clash was regarded as likely to produce the greatest embarrassment in connection with the program of aid to Britain. The military and naval advisers of the President were opposed to it, and said so again and again. Even on the eve of Pearl Harbor this was the case. In addition, Secretary Hull was opposed to it. Even the apostle of caution, he made his point of view quite clear almost up to the end. And as for the President, it is worth pointing out that on the occasion of the Japanese occupation of southern Indo-China he came forward with a proposal for the neutralization of that territory in the interests of peace, and that in August he frankly stated it to be his purpose to "baby the Japanese along." That he feared Japanese aggression is likely, almost certain; that he desired it is something that cannot be proved.

But let us look at the various specific actions which have awakened criticism on the part of the revisionists. In the first place I cannot see that staff conversations with the British were open to any objections whatsoever. If the object of the Roosevelt administration was to limit Japanese aggression in the Far East, then it seems wholly rational to take precautions against such aggression, and surely it could reasonably be expected that such precautions would serve as a deterrent rather than as an incitement to action. It is, in my judgment, rather distorted thinking that regards such action as provocation. This is precisely the point of view of the Kremlin today with regard to the North Atlantic treaty and the European defense pact, or, to take another example, very like the contention of the Germans when they invaded Belgium in 1914. Because the British had engaged in military conversations with the Belgians looking to the possible violation of the neutrality treaty of 1839, it was claimed by apologists for Germany that the violation of neutrality was defensible. Where is the possible justification for such reasoning?

There is more to be said with regard to the breaking off, by the United States, of commercial and financial relations with Japan on the heels of the Japanese occupation of southern Indo-China in the summer of 1941. Undoubtedly this created an extraordinarily difficult situation for the government in Tokyo. Undoubtedly the cutting off of the oil supply from the United States gave great additional force to the arguments of the militarists. Undoubtedly, in the absence of a far-reaching diplomatic arrangement, it presented a strong reason for "bursting out" of the circle, and going to war. If the administration put faith in this measure of economic coercion as a substitute for physical resistance, its faith was to turn out to be groundless. For myself, I have for a long time believed that economic coercion against a strong and determined power is more likely to produce war than to prevent it. But there are circumstances that ought to be mentioned in favor of the action of the administration. It is to be emphasized that the severance of commercial and financial relations resulted not in a breach of the negotiations with Japan but in a resumption of those negotiations. It is to be remembered that Prince Konoye's proposal for a personal conference with the President came after and not before the President's action. American policy by no means put an end to the efforts of those substantial elements in Japan who feared a clash with this country and who were laboring to prevent it. It must be pointed out, also, that the alternative was by no means a pleasant one. At a time when we were deeply engaged in the Atlantic, when we were being more and more deeply committed with regard to the war in Europe, when our domestic supply of oil might have to be substantially curtailed, the continuation of our exports to the Far East to assist Japan in possible projects of aggression was a very difficult policy to follow. It may even be that it would have proven to be totally impracticable from a political point of view.

We come in the third place to the efforts of Premier Konoye to establish direct contact with President Roosevelt. It is well known that Ambassador Grew believed at that time, and that he has more than once stated since, that a good deal was to be hoped from such a meeting. And it is by no means clear why, if the objective were the postponement of a crisis, the experiment should not have been tried. Secretary Hull brought to this problem, as it seems to me, a rigidity of mind which may properly be criticized. In insisting on a previous definition of the issues before the meeting was held, he was instrumental in preventing it. While we cannot know what the result of such a meeting would have been, we are entitled, I think, to wish that it had been held. All the more is this true since it would appear likely that Prince Konoye was sincere in the effort which he made to avoid war.

But there is another side to the matter. We cannot be absolutely sure of Konoye's good faith. We can be still less sure of the willingness of the Tokyo militarists to support him in the far-reaching concessions that would have been necessary. And in the final analysis we cannot be sure of the ability of the American government to make concessions on its own part.

And here we come, as it seems to me, to the crux of the matter. It was the American policy in China that created an impassable barrier in our negotiations with Japan. It is necessary to examine that policy. From one angle of vision the patience of the American government in dealing with the China incident seems quite remarkable. There was a good deal to complain of from 1935 onward, certainly from 1937 onward, if one were to think in terms of sympathy for an aggressed people and in terms of the traditional policy of the United States with regard to this populous nation. The Roosevelt administration moved very slowly in its opposition to Japan. It made its first loan to Chiang Kai-shek in the fall of 1938. It denounced the commercial treaty of 1911 with Nippon only in the summer of 1939. And it embarked upon a policy of really substantial aid to China only contemporaneously with the signing of the tripartite pact in the fall of 1940. Its increasing assistance to Chiang is intelligible on the ground that to keep the Japanese bogged down in China was one means of checking or preventing their aggressive action elsewhere.

The fact remains, however, that it was the Chinese question which was the great and central stumbling block in the long negotiations that took place in 1941. Though the Japanese had entered into an alliance with the Axis powers, it seems not unlikely that, in 1941, as the issue of peace or war defined itself more clearly, they would have been willing to construe away their obligations under that alliance had they been able to come to terms with the United States on the Chinese problem. But by 1941 the American government was so far committed to the cause of Chiang that it really had very little freedom of maneuver. The various Japanese proposals for a settlement of the China incident would have involved a betrayal of the Chinese Nationalist leader. The proposal for a coalition government, a government of the Nationalists and the puppet régime of Wang Ching-wei, could hardly have been accepted. The proposal that America put pressure on Chiang to negotiate, and cut off aid to him if he refused, was by this time equally impracticable. And the question of the withdrawal of the Japanese troops in China presented insuperable difficulties. True it is that in October of 1941 the idea of a total withdrawal seems to have been presented to Mr. Welles by Mr. Wakatsuki, Admiral Nomura's associate in the negotiations. But the idea was emphatically rejected by the militarists in Tokyo, and perhaps there was never a time when they would have agreed to any proposal that at the same time would have been acceptable to Chungking. The American government had been brought, by its policy of association with the Chinese Nationalists, to the point where understanding with Japan was practically impossible.

This fact is dramatically illustrated by the negotiations over the *modus vivendi* in November, 1941. At this time, as is well known, proposals were brought forward for the maintenance of the *status quo,* and a gradual restoration of more normal relations through the lifting of the commercial restrictions, and through the withdrawal of the Japanese from southern Indo-China. At first it seemed as if there were a possibility of working out some such proposal. But the Chinese objected most violently, and Secretary Hull dropped the idea. In the face of Chinese pressure, and of the possible popular indignation which such a policy of concession might produce, and acting either under the orders or at least with the assent of the President, he backed down. We must not exaggerate the importance of this. There is no certainty that the *modus vivendi* would have been acceptable to Tokyo, and, judging by the Japanese proposals of November 20, there is indeed some reason to think otherwise. But the fact remains that our close association with Chiang was a fundamental factor in making the breach with Japan irreparable. And it seems fair to say in addition that our hopes with regard to Nationalist China were at all times, in 1941 as later, very far removed from political reality.

Let us not, however, jump to absolute conclusions with regard to questions that, in the nature of the case, ought not to be a matter of dogmatic judgment. If there was a party in Japan, and a substantial one, which feared war with the United States and earnestly sought for accommodation, there was also a party which regarded the course of events in Europe as a heaven-sent opportunity for national self-aggrandizement. That this party might in any case have prevailed, whatever the character of American policy, does not seem by any means unlikely. It is significant that in July of 1941 the fall of Matsuoka brought no change in policy in the Far East, and that the so-called moderate, Admiral Toyoda, gave the orders for the crucial and revealing occupation of southern Indo-China in the summer of 1941.

Let us not forget, either, that after all it was the Japanese who struck. The ruthless act of aggression at Pearl Harbor was no necessary consequence of the breakdown of negotiations with the United States. If new oil supplies were needed, they were, of course, to be secured by an attack on the Dutch East Indies, not by an attack on Hawaii. Though there were strategic arguments for including America in any war-like move, there were strong political reasons for not doing so. No greater miscalculation has perhaps ever been made than that made by the militarists at Tokyo in December, 1941. By their own act, they unified American opinion and made their own defeat inevitable. It will always remain doubtful when the decisive involvement would have come for the United States had the bombs not dropped on Pearl Harbor on the 7th of December of 1941.

What, in conclusion, shall we say of revisionist history? There is a sense in which it is stimulating to the historian, and useful to historical science, to have the presuppositions, the conventional presuppositions, of the so-called orthodox interpreters of our foreign policy, subjected to criticism. There is surely some reason to believe that the candid examination of the views of these critics will, in the long run, result in a more accurate and a more objective view of the great events of the prewar years and in a better balanced judgment of President Roosevelt himself.

But there is another side of the question which, of course, must be recognized. It is fair to say that virtually all revisionist history (like some orthodox history) is written with a *parti pris*. It is hardly possible to speak of it as dictated by a pure and disinterested search for truth. It is, on the contrary, shot through with passion and prejudice, with passion and prejudice that may spring from comprehensible or even good motives, but which are passion and prejudice none the less. It also rests upon hypotheses which, in the nature of the case, cannot be demonstrated, and assumptions that will, it is fair to say, never be generally, or perhaps even widely, accepted. As to its practical effects, there are no signs that the isolationism of the present era has important political effects, so far as foreign policy is concerned. Conceivably, it provides some reinforcement for partisan Republicanism. But even here it seems considerably less effective than the unscrupulous campaign of Senator McCarthy and his colleagues to represent the previous administration as one saturated with Communists. The urgency of present issues may make revisionism less of a force in our time than it was two decades ago. As to this, we shall have to see what the future unfolds.

America in War and Peace

The New Deal had run its course — at all events, the first lap — by 1938. Stymied by a conservative coalition in Congress and then increasingly absorbed in the world crisis, the Roosevelt administration put aside its commitment to domestic reform. "Dr. Win-the-War" replaced "Dr. New Deal." There had been a coherence to the New Deal era: the Great Depression had then posed a clear challenge, the New Deal had offered the nation's response. But in the years that followed, domestic reform was beset by puzzling cross-currents. There was, first of all, the impact of World War II itself. Then peace brought economic problems that were very different from those of the prewar era — inflation, not depression; scarcity, not surpluses — and to come to grips with these proved, in some ways, more difficult. Now, too, black Americans, largely neglected by the New Deal, began to exert new pressures; civil rights became a major issue for the first time since Reconstruction. The New Deal reforms themselves were a force in the nation's political life. How should they be extended or redirected? A troubling new issue also now emerged. With the coming of the cold war, internal security became a rallying cry on the right. Over this complex scene, there presided — or rather, contended — Harry S Truman, very different as man and politician from Franklin D. Roosevelt. In the following essay Barton J. Bernstein, a leading historian of this period, assesses these problems. Though the limited scholarship as yet done on the 1940s makes his conclusions tentative, Bernstein's analysis successfully puts the decade into perspective.

The essay is valuable also as an example of the New Left approach to recent American history. A group of younger historians has taken issue with the "liberal" analysis of the New Deal and its consequences. While liberal historians have emphasized the advance of social reform and the redistribution of economic and political power under Roosevelt and Truman, the New Left historians stress the limits of those reforms, the exclusion from them of the least privileged Americans, and the preservation and indeed strengthening of the corporate business system.

What is distinctive about the New Left approach is not so much new analysis and fresh information. New Left writings have, in fact, said very little of a substantive nature about the New Deal that was not already said by the liberal historians. That holds, too, for the following essay on the 1940s. With one notable exception — the observation that the liberals' approach to internal security made them vulnerable to attack from the right — Bernstein provides little here of fact or insight that he and others had not already seen from a liberal perspective. The great difference is in the area of judgment. The New Left sets up a moral standard and, by it, measures every action. In the nature of the case, very little passes muster. Hence the querulous tone of Bernstein's essay. Hardly a paragraph passes without the notation of another shortcoming. This approach serves usefully to shake the liberal historians out of their complacency. But one still awaits the distinctive interpretation of the New Deal-Fair Deal that will presumably be forthcoming from New Left historians.

FOR FURTHER READING:

BERNSTEIN, BARTON J. and MATUSOW, ALLEN J., eds. *Truman Administration: A Documentary History.* New York: Harper & Row, Publishers, 1968.*

LUBELL, SAMUEL. *The Future of American Politics.* New York: Harper & Row, Publishers, 1952.*

POLENBERG, RICHARD, ed. *America at War: The Home Front.* Englewood Cliffs, N.J.: Prentice-Hall, 1968.*

Asterisk denotes paperback edition.

America in War and Peace: The Test of Liberalism   BARTON J. BERNSTEIN

The domestic events of the war and postwar years have failed to attract as much scholarly effort as have the few years of the New Deal. The reforms of the thirties and the struggle against depression have captured the enthusiasm of many liberal historians and have constituted the major themes shaping their interpretations. Compared with the excitement of the New Deal years, the events at home during the next decade seem less interesting, certainly less dramatic.

The issues of these years also seem less clear, perhaps because the period lacks the restrictive unity imposed upon the New Deal. Despite the fragmentary scholarship, however, the major issues are definable: economic policies, civil rights, civil liberties and social welfare policies. The continued dominance by big business, the consolidation of other groups within the economy, the challenge of racial inequality — these are the themes of the wartime Roosevelt administration. Toward the end of Roosevelt's years, they are joined by another concern, the quest for social reform, and in Truman's years by such themes as economic readjustment, the renewed struggle against inflation, and the fear of disloyalty and communism. These problems are largely the legacy of the New Deal: the extension of its limited achievements, the response to its shortcomings, the criticism of its liberalism.

It was during the war years that the nation climbed out of depression, that big business regained admiration and increased its power, and that other interests became effective partners in the political economy of large-scale corporate capitalism. While the major interests focused on foreign policy and on domestic economic problems — on mobilization and stabilization, later on reconversion and inflation — liberal democracy was revealing serious weaknesses. Opposing fascism abroad as a threat to democratic values, the nation remained generally insensitive to the plight of its citizens who suffered indignity or injury because of their color. Violating liberal values in the process of saving American democracy, Roosevelt's government, swept along by a wave of racism, victimized Japanese-Americans. Uncommitted to advancing the Negroes' cause, the war government resisted their demands for full participation in democracy and prosperity, and grudgingly extended to them only limited rights.

Though the New Deal had gone intellectually bankrupt long before Pearl Harbor

Source: Barton J. Bernstein, "America in War and Peace: The Test of Liberalism," in *Towards a New Past: Dissenting Essays in American History,* ed. Barton J. Bernstein (New York: Random House, 1968), pp. 289–312.

and reform energies were submerged during most of the war, they reappeared in the last years of the conflict. Reviving the reform spirit in 1944, Roosevelt called for an "Economic Bill of Rights" for postwar America. In his last year, however, he was unable to achieve his goals, and Truman's efforts were usually too weak to overcome the conservative coalition blocking his expanded reform program. Mobilized by apprehension, liberals wrongly believed that the conservative bloc wished to destroy unions, to reorganize the corporate economy, and to leave the nation without protection from depression. But as unions endured and the economy grew, the fears and energies of liberals waned. Exaggerating the accomplishments of past reforms and believing that widespread prosperity had been achieved, they lost much of their social vision: they came to praise big business, to celebrate pluralism, to ignore poverty. Yet to their surprise they fell under vigorous attack from the right, in a new assault on civil liberties. In viewing McCarthyism as an attack upon the reform tradition, however, liberals failed to understand that they and the Democratic administration, as zealous anticommunists, also shared responsibility for the "red scare."

During the war and postwar years, big business regained national admiration and received lavish praise for contributing to victory over fascism. Yet few realized that business had not initially been an enthusiastic participant in the "arsenal of democracy." Such firms as Standard Oil of New Jersey, Dow Chemical, United States Steel, Du Pont, General Motors, and the Aluminum Company of America had assisted the growth of Nazi industry and delayed America's preparation for war. Even after most Americans had come to condemn fascism, these corporations had collaborated with German business, sharing patents and often blocking production of defense materials in America. The general ideology of these firms was probably best expressed by Alfred Sloan, Jr., the chairman of the General Motors board, when he replied to a stockholder: ". . . an international business operating throughout the world should conduct its operations in strictly business terms without regard to the political beliefs in its management, or the political beliefs of the country in which it is operating."

In the two years before Pearl Harbor, major industries were also reluctant to prepare for defense. Though the aircraft industry ended its "sit-down" strike after the government had relaxed profit restrictions and improved terms for amortization other industries continued to resist expansion and production for defense. Sharing the common opinion that American intervention was unlikely, and painfully recalling the glutted markets of the depression decade, the steel industry and the aluminum monopoly (Alcoa) opposed growth, which might endanger profits. Nor were the automobile makers and larger producers of consumer durables willing to take defense contracts which would convert assembly lines from profitable, peacetime goods to preparation for a war that many believed, and President Roosevelt seemed to promise, America would never enter.

Fearful of bad publicity, the leaders of these industries never challenged the administration nor demanded a clear statement of their responsibility. They avoided a dialogue on the basic issues. Still suffering from the opprobrium of the depression, industrialists would not deny corporate responsibility to the nation. Though privately concerned about the welfare of their companies, industrialists never argued that they owed primary responsibility to their stockholders. Fearful of jeopardizing their firms' well-being, company officials did not publicly express their doubts. Yet they could have objected publicly to executive suasion and contended that the issues were so grave that a Congressional mandate was necessary. Instead, they publicly accepted their obligation to risk profits for American defense, but in practice they continued to avoid such risks. Often they made promises they did not fulfill, and when they resisted administration policy, they took refuge in evasion. They restricted the dialogue to matters of feasibility and tactics — that expansion in steel and aluminum was unnecessary, that partial conversion was impossible, and that available tools could not produce defense goods.

The government also avoided opening the dialogue. The prewar mobilization agencies, administered largely by dollar-a-year men, did not seek to embarrass or coerce recalcitrant industries. Protecting business from public censure, the directors of mobilization — such men as William Knudsen of General Motors and Edward Stettinius of United States Steel — resisted the efforts of other government officials to force prompt expansion and conversion. In effect, Knudsen, Stettinius, and their cohorts acted as protectors of "business as usual." Despite the protests of the service secretaries, Roosevelt permitted the businessmen in government to move slowly. Though he encouraged some assistants to prod business, and occasionally spurred the dollar-a-year men, he avoided exerting direct pressure on big business.

The President was following the strategy of caution. Reluctant to encourage public criticism of, or even debate on, his foreign policy, he maneuvered to avoid conflict or challenge. Because the nation respected big businessmen, he chose them to direct mobilization. He too had faith in their ability, and he hoped to win cooperation from the suspicious business community by selecting its leaders as his agents.

While many liberals criticized Roosevelt's reliance upon big business, the most direct, public challenge to business power came from Walter Reuther, vice-president of the recently formed United Automobile Workers, and from Philip Murray, president of the CIO and the United Steel Workers. Criticizing "business as usual" policies, they proposed a labor-management council to guide industry during war. The plan shocked industrialists. It was radicalism, an invasion of management's prerogatives, a threat to private enterprise, asserted business leaders. They would not share power or sanction a redefinition of private property. Having grudgingly recognized industrial unions shortly before the war, they remained suspicious of organized labor and were unwilling to invite its leaders into the industrial councils of decision making.

Despite these suspicions, the administration called upon labor leaders and their organizations for cooperation in the war effort. Needing their support, Roosevelt appointed union chiefs to positions in the stabilization, and mobilization agencies, and thus bestowed prestige upon organized labor. Calling for a labor-management partnership, he secured a wartime no-strike pledge. As junior partners in the controlled economy, labor leaders generally kept the pledge.[1] Cooperating with business leaders in the defense effort, union representatives, by their actions, convinced many businessmen that organized labor did not threaten large-scale corporate capitalism.[2] By encouraging labor-management cooperation, the war years, then, provided a necessary respite between the industrial violence of the thirties and sustained collective bargaining, and speeded the consolidation of the new organization of the American economy.

It was within a government-controlled economy (dominated by business) that the major interests struggled for economic advantages. Farmers, rescued from the depression by enlarged demand, initially battled price controls but soon acceded to them and tried simply to use political power to increase their benefits. Also reaping the gains of war, workers received higher incomes but bitterly criticized the tight restraints on hourly wage increases. Business, also recovering from the depression, complained about price controls, which indirectly limited profits. Though all interests chafed under the restraints, none disputed in principle the need for government-imposed restraints on wages and prices: all agreed that a free price system during war, when civilian demand greatly outstripped consumer goods, would have created inequity and chaos.

Despite price restrictions and the excess-profits tax, the major corporations prospered, benefitting from cost-plus contracts and the five-year amortization plan (which made the new plants partial gifts from the government). As dollar-a-year men poured into Washington, big firms gained influence and contracts. Smaller businessmen, unable to match the influence and mistrusted by procurement officers, declined in importance. In a nation that prized the large corporation, few had confidence in small business. Even the creation of a government agency to protect small business failed to increase significantly its share in the war economy.

The interests of big business were defended and advanced by the dollar-a-year men, and particularly by those on the War Production Board (WPB), the agency controlling resources. In many wartime Washington agencies, and especially on the WPB, the leaders of big business and the military served together and learned to cooperate. Burying earlier differences about preparation for war, they developed similar views of the national interest and identified it with the goals of their own groups. The reconversion controversy of 1944, which C. Wright Mills views as the beginning of the military-industrial alliance, is the outstanding example of this coalition of interests.

In early 1944, big business was experiencing large military cutbacks and withdrawing subcontracts from smaller firms, often leaving them idle. Temporarily proponents of strong controls, most of the WPB executives from industry and finance would not allow these smaller firms to return to consumer goods. They collaborated with representatives of the military to block the reconversion program. Desiring control of the wartime economy, such military leaders as Robert P. Patterson, Under Secretary of War, James Forrestal, Under Secretary of the Navy, and Major General Lucius Clay, Assistant Chief of Staff for Matériel, feared that reconversion would siphon off scarce labor and disrupt vital production. Joining them were such WPB executives as Charles E. Wilson, president of General Electric, Lemuel Boulware, a Celotex executive and later a General Electric vice-president, and financiers Arthur H. Bunker of Lehman Brothers and Sidney Weinberg of Goldman, Sachs. Sympathetic to military demands, they were also afraid that the earlier return of small producers to consumer markets would injure big business. While some may have acted to protect their own companies, most were simply operating in a value system that could not accept a policy which seemed to threaten big business. Through cunning maneuvering, these military and industrial leaders acted to protect the prewar oligopolistic structure of the American economy.

The war, while creating the limited prosperity that the New Deal had failed to create, did not disrupt the economic distribution of power. Nor did the extension of the wartime income tax significantly reallocate income and wealth, for the Congress even rebuffed Roosevelt's effort to limit the war incomes of the wealthy. Though the wartime measures and not the New Deal increased the tax burden on the upper-income groups, "the major weight," emphasizes Gabriel Kolko, "fell on income groups that had never before been subjected to the income tax."

Failing to limit business power or to reallocate wealth, the wartime government was more active in other areas. Yielding to pressures, Roosevelt slightly advanced the welfare of the Negro, but the President also bowed to illiberal pressures and dealt a terrible blow to civil liberties when he authorized the forced evacuation of 110,000 loyal Americans of Japanese descent.

It was the "worse single wholesale violation of civil rights" in American history, judged the American Civil Liberties Union. Succumbing to the anti-Japanese hysteria of Westerners (including the pleas of California Attorney-General Earl Warren and the Pacific coast congressional delegation under Senator Hiram Johnson) and the demands of the military commander on the coast, the President empowered the Army to remove the Japanese-Americans.[3] ("He was never theoretical about things. What must be done to defend the country must be done," Roosevelt believed, later wrote Francis Biddle, his Attorney-General.) "Japanese raids on the west coast seemed not only possible but probable in the first months of war, and it was quite impossible to be sure that the raiders would not receive important help from individuals of Japanese origin," was the explanation later endorsed by Secretary of War Henry Stimson.

Privately Stimson called the episode a "tragedy," but he supported it as War Department policy. Opposing the decision, Biddle could not weaken the resolve of Roosevelt. Though liberals protested the action, the Supreme Court later upheld Roosevelt and the War Department.[4] "The meaning of the decision," concludes Arthur Link, "was clear and foreboding: in future emergencies no American citizen would have any rights that the President and the army were bound to respect when, *in their judgment*, the emergency justified drastic denial of civil rights."

Though anti-Japanese feeling was most virulent on the Pacific coast, racism was not restricted to any part of America. In most of America, Negroes had long been the victims of hatred. Frequently lacking effective legal protection in the South, Negroes also encountered prejudice, fear, and hatred in the North. During the war there were racial clashes in Northern cities. New York narrowly averted a major riot. In Los Angeles whites attacked Negroes and Mexicans, and in Detroit whites invaded the Negro sector and pillaged and killed.[5]

Despite the evidence of deep racism, liberal historians have usually avoided focusing upon the hatred in white America and the resort to violence. Curiously, though emphasizing the disorganization of the Negro community, they have also neglected the scattered protests by organized Negroes — boycotts of white-owned stores in Negro areas of Memphis and Houston when they would not hire Negroes, a sit-in in a public library in Alexandria, Virginia, a Harlem boycott of a bus line to compel the hiring of Negro drivers.

Condemned to inferiority in nearly all sectors of American life, Negroes did not share in the benefits of the early defense economy. Denied jobs in many industries, they also met discrimination by the military. The Air Corps barred them, the Navy segregated them to the mess corps, and the Army held them to a small quota, generally restricting them to menial tasks. During the 1940 campaign, Negro leaders attacked the administration for permitting segregation and discrimination, and demanded the broadening of opportunity in the military. It is not "a fight merely to wear a uniform," explained *Crisis* (the NAACP publication). "This is a struggle for status, a struggle to take democracy off a parchment and give it life."

Negroes gained admission to the Air Corps when it yielded under White House pressure, but they failed to gain congressional support for wider participation in the military. At Roosevelt's direction the War Department did raise its quota of Negroes — to their proportion in the population. But the Army remained segregated. Though unwilling to challenge segregation, the administration still courted Negro leaders and the black vote. Rather than bestowing benefits upon the masses, Roosevelt maintained their allegiance by offering symbolic recognition: Colonel Benjamin O. Davis, the Army's highest ranking Negro, was promoted to Brigadier General, and some prominent Negroes were appointed as advisers to the Secretary of War and the Director of Selective Service. ("We asked Mr. Roosevelt to change the rules of the game and he countered by giving us some new uniforms," complained the editors of the *Baltimore Afro-American.* "That is what it amounts to and we have called it appeasement.")

As the nation headed toward war, Negroes struggled to wring other concessions from a president who never enlisted in their cause and would not risk antagonizing powerful Southerners. Discriminated against by federal agencies during the depression and denied an equal share of defense prosperity, Negroes were unwilling to acquiesce before continued injustice. In some industrial areas the NAACP and *ad hoc* groups organized local protests. After numerous unsuccessful appeals to the President, Negro leaders planned more dramatic action — a march on Washington.

Demanding "the right to work and fight for our country," the leaders of the March on Washington Movement — A. Philip Randolph, head of the Brotherhood of Sleeping Car Porters, Walter White, executive secretary of the NAACP, and Lester Granger, executive secretary of the Urban League — publicly requested executive orders ending racial discrimination in federal agencies, the military and defense employment. In private correspondence with the President they sought more: the end of segregation in these areas. So bold were their goals that some still have not been enforced by the government, and it is unlikely that Negro leaders expected to secure them.

Refusing to give up the march for the promise of negotiations, Negro leaders escaped the politics of accommodation. Though white liberals urged Randolph and his cohorts to call off the march, they would not yield. Applying pressure on an uncomfortable administration, they ultimately settled for less than they had requested (and perhaps less than they had anticipated) — an executive order barring discrimination in defense work and creating a Federal Employment Practices Committee (FEPC). Meager as the order was, it was the greatest achievement in American history for organized Negro action.[6]

FEPC did not contribute significantly to the wartime advancement of the Negro. His gains were less the results of federal efforts than of the labor shortage. Undoubtedly, the committee would have been more effective if Roosevelt had provided it with a larger budget, but the Negro's cause never commanded the President's enthusiasm. Yet he did protect FEPC from its enemies, and by maintaining the agency, stressed its symbolic importance.

It affirmed the rights of Negroes to jobs and focused attention on the power of the federal government to advance the interests of its black citizens. It did not smash the walls of prejudices; it only removed a few bricks. FEPC, concludes Louis Ruchames, "brought hope and a new confidence into their [Negro] lives. It gave them cause to believe in democracy and in America. It made them feel that in answering the call to their country's colors, they were defending, not the oppression and degradation, to which they were accustomed, but democracy, equality of opportunity, and a better world for themselves and their children."

Still relegated to second-class citizenship, Negroes had found new dignity and new opportunity during the war. Loyal followers of Roosevelt, loving him for the few benefits his government had extended, black Americans had become important members of the shifting Democratic coalition. By their presence in Northern cities, they would also become a new political force. For the Democratic party and the nation, their expectations and needs would constitute a moral and political challenge. By its response, white America would test the promise of liberal democracy.

When the nation joined the Allies, Roosevelt had explained that "Dr. Win-the-War" was taking over from "Dr. New Deal," and there were few liberal legislative achievements during the war years. Those benefits that disadvantaged groups did receive were usually a direct result of the labor shortage and the flourishing economy, not of liberal politics. By 1944, however, Roosevelt was prepared to revive the reform spirit, and he revealed his liberal vision for the postwar years. Announcing an "Economic Bill of Rights," he outlined "a new basis for security and prosperity": the right to a job, adequate food, clothing, and recreation, a decent home, a good education, adequate medical care, and protection against sickness and unemployment.[7]

Noble as was his vision of the future society, Roosevelt was still unprepared to move far beyond rhetoric, and the Congress was unsympathetic to his program. While approving the GI Bill of Rights,[8] including educational benefits and extended unemployment pay, Congress resisted most liberal programs during the war. Asserting its independence of the executive, the war Congress also thwarted Roosevelt in other ways — by rejecting a large tax bill designed to spread the cost of war and to reduce inflationary pressures) and by liquidating the National Resources Planning Board, which had originated the "second bill of rights" and also studied postwar economic planning.

By its opposition to planning and social reform, Congress increased the anxieties of labor and liberals about the postwar years and left the new Truman administration poorly prepared for the difficult transition to a peacetime economy when the war suddenly ended. Fearing the depression that most economists forecast, the administration did, however, propose a tax cut of $5 billion. While removing many low-income recipients from the tax rolls, the law was also of great benefit to large corporations. Charging inequity, organized labor found little support in Congress or the executive, for the government was relying upon business activity, rather than on consumer purchasing power, to soften the economic decline. Significantly, despite the anticipated $30 billion deficit (plus the $5 billion tax), no congressman expressed any fear of an unbalanced budget. Clearly fiscal orthodoxy did not occupy a very high place in the scale of values of congressional conservatives, and they accepted in practice the necessity of an unbalanced budget.

Before the tax bill passed, the wartime harmony of the major interest groups had crumbled: each struggled to consolidate its gains and advance its welfare before the anticipated economic collapse. Chafing under the no-strike pledge and restrictions on wage raises, organized labor compelled the administration to relax its policy and free unions to bargain collectively. Farmers, fearful of depression, demanded the withdrawal of subsidies which artificially depressed prices. Big business, despite anticipated shortages, secured the removal of most controls on the allocation of resources.

As the economic forecasts shifted in late autumn, the administration discovered belatedly that inflation, not depression, was the immediate economic danger. The President acted sporadically to restrain inflationary pressures, but his efforts were too occasional, often misguided, and too weak to resist the demands of interest groups and the actions of his own subordinates.

Beset by factionalism and staffed often by men of limited ability, Truman's early government floundered. By adopting the practice of cabinet responsibility and delegating excessive authority to department chiefs, Truman created a structure that left him uninformed: problems frequently developed unnoticed until they had swelled to crises, and the choice then was often between undesirable alternatives. Operating in a new politics, in the politics of inflation, he confronted problems requiring greater tactical skill than those Roosevelt had confronted. Seeking to maintain economic controls, and compelled to deny the rising expectations of major interest groups, his administration found it difficult to avoid antagonizing the rival groups. In the politics of depression, the Roosevelt administration could frequently maintain political support by bestowing specific advantages on groups, but in the politics of inflation the major interest groups came to seek freedom from restrictive federal controls.

So difficult were the problems facing Truman that even a more experienced and skilled president would have encountered great difficulty. Inheriting the hostile Congress that had resisted occasional wartime attempts at social reform, Truman lacked the skill or leverage to guide a legislature seeking to assert its independence of the executive. Unable to halt fragmentation of the Democratic coalition, and incapable of ending dissension in his government, he also found that conservative subordinates undercut his occasional liberalism. Though he had gone on record early in endorsing a reform program ("a declaration of independence" from congressional conservatives, he called it), he had been unsuccessful in securing most of the legislation — a higher minimum wage, public housing, expanded unemployment benefits, and FEPC. Even the employment act was little more, as one congressman said, than a license to look for a job. The President, through ineptitude or lack of commitment, often chose not to struggle for his program. Unable to dramatize the issues or to command enthusiasm, he was an ineffectual leader.[9]

So unsuccessful was his government that voters began jibing, "To err is Truman." Despairing of a resurgence of liberalism under Truman, New Dealers left the government in droves. By the fall of 1946, none of Roosevelt's associates was left in a prominent position. So disgruntled were many liberals about Truman and his advisers, about his unwillingness to fight for price controls, housing, benefits for labor, and civil rights, that some turned briefly to serious consideration of a new party.[10]

Achieving few reforms during his White House years, Truman, with the notable exception of civil rights, never moved significantly beyond Roosevelt. The Fair Deal was largely an extension of earlier Democratic liberalism, but Truman's new vigor and fierce partisanship ultimately made him more attractive to liberals who despairingly watched the GOP-dominated Eightieth Congress and feared a repeal of the New Deal.

Their fears were unwarranted, as was their enthusiasm for the Fair Deal program. In practice it proved very limited — the housing program only provided for 810,000 units in six years of which only 60,000 were constructed;[11] social security benefits were extended to ten million[12] and increased by about 75 percent, and the minimum wage was increased to 75 cents, but coverage was reduced by nearly a million. But even had all of the Fair Deal been enacted, liberal reform would have left many millions beyond the benefits of government. The very poor, the marginal men, those neglected but acknowledged by the New Deal, went ultimately unnoticed by the Fair Deal.[13]

While liberals frequently chafed under Truman's leadership and questioned his commitment, they failed generally to recognize how shallow were his reforms. As the nation escaped a postwar depression, American liberals gained new faith in the American economy. Expressing their enthusiasm, they came to extol big business for its contributions. Believing firmly in the success of progressive taxation, they exaggerated its effects, and congratulated themselves on the redistribution of income and the virtual abolition of poverty. Praising the economic system, they accepted big agriculture and big labor as evidence of healthy pluralism that protected freedom and guaranteed an equitable distribution of resources.

Despite the haggling over details and the liberals' occasional dismay at Truman's style, he expressed many of their values. Like Roosevelt, Truman never challenged big business, never endangered large-scale capitalism. Indeed, his efforts as well as theirs were directed largely to maintaining and adjusting the powers of the major economic groups.

Fearing that organized labor was threatened with destruction, Truman, along with the liberals, had been sincerely frightened by the postwar rancor toward labor. What they failed to understand was that most Americans had accepted unions as part of the political economy. Certainly most major industrialists had accepted organized labor, though smaller businessmen were often hostile. Despite the overwrought rhetoric of debates, Congress did not actually menace labor. It was not seeking to destroy labor, only to restrict its power.

Many Americans did believe that the Wagner Act had unduly favored labor and was creating unions indifferent to the public welfare and hostile to corporate power. Capitalizing on this exaggerated fear of excessive union power, and the resentment from the postwar strikes, businessmen secured the Taft-Hartley Act. Designed to weaken organized labor, it tried but failed to protect the membership from leaders; it did not effectively challenge the power of established unions. However, labor chiefs, recalling the bitter industrial warfare of the thirties, were still uneasy in their new positions. Condemning the legislation as a "slave-labor" act, they responded with fear, assailed the Congress, and declared that Taft-Hartley was the major political issue.

Within a few years, when unions discovered that they were safe, Taft-Hartley faded as an issue. But in 1948 it served Truman well by establishing the GOP's hostility to labor and casting it back into the Democratic ranks. Both the President and union chiefs conveniently neglected his own kindling of antilabor passions (as when he had tried to draft strikers). Exploiting Taft-Hartley as part of his strategy of patching the tattered Democratic coalition, Truman tied repeal of the "slave-labor" law to price controls, farm benefits, anticommunism, and civil rights in the campaign which won his election in his own right.

In courting the Negro the Truman administration in 1948 made greater promises to black citizens than had any previous federal government in American history. Yet, like many Americans, Truman as a senator had regarded the Negro's plight as peripheral to his interests, and with many of his generation he believed that equality was compatible with segregation. As President, however, he found himself slowly prodded by conscience and pushed by politics. He moved cautiously at first and endorsed only measures affirming legal equality and protecting Negroes from violence.

Reluctant to fragment the crumbling Democratic coalition, Truman, in his first year, had seemed to avoid taking positions on civil rights which might upset the delicate balance between Northern and Southern Democrats. While he endorsed legislation for a statutory FEPC that the Congress would not grant, his efforts on behalf of the temporary FEPC (created by Roosevelt's executive order) were weaker. Having already weakened the power of the temporary agency, he also acquiesced in the legislative decision to kill it. Despite the fears of Negro leaders that the death of FEPC would leave Negroes virtually unprotected from discrimination in the postwar job market, Truman would not even issue an order requiring nondiscrimination in the federal service and by government contractors.

Though Truman was unwilling to use the prestige or power of his great office significantly on behalf of Negroes, he did assist their cause. While sidestepping political conflict, he occasionally supported FEPC and abolition of the poll tax. When Negroes were attacked, he did condemn the racial violence. Though generally reluctant to move beyond rhetoric during his early years, Truman, shortly before the 1946 election, found conscience and politics demanding more. So distressed was he by racial violence that when Walter White of the NAACP and a group of white liberals urged him to assist the Negro, he promised to create a committee to study civil rights.

The promise of a committee could have been a device to resist pressures, to delay the matter until after the election. And Truman could have appointed a group of politically safe men of limited reputation — men he could control. But instead, after the election, perhaps in an effort to mobilize the liberals for 1948, he appointed a committee of prominent men sympathetic to civil rights. They were men he could not control and did not seek to control.

The committee's report, undoubtedly far bolder than Truman's expectations, confirmed charges that America treated its Negroes as second-class citizens. It called for FEPC, an antilynching law, an anti-poll tax measure, abolition of segregation in interstate transportation, and the end of discrimination and segregation in federal agencies and the military. By attacking Jim Crow, the committee had moved to a redefinition of equality and interpreted segregation as incompatible with equality.

Forced by the report to take a position, he no longer could easily remain an ally of Southern Democrats and maintain the wary allegiance of Negro leaders and urban liberals. Compelled earlier to yield to demands for advancement of the Negro, pressures which he did not wish fully to resist, Truman had encouraged these forces and they were moving beyond his control. On his decision, his political future might precariously rest. Threatened by Henry Wallace's candidacy on a third-party ticket, Truman had to take a bold position on civil rights or risk losing the important votes of urban Negroes. Though he might antagonize Southern voters, he foresaw no risk of losing Southern Democrats, no possibility of a bolt by dissidents, and the mild Southern response to the Civil Rights Report seemed to confirm this judgment.

On February 2, 1948, Truman asked the Congress to enact most of the recommendations of his Civil Rights Committee (except most of those attacking segregation). Rather than using his executive powers, as the committee had urged, to end segregation in federal employment or to abolish segregation and discrimination in the military, he *promised* only to issue orders ending discrimination (but not specifying segregation) in the military and in federal agencies. Retreating to moderation, the administration did not submit any of the legislation, nor did Truman issue the promised executive orders. "The strategy," an assistant later explained, "was to start with a bold measure and then temporize to pick up the right-wing forces. Simply stated, backtrack after the bang."

Truman sought to ease Southern doubts by inserting in the 1948 platform the party's moderate 1944 plank on civil rights. Most Negro leaders, fearing the taint of Wallace and unwilling to return to the GOP, appeared stuck with Truman and they praised him. Though they desired a stronger plank, they would not abandon him at the convention, for his advocacy of rights for Negroes was unmatched by any twentieth-century president. To turn their backs on him in this time of need, most Negroes feared, would be injuring their own cause. But others were prepared to struggle for a stronger plank. Urban bosses, persuaded that Truman would lose, hoped to save their local tickets, and prominent white liberals sought power and principle. Triumphing at the convention, they secured a stronger plank, but it did not promise social equality. By promising equality when it was still regarded as compatible with segregation, they were offering far less than the "walk forthrightly into the bright sunshine of human rights," which Hubert Humphrey, then mayor of Minneapolis, had pledged in leading the liberal effort.

When some of the Southerners bolted and formed the States Rights party, Truman was freed of any need for tender courtship of the South. He had to capture the Northern vote. Quickly he issued the long-delayed executive orders, which established a federal antidiscrimination board, declared a policy of equal opportunity in the armed forces, and established a committee to end military discrimination and segregation. (In doing so, Truman courted Negro voters and halted the efforts of A. Philip Randolph to lead a Negro revolt against the draft unless the military was integrated.) Playing politics carefully during the campaign, Truman generally stayed away from civil rights and concentrated on inflation, public housing, and Taft-Hartley.

In the new Democratic Congress Truman could not secure the civil rights program, and a coalition of Southern Democrats and Northern Republicans blocked his efforts. Though liberals were unhappy with his leadership, they did not question his proposed legislation. All agreed on the emphasis on social change through legislation and judicial decisions. The liberal way was the legal way, and it seldom acknowledged the depth of American racism or even considered the possibility of bold new tactics. Only occasionally — in the threatened March on Washington in 1941, in some ride-ins in 1947, and in the campaign of civil disobedience against the draft in 1948 — had there been bolder means. In each case Negroes had devised and carried out these tactics. But generally they relied upon more traditional means: they expected white America to yield to political pressure and subscribe to the dictates of American democracy. By relying upon legal change, however, and by emphasizing measures to restore a *modicum* of human dignity, Negroes and whites did not confront the deeper problems of race relations which they failed to understand.[14]

Struggling for moderate institutional changes, liberals were disappointed by Truman's frequent unwillingness to use his executive powers in behalf of the cause he claimed to espouse. Only after considerable pressure did he create a FEPC-type agency during the Korean War. His loyalty-and-security program, in its operation, discriminated against Negroes, and federal investigators, despite protests to Truman, apparently continued to inquire into attitudes of interracial sympathy as evidence relevant to a determination of disloyalty. He was also slow to require the Federal Housing Administration to stop issuing mortgages on property with restrictive covenants, and it continued, by its policies, to protect residential segregation.

Yet his government was not without significant achievements in civil rights. His special committee had quietly acted to integrate the armed forces, and even the recalcitrant Army had abolished racial quotas when the President secretly promised their restoration if the racial imbalance became severe. And the Department of Justice, despite Truman's apparent indifference, had been an active warrior in the battle against Jim Crow. Entering cases as an *amicus curiae,* Justice had submitted briefs arguing the unconstitutionality of enforcing restrictive covenants and of requiring separate-but-equal facilities in interstate transportation and in higher education. During the summer of 1952, the Solicitor-General's Office even won the administration's approval for a brief directly challenging segregated primary education.

The accomplishments of the Truman years were moderate, and the shortcomings left the nation with a great burden of unresolved problems. Viewed from the perspective of today, Truman's own views seem unduly mild and his government excessively cautious; viewed even by his own time he was a reluctant liberal, troubled by terror and eager to establish limited equality. He was ahead of public opinion in his legislative requests, but not usually in his actions. By his occasional advocacy, he educated the nation and held high the promise of equality. By kindling hope, he also may have prevented rebellion and restrained or delayed impulses to work outside of the system. But he also unleashed expectations he could not foresee, and forces which future governments would not be able to restrain.

Never as committed to civil rights as he was opposed to communism at home and abroad, Truman ultimately became a victim of his own loyalty-and-security policies. Mildly criticized in 1945 and 1946 for being "soft on communism," the administration belatedly responded after the disastrous election of 1946. Truman appointed a committee to investigate loyalty and security, promptly accepted its standard of judgment ("reasonable grounds of belief in disloyalty"), and created a system of loyalty boards.

Outraging many liberals, his loyalty program provoked vigorous criticisms — for its secret investigations, for the failure to guarantee the accused the right to know the identity of and cross-examine the accuser, for its loose standards of proof, for its attempt to anticipate disloyal behavior by inquiring into attitudes. In seeking to protect the nation, the government seemed to be searching for all who might be disloyal — "potential subversives," Truman called them.

Dangerously confusing the problems of loyalty and security, the administration, in what might seem a burst of democratic enthusiasm, decided to apply the same standards to diplomats and gardeners. Disloyalty at any level of government would endanger the nation. "The presence within the government of any disloyal or subversive persons constitutes a threat to democratic processes," asserted Truman in launching the program. Anxious to remove communism in government as a possible issue, Truman had exaggerated the dangers to the nation. And by assuming that disloyalty could be determined and subversives discovered, Truman seemed also to be promising *absolute* internal security.

Shocked by earlier lax security procedures and unwilling to rely exclusively upon counterintelligence to uncover spies, the administration had responded without proper concern for civil liberties. So extreme was the program that it should have removed loyalty and security as a political issue. But by failing to distinguish between radical political activity and disloyalty, the administration endangered dissent and liberal politics: it made present or past membership in organizations on the Attorney-General's list evidence of possible disloyalty. Thus, in justifying investigations of political activity, it also legitimized occasional right-wing attacks on the liberal past and encouraged emphasis on the radicalism of a few New Dealers as evidence of earlier subversion.

In their own activities, many liberals were busy combatting domestic communism. Taking up the cudgels, the liberal Americans for Democratic Action (ADA) came often to define its purpose by its anticommunism. As an enemy of those liberals who would not renounce association with Communists, and, hence, as vigorous foes of the Progressive party, the ADA was prepared to do battle. Following Truman's strategy, ADA members assailed Wallace and his supporters as Communists, dupes of the Communists, and fellow travelers. To publicize its case the ADA even relied upon the tactic of guilt by association and paid for advertisements listing the Progressive party's major donors and the organizations on the Attorney-General's list with which they were or had been affiliated. (Truman himself also red-baited. "I do not want and will not accept the political support of Henry Wallace and his Communists. . . . These are days of high prices for everything, but any price for Wallace and his Communists is too much for me to pay.") In the labor movement liberals like the Reuther brothers led anticommunist crusades, and the CIO ultimately expelled its Communist-led unions. ("Granting the desirability of eliminating Communist influence from the trade union movement," later wrote Irving Howe and Louis Coser, "one might still have argued that mass expulsions were not only a poor way of achieving this end but constituted a threat to democratic values and procedures.")

Expressing the administration's position, Attorney-General J. Howard McGrath proclaimed a "struggle against pagan communist philosophies that seek to enslave the world." "There are today many Communists in America," he warned. "They are everywhere — in factories, offices, butcher stores, on street corners, in private business. And each carries in himself the death of our society." ("I don't think anybody ought to be employed as instructors [sic] for the young people of this country who believes in the destruction of our form of government," declared Truman.)[15]

Calling for a crusade against evil, viewing communism as a virulent poison, the administration continued to emphasize the need for *absolute* protection, for *absolute* security. By creating such high standards and considering their fulfillment easy, by making success evidence of will and resolution, the administration risked assaults if its loyalty-and-security program was proved imperfect. To discredit the administration, all that was needed was the discovery of some red "spies," and after 1948 the evidence seemed abundant — Alger Hiss, William Remington, Judith Coplon, Julius and Ethel Rosenberg.

In foreign policy, too, Truman, though emphasizing the danger of communism, had promised success. Containment could stop the spread of communism: military expansion could be restrained and revolutions prevented. Since revolutions, by liberal definition, were imposed on innocent people by a small minority, a vigilant American government could block them. By his rhetoric, he encouraged American innocence and left many citizens little choice but to believe in their own government's failure when America could not thwart revolution — when the Chinese Communists triumphed. If only resolute will was necessary, as the administration suggested, then what could citizens believe about America's failure? Was it simply bungling? Or treason and betrayal?

By his rhetoric and action, Truman had contributed to the loss of public confidence and set the scene in which Joseph McCarthy could flourish. Rather than resisting the early movement of anticommunism, he had acted energetically to become a leader, and ultimately contributed to its transformation into a crusade which threatened his administration. But the President could never understand his own responsibility, and his failure handicapped him. Because he had a record of vigorous anticommunism, Truman was ill-prepared to respond to McCarthy's charges. At first the President could not foresee any danger and tried to dispense with McCarthy as "the greatest asset the Kremlin has." And later, as the Senator terrorized the government, Truman was so puzzled and pained that he retreated from the conflict and sought to starve McCarthy without publicity. Rather than responding directly to charges, the President tried instead to tighten his program. But he could not understand that such efforts (for example, revising the loyalty standard to "reasonable doubt as to the loyalty of the individual") could not protect the administration from charges of being soft on communism. He only encouraged these charges by seeming to yield to criticism, admitting that the earlier program was unnecessarily lax.

The President was a victim of his own policies and tactics. But bristling anticommunism was not simply Truman's way, but often the liberal way. And the use of guilt by association, the discrediting of dissent, the intemperate rhetoric — these, too, were not simply the tactics of the Truman administration. The rancor and wrath of these years were not new to American politics, nor to liberals. Indeed, the style of passionate charges and impugning opponents' motives may be endemic to American democratic politics. Submerging the issues in passion, using labels as substitutes for thought, questioning motives, these tactics characterized much of the foreign policy debate of the prewar and postwar years as well — a debate in which the liberals frequently triumphed. Developing a more extreme form of this rancorous style, relying upon even wilder charges and more flagrant use of guilt by association, McCarthy and his cohorts flailed the liberals and the Democratic administration.

In looking at the war and postwar years, liberal scholars have emphasized the achievements of democratic reform, the extension of prosperity, the movements to greater economic and social equality. Confident that big business had become socially responsible and that economic security was widespread, they have celebrated the triumph of democratic liberalism. In charting the course of national progress, they frequently neglected or minimized major problems, or they interpreted them as temporary aberrations, or blamed them on conservative forces.

Yet the developments of the sixties — the rediscovery of poverty and racism — suggest that the emphasis has been misplaced in interpreting these earlier years. In the forties and fifties white racism did not greatly yield to the dictates of American democracy, and the failure was not only the South's. The achievements of democratic liberalism were more limited than its advocates believed, and its reforms left many Americans still without adequate assistance. Though many liberal programs were blocked or diluted by conservative opposition, the liberal vision itself was dim. Liberalism in practice was defective, and its defects contributed to the temporary success of McCarthyism. Curiously, though liberalism was scrutinized by some sympathizers who attacked its faith in progress and by others who sought to trace McCarthyism to the reform impulses of earlier generations, most liberals failed to understand their own responsibility for the assault upon civil liberties or to respond to the needs of an "other America" which they but dimly perceived.

NOTES

1. . . . It was in response to the coal strikes led by John Lewis that Congress passed the Smith-Connally Act.
2. "With few exceptions throughout the war years, labor, not management, made the sacrifices when sacrifices were necessary," concludes Paul A. C. Koistinen, "The Hammer and the Sword: Labor, the Military, and Industrial Mobilization" (unpublished Ph.D. dissertation, University of California at Berkeley, 1965), p. 143.
3. Stetson Conn et al., *Guarding the United States and Its Outposts,* in *United States Army in World War II: The Western Hemisphere* (Washington, 1964), pp. 115–49. The Canadian government also moved Japanese away from the coast.
4. *Korematsu* v. *U.S.,* 323 US 214, at 219. The Court split and Justice Black wrote the opinion. Justices Roberts, Murphy and Jackson dissented. Also see *Hirabayshi* v. *U.S.,* 320 US 81.
5. Apparently Roosevelt refused to condemn the riots. Vito Marcantonio to Roosevelt, June 16, 1943, and reply, July 14, 1943, Vito Marcantonio Papers, New York Public Library. Also see Roosevelt's Proclamation No. 2588, in Samuel Rosenman, ed., *The Public Papers of Franklin D. Roosevelt* (13 vols.; New York, 1938–50), *XII,* 258–59.
6. For the notion that the events of the war years constitute the beginnings of the civil rights revolution, see Dalfiume, "Desegregation of the Armed Forces," pp. 177–89.
7. Message on the State of the Union, January 11, 1944, in Rosenman, ed., *Public Papers of Roosevelt, XIII,* p. 41. For some evidence that Roosevelt was at least talking about a new alignment of politics, see Samuel Rosenman, *Working with Roosevelt* (London, 1952), pp. 423–29. Probably this was a tactical maneuver.
8. President's statement on signing the GI Bill of Rights, June 22, 1944, in Rosenman, ed., *Public Papers of Roosevelt, XIII,* 180–82, and Rosenman's notes, pp. 183–84. The GI Bill has generally been neglected as an antidepression measure.
9. Lubell, *The Future of American Politics,* pp. 8–27, while emphasizing the continuation of the prewar executive-legislative stalemate and the strength of conservative forces in the postwar years, has also been critical of Truman. "All his skills and energies . . . were directed to standing still. . . . When he took vigorous action in one direction it was axiomatic that he would contrive soon afterward to move in the conflicting direction. . . ."
10. Curtis MacDougall, *Gideon's Army* (3 vols.; New York, 1965–66), *I,* 102–27. The National Educational Committee for a New Party, which would be explicitly anticommunist, included John Dewey, A. Philip Randolph, Daniel Bell, and Lewis Corey.
11. Richard O. Davis, *Housing Reform during the Truman Administration* (Columbia, Mo.) p. 136. The original measure aimed for 1,050,000 units in seven years, at a time when the nation needed more than 12,000,000 units to replace inadequate housing. During the Truman years, the government constructed 60,000 units of public housing. . . . Rather than creating programs to keep pace with urban needs, the government in these years fell further behind. In contrast, private industry was more active, and it was assisted by noncontroversial federal aid. Under Truman's government, then, the greatest achievement in housing was that private capital, protected by the government, built houses for the higher-income market.

12. Under the old law, the maximum benefit for families was $85 a month and the minimum was $15, depending on prior earnings. The new minimum was $25 and the maximum $150. (*Social Security Bulletin,* September 1950, p. 3). Unless couples also had other sources of income, even maximum benefits ($1,800 a year) placed them $616 under the BLS "maintenance" standard of living and $109 above the WPA-based "emergency" standard of living — the poverty level. (Calculations based on Kolko, *Wealth and Power,* pp. 96–98.) Since the payments were based on earnings, lower-income groups would receive even fewer benefits. They were the people generally without substantial savings or significant supplementary sources of income, and therefore they needed even more, not less, assistance.

13. Bernstein, "Economic Policies of the Truman Administration." Truman had achieved very little: improved unemployment benefits, some public power and conservation projects, agricultural assistance, and a National Science Foundation. He failed to secure the ill-conceived Brannan Plan and two programs suggested by Roosevelt: federal aid to education and health insurance. For his health insurance programs, see his messages of November 19, 1945, in *Public Papers of Truman* (1945), pp. 485–90, and of May 19, 1947, in *ibid.,* (1947), pp. 250–52. In 1951, when the BLS calculated that a family of four needed $4,166 to reach the "maintenance" level, 55.6 percent of the nation's families had incomes beneath that level (Bureau of the Census, *Income Distribution in the United States,* p. 16).

14. There was no urging of special programs to assist Negroes left unemployed (at roughly double the white rate) in the mild recession of 1949–1950, nor was there open acknowledgment of race hatred.

15. . . . In his veto of the McCarran Act, Truman failed to defend civil liberties effectively and instead emphasized that the act would impair the government's anticommunist efforts. Veto message of September 22, 1950, *Public Papers of Truman* (1950), pp. 645–53.

America in the World Arena

The cold war, however it began, was unmistakable in its consequences. Casting aside the last vestiges of its historic isolationism, the United States plunged headlong into the era of interventionism. Beginning with the Truman Doctrine of March 1947, the country committed itself to resisting the tide of Communist expansion. Economic aid began to flow, an elaborate structure of anti-Communist alliances emerged, and American military forces took up stations around the world. By 1967, almost 120 billion dollars in assistance had been expended, 700,000 American soldiers were encamped on foreign soil, four regional defense alliances and 42 mutual defense treaties committed the United States throughout the world, and the country was mired in a land war in Southeast Asia. That last fact, more than anything else, brought home to the United States the enormity of the task it had undertaken as the world's policeman.

This role, Ronald Steel argues in the following selection, began in a realistic response to the Soviet Union in the late 1940s. Since then, however, the undertaking has grown far out of hand, not so much from deliberate choice, Steel suggests, as by accident. But the underlying reasons for the interventionist course are hardly accidental. First, there was the moralism with which the New World had always viewed the Old World. Second, there was the enormous power that suddenly was America's to wield. These two circumstances conspired to a fatal conclusion: that the United States *should* and *could* work its will throughout the world. Now we are discovering our grievous error on both counts. American power is not unlimited. Nor is American idealism by any means a wonder-working ingredient in world affairs. Ronald Steel points to a further irony. The burdens of interventionism have grown insupportable at the very time that the world situation that called it forth is passing. The cold war as it seemed, say in 1950, is gone. The world is no longer divided into two camps. Western Europe is resurgent; the Communist bloc has fallen into disarray; the Third World has emerged; and nuclear weapons, fearful as they are, do not translate into applicable power. The United States, Steel stresses, finds itself in a world grown much more complex over the past two decades, and one peculiarly intractable before American-style interventionism. It remains to be seen whether America can bring its role into line with world realities and with its own real interests.

FOR FURTHER READING:

ALPEROWITZ, GAR. *Cold War Essays.* New York: Doubleday & Company, Anchor Books, 1969.*

BARNET, RICHARD J. *Intervention and Revolution.* Cleveland: World Publishing Company, Meridian Books, 1969.*

STILLMAN, EDMUND, and PFAFF, WILLIAM. *New Politics: America and the End of the Postwar World.* New York: Harper & Row, Publishers, 1961.*

Asterisk denotes paperback edition.

From *Pax Americana*   RONALD STEEL

"Sometimes people call me an idealist," Woodrow Wilson once said as he stumped the country trying to drum up support for the League of Nations. "Well, that's the way I know I am an American. America, my fellow citizens . . . is the only idealistic nation in the world." Wilson, whose career is a tragic example of what happens when idealism is divorced from political realism, never spoke a truer word. America is an idealistic nation, a nation based upon the belief that the "self-evident truths" of the Declaration of Independence should be extended to unfortunate peoples wherever they may be.

For the first 170 years of our national existence, however, we were content to make this a principle rather than a program of action. America was, in John Quincy Adams' phrase, "the well-wisher to the freedom and independence of all," but "the champion and vindicator only of her own." With the exception of Mexico, the Philippines and a few brief adventures in the Caribbean, our national idealism did not go abroad in search of new fields to conquer. The great European war of 1914–1918 entangled us more against our will than by design. We entered it under the banner of idealism when neutrality became difficult, and we left Europe in disillusionment when power politics reared its ugly head at Versailles. Never again, we said. And never again we did, until the Japanese dragged us into a global war by the attack on Pearl Harbor.

From that time on, American idealism was transformed into a plan. The Word was given Flesh by the mating of American military power to a native idealism. For the first time in its history the nation had the ability to seek its idealistic goals by active intervention rather than merely by pious proclamation. The result was twin crusades, one in Europe, one in Asia: one to restore freedom to the West, one to bring it to the East. But the passing of one tyranny in Europe saw the rise of another; the defeat of Japan gave way to the resurgence of China. The triumph of the Second World War marked not the end of our labors, but only the beginning. It transformed a philosophical commitment to the principles of freedom and democracy into a political commitment to bring them about. American idealism was the foundation; American power was the instrument to achieve the ideals. From 1945 on, we were no longer simply the "well-wisher" to the world; we were its "champion and vindicator" as well. The moral purity of American isolationism gave way to the moral self-justification of American interventionism.

The change from the old isolationism to the new interventionism flowed almost inevitably from the Second World War. The unavoidable war against fascism revealed the bankruptcy of isolationism and destroyed the illusion that America could barricade herself from the immoralities of a corrupt world. It also provided the means for the dramatic growth of American military power which made the new policy of global interventionism possible. As a result of her participation in the war, America became not only a great world power but *the* world power. Her fleets roamed all the seas, her military bases extended around the earth's periphery, her soldiers stood guard from Berlin to Okinawa, and her alliances spanned the earth.

The Second World War threw the United States into the world arena, and the fear

Source: Ronald Steel, *Pax Americana* (New York: The Viking Press, Compass Books, 1968), pp. 3–14, 28–49.

of communism prevented her from retreating. The old isolationism was buried and discredited. The crusade that was the war against fascism gave way to the new crusade that was the cold war against communism. Roused to a new sense of mission by the threat of Soviet communism, eager to bring her cherished values to the masses of mankind, a bit infatuated with the enormous power she possessed through the unleashing of the atom, America quickly accepted — and even came to cherish — her new sense of involvement in the fate of the world. The world of the early postwar era may not have been the One World of Wendell Willkie's dream, but America felt a unique sense of responsibility about its welfare.

A reaction to the old isolationism, the new globalism forced Americans to realize that they could no longer escape involvement in an imperfect world. But because the cold war, like the Second World War, was conceived as a moral crusade, it inflated an involvement that was essentially pragmatic into a moral mission. Since we were accustomed to victory in battle and were stronger than any nation had ever been in history, we believed that the world's problems could be resolved if only we willed hard enough and applied enough power. Convinced of the righteousness of our cause, we became intoxicated with our newly discovered responsibilities and saw them as a mandate to bring about the better world we so ardently desired. American military power, consecrated by the victory of the Second World War and reconfirmed by the development of the atomic bomb, joined forces with the power of American idealism to inaugurate a policy of global interventionism.

This policy of interventionism is not only military, although we have intervened massively throughout the world with our military power. Our intervention has also been economic and political. We have funneled nearly $120 billion of American money into foreign aid since the Second World War — to bring about changes in other countries that would reflect our ideals or advance our interests. We have intervened in the politics of other nations as well, trying to push some into new alignments, trying to remake the social structures of others, and helping to overthrow the governments of not a few. America, whether most of us realize it or not, has become the interventionist power par excellence. Whether we consider this to be commendable or deplorable, it is certainly undeniable.

For the past quarter-century the United States has — at a great financial, human, and even emotional cost — been pursuing a foreign policy designed to promulgate American values. This ambition inspired the policy of "containment" that followed the Second World War, and provided the rationale for a series of military involvements. Seeking universal peace and condemning war as a means for settling political grievances, America has, nonetheless, been an active belligerent in two major land wars since 1950 and the sponsor of a series of military interventions — a record unmatched by any other power. America did not enter these wars from a sense of adventure, or a quest for territorial gain, or an effort to retain distant colonies, but rather from a desire to contain communism and protect the values and boundaries of the "free world." "What America has done, and what America is doing now around the world," President Johnson declared at Catholic University a few months after he ordered the bombing of North Vietnam, "draws from deep and flowing springs of moral duty, and let none underestimate the depth of flow of those wellsprings of American purpose."

Who, indeed, would underestimate them? But to estimate them highly is not necessarily to understand them, or to find them always wise. The moral inspiration of America's involvement in foreign wars is undeniable. But it has also posed a terrible dilemma for American diplomacy, one which is rarely acknowledged openly and is often not even clearly recognized. It is the dilemma of how American ideals can be reconciled with American military actions — and, perhaps even more grave, of how American values can be made relevant to a world that seems not to want or even respect them. However deep the wellsprings of moral duty to which President Johnson refers, the means chosen to transfer these values to a recalcitrant and often unadmiring world has troubled many thoughtful Americans. The President and his advisers speak in the most noble rhetoric of the need to defend freedom wherever it may be threatened and of the indivisibility of our responsibility to protect other nations from external (and even internal) aggression. Yet the pursuit of this aspiration has frequently led others to believe that our motives may be self-justifying and tinged with hypocrisy.

The United States has become an interventionist power, indeed the world's major interventionist power, without most Americans quite realizing how it happened or its full implications. Intervention has been the dominant motif of American postwar foreign policy, but the purpose, and even the methods, of this intervention have been concealed in a miasma of rhetoric and confusion. In the belief that we were containing or repelling communism, we have involved ourselves in situations that have been morally compromising, militarily frustrating, and politically indecisive.

The commitment to interventionism as a guiding principle has made it exceedingly difficult to distinguish between necessary and spurious motives for interventions — to determine which actions have a direct relation to the nation's security, and which merely represent wish-fulfillment on an international scale. In this respect it reflects a traditional weakness in American policy — a penchant for grandiose principles at the expense of a cool assessment of national interests, which has led the nation into painful involvements as a result of bold gestures carelessly made. The warning of John Quincy Adams has lately been forgotten in the intoxication of heady moral obligations, obligations which no one asked us to assume, and whose purpose we do not often understand. This is not the fault of the public but of its leaders, who are often tempted to use slogans to justify their actions, and then become prisoners of them. "American statesmen," as the historian Dexter Perkins has written,

> have believed that the best way to rally American opinion behind their purposes is to assert a moral principle. In doing so, they have often gone far beyond the boundaries of expediency. And perhaps it is fair to say that in underemphasizing security, they have helped to form a national habit which unduly subordinates the necessities of national defense to the assertion of lofty moral principles.

The rhetoric of our cold-war diplomacy rests upon the indivisibility of freedom, the belief in self-determination, the necessity for collective security, and the sanctity of peaceful reform as opposed to violent change. These are not bad ambitions, but no where does this noble rhetoric seem to be in touch with the crass reality of the world as it is. Freedom, we have learned, is not only divisible between nations but subject to a hundred different interpretations. One man's freedom, all too often, is another man's exploitation. Self-determination can be a formula for political instability, and one which it may not always be in our interest to further. Collective security, as applied to our postwar military pacts, has never been much more than a polite word for a unilateral guarantee by the United States to protect her clients. Even this is now being shattered by the break-up of the cold-war alliances. The commitment to peaceful social change by constitutional processes has now collided with the reality of revolution and disorder throughout much of the world.

With every expansion of our commitments, there has been a corresponding expansion of our official rhetoric. Statesmen, unable to adjust our limited means to our unlimited ends, have committed us to goals beyond the capacity of the nation to carry out. They have done this not because they are knaves intent on foreign adventurism, but because they have been carried away by the force of their own rhetoric. Infused by the belief that nothing is unattainable so long as the cause is just, and fortified by reliance on America's awesome military power, they frequently confuse the desirable with the attainable. In doing so, they commit the nation to ends that cannot be achieved, and thereby breed a national frustration that nags at the roots of American democracy. "To some extent," in the words of a Senate committee dealing with problems of national security, "every postwar administration has indulged our national taste for the Grand and even the grandiose." Because the source of this comment is not one which is normally unreceptive to the application of American military power, its conclusions deserve quotation at greater length:

> The idea of manifest destiny still survives. Officials make sweeping declarations of our world mission, and often verbally commit the Nation to policies and program far beyond our capabilities. In this way expectations may be created at home and abroad that are certain to be disappointed and that may result in a squandering of our power and influence on marginal undertakings. We may also find ourselves entangled in projects that are incompatible with the real needs of other peoples, or are, in some cases, actually repugnant to them. To some extent every postwar administration has indulged our national taste for the grand and even the grandiose.
>
> Our ability to think up desirable goals is almost limitless; our capabilities are limited. We still have much to learn about the need to balance what we would like to do with what we can do — and to establish intelligent priorities.
>
> The "can do" philosophy accords with American folklore, but even the United States cannot do everything. In policymaking, also, the assumption tends to be made that "we can find a way." We can do a lot, but our power is limited and the first claimant on it is the American people. Accordingly, it must be rationed in accordance with a responsible ordering of national interests.

The alignment of national goals with national interests — of our desires with our needs — is the most pressing task facing American diplomacy. It is a task that has become increasingly urgent with each expansion of our commitments. These commitments are to be found in a tangle of regional alliances, military pacts, verbal agreements, and even unilateral decisions. They can all, to one degree or another, be traced back to the Truman Doctrine of March 1947, when the United States made the ambiguous offer to defend threatened nations from aggression, whether direct or indirect. This led, through the back door of the European Recovery Program, to NATO, under which the United States is pledged to the defense of most of Europe and even parts of the Near East — from Spitzbergen to the Berlin Wall and beyond to the Asian borders of Turkey. From there the commitments become more vague, the situations more ambiguous, the countries themselves less crucial to American security.

From the seeds of the Truman Doctrine and the precedent of NATO came the

Middle East Resolution, under which Congress gave President Eisenhower permission to protect the Arabs against communism; the CENTO and SEATO treaties that John Foster Dulles constructed to fill in the alliance gap from Iran to the Philippines; the ANZUS treaty with Australia and New Zealand; special defense arrangements with Japan and Korea; an unwritten obligation to protect India; the pledge for the defense of the entire western hemisphere under the Rio Pact; various peace-keeping functions under the United Nations; and, most recently, the Tonkin Gulf Resolution, a blank check given by Congress, allowing President Johnson to intervene as he sees fit in Southeast Asia. Early in 1968 the United States had 700,000 soldiers stationed in 30 countries, was a member of 4 regional defense alliances and an active participant in a fifth, had mutual defense treaties with 42 nations, was a member of 53 international organizations, and was furnishing military or economic aid to nearly 100 nations across the face of the globe. Put all this together and it leaves us, in James Reston's words, with "commitments the like of which no sovereign nation ever took on in the history of the world."

These entanglements happened more by accident than by design. The United States became involved in the defense of Western Europe because the defeat of Nazi Germany brought Stalin's armies into Central Europe. In Asia the disintegration of the Japanese Empire brought Russia into Manchuria and the United States into Japan, Okinawa, South Korea, and Taiwan. Later we advanced into Indochina when the French, despite our financial and military support, were unable to retain their Asian territories. We had no intention of virtually annexing Okinawa, of occupying South Korea, of preventing the return of Taiwan to China, of fighting in Indochina, or of remaining in Western Europe. If someone had said in 1947 that twenty years later there would be 225,000 American soldiers in Germany, 50,000 in Korea, and a half million Americans fighting in Vietnam, he would have been considered mad. Yet so accustomed are we to our global commitments that we take this remarkable situation for granted.

Although the postwar vacuums are receding — with the resurgence of China, the recovery of Japan, and the revival of Europe — our commitment remains unchanged. We are still playing the same role of guardian that we played twenty years ago, when America and Russia were the only important powers in the world. Our diplomacy has not kept pace with the changes in the world power structure, and we are engaged far beyond our ability to control events. The result has been a dangerous gap in our foreign policy between our involvements and our means — between what we would like to accomplish and what we can reasonably hope to accomplish.

In a way it could be said that our foreign policy has been a victim of its own success. In the decision to rebuild and defend Western Europe, the United States acted with wisdom, humanity, and an enlightened conception of her own interests. The military alliance with Western Europe worked successfully because there was a clear community of interests between America and her allies. When we built our bases in Europe and sent our own soldiers to man the front lines, it was in the knowledge that we agreed with our allies on the dangers they faced and on the means by which they should be met. We came not as an army of occupation or as foreign mercenaries, but as friends joined in a common cause. We turned our back on the isolationism of the 1930s, put the American frontier right up to the Brandenburg Gate in Berlin, pledged our atomic weapons to the defense of our allies, added our own soldiers as guarantors of this pledge, and accepted the risk of nuclear devastation. We took this terrible risk because we had to: because neither strategically nor culturally could we accept the loss of Western Europe to our adversaries. The goal we sought in Western Europe in the early postwar period had three qualities essential for military intervention: it was vital to our interests, it was within our means to achieve, and it had the support of those we were trying to protect.

The difficulty, however, arose when the principles underlying NATO and the Marshall Plan were applied indiscriminately throughout the world — when it was assumed that the success of the Atlantic alliance could be duplicated in countries which shared neither our traditions, nor our interests, nor even our assessment of the dangers facing them. Too often American diplomacy has been engaged in the effort to create miniature NATOs and Marshall Plans with countries that have only recently shaken off the yoke of Western rule, that are at a greatly inferior stage of economic and political development, that are as suspicious of us as they are of our adversaries, that are endemically poor and unstable, and that usually greet us as unwanted manipulators rather than as welcome friends.

If our policies were judged by a cold calculation of national interest, a good many of them might have been scrapped long ago. If the struggle with Russia were merely over geographical spheres of influence, if the cold war were nothing more than old-fashioned power politics on a global scale, our commitments could have been cut and our involvements drastically limited. But the cold war has not been simply a struggle of giants for supremacy; it has also been an ideological contest for the allegiance of mankind. Or so it has seemed to its leading participants. It is because we feel ourselves embroiled in a much greater struggle that we are involved in the sustenance and security of some hundred countries, that we have replaced the old isolationism with a sweeping policy of interventionism and are today fighting yet another land war in Asia.

We are there because we feel ourselves to be pledged to a worldwide struggle against communism, because we see ourselves as the defenders of freedom and democracy in the contest against tyranny, because we are, in President Kennedy's words, "by destiny rather than choice, the watchmen on the walls of world freedom." But this role of watchman is not, for all President Kennedy's noble rhetoric, imposed by destiny. It is imposed by ourselves and subject to whatever limitations we choose to put upon it. It can provide the excuse for our playing the role of global gendarme, or serve as a guideline for a measured calculation of the national interest. No task of global omniscience is imposed upon us that we do not choose for ourselves.

As we face the obligations of our global commitments, we are becoming aware of our inability to impose our will upon events or to structure the world into the form we believe it should take. We have the power to destroy most human life on the planet within a matter of minutes, yet we cannot win a guerrilla war against peasants in black pajamas. We are so rich that we can retain an army in Europe, fight a war in Asia, dispense billions in foreign aid, and increase our national wealth by $30 billion a year. Yet we cannot adequately deal with the decay of our cities, the pollution of our atmosphere, the disintegration of public services, the growing hostility between whites and blacks, and the inadequacy of our educational system. Nor, despite the fact that we have dispensed nearly $120 billion abroad during the past twenty years, have we been able seriously to alleviate the poverty and hopelessness in which most of the world's population lives. We have assumed the responsibility for creating Great Societies at home and abroad, but we have not been able to bring this goal into line with our interests or capacities.

As a nation we have what General de Gaulle has uncharitably labeled "a taste for intervention." Applied intelligently and with restraint, as in Western Europe after the war, this taste has done credit to our nation and served its interests. But expanded indiscriminately and without measure, it has involved us in struggles we do not understand, in areas where we are unwanted, and in ambitions which are doomed to frustration. Intervention is neither a sin nor a panacea. It is a method, and like all methods it must be directly related to the end in view. Otherwise it is likely to become an end in itself, dragging the nation down a path it never intended to follow, toward a goal it may find repugnant.

Too often our interventions have seemed to be imposed upon us by abstract theory rather than by a cold assessment of political realities. We have found ourselves involved in areas — the Congo the day before yesterday, Santo Domingo yesterday, Vietnam today, perhaps Thailand tomorrow — where our presence has sometimes exacerbated rather than alleviated the problem, and where it was not within out power to achieve a solution. Interventionism, as a principle of foreign policy, has not served us noticeably well in recent years. But it is a principle to which we are deeply committed: in NATO and its sister pacts, CENTO and SEATO; in the Alliance for Progress; in the Rio Pact and the OAS; in foreign aid; in Southeast Asia; and in any nation which may be taken over by communists, whether from the inside or the outside. It has fostered a staggering program of involvements and it could easily lead us, as it already has in Vietnam, into conflicts whose extent we cannot possibly foresee.

We we are in very deep in Europe, in Korea and Japan, in Thailand and Vietnam, in Latin America, and in the entire nexus of underdeveloped countries which are tottering between various forms of authoritarianism. Whether we are in too deep for our own good, and perhaps even for the good of those we are trying to help, is the problem that this book seeks to explore. The answer, however, will be found not here but in the attitude — in the modesty as well as in the wisdom — that we bring to this peculiarly American dilemma. And it is an American dilemma: the dilemma of how to use power — sometimes economic power in the form of tractors and dollars, sometimes raw military power in the form of soldiers and napalm — for the achievement of ends which American leaders declare to be morally desirable.

The answer to that dilemma has eluded us ever since we plunged wholeheartedly into the world arena a generation ago and acquired, in a bout of moral fervor, a string of dependencies stretching around the globe — an empire, in short. It is an accidental empire, the scope of which the world has never seen, and which we, to this day, have scarcely begun to recognize ourselves.

*　*　*

For the past two decades we have viewed the world and our place in it through the lenses of the cold war. A whole generation of Americans has come to maturity knowing incessant crisis and the threat of instant obliteration as the normal condition of everyday life. For those born in the cold war, and for those ushered into it by an implacable history, it has been the central political reality of our time. Inescapable, and seemingly inexhaustible, the cold war has become a permanent fixture of our mental vocabulary, limiting our horizons to questions of survival, security, and prestige.

The cold war has been both a stultifying and an exhilarating period in American life. It gave birth to the self-destructive hysteria of McCarthyism, but it also inspired the creation of an American empire and the euphoria of power that has gone with it. The cold war made us fear for our safety, but it also excited us with the knowledge that we were one of the arbiters of the world. With the passing of time we even, in a peculiar way, grew fond of the cold war. It became familiar, predictable, and almost comfortable, providing a rationale for actions that flattered our pride and augmented our influence over others.

The cold war has been a struggle for power, but more than that, it has also been a struggle over ideology: one, so the antagonists believed, for the soul of mankind. The Russians, while behaving in ways that augment their status as a great power, have nonetheless believed in the mythology of communism and their duty to spread it to nations oppressed by the "imperialists." The fact that they have rarely let their belief in the promulgation of the communist faith interfere with the security of Mother Russia does not diminish the fact that they conceive of themselves as a basically messianic power. They believe in communist dogma (although they persistently twist it to suit theur national needs), and they have managed to convince others that they are serious.

No nation needed persuading less than the United States, whose fear of Russian power was fortified by a deep-seated hostility to communist ideology. While America initially responded to the Soviet menace in terms of national interest — pouring her troops back into Europe after the Second World War in order to prevent the Russians from marching across the Elbe — she gradually came to look upon the Russian challenge as basically an ideological one. Thus the achievement of a military balance in Central Europe did not diminish the cold war. It simply changed it from a classical power rivalry to a primarily ideological struggle. This was because the United States matched the ideology of communism with a counter-ideology of its own: anti-communism. Around these twin poles of communism and anti-communism the cold war has raged for more than twenty years.

For a long time there was good reason to fear that the cold war might erupt into a hot one. The Berlin blockade, the Korean war, the fighting in Iran and Greece, the Hungarian revolt, the Berlin crisis of 1961, and the confrontation over Cuba all brought the world near the brink of war. Yet the nuclear giants, awed by the enormity of their own powers of destruction, have always pulled back before confrontation led to open conflict. They managed to keep the peace because they knew that total war in the nuclear age was intolerable. Provocations which in an earlier period would probably have led to a declaration of war were smoothed over and disguised. The great powers have shown a healthy concern for their own survival. The atomic bomb, by positing the threat of total obliteration, has helped to keep an uneasy peace. "By a process of sublime irony," as Churchill said in 1955, we "have reached a stage in this story where safety will be the sturdy child of terror and survival the twin brother of annihilation."

The longer the equilibrium between the two nuclear giants has lasted, the more it has been possible for the smaller powers to pursue their own separate paths and for the natural process of disintegration to develop within the great rival alliances. While America and Russia have been consumed by the struggle to restrain each other from attack and to spread their rival ideologies, the once-intimidated spectators have been straying off into the wings and setting up their own sideshows. In the process, the contest between the giants has lost much of its former virulence, as even the gladiators themselves have begun to realize. The cold war between Russia and the West is no longer a struggle for global supremacy so much as it is a kind of military gymnastics. Neither side has any intention of attacking the other, and each is content to let its rival rein supreme within its own sphere of influence. A relatively stable power balance has been achieved between Russia and the West, and the centers of danger have now shifted to Asia and the underdeveloped nations. What remain are lingering commitments to ideology and a political vocabulary formed during a postwar period that is now virtually over.

Thus, though the postwar world is passing into history, its mythology stays on in the form of conventional labels — the "communist bloc," the "free world" — which conceal the remarkable changes that have occurred since the mid-1950s: the convulsions in the Soviet empire, the defection of China, the shock of decolonialization, the revival of Europe, and the development of common interests between America and Russia. The cold-war labels conceal these because they are rooted in a view of the world that has not changed to any real degree since 1948, when we assumed that the Red Army was about to sweep Western Europe into its maw. From this assumption, which seemed valid at the time, but which virtually everyone agrees is now exceedingly unlikely, sprang the NATO alliance, the rearmament of Germany, the semi-permanent garrisoning of an American army on the Continent, and the vision of an Atlantic community knitting Europe and America together in "equal partnership." But with Europe no longer on her knees, with Russia no longer so menacing, and America no longer invulnerable, the conditions which originally inspired the Atlantic alliance, and America's presence in Europe, have largely disappeared. In their place are ambiguous and shifting relations between three changing powers: an interventionist America, a cautious Russia, and an evolving Europe. Today the whole focus of instability is switching away from Europe, where the containment of communism has been achieved, to a revolution-prone Third World. There the problems of development and the sudden transition from colonialism to independence have been accompanied by virulent nationalism and civil disorders into which the super-powers have been drawn.

Accustomed to think in the rhetoric of the cold war, we have seen these disorders as part of the global struggle between "freedom" and "communism." And because that struggle had begun in Europe, where the problem was one of defending weakened nations from the legions of the Red Army, we applied the same remedies elsewhere. Trying to reproduce NATO in contexts where virtually none of its elements applied, we created miniature alliances such as CENTO and SEATO, composed of nations which shared few of our assumptions about the dangers they faced and which had special uses of their own for the military aid we furnished.

The cold-war pacts have, for the most part, been largely forgotten by all but that handful of diplomats and generals whose job it is to attend their yearly conferences in such agreeable places as Teheran and Bangkok. But the dogma that inspired them lives on. The obsession with communism as an ideology, which burdened us for so long in Europe, has now switched its roost to Asia, and the specter of a global conspiracy directed from Moscow has been replaced by the specter of one directed from Peking. The focal point has changed: the obsession remains the same. It is one which is held with great tenacity even in the highest councils of our government.

The dogma has lingered on because it alone can justify a good many of our current involvements. Without the belief that popularly inspired revolutions are likely to fall into the hands of communists, how justify the intervention in Santo Domingo? Without the assumption that any communist government in Asia must automatically be subservient to Peking and manipulated by her, how justify the war in Vietnam? Without the dogma, how could there be public support for the policies of military intervention being pursued by the administration? Such policies are reasonable only if we assume that there is still a universal communist conspiracy and that all revolutions are master-minded by the same malevolent source — formerly Moscow, and now Peking. This assumption is the basis for current American diplomacy, and it rests upon the unexamined dogma of the cold war.

The irony of our present foreign policy, however, is that a workable power balance has been achieved between the nuclear giants, and it is now possible to speak openly of a real community of interests between Washington and Moscow. Ideological differences remain between America and Russia, but they have been reduced to secondary importance. In Asia, on the other hand, the ideological conflict between America and China is paramount, while the threat to national interest is very much secondary. Thus our relations with Russia are exactly the opposite of our relations with China, even though they are both communist powers and both theoretically dedicated to the triumph of their ideology. Paradoxically, China is considered to be a greater threat to the peace, although she is far weaker than Russia, because her ideological motivation appears so much stronger. Listening to what China says, rather than coldly judging what she has done and what she is capable of doing with her limited resources, we are terrified. Observing what Russia has done under her policy of "peaceful co-existence," rather than paying attention to her messianic vocabulary, we are reassured and believe an arrangement can be worked out with our leading adversary.

If the cold war means simply an ideological struggle between communism and anti-communism, that struggle goes on and will continue to go on so long as the major powers believe that these counter-ideologies are important. But if the cold war can be described as a power struggle between America and Russia for the allegiance of the world — one which began over the territory of Europe but which later embraced ideology — that struggle has been greatly diminished. It is highly unlikely to be resurrected in anything resembling its old form. There are at least four major reasons why this is so.

First, there is the recovery and growing independence of Western Europe. When the Second World War ended, Europe was not only in physical ruins, but in moral ruins as well. There was no talk of Europe as an independent power center because there was no conviction that the European states could ever again marshal sufficient power to stand by themselves on the world stage.

Yet as the work of economic recovery — made possible by generous American assistance through the Marshall Plan — proceeded, there was a corresponding growth of self-confidence in Western Europe. The defeat of the Italian Communist Party in the general election of 1948 brought an end to the fear that communism would come to Western Europe from within. The guarantee of American protection under the NATO alliance, signed in the spring of 1949, convinced most Europeans that communism was blocked from without as well. From that time on, the tide turned in Western Europe. The Czech coup had shown both the extent and the limitations of Russian power. The line of political demarcation was fixed in Central Europe and, except for the independence of Austria, it has remained untouched ever since.

The division of Europe was cruel and arbitrary, but it also provided stability on both sides of the Iron Curtain. It showed where communism was going to remain, and where it was unable to expand. With the eastern part of the continent under

Soviet domination for an indeterminate time, something radically new was undertaken in compensation: the construction of a *Western* European community. Inspired by visions of political unification that would submerge old national rivalries, the leaders of postwar Europe launched a series of remarkable experiments: the European Coal and Steel Community, the European Defense Community, Euratom, and the Common Market. Today the economies of the six nations of the Common Market are so intertwined and interdependent that they could not be severed without causing severe damage to all the nations involved. Integration has worked, and the member nations of the EEC have a vested interest in its survival.

The resurgence of European self-confidence has been one of the most unexpected phenomena of the postwar era. The nightmare of the Nazi period has been largely forgotten, the social and economic stagnation of prewar times has been relegated to the history books, and the sense of political impotence that followed Europe's collapse is also passing. The narrow chauvinism of the past is being replaced by a growing spirit of intra-European cooperation, and the old despair has given way to a belief that Europeans must be masters within their own house. This is not so much a new chauvinism as it is the expression of a European personality. Europe has been divided and occupied by two foreign giants for nearly a quarter-century. The American occupation, while it has been a benevolent one, is now considered anachronistic. The Europeans are demanding a much greater voice not only within the Atlantic alliance but over all the decisions that affect their future.

The second factor marking the passing of the postwar world has been the desintegration of the communist bloc and the rise of a second Rome in Peking. The Soviet empire in eastern Europe, imposed by the Red Army at the end of the Second World War and maintained by regimes subservient to Moscow, has been splintered, probably irrevocably. It is no longer accurate to speak of "satellites" when referring to such nations as Hungary, Rumania, and Poland. Solidly within the Soviet orbit, they are nonetheless free to pursue their own internal policies, often over the objections of the Kremlin. "Communism," as George Kennan has written, "has come to embrace so wide a spectrum of requirements and compulsions on the part of the respective parties and regimes that any determined attempt to reimpose unity on the movement would merely cause it to break violently apart at one point or another."

Neither as a political-economic system nor as an ideology has communism been able to overcome the power of nationalism. This failure has been endemic in communism ever since the creation of the Soviet state, when Lenin waited for the workers of the West to join the Russian example, and instead faced a wall of iron hostility. If there has been any single lesson in Eastern Europe during the past twenty years, it has been that communism has failed while nationalism has triumphed. A sense of national identity which transcends ideology is as strong today in Eastern Europe as it ever was, and far stronger than it is in the West. When one considers the excesses of East European nationalism in the past, this revival is not necessarily a welcome phenomenon. But it is a fact, and a fact that communism has done nothing to alleviate.

Even the old territorial grievances are beginning to be heard again as the Rumanians aspire for the return of Bessarabia from the Soviet Union, and as the Albanians file their claim on the parts of Macedonia held by Yugoslavia. Today there is no Soviet bloc. There is simply an association of states proclaiming formal allegiance to the same ideology and dependent upon Russian power for protection against external enemies. "Polycentrism" is the word used to describe this loosening of Moscow's hold upon the other communist nations. What it means precisely is the creation of rival centers of power within the communist orbit. The heresy of the Yugoslavs and of the Italian Communist Party has now become the hallmark of the communist movement. Instead of a single communist church with the Pope sitting in Moscow, the Marxist-Leninist churches are now autocephalous. It is no longer possible to know what is the line of communist orthodoxy, because there no longer is a single orthodoxy. The Communist Party of Czechoslovakia is equal in authority to the Communist Party of the Soviet Union over questions of Marxist-Leninist dogma and, in practice, over all questions which do not involve the security of the Soviet state.

As a result of this fission within the communist bloc, communist groups throughout the world are behaving in terms of local conditions rather than along lines laid down by Moscow. The Czechs are imposing a market economy, the Yugoslavs are experimenting with mixed enterprise, the Rumanians are inviting capitalist investment, the Italian communists ponder dissolving themselves in a Popular Front movement, the Albanians daily proclaim the perfidy of Moscow, and the Chinese accuse the Russians of betraying the proletarian revolution. Heresy is now everywhere, which means that there is no longer any orthodoxy.

The break-up of communist orthodoxy has, of course, been stimulated by the rupture between China and Russia. Whatever hopes Moscow had for dominating the world communist movement were shattered by the establishment of an independent communist government in Peking. The Russians could not have foreseen the precise form the Chinese revolt against their authority would take, but they had a clear premonition of its coming. The Chinese revolution was basically an indigenous affair, and the Chinese leaders have never concealed their demand for full equality with the Russians within the world communist movement.

Caught in the flush of their revolution, and eager to reassert their national pride, the Chinese are challenging the Russians not only over the interpretation of communist scripture, but also over the disputed territories along their common frontier. The roots of this conflict extend deep into the past. If the West had not been so blinded by its own ideological blinkers it would long ago have realized that Sino-Soviet solidarity was nothing but a myth which could not long survive the test of time and clashing national interests.

Two giant nations sharing a common frontier — one committed to "peaceful coexistence" and the pursuit of affluence, the other mired in poverty and demanding world revolution — China and Russia are natural adversaries, regardless of what ideology they may share. A common dedication to Marxism-Leninism, such as they separately interpret it, has, if anything, only intensified their conflict. The open break between China and Russia has been of vital importance to the West, for it has eliminated the danger that the world communist movement could be placed at the service of the Soviet state. In this dramatic triumph of nationalism over communist unity, ideology has been relegated to the back seat. As a result of the Chinese challenge to Moscow, the smaller communist nations throughout the world now have an unprecedented freedom to pursue their own separate paths. Orthodoxy cannot be reimposed without shattering the bloc completely. The cold-war trauma of a communist monolith has been broken. In its place is a hydra with as many heads as there are communist parties.

In the world of independent states, every government — communist or non-communist — must look after its own interests. In doing so it may find, as several communist governments have found already, that its major adversary shares its ideology. Although alliances of various communist nations in the future cannot be precluded, they are unlikely to be permanent. An indigenous communist revolution in any new country can no longer be assumed to augment the power or influence of any other communist state. A communist Yugoslavia did not augment Russian power. On the contrary, it decreased it by defying Russia's sole right to speak for the communist world. By the same token, a communist North Vietnam or North Korea has not increased China's power. Here a common ideology has been allowed to mask the conflict of national interests. By refusing to recognize this, we have been the victims of a mythology that the communists themselves no longer believe in.

The third factor which has signaled the end of the postwar world has been the spectacular appearance of Africa, Asia, and Latin America in the center of the world arena. Twenty years ago the movement from colonialism to independence had barely begun. Today it has been virtually completed. Except for a few enclaves which are unlikely to hold out much longer against the tide, European colonialism is now a thing of the past. With a speed that has dazzled even the most enthusiastic spokesmen of independence, the European powers have pulled out of Asia and Africa — sometimes, indeed, too soon. In the vast underdeveloped areas that were once their colonies, some threescore newly independent states have demanded their rights to equality, prosperity, and seats in the United Nations.

This is, by any standard, one of the great revolutions of modern times, even more important than the Russian revolution of 1917. By their assertion of equality with the older nations of the West, the underdeveloped states of the Third World have transformed the world power structure. They have reduced the Russo-American cold war to a parochial power conflict and rephrased the problems of world politics in a new vocabulary. To these nations the question of communism versus anti-communism is peripheral or even irrelevant. Their concern is with economic development, political influence, and racial equality. They envy the West (in which they include Russia) its material prosperity, its economic techniques, its social discipline. They are interested in political ideology only insofar as it can be used to achieve the goals they value. They all proclaim their allegiance to "socialism," but the word itself covers such a variety of experiences and abuses that it can no longer even be defined in Western terms.

The rise to independence of the submerged peoples has undermined most of our assumptions about the world power struggle. It has demonstrated that the real struggle is not between communists and anti-communists but between haves and have-nots; not between Russians and Americans, but between economically developed societies and economically primitive ones. By rephrasing diplomacy in terms of economic development (and thus economic power) the underdeveloped nations of the Third World have taken the ideological sting out of the cold war. As their demands upon the rich nations increase, they have forced America and Russia to realize that they share a real community of interests. Prosperous, technologically advanced, politically stable societies, they have more in common with each other than with the clamorous poor in the southern hemisphere who demand their attention and their help. Compared to the new nations of Asia and Africa, the Soviet Union emerges as a status-quo power, affluent, conservative, and more interested in increasing its wealth than in spreading the world revolution.

Insofar as the new nations can find a major power that shares their problems, that power is China, the underdeveloped nation par excellence. A country that has only recently shaken off the domination of technologically advanced foreign powers, facing all the problems of a galloping rise in population, insufficient natural resources, an inadequate industrial base, and the hostility of both Russia and America, China would seem to be the ally of all the impoverished nations of the world. Hoping to win allies where they can find them, the Chinese have zealously — but with astonishing ineptitude — tried to rally the Africans, Asians, and Latin Americans into a holy alliance of the poor against the rich. Indeed, they have so twisted Marxist doctrine from its original intentions that they are using it as an instrument of class warfare between rich and poor nations, rather than between economic classes *within* nations. They have tried to make it a tool by which the poor nations may demonstrate their superiority over the rich nations and the "historical inevitability" of their triumph.

While the Chinese have proclaimed themselves the leaders of the new world revolution, they have had little success in winning anyone's allegiance. This is because the new nations are as suspicious of the Chinese as they are of the super-powers. They are basically uninterested in the ideological pretensions of communism particularly when, as in China's case, these are not even combined with large doses of foreign aid. These nations are determined to stay out of the quarrels of the great powers and are much too absorbed in their own problems of nationalism and economic development to play an active role in the cold war.

The fourth factor to diminish the cold war has been the declining importance of nuclear weapons in the world power balance. Although it may seem anomalous, experience has shown that atomic weapons have been of virtually no value in settling political disputes. Among nuclear powers, atomic weapons serve as a deterrent which inhibits direct combat. Had it not been for the atom bomb, it is likely that Russia and America would have been at war long ago over one of their many areas of dispute. The Bomb has helped them keep the peace, but it has not allowed them to settle their grievances. The grievances, in fact, remain virtually the same as they have been since the rivalry began: the partition of Germany and the division of Europe. The Bomb, in other words, has frozen the political status quo.

Similarly, between a nuclear and a non-nuclear power, atomic weapons seem to have been of little use. They have not allowed their possessors to intimidate those without such weapons, nor even to win a battle once it was engaged. What they have done, surprisingly, is to force the great to descend to the level of the small, to compel the atomic powers to fight with conventional weapons. This has been the experience of the French in Algeria, and of the British in Cyprus, Kenya, and Aden. The United States too has discovered that her atomic weapons are not really relevant in areas of limited war such as Korea and Vietnam. Despite her vast technological superiority, she has been obliged to fight guerrilla warfare on the terrain chosen by the guerrillas, not because she wants to, but because there is no alternative. Although she possesses greater power than any nation in history, the United States cannot impose her will even on a technologically backward society of a few million people. Nor can the Russians, for that matter, bend the defiant Albanians to their will. When she was kicked out of her submarine base on the Adriatic, and when her embassy in Tirana was seized, the world's second mightiest military power could do little more than issue a diplomatic protest.

Atomic bombs, it has now become apparent, exist only to deter other atomic bombs. They cannot be used even in limited combat, lest they trigger off an unlimited war. They cannot be brandished as a bluff against another atomic power, because nobody would believe a bluff that involved the threat of national suicide. They cannot be disposed of — unless both nuclear powers could reach an agreement to dispose of them at once. And even if they did, neither could be sure that the other didn't have some weapons hidden which it would use for atomic blackmail, or that a third power might not arise to threaten them both. Paradoxically, then, the atomic bomb has kept the peace between the two great powers, while providing the cover behind which lesser powers — and indeed even they themselves — carry on low-key rivalries. It has, in one sense, made the world a safer place for the nuclear powers and their allies. But it has also reduced the necessity for them to resolve their major outstanding grievances.

The irony of the Bomb is that it is really the enemy of the super-powers. So long as it remains in their hands alone, a balance can be maintained. But if it is dispersed to a host of minor powers, it will deprive the giants of the great advantages they have over their rivals: their physical size and their economic strength. Russia and America, spreading over entire continents and marshaling the most powerful economies the world has ever known, do not need nuclear weapons to be great. Without them, they are still the strongest and richest nations in the world. Because of their geography they are also the most secure from attack. But the atom has diminished the advantage of size, and the intercontinental missile has annihilated the protection of the oceans. Together these two weapons have upset the classic relationships between great powers and small ones. They have endowed the latter with a strength that belies their size and robbed the former of their power superiority. They have not made the small the equal of the great, but they have narrowed the gap between them. France, for example, will always remain inferior to Russia on any power scale. But the French Bomb has now become a serious consideration in any designs the Russians may have on Western Europe. Similarly, the Chinese Bomb will not, for a long time at least, pose any direct danger to the United States. But when China develops an effective delivery system she will be far safer from an American attack than if neither side had ever developed a bomb.

Thus has the Bomb served as an equalizer between the small and the great. It is, to be sure, a symbolic equalizer, since it would serve nobody's purpose if it were ever used. But in the strange world of atomic deterrence it has a certain psychological utility. No one is happy that it has been invented. But now that it is among us, no nation aspiring to major-power status feels fully armed without it. Even those nations such as West Germany, for whom the possession of a Bomb means political disaster, cannot refrain from expressing their inferiority feelings because they do not have one. And technologically advanced mini-powers, such as Israel and Switzerland, contemplate the eventual acquisition of nuclear arsenals.

American and Russia both have "overkill" power to destroy one another as organized socieites, with enough weapons left over to obliterate the rest of mankind as well. But neither can shame the other into surrendering anything it considers vital. Khrushchev issued ultimatums for three years in Berlin, threatening the most dire happenings if the West did not retreat. Yet there was no retreat and there were no dire happenings because the Russians had no intention of launching a nuclear war over the status of Berlin. Even the Cuban missile crisis, which brought the world closer to the nuclear abyss than it has been at any other point in the cold war, was not resolved because President Kennedy threatened to use American nuclear weapons. On the contrary, the successful resolution of that crisis was due in large part to the fact that the United States used her non-nuclear superiority in the Caribbean — her sea and air power — to induce the Russians to withdraw their missiles.

The present hard-won nuclear balance has not only reduced the threat of atomic war and virtually nullified the advantages of atomic weapons, but also made both sides realize that they have a vital common interest in preserving the peace. To do so they must prevent lesser powers, whether allies or adversaries, from upsetting the balance and forcing them into nuclear confrontation against their will. Thus the covert collusion between the super-powers to close the nuclear club to new members. The non-proliferation treaty, however desirable, is designed to stabilize the peace by preserving their nuclear duopoly. Everybody knows this, but the small powers are mostly willing to tolerate it because it is to their advantage. The only important nations to oppose it are those that aspire to major-power status: so far, France and China.

With the recognition by both sides that virtually nothing is worth a nuclear war, a good deal of air has gone out of the Russo-American confrontation. Fanatics in both camps — whether Birchites of Maoists — may still speak of victory, but responsible political leaders know better. President Eisenhower summed up the grim truth about the atomic balance when he said that there is "no alternative to peace." And Khrushchev, in his own vivid way, put the Chinese fanatics in their place when he said: "Is there a madman or a clever man who could tell what would happen after a nuclear war? It's stupid, stupid, stupid. . . . And there are people among communists who believe that war is good for revolution. Those who call for revolution now should go to see a psychiatrist." The revolution, in case anyone had any doubts, clearly takes a back seat to the preservation of the Russo-American nuclear balance.

These, then, are the major factors which have served to topple the ideological superstructure of the cold war and replace it by perplexing and constantly shifting relationships among the great and not-so-great powers. The postwar world has been shattered beyond recognition, and much of what we have taken for granted during the past twenty years is no longer true. Strange combinations are in process of forming: unlikely alliances among long-standing foes, unexpected rivalries among close allies. There is a new freedom, and even a new anarchy, at large in the world, an anarchy that neither of the great powers is capable of mastering.

Traditionally anti-communist Spain has strengthened her diplomatic and economic ties with communist Cuba, has tried to blackmail the United States over the use of bases on her territory, has signed a consular pact with Rumania, and is moving toward full diplomatic ties with the Soviet Union. Pakistan, the fulcrum of both the CENTO and the SEATO pacts and the recipient of billions of dollars in American aid, has formed an unofficial alliance with China in a squeeze play against India. The Turks, historically anti-Russian, but bitter over the refusal of United States support in the crisis over Cyprus, contemplate a rapprochement with the Soviets. Britain, blocked in her bid to enter the Common Market and plagued by a stagnant economy, has relinquished the political leadership of Europe to Gaullist France. Indonesia, after flirting with communism, has wandered back into the neutralist camp, but remains profoundly unstable. India, still incapable of coping with her own economic needs, contemplates the acquisition of an atomic arsenal to balance off China. Israel and Egypt threaten to follow suit and by their action induce a wholesale proliferation of nuclear weapons among the mini-powers. West Germany, the most powerful non-nuclear power on the Continent, is straying from her old policy of rigidity toward the East, and is contemplating potentially disturbing paths to reunification. Gaullist France, eager to reunite Europe under her leadership and resentful of American "Hegemony," simultaneously establishes ties with Peking and flirts with Moscow. Latin America, once a secure haven for United States investment and a faithful supporter of United States diplomacy, is trying to loosen the grip of the Yankee colossus by overtures to Europe, thereby turning the Monroe Doctrine on its head. The uncommitted new states of Africa and Asia, rather than emulate either of the super-powers, have tried to play them off against each other for their own advantage. The United Nations, by the admission of scores of former colonial states, has been transformed from a tool by which the super-powers could police the world into an instrument by which the mini-powers can exert pressure on the giants. Even Russia, once the world's leading provocateur, has lately been playing the role of peacemaker in the dispute between India and Pakistan.

The shattering of the old alliances and the rise of new political constellations have threatened the dominance the two nuclear giants have enjoyed for the past quarter-century. Control is slipping out of their grasp, and the days of their hegemony now seem to be numbered. For a long time to come they will remain the most powerful nations in the world. But their ability to cajole, intimidate, or speak for others is diminishing steadily. A world which for more than two decades revolved around the rival poles of Moscow and Washington has now fragmented into scores of pieces. It is no longer One World, to be fought over between the communists and the anti-communists; or even two worlds to be divided between them. Rather it is a series of interlocking and constantly shifting relationships between great and small powers who use one another for their own temporary advantage.

With the diminishing of the ideological conflict that has given the cold war its particular virulence and meaning, America and Russia are no longer powers with a major source of conflict between them. The only place their vital interests ever collided was in Central Europe. But now that they have reached a *de facto* accord to leave well enough alone, Europe is not a major source of contention. Two great powers on opposite sides of the world, Russia and America are learning to carry on their competition in terms of a traditional power rivalry. Each remains committed to its ideology, but since neither can enforce it upon the other without inducing a nuclear war, dialogue, compromise, and even agreement are possible. The contest for the soul of the world can be carried on in a muted key.

Already a tacit cooperation between the super-powers has begun. It cannot be openly admitted, for the extremists on both sides would point out that the emperors had been shorn of their ideological clothes. But it is going on nonetheless. The nuclear-test-ban treaty of 1963, the efforts to agree on a non-proliferation treaty to close the nuclear club, and the restraint both powers have shown in Vietnam, are simply the most obvious examples of this cooperation. Self-restraint where rival spheres of influence are concerned has been the hallmark of the Russo-American competition. This has been enforced upon them by the fear that a direct clash might ignite a nuclear war. The United States refrained from supporting the 1953 revolt in East Berlin, let the Hungarian rebellion be crushed in 1956, and accepted the construction of the Berlin Wall in 1961. The Soviet Union, for its part, has respected the security of West Berlin and has tolerated our devastation of communist North Vietnam. In Suez and Iraq, the Congo and Laos, Cyprus and Kashmir, the super-powers have collaborated to limit conflicts into which they might be drawn as participants.

This is true even in such a chronic trouble spot as the Middle East, where America and Russia have been engaged in the dangerous game of arming rival protégés. When hostility between Israel and her Arab neighbors again erupted into war in June 1967, the two super-powers showed a common desire to prevent the conflict from spreading. The Russians, while courting the Egyptians with advanced military hardware, had no desire to unleash a general war in the Middle East. Nor did the United States, already overextended in Vietnam, want to get involved in such a war. Indeed, the Israeli blitzkrieg spared Washington the agonizing choice of either abandoning the Jewish state to possible extinction, or sending in the Sixth Fleet and risking a confrontation with Russia. The very brevity of the six-day war gave Washington and Moscow a chance to pull back from an explosive situation they had allowed to get out of hand. Behind the scenes they set about to defuse the Middle East crisis and prevent another eruption of hostilities that could imperil their détente.

In other areas their co-operation has been even more marked. After the mutually dissatisfying experience of the Congo, they have tried to keep the cold war out of Africa. As Russia has been notably restrained in Latin America since the Cuban debacle, so the United States has refrained from exploiting the explosive nationalism in Eastern Europe. Both have agreed to demilitarize the Antarctic, ban nuclear weapons from outer space, try to stabilize the arms race, share the burden of building up India as a potential rival to China, and keep Fidel Castro on a short leash. Two great powers with a vested interest in the status quo and the perpetuation of their nuclear duopoly, they have discovered that collaboration may be exceedingly beneficial to both of them.

The fear that America and Russia may be drawn into a nuclear war by some precipitous action of their allies, such as China or Germany, has led both sides to reconsider the value of their alliances. They are beginning to realize that the alliances may be important less as a means of confronting each other than as a means of keeping some of the smaller powers in line. This desire of Russia and America to seek rapprochement through their rival power blocks is a clear repudiation of the theory on which the cold-war alliances have been based. These alliances are no longer directed against each other, but are, in effect, instruments by which the super-powers seek to maintain a balance. Whether they will be able to sustain their alliances once their purpose becomes apparent is exceedingly problematical. But in this interim period there is a growing belief in both rival capitals that Russian-American dominance should be maintained as long as possible in order to prevent other countries from intruding on the scene.

Faced with the growing insubordination of their allies and the obduracy of the neutrals, America and Russia are in the declining days of their condominium. Like generals of two mutinous armies, they are becoming aware of the fact that, although they are on opposite sides, the problems they face are strikingly similar, and that what is to the advantage of one is not necessarily to the disadvantage of the other. Indeed, their interests in many cases are surprisingly parallel. Trying to maintain a nuclear balance, keeping restless allies in check, paying blackmail to the underdeveloped nations, and seeking to prevent Third World revolutions from spilling over into conflagrations that might involve them, the super-powers are being drawn together into an unacknowledged, and still rather embarrassing, cooperation.

For the first time since 1945 Franklin Roosevelt's idea of a great-power directorship over the world has become theoretically possible. America and Russia now realize that it is to their interests. But is it not already too late? The time has passed when Washington could decree a German settlement without the accord of Bonn, or when Moscow could impose a solution upon Pankow. Washington cannot speak for Paris, or even for Saigon, any more than Russia can speak for Peking, or even for Bucharest. The break-up of the old alliances and the entry upon the world scene of other powers — a resurgent Europe, an ambitious China — have destroyed the ability of the nuclear giants to impose their own conceptions of order. The agreements they can reach are limited not only by the fear and suspicion induced by the cold war, but also by their declining power over their allies.

With pretensions to world leadership they cannot easily shed, with global responsibilities that flatter their national egos, with ideological beliefs that confirm their sense of mission, and with restless allies who could throw the hard-earned détente into doubt, the super-powers remain victims of their obsessions, their fears, and their fantasies. They cannot turn their covert collaboration into an open entente because they remain committed to inherited postures and nagging ideologies. For some time to come they will remain publicly committed to the ideological goals of the cold war, even though they may privately recognize that these are unattainable (as in the case of world communism) or perhaps even undesirable (as in the case of German reunification). Thus it may be that America and Russia will try to solidify their détente, even while protesting that no collaboration is taking place. This protest is necessary not only to soothe their allies, but also to lessen the shock of such a reversal of attitudes. It also, paradoxically, may give them a certain freedom of maneuver. This is particularly true of an ideologically oriented government like that of the Soviet Union. "The continued use of the symbols 'world communism' and 'revolution'," as one historian has observed,

satisfies . . . those who desire whatever they think these symbols represent. . . . It may fill their needs as adequately as, or more so than, an actual realization of world communism and the revolution could. . . . One may expect that the more the Soviet government changes its policies from those that were once associated with the goal of world communism, the less can it afford to stop insisting that it continues to stand for this goal. It is therefore unreasonable to expect a Soviet policy change to be initiated or accompanied by an open renunciation of the Soviet goals of burying capitalism and establishing world communism. Such a renunciation can only be one of the last, rather than one of the first, concomitants of a policy change and will for a long time be as impossible psychologically and politically as a statement by an American President (no matter what his foreign policy) that he is no longer interested in fighting communism.

Symbol and myth still play a predominant role in the relations between the superpowers. This is clearly true for the Russians. It is equally true, though less obviously so, for ourselves. We are not only chained to the recitation of the old dogma in order to please the fundamentalists within our own camp; we are all too often convinced that the dogma is true. We have repeated it so often and lived with it for so long that we have ended up taking it at face value. There are, of course, real points of conflict between ourselves and the Russians, between ourselves and the Chinese, between ourselves and our own allies. These are unavoidable and to be expected in the relations among nations. But they are not conflicts which can be defined within the traditional vocabulary of the cold war. The insistence on doing so has hobbled our diplomacy and made much of it irrelevant to the world in which we now live.

The Politics of the Radical Right

With the onset of the cold war, there emerged a strong right-wing thrust in American politics. Twice in the past two decades — during the early 1950s in the heyday of Senator Joseph R. McCarthy of Wisconsin, and again with the Presidential candidacy of Senator Barry Goldwater on the Republican ticket in 1964 — the Right has emerged as a major challenge to the liberal consensus in American politics. Although both McCarthy and Goldwater failed, the Radical Right has established itself as a major and continuing force on the political scene.

From the very first, the Radical Right attracted unusual attention from historians and social scientists, partly because they were among its targets, partly because of its clear importance, and, perhaps most of all, because the phenomenon posed fascinating problems of analysis. McCarthyism seemed to violate the central assumption about American politics: that men acted in rational relationship to economic interests and needs. What were the sources of the Radical Right? What were its character and purposes?

No one responded more brilliantly to these questions than the historian Richard Hofstadter. In his book *The Age of Reform* he attempted to trace the roots of the New Right back to characteristics of populist and progressive reform. His essay "The Pseudo-Conservative Revolt" confronted the contemporary situation directly. The thrust of Hofstadter's argument was that the new American Right had to be seen, not in the context of conventional "interest" politics, but rather as an expression of "status" politics — "a product of the rootlessness and heterogeneity of American life and, above all, of its peculiar scramble for status and its peculiar search for secure identity." The groups hardest hit by social anxiety were old-family Americans in decline and ethnic Americans on the rise, and these, Hofstadter argued, formed the backbone of McCarthyism. Hofstadter termed the movement "pseudo-conservative" to set it apart from the reasoned conservatism of such men as Senator Robert A. Taft and to emphasize its psycho-social character.

Hofstadter's thesis came under sharp scholarly criticism in succeeding years, both on empirical and analytical grounds. With the passage of time, too, it became clear that the character, if not the inner dynamics, of the Radical Right was changing. In the following essay, written in 1965, Hofstadter comes to grips with these two challenges to his earlier thesis. The essay is most interesting on both counts. It is a fine example of how a first-rate historian can refine an initial hypothesis to take into account criticism and fresh data. And it analyzes, in a more penetrating way than he had earlier, the nature of the Radical Right of the 1960s. The crucial substantive change is in Hofstadter's emphasis on fundamentalism, now transferred to America's suburbs, as the source of current right-wing politics. Hofstadter traces the roots of the Radical Right back to the cultural politics of the 1920s and shrewdly delineates its characteristics in fundamentalist terms. Critics will not have so easy a time with this reformulation.

FOR FURTHER READING:

BELL, DANIEL. *The Radical Right*. New York: Doubleday & Company, Anchor Books, 1963.*
GOLDWATER, BARRY M. *The Conscience of a Conservative*. New York: Macfadden Books, 1960.*
ROVERE, RICHARD. *Senator Joe McCarthy*. Cleveland: The World Publishing Company, Meridian Books, 1957.*

Asterisk denotes paperback edition.

Pseudo-Conservatism Revisited—1965

RICHARD HOFSTADTER

The Goldwater campaign showed that the ultra-right has grown considerably in organization and influence, if not in numbers, over the past ten years, and the effort to understand it has lost none of its urgency. Although a decade of experience and inquiry, climaxed by the Goldwater movement, which is itself almost an ideal test case for the nature of pseudo-conservatism, has confirmed some of the suggestions advanced in "The Pseudo-Conservative Revolt" and similar ventures in explanation, these ideas appear at other points to need revision.

There are four general matters on which I believe my own essay now demands qualification or correction. The first and most complex has to do with the place of status anxieties and status resentments in the right-wing ferment of the McCarthyist era. At the time I wrote, the status factor had been largely ignored and therefore needed emphasizing, but I have no doubt that an essay devoted rather single-mindedly to this one element in a complex situation inevitably had the effect of giving it disproportionate weight. Also, the term "status" was used in an uncommonly wide sense, and needed more definition than it got. But this is not to be taken as a retraction of what I had to say about the importance of status considerations; it is a preface to some refinements of my original statement. The distinction made in the earlier essay between status politics and interest politics seems to me to be of fundamental significance, and to have a general usability in understanding our political history that goes far beyond the issues of the 1950's which it was invoked to explain.

The other points are more easily dealt with. I think that in portraying the pseudo-conservative type, my essay overstressed clinical findings by failing to supplement them sufficiently with a more conventional historical analysis of the rhetoric, arguments, and tactics of the pseudo-conservatives. I hope I have made amends in the next essay, which deals with the Goldwater campaign. Again, I believe now that I overstated the role of certain ethnic minorities in the right wing. To be sure, these were present, as additional data have since shown; but they have turned out to be more a receding than an advancing element, and it is probably the native American side of the right wing that demands our primary attention. Finally — and this point is related to the preceding one — I made only passing reference in a footnote to the role of fundamentalism, and it is plain that this is one of the salient elements in the right wing, an element whose importance has become increasingly evident in the past decade.

Source: Richard Hofstadter, *The Paranoid Style in American Politics* (New York: Alfred A. Knopf, 1966), chap. 3, "Pseudo-Conservatism Revisited — 1965," pp. 66–93.

The last two points can best be discussed in connection with the significant changes that have recently taken place in the right wing, which, despite some continuity in ideas and in leadership, render any static account of it somewhat misleading. In this respect, my emphasis on ethnic factors in the pseudo-conservatism of 1954 now seems to me analogous to the strategy of generals who are prepared to fight the last war. What was true about it, I believe, is that the extreme right did draw somewhat on the older isolationism, in which the attitudes of German and Irish Americans were important, and also, to a degree, upon the feelings of Americans linked to Eastern European countries under Soviet domination. Our role in the Second World War temporarily stirred the feeling of national dislocation and the Anglophobia of these groups, feelings which were duly exploited by McCarthy. But the radical rightism of the 1960's is predominantly a movement of white Anglo-Saxon Protestant Republicans, with only a fringe of ethnic support. German Anglophobia now appears to be of less consequence than it once was and the election of an Irish Catholic President in 1960 may have helped to quiet the sense of incomplete cultural acceptance that has troubled the American Irish since 1928. In retrospect, it seems that even by 1954 ethnic factors in American pseudo-conservatism were waning, not rising.

Over the past three decades, right-wing movements have appealed to segments of the public which, though overlapping, have been significantly different. In the 1930's the chief vehicle of right-wing discontent was Father Coughlin's Social Justice movement, a depression phenomenon drawing the bulk of its support from those who suffered most from bad times — the working class and the unemployed, farmers and some of the lower middle class. Its tone was more pseudo-radical than pseudo-conservative. It played on old Populist themes, attacked international bankers, demanded free silver and other changes in the money and credit system, and resorted to an anti-Semitic rhetoric far more virulent than anything the Populists would have dreamed of. It was stronger in rural areas and small towns than in cities, and much stronger among Catholics, particularly Irish Catholics, than among Protestants. Its isolationist and Anglophobic note drew support from Germans, both Catholic and Lutheran. It was strongest in two areas: the West Central states, where its appeal was both ethnic and agrarian, and in New England, where it attracted Irish Catholics. That Coughlin had little strength in the South is perhaps an interesting token of surviving religious prejudice; also, up to the time of Huey Long's assassination, the South had its own native and more appealing messiah.

Coughlinism died with the war and the subsequent prosperity. The new right wing of the McCarthy era showed both continuity and discontinuity with Coughlinism. McCarthy, as an Irish Catholic, picked up much of the ethnic and religious following that had once been Coughlin's, as well as some support from ethnic groups drawn from the "captive" nations of Eastern Europe. But as a phenomenon of prosperity McCarthyism was almost entirely devoid of economic content and had no economic program. Since McCarthy appealed both to Republicans who resented their party's continuing domination by its eastern wing and to those in both parties who were swept up by the anti-Communist passions of the cold war, his following was much greater than Coughlin's. On the whole, he received a measure of support disproportionate to their numbers in the general population from Catholics and from the ill-educated, but also from Republicans, Irish Americans, the lower classes, and the aged. Along with economic issues, McCarthy abruptly dropped the old right-wing appeal to anti-Semitism.

Part of McCarthy's strength lay in his ability to combine a mass appeal with a special appeal to a limited stratum of the upper classes. As compared with Coughlin, whose following had been almost entirely a low-status public, McCarthy was able to win considerable support from the middle and upper ranks of society, mobilizing Republicans who had never accepted the changes brought by the New Deal and whose rage at the long exclusion of the party from presidential power was reaching a peak. There is evidence also that McCarthy had a special appeal to the postwar newly rich. Most prophetic too of the future of the right wing was his strong appeal for fundamentalist-oriented Protestants, who now took a significant place along with their Catholic counterparts.[1]

This is strikingly illustrated by the changing views of Baptists. Probably because of Coughlin's priestly vocation, Baptists had ranked low among the evangelical denominations that supported him, but McCarthy, though a lay Catholic, commanded more support from them than from any other Protestant denomination. It is in the McCarthyist era that the anti-Communist issue becomes so salient for members of this evangelical denomination (and presumably others) that they abandon their traditional anti-Catholic animus in order to take part in right-wing ecumenical anti-Communism.

The right wing of the 1960's, whose leadership has fallen to the John Birch Society, continues to move up the socio-economic ladder. With its strong commitment to ultraconservative economic ideas, the Birch Society makes little appeal to the economically deprived. It is primarily an organization of well-educated, middle- and upper-status Republicans who are deviants among the educated strata in several ways — including a greater disposition to ethnic prejudice than the population as a whole.[2] As an elite corps, the Birch Society is, of course, much better educated than the members of other right-wing groups. It has also brought out an interesting polarity within the educated upper classes of American society, which is related to party affiliation. Among Democrats, increasing education is correlated with increasing disapproval of the Birch Society; but among Republicans, increasing education is correlated with increasing support for the society.

Although the Birch Society as a whole draws its most vital public support from affluent Republican Protestants, it has some special appeal, when party affiliation is held constant, to Catholics. Its sociological profile is that of a group enjoying a strong social position, mainly well-to-do and educated beyond the average, but manifesting a degree of prejudice and social tension not customarily found among the affluent and the educated.

Although it is doubtful that extreme rightists in the 1960's are any more numerous than they were in the McCarthyist period, the right wing has learned the secret of organization, which largely accounts for its greater successes. Coughlinism and McCarthyism were largely the creation of astute and voluminous publicity on the radio and in the press, which was not matched by their organizational efforts. Coughlin's organized groups were of relatively little consequence, and McCarthy could barely organize his own files, much less a national movement. The John Birch Society, with only a fraction of McCarthy's support among the public, has won its successes through tightly organized and militant cadres of workers, operating in a manner resembling that of Communist cells, and linked to the Republican party not through publicity but by active work in district, precinct, and community organizations where ideological affinities can be translated into power.

At the grass roots the extreme right now draws its primary support from two basic (and at points overlapping) social types: first, the affluent (perhaps newly affluent) suburban educated middle class, largely outside the Northeast, which responds to ultra-conservative economic issues as well as to militant nationalism and anti-communism, and which seeks to win a place in the political structure proportionate to the secure place it has won in society; and second, a large lower middle class, somewhat less educated and less charmed than the first group by old-fashioned economic liberalism but even more fearful of communism, which it perceives rather abstractly in the light of a strong evangelical-fundamentalist cast of thought.

The reemergence of fundamentalism in politics, invigorated by the conditions of the cold war and the stimulus of the affluent society, is a notable development of the past fifteen years. Of necessity I use the term "fundamentalism" in a rather extended way to describe a religious style rather than firm doctrinal commitments, since no one knows how many evangelical right-wingers adhere to a literal view of Scripture and other fundamentalist tenets. Two other qualifications should be made: first, there are large numbers of fundamentalists who interpret their religious commitment as a reason to withdraw from worldly politics, in which they see no more hope than they do in the other things of this world; and second, many fundamentalists have inherited generous views on domestic economic reforms which they do not easily give up. But on certain issues of cultural politics fundamentalists have always been rigid, and when such issues become more salient the fundamentalists become more responsive to the blandishments of pseudo-conservative prophets. Moreover, the Manichean and apocalyptic style of thought prevalent in the fundamentalist tradition can easily be carried over into secular affairs and transmuted into a curiously crude and almost superstitious form of anti-communism.

Not only is the entire right-wing movement infused at the mass level with the fundamentalist style of mind, but the place in its ranks of fundamentalist preachers, ex-preachers, and sons of preachers is so prominent as to underline the mutual congeniality of thought. Leading right-wing spokesmen have brought into politics the methods and the style of the evangelical revivalists, just as many preachers have discovered that they can arouse more fervor and raise more cash by politicizing their message than they can by appealing solely to the religious sensibilities of their audiences.[3]

Under the aegis of right-wing politics, rigid Protestants of a type once intensely anti-Catholic can now unite with Catholics of similar militancy in a grand ecumenical zeal against communism and in what they take to be a joint defense of Christian civilization. The malevolent energy formerly used in the harassment of Catholics can now be more profitably spent in the search for Communists, or even in attacks on the alleged subversiveness of liberal Protestant denominations. The Manichean conception of life as a struggle between absolute good and absolute evil and the idea of an irresistible Armageddon have been thinly secularized and transferred to the cold war. The conflict between Christianity and communism is conceived as a war to the death, and Christianity is set forth as the only adequate counterpoise to the communist credo.

Fundamentalist leaders play a part in right-wing organizations far out of proportion to the strength of fundamentalism in the population at large. Among them are

Robert H. Welch, Jr., the founder of the John Birch Society; Dr. Fred C. Schwarz, the head of the Christian Anti-Communism Crusade; and Reverend Billy Hargis, of the Christian Crusade, which flourishes in the Southwest.[4]

A large part of the rise of fundamentalist ultra-conservatism may be linked with the astonishing growth of the Southern Baptist Church, which increased from 2,300,000 members in 1936 to 10,000,000 in 1962. A comparable growth has also been enjoyed by the right-wing Churches of Christ. The increase in these groups has far outstripped that of more moderate Protestant denominations in the same period. Such church groups have created a vast religious public, once poor and depression-ridden but now to a large degree moderately prosperous, whose members sometimes combine the economic prejudices of the newly well-to-do with the moral prejudices of the revolt against modernity.

We know more, of course, about the role of fundamentalist leaders in right-wing groups than we do about fundamentalism among the mass following. The presence of two kinds of subcultures in the Christian Anti-Communism Crusade is suggested in a study by Raymond E. Wolfinger and his associates of a sample of its members in Oakland, California. Their findings point to a bifurcation between a relatively affluent, educated, and "sophisticated" wing, concerned most intensely with the economic content of ultra-conservatism, and a more deeply religious wing, leaning toward fundamentalism, primarily concerned with religious and moral issues. Among 308 people who consented to be interviewed, persons belonging to fundamentalist churches constituted 20 per cent (they would be a larger proportion in southern California). Those who reported that they came to the "schools" of this right-wing movement because of church influence differed from the whole sample in important respects: they were more fundamentalist, more active as church members, less affluent, less educated, and less active in politics. They were more favorably disposed than other respondents to such reforms as medicare and federal aid to education, and were more willing to accept the legitimacy of trade unions. Their more intense Christian convictions were perhaps also reflected in their taking a less sympathetic view than other members of the South's position on racial integration. But they were more anti-evolution, more disturbed about the threat of communism to theistic belief, and more anxious about the alleged internal threat of communism to the nation. An impressionistic study by participant observers of the membership of the same movement in a small midwestern industrial city found the members predominantly Baptist-fundamentalist, educated, with few exceptions, only to the high-school level, aggressively anti-intellectual, anxious about the preservation of the old-fashioned moral virtues, and rather disposed to see the world in the paranoid style.

One way of adding to our understanding of the politics of the 1950's and 1960's is to compare it with that of the 1920's. During the 1920's our political life was profoundly affected, and at times dominated, by certain cultural struggles, which were interrupted and deflected by the depression, the New Deal, and the war, but which have in a measure reasserted themselves in the different setting of the postwar decades. Both the 1920's and the postwar years, as periods of relative prosperity, saw some diminution in the force of economic issues and an upsurge in the issues of status politics — issues of religion, morals, personal style, and culture. It is significant that the election campaign which, of all the campaigns in our history, was most completely dominated by status politics was the Smith-Hoover campaign of 1928, conducted when the ill-fated boom of the twenties was nearing its peak. In 1964, again under prosperous conditions, the issues of status politics once more played an unusually significant part.

During the 1920's small-town and rural Protestants were waging a vigorous defense of their cultural values against their rapidly gaining foes — the advancing Catholics and minority ethnic groups on one side and the modernists in religion and secularists in intellectual culture on the other. The Ku Klux Klan, Prohibitionism, the campaign against evolution in the schools, anti-Catholicism and the whispering campaign against Al Smith were all aspects of this struggle. On one count, immigration restriction, the old guard scored an important and permanent victory, and on another, Prohibition, they scored a gratifying if temporary success. But on the others they continued to lose ground. They substantially lost the fight against teaching evolution in the public schools, which exposed them to humiliating ridicule throughout the world. Lost, too, was the fight against modern relaxation in manners, morals, and censorship. Again the effort to contain the influence of immigrants in politics was lost within the Democratic party. The rural Protestant Democrats fought in 1924 to keep their party free of urban ethnic domination, and the two factions nearly tore the Democratic party apart at its 1924 convention. By 1928 the enemy was in control and Smith was nominated. He paid a heavy price for his religion and his defiance of establishment manners and morals, but he did succeed, partly by mobilizing the ethnic Catholic vote, in rehabilitating his party and raising it from the desperate condition it had reached in the two previous elections. The Democratic party became the coalition party of the new urban polyglot America. What Smith had begun, Roosevelt completed; F.D.R.'s consolidation of the ethnic and working-class elements in the country into an effective political force was almost as important as his economic reforms.

The problems of the depression and the Second World War somewhat eclipsed these cultural antagonisms, though they were often visible beneath the surface. Fundamentalist-evangelical America was, in fact, so long divided or quiescent as a political force that many intellectuals have forgotten that it still exists. Nor has it surrendered its commitment to Prohibitionism or its dislike of evolution in popular education. Even as recently as 1959, according to a Gallup poll, 34 per cent of all Protestants favored national Prohibition. Three-fifths of all Protestant farmers and two-fifths of all Protestants living in towns of less than 10,000 population took this view. Again, only a few years earlier, another survey showed the effects of a resolute if quiet effort being made to protect the young against Darwinism and secularism. In a poll of adolescents based on an unusually large sample, only 35 per cent responded by checking "Yes" alongside the statement: "Man was evolved from lower forms of animals." As many as 40 per cent marked "No," and 24 per cent "Don't know."

Now the point of all this is not to say that the old cultural issues of the 1920's are important manifest issues under present conditions, but rather that ascetic Protestantism remains a significant undercurrent in contemporary America, and that its followers have found newfangled ways of reaffirming some of their convictions. They cannot bring back Prohibition or keep evolution entirely out of the schools. They have been unable even to defend school prayer or prevent *Life* magazine from featuring the topless bathing suit. But they can recriminate against and punish the new America that outrages them, and they have found powerful leaders to echo their views. As the old fight against immigration has waned in significance, the

Negro "revolution" has frightened many of them, and has given a new focus to ethnic conflict. The participants in this revolt against modernity are no longer rubes and hicks, and they have gained something both in sophistication and in cohesiveness through modern urbanization. They too live in the cities and the suburbs, at closer and more irritating range to the things that disturb them, but also closer to each other, and more susceptible to organization.

Above all, they have found a fighting issue that helps them to surmount their previous isolation, an issue on which at last they have common ground with all America: they are implacably and consumingly anti-Communist, and in the grand ecumenicism of their anti-Communist passion they welcome all allies. They are particularly happy to have made terms with the Catholics and to accept members of minority ethnic groups as comrades-in-arms. That the Whore of Babylon now sits in Moscow, not Rome, is to their incalculable advantage, for they have been able to turn a powerful domestic foe, the Church, into an ally, and in its former place they have installed the impotent American Communist. Nor does it trouble them that genuine Communists are all but impossible to find. Liberals, pacifists, beatniks, agitators for racial justice, radicals of other persuasions — what Robert Welch calls "comsymps" — will do as well.

People who share this outlook have a disposition to interpret issues of secular politics as though they were solely moral and spiritual struggles. They are less concerned with the battle against communism in the world theater than they are with the alleged damage it does to politics and morals at home. The cold war serves as a constant source of recriminations about our moral and material failure, but as an objective struggle in the arena of world politics it is less challenging to them than it is as a kind of spiritual wrestling match with the minions of absolute evil, who, as is so often the case with Satanic powers, exercise an irresistible attractiveness. Those who look at the world in this way see their fundamental battle as one to be conducted against other Americans at home, and they respond eagerly to the notion, so pervasive in the right wing, that the worst enemy of American liberties is to be found in Washington. Moreover, whereas in the past only an occasional wealthy crank was interested in subsidizing attacks on Catholicism, the anti-Communist crusade brings lavish outpourings from right-wing foundations and from some of the nation's large business firms.

Though many Americans with fundamentalist leanings have traditionally been sympathetic to economic and social reforms, there is one aspect of right-wing thought that invariably attracts them — the moralistic quality of its economic ideas. Christian economic moralism, to be sure, has often buttressed benevolence and inspired social reform. But it has another side: insofar as economic life is regarded as a sphere for the fulfillment of the ascetic Protestant virtues, Christian moralism has worked for right-wing discontent. One strain in Protestant thinking has always looked to economic life not just for its efficacy in producing goods and services but as a vast apparatus of moral discipline, of rewards for virtue and industry and punishments for vice and indolence. In the past, vocational life was supposed to inculcate prudence, economy, and diligence — and many writers seem to have felt that economic discipline would be more effective in this task than sermons and exhortations. The vocational life was a moral testing ground. Today these assumptions have been flouted. The modern economy, based on advertising, lavish consumption, installment buying, safeguards to social security, relief to the indigent, government fiscal manipulation, and unbalanced budgets, seems reckless and immoral, even when it happens to work. In the intellectual synthesis of contemporary ultra-conservatism, the impulses of Protestant asceticism can thus be drawn upon to support business self-interest and the beautiful mathematical models of neo-classical economists.

We can now return to our original interest: to what extent are the newly affluent, the fundamentalist, and the other constituent elements of the modern American right animated by status resentments and anxieties? This question does not seem to have the same urgency it had ten years ago, because the point which the various authors of *The Radical Right* then sought to make has been widely accepted. At that time we were all struck by a salient fact: the literature of the American right was a literature not of those who felt themselves to be in possession but of those who felt dispossessed — a literature of resentment, profoundly anti-establishment in its impulses.[5] We were all struck by the flimsiness of its pretensions to conservatism, and by its profound hostility to the culture and institutions by which it was surrounded.

If the essays in *The Radical Right* dwelled on status resentments, it was not because the authors thought they had found a final, single explanation of the right-wing line of thought, but because we had come upon a hitherto neglected and unexplained side of the movement. Our ideas were offered as an addition to the store of what was already known about the right wing, not as an attempt to displace the undeniable structural and historical setting in which the right wing arose. We were, in short, not trying to deny the obvious, but to go beyond it.

Our emphasis, then, on certain social and psychological forces at work in American society was not intended to deny the plurality of circumstances that gave birth to the right-wing resurgence — the shock of the Korean War, the failures of our foreign policy, the frustrations of Republicans too long defeated in presidential politics, the traditional irritations of big money, the continued high taxes, the impact of inflation, revelations of Communist espionage and of political corruption, the long-standing pent-up resentment against the New Deal and the social reforms it had established, the dislike of the type of national leadership that it had installed. We were trying to bring to the surface the additional sociological and psychological forces that helped all these circumstances come to a center and find a rhetorical form, and that gave to their anti-establishment animus its particular edge. We were impressed by the way in which the processes of prosperity yield their own kind of discontent, which, if not so widely shared as that of hard times, is nonetheless as bitter.

The emphasis given to status resentments and anxieties in the essays in *The Radical Right* was based partly on inferences from poll data about the socio-economic status and the education of McCarthyists, partly from impressionistic observation of contemporary social changes, and partly from the rhetoric of McCarthyism and the social objects against which its grievances were directed. What seemed important was not only the wrongs the McCarthyist right-wingers thought had been committed but who they thought had committed them; and repeated denunciations of "striped-pants diplomats," Ivy League graduates, high-ranking generals, college presidents, intellectuals, the Eastern upper classes, Harvard professors, and members of Phi Beta Kappa seemed to be serving psychological purposes which had little to do with arriving at a realistic historical account of the nation's difficulties and failures. As McCarthy put it in his famous speech at Wheeling, the nation had been sold out by "those who have had all the benefits that the wealthiest nation on earth has to offer — the finest homes, the finest college education, and the finest jobs in Government. . . . The bright young men who are born with silver spoons in their mouths are the ones who have been worst."

This seemed to voice certain status resentments, but it was hard to gauge them quantitatively or to measure their place among the many forces that were at work. To my knowledge only one study has been made to try to define felt status grievances in such a way as to put the notion to the test, and it reports a modest confirmation of the hypothesis of *The Radical Right.* Other empirical studies have stressed quite correctly the large number of variables that have gone into the making of the right wing, but have not effectively argued that status resentments should be excluded from them.

The essays in *The Radical Right* were prompted by a curiosity about certain facts hitherto taken for granted. We wanted to know why Americans who were affected in a similar way by many events reacted to them so differently. Of course, party affiliation, socio-economic status, and geographical region always affect political opinions, but in this case the aggregate of these readily perceptible factors did not yield a satisfactory or exhaustive answer. There was a wide range of reaction to the events of the 1950's, for example, among people in the same social class and in the same political party. People responded to political events, as they always do, not merely with profoundly different opinions about the policies that should be pursued but in strikingly different mental and rhetorical styles. It was understood that the Korean War and the overlong exclusion of Republicans from the White House had much to do with the temper of the times, but why did some Republicans welcome the peace in Korea while others branded the Republican President who made it as a traitor? Again, millionaires cannot be expected to like progressive taxation, but how could we account for the political differences between a first- or second-generation oil millionaire in Texas and a third-generation oil millionaire in New York? Why did taxpayers enjoying the same income and belonging to the same political party have such profoundly different views of the social reforms inherited from the New Deal?

I confess to mixed feelings about the term "status politics" as a means of explaining the discontents animated by the right wing. On one hand, I have no desire to overstate the role of status, narrowly defined, in the right wing of the 1950's or of today. There are a large number of factors, social and economic, that enter into the composition of the right wing, and, like any other single explanation, this one is bound to have its limitations. Yet I should be sorry if, because of its limited utility in this context, the fundamental importance of the distinction between status politics and interest politics should be lost. I chose the term "status politics" because I was looking for a way to designate an impulse held in common by a variety of discontented elements. If there is something misleading in the word "status," it is because its meaning is somewhat too specific to account for what it attempts to describe, and takes the part for the whole. Few critics have denied the presence or significance of what is intended, but it has been suggested that such terms as "cultural politics" and "symbolic politics" will serve better.

In my original essay I used the term "status politics" to refer to three things that are related but not identical: first is the problem of American identity, as it is complicated by our immigrant origins and the problems of ethnic minorities; second, the problem of social status, defined as the capacity of various groups and occupations to command personal deference in society; and, finally, the effort of Americans of diverse cultural and moral persuasions to win reassurance that their values are respected by the community at large. The purpose of the term was to heighten our awareness of a constant political struggle arising not out of the real or imagined contest for gain that is familiar in our interest-group politics — that is, the historical struggles for cheap land, cheap credit, higher farm prices, larger profits, market protection of various kinds, more jobs, more bargaining power, economic security — but out of commitments to certain other values, which are taken by the persons who share them to be ultimate moral goals, disinterestedly pursued. Such persons believe that their prestige in the community, even indeed their self-esteem, depends on having these values honored in public. Besides their economic expectations, people have deep emotional commitments in other spheres — religion, morals, culture, race relations — which they also hope to see realized in political action. Status politics seeks not to advance perceived material interests but to express grievances and resentments about such matters, to press claims upon society to give deference to non-economic values. As a rule, status politics does more to express emotions than to formulate policies. It is in fact hard to translate the claims of status politics into programs or concrete objectives (national Prohibition was an exception, though ultimately an unsuccessful one); and for the most part the proponents of such politics, being less concerned with the uses of power than with its alleged misuse, do not offer positive programs to solve social problems. The operative content of their demands is more likely to be negative: they call on us mainly to prohibit, to prevent, to censor and censure, to discredit, and to punish.

The most useful attempt to apply the concept of status politics to an aspect of our history is Joseph R. Gusfield's recent book on the temperance movement, *Symbolic Crusade: Status Politics and the Temperance Movement.* Defining status politics rather sharply as "political conflict over the allocation of prestige," he argues that its importance "lies precisely in identifying non-economic segments as crucial in certain social and political conflicts." Gusfield distinguishes between the political aims of those he calls "cultural fundamentalists" and "cultural modernists" — the fundamentalists having a character more rigidly and exclusively oriented toward production, work, and saving, while the modernists are more concerned with consumption and enjoyment. The fundamentalists are "locals" in Robert Merton's terminology: that is, they take their values from the traditions of local society; the modernists are "cosmopolitans" in that they are more *au courant* with what is going on in the nation-wide mass society, whether or not they approve of it. Both are engaged with politics, but the fundamentalists have a special edge because they want to restore the simple virtues of a bygone age and they feel themselves to be fighting in a losing cause.

This is exemplified by the temperance movement, whose political commitments Gusfield traces from the early days of the Republic to recent times. The temperance movement of the late nineteenth and the early twentieth century, he points out, was often associated with progressive causes — feminism, Christian pacifism, the Progressive movement of the Roosevelt-Wilson era — but as its members have felt an increasing sense of alienation from modernity, and as its more moderate adherents have been drawn away into the orbit of cosmopolitan society, temperance advocates have become more and more embittered. They know that they are regarded as oddities and that the most respectable and honored people no longer support their cause. Since the New Deal — a heavily urban and cosmopolitan administration

— gave the *coup de grâce* to national Prohibition, the members of the movement have moved to the political right. The Prohibition party no longer attempts, as it did a generation ago, to appeal to reformers and liberals, but, as Gusfield concludes, "has moved toward an open appeal to the right-wing elements of both major parties."

In many areas of life, the style of status politics has been shaped in large measure by rigid moral and religious attitudes, and those who are moved by the issues of status politics transfer these attitudes to social and economic questions. On many occasions they approach economic issues as matters of faith and morals rather than matters of fact. For example, people often oppose certain economic policies not because they have been or would be economically hurt by such policies, or even because they have any carefully calculated views about their economic efficacy, but because they disapprove *on moral grounds* of the assumptions on which they think the policies rest.

A prominent case in point is the argument over fiscal policy. Deficit spending is vehemently opposed by great numbers of people in our society who have given no serious thought — indeed, are hardly equipped to do so — to the complex questions bearing on its efficacy as an economic device. They oppose it because their personal experience or training in spending, debts, and prudential management leads them to see in deficit spending a shocking repudiation of the moral precepts upon which their lives have been based. As a matter of status politics, deficit spending is an affront to millions who have been raised to live (and in some cases have been forced by circumstances to live) abstemious, thrifty, prudential lives. As a matter of interest politics, deficit spending might work to their advantage; but the moral and psychological effect, which is what they can really understand and feel, is quite otherwise: when society adopts a policy of deficit spending, thrifty small-businessmen, professionals, farmers, and white-collar workers who have been managing their affairs by the old rules feel that their way of life has been officially and insultingly repudiated.

Historians and social critics of the present generation have a particularly urgent need for such an analytical instrument as status politics: it serves to keep their conception of political conflict from being imbued with the excessive rationalism that infused the work of the two preceding generations of historians and political scientists. Under the guidance of such writers as Charles A. Beard, Frederick Jackson Turner, V. L. Parrington, Arthur F. Bentley, and others, we used to think of political man basically as a rational being who reckons as well as he can what his economic interests are, forms pressure groups and parties to advance these interests, and as a citizen casts his vote in order to see them realized.

Of course, the writers of this school understood that men can make miscalculations as to the nature of their interests and the best ways of pursuing them, and they also knew that at times non-economic factors entered significantly into political behavior. But they persisted in seeking fundamental economic motives in almost all political conflict. When they dealt with non-economic factors, as their sense of reality compelled them to do, they tended to discount the significance of these factors and to look upon them as momentary aberrations, and felt no need to develop a theory that would take adequate account of them. They were strongest when writing about those political conflicts that did in fact rest squarely on economic issues, and weakest when other issues came to the foreground. Their conceptions of historical change were least suited to deal with the kind of discontents that have developed during prosperity and which to a significant degree cut across class lines.

This rationalistic bias has very largely broken down in our time, partly under the impact of political events, partly because of what has been learned through public-opinion polling and depth psychology.[6] A conception of politics which dealt with the public largely as a set of economic blocs had no adequate way of coping with the variety of other factors that have entered into our political history — among them the sheer weight of habit and party loyalty, ethnic origins and traditions, religious affiliations and religious styles, racial and ethnic prejudices, attitudes toward liberty and censorship, feelings about foreign policy quite unrelated to commercial goals and of dubious relationship to the national interest. In American history the combined effect of such forces has been singularly large. The wealth of the country and the absence of sharp class-consciousness have released much political energy for expression on issues not directly connected with economic conflict; and our unusually complex ethnic and religious mixture has introduced a number of complicating factors of great emotional urgency.

Significantly, the periods in which status politics has been most strikingly apparent have been the relatively prosperous 1920's and the 1960's. In periods of prosperity, when economic conflicts are blunted or subordinated, the other issues become particularly acute. We have noticed that whereas in depressions or during great bursts of economic reform people vote for what they think are their economic interests, in times of prosperity they feel free to vote their prejudices. In good times, with their most severe economic difficulties behind them, many people feel that they can afford the luxury of addressing themselves to larger moral questions, and they are easily convinced that the kind of politics that results is much superior to the crass materialism of interest politics. They have fewer inhibitions about pressing hard for their moral concerns, no matter how demanding and ill-formulated, as an object of public policy, than they have in pressing for their interests, no matter how reasonable and realistically conceived. In the following essay, I will try to show that Barry Goldwater was one campaigner who saw with considerable clarity the distinction between interest politics and status politics, and went out of his way in his campaign to condemn the immorality of the first and to call for an intensification of the second.

NOTES

1. McCarthyism, it must also be remembered, was a phenomenon of much broader significance than the far right itself. During 1953 and 1954, when McCarthy was at the peak of his influence, there was no poll in which less than 34 per cent of the public was found approving him, and at one point, January 1954, the figure rose to 50 per cent. No sensible observer has ever imagined that extreme right-wing ideas command the loyalty of one third, much less one half, of the American public. In July 1964, for example, at a time of great right-wing ferment, a major national poll found that only 4 per cent of the public would be influenced to vote for a presidential candidate because he was endorsed by the John Birch Society, as against 47 per cent who would be more disposed to vote against him; the remainder would have been unaffected or expressed no opinion. *The New York Times,* July 31, 1964. Characteristically, from about 5 to 10 per cent of the public will express approval of the Birch Society . . . though right-wing positions often receive the endorsement of as much as 15 per cent of the public.
2. Birchite prejudice, it should be said, is directed more significantly against Negroes, Mexicans, and Orientals than it is against Jews. Birchites are a shade *less* prejudiced against Catholics than anti-Birchites. . . . Though all polls agree on the relatively high level of formal education among Birchites, they do not provide information about the kind of colleges they attended, and it would be interesting to know to what extent these were the great cosmopolitan universities and colleges or denominational institutions.

3. This is not the first period in our history in which fundamentalist leaders, anguished over the general repudiation of their beliefs and values, lent their energies to political reaction. During the 1920's they gave heavy support to the Ku Klux Klan, particularly in the South. During the years 1922 to 1928, 26 of 39 anti-Catholic lecturers employed by the Klan were Protestant ministers of the fundamentalist type, and 16 of such ministers were Klan officials. Klansmen were regularly entertained in the homes of such ministers, and churches were used for Klan meetings. The two chief leaders of the new Klan had fundamentalist backgrounds — its initiator, Colonel William J. Simmons, had been a religious camp meeting exhorter, and its most successful promoter, Edward Y. Clarke, went into the fundamentalist movement after giving up his efforts in the Klan. In return, the Klan often fought for passage of the anti-evolution laws. . . .

4. Welch, who was raised as a pious fundamentalist Baptist in North Carolina, chose to name his organization after a young fundamentalist Baptist preacher from Macon, Georgia, who was killed by the Chinese Communists. As a prosperous candy manufacturer, once very active in the National Association of Manufacturers, Welch embodies the union of fundamentalist inspiration and small-business parochial conservatism that animates the extreme right. Schwarz is the son of an Australian pentecostal preacher; he had considerable experiences in his native country as a lay preacher before coming to the United States on the invitation of some anti-modernist preachers. He began his American career with an evangelical-style tour. Preachers and ex-preachers figure prominently in the "faculty" he has recruited for his anti-Communist "schools." Hargis moved on from evangelism to right-wing politics in much the same way as such predecessors as Gerald L. K. Smith, Gerald Winrod, and J. Frank Norris. He is the product of Ozark Bible College in Arkansas and of the Disciples of Christ, though his ministry is now independent. Another successful southwestern leader is Dr. George Benson, a former Church of Christ missionary in China, now president of the church-affiliated Harding College in Searcy, Arkansas. This organization still holds forth against Darwin, but its main claim to fame is its role as the source of right-wing political radio broadcasts and films, on the strength of which it has attracted munificent contributions from businessmen. In the East, the Reverend Carl McIntire of the Bible Presbyterian Church in Collingswood, New Jersey, reaches large audiences with his radio broadcasts. A former disciple of the highbrow fundamentalist H. Gresham Machen, McIntire set up on his own after being expelled from the General Assembly of the Presbyterian Church, and he has been vociferous in fighting modernist Christianity and the ecumenical movement. Finally, there is the Church League of America, founded in 1937 to fight liberal Protestantism but now a right-wing organization managed by Edgar Bundy, a minister ordained in the Southern Baptist Convention.

5. One is struck also by the disparity between the actual social position of these segments of the population and the intensity of their discontent. As Daniel Bell observes, they come from disparate groups many of which are doing very well. "In identifying 'the dispossessed,' it is somewhat misleading to seek their economic location, since it is not economic interest alone that accounts for their anxieties. . . ."

6. Even the pollsters, however, were slow to break away from the older pattern of thought. The realization that socio-economic status was a fundamental category was at the very foundation of commercial polling, but the importance of religious affiliation was not realized. George Gallup found it hard to believe when Paul Larzarsfeld first told him that religious affiliation has a powerful and independent relation to voting habits; and even as recently as 1959 Elmo Roper asserted that there is no relation between religious affiliation and voting. . . . On religion as an independent force in American politics, and on the conservative drive of ascetic Protestantism, see Benton Johnson: "Ascetic Protestantism and Political Preference," *Public Opinion Quarterly, XXVI* (Spring 1962), 35–46.

Black Power: Two Views

The cry for "Black Power," first heard in the land in June 1966, signaled a major turning point in the Negro's struggle for equality in America. Until then, the essential thrust had aimed at civil rights objectives: the elimination of segregation and discrimination and the protection of the right to vote. When the Supreme Court, in 1954, declared unconstitutional laws requiring segregated public schools, the civil rights movement received a powerful boost. This, clearly, marked the opening of a decisive shift in public policy, the precedent for ending the legal barriers to equal treatment and integration. Blacks, for their part, mobilized to help accomplish those objectives. Beginning with the Montgomery bus boycott of 1955, Martin Luther King's doctrine of nonviolent resistance was employed persistently and courageously in the hostile South.

But, despite a record of considerable surface success as measured by its original aims, the civil rights movement suffered a loss of hope by the mid-1960s, especially among its younger adherents. For one thing, nonviolence in the violent South took a terrific psychological toll on civil rights workers. For another, they discovered that formal rights did not lead automatically to actual equality; nor did it seem that the North was any more willing in practice to accept integrated schooling and open housing than the South. There was, too, a growing disillusionment with liberal white allies whose rhetoric often outstripped their actions: the Democratic convention of 1964 was a case in point. Finally, there was the growing realization that civil rights had little relevance to the problems of the poor blacks anyway. Ghetto unrest was mounting in the early 1960s; in the summer of 1965 Watts exploded in riot. The following May, the Student Nonviolent Coordinating Committee called on "black Americans to begin building independent political, economic, and cultural institutions that they will control and use as instruments of social change in this country." The following month, during the tense march to Jackson, Mississippi, after the shooting of James Meredith, Stokely Carmichael, the new SNCC chairman, denounced nonviolent tactics and issued the call for Black Power.

At first merely a slogan used in anger, Black Power quickly came to designate the militants' search for an authentic alternative to the civil rights movement. In the following months, Stokely Carmichael and others attempted to define, in a thoroughgoing way, the meaning of Black Power. The following essay is one such effort. Starting with the assumption that groups in America have always advanced by developing collective power, Carmichael argues that this has been the fundamental failing of black Americans. In trying to trace the reasons, Carmichael finds one in integrationism, which siphons off some blacks into middle-class America, leaving the black community the poorer and, by this form of tokenism, assuaging white guilt.

For their part, many white liberals deplored this turn in black thinking. As Milton Mayer observed in his response to Carmichael's essay, Black Power sacrificed the redemptive nature of the civil rights movement; instead of rejecting America's emphasis on power, as Martin Luther King had attempted to do, the Black Power advocates merely wanted to join the power system. Nor, Mayer feared, were they likely to succeed, for the black man confronted obstacles faced by no other American.

Since 1966, the Black Power issue has not become clearer; indeed, the ambiguities and unanswered questions have increased. Given their economic marginality, how are the black ghettos to develop viable economic institutions? Is it possible to reconcile the tendencies toward class action, which advocates an alliance with poor whites, with black nationalism and separatism? Does Black Power accept the system, as Carmichael seems to say in the following essay, or does it aim for revolution, as his public rhetoric and identification with Maoism would seem to indicate? And what of violence? Is it to be an instrument of defense or, as seems more and more the case, or attack? The lack of clear answers in part reflects insufficiently hard thinking by Black Power advocates, but in part too it reflects the unyielding dilemmas they face. But, if so much about Black Power remains cloudy, the underlying import seems clear enough: the civil rights movement, with its tactics of nonviolence, its focus on legal barriers, its integrationist ends, has fallen short and is being replaced by new forms of black protest.

FOR FURTHER READING:

CARMICHAEL, STOKELY, and HAMILTON, CHARLES V. *Black Power.* New York: Random House, Vintage Books, 1967.*
Report of the National Advisory Commission on Civil Disorders. New York: Bantam Books, 1968.*
SILBERMAN, CHARLES E. *Crisis in Black and White.* New York: Random House, Vintage Books, 1964.*

Asterisk denotes paperback edition.

Toward Black Liberation

STOKELY CARMICHAEL

One of the most pointed illustrations of the need for Black Power, as a positive and redemptive force in a society degenerating into a form of totalitarianism, is to be made by examining the history of distortion that the concept has received in national media of publicity. In this "debate," as in everything else that affects our lives, Negroes are dependent on, and at the discretion of, forces and institutions within the white society which have little interest in representing us honestly. Our experience with the national press has been that where they have managed to escape a meretricious special interest in "Git Whitey" sensationalism and race-war-mongering, individual reporters and commentators have been conditioned by the enveloping racism of the society to the point where they are incapable even of objective observation and reporting of racial *incidents*, much less the analysis of *ideas*. But this limitation of vision and perceptions is an inevitable consequence of the dictatorship of definition, interpretation, and consciousness, along with the censorship of history that the society has inflicted upon the Negro — and itself.

Our concern for the black power addresses itself directly to this problem, the ne-

Source: Stokely Carmichael, "Toward Black Liberation," in *Black and White in American Culture,* eds. Jules Chametsky and Sidney Kaplan (Amherst, Mass.: University of Massachusetts Press, 1969), pp. 76–87.

cessity to reclaim our history and our identity from the cultural terrorism and depredation of self-justifying white guilt.

To do this we shall have to struggle for the right to create our own terms through which to define ourselves and our relationship to the society, and to have these terms recognized. This is the first necessity of a free people, and the first right that any oppressor must suspend. The white fathers of American racism knew this — instinctively it seems — as is indicated by the continuous record of the distortion and omission in their dealings with the red and black men. In the same way that Southern apologists for the "Jim Crow" society have so obscured, muddied, and misrepresented the record of the reconstruction period, until it is almost impossible to tell what really happened, their contemporary counterparts are busy doing the same thing with the recent history of the civil rights movement.

In 1964, for example, the National Democratic party, led by L. B. Johnson and Hubert H. Humphrey, cynically undermined the efforts of Mississippi's black population to achieve some degree of political representation. Yet, whenever the events of that convention are recalled by the press, one sees only that aversion fabricated by the press agents of the Democratic party. A year later the House of Representatives, in an even more vulgar display of political racism, made a mockery of the political rights of Mississippi's Negroes when it failed to unseat the Mississippi Delegation to the House which had been elected through a process which methodically and systematically excluded over 450,000 voting-age Negroes, almost one half of the total electorate of the state. Whenever this event is mentioned in print it is in terms which leave one with the rather curious impression that somehow the oppressed Negro people of Mississippi are at fault for confronting the Congress with a situation in which they had no alternative but to endorse Mississippi's racist political practices.

I mention these two examples because, having been directly involved in them, I can see very clearly the discrepancies between what happened and the versions that are finding their way into general acceptance as a kind of popular mythology. Thus the victimization of the Negro takes place in two phases — first it occurs in fact and deed, then, and this is equally sinister, in the official recording of those facts.

The "Black Power" program and concept which is being articulated by SNCC, CORE, and a host of community organizations in the ghettoes of the North and South has not escaped that process. The white press has been busy articulating their own analyses, their own interpretations, and criticisms of their own creations. For example, while the press had given wide and sensational dissemination to attacks made by figures in the civil rights movement — foremost among which are Roy Wilkins of the NAACP and Whitney Young of the Urban League — and to the hysterical ranting about black racism made by the political chameleon that now serves as vice-president, it has generally failed to give accounts of the reasonable and productive dialogue which is taking place in the Negro community, and in certain important areas in the white religious and intellectual community. A national committee of influential Negro churchmen affiliated with the National Council of Churches, despite their obvious respectability and responsibility, had to resort to a paid advertisement to articulate their position, while anyone shouting the hysterical yappings of "Black Racism" got ample space. Thus the American people have gotten at best a superficial and misleading account of the very terms and tenor of this debate. I wish to quote briefly from the statement by the national committee of churchmen which I suspect that the majority of Americans will not have seen. This statement appeared in *The New York Times* of July 31, 1966.

We an informal group of Negro Churchmen in America are deeply disturbed about the crisis brought upon our country by historic distortions of important human realities in the controversy about "black power." What we see shining through the variety of rhetoric is not anything new but the same old problem of power and race which has faced our beloved country since 1619.

. . . The conscience of black men is corrupted because, having no power to implement the demands of conscience, the concern for justice in the absence of justice becomes a chaotic self-surrender. Powerlessness breeds a race of beggars. We are faced now with a situation where powerless conscience meets conscience-less power, threatening the very foundation of our Nation.

. . . We deplore the overt violence of riots, but we feel it is more important to focus on the real sources of these eruptions. These sources may be abetted inside the Ghetto, but their basic cause lies in the silent and covert violence which white middleclass America inflicts upon the victims of the inner city.

. . . In short; the failure of American leaders to use American power to create equal opportunity *in life* as well as *law,* this is the real problem and not the anguished cry for black power.

. . . Without the capacity to *participate with power, i.e.,* to have some organized political and economic strength to really influence people with whom one interacts — integration is not meaningful.

. . . America has asked its Negro citizens to fight for opportunity as *individuals,* whereas at certain points in our history what we have needed most has been opportunity for the *whole group,* not just for selected and approved Negroes.

. . . We must not apologize for the existence of this form of group power, for we have been oppressed as a group and not as individuals. We will not find our way out of that oppression until both we and America accept the need for Negro Americans, as well as for Jews, Italians, Poles, and white Anglo-Saxon Protestants, among others to have and to wield group power.

Traditionally, for each new ethnic group, the route to social and political integration into America's pluralistic society has been through the organization of their own institutions with which to represent their communal needs within the larger society. This is simply stating what the advocates of black power are saying. The strident outcry, *particularly* from the liberal community, that has been evoked by this proposal can only be understood by examining the historic relationship between Negro and white power in this country.

Negroes are defined by two forces, their blackness and their powerlessness. There have been traditionally two communities in America. The white community, which controlled and defined the forms that all institutions within the society would take, and the Negro community which has been excluded from participation in the power decisions that shaped the society, and has traditionally been dependent upon, and subservient to, the white community.

This has not been accidental. The history of every institution of this society indicates that a major concern in the ordering and structuring of the society has been the maintaining of the Negro community in its condition of dependence and oppression. This has not been on the level of individual acts of discrimination between individual whites against individual Negroes, but as total acts by the white community against the Negro community. This fact cannot be too strongly emphasized — that racist assumtpions of white superiority have been so deeply ingrained in the structure of the society that it infuses its entire functioning, and is so much a part of the national subconscious that it is taken for granted and is frequently not even recognized.

Let me give an example of the difference between individual racism and institutionalized racism, and the society's response to both. When unidentified white terrorists bomb a Negro church and kill five children, that is an act of individual racism, widely deplored by most segments of the society. But when in that same city, Birmingham, Alabama, not five but five hundred Negro babies die each year because of a lack of proper food, shelter, and medical facilities, and thousands more are destroyed and maimed physically, emotionally, and intellectually because of conditions of poverty and deprivation in the ghetto, that is a function of institutionalized racism. But the society either pretends it doesn't know of this situation, or is incapable of doing anything meaningful about it. And this resistance to doing anything meaningful about conditions in that ghetto comes from the fact that the ghetto is itself a product of a combination of forces and special interests in the white community, and the groups that have access to the resources and power to change that situation benefit, politically and economically, from the existence of that ghetto.

It is more than a figure of speech to say that the Negro community in America is the victim of white imperialism and colonial exploitation. This is in practical economic and political terms true. There are over twenty million black people comprising ten per cent of this nation. They for the most part live in well-defined areas of the country — in the shanty-towns and rural black belt areas of the South, and increasingly in the slums of northern and western industrial cities. If one goes into any Negro community, whether it be in Jackson, Mississippi, Cambridge, Maryland, or Harlem, New York, one will find that the same combination of political, economic, and social forces are at work. The people in the Negro community do not control the resources of that community, its political decisions, its law enforcement, its housing standards; and even the physical ownership of the land, houses, and stores *lie outside that community.*

It is white power that makes the laws, and it is violent white power in the form of armed white cops that enforces those laws with guns and nightsticks. The vast majority of Negroes in this country live in these captive communities and must endure these conditions of oppression because, and only because, *they are black and powerless.* I do not suppose that at any point the men who control the power and resources of this country ever sat down and designed these black enclaves and formally articulated the terms of their colonial and dependent status, as was done, for example, by the apartheid government of South Africa. Yet, one can not distinguish between one ghetto and another. As one moves from city to city it is as though some malignant racist planning unit had done precisely this — designed each one from the same master blueprint. And indeed, if the ghetto had been formally and deliberately planned, instead of growing spontaneously and inevitably from the racist functioning of the various institutions that combine to make the society, it would be somehow less frightening. The situation would be less frightening because, if these ghettoes were the result of design and conspiracy, one could understand their similarity as being artificial and consciously imposed, rather than the result of identical patterns of white racism which repeat themselves in cities as distant as Boston and Birmingham. Without bothering to list the historic factors which contribute to this pattern — economic exploitation, political impotence, discrimination in employment and education — one can see that to correct this pattern will require far-reaching changes in the basic power relationships and the ingrained social patterns within the society. The question is, of course, what kinds of changes are necessary, and how is it possible to bring them about?

In recent years, the answer to these questions which has been given by most articulate groups of Negroes and their white allies, the "liberals" of all stripes, has been in terms of something called "integration." According to the advocates of integration, social justice will be accomplished by "integrating the Negro into the mainstream institutions of the society from which he has been traditionally excluded." It is very significant that each time I have heard this formulation it has been in terms of "the Negro," the individual Negro, rather than in terms of the community.

This concept of integration had to be based on the assumption that there was nothing of value in the Negro community and that little of value could be created among Negroes, so the thing to do was to siphon off the "acceptable" Negroes into the surrounding middle-class white community. Thus the goal of the movement for integration was simply to loosen up the restrictions barring the entry of Negroes into the white community. Goals around which the struggle took place, such as public accommodation, open housing, job opportunity on the executive level (which is easier to deal with than the problem of semi-skilled and blue-collar jobs which involve more far-reaching economic adjustments), are quite simply middle-class goals, articulated by a tiny group of Negroes who had middle-class aspirations. It is true that the student demonstrations in the South during the early sixties, out of which SNCC came, had a similar orientation. But while it is hardly a concern of a black sharecropper, dishwasher, or welfare recipient whether a certain fifteen-dollar-a-day motel offers accommodations to Negroes, the overt symbols of white superiority and the imposed limitations on the Negro community had to be destroyed. Now, black people must look beyond these goals, to the issue of collective power.

Such a limited class orientation was reflected not only in the program and goals of the civil rights movement, but in its tactics and organization. It is very significant that the two oldest and most "respectable" civil rights organizations have constitutions which *specifically* prohibit partisan political activity. CORE once did, but changed that clause when it changed its orientation toward black power. But this is perfectly understandable in terms of the strategy and goals of the older organizations. The civil rights movement saw its role as a kind of liaison between the powerful white community and the dependent Negro one. The dependent status of the black community apparently was unimportant since — if the movement were successful — it would blend into the white community anyway. We made no pretense of organizing and developing institutions of community power in the Negro community, but appealed to the conscience of white institutions of power. The posture of the civil rights movement was that of the dependent, the suppliant. The theory was that without attempting to create any organized base of political strength itself, the civil rights movement could, by forming coalitions with various "liberal" pressure organizations in the white community — liberal reform clubs, labor unions, church groups, progressive civic groups — and at times one or other of the major political parties — influence national legislation and national social patterns.

I think we all have seen the limitations of this approach. We have repeatedly seen that political alliances based on appeals to conscience and decency are chancy things, simply because institutions and political organizations have no consciences, outside their own special interests. The political and social rights of Negroes have been and always will be negotiable and expendable the moment they conflict with the interests of our "allies." If we do not learn from history, we are doomed to repeat it, and that is precisely the lesson of the Reconstruction. Black people were allowed to register, vote, and participate in politics because it was to the advantage of powerful white allies to promote this. But this was the result of white decision, and it was ended by other white men's decision before any political base powerful enough to challenge that decision could be established in the Southern Negro community. (Thus at this point in the struggle Negroes have no assurance — save a kind of idiot optimism and faith in a society whose history is one of racism — that if it were to become necessary, even the painfully limited gains thrown to the civil rights movement by the Congress would not be revoked as soon as a shift in political sentiments should occur.)

The major limitation of this approach was that it tended to maintain the traditional dependence of Negroes and of the movement. We depended upon the goodwill and support of various groups within the white community whose interests were not always compatible with ours. To the extent that we depended on the financial support of other groups, we were vulnerable to their influence and domination.

Also, the program that evolved out of this coalition was really limited and inadequate in the long term and one which affected only a small select group of Negroes. Its goal was to make the white community accessible to "qualified" Negroes, and presumably each year a few more Negroes armed with their passports — a couple of university degrees — would escape into middle-class America and adopt the attitudes and life styles of that group; and one day the Harlems and the Wattses would stand empty, a tribute to the success of integration. This is simply neither realistic nor particularly desirable. You can integrate communities, but you assimilate individuals. Even if such a program were possible, its result would be, not to develop the black community as a functional and honorable segment of the total society, with its own cultural identity, life patterns, and institutions, but to abolish it — the final solution to the Negro problem. Marx said that the working class is the first class in history that ever wanted to abolish itself. If one listens to some of our "moderate" leaders, it appears that the American Negro is the first race that ever wished to abolish itself. The fact is that what must be abolished is not the black community, but the dependent colonial status that has been inflicted upon it. The racial and cultural personality of the black community must be preserved and the community must win its freedom while preserving its cultural integrity. This is the essential difference between integration as it is currently practised and the concept of black power.

What has the movement for integration accomplished to date? The Negro graduating from M.I.T. with a doctorate will have better job opportunities available to him than to Lynda Bird Johnson. But the rate of unemployment in the Negro community is steadily increasing, while that in the white community decreases. More educated Negroes hold executive jobs in major corporations and federal agencies than ever before, but the gap between white income and Negro income has almost doubled in the last twenty years. More suburban housing is available to Negroes, but housing conditions in the ghetto are steadily declining. While the infant mortality rate of New York City is at its lowest rate ever in the city's history, the infant mortality rate of Harlem is steadily climbing. There has been an organized national resistance to the Supreme Court's order to integrate the schools, and the federal government has not acted to enforce that order. Less than fifteen per cent of black children in the South attend integrated schools, and Negro schools, which the vast majority of black children still attend, are increasingly decrepit, overcrowded, under-staffed, inadequately equipped and funded.

This explains why the rate of school dropouts is increasing among Negro teenagers, who then express their bitterness, hopelessness, and alienation by the only means they have — rebellion. As long as people in the ghettoes of our large cities feel that they are victims of the misuse of white power without any way to have their needs represented — and these are frequently simple needs: to get the welfare inspectors to stop kicking down your doors in the middle of the night, the cops from beating your children, the landlord to exterminate the vermin in your home, the city to collect your garbage — we will continue to have riots. These are not the products of "black power," but of the absence of any organization capable of giving the community the power, the black power, to deal with its problems.

SNCC proposes that it is now time for the black freedom movement to stop pandering to the fears and anxieties of the white middle class in the attempt to earn its "good-will," and to return to the ghetto to organize these communities to control themselves. This organization must be attempted in northern and southern urban areas as well as in the rural black belt counties of the South. The chief antagonist to this organization is, in the South, the overtly racist Democratic party, and in the North, the equally corrupt big city machines.

The standard argument presented against independent political organization is "But you are only ten per cent." I cannot see the relevance of this observation, since no one is talking about taking over the country, but taking control over our own communities.

The fact is that the Negro population, ten per cent or not, is very strategically placed because — ironically — of segregation. What is also true is that Negroes have never been able to utilize the full voting potential of our numbers. Where we could vote, the case has always been that the white political machine stacks and gerrymanders the political subdivisions in Negro neighborhoods so the true voting strength is never reflected in political strength. Would anyone looking at the distribution of political power in Manhattan, ever think that Negroes represented sixty per cent of the population there?

Just as often the effective political organization in Negro communities is absorbed by tokenism and patronage — the time honored practice of "giving" certain offices to selected Negroes. The machine thus creates a "little machine," which is subordinate and responsive to it, in the Negro community. These Negro political "leaders" are really vote deliverers, more responsible to the white machine and the white power structure than to the community they allegedly represent. Thus the white community is able to substitute patronage control for audacious black power in the Negro community. This is precisely what Johnson tried to do even before the Voting Rights Act of 1966 was passed. The National Democrats made it very clear that the measure was intended to register Democrats, not Negroes. The President and top officials of the Democratic party called in almost one hundred selected Negro "leaders" from the Deep South. Nothing was said about changing the policies of the racist state parties, nothing was said about repudiating such leadership figures as James Eastland and Ross Barnett in Mississippi or George Wallace in Alabama. What was said was simply "Go home and organize your people into the local Democratic party — *then* we'll see about poverty money and appointments." (Incidentally, for the most part the War on Poverty in the South is controlled by local Democratic ward heelers — and outspoken racists who have used the program to change the form of the Negroes' dependence. People who were afraid to register for fear of being thrown off the farm are now afraid to register for fear of losing their Head Start jobs.)

We must organize black community power to end these abuses, and to give the Negro community a chance to have its needs expressed. A leadership which is truly "responsible" — not to the white press and power structure, but to the community — must be developed. Such leadership will recognize that its power lies in the unified and collective strength of that community. This will make it difficult for the white leadership group to conduct its dialogue with individuals in terms of patronage and prestige, and will force them to talk to the community's representatives in terms of real power.

The single aspect of the black power program that has encountered most criticism is this concept of independent organization. This is presented as third-partyism, which has never worked, or a withdrawal into black nationalism and isolationism. If such a program is developed it will not have the effect of isolating the Negro community but the reverse. When the Negro community is able to control local office and negotiate with other groups from a position of organized strength, the possibility of meaningful political alliances on specific issues will be increased. That is a rule of politics and there is no reason why it should not operate here. The only difference is that we will have the power to define the terms of these alliances.

The next question usually is: "So — can it work, can the ghettoes in fact be organized?" The answer is that this organization must be successful, because there are no viable alternatives — not the War on Poverty, which was at its inception limited to dealing with effects rather than causes, and has become simply another source of machine patronage. And "Integration" is meaningful only to a small chosen class within the community.

The revolution in agricultural technology in the South is displacing the rural Negro community into northern urban areas. Both Washington, D.C. and Newark, New Jersey, have Negro majorities. One third of Philadelphia's population of two million people is black. "Inner city" in most major urban areas is already predominantly Negro, and, with the white rush to suburbia, Negroes will in the next three decades control the hearts of our great cities. These areas can become either concentration camps with a bitter and volatile population whose only power is the power to destroy, or organized and powerful communities able to make constructive contributions to the total society. Without the power to control their lives and their communities, without effective political institutions through which to relate to the total society, these communities will exist in a constant state of insurrection. This is a choice that the country will have to make.

By Power Possessed   MILTON MAYER

Morris Cohen of C.C.N.Y. was lecturing at Chicago in 1941 (prior to December 7), and his old friend Irving Salmon (like Cohen a Jew) was giving a reception for

Source: Milton Mayer, "By Power Possessed," in *Black and White in American Culture,* eds. Jules Chametsky and Sidney Kaplan (Amherst, Mass.: University of Massachusetts Press, 1969), pp. 88–93.

him at the University. The small talk was large and loud with the European war. Salmon, a rabid interventionist, was saying, "I just want to bash in a few Nazi heads before I die." "It seems to me, Irving," said Cohen, "that bashing heads is for the ninety-six per cent — not for the four per cent."

Now Stokely Carmichael is not for bashing in heads — though I don't suppose it's excluded, since White Power doesn't exclude it. And I think I comprehend what he means by Black Power. What I don't apprehend is how he thinks Black Power will be come by and what he thinks it will do. His counsel of desperation is no better counsel for being a reflexive response to a condition he and I find unendurable; any more than the starving man's theft of bread is a meaningful attack on *his* condition.

Nor do Stokely Carmichael's references (outside his essay) to Irish Power enlighten me. The Kennedys could shuck their Irish skins — even their Catholic skins, which, incidentally, put them into the twenty-five to thirty per cent Power bracket — and emerge as rich and beautiful young Americans with plenty of everything. Rich, young, beautiful — and white. The Negro has plenty of nothing, and when he has plenty of everything — jobs, houses, schools, votes — he will still be black: the one discernible *other* in a society whose Know-Nothings were never able to close the door altogether against the "Irish." The discriminable Negro is the uniquely irresistible object of discrimination.

The Kennedys represent a majority amalgam of special interests. The Carmichaels represent the Negro (who is poor) and nobody else; least of all the poor white. The Negro's is a special interest in which nobody else is interested. His special interest is, to be sure, *intelligible* to a rich society which rocks along without any consuming concern for the common good, but the small special interest (like the corner grocer's) is increasingly inconsequential in the age of amalgamation.

Irish Power never mobilized the white Anglo-Saxon Protestants, except sectionally and sporadically; and they were so sharply divided among themselves that they could not focus their hostility on the Irish. But Black Power mobilizes the whites in an ad hoc alliance in which (as is usual in such situations) they sink their differences and gang up. If Stokely Carmichael means to pit the ten per cent's Power against the ninety per cent's, the ninety per cent will be delighted to accommodate him and see what it can do against the ten in a fair and free contest. "It is white power that makes the laws," he says, as if he were somehow arguing *for* his position, "and it is violent white power in the form of armed white cops that enforces those laws with guns and nightsticks."

Let us suppose, contrary to likelihood, that the ten per cent comes out on top in the contest. What will it be and do then? It is not beyond a reasonable doubt that coercive triumph, over the centuries, has improved the triumphant Wasps. Nor has modern triumph over the Wasps much improved the Irish beyond putting lace curtains in their windows. Whatever the Wasps did in their day, the Irish (and the Portuguese, the Poles, and the Patagonians) do in theirs; and this is not necessarily improvement. Socrates, Acton, and Fulbright all seem to be saying that Power is not an unmixed blessing, and the statesman of ancient days said of the horrors of his triumphant Rome, "All that we do, we do because Power compels us."

What makes Stokely Carmichael think that the Negroes will use Power to better advantage than the whites have been able to use it? I know there is no great point in describing the disappointments of freedom to the untutored slave. But Stokely Carmichael is a tutored slave. He may hope that the Negro would master Power rather than be mastered by it, but his tutoring must have acquainted him with the dictum of Confucius: "He who says, 'Rich men are fools, but when I am rich I will not be a fool,' is already a fool."

I say "would," rather than "will," because I cannot see how Black Power, as I understand it, will come into its own until blacks are thirty, or forty, or fifty-one per cent of the whole society. It will elect a sheriff where it is fifty-one per cent of the electorate; but there are not many such counties, and still fewer states. White Power will fight for its commercial control of the "inner city" — where the Negro already has fifty-one (or eighty-five) per cent of the overnight populace; and when it surrenders what will we have then, except the ghetto unpolluted, with the Negro completing the wall the white began?

The exploitation of the huddled "nationality" neighborhoods, Irish, Italian, Jewish, German, Polish, Swedish, and Bohemian, tore our metropolitan communities to pieces three-quarters of a century ago. Their "leaders" delivered them en bloc to the boodlers and got them a statue of Kosciusko in exchange. Stokely Carmichael has to convince us that his high hope will be realized; that the Negroes will be an exception to the upper class pattern and their inner city serve the welfare of its inhabitants and the general welfare on which the particular ultimately depends. It will not be radical idealists like Stokely Carmichael or Martin King who will do what has always had to be done to win American elections. It is much more likely that the present congressman from Harlem will be the mayor of Stokely Carmichael's *new* New York.

Stokely Carmichael is righter than he is wrong. Integration does mean what he says it means — the assimilation of the psychologically suicidal Negro into the white man's society on the white man's intolerable and unenviable terms. And he is right in suggesting that the white's guilt is collective — I and all the other "friends of the Negro" have exploited him; and not through our grandfathers, either. We travel as effortlessly as we do because we, not our grandfathers, are riding on the black man's back.

Stokely Carmichael is righter than he is wrong; but he is mortally wrong. He is mortally wrong because he accepts the white definition of Power and ignores the demonstrable (if mystifying) fact that there is a kind of power that a majority (be it all men but one) cannot handily dispose of. I speak of nonviolent noncooperation, nonviolent resistance, and nonviolent action undertaken in a nonviolent spirit.

Even on the white man's view of power, the Negro may get some mileage out of nonviolence. American society can live easier every year without menial labor, but for a few years or decades yet it cannot live in the manner to which it is accustomed without the Negro ten per cent. They perform its filthiest jobs and return the profit on its filthiest property. At excruciating cost to themselves, but in solid self-interest, they can leave some of its filth unswept and unprofitable. They still have a small margin of muscle in noncooperation, and by muscle I mean nothing more exalted than Stokely Carmichael or the white man means.

But the margin, in a society which cannot employ its whites, and does not need to, is shrinking. It is the powerlessness inherent in nonviolent noncooperation that the Negro can, perhaps — I say only "perhaps" — turn to account as a peculiar form of power. The whites are guilty. And they would rather fight than switch to expiation. If the Negro can find a weapon that will take the fight out of them, the whites' only remaining course may be justice, not only for the Negro but for every other oppressed minority.

In his *Massachusetts Review* statement, where he purports to present the essentials of the matter, Stokely Carmichael seems never to have heard of Martin King, or of Greensboro. Or of Rosa Parks — who brought Martin King and Greensboro *and Stokely Carmichael* into being. Rosa Parks had something less than ten per cent of the Power (as Stokely Carmichael reckons it) when she could not bring herself to move to the back of the bus in Montgomery. But without the strange power she exercised that day in 1955, Stokely Carmichael would not have the familiar power he has now.

Her power wasn't black. It was human (and, for all any of us know, divine by virtue of its being human). It was the power to heap coals of fire on the heads of the Powerful until they would *want* to do differently than they were doing. It was the power of redemption, and it came out of the most impotent segment of American society, the psalm-singing Southern Negro with his childlike power to believe that he would overcome some day. Out of that power came the Movement; out of the Movement came all that came in the next decade; and out of the deliquescence of the Movement, as it went North to the unbelieving Negro, comes the present vacuum into which Stokely Carmichael would proceed with hopeless weapons instead of none. The analogy with India is colossally imperfect, but it has this much application: We do not *know* that the American white man is less susceptible of being civilized than the British were at Amritsar.

Stokely Carmichael pointedly ignores the power that gave him birth, and he divides the Negroes into the unaccepting (like himself) and the acceptable "passers." He cannot possibly be unconscious of the singular phenomenon of our time and of all time — the power of one powerless person, neither murderer nor victim, neither combatant nor suppliant, to overcome; and, what is more, to win supporters from the ranks of the enemy. Until Montgomery nothing else had ever moved the white man's church at all. And without moved and uncoerced allies the ten per cent will never make it in the halls of Congress or the streets of Selma or any other center of Stokely Carmichael's kind of power.

The Movement is failing, if it is failing, because it has gone North, where the Negro is who doesn't see why he, of all people, should have to be better than the White man. The primitive Negro of the South sees why. Washed in the blood of the Lamb, he sees why he has to be responsible, not for the Negro, not for the white man, but for Man and the salvation of Man through sorrow and suffering and endurance to the end. But moving mountains is slow going, and Stokely Carmichael sounds like Marx's London businessman who would cut off his own right arm for a short-term profit. The short-term Negro will not even get the profit; he hasn't enough to invest.

The redemptive love to which men are called — and to which the psalm-singing Negro responded — is not assured of a profit either. Its prospect of short-term success is slight, but the slightest prospect is better than no prospect at all, and Stokely Carmichael's way has been tried (by the white man) again and again and again. It has failed.

Its very failure may be a sign that men are not bad, and that treating them (and oneself) as if they were is therefore inefficacious. "We have repeatedly seen," says Stokely Carmichael, "that political alliances based on appeals to conscience and decency are chancy things, simply because institutions and political organizations have no consciences outside their own special interests." ("Men are bad," says Machiavelli, "and if you do not break faith with them, they will break faith with you.")

If Stokely Carmichael is right, his way is no worse than Martin King's, only more tiresome as a spectacle; except that Martin King's is directed to the refinement of our sensibilities and Stokely Carmichael's is not.

The issue between them is the issue of knowing. Stokely Carmichael knows, and Martin King doesn't. Martin King doesn't know what power may be within us, or working through us, or what we can and cannot do. William Penn was the first white man the Indians had ever seen without a gun. He went to them, saying to his followers, "Let us try what love will do, for if they see that we love them they will not want to injure us," and on that occasion, and as long as Penn and his successors governed Pennsylvania, and in Pennsylvania alone, the prospect proved to have been splendidly justified. But it was so slight that it took faith above all knowing.

Stokely Carmichael does not display that faith. For all the good his having become a Southern Negro has done him, he might as well have been a white man. He appropriates the white man's racism as the black's and adopts the white man's Power without either God *or* the big battalions. So far is he from supposing that there may be an omnipotence which empowers its votaries, that he has got to settle in the end, not for God, or even for man, but for brute. Count clubs or noses — and if men are brutes, it matters not which — coercion carries the day in the jungle. Whoever chooses the jungle had better be a lion.

Deprivation in an Affluent Society

In the years after World War II, the American economy performed with immense success. The terrible shadow of depression, which had hung over the country during the 1930s, seemed permanently dissipated. But the level of economic activity was not the only measure of economic performance. Who had benefited from the quadrupling of the Gross National Product between 1945 and 1965? For a decade and more following the war, a genuine redistribution of income seemed to be in process. Existing data indicated that, since 1929, the share going to the top 5 percent had been shrinking, while the bottom 20 percent had been gaining a larger share. With total income growing and redistribution taking place, it seemed in the 1950s as if America was reaching the economic millennium — the point at which poverty would become unknown. It came, therefore, as a rude shock to discover that poverty, even if invisible to affluent Americans, was not disappearing, that it in fact was persistent and that it covered fully a quarter of the population. That was the dismal message of Michael Harrington's *The Other America,* and other investigators following him. The "rediscovery" of America's poor, plus the eruption of the black ghettos, had a powerful effect on the nation's politics: it made "the war on poverty" the primary domestic issue of the 1960s.

In the following essay Richard Parker, a Junior Fellow at the Center for the Study of Democratic Institutions, examines the subject from the perspective of the decade's end. He takes a far dimmer view of income redistribution than had his predecessors in the 1950s. The share of the poverty-stricken bottom has not changed significantly since 1910, Parker concludes. The share of the top 5 percent may have fallen slightly but, for reasons Parker explains, it fell a good deal less than earlier statistics had indicated. More striking yet are Parker's conclusions regarding the economic middle. Long-term redistribution of income has actually favored the upper-middle income group — the technocratic elite. As one goes down the economic ladder, distribution gains consistently lessen. And, what is more, the lower-middle class, a full third of the population, lives in a state of deprivation, lacking an income that is adequate for a standard of decent comfort.

Why has the nation so persistently blinded itself to these harsh realities? Why have its efforts at reform so consistently fallen short? Parker addresses himself to these questions in a thoughtful and imaginative way. If his answers seem to foreclose too definitely the possibility of change, assuredly they do express the pessimism of the intellectual generation now coming of age.

FOR FURTHER READING:

Caudill, Harry M. *Night Comes to the Cumberlands.* Boston: Little, Brown & Company, Atlantic Monthly Press, 1963.*
Galbraith, John K. *The Affluent Society.* New York: New American Library, Mentor Books, 1959.*
Harrington, Michael. *The Other America.* Baltimore: Penguin Books, Pelican Books, 1962.*

Asterisk denotes paperback edition.

The Myth of Middle America

RICHARD PARKER

It was a tenet of both liberal and conservative dogmas following World War II that, economically, life in America was getting better all the time. Aside from the political flurry of McCarthyism in the early nineteen-fifties, the economy was everyone's favorite topic of discussion. After economists had predicted a major postwar recession, the American economy fooled them and began what seemed like a skyrocket burst. Between 1945 and 1965, the Gross National Product quadrupled, and disposable personal income increased two-and-a-half-fold. Postulating a "trickle-down" theory of income distribution, economists assumed that it was only a question of time before poverty was eliminated in America.

Suckled on the Horatio Alger myth and teethed on depression and war, the American public was glad to hear the news. Madison Avenue blared the New Affluence across front pages, and invited all of us to join the feast of consumption. The new symbol of America was the suburb, the grassy, tree-shaded Eden of responsible Americans. There a family was safe and happy with its two cars, two children, dog, and barbeque pit. Social science and the academy in general took over the affluence myth virtually *in toto*, declaring the end of scarcity, and with it the end of ideology, and the dawn of a new technocratic age where abundance, rather than scarcity, would be our bane. A Gallup Poll would most likely have found wide acceptance of David Lilienthal's views that "one finds the physical benefits of our society distributed widely, to almost everyone, with scant regard to status, class, or origin of the individual."

But the myth of the New Affluence was a cruel distortion of reality. Composed of half-truths, it closed our eyes, cut us off from a recognition of America, and blocked off political and social alternatives. Today, poverty in the midst of prosperity seems almost characteristic of mature capitalism. Moreover, deprivation also seems characteristic and, together with poverty, describes the living conditions of nearly half the American people. What once appeared to be a New Affluence, I contend, is in fact an expansion of the economy which has disproportionately benefited the upper and upper-middle classes, while it has left the poor and the deprived to gather what crumbs fall from the table.

Marx contended in *Das Kapital* and elsewhere that poverty was a normal condition of capitalism even in the best of times. He argued that even if workers' actual wages rose, the differential between their wages and the income of the rich would continue to increase. The issue was settled to the satisfaction of most American economists by the performance of their own economy after the Second World War. A number of them had their faith in capitalism shaken by the Depression, but the postwar boom quickly allayed most of their doubts. The original Marxian criticism that wages might rise but differentials between classes grow larger was lost sight of in the general euphoria of the nineteen-fifties.

The euphoria, moreover, was not limited to the traditional, or laissez-faire, economists. Liberal interventionists and Keynesians alike joined with conservatives to announce the death of poverty in mature capitalism. John Kenneth Galbraith, for

Source: Richard Parker, "The Myth of Middle America," *The Center Magazine* (March 1970), pp. 61–70.

example, claimed that by the late fifties American poverty was limited to "the insular poor" and "the case poor." The former were the inhabitants of areas like Appalachia and the rural South, where shifting employment patterns were causing "painful, but temporary hardship." The "case poor" were the alcoholics, invalids, and elderly who could not, or would not, get ahead. Keynes himself (like Marx) had, of course, foreseen no such amelioration, even in Keynesian capitalism. As Paul Mattick notes in his book *Marx and Keynes,* "Keynesian interventions in the economy necessarily adjust production and consumption in favor of investments. Such adjustments cannot end the paradox of poverty in the midst of plenty, and are not designed to do so." The problem of economists was to explain *why* poverty was disappearing at such a rapid rate. Census statistics indicated that families with incomes below three thousand dollars had declined from twenty-eight to fourteen per cent between 1947 and 1966. But why? Obviously prosperity in general, and unionization in particular, had improved the lot of the workingman. But raw data, as well as a few highly sophisticated studies, indicated not only that the economic pie was getting bigger but that a significant reallocation was taking place. It appeared that, for some poorly understood reasons, a real change was taking place in the economy. Arthur Burns, then an Eisenhower adviser, rejoiced: "The transformation in the distribution of our national income . . . may already be counted as one of the great social revolutions of history." Paul Samuelson spoke for the liberals when he said,"The American income pyramid is becoming less unequal."

Though still lacking an explanation, the economists' statistical foundations seemed eminently solid. Simon Kuznets' massive study, *Shares of Upper Income Groups in Income and Savings,* indicated a major decline in the percentage of personal income controlled by the upper strata of the society, a decline that "would continue." The late Selma Goldsmith and her associates showed that the share of personal income received by the top five per cent declined from thirty per cent in 1929 to 26.5 per cent in 1936–37, and to 20.7 per cent by 1944. Similarly, she showed that the share of the top twenty per cent declined from 54.4 to 51.7 to 45.8 per cent in the same periods. At the other end of the spectrum, the bottom twenty per cent began to show some, if sizably smaller, gains.

Using these data, plus rawer data collected by the Bureau of the Census and other government agencies, economists postulated a theory for income distribution. According to the theory, income was slowly but irreversibly "trickling down" the income scale from the rich to the poor, to result finally in Samuelson's "flattened pyramid." It was presumed to be only a question of time before the last vestiges of poverty would disappear entirely; by the late fifties, Galbraith declared calmly, poverty in America was no longer "a massive affliction but more nearly an afterthought."

As a consequence, the study of income distribution as an economic discipline rapidly declined throughout the fifties. The university, like the nation at large, mesmerized by the new Affluent Society, was content to rest its discussions of poverty on clichés and rudimentary data. In economics, the new interest was in "value-free" econometrics; in the popular consciousness, it was in *The Organization Man* and *The Man in the Gray Flannel Suit.* Affluence was the presumed condition of almost all, and discussion centered on suburbia, Martinis, and psychoanalysis. Maladies were the result of too much rather than too little.

The "rediscovery" of poverty in America, then, came as a rude awakening to most. Michael Harrington's *The Other America,* which got widespread attention in the early sixties, provided graphic portrayals of the personal impact as well as the extent of poverty. It inspired a major reëxamination of the country's goals. Harrington's estimation that one-quarter of the American people lived in poverty shattered not only national pride but also the sublime self-confidence of the economics establishment. To them, his words were heresy.

Discomfiture was not limited to economists. It spread through the social sciences. Two sociologists, S. M. Miller and Martin Rein, looking back on their colleagues' embarrassing mistakes, described the general theory that had governed sociological thinking in the fifties: "The expansion of production and productivity resulted in a much greater economic pie. The graduated income tax, expanded welfare services, and education were more equitably distributing this larger pie. Continued increase in aggregate economic wealth would invariably filter down, more or less equitably, to all income groupings. Marginal economic groups, it was assumed, would in time 'gracefully succumb' to continued economic growth and that small residual group not covered by expanded welfare and social security programs would be handily cared for by the public dole."

But even after Harrington pricked the popular balloon, air leaked out with surprising slowness. Those running the federal government's War on Poverty (and many social scientists) agreed to define as poor only those families with annual incomes below three thousand dollars. This swift bit of statistical legerdemain immediately shrank Harrington's one-quarter to a less frightening one-fifth. The effect was not only to minimize the poverty in America but to ignore the basic contradictions in the myth of prosperity.

A reëvaluation of postwar prosperity leads to major second thoughts about "trickle down" theories of income distribution. As early as 1957, Robert Lampman, of the University of Michigan, noted that initial gains by the poor to increase their share of the wealth had not only stopped but were reversing. By the early sixties, the rich were again increasing their control of the lion's share of personal income.

The premature optimism of economists like Burns lay in statistics that took no official notice of their unusual circumstances. During the war and shortly thereafter, the income of laborers and service workers increased almost twice as fast as that of professionals and managerial workers. But this was due chiefly to war-related factors that would be unlikely in a peacetime economy, such as full employment mixed with a shortage of non-skilled labor. By the late fifties, the lower categories no longer showed high-rate gains: laborers' and service workers' income increased only forty-eight per cent while managerial income increased seventy-five per cent. Joseph Pechman concluded in 1969 that "the distribution of income in the nineteen-fifties period may not have been very different from what it was in the early nineteen-twenties."

These gross figures, some would argue, are misleading because of shifts in the labor market. Thus the small gains for laborers might be offset by the diminishing number of common laborers, or the high incidence of poverty among farmers offset by decreasing numbers of farmers. But Herman Miller, an economist with the Census Bureau, disagreed. Writing in a Bureau monograph, *Income Distribution in the United States,* he concluded that shifts in job distribution did not substantially affect patterns of income distribution. "Of course it could still be argued that the over-all stability of income distribution for the urban population masks important changes which have taken place for various subgroups within the population. But this hypothesis . . . does not appear to be supported by the facts. Income distribution within the urban population has not shifted even when that population is further classified by labor force status of wife, age of head, or size of family."

Miller, however, does underline one important trend: the increasing number of families in which both husband and wife work. "It should be noted that incomes are much more equally distributed among families where the wife is working than where she is not working; the sizable increase in the proportion of families with working wives has therefore tended to decrease income inequality during the past decade." Moreover, Census projections show that the proportion of women in the labor force will continue to grow over the next two decades.

Yet even the increased family income provided by a second earner was unable to offset the gains by upper and upper-middle classes in control of personal income. Using Census data as well as studies by various economic agencies, Joseph Pechman acknowledged that the rich, but not the poor, had prospered in the postwar era. He pointed out that the simplest Census tables, those most often cited, exclude capital gains and therefore grossly misrepresent income trends in the upper fifth of the economy. For example, the following table shows the standard before-tax income shares of the rich, according to Census data:

Year	Top 5% of Families	Top 20% of Families
1952	18%	42%
1957	16	40
1962	16	42
1967	15	41

What this table indicates obviously is confirmation of Burns' "great revolution." But are the figures accurate?

Tax data are needed to push the analysis further. These data are more useful, because they show the realized capital gains of these families and net income after federal taxes. The salient observation here is that, contrary to another popular myth now also on the wane, the federal income tax is *not* progressive in its effect. Computing total disposable (i.e. after-tax) income, we find the following:

Year	Tax Units Top 5%	Tax Units Top 15%
1952	16%	30%
1963	17	33
1967	17	34

However, this table itself can only be considered an estimate that falls to the low side. Since the Second World War, innumerable tax benefits and payment forms have grown up which benefit only the rich. Pechman names tax-exempt interest and depletion allowances as sources of income, then adds: "During World War II, methods of compensation were devised to funnel income to business executives in nontaxable forms. The devices used are well known: deferred compensation and pension plans, stock option arrangements, and direct payment of personal consumption expenditures through expense accounts." Having listed these varieties of unreported income, he prefers caution, and concludes, "Little is known about the impact on the distribution of income."

Gabriel Kolko is not so timorous. In *Wealth and Power in America,* Kolko announced that "the impact of the federal income tax on the actual distribution of income has been minimal, if not negligible." Drawing on a number of sources for his data, he deduced that adding the uncomputed income of the upper classes would raise their total disposable income two or three percentage points above Pechman's own figures. (Thus the top five per cent received about twenty per cent of the personal income, and the top one per cent about ten per cent of that income.) Since 1952, the effective federal tax rate on the upper one per cent of the population has *dropped* from thirty-three to twenty-six per cent.

What may be said of the federal tax structure can be repeated *ad nauseam* for state and local tax structures. The impact of property and sales taxes is clearly regressive, and, as one economist put it, this is "disturbing because the state-local tax system is the growing element of the national system." Federal tax revenues have remained fairly constant as a proportion of Gross National Product, hovering around twenty per cent since 1951. State and local taxes, by contrast, have risen from 7.1 per cent of the Gross National Product in 1951 to 11.9 per cent in 1968. "Assuming that state-local taxes respond more or less proportionately to the rise in the national product . . . the states and local governments must have increased rates by sixty-eight per cent in these seventeen years to push up their tax yields to current levels." The motivation is obviously not simple greed, but a reflection of increased demand on public services and increasing population concentration in metropolitan areas. Nonetheless, the burden of these social changes falls most heavily on those least able to pay.

The Economic Report of the President, 1969 shows the following:

Income Classes	State and Local Taxes (Percentage of Income)
Under $2,000	25%
2,000–4,000	11
4,000–6,000	10
6,000–8,000	9
8,000–10,000	9
10,000–15,000	9
15,000 and over	7

Analysis of income alone, in the case of the rich, obviously also misrepresents the actual concentration of economic well-being in the country. Affluence for the rich, unlike income for the middle and lower classes, is rarely limited to wages and salaries. Rents, dividends, interest, all go into the total wealth of the upper class. James D. Smith, of the Office of Economic Opportunity, in analyzing data of persons with gross assets in excess of sixty thousand dollars, found a highly concentrated wealth structure. This group, representing the top 1.5 per cent of the wealth-holders in the country, received the following amounts of income:

Type	Billions	Per Cent of Total (Each Type)
Wages and salaries	$25.9	10.8%
Dividends	8.0	74.8
Interest	3.1	27.9
Rent	6.4	52.5
Capital gains	57.6	71.4

Furthermore, this table is an understatement of concentration. It excludes $1.7 billion in dividends paid to trust funds and non-profit foundations; it assumes only average yields on assets, rather than optimum figures to be obtained through the advice of investment counselors; finally, its data are for 1958, and all subsequent information shows increasing pyramiding of the wealth structure.

Gabriel Kolko also contributes significant figures on the concentration of total wealth in the upper brackets which supplement Smith's own research. For example, in 1960 the top ten per cent controlled two-thirds of all liquid assets, while fifty-one per cent of the spending units headed by unskilled or service workers had no assets. Other, more shocking data suggest that between .2 and .3 of one per cent of the population control twenty-two per cent of the personal wealth and sixty to seventy per cent of all privately held corporate wealth.

What in fact was the condition of the poor through the fifties and into the sixties? First of all, we must have a definition of poverty. The federal government has chosen the income-line method, with all families falling below three thousand dollars (now thirty-seven hundred, because of inflation) defined as poor, and therefore eligible for charitable assistance. Before 1962, little was known about this group; since then, a veritable anti-poverty industry has dredged up quantities of information about these people, from their illiteracy rates to their reproduction out of wedlock.

Given all this information, what have we learned? First of all, the income-line method is misleading. It fails to account for assets, temporary impoverishment, and several other factors. Second, and more important, the three thousand dollars has been recognized as ridiculously, if not criminally, low.

How in fact was the government's poverty budget originally arrived at? Politically, several factors interacted; methodologically, the explanation is simple. An annual food budget was prepared, and then that figure was tripled. The budget followed Department of Agriculture guidelines that included the notion that food occupies about one-third of normal expenditures. But simple methodology belied the gross underestimation of need. Oscar Ornati, in *Poverty Amid Affluence,* summarized a typical 1960 "adequate minimum" budget for a family of four:

"It provides for simple clothing to protect against the weather and maintain cleanliness. A woman's coat, for instance, must last five years. Leftover food must be retrieved. A cup of flour spilled means no thickening that week; a blown bulb, no light for that month; and a chair broken in anger cannot be replaced for a year. The meat budget allows for stewing lamb, beef liver, or heart, picnic shoulder, fillet of haddock, or perhaps a boned veal roast. No frozen foods are provided for. It allows nothing for an occasional glass of beer, tobacco, or telephone calls. The budget assumes a small rented five-room flat. The family living room might have two chairs. A mattress and spring on legs may serve as a couch, a dropleaf table for eating; two straight chairs may also be there. Linoleum may cover the floor, and there can be a lamp or two. An electric refrigerator and iron are allowed. The family may listen to the radio an hour a day, but television is not included in the budget. There will be money to buy aspirin but none for 'miracle' drugs. The husband may get a haircut once a month, and the wife a home permanent once a year. She can use a self-service launderette. There will be no money to buy the children candy or ice cream, or to go to the movies, or to offer a visitor a cup of coffee."

The government's budget is unrealistic on other scores. It fails to take account of the overpricing and shoddy quality of food in poor areas, as documented in books like David Caplovitz' *The Poor Pay More.* It ignores the high cost of other items such as housing and furniture, etc. (usually ten to twenty-five per cent overpriced, according to one Bureau of the Census economist) that drives up maintenance costs in the other two-thirds of its budget. In farm areas, it still relies heavily on the presumption that the rural families produce much of their own food, although as a percentage of the total food consumed, home-grown items have fallen from seventy to thirty-six per cent in the past twenty years. It makes no allowances for the higher education of the children, unless one presumes they will receive full scholarship aid, which is highly unlikely. Finally, it assumes no major medical expenses in the family, although over half of the poor are not covered by medical insurance.

The actual meals upon which the entire budget is based inspire greater disbelief. The words of the Census that "assuming the homemaker is a good manager and has the time and skill to shop wisely, she may prepare nutritious, palatable meals . . . for herself, a husband, and two young children" on a budget of seventy cents per day per person inspired one pundit to comment that "Betty Crocker herself would starve." A statistician for H.E.W. describes how a housewife must spend her money:

"For a meal all four of them ate together, she could spend on the average only ninety-five cents, and to stay within her budget she must allow no more a day than a pound of meat, poultry, or fish altogether, barely enough for one small serving for each family member at one of the three meals. Eggs could fill out her family fare only to a limited degree because the plan allows less than two dozen a week for all uses in cooking and at the table, not even one to a person a day. And any food extras, such as milk at school for the children or the coffee her husband might buy to supplement the lunch he carries to work, have to come out of the same food money or compete with the limited funds available for rent, clothing, medical care, and all other expenses. Studies indicate that, on the average, family members eating a meal away from home spend twice as much as the homemaker would spend for preparing one for them at home. The twenty-five cents allowed for a meal at home in the economy plan would not buy much even in the way of supplementation."

Despite the obvious sub-minimal character of this "minimum budget," some optimism has been generated by the War on Poverty and a booming economy, inducing people to believe that the poor are "disappearing." But this optimism needs closer scrutiny. First of all, a three-thousand-dollar limit is a ridiculously low level separating the poor from the non-poor. Second, the government has continued to play games with its own figures ever since the War on Poverty began. For example, the cutoff limit of poverty is measured by pre-tax income figures, although the poverty budget was constructed on an after-tax basis. Third, politics has taken a heavy toll on the poor. According to the McGovern Committee: "In 1968, government statisticians estimated there were between twenty-two and twenty-seven million Americans living in poverty." But at the beginning of 1969 "the higher of these two figures was dropped without explanation" and the twenty-two million used as the official estimate. Finally, government economists have consistently underestimated the effect of taxes and inflation on the poor, or so say a group of non-government economists (writing in *Life,* August 15, 1969). Since fixture of the three-thousand-dollar figure in 1960–61 dollars, inflation and taxes have required a gain of forty-one per cent in actual income to maintain a real income equivalent. This would require a present definition of the poverty level at $4,240, or $540 more than the government now allows. Such an adjustment would add several million more families to the rolls of the poor.

For the extremely poor, times are now even harder. As the Southern Rural Research Project reported: "The poor and the hungry had their brief moment in the sun: America may lionize its victims, but the vogue of compassion passes quickly on; the hungry have now become somewhat passé. Americans seem to take it for granted that once such alarming conditions are publicly known, the appropriate authorities will automatically step in and clear the matter up." Dr. Arnold Schaefer, who headed the Public Health Service's National Nutrition Survey, had been among the first to document malnutrition in sample counties in Texas and Louisiana; now the survey has been discontinued, and Dr. Schaefer has passed quietly from the scene. One wonders if the fifteen million malnourished have disappeared as quietly.

The Nixon Administration's response to the crisis of poverty remains to be seen, since its proposed revamping of the welfare system has yet to pass Congress. The central feature of minimum income is an advance over existing programs, since it recognizes working as well as non-working poor; but its own ceilings of aid are so low as to offset the extension in coverage. His proposals to tie Social Security to cost-of-living indices also seem designed to benefit one segment of the poor, but this was rejected in favor of a one-shot fifteen-per-cent bonus.

The central fallacy, or perhaps the central design, in the government's designation of the poor is its narrowness. Given the present definition of the poor, we avoid the larger contours of our social reality. Compared with the wealthy or near-wealthy, the gains of the poor have been almost immaterial. In 1946, the bottom twenty per cent of all families (the government estimate of the "poor" hovers around sixteen per cent) received five per cent of the income; by 1967, the same fifth — now forty million people — received 5.4 per cent. In other words, the intonations of "trickle down" by economists of the fifties now sound hollow indeed.

Crucial to the isolation of the poor is not only the government's action, but the basic American myth. We are people of the *middle* class, bourgeois, home folks, people who still like Norman Rockwell and live decent, unextravagant lives. De Tocqueville did not instigate the myth, but *Democracy in America* certainly strengthened it. His comments on the "tendencies toward the equalization of the conditions of life" set the pattern for all later social scientists and historians who sought to capture the fundamental character of the country. Louis Hartz, as recently as the middle nineteen-fifties, still wrote of "irrational Lockeanism" as the controlling factor in American political life, and saw this as a reflection of the dominant "middle class."

The belief in progress has always caused Americans to see their past in an ambivalent light. They have viewed the past romantically, choosing to see our problems as smaller and our victories larger than life. What is imperialism to some has been Manifest Destiny in America. What for some was genocide directed toward the Indian was only "resettlement" of the natives. Even when we made mistakes, there was seldom an accusation of guile or willfulness on our part. The Spanish-American War was "misguided," but it was fought with the best of intentions.

By this kind of logic, our poor today are still better off than ninety per cent of the world, and certainly in a better state than they were fifty years ago. The discomfort that greeted disclosures by the muckrakers and writers of the naturalist school at the turn of the century has been replaced today by a comfortable agreement that "things were bad then, but just look at them now." After all, the middle class has always been America's strength and salvation. If we do have poor, well, either they are lazy and inefficient (the conservative view) or they are victimized minorities — blacks, the old, unwed welfare mothers (the liberal view). In any case, nobody opposes welfare anymore — Nixon is pushing the guaranteed income — and besides, as liberal economist Alan Batchelder has assured us, "the poor will continue to disappear as the economy expands."

The fundamental misdirection of all this is away from analysis of the "middle class" to a blind invocation of the myth itself. As recently as October, 1969, *Newsweek,* for example, ran an otherwise perceptive article entitled simplistically: *The Troubled American — A Special Report on the White Majority.* Studded with references to "America's vast white middle-class majority," it intoned the familiar lauds: "America has always been the most middle class of nations, the most generous and the most optimistic." But what in fact the article showed most clearly is that for an enormous proportion of the "middle class," embourgeoisement has been a half-filled dream, a set of unsatisfied hopes. These are the people Leon Keyserling has called not the poor but "the deprived Americans" — "above poverty but short of the minimum requirements for a modestly comfortable level of living." In 1964, Keyserling estimated their number at seventy-seven million men, women, and children.

Keyserling's distinction between a family income of thirty-five hundred dollars ("poverty") and forty-five hundred ("deprivation") should be clear to an economist: the "deprived" all work. Unlike the poor, whose ranks are swelled by the elderly, the infirm, and the blacks, the "deprived" cannot be dismissed as victims of "non-market forces." The "deprived" are functioning, productive members of our economic system: the manual laborers, the clerks, the launderers, the hospital workers of our society. They may have their own home, but it is heavily mortgaged; they may have a late-model car, but it has been financed at steep rates. Their savings, which form a family's cushion against disaster, are marginal: forty per cent are either in debt or have savings of less than one hundred dollars. Liquid assets show even less room for error: twenty per cent of all families own no assets, and forty-eight per cent own less than five hundred dollars' worth. Yet, as Kolko rightly points out: "Liquid assets — such as checking and savings accounts, shares in savings-and-loan associations and credit unions, and government savings bonds — are of decisive importance to low- and even middle-income families exposed to layoffs, unemployment, or medical and other emergencies. Often they represent the entire margin between security and the relief rolls."

The myth of the middle class serves as a permanent leash on the deprived. Lacking the income, they are still expected to provide their families with the amenities that advertising, television, and the academic mythmakers have told them the "middle class" enjoys. Constantly under pressure, they retain all the old American virtues as a desperate bulwark against the encroachment of the "shiftless poor."

They, like the poor, bear a heavy burden of the taxation because of regressive tax structures. They aspire to better education for their children, their own home, and more leisure. Yet, in a great many cases, both father and mother must work simply to maintain their present condition.

The disparities within the "middle class" and the number of the "deprived" are brought out most clearly when one examines the data of income growth over the past half-century. The accompanying table shows control of the income shares by population tenths since 1910. Omitting the top tenth as "upper class" and the bottom two-tenths as "poor," analysis of the remaining "middle class" yields striking results.

Percentage of National Personal Income, Before Taxes,
Received by Each Income-Tenth*

	Highest Tenth	2nd	3rd	4th	5th	6th	7th	8th	9th	Lowest Tenth
1910	33.9	12.3	10.2	8.8	8.0	7.0	6.0	5.5	4.9	3.4
1918	34.5	12.9	9.6	8.7	7.7	7.2	6.9	5.7	4.4	2.4
1921	38.2	12.8	10.5	8.9	7.4	6.5	5.9	4.6	3.2	2.0
1929	39.0	12.3	9.8	9.0	7.9	6.5	5.5	4.6	3.6	1.8
1934	33.6	13.1	11.0	9.4	8.2	7.3	6.2	5.3	3.8	2.1
1937	34.4	14.1	11.7	10.1	8.5	7.2	6.0	4.4	2.6	1.0
1941	34.0	16.0	12.0	10.0	9.0	7.0	5.0	4.0	2.0	1.0
1945	29.0	16.0	13.0	11.0	9.0	7.0	6.0	5.0	3.0	1.0
1946	32.0	15.0	12.0	10.0	9.0	7.0	6.0	5.0	3.0	1.0
1947	33.5	14.8	11.7	9.9	8.5	7.1	5.8	4.4	3.1	1.2
1948	30.9	14.7	11.9	10.1	8.8	7.5	6.3	5.0	3.3	1.4
1949	29.8	15.5	12.5	10.6	9.1	7.7	6.2	4.7	3.1	0.8
1950	28.7	15.4	12.7	10.8	9.3	7.8	6.3	4.9	3.2	0.9
1951	30.9	15.0	12.3	10.6	8.9	7.6	6.3	4.7	2.9	0.8
1952	29.5	15.3	12.4	10.6	9.1	7.7	6.4	4.9	3.1	1.0
1953	31.4	14.8	11.9	10.3	8.9	7.6	6.2	4.7	3.0	1.2
1954	29.3	15.3	12.4	10.7	9.1	7.7	6.4	4.8	3.1	1.2
1955	29.7	15.7	12.7	10.8	9.1	7.7	6.1	4.5	2.7	1.0
1956	30.6	15.3	12.3	10.5	9.0	7.6	6.1	4.5	2.8	1.3
1957	29.4	15.5	12.7	10.8	9.2	7.7	6.1	4.5	2.9	1.3
1958	27.1	16.3	13.2	11.0	9.4	7.8	6.2	4.6	3.1	1.3
1959	28.9	15.8	12.7	10.7	9.2	7.8	6.3	4.6	2.9	1.1

* In terms of "recipients" for 1910–37 and "spending units" for 1941–59.

SOURCE: Data for 1910–37 are from National Industrial Conference Board, *Studies in Enterprise and Social Progress* (New York: National Industrial Conference Board, 1939), p. 125. Data for 1941–59 were calculated by the Survey Research Center. Figures for 1941–46 are available in rounded form only.

The most interesting observation is that there are two distinct strata in the "middle class," the upper of the two having gained markedly greater control of income. Between 1910 and 1959, the second, third, and fourth deciles increased their percentage of the total income more than one-quarter, while the fifth, sixth, seventh, and eighth deciles were able to advance only from 26.5 per cent to 27.9 per cent in the same period.

This information sheds light on much of the writing over the past two decades on the Affluent Society. The "middle class," as a homogeneous group, has done well; but closer examination reveals that that success becomes smaller and smaller as one moves down the income scale within that class. The astigmatic concern of the social scientists for suburbia, executive anomy, and the crises of "the abundant society" has proceeded from myths that now seem badly worn — from the myth of the New Affluence, from the myth of "trickle-down" income and wealth redistribution and the omnipotence of Keynes, and from the capstone myth of them all — the myth of the American middle class.

As a matter of fact, the "middle class" may have escaped the grasp of more than the poor and the deprived. If by "middle class" one means a decent, modest standard of living, it seems that perhaps sixty to seventy per cent of the country have difficulty in reaching it. In 1966, the Bureau of Labor Statistics announced that the average urban family required $9,191 per year to live comfortably; yet the median income that same year was fourteen hundred dollars less than that figure.

At this point, it seems wise to stop and make two observations: the first an estimation of some present and possibly future realities; the second, an historical speculation.

The first observation is about the "unmentioned middle class," the professional, technical elite and its immediate support structure. These people are the true beneficiaries of the Affluent Society, and are the class which has sought to reshape the American myths in its image. College-educated, employed as lawyers, engineers, advertisers, and real-estate dealers, these people are the upper strata of the middle class that experienced the greatest gains in postwar years. The suburban crises of the fifties were *their* crises, the suburban malaise was drowned in *their* Martini glasses. If one were to seek a paradigm for their group, one would find it during the Kennedy era, in the bright young men around the seat of power; but one could also find it in the older and younger men, in corporations and universities. They are those whom Daniel Bell described as the "technocratic elite."

An attack on this group here is not immediately relevant. The Vietnam war has already prompted a number of incisive critiques of them, particularly on the university level. However, critique and solution are not synonymous. It seems likely that the import of young people's radicalism will be diffused and co-opted back into electoral party politics, and the thrust of radical restructuring lost, as it was in the New Deal. Already the "beautiful people" seem to be emerging as the new archetype of this social caste . . . human beings who span Establishment and anti-Establishment factionalism, who work for corporations by day, yet smoke dope by night.

The problem is that their amorality is more difficult to detect because it so often hides behind a veil of rhetorical concern. Unlike the industrial captains of the last century, their contemporary lieutenants feign not indifference but impotence. After all, they *are* concerned, God knows, but they are only vice-presidents or mere managers. They may give occasionally to the political *outré* or talk of "repressive tolerance" at cocktail parties, but those gestures mark the boundaries of their social concern.

One index of that social indifference emerges in an ironic place: Michael Harrington in January had an article in *The Atlantic* entitled "The Betrayal of the Poor." The irony is that *The Atlantic*, for all its enlightenment, is still an organ of that upper-middle class who have not so much resisted, as they have ignored, social change.

The article begins: "For all the rhetoric of recent years about the war on poverty, the poor in America are almost as numerous as ever. . . . Unless the government makes immensely greater commitments of resources and planning, the country is doomed to a social explosion in the seventies that will make the turbulent sixties seem tranquil by comparison." The article, like articles on the malnourished, on housing conditions, on the quality of education in the ghetto, will be read and then lost in the comfortable notion that once federal programs are established, everything will be taken care of. Enter the New Deal, Phase II.

The error in this remains the presumption of the liberal upper-middle class since the first decade of this century: that social legislation by the federal government will cure what ails us. Jane Addams suggested it; Ralph Hunter, one of the nation's first social welfare workers, endorsed it; the New Deal itself put the seal of approval on it; and now even Republicans have begun to see merit in the idea. Unfortunately, the theory has never worked.

The critical assumption behind liberal optimism about coalition between the federal government and corporate capitalism has been that things keep getting better all the time. There are more cars, more homes, better schools, etc., than ever before and, in the midst of this prosperity, the distribution of all this largesse has been getting better as well.

Taking the first half of this claim — that the total quantity of goods has increased — there is no dispute. But one *can* make some comparisons between the United States and other industrialized nations. Fifteen nations have higher literacy rates. Ten nations have lower infant mortality rates. To my knowledge, the United States is the only industrialized nation that does not offer comprehensive medical insurance for all its people. It offers perhaps the worst unemployment protection and the worst welfare system among the developed countries. It has fifteen million malnourished. It has thirty million poor. It has seventy-seven million deprived. Few other nations can claim such tawdry conditions amid such phenomenal growth.

On the second half of the comfortable liberal optimism — that distribution has been getting better and better — there is a fundamental error in the assumption. Since the Second World War, the only significant redistribution of income in the United States has been between the upper and the upper-middle classes. Overall, distribution has remained essentially stable not only over the past twenty years but over the entire twentieth century.

There are three sources for this statement. The first is the chart on income distribution (see p. 491) that shows the limits of change. The second is from Joseph Pechman, a conventionally liberal economist, writing in *The Public Interest,* who states: "The year 1929 must have been the high point of inequality during the nineteen-twenties, so that distribution of income in the more recent period may not have been very different from what it was in the early twenties if account is taken of undistributed profits." The third is a much earlier source. Published in 1904, Robert Hunter's *Poverty* is probably the first attempt made to estimate the number of poor in America. Highly sympathetic to the poor, it uses the data of state and private welfare agencies (since federal data were nonexistent). While emphasizing the wretched conditions of the poor, Hunter limits their number to only twelve per cent of the population. Today economic historians agree that Hunter's estimate was off the mark by six per cent, thus leaving at the turn of the century a minority poor of eighteen per cent. Yet eighteen per cent was the government's estimate of the poor sixty years later!

None of these three estimates is perfect (none ever can be, because crucial data are lacking); but they can give a newer and perhaps more accurate contour of poverty and affluence in America. We are, as De Toqueville said, and as American social scientists have reaffirmed ever since, "a people of the middle class." But to be middle class is both a social-psychological and economic problem. Among those who call themselves "middle class," perhaps a majority have always lacked the money to be in fact what they believe they are. Not only are the poor still with us, but they have been there for years. Michael Harrington's announcement that our poor are the "first minority poor in history" has been misunderstood; the poor have always been a minority in America, but a stubborn minority that refuses to decrease and disappear. The rich in America just keep getting richer. All the talk of income distribution, of flattening pyramids, and of peaceful economic revolutions has been nonsense, fabricated in part out of optimism, in part out of a myopia in the professional classes who themselves gained so rapidly after the Second World War.

At the end of an account such as this, it is usually expected that the author will offer remedies, specific reforms such as tax legislation or welfare payments — or at least see reason for hope on the horizon. I cannot. First, because "reform" has become the province of politicians and electoral platforms, and deals with our needs about as realistically as someone using a Band-Aid on a compound fracture. Yet, even liberals accept reformism, as they did when they quietly applauded the Nixon proposal of a guaranteed annual income for the poor, despite the dire (and probably accurate) warning of Michael Harrington that "a guaranteed annual income could be a way to institutionalize poverty at the subsistence level in the United States."

Second, and more important, I do not seek "reform" because, at age twenty-three, I have lost faith in the willingness of America to "reform." I have lived with the poor, eaten their food, slept in their beds, and taught their children, in Alabama, in Vermont, in Watts. I know their bitterness, and I share it. John Kenneth Galbraith observed recently that "liberalism has been excessively tender toward the rich." A surprise to liberals, but a fact of life for the poor. Attempts at reform have delivered to the poor nothing but promises. They have watched the War on Poverty beaten into ineffectual irrelevance. They have listened to America's liberal politicians promise food as they stare at empty plates. They know the sham of reform.

A College Generation in Rebellion

The nation's campuses have never quite matched the fond stereotypes of old grads and TV writers. Varying from college generation to generation, there has always been student engagement with the issues agitating the larger society. The 1950s marked a low point of student activism; it was the "silent" generation. The 1930s, on the other hand, saw intense student militancy on many campuses. Then as now, vocal radicals took the lead and, antiwar sentiment was powerful — in 1937 students took a pledge nationwide not to participate in any future war. Then as now, demonstrating students attracted national attention and infuriated their elders. But the similarities should not be permitted to mask what is new in the current unrest. Never before has an American student movement been so widespread and deeply felt, never has it confronted in so fundamental a way the shortcomings of the society, never has it been so violent and disruptive. From rather modest beginnings, as it now seems, in the Free Speech Movement at Berkeley in 1964, student activism gathered force until, triggered by the invasion of Cambodia and the killing of six students at Kent State University and Jackson State College, it paralyzed virtually the entire system of higher education in May 1970 and had profound repercussions throughout the nation. Something seems to be happening that has never before occurred in our history: college students are becoming a force for social change in America.

In the following essay, Yale psychologist Kenneth Keniston examines the roots of contemporary student unrest. The primary source he locates in the "postindustrial" stage of our development, that is, the point at which the objectives of industrialism have essentially been accomplished. This has served, first, to undermine the very values — industrial ethic — that brought about that success; and, second, to create a student population unique in numbers and development and by definition idealistic and questioning in its view of the world. So, paradoxically, student activism arises more from the successes of the system than from its failures. (The specific evils under student attack, Keniston notes, are not any worse than in the past, and some are hardly as bad.) From the two above conditions, the characteristics of student unrest follow: fury at the shortcomings in the old order — judged by its own standards — and, at once, an insistence on an educational system and style of life that rejects the ethic of the old order.

The thrust of Keniston's analysis is to emphasize the significance of student activism as a social phenomenon rather than merely as a response to specific provocations or as an expression of personal disorders. By so doing, Keniston gives new importance to the rebellion of youth. It is likely to endure and to leave a permanent mark on contemporary America.

FOR FURTHER READING:

FEUER, LEWIS. *Conflict of Generations.* New York: Basic Books, 1969.
KENISTON, KENNETH. *The Uncommitted: Alienated Youth in American Society.* New York, Dell Publishing Company, Delta Books, 1967.*
————. *Young Radicals.* New York: Harcourt, Brace & World, 1968.
KUNEN, JAMES S. *Strawberry Statement: Notes of a College Revolutionary.* New York: Random House, 1969.*

Asterisk denotes paperback edition.

You Have to Grow Up in Scarsdale to Know How Bad It Is

KENNETH KENISTON

The recent events at Harvard are the culmination of a long year of unprecedented student unrest in the advanced nations of the world. We have learned to expect students in underdeveloped countries to lead unruly demonstrations against the status quo, but what is new, unexpected and upsetting to many is that an apparently similar mood is sweeping across America, France, Germany, Italy and even Eastern European nations like Czechoslovakia and Poland. Furthermore, the revolts occur, not at the most backward universities, but at the most distinguished, liberal and enlightened — Berkeley, the Sorbonne, Tokyo, Columbia, the Free University of Berlin, Rome and now Harvard.

This development has taken almost everyone by surprise. The American public is clearly puzzled, frightened and often outraged by the behavior of its most privileged youth. The scholarly world, including many who have devoted their lives to the study of student protest, has been caught off guard as well. For many years, American analysts of student movements have been busy demonstrating that "it can't happen here." Student political activity abroad has been seen as a reaction to modernization, industrialization and the demise of traditional or tribal societies. In an already modern, industrialized, detribalized and "stable" nation like America, it was argued, student protests are naturally absent.

Another explanation has tied student protests abroad to bad living conditions in some universities and to the unemployability of their graduates. Student revolts, it was argued, spring partly from the misery of student life in countries like India and Indonesia. Students who must live in penury and squalor naturally turn against their universities and societies. And if, as in many developing nations, hundreds of thousands of university graduates can find no work commensurate with their skills, the chances for student militancy are further increased.

These arguments helped explain the "silent generation" of the nineteen-fifties and the absence of protest, during that period, in American universities, where students are often "indulged" with good living conditions, close student-faculty contact and considerable freedom of speech. And they helped explain why "super-employable" American college graduates, especially the much-sought-after ones from colleges like Columbia and Harvard, seemed so contented with their lot.

But such arguments do not help us understand today's noisy, angry and militant students in the advanced countries. Nor do they explain why students who enjoy the greatest advantages — those at the leading universities — are often found in the revolts. As a result, several new interpretations of student protest are currently being put forward, interpretations that ultimately form part of what Richard Poirier has termed "the war against the young."

Many reactions to student unrest, of course, spring primarily from fear, anger, confusion or envy, rather than from theoretical analysis. Governor Wallace's at-

Source: Kenneth Keniston, "You Have to Grow Up in Scarsdale to Know How Bad It Is," *The New York Times Magazine* (April 27, 1969), pp. 27–28, 122–129.

tacks on student "anarchists" and other "pin-headed intellectuals;" for example, were hardly coherent explanations of protest. Many of the bills aimed at punishing student protesters being proposed in Congress and state legislatures reflect similar feelings of anger and outrage. Similarly, the presumption that student unrest *must* be part of an international conspiracy is based on emotion rather than fact. Even George F. Kennan's recent discussion of the American student left is essentially a moral condemnation of "revolting students," rather than an effort to explain their behavior.

If we turn to more thoughtful analyses of the current student mood we find two general theories gaining widespread acceptance. The first, articulately expressed by Lewis S. Feuer in his recent book on student movements, "The Conflict of Generations," might be termed the "Oedipal Rebellion" interpretation. The second, cogently stated by Zbigniew Brzezinski and Daniel Bell, can be called the theory of "Historical Irrelevance."

The explanation of Oedipal Rebellion sees the underlying force in all student revolts as blind, unconscious Oedipal hatred of fathers and the older generation. Feuer, for example, finds in all student movements an inevitable tendency toward violence and a combination of "regicide, parricide and suicide." A decline in respect for the authority of the older generation is needed to trigger a student movement, but the force behind it comes from "obscure" and "unconscious" forces in the child's early life, including both intense death wishes against his father and the enormous guilt and self-hatred that such wishes inspire in the child.

The idealism of student movements is thus, in many respects, only a "front" for the latent unconscious destructiveness and self-destructiveness of underlying motivations. Even the expressed desire of these movements to help the poor and exploited is explained psychoanalytically by Feuer: Empathy for the disadvantaged is traced to "traumatic" encounters with parental bigotry in the students' childhoods, when their parents forbade them to play with children of other races or lower social classes. The identification of today's new left with blacks is thus interpreted as an unconscious effort to "abreact and undo this original trauma."

There are two basic problems with the Oedipal Rebellion theory, however. First, although it uses psychoanalytic terms, it is bad psychoanalysis. The real psychoanalytic account insists that the Oedipus complex is universal in all normally developing children. To point to this complex in explaining student rebellion is, therefore, like pointing to the fact that all children learn to walk. Since both characteristics are said to be universal, neither helps us understand why, at some historical moments, students are restive and rebellious, while at others they are not. Second, the theory does not help us explain why some students (especially those from middle-class, affluent and idealistic families) are most inclined to rebel, while others (especially those from working-class and deprived families) are less so.

In order really to explain anything, the Oedipal Rebellion hypothesis would have to be modified to point to an unusually *severe* Oedipus complex, involving especially *intense* and unresolved unconscious feelings of father-hatred in student rebels. But much is now known about the lives and backgrounds of these rebels — at least those in the United States — and this evidence does not support even the modified theory. On the contrary, it indicates that most student protesters are relatively *close* to their parents, that the values they profess are usually the ones they learned at the family dinner table, and that their parents tend to be highly educated, liberal or left-wing and politically active.

Furthermore, psychological studies of student radicals indicate that they are no more neurotic, suicidal, enraged or disturbed than are non-radicals. Indeed, most studies find them to be rather more integrated, self-accepting and "advanced," in a psychological sense, than their politically inactive contemporaries. In general, research on American student rebels supports a "Generational Solidarity" (or chip-off-the-old-block) theory, rather than one of Oedipal Rebellion.

The second theory of student revolts now being advanced asserts that they are a reaction against "historical irrelevance." Rebellion springs from the unconscious awareness of some students that society has left them and their values behind. According to this view, the ultimate causes of student dissent are sociological rather than psychological. They lie in fundamental changes in the nature of the advanced societies — especially, in the change from industrial to post-industrial society. The student revolution is seen not as a true revolution, but as a counterrevolution — what Daniel Bell has called "the guttering last gasp of a romanticism soured by rancor and impotence."

This theory assumes that we are moving rapidly into a new age in which technology will dominate, an age whose real rulers will be men like computer experts, systems analysts and technobureaucrats. Students who are attached to outmoded and obsolescent values like humanism and romanticism unconsciously feel they have no place in this post-industrial world. When they rebel they are like the Luddites of the past — workers who smashed machines to protest the inevitable industrial revolution. Today's student revolt reflects what Brzezinski terms "an unconscious realization that they [the rebels] are themselves becoming historically obsolete"; it is nothing but the "death rattle of the historical irrelevants."

This theory is also inadequate. It assumes that the shape of the future is already technologically determined, and that protesting students unconsciously "know" that it will offer them no real reward, honor or power. But the idea that the future can be accurately predicted is open to fundamental objection. Every past attempt at prophecy has turned out to be grievously incorrect. Extrapolations from the past, while sometimes useful in the short run, are usually fundamentally wrong in the long run, especially when they attempt to predict the quality of human life, the nature of political and social organization, international relations or the shape of future culture.

The future is, of course, made by men. Technology is not an inevitable master of man and history, but merely provides the possibility of applying scientific knowledge to specific problems. Men may identify with it or refuse to, use it or be used by it for good or evil, apply it humanely or destructively. Thus, there is no real evidence that student protest will emerge as the "death rattle of the historical irrelevants." It could equally well be the "first spark of a new historical era." No one today can be sure of the outcome, and people who feel certain that the future will bring the obsolescence and death of those whom they dislike are often merely expressing their fond hope.

The fact that today's students invoke "old" humanistic and romantic ideas in no way proves that student protests are a "last gasp" of a dying order. Quite the contrary: *All* revolutions draw upon older values and visions. Many of the ideals of the French Revolution, for example, originated in Periclean Athens. Revolutions do not occur because new ideas suddenly develop, but because a new generation begins to take *old* ideas seriously — not merely as interesting theoretical views, but as the basis for political action and social change. Until recently, the humanistic vision of human fulfillment and the romantic vision of an expressive, imaginative and passionate life were taken seriously only by small aristocratic or Bohemian groups. The fact that they are today taken as real goals by millions of students in many nations does not mean that these students are "counterrevolutionaries," but merely that their ideas follow the pattern of every major revolution.

Indeed, today's student rebels are rarely opposed to technology *per se*. On the contrary, they take the high technology of their societies completely for granted, and concern themselves with it very little. What they *are* opposed to is, in essence, the worship of Technology, the tendency to treat people as "inputs" or "outputs" of a technological system, the subordination of human needs to technological programs. The essential conflict between the minority of students who make up the student revolt and the existing order is a conflict over the future direction of technological society, not a counterrevolutionary protest against technology.

In short, both the Oedipal Rebellion and the Historical Irrelevance theories are what students would call "put-downs." If we accept either, we are encouraged not to listen to protests, or to explain them away or reject them as either the "acting out" of destructive Oedipal feelings or the blind reaction of an obsolescent group to the awareness of its obsolescence. But if, as I have argued, neither of these theories is adequate to explain the current "wave" of student protest here and abroad, how can we understand it?

One factor often cited to explain student unrest is the large number of people in the world under 30 — today the critical dividing line between generations. But this explanation alone, like the theories just discussed, is not adequate, for in all historical eras the vast portion of the population has always been under 30. Indeed, in primitive societies most people die before they reach that age. If chronological youth alone was enough to insure rebellion, the advanced societies — where a greater proportion of the population reaches old age than ever before in history — should be the *least* revolutionary, and primitive societies the *most*. This is not the case.

Most relevant factors are the relationship of those under 30 to the established institutions of society (that is, whether they are engaged in them or not); and the opportunities that society provides for their continuing intellectual, ethical and emotional development. In both cases the present situation in the advanced nations is without precedent.

Philippe Aries, in his remarkable book, "Centuries of Childhood," points out that, until the end of the Middle Ages, no separate stage of childhood was recognized in Western societies. Infancy ended at approximately 6 or 7, whereupon most children were integrated into adult life, treated as small men and women and expected to work as junior partners of the adult world. Only later was childhood recognized as a separate stage of life, and our own century is the first to "guarantee" it by requiring universal primary education.

The recognition of adolescence as a stage of life is of even more recent origin, the product of the nineteenth and twentieth centuries. Only as industrial societies became prosperous enough to defer adult work until after puberty could they create institutions — like widespread secondary-school education — that would extend adolescence to virtually all young people. Recognition of adolescence also arose from the vocational and psychological requirements of these societies, which needed much higher levels of training and psychological development than could be guaranteed through primary education alone. There is, in general, an intimate relationship between the way a society defines the stages of life and its economic, political and social characteristics.

Today, in more developed nations, we are beginning to witness the recognition of still another stage of life. Like childhood and adolescence, it was initially granted only to a small minority, but is now being rapidly extended to an ever-larger group. I will call this the stage of "youth," and by that I mean both a further phase of disengagement from society and the period of psychological development that intervenes between adolescence and adulthood. This stage, which continues into the 20s and sometimes into the 30s, provides opportunities for intellectual, emotional and moral development that were never afforded to any other large group in history. In the student revolts we are seeing one result of this advance.

I call the extension of youth an advance advisedly. Attendance at a college or university is a major part of this extension, and there is growing evidence that this is, other things being equal, a good thing for the student. Put in an oversimplified phrase, it tends to free him — to free him from swallowing unexamined the assumptions of the past, to free him from the superstitions of his childhood, to free him to express his feelings more openly and to free him from irrational bondage to authority.

I do not mean to suggest, of course, that all college graduates are free and liberated spirits, unencumbered by irrationality, superstition, authoritarianism or blind adherence to tradition. But these findings do indicate that our colleges, far from cranking out only machinelike robots who will provide skilled manpower for the economy, are also producing an increasing number of highly critical citizens — young men and women who have the opportunity, the leisure, the affluence and the educational resources to continue their development beyond the point where most people in the past were required to stop it.

So, one part of what we are seeing on campuses throughout the world is not a reflection of how bad higher education is, but rather of its extraordinary accomplishments. Even the moral righteousness of the student rebels, a quality both endearing and infuriating to their elders, must be judged at least partially a consequence of the privilege of an extended youth; for a prolonged development, we know, encourages the individual to elaborate a more personal, less purely conventional sense of ethics.

What the advanced nations have done is to create their own critics on a mass basis — that is, to create an ever-larger group of young people who take the highest values of their societies as their own, who internalize these values and identify them with their own best selves, and who are willing to struggle to implement them. At the same time, the extension of youth has lessened the personal risks of dissent: These young people have been freed from the requirements of work, gainful employment and even marriage, which permits them to criticize their society from a protected position of disengagement.

But the mere prolongation of development need not automatically lead to unrest. To be sure, we have granted to millions the opportunity to examine their societies, to compare them with their values and to come to a reasoned judgment of the existing order. But why should their judgment today be so unenthusiastic?

What protesting students throughout the world share is a mood more than an ideology or a program, a mood that says the existing system — the power structure — is hypocritical, unworthy of respect, outmoded and in urgent need of reform. In addition, students everywhere speak of repression, manipulation and authoritarianism. (This is paradoxical, considering the apparently great freedoms given them in many nations. In America, for example, those who complain most loudly about being suffocated by the subtle tyranny of the Establishment usually attend the institutions where student freedom is greatest.) Around this general mood, specific complaints arrange themselves as symptoms of what students often call the "exhaustion of the existing society."

To understand this phenomenon we must recognize that, since the Second World War, some societies have indeed begun to move past the industrial era into a new world that is post-industrial, technological, post-modern, post-historic or, in Brzezinski's term, "technectronic." In Western Europe, the United States, Canada and Japan, the first contours of this new society are already apparent. And, in many other less-developed countries, middle-class professionals (whose children become activists) often live in post-industrial enclaves within pre-industrial societies. Whatever we call the post-industrial world, it has demonstrated that, for the first time, man can produce more than enough to meet his material needs.

This accomplishment is admittedly blemished by enormous problems of economic distribution in the advanced nations, and it is in terrifying contrast to the overwhelming poverty of the Third World. Nevertheless, it is clear that what might be called "the problem of production" *can,* in principle, be solved. If all members of American society, for example, do not have enough material goods, it is because the system of distribution is flawed. The same is true, or will soon be true, in many other nations that are approaching advanced states of industrialization. Characteristically, these nations, along with the most technological, are those where student unrest has recently been most prominent.

The transition from industrial to post-industrial society brings with it a major shift in social emphases and values. Industrializing and industrial societies tend to be oriented toward solving the problem of production. An industrial ethic — sometimes Protestant, sometimes Socialist, sometimes Communist — tends to emphasize psychological qualities like self-discipline, delay of gratification, achievement-orientation and a strong emphasis on economic success and productivity. The social, political and economic institutions of these societies tend to be organized in a way that is consistent with the goal of increasing production. And industrial societies tend to apply relatively uniform standards, to reward achievement rather than status acquired by birth, to emphasize emotional neutrality ("coolness") and rationality in work and public life.

The emergence of post-industrial societies, however, means that growing numbers of the young are brought up in family environments where abundance, relative economic security, political freedom and affluence are simply facts of life, not goals to be striven for. To such people the psychological imperatives, social institutions and cultural values of the industrial ethic seem largely outdated and irrelevant to their own lives.

Once it has been demonstrated that a society *can* produce enough for all of its members, at least some of the young turn to other goals: for example, trying to make sure that society *does* produce enough and distributes it fairly, or searching for ways to live meaningfully with the goods and the leisure they *already* have. The problem is that our society has, in some realms, exceeded its earlier targets. Lacking new ones, it has become exhausted by its success.

When the values of industrial society become devitalized, the élite sectors of youth — the most affluent, intelligent, privileged and so on — come to feel that they live in institutions whose demands lack moral authority or, in the current jargon, "credibility." Today, the moral imperative and urgency behind production, acquisition, materialism and abundance has been lost.

Furthermore, with the lack of moral legitimacy felt in "the System," the least request for loyalty, restraint or conformity by its representatives — for example, by college presidents and deans — can easily be seen as a moral outrage, an authoritarian repression, a manipulative effort to "co-opt" students into joining the Establishment and an exercise in "illegitimate authority" that must be resisted. From this conception springs at least part of the students' vague sense of oppression. And, indeed, perhaps their peculiar feeling of suffocation arises ultimately from living in societies without vital ethical claims.

Given such a situation, it does not take a clear-cut issue to trigger a major protest. I doubt, for example, that college and university administrators are in fact *more* hypocritical and dishonest than they were in the past. American intervention in Vietnam, while many of us find it unjust and cruel, is not inherently *more* outrageous than other similar imperialistic interventions by America and other nations within the last century. And the position of blacks in this country, although disastrously and unjustifiably disadvantaged, is, in some economic and legal respects, better than ever before. Similarly, the conditions for students in America have never been as good, especially, as I have noted, at those élite colleges where student protests are most common.

But this is *precisely* the point: It is *because* so many of the *other* problems of American society seem to have been resolved, or to be resolvable in principle, that students now react with new indignation to old problems, turn to new goals and propose radical reforms.

So far I have emphasized the moral exhaustion of the old order and the fact that, for the children of post-industrial affluence, the once-revolutionary claims of the industrial society have lost much of their validity. I now want to argue that we are witnessing on the campuses of the world a fusion of *two revolutions* with distinct historical origins. One is a continuation of the old and familiar revolution of the industrial society, the liberal-democratic-egalitarian revolution that started in America and France at the turn of the 18th century and spread to virtually every nation in the world. (Not completed in any of them, its contemporary American form is, above all, to be found in the increased militancy of blacks.) The other is the new revolution, the post-industrial one, which seeks to define new goals relevant to the 20th and 21st centuries.

In its social and political aspects, the first revolution has been one of universalization, to use the sociologist's awkward term. It has involved the progressive extension to more and more people of economic, political and social rights, privileges and opportunities originally available only to the aristocracy, then to the middle class, and now in America to the relatively affluent white working class. It is, in many respects, a *quantitative* revolution. That is, it concerns itself less with the quality of life than with the amount of political freedom, the quantity and distribution of goods or the amount and level of injustice.

As the United States approaches the targets of the first revolution, on which this society was built, to be poor shifts from being an unfortunate fact of life to being an outrage. And, for the many who have never experienced poverty, discrimination, exploitation or oppression, even to *witness* the existence of these evils in the lives of others suddenly becomes intolerable. In our own time the impatience to complete the first revolution has grown apace, and we find less willingness to compromise, wait and forgive among the young, especially among those who now take the values of the old revolution for granted — seeing them not as goals, but as *rights.*

A subtle change has thus occurred. What used to be utopian ideals — like equality, abundance and freedom from discrimination — have now become demands, inalienable rights upon which one can insist without brooking any compromise. It is noteworthy that, in today's student confrontations, no one requests anything. Students present their "demands."

So, on the one hand, we see a growing impatience to complete the first revolution. But, on the other, there is a newer revolution concerned with newer issues, a revolution that is less social, economic or political than psychological, historical and cultural. It is less concerned with the quantities of things than with their qualities, and it judges the virtually complete liberal revolution and finds it still wanting.

"You have to have grown up in Scarsdale to know how bad things really are," said one radical student. This comment would probably sound arrogant, heartless and insensitive to a poor black, much less to a citizen of the Third World. But he meant something important by it. He meant that *even* in the Scarsdales of America, with their affluence, their upper-middle-class security and abundance, their well-fed, well-heeled children and their excellent schools, something is wrong. Economic affluence does not guarantee a feeling of personal fulfillment; political freedom does not always yield an inner sense of liberation and cultural freedom; social justice and equality may leave one with a feeling that something else is missing in life. "No to the consumer society!" shouted the bourgeois students of the Sorbonne during May and June of 1968 — a cry that understandably alienated French workers, for whom affluence and the consumer society are still central goals.

What, then, are the targets of the new revolution? As is often noted, students themselves don't know. They speak vaguely of "a society that has never existed," of "new values," of a "more humane world," of "liberation" in some psychological, cultural and historical sense. Their rhetoric is largely negative; they are stronger in opposition than in proposals for reform; their diagnoses often seem accurate, but their prescriptions are vague; and they are far more articulate in urging the immediate completion of the first revolution than in defining the goals of the second. Thus, we can only indirectly discern trends that point to the still-undefined targets of the new revolution.

What are these trends and targets?

First, there is a revulsion against the notion of quantity, particularly economic quantity and materialism, and a turn toward concepts of quality. One of the most delightful slogans of the French student revolt was, "Long live the passionate revolution of creative intelligence!" In a sense, the achievement of abundance may allow millions of contemporary men and women to examine, as only a few artists and madmen have examined in the past, the quality, joyfulness and zestfulness of experience. The "expansion of consciousness"; the stress on the expressive, the aesthetic and the creative; the emphasis on imagination, direct perception and fantasy — all are part of the effort to enhance the quality of this experience.

Another goal of the new revolution involves a revolt against uniformity, equalization, standardization and homogenization — not against technology itself, but against the "technologization of man." At times, this revolt approaches anarchic quaintness, but it has a positive core as well — the demand that individuals be appreciated, not because of their similarities or despite their differences, but because they *are* different, diverse, unique and noninterchangeable. This attitude is evident in many areas: for example, the insistence upon a cultivation of personal idiosyncrasy, mannerism and unique aptitude. Intellectually, it is expressed in the rejection of the melting-pot and consensus-politics view of American life in favor of a post-homogeneous America in which cultural diversity and conflict are underlined rather than denied.

The new revolution also involves a continuing struggle against psychological or institutional closure or rigidity in any form, even the rigidity of a definite adult role. Positively, it extols the virtues of openness, motion and continuing human development. What Robert J. Lifton has termed the protean style is clearly in evidence. There is emerging a concept of a lifetime of personal change, of an adulthood of continuing self-transformation of an adaptability and an openness to the revolutionary modern world that will enable the individual to remain "with it" — psychologically youthful and on top of the present.

Another characteristic is the revolt against centralized power and the complementary demand for participation. What is demanded is not merely the consent of the governed, but the involvement of the governed. "Participatory democracy" summarizes this aspiration, but it extends far beyond the phrase and the rudimentary social forms that have sprung up around it. It extends to the demand for relevance in education — that is, for a chance for the student to participate in his own educational experience in a way that involves all of his faculties, emotional and moral as well as intellectual. The demand for "student power" (or, in Europe, "co-determination") is an aspect of the same theme: At Nanterre, Columbia, Frankfurt and Harvard, students increasingly seek to participate in making the policies of their universities.

This demand for participation is also embodied in the new ethic of "meaningful human relationships," in which individuals confront each other without masks, pretenses and games. They "relate" to each other as unique and irreplaceable human beings, and develop new forms of relationships from which all participants will grow.

In distinguishing between the old and the new revolutions, and in attempting to define the targets of the new, I am, of course, making distinctions that students themselves rarely make. In any one situation the two revolutions are joined and fused, if not confused. For example, the Harvard students' demand for "restructuring the university" is essentially the second revolution's demand for participation; but their demand for an end to university "exploitation" of the surrounding community is tied to the more traditional goals of the first revolution. In most radical groups there is a range of opinion that starts with the issues of the first (racism, imperialism, exploitation, war) and runs to the concerns of the second (experiential education, new life styles, meaningful participation, consciousness-expansion, relatedness, encounter and community). The first revolution is personified by Maoist-oriented Progressive Labor party factions within the student left, while the second is represented by hippies, the "acid left," and the Yippies. In any individual, and in all student movements, these revolutions coexist in uneasy and often abrasive tension.

Furthermore, one of the central problems for student movements today is the absence of any theory of society that does justice to the new world in which we of the most industrialized nations live. In their search for rational critiques of present societies, students turn to theories like Marxism that are intricately bound up with the old revolution.

Such theories make the ending of economic exploitation, the achievement of social justice, the abolition of racial discrimination and the development of political participation and freedom central, but they rarely deal adequately with the issues of the second revolution. Students inevitably try to adapt the rhetoric of the first to the problems of the second, using concepts that are often blatantly inadequate to today's world.

Even the concept of "revolution" itself is so heavily laden with images of political, economic and social upheaval that it hardly seems to characterize the equally radical but more social-psychological and cultural transformations involved in the new revolution. One student, recognizing this, called the changes occurring in his California student group, "too radical to be called a revolution." Students are thus often misled by their borrowed vocabulary, but most adults are even more confused, and many are quickly led to the mistaken conclusion that today's student revolt is nothing more than a repetition of Communism's in the past.

Failure to distinguish between the old and new revolutions also makes it impossible to consider the critical question of how compatible they are with each other. Does it make sense — or is it morally right — for today's affluent American students to seek imagination, self-actualization, individuality, openness and relevance when most of the world and many in America live in deprivation, oppression and misery?

The fact that the first revolution is "completed" in Scarsdale does not mean that it is (or soon will be) in Harlem or Appalachia — to say nothing of Bogotá or Calcutta. For many children of the second revolution, the meaning of life may be found in completing the first — that is, in extending to others the "rights" they have always taken for granted.

For others the second revolution will not wait; the question. "What lies beyond affluence?" demands an answer now. Thus, although we may deem it self-indulgent to pursue the goals of the new revolution in a world where so much misery exists, the fact is that in the advanced nations it is upon us, and we must at least learn to recognize it.

Finally, beneath my analysis lies an assumption I had best make explicit. Many student critics argue that their societies have failed miserably. My argument, a more historical one perhaps, suggests that our problem is not only that industrial societies have failed to keep all their promises, but that they have succeeded in some ways beyond all expectations. Abundance was once a distant dream, to be postponed to a hereafter of milk and honey; today, most Americans are affluent. Universal mass education was once a Utopian goal; today in America almost the entire population completes high school, and almost half enters colleges and universities.

The notion that individuals might be free, en masse, to continue their psychological, intellectual, moral and cognitive development through their teens and into their 20's would have been laughed out of court in any century other than our own; today, that opportunity is open to millions of young Americans. Student unrest is a reflection not only of the failures, but of the extraordinary successes of the liberal-industrial revolution. It therefore occurs in the nations and in the colleges where, according to traditional standards, conditions are best.

But for many of today's students who have never experienced anything but affluence, political freedom and social equality, the old vision is dead or dying. It may inspire bitterness and outrage when it is not achieved, but it no longer animates or guides. In place of it, students (and many who are not students) are searching for a new vision, a new set of values, a new set of targets appropriate to the post-industrial era — a myth, an ideology or a set of goals that will concern itself with the quality of life and answer the question, "Beyond freedom and affluence, what?"

What characterizes student unrest in the developed nations is this peculiar mixture of the old and the new, the urgent need to fulfill the promises of the past and, at the same time, to define the possibilities of the future.

A B C D E F G H I J   9 8 7 6 5 4 3 2 1

DATE D